CRIMINOLOGY

A Contemporary
Handbook

CRIMINOLOGY

A Contemporary Handbook

SECOND EDITION

JOSEPH F. SHELEY

Wadsworth Publishing Company
I(T)P™ An International Thomson Publishing Company

Belmont • Albany • Bonn • Boston • Cincinnati • Detroit • London • Madrid • Melbourne
Mexico City • New York • Paris • San Francisco • Singapore • Tokyo • Toronto • Washington

Dedication

For Bernadette and Claire

Editor: Serina Beauparlant
Editorial Assistant: Jason Moore
Production Editor: Angela Mann
Managing Designer: Ann Butler
Print Buyer: Karen Hunt
Permissions Editor: Jeanne Bosschart

Copy Editor: Robert Fiske
Technical Illustrator: Craig Hanson
Cover: Image House Inc./Stuart Patterson
Compositor: ColorType, San Diego
Printer: Arcata Graphics/Fairfield

For more information, contact:

Wadsworth Publishing Company
10 Davis Drive
Belmont, California 94002

International Thomson Publishing
Berkshire House 168-173
High Holborn
London, WC1V 7AA
England

Thomas Nelson Australia
102 Dodds Street
South Melbourne 3205
Victoria, Australia

Nelson Canada
1120 Birchmount Road
Scarborough, Ontario
Canada M1K 5G4

International Thomson Publishing GmbH
Königwinterer Strasse 418
53227 Bonn
Germany

International Thomson Publishing Asia
221 Henderson Road #05-10
Singapore 0315

International Thomson Publishing - Japan
Hirakawacho-cho Kyowa Building, 3F
2-2-1 Hirakawacho
Chiyoda-ku, 102 Tokyo,
Japan

1 2 3 4 5 6 7 8 9 10 — 01 00 99 98 97 96 95

Library of Congress Cataloging-in-Publication Data

Criminology: a contemporary handbook/Joseph F. Sheley [editor]. — 2nd ed.
   p.   cm.
Includes bibliographical references and index.
ISBN: 0-534-24438-6 (acid free)
1. Criminology — United States I. Sheley, Joseph F.
HV6025.C738   1995
364.973 — dc20   94–11961

CONTENTS

◆

◆   v

FOUR
_____

CRIMINAL BEHAVIOR: GENDER AND AGE 83
Darrell Steffensmeier and Emilie Allan

FIVE
_____

CRIMINAL BEHAVIOR: RACE AND CLASS 115
Anthony R. Harris and Lisa R. Meidlinger

SIX

CRIME VICTIMS 145
Andrew A. Karmen

ELEVEN

RESPECTABLE CRIME 249
James W. Coleman

FOURTEEN

CONTROL AND DETERRENCE THEORIES OF CRIMINALITY 329
Marvin Krohn

FIFTEEN

ALTERNATIVE APPROACHES: LABELING AND CRITICAL PERSPECTIVES 349
Gray Cavender

PART FIVE

CRIMINAL JUSTICE 369

SIXTEEN

THE POLICE 373
Stephen D. Mastrofski

NINETEEN

CORRECTION BEYOND PRISON WALLS   453
Todd Clear

TWENTY-TWO

TWENTY-THREE

TWENTY-FOUR

THE DEATH PENALTY IN AMERICA 557
M. Dwayne Smith

PREFACE

◆

As with the first edition of *Criminology: A Contemporary Handbook*, this revision serves as a vehicle by which to transmit many criminologists' thoughts about their specialties in a relatively consistent style and format. The chapters represent their authors' ideas about the current state of the research and theory in their respective areas of expertise. The reader receives more than a summary from each. There are ideas in these chapters that no one author of a text could have provided. The present revision contains three new chapters as well as updated versions of most of the chapters in the original edition. It also contains an expanded introductory discussion of the nature and basic concepts of criminology.

For me, the editor, production of the text was a powerful and gratifying learning experience—much like going back to school. I became a better criminologist through the dialogue I had with the authors over their chapters. I asked them to write within the general framework I sought, but beyond that, the chapters were theirs. Editor and author did not always see eye to eye. In some instances, critical exchanges provided clearer thinking; in other instances, space constraints limited authors. But within space limits, each author was the arbiter of substance. The level of cooperation from, and the extent of consultation with, the authors exceeded every expectation. Each recognized the need for restraint and direction. *Criminology: A Contemporary Handbook* thus became a structured team effort that allowed team members to display their considerable individual talents.

I am unsure which was more difficult for the writers of this book's chapters—bowing to my stylistic demands or working within the framework I requested. Stylistically, I sought a consistency that assured instructors that their students would not be jerked to and fro by uneven prose as they worked their way through the book. This was no small task, but I feel we succeeded overall. There is a uniformity in presentation here that generally is absent in the standard collection of articles that only secondarily might suit the classroom.

In terms of a framework around which to structure the chapters, I asked the authors to step outside what they perceived as the academic concerns of their discipline and to put themselves in the students' place. Most students enter the criminology course with very serious concerns about crime and their welfare in this society. They believe they have a stake in discussions of crime by virtue of their images, fears, experiences, perceived risks, outrage, and advocated policies regarding it. Given this, *Criminology: A Contemporary Handbook* employs as its theme the notion that crime must be understood as a "social problem." Social conditions become social problems when they are defined as such by significant numbers of people. The perception may not be accurate, but the concern it generates is real. The social construction of perceptions and fears—the sources of ideas about crime and its causes, the likelihood of victimization—is itself a complex problem for study. Equally complex is how people respond to perceptions and fears. Whether at the personal or governmental level, anticrime policies carry potentially costly consequences. The decision to place bars on one's window makes entrance more difficult, but exit becomes harder as well. Eliminating the exclusionary rule might make it easier to catch crooks (although research suggests it would not), but it also opens the door to greater levels of state intrusion in our lives. In this sense, the accuracy of the perceptions that inform such decisions obviously becomes important. The authors of the book's chapters were asked to address this problem—to link their themes to the larger issue of challenging readers' ideas about crime and to convey to them the complexity and, more often than not, the futility of most crime control efforts. This framework links the twenty-three chapters that constitute *Criminology: A Contemporary Handbook*.

Part One includes two chapters meant to encourage readers to think about crime in terms other than "good guy–bad guy." Chapter One reviews the content and sources of public notions of contemporary crime and punishment. Chapter Two examines the role of major interest groups in determining who and what come to be labeled criminal in this society and in shaping the content of our perceptions of crime as a social problem.

Part Two explores various dimensions of criminal activity, including a critical look in Chapter Three at the statistics we use to gain a sense of crime in America. Chapters Four and Five offer detailed analyses of four correlates of criminal activity: gender, age, race, and class. Chapter Six profiles victims of crime.

Part Three explores five types of crime, some of which the public knows well, others of which the public is relatively ignorant. Chapters Seven and Eight examine violent crime and property crime, respectively, and challenge readers' stereotypes of these most feared offenses. Chapter Nine covers vice crime—about which readers will be surprised how little they know. Chapter Ten, on organized crime, and Chapter Eleven, on white collar crime, both are designed to turn readers' attention away from street crime and toward other costly criminal endeavors more intimately intertwined with conventional business pursuits.

Part Four addresses a more traditional criminological concern: explaining criminal behavior. Chapter Twelve provides a critique of contemporary notions of biological links to offense behavior. Chapters Thirteen and Fourteen offer fresh looks at old causal themes—strain and subcultural theories and control and deterrence theories. Chapter Fifteen explores two relatively contemporary challenges to mainstream causal theorizing—the labeling and critical perspectives.

The final two parts of the book deal with crime control. Part Five studies the criminal justice system. The institution of policing is described in terms of its bare essentials in Chapter Sixteen, and the prosecution and sentencing elements of the court system are addressed in Chapter Seventeen. Correction within and without prison walls is investigated in Chapters Eighteen and Nineteen. And in Part Six, Chapters Twenty through Twenty-Four examine five contemporary, and highly controversial, crime control issues: drugs and crime, gun control, career offenders, civil liberties, and capital punishment.

The theme and format of *Criminology: A Contemporary Handbook* notwithstanding, the book is both comprehensive and flexible. No two instructors design their courses in precisely the same manner. Hence, I have tried to give users of this text many options. If instructors so choose, they can work through the several self-contained sections of the book in order. Or, given the number and diversity of chapters, instructors easily can adapt them to nearly any course outline.

ACKNOWLEDGMENTS

The people who have contributed chapters to this book obviously merit my sincere gratitude — not just for the written page but for teaching me so much. As well, Wadsworth Editor Serina Beauparlant's level of insight into the difficulties of editing a book like this remains a source of amazement. Angela Mann and Robert Fiske provided expert copyediting of a book with so many authors that one wonders how they did it. Special thanks to Stephen Feiler for bibliographic assistance and to Rhoda Carr and Victoria Brewer for indexing help. Finally, very helpful reviews of the book at various stages came from the following individuals: Robert G. Culbertson, Northwest Missouri State University; Martin Dosick, Springfield College; Travis Hirschi, University of Arizona; Eleanor M. Miller, University of Wisconsin; Daniel M. Schores, Austin College; and Harwin L. Voss, University of Kentucky.

ABOUT THE AUTHORS

◆

ROBERT AGNEW received the Ph.D. in sociology from the University of North Carolina. He is a member of the Department of Sociology at Emory University. His research interests focus on the causes of delinquency. He has published widely on this topic in such journals as *Social Problems*, *Journal of Quantitative Criminology*, *Journal of Marriage and the Family*, and *Social Forces*. At present, he is developing and testing several revisions of strain theory.

JAY S. ALBANESE is Chair of the Department of Political Science and Criminal Justice at Niagara University. He received the Ph.D. in criminal justice from Rutgers University. Among the seven books he has published are *Organized Crime in America* (Anderson Publishing), *Dealing with Delinquency* (Nelson-Hall), and *Crime in America* (with Robert Pursley; Prentice Hall). He has authored numerous articles on organized crime and other criminal justice topics in professional journals and edited volumes.

EMILIE ANDERSEN ALLAN received the Ph.D. in sociology from Pennsylvania State University and currently is a member of the Sociology faculty at Saint Francis College of Pennsylvania. Her research focuses on crime and the labor market, social costs and benefits of incarceration, and variations in criminal behavior across age, gender, and race categories. Her publications have appeared in *American Sociological Review*, *American Journal of Sociology*, and *Social Forces*.

ROBERT J. BURSIK, JR., is a faculty member in the Department of Sociology and Co-Director of the Center for the Study of Crime, Delinquency, and Social Control at the University of Oklahoma. His Ph.D. in sociology is from the University of Chicago. His research pertains primarily to testing aspects of social disorganization theory, and he is interested in the movement by which traditional theoretical paradigms, once thought contradictory, now are being integrated in criminology. He has published articles in *American Journal of Sociology*, *Social Forces*, *Criminology*, and many other professional journals.

GRAY CAVENDER is on the faculty of the School of Justice Studies at Arizona State University. He holds the Ph.D. in criminology from Florida State University and the J.D. from the University of Tennessee. In addition to his interest in criminological theory, he has focused his research on the media. His work-in-progress includes an analysis of media coverage and political language in the Iran/Contra affair. He has published widely in such journals as *Criminology* and *Sociological Quarterly*. He co-authored *Corporate Crime Under Attack: The Ford Pinto Case and Beyond* (Anderson Publishing).

WILLIAM J. CHAMBLISS, past President of the American Society of Criminology, has received the Lifetime Achievement Award of the American Sociological Association's Criminology Section and the Bruce Smith Sr. Award of the Academy of Criminal Justice Sciences. He holds the Ph.D. in sociology from the University of Indiana, and is a member of the Sociology faculty at George Washington University. He has published twelve books and numerous articles on the sociology of law and criminology, including *Law, Order, and Society* (Addison-Wesley) and *On the Take* (Indiana University Press).

TODD R. CLEAR is a member of the Criminal Justice faculty at Rutgers University, Graduate School of Criminal Justice. He received the Ph.D. in criminal justice from the State University of New York at Albany. He has won the Nelson A. Rockefeller Award from the State University of New York at Albany and the Cincinnati Award from the American Probation and Parole Association. Co-author of *Controlling the Offender in the Community* (Lexington Books), he has written numerous books and articles on correctional policy. He is currently continuing his work on classification systems in corrections.

JAMES W. COLEMAN earned the Ph.D. from the University of California, Santa Barbara, and is on the Sociology faculty at California Polytechnic Institute, San Luis Obispo. His principal research interests are white collar crime, the sociology of religion, and political economy. He has authored *The Criminal Elite: The Sociology of White Collar Crime* (St. Martin's Press) and has published numerous articles in such journals as *American Journal of Sociology* and *Social Problems*. He is presently at work on a study of Zen Buddhism in North America.

CYNTHIA S. GENTRY received the Ph.D. in sociology from Tulane University and is now a member of the Department of Sociology at Trinity University. She has focused her research on culture and crime, sexual harassment, and the relationship between pornography and levels of violence against women. She currently is investigating theoretical and measurement issues regarding community-level models of crime. Her written work has appeared in such journals as *Sociological Inquiry* and *Journal of Social Psychology*.

ANTHONY R. HARRIS is a member of the Department of Sociology at the University of Massachusetts at Amherst and holds the Ph.D. in sociology from Princeton University. He has been Invited Fellow, Netherlands Institute for Advanced Studies, and Visiting Scholar, Harvard University. His research has focused on the empirical and theoretical links between crime and the major demographic correlates of self-identity, including gender and race. His articles have appeared in *American Sociological Review*, *Social Science Quarterly*, and *Social Problems*.

SUSAN N. HERMAN is on the faculty of Brooklyn Law School, where she teaches courses in criminal law, constitutional procedure, and constitutional law. She received the J.D. from New York University. She is a member of the National Board of Directors of the American Civil Liberties Union and Reporter for the Criminal Procedure Committee of the United States District Court for the Eastern District of New York. She has published extensively in the area of criminal justice and the Supreme Court.

JAMES INVERARITY is a member of the Department of Sociology at Western Washington University. His professional writing has appeared in numerous journals. He has co-authored *Law and Society* (Little, Brown) and most recently has published several papers on the linkages between labor markets and imprisonment in the United States.

ANDREW A. KARMEN received the Ph.D. in sociology from Columbia University. He is now a member of the Department of Sociology at John Jay College of Criminal Justice of the City University of New York. He is author of *Crime Victims: An Introduction to Victimology* (Brooks/Cole) and co-editor of *Deviants: Victims or Victimizers?* (Sage). In addition, he has written articles and chapters on research taboos, news media ethics, the Rosenberg spy case, agent provocateurs, use of deadly force by police, and vigilantism.

JANET KATZ received the Ph.D. in criminal justice from the State University of New York at Albany. She is currently chair of the Department of Sociology and Criminal Justice at Old Dominion University. Her research interests lie in the areas of biology and crime and women and crime. She co-edited *Biology, Crime and Ethics* (Anderson Publishing) and has published papers on attitude-behavior inconsistency and on the eugenics movement in such journals as *Contemporary Crises* and *Applied Social Psychology*.

MARVIN D. KROHN is chair of the Department of Sociology at the State University of New York at Albany. He received the Ph.D. in criminology from Florida State University. His research has focused primarily on the causes of adolescent substance abuse and juvenile delinquency. Recently, he has been developing a social network theory of delinquency that integrates aspects of social control and differential association theories. He has authored or co-authored numerous books and articles, including *Delinquent Behavior* (Prentice-Hall) and *Theoretical Integration in the Study of Deviance and Crime* (SUNY Press).

HENRY R. LESIEUR holds the Ph.D. in sociology from the University of Massachusetts at Amherst. Presently, he is chair of the Department of Criminal Justice Sciences at Illinois State University. Author of *The Chase: Career of the Compulsive Gambler* (Schenkman), he is editor of *Journal of Gambling Studies* and has written many articles and book chapters on crime and pathological gambling. His current research centers on gambling and addictions. He has published in such journals as *Social Problems* and *The British Journal of Addictions*.

STEPHEN D. MASTROFSKI earned the Ph.D. at the University of North Carolina. He is a member of the Department of Administration of Justice at the Pennsylvania State University and a Visiting Fellow at the National Institute of Justice. Currently conducting an observational study of police patrol officers in a community policing context, he has published on a variety of topics regarding police organizations, behavior, performance, and reform. His work has appeared in such outlets as *Law and Society Review*, *Justice Quarterly*, and *Journal of Research in Crime and Delinquency*.

LISA R. MEIDLINGER is a Ph.D. candidate in Sociology at the University of Massachusetts at Amherst. Her research interests lie in the area of delinquency and social psychology, specifically, the processes of identity formation in adolescents. She is currently studying the reporting and documentation of sexual assault on college campuses.

MARTHA A. MYERS won the Outstanding Scholarship Award from the Crime and Delinquency Division of the Society for the Study of Social Problems for her co-authored book *The Social Contexts of Criminal Sentencing*. She holds the Ph.D. from Indiana University and is a member of the Sociology faculty at the University of Georgia. Her published work has appeared in such journals as *Criminology*, *Social Forces*, and *Law and Society Review*. Her most recent research explores the relationship between social structure and punishment in the postbellum South.

ROBERT M. O'BRIEN is head of the Department of Sociology at the University of Oregon. He received the Ph.D. in sociology from the University of Wisconsin. He publishes in the area of criminology, measurement, and stratification. He has authored *Crime and Victimization Data* (Sage) and co-authored *Urban Structure and Victimization* (with David Decker and David Shichor). Much of his recent work in criminology examines the relationship between macrostructural variables and crime rates.

ROBERT NASH PARKER holds the Ph.D. in sociology from Duke University and is a Senior Research Scientist and Study Director at the Prevention Research Center in Berkeley, California. His published work has appeared in such journals as *American Journal of Sociology*, *Social Forces*, and *Journal of Quantitative Criminology*. His current research interests focus on the relationship between violent crime victimization risk and alcohol-related behavior. He is the author of the forthcoming book, *Alcohol and Homicide: A Deadly Mix of Two American Traditions* (SUNY Press).

JOSEPH F. SHELEY is a faculty member of the Department of Sociology at Tulane University. He received the Ph.D. in sociology from the University of Mass-achusetts. He is the author of *Understanding Crime* (Wadsworth), *America's "Crime Problem"* (Wadsworth), and numerous articles in such journals as *American Sociological Review*, *Social Problems*, *Social Forces*, and *American Journal of Public Health*. His research interests center on criminal justice and law, control theories of deviance, and the relationship between normative beliefs and criminal behavior. At present, he is studying patterns of firearms acquisition and use by juveniles.

NEAL SHOVER holds the Ph.D. in sociology from the University of Illinois and is a member of the Sociology faculty at the University of Tennessee. His major research interests lie in corporate crime and the social psychology of criminal careers. He has authored or co-authored four books and has published numerous articles and chapters in professional books and journals. His *Great Pretenders*, an analysis of the pursuits and careers of persistent thieves, will be published by Westview Press in 1994.

M. DWAYNE SMITH is chair of the Department of Sociology at Tulane University. He received the Ph.D. in sociology from Duke University. His primary research interest is in social-structural influences on violent crime. He has authored articles on this general topic in such journals as *American Sociological Review*, *American Journal of Sociology*, and *Social Forces*. His research on discriminatory patterns of death sentencing in Louisiana was published in *Journal of Criminal Justice*. He is now at work on a study of differential urban homicide rates.

DARRELL STEFFENSMEIER, a member of the Sociology faculty at Pennsylvania State University, received the Ph.D. in sociology from the University of Iowa. He has published widely concerning the relationship between gender and crime and between age and crime. His work on these topics has appeared in such journals as *American Sociological Review*, *American Journal of Sociology*, and *Social Forces*. On the basis of his book on trade in stolen property, *The Fence: In the Shadow of Two Worlds* (Rowman & Littlefield), he was given the 1987 Award for Outstanding Scholarship by the Crime and Delinquency Division of the Society for the Study of Social Problems.

CHRISTY A. VISHER received the Ph.D. in sociology from Indiana University. She is now Senior Research Associate at the National Institute of Justice, where she conducts research on issues related to criminal justice policy. Interested primarily in the area of drugs and criminal careers, she has also published widely on such aspects of the criminal justice system as the arrest process, jurors' decisions in criminal trials, incapacitation, and drug testing. Her work has appeared in such journals as *Criminology, Social Problems,* and *American Sociological Review.*

MARK WARR is a faculty member in the Department of Sociology at the University of Texas at Austin. He obtained the Ph.D. in sociology from the University of Arizona. His research interests include deterrence, rape, and opportunity theories of crime. He has written extensively on public perceptions of and reactions to crime and, particularly, on fear of crime. His articles have appeared in such journals as *Social Forces, Criminology,* and *Social Problems.*

MICHAEL WELCH received the Ph.D. in sociology from the University of North Texas. Presently, he is on the faculty of the Administration of Justice at Rutgers University. He has focused his research on corrections, deviance, and social control. He has published book chapters and articles in such journals as *American Journal of Criminal Justice* and *Journal of Crime and Justice.* He is also author of *Corrections: A Critical Approach* (McGraw-Hill).

JAMES D. WRIGHT holds the Ph.D. in sociology from the University of Wisconsin. He is now the Charles A. and Leo M. Favrot Professor of Human Relations in the Department of Sociology at Tulane University. Among his twelve books are two dealing with firearms ownership and gun control issues: *Under the Gun* (Aldine) and *Armed and Considered Dangerous* (Aldine). A recent book, *Homelessness and Health* (McGraw-Hill), was selected for commendation by the National Press Club. He has published articles in such journals as *Science, American Sociological Review,* and *Social Problems.*

- The Study of Crime
- Sociological Interests
- Issues for Study
- Basic Concepts
- Substantive Law
  Self-Defense
  Insanity
  Age

- Procedural Law
- Contemporary Criminology

A Brief
Introduction to
Criminology

THE STUDY OF CRIME

First-time readers of a book about criminology often are surprised at how little the text contains about cops and robbers and about criminal modus operandi. Instead, in one or another fashion, the book is about the larger social contexts shaping every facet of the issue of crime — law, criminal behavior, the organization of criminal justice, correction of offenders. More formally, *criminology is the scientific study of crime as a social phenomenon* (as opposed, for example, to a legal or forensic phenomenon). That is, crime is a matter of sociological interest because it is defined within a social arena, it violates social rules, and it draws a social response. A criminal act is a social, though generally not sociable, act occurring in a social setting and implicated in a society's cultural and structural framework.

The claim to scientist sets the criminologist apart from others — journalists and social commentators, for example — who think and write about crime. Criminologists employ the scientific method in their work: testable hypotheses, rigorous and replicable forms of direct observation of the empirical world, and care to the control of biases in the formation and interpretation of the outcomes of a study. The discipline seeks to establish a general, verified body of knowledge about the social aspects of crime, its definition, and responses to it.

SOCIOLOGICAL INTERESTS

Criminologists usually are sociologists though their ranks include economists, historians, psychologists, and others. Criminal behavior is central to the most basic of sociological problems, that of order and disorder. The sociologist is concerned with the collective aspects of human life, how one collective aspect (rapid social change, for example) influences another (suicide rates, for example).

In a more social psychological vein, the sociologist seeks to know how societal conditions influence individuals so that they engage in behaviors that produce societal rates of behavior — how poverty influences individuals' perceptions of the world to the extent that they contribute to the society's crime rate or how level of racial integration influences the extent of white citizens' pressure on police to combat crime, for instance.

These interests translate into general questions about order and disorder: What is social order? How is order created? How is it maintained and to whose benefit? What spells the difference between orderly social change and collapse into disorder?

The study of criminal behavior springs directly from these questions. Some sociologists have viewed crime as a sign of a weakened or socially disorganized society. Others have noted that, paradoxically, criminal behavior in tolerable amounts may serve to strengthen the existing social order or specific groups' hold over it. Others have studied crime as the vehicle toward understanding societal members' assumptions about order, the assumptions on which those members base decisions that contribute to everyday order and disorder. Finally, some sociologists have viewed social order as the socially constructed result of competition and conflict among various groups in society. Crime thus is understood as endangering the interests of some groups while promoting the interests of others.

ISSUES FOR STUDY

Within this framework, criminologists study these more specific issues:

1. *The creation and use of laws.* Criminology is concerned in part with the development of laws, the roles of law in a society, law as an instrument of social change, and the functions of legislation and law enforcement for interest groups within a society.

2. *Patterns of crime.* Some criminologists study patterns of crime for a society or community at a given point in time and over various periods. This area of criminology involves the study of trends and the impact of crime on a population. It examines as well the way criminal behavior is distributed among us — by gender, age, race, and so forth.

3. *Causes of crime and criminality.* Criminologists also study the conditions affecting societal crime rates and the causes of individual and group involvement in crime. This study of causes also attempts to identify distinctive types of criminal careers and their development. Traditionally, a major goal of causal analysis has been the formulation of strategies for crime prevention.

4. *The societal reaction to crime.* Criminological theory and research focus on the forces influencing a society's definitions of certain behaviors as criminal, the ways in which a society reacts to individuals and their acts, the process by which individuals come to be called criminals, and individuals' reactions to society's definition of them.

5. *Criminal justice administration.* Many criminologists are interested in the criminal justice system and its organizational and bureaucratic processes, the police and the legal profession as occupational categories, and the criminal justice system as the primary producer of a community's criminal population and crime rates.

6. *Custody, punishment, and rehabilitation of criminals.* A final branch of criminology is the study of society's methods of dealing with criminals. Most research in this area is designed to evaluate the success and deterrent effects of correctional programs, from the point of view of both the public and the individual offender. Much of this research concerning prisons and other correctional agencies also is used in developing theories of bureaucracy.

BASIC CONCEPTS

Throughout this book, and certainly in the discussions it provokes, a number of terms will appear that require brief definition and conceptualization. Among these terms is *social control*, the subordination of individual interests to those of a collectivity. Stated more practically, social control involves convincing or coercing individuals to align their behavior with the *norms*, or rules, of a group. In relatively small homogeneous societies, norms are nearly universally shared, and norm violation, or *deviance*, offends the larger group to which the individual belongs. In the larger heterogeneous society, social control may also take the form of bringing the individual's behavior into line with what are nearly universally shared ideas about right and wrong; murder is an act that generally is not tolerated by the vast majority of the larger society's members. Yet, social control in the larger society also may take the form of one group's domination of an individual or another group in ways that maintain or enhance the interests of the coercive faction but are detrimental to those of the coerced faction.

Social control is accomplished primarily through *socialization*, the process by which individuals come to internalize, or form a commitment to, the values, customs, and norms of the collectivity. Collectivities apply or threaten to apply *sanctions*, or punishments, to individuals who deviate from societal or dominant group norms. The application of sanctions often has as its goal *justice* by which the collective sentiment is "set right" in knowing that a deviant has been made to suffer, at the hands of the collectivity and in terms of some generally agreed-on standard, a penalty for the norm violation. The application of a sanction is sometimes aimed at *specific deterrence* by which offending individuals are convinced not to repeat their deviant behavior. Finally, sanctions are sometimes applied or threatened to accomplish a measure of *general deterrence*, that is, to convince those who have not yet violated a norm to forego the temptation to do so.

In all societies, socialization remains the primary mechanism by which to achieve social control; reliance on sanction seems to increase in importance as societies grow larger and more diversified—and, thus, as the socialization process loses its uniformity of application.

In some societies, especially in larger ones, many norms are made highly explicit and come to be enforced by the state as *laws*. Laws generally proscribe behavior; they specify acts that individuals are forbidden to do. They also generally list the sanctions that accompany law violations. Pertinent to our present interests, we distinguish *civil* from *criminal* law. The former primarily concerns disputes between parties (individual versus individual, individual versus group, group versus group), one or both of whom claim to have been wronged by the other to the extent that a loss is demonstrable. A divorce action is an example of a civil law case, as is the suit brought by the residents of a neighborhood against their city for failure to enforce environmental codes. In civil law, the court is essentially a referee whose task it is to settle the dispute in the manner fairest to both parties.

Criminal law pits the individual charged with a law violation against the state. That is, though an individual may have suffered at the hands of another, criminal law treats the violation as an affront to the collectivity; by his or her actions, the offender has threatened the stability and the welfare of the people. Alleged offenders are tried in court by and in behalf of the state; those found guilty are punished by and in behalf of the state. Much stricter rules of evidence are employed in criminal courts. In criminal court proceedings, guilt must reflect the judgment that there is no reasonable doubt that the defendant violated the law in question; in civil court proceedings, a decision favoring one party over another need reflect only a "preponderance of evidence."

SUBSTANTIVE LAW

Criminal law takes two forms, one clearly recognized by most people, the other less so. The better known form is *substantive law*. Substantive law defines acts that members of this society may not perform, for example, assault, possession of heroin, corporate price fixing. Substantive law also includes descriptions of the specific range of penalties for violation of any given statute. Violations of criminal statutes are classified as *felonies* or *misdemeanors*. The former are considered more serious and include such acts as homicide and burglary. The latter, less serious, include acts such as soliciting for prostitution and disorderly conduct.

In determining guilt or innocence, criminal law burdens the state, rather than the accused, with the obligation to demonstrate that the accused indeed violated substantive law and that he or she possessed *mens rea* — a "guilty mind" — or, in other words, *intended* to break the law. Practically speaking, in the vast majority of cases, proof that the individual violated the law carries with it the assumption of intent. Yet, it is possible to violate a law without intent, and the courts recognize this. Children who have not yet attained the age of reason cannot commit a crime in the legal sense because they cannot appreciate the consequences of their own behavior; senile persons cannot commit crimes for the same reason. If one is physically coerced to violate the law or injures another in self-defense, one is not a criminal, for criminal intent is lacking. Accidents and mistakes cannot be crimes, for intent is not present (though we are responsible for the foreseeable consequences of our actions, such as accidents resulting from speeding). Finally, legal insanity can relieve one of the responsibility for a criminal act. Three of these factors—self-defense, insanity, and age—have received considerable public attention in recent years.

SELF-DEFENSE

To claim self-defense successfully, the defendant must show that, in terms of any reasonable person's perception of the situation, there was no avenue by which to avoid injuring another individual. If one could have avoided the danger by flight (if that could have been accomplished safely) or by calling the police, for example, then self-defense claims do not apply. What's more, the amount of force used to defend oneself must not exceed that necessary to prevent the threatened harm. Nor can one defend property with deadly force if the situation does not also include the threat of personal harm.

With this in mind, we begin to understand the controversy surrounding the 1984 New York subway shootings by Bernard Goetz of four teenagers attempting to rob him—after the robbers already had been downed by Goetz. The case against Goetz hinged on the jury's perception that such force was necessary because he reasonably felt himself in danger of being the victim of a violent felony. We also begin to understand the controversy surrounding the many recent cases in which women have shot or otherwise injured abusive husbands while they were sleeping. With differing degrees of success, the defendants in such cases have argued that, over long periods, they *had* attempted to avoid such lethal action by running away and by seeking criminal justice intervention; it was only in the face of the failure of such attempts at avoidance and in the face of threats by their husbands to hunt them down should they flee, that such planned violence became necessary.

INSANITY

The same level of controversy has attached to the plea of legal insanity, especially following John Hinckley's successful use of the plea after he shot President Reagan in 1982. At issue always is the fear that criminals "fake" insanity and are set "scot-free" by gullible juries. Let us look at this complex problem.

Insanity is a legal, not a medical, concept. It means in simplest terms that a person could not avoid committing the crime in question because he or she had a mental defect. Exactly how insanity is defined in court trials varies by court system. About a third of the states utilize a formula based on the *M'Naghten Rule*, a definition of insanity established in England in 1843 during a murder trial. In essence, the M'Naghten rule states that a person is legally insane if he or she could not understand the nature and quality of the act in question or could not understand that the act was wrong at the time it was committed. Over the years, some states have added an "irresistable impulse" rule whereby criminal responsibility is negated if the person who committed the act can demonstrate that he or she was unable to control an impulse to act in a manner he or she knew was illegal. The M'Naghten rule is known as the *prosecutor's rule* since it is extremely difficult for a defendant to demonstrate insanity under its terms.

The 1940s and 1950s witnessed a growing national respect for psychiatry and with it some doubts about the fairness of M'Naghten-type formulas. These formulas cannot accommodate the person who can distinguish right from wrong and is not acting under impulse, but who is somehow emotionally compelled to violate a law. The mad bomber who cannot help himself, or a "Son of Sam" who is driven to kill for years, even though knowing that killing is wrong, serve as examples. Thus, in 1954, a judge for the U.S. Court of Appeals in the District of Columbia handed down the *Durham formula* whereby persons may be found insane if their criminal act is a product of a mental disease or defect. Knowing right from wrong and acting impulsively are not necessary elements within this formula.

Only one state actually utilizes the Durham formula now. About half the states have adopted a formula called the *Substantial Capacity Test* proposed in 1955 by the American Law Institute. Under this proposal, criminal responsibility is negated if, because of mental defect or disease, persons cannot appreciate the nature of their criminal behavior or cannot act in accord with the law. Mental defect or disease must be demonstrated independent of the criminal act. This formula rule is known as a *defendant's rule* because critics argue that it is too easily employed in the defendant's behalf. The rule makes the state's case more difficult. Defendants can attempt to link their crimes to more nebulous mental problems. Prosecutors find such pleas harder to rebut "beyond a reasonable doubt." Where once psychiatrists simply could state whether, in their opinions, a defendant could distinguish right from wrong, psychiatrists now deal in far fuzzier diagnoses of mental defect and even fuzzier links to criminal behavior. Defense attorneys may call several psychiatrists to establish insanity. Because psychiatry is a highly inexact science marked by disagreement among its practitioners, the prosecution can find an equal number of psychiatrists to contradict those employed by the defense. The jury, a group of lay persons, is left to decide which of these experts is correct.

A number of solutions have been offered to remedy the problems associated with insanity pleas. Some states have eliminated the plea altogether; others allow the jury to return a verdict of "guilty but insane." Others allow the defendant to enter a plea of "diminished capacity" (the inability fully to premeditate the offense) and be found guilty of a lesser offense. Most critics simply call for a return to the narrower M'Naghten rule. In fact, insanity is a rarely employed plea under any formula for its determination; the majority of those using it are charged with lesser offenses, and most do not use the plea successfully (Maeder, 1985). Choice of formula for the few cases using the plea must rest with one's priorities: a legal net so tight that it catches all who enter it, both guilty and not guilty, or a net so loose that some guilty escape along with those who are not guilty.

AGE

The notion that age of the person violating the law mitigates intent is at the heart of this country's decision to separate adult and juvenile court systems. Although different states employ different ages by which to designate juveniles (generally sixteen through nineteen years), all consider juveniles unable to appreciate the consequences of their acts in the same manner that adults appreciate them. With rare exceptions (most states permit the prosecution of juveniles as adults for selected offenses), children who break the law are not considered criminals but, instead, as persons in need of protection and treatment. Juvenile court proceedings are usually informal and conducted behind closed doors though juveniles generally have the same rights as do adults (save the right to a jury trial). Juveniles involved in such legal proceedings cannot be identified to the press. Juvenile offenders technically are not punished but, again technically, are placed in rehabilitative situations; these include the youth's family so far as possible. When juveniles reach the age of majority, their juvenile court records are sealed and cannot be used in criminal court proceedings.

The juvenile justice system has become controversial as the public increasingly perceives juveniles as responsible for highly serious, assaultive acts. Many believe that the juvenile's awareness that he or she likely will not be punished for an act and that a new lease on legal life will begin at the age of majority translates to the relative freedom to commit acts for which adults would be punished severely. In fact, many argue that increases in crime in the past few decades in large part are attributable to government's failure to "get tough" with juveniles. Yet, most states continue to adhere to traditional juvenile justice philosophy, separating juvenile from adult cases though the use of criminal courts to deal with especially serious juvenile offenders is increasingly common.

PROCEDURAL LAW

The form of criminal law less known to the public is *procedural law*, which governs actions of state officials in dealing with persons suspected or found guilty of criminal acts. This kind of law covers such phenomena as searches and arrests, the right to a fair and speedy trial, the right to counsel, admissibility of evidence, and the right to appeal. Through television crime shows, most people are familiar with at least one procedural law, the *Miranda rule*, whereby police must inform suspects of their legal rights at the time of the arrest.

There is an inherent tension between substantive and procedural law. Substantive law strives for order (the absence of crime) through control of the population. It is prevented from doing so completely by procedural law, or the rule of law, which traditionally in the United States has been placed above the enforcement of substantive law. Hence, total order is beyond reach, and perhaps the popular phrase "law and order" should read, "law and a degree of disorder." We cannot presently have both total enforcement of substantive law and full protection of individual rights. Currently procedural law takes precedence, and until detection, prevention, and prosecution techniques are developed that work without violating individual rights, or until our priorities change, some apparent criminals indeed will go unpunished.

Because laws, both substantive and procedural, are essentially social definitions of, or meanings given to, certain activities, they always are changeable. What currently is not considered a right later may be defined as such. In addition, many laws are not written clearly and therefore constantly are open to changes in interpretation. Thus, rights may be affirmed totally (no restrictions), liberally affirmed (limited restrictions), conservatively affirmed (major restrictions), or abolished. Many now view crime as uncontrollable and define procedural laws as "technicalities" that give criminals the freedom to violate the law without fear of punishment. Others argue that procedural law is all that hinders the creation of a police state, a specter more dangerous than crime as we know it now.

The tension between substantive and procedural law in many ways is the stuff of a contemporary criminology. For it brings to the fore matters like the importance of freedom from state dominance as well as from the predations of fellow citizens. More sociologically, this is the heart of the issue of social control in the larger society. More pragmatically, it is a point of entry for criminology's input into crime-control policy. No matter how seemingly academic the criminologist's subject for study, it likely is at least indirectly implicated in both sociological and pragmatic aspects of social control.

CONTEMPORARY CRIMINOLOGY

Apart from rough agreement concerning the basic concepts just discussed, there seems to be little consensus among criminologists about what members of their discipline should be doing today. Indeed, there seem to be nearly as many definitions of *contemporary criminology* as there are criminologists. Some decry the loss of traditional theoretical orientation among criminologists today—the lack of more than superficial attention to Durkheim and Simmel, for example. Others argue that quantitative research fails to capture the essence of criminal and social control endeavors. How, for instance, can the study of crime and unemployment rates tell us anything about the meaning of either issue for the person violating the law? Still others view both these matters as distractions from the applied research that criminologists "should be doing." What is the need for theory, they ask, when meaningful criminological contributions involve practical answers to today's street crime problem? Sociobiologists implore colleagues to become more interdisciplinary and to recognize the potential role of biological factors in the etiology of criminal behavior. More Marxian criminologists argue that all these issues camouflage the conflicting class interests that underpin all social problems.

This book does not try to resolve these debates (it could never do so). Nor does it seek to be all things to all readers by trying to address every possible issue. Rather, it defines *contemporary criminology* broadly: a criminology that tempers tradition with current dues-paying. Criminology is not just a technical discipline that addresses today's criminal justice issues and will reshape itself when tomorrow's criminal justice issues weigh on us. Yet, it is also not what it was two or five or ten decades ago. Theoretical issues that informed the discipline early in this century (for example, criminological themes in social disorganization theory) should inform it still—but should not constitute all it does. Recent sociobiological and Marxian issues cannot be ignored; nor are they sufficiently articulated by their adherents that we can exclude all else from discussion. Contemporary criminologists should seek to make contributions to criminal justice policy issues (though we may dispute what constitutes a contribution) within some traditional criminological framework (from among many).

In what manner, then, is this book contemporary? First, it seeks a theme that integrates academic criminology with contemporary social concerns about crime. The chapters are structured so that they address the worries of the average reader—a student in a criminology or criminal justice course. Most people reading this book are neither perpetrators nor victims of serious crime. However, like most members of our society, they exhibit a great deal of fear of "street crimes," both attitudinally and behaviorally. Most make personal anticrime decisions that are conceivably problematic—to keep a gun in the house and risk an accidental shooting, for example. Equally important, fear of crime leads to demands for law and order, encouragement of legislation and criminal justice system efforts to curb crime through restraints on individual rights, and approval of tax spending for anticrime research and programs. Because all these carry potentially serious costs, we owe it to ourselves to formulate as accurate a picture of crime as possible before supporting various anticrime measures. The authors of the chapters in this book were asked to write them in a manner that addresses the average citizen's concerns and (mis)conceptions about crime—to challenge the reader's stereotypes of victim profiles or to review the evidence that bears on the reader's beliefs about the deterrent effect of the death penalty, for example.

Second, although the book addresses the contemporary reader's concerns about crime, it provides a sense of what criminology is about more generally. There is, for instance, a considerable amount of theory in this book, not only in the theory chapters of Part Four, but in most other chapters as well—all aimed at showing readers that theory is not irrelevant to their fears of crime. The discussions of violent and property crimes introduce the reader to "routine activities" theory. The chapter on gender and crime relies considerably on social control theory. The themes that are covered are not traditional in all instances. The reader is introduced to Marxian criminological thought and to the current controversy over biological explanations of criminal behavior in various chapters, for example. Nor have the authors focused solely on crimes of traditional interest, that is, street crimes. Chapters address vice crime, organized crime, and white collar crime, again with an eye to challenging the reader's taken-for-granted ideas about these activities and their importance as social problems.

Finally, as we noted, criminologists should pay their dues. This means moving beyond the academic side of criminological questions and addressing aspects of contemporary anticrime policy. As public concern about crime has grown, public patience with searches for long-range solutions to the problem of crime has worn thin. Shifting with public sentiment in recent years (and spurred in the 1970s by the availability of government and private foundation grants—money that all but disappeared in the 1980s), criminologists now are more willing to address more contemporary crime questions, with an eye to more immediate crime control strategies, than was once the case. Research of this type attempts to identify or conceptualize crime issues better, to map strategies to combat crime, and to evaluate the costs and the effects of the strategies. It assumes that criminologists can, and should, make immediate, significant contributions to the solution of crime without becoming mere technicians for hire by policy planners.

Most chapters in this book discuss policy issues—the potential for controlling violent or white collar crime, for example. Most point out the complexity of the problems we face and the attendant difficulty in combating them. The chapters on the elements of the criminal justice system (Part Five) are especially important in this regard. They make clear in short order that the system is not a simple reactive machine that needs only to be geared better to catch and punish offenders. The message in all these chapters is one of system frustration at having underconceptualized the crime problem and having failed to deliver in terms of controlling it. The five chapters that conclude the book exemplify good, policy-oriented research that is not simply technical work. Each takes on a major contemporary crime control issue (drugs and crime, gun control, due process, selective incapacitation, capital punishment) and dissects it in a manner that permits readers to make the informed choices they should be making—exactly the goal of this book.

DISCUSSION QUESTIONS

1. Define criminology and describe the issues on which criminologists characteristically focus their attention. With these in mind, in what ways is the study of crime *sociological*?

2. Discuss the concept of social control. With what mechanisms is social control generally accomplished within a society?

3. Distinguish criminal from civil law and substantive from procedural law. Include in the description of substantive law the factors that negate criminal liability for an act. In what ways are procedural and substantive law related, and what bearing does the relationship have on the public's interest in "law and order"?

PART ONE

STRUCTURING VIEWS OF CRIME

Public opinion polls consistently indicate that most Americans believe our society has a crime problem of very serious proportions. The majority of those expressing such sentiments have not themselves been victims of violent crimes, but nevertheless have come to consider such crimes rampant. This perception of crime as a social problem is the product of various bits of information the individual receives from others—some from relatives and friends, most from more impersonal sources. Our commonly held beliefs about crime are based on what we are told by groups trying to influence legislation, by political office seekers, by the media, and by those who publish official crime statistics.

In this sense, our notion of crime is socially constructed. No matter how many crimes actually are committed in our society, our beliefs about crime generally are structured by the information we receive about it. In Part One, we explore this phenomenon from two angles. First, we examine the many aspects of people's perceptions of and opinions about crime in this society. Second, we explore the many interests behind crime legislation and law enforcement—the defining of the types of acts that come to be called "criminal."

In Chapter 1, "Public Perceptions of Crime and Punishment," Mark Warr analyzes the public's sources of information about crime and the effects of views of crime on citizens' lives. Warr examines many seeming contradictions regarding crime victimization and fear. He looks to sensitivity to risk and to perceived seriousness of various types of crime to explain such contradictions. Warr extends his analysis by studying public conceptions of appropriate punishment for crime. He finds that desired levels of punishment are structured by more than one "theory" of punishment. He also finds that Americans inaccurately perceive the penalties currently assigned to various crimes and examines potential problems in linking actual punishment to public notions of what punishment should be. The latter half of Warr's chapter investigates media coverage of crime. He documents the media's distortion of the overall picture of crime in this society and the ways in which that distortion occurs. Most important, he emphasizes the link between distortions and misperceptions and the "politics of crime."

The political nature with which Warr concludes his chapter leads into Chapter 2, "Crime, Law, and Social Conflict," by Joseph Sheley. Sheley explores criminal status as a definitional problem through discussion of interest groups, ruling classes, and definitions of crime. The vehicle that binds the elements of this discussion together is the conflict perspective. Sheley begins by introducing the more traditional consensus framework by which definitions of crime are viewed as reflections of underlying social values concerning right and wrong. He notes that the consensus model encounters problems addressing the issues of legislation and enforcement in the larger, more heterogeneous society. In shifting to a conflict model, by which definitions of crime are viewed as reflections of power groups trying to enhance their economic and other interests, the complexity and the political nature of "crime problems" in societies like ours is better appreciated. Three themes are emphasized: (1) the relativity of criminal definitions, (2) the control of major social institutions as a factor in determining criminal definitions, and (3) the status of law as an instrument of power. The issue ultimately pondered is the shape of the interests behind law and much of our notion of crime in this society. Are legislation and law enforcement structured by elite powerful groups in this society or by a plurality of interest groups? What role do state agents play in defining who and what are called criminal in this society?

In conclusion, Part One suggests that our "crime problem" is no simple issue. It is not just the sum total of bad guys attacking good people and of law responding to these attacks. Instead, it reflects an ongoing social structuring of a picture of life in America by various parties.

CHAPTER 1

◆

PUBLIC PERCEPTIONS OF CRIME AND PUNISHMENT

Mark Warr
University of Texas at Austin

CRIME IS A PHENOMENON that Americans routinely hear about, read about, talk about, and, particularly through the medium of television, watch. Consider the sources of information on crime that an average citizen may encounter on any given day. When the television set is turned on, reports of crime are likely to appear on the local or national news. Prime-time television presents a variety of crime or "cop" shows. Bookstores frequently offer crime-related books among the bestsellers and devote entire sections of the store to crime fiction. Movies that are rented or viewed in a theater stand a good chance of having a crime-related plot. Newspapers and radio, like television, devote considerable space and time to reports of crime. The topic of crime is even likely to find its way into our daily conversations (Skogan and Maxfield, 1981).

Even though they are exposed to an abundance of communications about crime, most Americans will not become victims of serious personal crimes like murder, rape, or robbery (see Chapter 6). Consequently, most of the information that people acquire about crime is based, not on direct experience with crime (that is, as victims), but rather on indirect or vicarious information that they acquire from the mass media or through social networks. Such information, however, may be far from accurate, as we will see later. Although false information may be of little consequence in some domains of life, false information about crime can be dangerous (when people fail to take necessary precautions) or tragic (when people needlessly limit their lives due to fear).

All the topics that we will consider in this chapter fall within a general area of theory and research that is most properly called the social psychology of crime and punishment. This area focuses on the beliefs and attitudes of a population as they pertain to crime and punishment, and the reactions that these beliefs and attitudes evoke. Among other topics, we examine such issues as fear of crime, the media and crime, and public opinion on crime and punishment.

THE FEAR OF CRIME

When we think of the consequences that crime has for individuals, we normally focus on the physical, emotional, and financial damage that victims suffer during or following the commission of a crime. Yet, crime has consequences not only for victims but also for the large majority of individuals who have never themselves been victims of truly serious crime. The reason is that the prospect of becoming a victim can produce intense fear in people, and fear of crime is capable of shaping individuals' lifestyles and habits. Indeed, fear of crime must be understood as one of the broadest social consequences of crime because the number of fearful individuals at any one point in time greatly exceeds the number of actual victims. That is, fear may affect a large portion of a population even when crime does not.

Fear of criminal victimization is quite prevalent in the United States. According to the General Social Survey (National Opinion Research Center, 1991), a national survey conducted annually in the United States, 43 percent of Americans surveyed in 1991 answered affirmatively to the question, "Is there anywhere near your home—that is, within a mile—where you would be afraid to walk alone at night?" In a survey of American cities conducted as part of the National Crime Victimization Survey (an annual victimization survey conducted in the United States), 46 percent of respondents reported they had limited or changed their activities because of crime, and only 55 percent said they felt very safe or reasonably safe about being out alone at night (Hindelang et al., 1978). One investigation (Warr, 1985) found that fear of one particular crime—rape—is remarkably common among younger women. In a survey of Seattle residents, women were asked to indicate how afraid they were in their everyday life of being raped, using a scale ranging from 0 (not afraid at all) to 10 (very afraid). Among women ages 19–35, two-thirds scored above 5 on the scale, and a startling 31 percent scored a 10.

AGE, SEX, AND FEAR

One of the most distinctive features of fear of victimization is that it is not uniformly distributed in the population, but rather is strongly related to age and sex. In general, the young are less fearful than the old, and males less fearful than females. At first glance, this pattern might seem to reflect the actual probabilities of victimization. That is, females and the elderly could be more afraid simply because they are more likely to be victims of crime than are males and the young. In fact, as we indicate in Chapter 6, exactly the opposite is true. Although they have the greatest fear, females and the elderly are actually at substantially lower risk of victimization for most crimes than are males and the young (see, for example, Stafford and Galle, 1984).

How, then, can we explain the greater fear of females and older individuals? One major reason is that females and the elderly exhibit substantially greater *sensitivity to risk*. In other words, when exposed to the same risk of victimization, females are more afraid than males, and older persons are more afraid than the young. Why? Apparently, women and the elderly perceive crime quite differently than do males and the young. Specifically, among women and older individuals, different crimes are subjectively linked in a way that is not true for males and the young. For example, a substantial correlation exists between fear of burglary and fear of murder among women, suggesting that for them, murder is viewed as a likely outcome of burglary. Among men, however, the correlation is much lower, suggesting that for men, the two crimes are not cognitively linked. In the same way, a strong correlation exists between fear of "being approached by a beggar" and fear of robbery among women, but not men. These sorts of subjective linkages between different types of crimes (referred to as perceptually contemporaneous offenses) appear more frequently and more strongly among women and the elderly. The implication is that many situations that appear relatively innocuous to men and young persons are likely to be viewed as much more dangerous by women and the elderly because of the offenses they portend (Warr, 1984).

As we noted, one offense that looms large for women but not men is, of course, rape. According to a study of fear of rape (Warr, 1985), (1) rape is feared more than any other crime among younger women, (2) rape is viewed as approximately equal in seriousness to murder by women, (3) the highest sensitivity displayed by any age or sex group to any crime is that of young women to rape, (4) fear of rape is closely associated with a variety of other offenses for which rape is a logical (though not necessary) outcome (for example, burglary, robbery, receiving an obscene phone call) or precursor (for example, homicide), and (5) fear of rape is strongly associated with certain lifestyle precautions (for example, not going out alone). Clearly, then, rape is at the heart of fear of crime for many women.

PERCEIVED RISK VERSUS SERIOUSNESS OF CRIMES

Setting aside age and sex differences in fear of crime, let us consider another question: In any given society or population, which crimes are feared most and which least? If members of a society were subject to, say, 100 different offenses, which offense would head the list as the most feared, and how would the remaining crimes be arranged? At first glance, the answer to the question seems obvious: The greater the perceived seriousness of a crime, the more it is feared. Hence, at the top of the list would be the most serious offenses (forms of homicide), and at the bottom truly petty crimes. That answer, however, immediately raises a problem. As a general rule, the more serious an offense, the less frequently it occurs. Hence, if seriousness were the only determinant of fear, then individuals would most fear precisely those offenses that were least likely to happen to them. To use an analogy, this is a little like fearing injury from falling meteors more than from rush-hour traffic.

To understand this problem better, let us examine a model of fear (Warr and Stafford, 1983): The degree to which any crime is feared depends on two factors: (1) the perceived seriousness of the offense and (2) the perceived risk of the offense (that is, the subjective probability that it will occur). Neither of these factors, however, is itself a sufficient condition for fear. A serious crime will not be highly feared if it is viewed as unlikely, nor will a seemingly inevitable offense be highly feared if it is not perceived to be serious. In order to provoke high fear, an offense must be viewed as both serious *and* likely to occur, meaning that fear is a multiplicative function of perceived risk and perceived seriousness. Data obtained in a survey of Seattle residents show that the multiplicative model of fear does in fact accurately predict the degree to which different crimes are feared (Warr and Stafford, 1983).

Table 1.1 displays the mean fear scores (on a scale ranging from 0 to 10) of the sixteen offenses rated by respondents in the Seattle study, along with the perceived risk and perceived seriousness of the offenses (also rated on scales of 0 to 10). Observe that murder, although viewed as the most serious offense by Seattle residents, is not highly feared because it is viewed as quite unlikely to occur to them. On the other hand, the most feared offense—a residential burglary that occurs when no one is home—is not even a violent crime; it is strongly feared because it is seen as moderately serious and very likely. So it is the balance between risk and seriousness that determines the fear attached to any given crime.

If perceived risk is a critical factor in producing fear, what features of the environment suggest to people that they are in danger of becoming victims of crime? In a survey of Dallas residents (Warr, 1990), respondents were provided with a set of vignettes describing situations that occur in everyday life and were asked to indicate (using a scale from 0 to 10) how afraid they would be of becoming a victim of crime in each situation. Characteristics of the situations were varied systematically in order to determine those features of the situations that were most fear provoking. Three factors proved to be critical. To illustrate these factors, imagine yourself sitting on a bench in a crowded park during the afternoon in an area you know well. Now imagine sitting on a bench alone at night in an area where you have never been before. Why is the latter situation more frightening? One factor is novelty—novel (that is, unfamiliar) environments are more frightening to individuals than are environments they have experienced before. A second factor is time—nighttime is clearly perceived as much more dangerous than daytime. And the final factor is the presence of other people—the presence of bystanders or crowds is usually reassuring, whereas being alone is frightening. None of these cues can, by itself, produce intense fear, but their cumulative effect is very large. Furthermore, none of the cues has any significant effect on fear once a crime actually appears imminent or is under way, and the effect of the cues is stronger or weaker according to the age and sex of the individual. Finally, the presence of others is reassuring only if those others are not themselves perceived as threatening. One group that is consistently viewed as potentially dangerous is young males. Young males are particularly frightening to females, but even young males are frightened of young males.

TABLE 1.1

**MEAN FEAR, PERCEIVED RISK, AND PERCEIVED SERIOUSNESS
OF SIXTEEN OFFENSES AMONG SEATTLE RESPONDENTS**

Offense Descriptions	Fear		Perceived Risk		Perceived Seriousness	
	Mean	*Rank*	*Mean*	*Rank*	*Mean*	*Rank*
1. Having someone break into your home while you're away	5.86	1	4.50	2	7.20	8
2. Being raped*	5.62	2	2.51	11	9.33	2
3. Being hit by a drunken driver while driving your car	5.11	3	3.57	6	7.66	5
4. Having someone break into your home while you're home	4.49	4	2.72	8	7.72	4
5. Having something taken from you by force	4.05	5	2.61	9	7.48	7
6. Having strangers loiter near your home late at night	4.02	6	3.83	5	4.35	13
7. Being threatened with a knife, club, or gun	4.00	7	2.57	10	8.25	3
8. Having a group of juveniles disturb the peace near your home	3.80	8	4.25	3	4.30	14
9. Being beaten up by a stranger	3.59	9	2.12	14	7.63	6
10. Being murdered	3.39	10	1.29	15	9.66	1
11. Having your car stolen	3.35	11	2.72	8	5.77	10
12. Being cheated or conned out of your money	2.50	12	2.16	13	5.55	11
13. Being approached by people begging for money	2.19	13	6.73	1	2.15	16
14. Receiving an obscene phone call	2.07	14	3.87	4	3.18	15
15. Being sold contaminated food	1.96	15	2.24	12	5.53	12
16. Being beaten up by someone you know	1.04	16	.83	16	6.17	9

SOURCE: Warr and Stafford, 1983.

*Female respondents only.

PERSONAL VERSUS ALTRUISTIC FEAR

Although people commonly fear for their own safety, they also fear for the safety of others, including their children, spouses, and friends. The distinction between *personal* fear (fear for oneself) and *altruistic* fear (fear for others) is fundamentally important because the two forms of fear display quite different characteristics. Respondents in a Dallas survey were asked about their fear for other household members (Warr, 1992). Surprisingly, husbands were more likely than wives to express altruistic fear, and the reasons are intriguing.

Whereas women often expressed fear for their children, relatively few women reported fear for their husbands. Evidently, many women believe that their husbands are sufficiently able to take care of themselves. Husbands, on the other hand, were less likely than wives to express fear for their children, but husbands were much more likely to express fear for their wives than vice versa. There appears, then, to be a rather clear and common division of labor in American families when it comes to altruistic fear. Warr also found that altruistic fear, unlike personal fear, is more common among younger age groups than older age groups, due, perhaps, to the fact that younger households are generally larger and contain more young children. And he found evidence that the protection of loved ones may be as powerful a motivating force as self-protection. Males who reported altruistic fear were more than five times more likely than other males to have purchased a weapon for protection against crime.

THE CONSEQUENCES OF FEAR

We cannot leave the topic of fear without considering the consequences of fear. Fear of crime (more specifically, personal fear) has been linked to a number of avoidance or precautionary behaviors, including, for example, avoiding going out alone, avoiding going out at night, or most commonly, avoiding certain places in a city, such as downtown or the subways (see, for example, DuBow et al., 1979; Skogan and Maxfield, 1981; Warr, 1985). Such precautionary behaviors are much more frequent among women than men (Warr, 1985). Fear also has an effect on transportation choices, participation in neighborhood crime watches and other crime-prevention associations, and not surprisingly, on the use of home security precautions (DuBow et al., 1979; Skogan and Maxfield, 1981). Skogan and Maxfield (1981) report that fully 96 percent of households interviewed in San Francisco, Chicago, and Philadelphia reported at least one home security precaution. In accordance with other research (DuBow et al., 1979; Research and Forecasts, 1980), they found that the most common precautions were such simple steps as locking doors, leaving a light on, asking neighbors to watch the house, identifying persons before letting them in, or stopping mail delivery when away for extended periods. Such precautions, of course, require little financial investment or time. Yet, more expensive and time-consuming precautions are not rare. Although estimates vary, roughly 25–40 percent of American households have invested in such measures as window bars or grates, improved locks, property engraving, alarm systems, improved lighting, or theft insurance (see, for example, DuBow et al., 1979; Research and Forecasts, 1980; Skogan and Maxfield, 1981).

THE SERIOUSNESS OF CRIMES

Crimes come in an enormously wide variety, from homicide to forgery, shoplifting to auto theft, and terrorism to desecration of a corpse. When we think about different types of crime, one of the most immediate and obvious differences is their *seriousness*. Although any two crimes will differ in many ways (for example, in their frequency, periodicity, and typical location), differences in seriousness are most readily apparent.

At first glance, seriousness appears to be an objective property of crimes, in the same way that weight and mass are objective properties of physical objects. Seriousness, however, is actually a perceptual property of crimes, meaning that it is a matter of opinion. Thus, two individuals or cultures may disagree on the seriousness of any particular crime. Given this perceptual quality, the seriousness of crimes can be measured only by soliciting the opinions of some population, such as a city or nation. The first major such investigation was conducted by Sellin and Wolfgang and described in their book *The Measurement of Delinquency* (1978). The authors measured and compared the perceived seriousness of crimes among different groups, including judges, university students, and police. Since the publication of this study, research on the perceived seriousness of crimes has continued unabated and has grown to include cross-cultural comparisons. One of the most consistent findings of this research has been that there is strong social consensus within the United States, as well as between our society and several other surveyed societies, about what constitutes serious crimes (see, for example, Rossi et al., 1974b; Normandeau, 1966; Wolfgang et al., 1985). Although there is less consensus about some crimes (for example, homosexual acts) than about others, the evidence indicates that Americans rank crimes in much the same way in terms of seriousness.

Table 1.2 presents the seriousness scores of selected crimes from a 1985 national survey of crime seriousness in which a sample of 60,000 Americans rated the seriousness of more than 200 offenses (Wolfgang et al., 1985). The seriousness scores range from a low of 0.2 for "A person under 16 years old plays hooky from school" to a high of 72.1 for "A person plants a bomb in a public building. The bomb explodes and 20 people are killed." As a general rule, crimes against persons (homicide, rape, robbery, assault, kidnapping) receive the highest scores, followed by crimes against property (burglary, fraud), and finally public order offenses (loitering, disturbing the peace), victimless offenses (prostitution, homosexual behavior), and various forms of petty crime. White collar offenses (such as price-fixing or bribery of a public official) receive relatively low scores, but at least one drug-related offense ("A person runs a narcotics ring") is seen to be roughly as serious (33.8) as some forms of homicide.

Why is the seriousness of crimes important? One reason is that social judgments about the seriousness of crimes are a fundamental aspect of human cultures. Most Americans, for example, would probably feel strange living in a society where the taking of another person's property was not regarded as a serious matter. Another reason is that the sentences imposed on offenders under our judicial system are generally predicated on the seriousness of the crime of which they have been convicted. Because seriousness has become a principal criterion of sentencing in the United States, the need for careful measurements of the seriousness of crimes is obvious. Public perceptions of the seriousness of crimes, however, are also crucial to understanding the social psychology of crime. For example, people appear to estimate the relative frequencies of different crimes on the basis of their seriousness (Warr, 1980). That is, most

TABLE 1.2   **PERCEIVED SERIOUSNESS OF SELECTED OFFENSES**

Offense Descriptions	Perceived Seriousness
A person plants a bomb in a public building. The bomb explodes and 20 people are killed.	72.1
A man forcibly rapes a woman. As a result of physical injuries, she dies.	52.8
A person robs a victim at gunpoint. The victim struggles and is shot to death	43.2
A man stabs his wife. As a result, she dies.	39.2
A person runs a narcotics ring.	33.8
An armed person skyjacks an airplane and holds the crew and passengers hostage until a ransom is paid.	32.7
A person intentionally sets fire to a building causing $100,000 worth of damage.	24.9
A person robs a victim of $1,000 at gunpoint. The victim is wounded and requires hospitalization.	21.0
A person sells heroin to others for resale.	20.6
A company pays a bribe of $100,000 to a legislator to vote for a law favoring the company.	14.5
A doctor cheats on claims he makes to a federal health insurance plan for patient services.	14.1
Ten high school boys beat a male classmate with their fists. He requires hospitalization.	11.7
A person steals a locked car and sells it.	10.8
A person operates a store where he knowingly sells stolen property.	10.3
A person breaks into a department store, forces open a safe, and steals $1,000.	9.7
A person breaks into a home and steals $1,000.	9.6
Several large companies illegally fix the retail prices of their products.	9.2
A person performs an illegal abortion.	8.6
A person sells marijuana to others for resale.	8.5
A person signs someone else's name to a check and cashes it.	7.2
A person uses heroin.	6.5
A person gets customers for a prostitute.	6.4
An employee embezzles $1,000 from his employer.	6.2
A person cheats on his federal income taxes and avoids paying $10,000 in taxes.	6.1
A theater owner knowingly shows pornographic movies to a minor.	5.7
A man exposes himself in public.	4.7
A person picks a victim's pocket of $100.	4.4
A person turns in a false fire alarm.	3.8
A person breaks into a school and steals $10 worth of supplies.	3.1
A woman engages in prostitution.	2.1
A person is a customer in a place where he knows gambling occurs illegally.	1.7
A male, over 16 years of age, has sexual relations with a willing female under 16.	1.6
A person smokes marijuana.	1.4
Two persons willingly engage in a homosexual act.	1.3
A person disturbs the neighborhood with loud, noisy behavior.	1.1
A person is drunk in public.	0.8
A person under 16 years old plays hooky from school.	0.2

SOURCE: Wolfgang et. al., 1985.

individuals correctly assume that murder occurs less frequently than burglary, robbery less frequently than shoplifting, and so on. Similarly, the central criterion used by Americans to judge the appropriate penalty for different crimes is the seriousness of the crime (see, for example, Hamilton and Rytina, 1980; Warr et al., 1983). And, as we noted previously, one of the factors that determines the degree to which a crime is feared is the perceived seriousness of the crime. Seriousness, then, is clearly a key perceptual property of crimes.

PUBLIC OPINION ON PUNISHMENT

A central area of the social psychology of crime and punishment is public opinion concerning punishments for crimes. What punishments, for example, does the general public consider appropriate for any particular crime? Among other uses, data on publicly preferred punishments for crimes permit an assessment of the mood of a nation or other social unit when it comes to dealing with crime. To illustrate, since reaching a low point in the 1960s, public support for the death penalty in the United States has been increasing steadily, and is now at unprecedented levels (see Chapter 24). Approximately three-quarters of Americans have expressed support for the death penalty in recent years (Jamieson and Flanagan, 1987: 2). Whatever the causes of this phenomenon, Americans clearly have little tolerance for crime or criminals at the present time.

In deciding how severe a punishment should be for any particular crime, does the general public rely on any discernible rule or principle? The answer is yes. A number of studies (see, for example, Hamilton and Rytina, 1980; Warr et al., 1983) indicate that, in deciding what punishment is appropriate for different crimes, individuals typically rely on a maxim: Let the punishment fit the crime. That is, they match the severity of the punishment to the seriousness of the crime. At first glance, this might seem to be evidence that the general public is guided by a desire for retribution because a central tenet of retribution is the principle of proportionality between offense seriousness and sanction severity. Although retribution is indeed a popular justification for punishment, it is not the only one to which Americans subscribe, and individuals may be guided by more than one theory of punishment in assigning penalties to crimes (Warr and Stafford, 1984; Warr, 1981; Vidmar and Ellsworth, 1982).

One consistent finding in the literature on public preferences concerns the form of punishment that the public desires. Simply put, Americans overwhelmingly regard imprisonment as the appropriate form of punishment for most crimes. Although the proportion who prefer prison increases with the seriousness of the crime (Blumstein and Cohen, 1981; Warr, et al., 1982), imprisonment is by far the most commonly chosen penalty across crimes. For example, in their report on the National Survey of Punishment for Criminal Offenses, Jacoby and Dunn (1987: 1–2) state that "respondents overwhelmingly supported the use of imprisonment as the most appropriate punishment for criminal offenses. Over all offense types, 71 percent of respondents said the appropriate punishment included prison. Other types of punishments (probation, a fine, or restitution) were most often combined with imprisonment, rather than being substitutes for imprisonment." Similar findings come from Warr et al. (1982) and Blumstein and Cohen (1980). It seems clear, then, that the Enlightenment conception of prison as a general or "all-purpose" form of punishment continues to hold sway among the American public.

Setting aside public preferences about criminal sanctions, consider this question: How accurate is public knowledge of existing criminal punishments? Could most Americans name the statutory punishment in their state for, say, murder or burglary? The evidence suggests that public knowledge of statutory punishments is quite limited; most individuals simply have no clear idea of what the punishments for different crimes are (Gibbs and Erickson, 1979; California Assembly, 1968; Williams et al., 1980). This is not to say that most individuals are entirely ignorant of the law; they seem to have a rough idea of which crimes receive the most severe sanctions. But even this information appears to stem not from knowledge of the law but rather from a presumption that the penalties assigned to crimes are proportional to their seriousness (Williams et al., 1980).

Public knowledge of criminal sanctions is not a minor matter. Legislatures often attempt to control crime through general deterrence, meaning that they increase or alter the penalty for an offense in order to deter persons who might commit the offense. But changes in criminal sanctions can scarcely have a deterrent effect if the public is unaware of them. Hence, publicizing a new sanction can be as critical as enacting it.

One possible use of public opinion data on punishment is to make criminal sanctions conform to public opinion. For example, if citizens of a state believed that armed robbery should carry a penalty of no less than ten years in prison, then the state legislature could amend the law to conform to public sentiment. Yet, as appealing as that idea might seem in a democratic society, it raises serious philosophical and practical problems. It can be argued, for example, that one purpose of law is precisely to protect individuals from the actions and beliefs of the general public, who may be guided more by anger and other passions than by reason, particularly when it comes to crime and punishment.

On a practical level, the use of public opinion data to determine criminal sentences is complicated by the fact that public opinion is subject to large and sometimes rapid fluctuations. Should the law therefore be changed with each new survey? Furthermore, public opinion is not necessarily informed opinion. For example, if the general public wished to send burglars to prison for, say, a minimum of eight years, would they understand the implications of that decision for the size of the prison population? And would they be willing to pay for new prisons? Similarly, the sentencing discretion historically given to judges by legislatures reflects the belief that each case must be treated individually. Within this framework, the burglar who shows remorse, for example, should not be treated as harshly as one who shows contempt for the court and the law. These sorts of details are apt to be lost if sentencing is turned over to public opinion.

THE MEDIA AND CRIME

A major source of information on crime in the United States is the mass media, including television, radio, newspapers, newsmagazines, books, and movies (see Graber, 1980; Conklin, 1975; Skogan and Maxfield, 1981). The depiction of crime in the mass media occurs under one of several formats. One of the most prominent formats is news coverage of crime. Even a casual viewer of the evening news (local or national) cannot fail to observe that crime stories are a staple of the news diet. In a media-saturated society such as ours, reports of particular crimes can reach a local or national audience almost instantly. Crime is routinely covered in the news not only because it occurs so frequently in our society but also because its inherent human-interest quality makes crime more "newsworthy" than many other topics.

Many critics argue that news coverage of crime, though seemingly factual and objective, actually presents a badly distorted picture of crime. Some of these criticisms date back to the days of nineteenth-century yellow journalism although they can be applied to modern media of mass communication as well. Let us examine some of the criticisms.

"NEWSWORTHINESS" AND NEWS DISTORTION

Although crime statistics are sometimes reported in the news, most crime news consists of reports of particular crimes, either as they are occurring (as in the case of a bank robbery in progress) or shortly after they have occurred (Graber, 1980; Fishman, 1981). Because the "supply" of crimes is virtually unlimited, choices must be made on which crimes to report. As with any other kind of potential news material, the central criterion for choosing crime stories is "newsworthiness." In the case of crime, a key element of newsworthiness is seriousness: The more serious a crime, the greater the chance it will appear as a news story. The brutal homicide, for example, is more likely to be reported than the nonviolent residential burglary. This standard is not in itself unreasonable, but it is at odds with a sociological reality. Recall that, as a general rule, crimes occur in inverse proportion to their seriousness: The more serious the crime, the less frequently it occurs (Erickson and Gibbs, 1979). Thus, whereas thousands of homicides occur annually in the United States, millions of burglaries are committed. Hence, by using seriousness as a criterion, the media are most likely to report precisely those crimes that are least likely to occur (Skogan and Maxfield, 1981; Sherizen, 1978; Sheley and Ashkins, 1981; Roshier, 1973).

The image of crime presented in the media is thus a reverse image of reality: The most frequent crimes are the least frequently reported, and the least frequent crimes are the most frequently reported. For example, Graber (1980) reports that murders constituted only 0.2 percent of offenses in Chicago in 1976, but they accounted for 26 percent of crime stories in the *Chicago Tribune*. Sheley and Ashkins (1981), in a study of media crime coverage in New Orleans, found much the same pattern. Table 1.3, taken from their study, lists the relative frequencies of offenses according to police data, and as they were

TABLE 1.3

**INDIVIDUAL INDEX OFFENSES
AS PERCENT OF TOTAL INDEX OFFENSES
REPORTED BY POLICE AND MEDIA**

Offense	Police	Times Picayune	TV 4	TV 6	TV 8
Homicide	.4%	12%	49%	50%	46%
Robbery	12	33	31	30	32
Rape	.6	6	3	3	4
Assault	7	17	2	4	1
Burglary	23	23	3	4	6
Larceny	46	8	12	9	11
Vehicle theft	11	1	0	0	0
Total	100	100	100	100	100
Violent	20	68	85	87	83
Property	80	32	15	13	17
Total	100	100	100	100	100

SOURCE: Sheley and Ashkins, 1981.

reported in one newspaper (the *Times-Picayune*) and on three television stations. As the table shows, no close correspondence exists between the police data and media reports, with the media, particularly television, focusing disproportionately on homicide and robbery. The bottom panel of the table reveals that although, according to the police, violent crime constituted only 20 percent of offenses, it accounted for 68–87 percent of the media crime stories. An outsider who knew our world only through news coverage might have a peculiar idea of the relative frequency of different crimes. The point is not that the presentation of crime news is deliberately distorted but that a standard editorial practice has an inadvertent consequence.

Aside from seriousness, another element of newsworthiness in crime stories is what Ericson et al. (1987) call "personalization." Here, a crime story becomes newsworthy because of the identity or plight of the person or persons involved. A crime that might not otherwise make the papers becomes news, for example, when the victim or offender is the mayor, a television celebrity, or the daughter of the chief of police. In large cities where serious crimes are commonplace, even murders and rapes will not necessarily make the news unless they involve prominent persons or public figures. Stories selected according to such criteria, however, may be quite unrepresentative of crimes in general.

DISTORTION IN PRINT AND BROADCAST MEDIA

Another source of distortion that may appear in media crime coverage, including both broadcast and print media, is the practice of using crime news as filler (see, for example, Graber, 1980; Gordon and Heath, 1981; Ericson et al., 1987). As we noted previously, crime news is seldom in short supply, and so, on a slow news day, column space or airtime may be filled in with crime stories. If crime news is routinely employed in this way, the amount of time or space devoted to crime from day to day will not accurately reflect the actual number of crimes. Crime news may also be increased in an effort to raise circulation or viewership, or be heavily featured in order to appeal to a certain kind of audience (Gordon and Heath, 1981; Dominick, 1978).

In one of the more carefully documented cases of media distortion, Fishman (1978) reported on a "crime wave" that occurred in New York City. A series of stories pertaining to crimes against the elderly first appeared in a New York newspaper. The theme was picked up in another paper and on television, adding to the number of stories on this topic. Fishman plotted the number of stories over several weeks, showing that the number of stories suddenly rose sharply, remained high for several weeks, and then declined. Police statistics, however, did not reveal any similar pattern in the number of crimes against the elderly. What had occurred was in fact not a crime wave but rather what Fishman called a "media wave." That is, a journalistic theme — "crimes against the elderly" — had been created, and instances fitting this theme were pulled selectively from the large daily pool of crimes (see also Ericson et al., 1987).

Wittingly or not, the media may present a distorted image of crime through news coverage in many other ways as well. Annual increases in the number of crimes in a city, for example, may be reported without converting the figures into rates or without reporting changes in population. To illustrate, a reported 10-percent increase in the number of crimes in a city, although a frightening statistic, would be considerably less frightening if it were noted that the population of the city had also grown by 10 percent, meaning that the probability of being victimized had in fact remained constant (Biderman et al., 1967). Similarly, a television story announcing a 20-percent increase in crime might be unnecessarily alarming if it did not also inform viewers of the *types* of crime that had actually increased. An increase in shoplifting, for example, is not the same as an increase in robbery or homicide. And the media, which frequently rely on FBI crime figures, do not always inform readers of well-known problems with those data (see Chapter 3).

DISTORTION IN TELEVISION PROGRAMS

Quite apart from the daily presentation of crime news is the depiction of crime in television drama and printed fiction. Crime fiction has been a major topic of Western literature at least since Holmes and Watson appeared in the late nineteenth century and continues today in the popular books of writers as disparate as Agatha Christie and Umberto Eco. The market for crime fiction, however, pales in comparison to that of television crime dramas, which may draw audiences in the tens of millions on a single night. Crime and cop shows have been a staple of prime-time television fare almost since the advent of television itself, owing, no doubt, to immense public demand for such shows and to the fact that crime shows, with their emphasis on action, tension, and moral dilemma, represent ideal dramatic vehicles for writers and producers.

In television crime dramas, no official claim to objectivity is made although some shows are praised for their "realism." Like news coverage of crime, crime dramas on television have been subjected to withering criticism for misrepresenting the realities of crime and law enforcement. In one study, for example, investigators coded information on every prime-time crime-related program that appeared during a six-week period of the 1980–1981 television season (Lichter and Lichter, 1983). Among other things, they found that murder is by far the most commonly portrayed crime on television and that television crime, in the aggregate, is much more violent than real-world crime. Offenders were correctly shown to be typically male, but the television offender was substantially older (usually over 30) than were real-world offenders and was frequently portrayed as either a businessman (or his flunky) or a professional criminal. Private detectives were given considerable prominence as law enforcement agents, and were frequently portrayed as more effective than the police in controlling crime. And, quite unlike the real world, virtually all offenders were caught and punished. Other research has supported these findings, as well as identifying other forms of distortion that appear in crime dramas (Elias, 1986; Dominick, 1973).

THE EFFECTS OF DISTORTION

As we have seen, there is a good deal of evidence that the image of crime presented in the media, whether in news coverage or dramatic presentations, does not closely conform to reality. Even so, some caution is necessary in interpreting this evidence. Critics of the media often seem to assume that the images of crime that appear in the media are readily accepted and adopted by the general public. This presumption rests on what is sometimes called the "hypodermic syringe" model of mass communication. According to this model, information or images that appear in the mass media are directly injected, so to speak, into the brains of the audience and become part of its members' storehouse of information or beliefs. Researchers in mass communication, however, have generally rejected this model as much too simplistic. Information or images that appear in the media, rather than simply entering the mind directly, are "filtered" in many ways. In the case of television, for example, the impact of a message depends on such factors as the personality and social characteristics of the viewer, who is in the room as the television is being viewed (for example, whether it is family viewing or lone viewing), what the viewer's previous attitudes and experiences with the topic have been, and so on (see DeFleur and Ball-Rokeach, 1975; Kline and Tichenor, 1972).

To say that the media distort crime, then, is not necessarily to say that public beliefs about crime also are distorted. In order to reach any conclusions concerning the accuracy of public beliefs about crime, direct measurements of public beliefs and knowledge about crime are necessary. Although relatively few in number, such studies suggest that the general public does not accept crime news uncritically (Graber, 1980) and that public beliefs about crime may be more accurate than commonly supposed (Warr, 1980, 1982).

In order to provide compelling evidence, studies designed to measure the impact of media messages require simultaneous measurement of both media content and the reactions of the persons exposed to that content. Such research is difficult to conduct in natural settings because of the large number of media sources and because of the problems involved in attempting to isolate, let alone control, the media messages to which individuals are exposed. One study that approaches an ideal design was conducted by Heath (1984), who questioned samples of newspaper readers in thirty-six cities, examining their fear of crime in light of characteristics of the newspapers they read. She found that individuals who read newspapers that printed a high proportion of local crime news were more afraid if the reported crimes were predominantly sensational (bizarre, violent) or random (the victim in no way provoked or precipitated the crime). However, these same factors *reduced* fear if the newspaper stories were predominantly nonlocal. Evidently, readers were reassured by the knowledge that random and sensational crimes were happening to other people in other places.

PUBLIC POLICY QUESTIONS

We have examined some of the major topics within the social psychology of crime and punishment, particularly those areas with well-established traditions of research. However, much of the research in this area consists of survey research on public attitudes concerning specific issues that have become matters of national controversy or that constitute major political issues of the time. These include such issues as gun control, prison overcrowding, the debate over the exclusionary rule (the rule that illegally obtained evidence cannot be used in court), the insanity defense, the legalization of some drugs, police corruption or brutality, the putative leniency of American criminal courts, and a host of other issues. Controversies like these are constantly fueling American public discourse, occasionally as a result of enormous publicity over particular events, such as the police beating of Rodney King in Los Angeles or the trial of Bernard Goetz in New York (for shooting several black teenagers in a subway car). In other instances, apparent crises in the criminal justice system (for example, prison overcrowding) force an issue to the forefront of public attention.

Although public interest in such issues often is transitory, it is important nonetheless because of its heavy influence on American politics. For example, political commercials featuring Willie Horton, who committed rape and murder while on furlough from prison, were a prominent feature of the 1988 presidential campaign, and the drug problem in the United States was an important issue in the 1992 presidential election. Crime rarely has achieved more prominence as a campaign issue than in the 1968 presidential campaign, in which Richard Nixon ran (ironically, in retrospect) on a strong "law and order" platform. At the local level, public concern about crime, or a loss of confidence in the police or courts, can affect the outcome of mayoral and other elections, as well as political appointments (for example, police chiefs) and elections of members of the legal system (for example, judges and district attorneys). In the United States, then, crime and politics are closely intertwined.

CONCLUSION

Criminology is sometimes thought to consist solely of the study of criminal behavior or the criminal justice system. Under this conceptualization, crime is understood to be merely a dependent variable, that is, a phenomenon to be explained. As we have seen in this chapter, however, crime is also an independent variable, a cause of beliefs and events. In the United States, crime affects our literature, our politics, our entertainment, and our everyday conversations. Fear of crime affects our lifestyles in both subtle and profound ways. To think of crime as merely an isolated element of our culture is to miss the point. If, as some have argued, abundant crime is a consequence of American culture (Merton, 1938), it is also true that American culture is shaped by crime. Those who doubt that proposition might wish to turn on a television set or radio, visit a newstand, or check the movie listings.

DISCUSSION QUESTIONS

1. How prevalent is fear of crime in the United States? Does crime fear affect people equally, or are there some groups displaying more fear than others? What accounts for such differences?

2. Are the members of this society roughly in agreement concerning the seriousness of most crimes? How about concerning the punishments for crime? What types of information are needed and what kinds are available to answer these questions?

3. Distinguish personal from altruistic crime fear. Are there differences in various groups' levels of altruistic fear? Describe these.

4. How accurate are public perceptions of the dimensions of crime in this society? To what extent are these perceptions shaped by the media? In what ways do the media distort the picture of crime?

CHAPTER 2

◆

CRIME, LAW, AND SOCIAL CONFLICT

Joseph F. Sheley
Tulane University

PERSISTENT CONFLICT over issues like abortion, pornography, and drug possession indicates a lack of consensus in this society about the morality and legality of *some* types of behavior. However, many criminologists are directing our attention to the seeming consensus behind other forms of behavior, those not currently the subject of debate. They ask us to consider what lies behind our seeming agreement to label certain acts (burglary, for example) and certain people "criminal"?

At first blush, this challenge poses little difficulty. We call acts crimes when they pose a threat to society, and we label people criminal when we catch them committing these acts. Yet, such definitions are not as instructive as they might seem, for they leave a number of questions unanswered. For example: Can we speak of society as if all members are affected similarly by crime? Can we easily say what constitutes a threat to society or groups within it? Is breaking the law the only criterion for gaining criminal status? Will it assure this status?

Having raised such questions, in this chapter, we will examine criminal status as a definitional problem through discussions of interest groups, ruling classes, and designations of acts and people as criminal. We will explore the possibility that the worth or quality of acts and persons is primarily a function of the meanings we give them and that these meanings are subject to change. Thus, who or what is labeled criminal at a given time may not depend on some abstract definition but rather may reflect the social, political, and economic situation of that time (Chiricos and Delone, 1992; Lessan, 1991).

THE CONSENSUS APPROACH: DEVIANCE AND SOCIAL UNITY

Until relatively recently, most sociological and criminological theory assumed that definitions of acts and persons as deviant or criminal reflected a value consensus within society. People were thought to hold much the same views of right and wrong because societies could not continue to function in a state of constant moral conflict. Thus, law was viewed by traditional theorists as a reflection of custom and a codification of societal values, as an institution functioning to settle disputes that arise when values and norms occasionally become cloudy, and as an expression of social control when an individual deviates too far from the normatively acceptable (see Parsons, 1962; Pound, 1943; Rich, 1978). Indeed, deviance itself and the ensuing application of the legal process were seen by some as necessary to the proper functioning of a society. Durkheim ([1895] 1958: 67; [1893] 1933: 102) provided some classic statements in this vein:

> Crime is a factor in public health, an integral part of all healthy societies.

> Crime brings together upright consciences and concentrates them. We have only to notice what happens, particularly in a small town, when some moral scandal has just been committed. They stop each other on the street, they visit each other, they seek to come together to talk of the event and to wax indignant in common. From all the similar impressions which are exchanged, for all the temper that gets itself expressed, there emerges a unique temper, more or less determinate according to the circumstances, which is everybody's without being anybody's in particular. That is the public temper.

Both Durkheim and, later, Mead (1918) were pointing up a paradox about crime. Although crime obviously is dysfunctional for a community in some ways—financial costs, personal injury, property damage, social disruption—it also may be functional in some important ways. Crime and other forms of deviance tend to remind members of a community about the interests and values they share. Community bonds are strengthened in the common outrage and indignation inspired by a deviant act. Further, deviance reassures individual members of a community of their own moral normality and forthrightness.

Some authors have cautioned us not to overemphasize the functions of deviance to the exclusion of problems it may create. While noting the unifying functions of punishment, Mead (1918: 91) also pointed out that punitive reactions to deviance may lead to repressive societal conditions that stifle the creativity that deviance often represents. Repressive hostility also may prevent societal self-examination and subsequent attempts at improvement. Finally, Coser (1956: 87–95) noted that if solidarity is weak in the first place, deviance and reactions to it can further divide a community into factions.

The "functions of deviance" theme continues to be explored, however. Some students of Durkheim suggest that a society actually encourages, or at least allows, a certain amount of deviance for its functional aspects. Obviously, the balance between functional and dysfunctional amounts of deviance is delicate—too much would destroy a society, yet too little would mean the loss of the societal unity derived from deviance. This unification function is considered so imperative that Durkheim ([1895] 1958: 67) once noted that if all present forms of criminal activity suddenly were eliminated, a society immediately would create new forms. Even in a society of saints, he wrote, "Faults which appear venial to the layman will create the same scandal that the ordinary offense does in ordinary consciousness."

Erikson's study (1966) of deviance in the early Puritan colonies supported Durkheim's conclusions. Erikson discovered three "crime waves" during the first sixty years of settlement in Massachusetts: the Antinomian controversy (a challenge to the community's religious establishment), the arrival of the Quakers from Pennsylvania, and the Salem witches hysteria. Each crime wave occurred at a time when unity in the colonies was waning, and each precipitated considerable turmoil. Erikson noted, however, that these crime waves were matters of shifts of public attention from one form of trouble to another — other problems were forgotten as each new crime problem arose. In fact, despite the crime waves, crime rates remained relatively stable over the six decades. For Erikson, this suggested a deviance "quota" — that is, the encouragement or allowance by the social system of a sufficiently functional amount of deviance to produce unity through creation of a response to a "common enemy."

Erikson's study of the three Puritan crime waves also led him to extend Durkheim's notion of the unification functions of deviance. He argued that crime in the colonies served certain boundary definition and maintenance functions. More generally, he believed that deviance and reactions to it help set the boundaries of acceptable behavior and provide a sense of stability and direction for a fledgling society. As time passes, these boundaries tend to become somewhat vague, and new possibilities for societal growth arise. Deviance again causes the society to refocus on its character and mission, to reemphasize the common beliefs and interests of its members. Deviance thus serves to maintain the social and moral boundaries of societies (Lauderdale, 1976).

Inverarity (1976) attempted to extend Erikson's work through a study of lynchings in Louisiana between 1889 and 1896. His thesis essentially was a restatement of Erikson's: As a united group begins to lose its sense of solidarity, it seeks out and represses "enemies," thus reunifying itself. According to Inverarity, prior to the late 1800s, the South was a white-dominated, relatively closed, united society. Two general white classes existed, a wealthy planter–merchant–industrialist class and a larger, poorer, farmer–laborer class. Their relationship was fairly harmonious, even if economically inequitable. Although blacks at this time were considered inferior by both white classes, they were able to vote. (Laws created to exclude the black vote did not become widespread until the early 1900s.)

In the late 1800s, the black vote was controlled by the wealthy class, who utilized this control to solidify its power position. White solidarity collapsed briefly in the early 1890s, however, with the advent of the Populist revolt, an abortive attempt to capture economic and political power by some members of the lower classes. Inverarity pointed out that this disunity coincided with an increase in lynchings, primarily of blacks but also of whites, in Louisiana parishes (counties). He posited that the lynchings were a societal mechanism to counter the lack of social unity by rallying people against their "common enemies." After the Populist movement collapsed in the 1890s, the white South reunited and lynchings declined in Louisiana. In Inverarity's opinion, the decline reflected the lessened need for a unifying mechanism—that is, a decreased necessity to search out a common threat. In short, as Erikson had suggested in his study of the early Massachusetts colonies, the societal response to deviance had functioned to strengthen a social system whose unity was threatened.

CRITICISMS OF THE CONSENSUS MODEL

Erikson's Puritan colonies and, to some extent, Inverarity's southern communities represented small, apparently highly homogenous societies. In general, the "functions of crime" thesis seems to apply far better to smaller societies than to larger, heterogeneous ones. As a society expands and becomes more differentiated, it tends to form clusters, smaller subcultures or groups that differ from one another in world view, social status, and economic interests. Generally, these groups compete for various scarce economic and status rewards in society. Crime and deviance within these smaller *segments* of a society may serve the same unification and boundary maintenance functions as did crime in smaller societies such as the Puritan colonies. More important, however, definitions of and reactions to crime and deviance in the larger society are tied integrally to competition and conflict *among* the smaller segments or interest groups.

But many critics of the consensus approach will not accept the notions of value consensus and functions of deviance even for the smaller society (see Chambliss, 1974; Turk, 1976). They argue that were consensus in the small society really present, deviance would be rarer and the use of legal threats to deter deviance rarer still. They note that "societal needs" and the functioning of social phenomena like deviance to meet those needs are impossible to document; they must be accepted on faith alone. According to these critics, the argument that laws are created in the interests of a few and then shape public values is as plausible as the belief that public values shape law (see Michalowski, 1985). Thus, whereas the consensus position assumes that the state (specifically, legal mechanisms and processes) represents the interests of the majority, many historical studies trace a given law to the interests of a powerful minority. By contrast, no studies have tied a law directly to the expressed will of a majority independent of the influence of some interested minority.

The possibility that the consensus approach may underestimate the role of political and economic conflict within smaller societies gains legitimacy with a second look at Erikson's study of crime waves in the Puritan colonies. As Chambliss and Seidman (1982: 197–201) note, in each of the crime situations studied by Erikson, the interests of the major political figures in the community were at stake. The Antinomian controversy became a "crime problem" when the "different" religious views of a woman and a few of her followers began to be taken seriously enough that large numbers of people sought her counsel rather than that of established church leaders. The result? The leaders accused their rivals not only of heresy but also of trying to overthrow the government. Similarly, Quakers became a "criminal element" rather than simply a nuisance when they began gaining converts to their belief that individuals should form their own covenant with God rather than seek that covenant through the intercession of church leaders. The result? Being a Quaker became a severely punishable criminal offense. Finally, Chambliss and Seidman note, the Salem witch problem was interwoven with a power dispute between political magistrates and leading clergymen.

Similar comments pertain to Inverarity's study of lynchings in Louisiana during the Populist revolt (Pope and Ragin, 1977; Wasserman, 1977). At the very least, his findings are open to other interpretations as plausible as his consensus thesis. For example, Inverarity's (1976) data indicate that 65 percent of the lynchings were responses to alleged homicides and rapes. If a rise in such serious crime coincided with the Populist revolt, it is difficult to link the two. The lynchings may have represented a common frontier–rural response to perceived heinous crimes. If lynchings declined after the Populist failure, it is possible that crime coincidentally declined or, more likely, was deterred by the lynchings. More important is the possibility of the political use of a "crime problem" by members of either or both white classes. The wealthier class, fearing success in the Populist's drive to unite blacks and poor whites as one working class, could easily have fomented racial unrest. More influential members of the poorer white class, whose status and economic opportunities were being eroded by the new Populism, could have countered the erosion as easily by stirring up racial hatred (Beck and Tolnay, 1990). More important, recent research ties lynching and incarceration of blacks in Georgia at the turn of the century to changes in the supply and location of black male labor (Myers 1990; Soule, 1992). Rates of lynching—as a social control device—varied with level of competition between blacks and whites in both agriculture and manufacturing. Indeed, beyond the social control aspects of the punishment of blacks, the incarceration rate of blacks was influenced by demands for convict labor, especially in the agrarian sector (Myers and Massey, 1991).

Finally, we note that, to date, most empirical grounding of the notion of "functions of deviance" relies on historical or field observation studies. The major exception is the work of Liska and Warner (1991) who employ data concerning crime, victimization, and social interaction among respondents in a twenty-six-city survey. They find that, in urban societies, the reaction to high crime rates increases the social isolation of citizens rather than bringing them closer together in common indignation. Ironically, in many cases the effect of the decrease in social interaction is to *lower* the crime rate. Crimes like robbery intensify fears and, therefore, constrain social activity; this in turn reduces the number of targets for robbers.

In general, then, we can find little evidence of a "solidarity effect" of crime—at least in the larger society. Few cases raised by consensus theorists are resistant to equally valid reinterpretations that focus on conflicts among interested or threatened parties. These alternative interpretations do not depend on the undocumentable notion of "societal need." Rather, they rest on potentially documentable economic and political interests of specific persons and groups, and form the basis of what is known as the *conflict perspective*.

THE CONFLICT APPROACH

If power struggles characterize smaller societies and shape law and its enforcement to the extent critics of the consensus model claim, it seems unlikely that the consensus model can describe accurately the sources of criminal definitions in larger societies. For this reason, an alternative approach is increasingly popular among criminologists: the conflict model. Although not all conflict models are alike, three themes cut across all models: (1) the relativity of criminal definitions, (2) the role of control of major social institutions in maintaining interests, and (3) the definition of law (legislation and enforcement) as an instrument of power.

CRIMINAL DEFINITIONS AS RELATIVE

Basically, the conflict perspective argues that no act or individual is intrinsically moral or immoral, criminal or noncriminal. If a criminal label is attached to an act or a person, there is an underlying reason—such definitions serve some interests within society. If these labels are tied to interests, then they are subject to change as interests change. Thus, every definition of an act as immoral, deviant, or criminal (or the converse) must be viewed as tentative, always subject to redefinition.

Prime examples of the definition–redefinition process are seen in our perpetually changing attitudes, laws, and law enforcement patterns concerning "vices" (see Chapter 9). Several states, for example, have decriminalized certain sexual acts between consenting adults (Cohn and Gallagher, 1984). At one time, possession of marijuana was legal in this country; currently, it is not though the debate over whether it should be continues. Abortion, once illegal, has been granted a status of legality that is challenged constantly (Davis, 1986). Gambling once was illegal in Atlantic City, New Jersey; it is now legal. Prostitution is legal in certain counties in Nevada, but outlawed elsewhere in the state as well as in all other states. Being the customer of a prostitute likewise is legal in some states but not in others (Roby, 1969). For all these acts, we may wonder which definition reflects their "true" quality or nature: evil (illegal) or good (legal). In practice, we must treat current meanings as "truth," for they are the meanings employed in a court of law. From a conflict perspective, however, we soon realize that nothing is inherently sacred or sacrilegious—all definitions are subject to change.

Some may argue that the emphasis of the conflict perspective on the relativity of moral and legal definitions is demonstrated easily with respect to vices, about which there is little societal consensus, but may not apply so easily to acts that seem uniformly defined by most people over time. For example, cannot murder be called intrinsically wrong if nearly everyone considers it to be and has done so for a very long time?

The conflict theorist likely will counter that universal acceptance of a criminal definition, even over a long period, may be mere coincidence. Whether or not universally accepted, a criminal definition almost certainly has its origins in the protection of some power group's interests. And the definition certainly need not be permanent. Radical structural changes such as those created by a severe famine or cultural changes like those fomented in Nazi Germany in the 1930s could cause changes in the value placed on human life (Hughes, 1962). Further, the conflict theorist might argue that definitions of homicide currently are being negotiated. Continual legislative and courtroom debates over the legal status of abortion and euthanasia are, at heart, debates about the limits of acceptable life-taking versus criminal homicide. The same holds for the fight over capital punishment. Finally, history suggests that a revolutionary political assassin's status as hero or murderer depends on the success of the revolution, not on the intrinsic value of the act of assassination.

CONTROL OF INSTITUTIONS

Conflict theorists argue that there are three basic means of maintaining and enhancing interests in a society: force, compromise, and dominance of social institutions. Force is the least desirable, for it calls attention directly to interest preservation and basically dares others to summon enough counterforce to alter the power structure. Compromise is preferred because all parties involved somehow benefit; yet, compromise still carries liabilities. The granting of concessions indicates the absence of absolute power in the hands of any one interest group. It points up the weaknesses of certain parties and encourages others to organize further to exploit those weaknesses.

The strongest mechanism for gaining or holding power is dominance of social institutions. Control of such institutions as the law, religion, education, government, economics, and science means control of the world views of members of society, especially regarding questions of interests and power. With respect to the problem of crime and criminals, control of legal institutions means that more powerful groups gain legal support for their interests by outlawing behavior and attitudes that threaten them or by focusing attention away from their own wrongdoings. Control of other institutions, such as religion and education, is used to promote the interests of the more powerful by shaping the opinions of the less powerful concerning the legitimacy of the economic, political, and legal status quo. For example, we note, without arguing its validity, that the religious belief that rewards in the afterlife await those who suffer in this life serves to discourage this life's less powerful from more aggressively seeking the earthly rewards now in the hands of the more powerful. Similarly, an examination of textbooks used in most of our public and private elementary and secondary schools indicates how rarely serious questions are raised concerning the unequal distribution of wealth and power in this society. It should be noted that control of such institutions often exceeds mere instrumental use of them. Instead, the powerful, who control world views, also have their own world views shaped by these same institutions. Their efforts to shape law reflect not only perceptions of interests but a whole value set that labels such interests inherently right and necessary to the health of the collectivity.

LAW AS AN INSTRUMENT OF POWER

Whereas consensus theorists view law as an institution expressing common societal values and controlled by the majority in society, conflict theorists view law as an instrument of control or, in Turk's (1976) words, "a weapon in social conflict." Whoever owns the law owns power. Those who own it fight to keep it; those who want it fight to get it. Indeed, Turk argues, rather than simply reducing conflict, law also produces it by virtue of its status as a resource to be won by some combatants and lost by others. This point is illustrated by the importance given to nominations of Supreme Court justices. Presidents attempt to fill court vacancies with persons sympathetic to their views—that is, with persons more likely to decide cases in a manner protecting the interests of a given president and the parties that president represents.

The value of law as an instrument of power should be quite evident. Most obviously, control of the legal order represents the ability to use specified agents of force to protect one's interests. Beyond this, Turk notes that decisions concerning economic power are made and enforced through law; that is, control of the legislature represents control of the process that determines in part the distribution of economic rewards through such vehicles as tax laws. Further, control of the legal process means control of the organization of governmental decisions in general—decisions concerning the structure of public education, for example. Control of the law aids in determining much of culture; law legitimizes "right" views of the world and delegitimizes "wrong" views. Finally, Turk points out that the attention commanded by the workings of law (police, trials, and so forth) serves to divert attention from more deeply rooted problems of power distribution and interest maintenance. In sum, as Quinney (1970: 13) suggests, laws that forbid particular behaviors and make others mandatory are passed by legislators who have gained office through the backing of various interest groups. The ability to have one's interests translated into public policy is a primary indicator of power.

If law is an instrument sought after and employed by powerful interest groups to enhance their position in society, and if criminal law forbids certain acts, we can reasonably define *crime* as acts perceived by those in power as direct or indirect threats to their interests. Conflict theorists (Chambliss and Seidman, 1982: 174–175; Michalowski, 1985: 69–96) note that most of our current criminal law derives directly from English common law. Jeffrey (1957) argues that acts such as murder, theft, and robbery, once considered dispute problems to be settled within or between families, became crimes against the state (wrongs against society) when Henry II, king of England, attempted to centralize his power in a politically divided country by declaring them wrongs against the crown. Hall (1952) has traced theft laws in their present form to their origin in the change from a feudal economy to a capitalist–mercantile economy. As a new economic class of traders and industrialists developed, the need to protect their business interests grew. Hall (1952: 66) describes the creation of embezzlement laws:

> The patterns of conditions which gave rise to embezzlement may therefore be delineated as follows: (1) the expansion of mercantile and banking credit and the use of credit mechanisms, paper money, and securities; (2) the employment of clerks in important positions with reference to dealing with and, in particular, receiving valuables from third persons; (3) the interests of the commercial classes and their representation in parliament; (4) a change in attitude regarding the public importance of what could formerly be dismissed as merely a private breach of trust; and (5) a series of sensational cases of very serious defalcation which set the pattern into motion and produced immediate action.

The same conditions spawned laws governing the receipt of stolen property and obtaining goods under false pretenses. The conflict theorists' point is that our definitions of crime have their roots less in general beliefs about right and wrong than in perceived threats to groups with the power to legislate their interests.

CONTROL OF LAW ENFORCEMENT

Law enforcement patterns as well as legislation reflect the attempts of the more powerful to protect their interests. Yeager (1987) notes the tendency of the U.S. Environmental Protection Agency to focus on smaller rather than larger firms when enforcing its regulations. Szasz (1984) describes industry attempts to control Office of Safety and Health Administration regulation activity— though Freitag (1983) notes that corporations generally do not dominate regulatory commissions by placing their agents on them. Likewise, Pontell et al. (1982) note the manner in which the structure of the medical profession thwarts efforts to police physicians' fraud and abuse. More recently, Smith and Jepson (1993) detail the transfer of influence over the regulation of Florida's marine resources from a once powerful interest group (commercial fishing families) to other economic and political interests like the recreational fishing industry.

Turning to the issue of street crime, Jacobs (1979: 914) writes:

> The more there are inequalities in the distribution of economic power and economic resources, the more one can expect that the social control apparatus of the state will conform to the preferences of monied elites. In this society, the major institution responsible for the coercive maintenance of stability and order is the police.

Jacobs argues that the greater the economic differences in a community, the more likely poorer community members are to attempt forcefully to alter the inequality. Thus, economic elites utilize the police for protection and as a general stabilizer within a community. Jacobs's analysis of police strength in metropolitan areas appears to support his thesis: Law enforcement personnel are more numerous in metropolitan areas where economic inequality is most pronounced.

In the same vein, Liska et al. (1981) report that following civil disorders in the South in the 1950s, 1960s, and early 1970s, whites in cities with larger percentages of nonwhite residents and less residential segregation perceived chances of crime victimization to be greater whether or not actual crime rates changed. Hence, the more powerful whites demanded and received greater police protection. Jackson and Carroll (1981; see Greenberg et al., 1979, for qualifying remarks) confirm this finding in their study of ninety nonsouthern cities, though Jackson's (1986) subsequent work suggests that the finding pertains more to larger than to smaller cities. To the extent that black population and political mobilization increased in cities in the late 1960s and early 1970s, cities' expenditures on police services increased—regardless of their crime rates. The authors conclude that police expenditures are a resource that is mobilized when minority groups appear to threaten the political and economic position of more dominant groups (see also Liska and Chamblin, 1984). They therefore echo Silver's (1967) characterization of the police as a mechanism designed to control "dangerous classes" in a way that protects wealthier classes but does so in a manner not directly orchestrated by the wealthy. That is, police protect the wealthy while appearing to protect the poor as well—all under a "war on crime" umbrella.

THE ELITE DOMINANCE APPROACH

Thus far, we have reviewed characteristics common to conflict theories. However, conflict theorists hold significantly differing views concerning the distribution and use of power in our society. The clearest difference revolves around the question of who is behind legislation and law enforcement: a single dominant class or a number of relatively powerful, competing interest groups. In this section, we examine the dominant role of owner-capitalists in our society; in the next section, we focus on a number of different groups, each of which wields varying amounts of power.

CLASS CONFLICT

A number of prominent conflict theorists argue that law in this society is rooted in class conflict (see Michalowski, 1985). Underlying this approach is the Marxian thesis of perpetual conflict between the two primary economic classes of capitalist societies, those who own or control the means of production (factories, machinery, investment capital) and those who work for these owners turning raw materials into salable goods. Owner-capitalists strive to minimize labor and production costs in order to increase the surplus value of production (profit), which then becomes capital to be invested in other capital-producing markets. If unchecked, the capitalist instinctively and constantly works to mechanize labor, thereby reducing the costs of production, and to monopolize the production market, thereby eliminating competition and increasing the pricing potential of goods in the consumer market. This same instinct drives capitalists constantly to expand both the range of goods they produce and the markets to which they ship these goods.

To the extent that they possess a class consciousness—that is, understand the capitalists' interests vis-à-vis their own—workers find themselves in conflict with owners. Both can lay claim to a portion of the profits from production—the owners by virtue of risked capital and the workers by virtue of their actual transformation of raw materials into usable and salable items. Because capitalists in our society have always, to varying degrees, controlled this process, it is clearly in their interest to keep workers unaware of their potential to enjoy a greater share of the surplus value of production. In terms of its sheer advantage in numbers, an aware and organized worker population could dictate the terms of profit distribution and, by moving one step further, seize the means of production from the owners.

LAW AND THE CAPITALISTS

Previously we mentioned the methods by which owners maintain their advantage over workers: force, compromise when necessary, and, most important, control of social institutions that shape the world view of workers, especially regarding their rights and duties within the capitalist system. Owners do not use any set combination of force, compromise, and control, however, to preserve their superior economic position. Crises within capitalism (unemployment due to increased mechanization, for example) constantly arise, forcing owners to devise new and varied solutions. The solutions in turn spawn new problems and crises (heavy government borrowing to support welfare programs designed to placate the unemployed, for example; see Devine et al., 1988). Thus, the conflict between owners and workers is dynamic, that is, characterized by constant change.

Because it would invite worker wrath during capitalism's sporadic major crises, however, capitalists seek to avoid the appearance of controlling directly the political economy. Thus, capitalists require a mechanism that appears free of direct owner influence, legitimizes the economic system, "holds things together" by defusing crises, and represses rebellion in the name of maintaining the general order. Some argue that the *state* is such a mechanism (for recent discussions of this thesis, see Allen, 1991; Campbell and Linberg, 1990; and Prechel, 1990). Its role is to organize and integrate economic, political, legal, and, occasionally, religious systems and processes. In this context, the legal order may be viewed as protector and enhancer of capitalist interests through tax legislation and incentives and through organization of and arbitration among various capitalist subgroups. At the same time, the apparent neutrality, as well as the mystical quality provided by complicated legal ritual, serves to convince workers that their general interests are maintained and protected. The legitimation given to the "law" by the workers allows capitalists to structure workers' attempts to protest or alter their situations. Thus, political and labor activism is held in check by laws governing the shapes such activism may take. Violations of these laws are addressed by the state for the "common good" — that is, because "no cause justifies illegal activity." Workers in general come to view the law as sacred and fail to appreciate the interests and forces underlying both the law and the crises it addresses.

INSTRUMENTALISTS AND STRUCTURALISTS

Clearly, as we have noted, law is an important tool in the preservation of economic interests, a resource worth fighting to gain and to keep. Yet, some Marxian conflict theorists disagree about the extent to which the law or, more generally, the state is controlled by capitalists. One camp, known as *instrumentalists*, argues that a core of "monopoly capitalists" — those heading the most powerful corporate and banking interests — totally control the state, orchestrate its every action, and utilize legal processes directly to preserve their interests. This approach is rooted in the writings of such theorists as Mills (1956) and Domhoff (1967, 1978), who have demonstrated empirically very strong economic and social ties among industrial leaders and those appointed to high-level government positions regulating business, education, financing, and media (Berkowitz and McQuaid, 1980). Quinney (1980: 84) describes the ruling class:

> The capitalist class also is divided into several fractions. Two major fractions are those capitalists who own major units of the economy and those whose holdings and power are less than that of the uppermost sector of the capitalist class. The upper division, the "monopoly sector," as contrasted to the "lieutenant sector," owns the largest corporations and financial institutions. . . . The other segment is largely delegated power by the monopoly sector.

So powerful are these major capitalists, in the eyes of instrumentalists, that they are able to avoid public scrutiny. Hill (1975) argues that monopoly capitalists

> use all the resources at their command to keep secret the extent of their power, their decisions, who they are, etc. . . . [They] desire to perpetuate the myth that America is a free, classless society. As long as the existence of a ruling class is hidden, the chances of rebellion against it are small. The myth that America is a "pluralistic democracy" is one of the greatest weapons in the arsenal that maintains their class rule.

And so extensive is monopoly capitalists' control of the political process, in the opinion of some instrumentalists (for example, Balkan et al., 1980: 8), that

> we can understand how even as powerful a person as President Nixon could have been forced to resign from the presidency. In spite of continued resistance from many powerful people to label the president a criminal, a sizeable majority of power elites came to the conclusion that, given the public knowledge of the president's "questionable" activities, it would be better for the long-term maintenance of their power to replace him with someone who inspired more public confidence.

The instrumentalist's position often is criticized on several grounds. For example, it fails to consider noneconomic influences on political and legal processes. It cannot account for the outlawing of certain behaviors seemingly in the interests of capitalists, such as price-fixing. It cannot explain why, if capitalists control the law, they do not simply change it to correspond to their interests rather than sometimes violating it themselves. Finally, it fails to consider disagreements and conflict among capitalists.

To counter these criticisms, a number of Marxian theorists espouse a less "vulgar," more complex brand of ruling class theory. These theorists, called *structuralists* (see Chambliss and Seidman, 1982; Greenberg, 1981; Stone, 1985), argue that the state and the law reflect more than simply ruling class interests. Instead, the role the state plays in furthering and legitimating capitalism negates its strict attachment to the monopoly capitalist sector. In short, structuralists believe the state is relatively autonomous (though they dispute the degree of autonomy; see Quadagno, 1984, and Skocpol, 1980) and, as such, protects the long-term interests of capitalists though not always their short-term interests. Thus, the state indeed often does execute the law fairly and against specific capitalists' concerns. Chambliss and Seidman (1982: 308) write:

> The state and government must legitimize the existing political and economic arrangements in order to provide an atmosphere in which capitalist accumulation and production can continue. . . . To serve the interests of the ruling class, the state must create [a sense of fairness] among the people. . . . [T]he state and legal order best fulfill their function as legitimizers when they appear to function as value neutral organs fairly and impartially representing the interests of everyone.

Structuralists as well as instrumentalists are open to criticism, however. For example, while they have begun to document the development of the short-term neutrality or impartiality of the state, they have yet to link short-term autonomy with the hypothesized long-term bias of the state toward capitalism. Structuralists seem as well to underemphasize legal discrimination against segments of the worker population (for example, blacks and women). They tend often to reify the "state," as if it has a life of its own, though Chambliss and Seidman (1982: 309–316) address this problem by refining the concepts of state and autonomy. In short, whereas instrumentalists have given us a conspiratorial ruling class whose existence is difficult to prove, structuralists have given us *two* powerful interests whose relationship is equally difficult to document: capitalists and the state (Allen, 1991; Prechel, 1990).

PLURALIST THEORIES

Though essentially agreeing with Marxian theorists that legislation and law enforcement have their roots in group conflict, another cadre of conflict theorists offers a broader explanation of the legal process. *Pluralist theorists* argue that the legal process is not controlled by one specific interest group but emerges from or is shaped by the conflicting interests of a multiplicity of groups, all seeking something different from a given legal issue (Troyer and Markle, 1982). The object of conflict is not always economic interest; it may also reflect status concerns and moral and ideological commitments. Hence, much of what occurs in legal conflicts is symbolic rather than purely instrumental.

Pluralist theories have their roots in historical studies of the process by which issues are contested and resolved rather than in identification of specific key parties involved in conflict (a theme pursued by Marxian theorists). Although pluralists recognize the unequal distribution of wealth and power in this society and its importance in the negotiation of conflict, they do not accord it the degree of significance that Marxian theorists do (Friedman, 1972). Like Marxian theorists, pluralists consider conflict ongoing and ever-changing as new groups vie for power and as groups in power err through oversight, misdefinition of the situation, and miscalculation of policy effects. Like the Marxian approach, the pluralist approach stresses the importance of gaining and preserving power through control of the world view of groups whose explicit or implicit support is required. Pluralists also vary in the degree to which they believe the state has become an autonomous, interested party in the conflict process rather than simply a sought-after resource.

MULTIPLE INTEREST GROUPS

Pluralists view society as composed partly of groups with varying awareness of their interests, and who organize to differing degrees to maintain and enhance these interests, and partly of groups unaware of their interests and, therefore, unorganized. Although more organized groups vary in their power to benefit themselves, none is so well organized that it enjoys total freedom to promote its interests. Power relationships and, therefore, the positions of interest groups in the power structure continually are subject to threat of change as groups increase or decrease in awareness and organizational might. New groups constantly are becoming conscious of and organizing around their interests and are posing threats to the traditional power structure. (The women's movement is a recent clear case in point.) All powerful groups require the support of other powerful groups above and below them in the power hierarchy. Further, no group can afford to arouse direct opposition from the unorganized; failure to placate this latter group may lead to discontent, which in turn breeds awareness of interests and leads to organized threats to the status quo. This same unorganized group also provides a pool of potential support for the various organized and organizing groups.

Roby (1969) offers a detailed example of law shaped by competition among diverse interest groups. In September 1967, a law took effect in the state of New York that made prostitution and patronizing a prostitute violations — that is, acts less serious than crimes yet still illegal — punishable by a maximum of fifteen days in jail, as opposed to the maximum one-year jail term for prostitution under the previous state law. Prior to the 1967 revision, patronizing a prostitute was not illegal.

According to Roby, the new law emerged from the work of a state governor's commission appointed in 1961 to revise the state's penal code. Following the example set by other states' penal code revisions, and at the urging of a former Supreme Court justice, the commission proposed that prostitution be considered a violation though they did not address the issue of patronizing prostitutes. However, when the proposed revision was presented at a public hearing, certain interested parties apparently caught opponents unaware and persuaded the commission to amend the proposal. An organization called the American Social Health Association argued that patronizing prostitutes should be outlawed in an effort to help prevent the spread of venereal disease. Others argued that patronizing should be outlawed for reasons of fairness — if prostitution is wrong, both parties to it are wrong. The new law, enacted in 1965 and effective as of September 1967, radically altered the legal status of prostitutes and their customers.

Before the new law took effect, however, another interest group exerted itself. Police and prosecutors argued that they would not be able to combat prostitution because customers of prostitutes would now be unwilling to testify against them in court and plainclothes officers would now face legal problems in arresting prostitutes. To force the issue, the police apparently relaxed their enforcement of prostitution laws in downtown Manhattan just before the new law was to take effect. Rumors flew concerning an "invasion" of prostitutes into the area, and this brought yet another group into the legal battle — downtown merchants and hotel owners, who claimed that businesses were being hurt by rampant street prostitution. Their political representatives began pressuring the police for more arrests. At this point, the commission that drafted the new law reentered the fray to defend it.

Just as the new law went into effect, the police flooded the courts with women charged with loitering. They argued that this was their only means to combat prostitution. This tactic brought yet other interest groups into the conflict: the New York Civil Liberties Union and the Legal Aid Society, who protested the dragnet as a violation of the arrested women's civil rights. To end the conflict, the New York City mayor appointed a new committee that accepted the police and prosecutors' proposal that prostitution be made a misdemeanor (a crime) punishable by up to a year in jail. The new proposal was presented to the appropriate state senate committee for review.

In a surprise move, the state senate committee effectively killed the proposed revision for at least a year, ostensibly because it felt a year in jail too harsh a penalty for prostitution. Yet, Roby notes that members of the senate committee had very close ties to the original commission that drafted the prostitution statute causing the conflict. One coalition had outfought the other.

STATE AGENTS

No law exists in a vacuum. Every law represents the intersection of interests of many groups, some cutting across socioeconomic classes. Among interested parties, many pluralists argue, are groups (or agencies) within the state. Legislators themselves have career interests in the legislation they initiate (Hollinger and Lanza-Kaduce, 1988). The creation of laws necessitates the creation of law enforcers (regulatory bureaus, prosecutors' offices, police departments, and so on). Once formed, law enforcement agencies themselves become interest groups whose existence may be threatened by other groups' attempts to decriminalize the behaviors they police, or strengthened through their own attempts to expand the realm of activities they monitor and the procedural powers needed for monitoring. Hence, law enforcement lobbies and public relations divisions attempt to sway legislators and public opinion to preserve or strengthen laws against such activities as drug use, prostitution, and gambling.

IDEOLOGICAL INTERESTS

Pluralists note that the multiplicity of groups involved in a given legislative conflict often indicates a variety of *types* of interest in a given issue. The most obvious of these are economic concerns: Certain groups may stand to lose or to gain economically if a given law is enacted (Graham, 1972). For example, the passage of antipollution laws clearly threatens some corporate financial interests. Laws allowing attorneys to advertise and set their own fee schedules threaten the economic interests of certain established law firms, but enhance the financial interests of other law firms as well as the general public.

Ideological concerns also influence law, in that laws often express political and moral values. The antipollution laws mentioned may reflect the political ideologies of groups who believe corporations should be held accountable for the condition of the environment that they in part shape. Laws governing freedom to protest politically obviously are political. The abortion issue now contested in the political arena is largely a moral issue.

Related to the ideology question is the issue of status in the legal process. Certain groups obtain sufficient power to define in large part the character of our culture (the degree to which it is a religious or a secular culture, for example). Some are able to maintain that powerful status, whereas others lose it and new groups gain it. Thus, the passage of a given law may reflect the rising or falling sociopolitical fortunes of these various groups. The movement toward increased criminalization of "hate crimes" (offenses committed against persons because of their race or sexual orientation, for example) demonstrates the growing political clout of groups that have traditionally lacked such influence (Herek and Berrill, 1992). The study by Zurcher et al. (1971) of antipornography campaigns, for example, indicates that those opposing pornography are fighting for a change in lifestyle or social climate, that is, for the power to define the cultural character of their region. Their success is, therefore, a comment on their sociopolitical status of these crusaders.

Of course, in line with the pluralist's view of intersecting types of interests, it must be pointed out that the economic interests of producers and sellers of pornography also are at stake in such campaigns. Similarly, those strongly opposed to censorship have an ideological interest in the issue. Local politicians — district attorneys, legislators, and so on — may also be party to an antipornography campaign in order to better their election interests. Finally, we should note that status interests at stake in legislation need not involve large groups of persons or status within the larger society. Pfohl (1977), for example, traces modern child abuse laws to the attempt of pediatric radiologists, a low-status specialty group in medicine, to carve out their own sphere of influence within medicine. Rather than working in an area of specialization supplementary to that of the pediatrician, pediatric radiologists now can enhance their status by becoming partners with pediatricians and psychiatrists in the fight against an important illness syndrome.

SYMBOLISM

The ideological and status interests behind some laws call attention to an important issue in most pluralist theories: *symbolic interests* (Edelman, 1964; Gusfield, 1963). Often, the surface issue that is contested is less important to the parties involved than is some underlying, broader issue. Underlying issues cannot always be contested directly in legislatures and courts because they may be too vague to state in legal terms. Instead, some more specific issue, perhaps only loosely tied to the underlying conflict, often becomes symbolic of the contest, mapping out an arena where it can be fought. At times, the groups involved are concerned only with legislation. They care not whether a law can be or is enforced (though the enforcement issue eventually may become symbolic as well) but only that their view of social, moral, or economic order be given the sacred stamp of the law.

Galliher and Cross (1983) provide an excellent illustration of the symbolic theme in their analysis of Nevada's penalty for possession of marijuana. The state's residents feel the need to convince the outside world, and perhaps themselves, that theirs is not a lawless and immoral world even though it permits casino gambling, prostitution, and "quicky" marriages and divorces. Further, the state wishes to show the federal government that it can control unwanted consequences of its liberal laws, such as the intrusion of organized crime. Nevada's tough marijuana law addresses both needs. Nevada is the only state in which first-offense possession of even the smallest quantity of the drug constitutes a felony punishable by up to six years in prison. Yet, Galliher and Cross point out that the law seldom is enforced. They argue that its presence on the books signifies less a desire to stamp out marijuana than a symbolic statement to the outside world concerning Nevada's lawfulness and moral character.

INFLUENCING LEGAL OUTCOMES

Within the pluralist model of the creation of law, the goal of any given group seeking to maintain or enhance its interests is to influence legislators to write laws and law enforcers to administer laws as the interest group sees fit. Because legislators and law enforcement officials are political beings whose jobs depend on a satisfied constituency, an interest group's immediate aim is to bring constituency pressure to bear on the officeholder to the extent necessary to accomplish the desired outcome. Thus, an interest group must sway a public that is indifferent or hostile to a position to accept that position as valid and to pressure its political representatives to legitimate it.

Social identity clearly plays a key role in swaying public opinion (Spector and Kitsuse, 1977; Turner, 1969). Discredited individuals and groups find it difficult to gain a sympathetic ear, whereas prominent and "legitimate" persons (for example, scientific experts and religious leaders) more easily capture an audience. Those attempting to reverse a criminal stigma — that is, to alter the public's definition of a given practice, such as marijuana use or prostitution — find the task extremely difficult, for they appear to have a self-serving interest in changing the public's mind (Jenness, 1990).

Assuming equal social respectability among interested parties in a contest to influence the legal process, the decisive factor is the propaganda effort. Quality of organization and resources utilized in capturing media attention and in directing public sentiment to lawmakers and law enforcers are extremely telling variables (Cohn and Gallagher, 1984; Hollinger and Lanza-Kaduce, 1988; Tierney, 1982). Interest groups attempt to employ symbols of the problem at hand — definitions and pictures of the problem and the people implicated in it that easily capture the public imagination. Thus, stereotypes are promoted (of the drug user, the rapist, the psychopath, the pornographer, and so forth) that fit the general public conception of evil and danger. Edelman (1977: 14) argues that the ability to create a "personified" danger — that is, to put a face to the problem even if that face is in reality only a mask — "marshals public support for controls over a much larger number of ambiguous cases symbolically condensed into the threatening stereotype."

Vocabularies also are created that subtly (and at times not so subtly) seek to influence the public (Edelman, 1977: 26, 1988). For example, proabortion-rights groups choose to characterize themselves as prochoice, whereas antiabortion groups label themselves prolife. Homosexuals present themselves as gay, whereas their opponents call them "perverts" (Spector and Kitsuse, 1977: 13–16). Such tactics accomplish more than simply gaining a public forum for an issue; they transform the issue into a "good versus evil" contest or from a personal trouble to a social problem whereby the public can more easily take a stand (Coltrane and Hickman, 1992).

The result of the propaganda activity of groups contesting an issue often is public indignation about a fiction that has emerged from the competitive propaganda process. For the interest groups, the creation is symbolic; for the public, it is real. Gusfield (1981) offers an illustration in his study of "drinking-driving" laws, or laws governing driving under the influence of alcohol. So effective were the "anti-drunk-driver" campaigns by interested parties that the public now equates the image of "drinking driver" with that of "killer." Gusfield argues that this conception is at odds with reality, at least as it is measured by the types of cases brought before the courts, most of which are treated leniently. Gentry (1988) makes the same point in her discussion of the issue of abducted children as a social problem. So skillful were interested parties in framing this issue that the public came to view the "problem" as one of over 50,000 abductions annually of children by strangers. In fact, evidence indicates that such kidnappings total less than 100 per year.

CRITICISMS OF PLURALIST THEORIES

The strength of the pluralist approach is essentially the weakness of the Marxian theories we discussed previously. Pluralists are able to demonstrate that much of the use of legal process involves the competing interests of many parties, not simply the maneuverings of an economic elite or of the state looking out for the long-term interests of that elite. Countering the pluralists, more radical instrumentalists argue that intergroup competition for both instrumental and symbolic legal support is a mirage, that ruling elites "allow" such competition (as long as it does not threaten specific ruling elite interests) in order to promote the impression that ours is a diversified, democratic society (Calevita, 1983). Of course, this claim is untestable. Yet, pluralists may be open to the more modest criticism that they do not listen closely enough to the Marxian theorists' message. Thus, although they pay lip service to power differentials, to the economic clout of corporations, and to a semiautonomous state, they exclude these elements from most of their analyses.

In part, the absence of attention focused by pluralists on elites is due to the types of law creation studied by pluralists. Pornography laws, for example, reflect the activity of groups of roughly equal power and organization, and such laws tend not to threaten any specific corporate interests. But how might pluralists explain tax law structure or weak legal control of corporations responsible for oil spills on our coasts despite very organized and strong efforts to gain such control (Molotch, 1970)? The answer lies in the pluralist penchant for defining elite involvement in the legal process as defensive, that is, as reacting only to direct economic threat. Surely, elites are sufficiently aware of their interests and sufficiently organized to pursue them that much of their activity is anticipatory and aimed at enhancement as well as at protection of interests.

Coleman (1985a) also argues that the pluralist model pays insufficient attention to the outcomes of conflicts—as opposed to the process by which conflicts occur. He focuses his claim on the effects of the Sherman Antitrust Act on the petroleum industry. On the one hand, antitrust legislation would seem to epitomize the tenets of the pluralist model: an amalgam of populist forces able to constrain major corporate interests. Yet, the resources of the petroleum companies permitted them to dodge the effects of the legislation aimed at them. Companies were able to delay legal proceedings until the political climate changed; they contributed substantially to the campaigns of politicians who could influence their situations; they concealed their holdings and their activities from public and government view; and they threatened state and local economies with plant closings. In short, Coleman argues, antitrust laws have been enforced against petroleum interests rarely and poorly. Pluralism, in this instance, is a mirage.

CONCLUSION

In sum, the conflict perspective seems to address more aggressively and more convincingly the issue of the workings of the legal process than does the consensus model. Despite criticisms of elements of the instrumentalist and structuralist Marxian theories and of pluralist theories, the conflict perspective's basic argument cannot be ignored: Laws do not simply appear miraculously on our law books and do not reflect "society's" values. Instead, the acts and people we call criminal and our concern with crime at any given time reflect the activity of groups in this society seeking legal support for economic, ideological, and status interests. Sometimes, only a few groups are involved in the struggle for legal support; other times, many groups compete. The issue contested in a legal struggle may be explicit and instrumental, or it may be symbolic of some greater conflict. The ebb and flow of law reflects the ebb and flow of interest groups, and laws emerging from this process must be viewed as tentative and negotiable. The key issue for conflict theorists, then, concerns the political strength of the major economic interests in this society: Do they stand alone, or do they share power with other, relatively weaker groups?

DISCUSSION QUESTIONS

1. Discuss the "functions of deviance" thesis. How well does it apply to both smaller and larger societies? What are the major criticisms of the thesis?

2. Discuss the major assumptions that underlie the conflict perspective concerning the criminality of acts and individuals. How do these differ from the assumptions of the consensus approach?

3. According to the conflict perspective, how are the interests of various groups maintained and enhanced in most societies? What role does law play in this process?

4. Distinguish the instrumentalist from the structuralist camp within the conflict perspective. In what ways do these camps differ from another within the conflict perspective, the pluralist approach.

PART TWO

DIMENSIONS OF CRIMINAL ACTIVITY

For most people, the "reality" of crime consists in great part of news media summaries of official crime statistics. But the public really knows very little about the statistics that inform those summaries—crimes reported; persons arrested, convicted, and imprisoned; and so forth. Further, most official crime statistics are quite problematic, so much so that other measures of amounts of crime have been developed. These include surveys of the general population concerning the number and types of crime victimization they have experienced and surveys of select samples of the population regarding number and types of crimes they have committed. These measures, however, have problems as well. In Chapter 3, "Crime and Victimization Data," Robert O'Brien examines the pros and cons of each type of statistic used to tell us something about crime. This balanced evaluation makes it clear that we can never rely solely on one source for the information we need about crime.

Another form of information that may structure our views of crime concerns who commits offenses. This knowledge is important, obviously, for social scientists seeking to explain criminal activity. However, it is also important for the average citizen who carries stereotypes about offenders that shape everyday decisions. In some ways, the basic correlates of criminal activity contain no real surprises: Women commit less crime than do men; younger persons are more active criminally than are their elders. But in Chapter 4, "Criminal Behavior: Gender and Age," Darrell Steffensmeier and Emilie Allan note that the gender–age–crime link is anything but simple to explain. Only when we begin to weave together notions of culture, social constraints, and differential opportunity—that is, unequal access to the chance to commit a crime—do we understand why males are criminally active or, more precisely, why women are not. Similar factors enter into considerations of age differences and rate of offending. In addition, the sheer power of changes in the age composition of the population over time not only influences levels of criminal behavior across age groups but also dictates to a large degree how much crime we will have to deal with as a society.

Perhaps even more difficult to understand is the interrelationship among crime, class, and race. Intuitively, we assume that the lower classes are the more criminal and that, because they are overrepresented among those classes, blacks have higher rates of offending than do whites. In one sense, intuition serves well here, but as Anthony Harris and Lisa Meidlinger point out in Chapter 5, "Criminal Behavior: Race and Class," the issue is not quite that simple. Race matters above and beyond class; the question is, why? The authors are careful to examine first the possibility that bias in the criminal justice system accounts for differential rates of offending across races. They dismiss this as the prime explanatory factor, as well as other commonsense explanations, not the least of which is that crime differences mirror biological variation. They look instead at some ironies of class and family composition and at subcultural differences in degree of proscription of certain offenses across races. Harris and Meidlinger close with a sensitive look at what too many people now believe is irrelevant to discussions of crime and other social problems: the historical *recency* of slavery and its cultural and psychological legacy.

Part Two concludes by shifting from profiles of offenders to profiles of victims—ultimately very similar pictures. In Chapter 6, "Crime Victims," Andrew Karmen discusses changing victimization trends in recent years and presents some findings that may surprise the average reader of this book. In explaining differences in rates of victimization, Karmen turns to the concept of differential risk; that is, the chances of being a crime victim are far from evenly distributed across our population. Population groups differ in lifestyle (exposure to crime situations) and in means to assure protection from crime. Within groups, individuals differ along much the same lines. Does this mean that the victim is to blame for the crime? Karmen cautions against this conclusion in his examination of the poorly conceived notion of victim precipitation of crime. He closes with a discussion of a related policy question: How and to what extent should victims of crime be compensated for their losses?

CHAPTER 3

CRIME AND VICTIMIZATION DATA*

Robert M. O'Brien
University of Oregon

FEDERAL, STATE, and local governments in the United States spend tens of millions of dollars compiling and analyzing crime statistics each year. This effort involves hundreds of thousands of person hours. The uses for these data range from influencing the allocation of resources within local law enforcement agencies to testing criminological theories. Crime statistics help establish the basic "social facts" of crime: How does the crime rate vary by age, sex, race, and income level of offenders and victims? How does it vary by the time of day, area of the city, or region of the country? How are the relationships between individuals (for example, strangers, friends, and relatives) related to the rates at which crimes are committed? These social facts form the building blocks for theories of criminal behavior and provide evidence by which these theories may be evaluated. There would be no reason to speak of teenagers "aging out of crime" if the rates of street crime were the same for seventeen- and forty-four-year-olds. If southern and northeastern states had the same rates of homicide, there would be no theory of a southern "culture of violence."

This chapter describes, evaluates, and compares the three major sources of crime data in the United States: the *Uniform Crime Reports*, the National Crime Victimization Survey, and self-report surveys. For each of these, we briefly describe how and what sorts of data are collected and some prominent problems and uses for these data. We then compare the data from these sources to see if they give us a similar picture of crime and victimization in the United States.

---

*Parts of this chapter are based on *Crime and Victimization Data* (O'Brien, 1985).

UNIFORM CRIME REPORTS: POLICE REPORTS OF CRIME

The most widely publicized criminal statistics in the United States are those based on the *Uniform Crime Reports* (UCR). When we read in a newspaper that the homicide rate in California is higher than the national average or that Detroit has the highest rate of homicide for any city over one million population in the United States, these figures are almost certainly based on UCR data.

The Uniform Crime Reporting program was initiated in the 1930s in order to obtain more reliable and comparable crime statistics. Nonuniform definitions of crimes from state to state and sometimes even between law enforcement jurisdictions within the same state presented a major obstacle to obtaining such data. In order to make the criminal statistics more comparable, the Uniform Crime Reporting program was developed to provide uniform definitions of crimes. Law enforcement agencies in the program report crimes on the basis of procedures for classifying and scoring offenses that are contained in the *Uniform Crime Reporting Handbook* (FBI, 1985). The purpose of these procedures is to make data on crimes as comparable as possible from one jurisdiction to another.

Local law enforcement agencies (police departments, sheriffs' departments, and so on) tabulate data collected under the Uniform Crime Reporting program using rules specified in the crime reporting handbook. These tabulations are then sent either directly to the FBI or to a state-level UCR program. In 1991, there were forty-two state-level programs. These programs, as well as the FBI, are responsible for providing some degree of quality control for the data. These quality checks include examining each report for arithmetic accuracy, for patterns of rates that differ from similar reporting agencies, and for trends that are unusual. Participation in the UCR program is voluntary except that many states with state-level programs have mandatory reporting requirements. In 1991, law enforcement agencies active in the program represented 241 million U.S. inhabitants: approximately 96 percent of the population living in the United States.

COVERAGE

The UCR provides a wealth of data with wide geographic coverage. These data are often available only in aggregate form, for example, number and rates of crimes for regions, states, Metropolitan Statistical Areas, cities, and counties. The UCR separates crimes into two parts. Part I crimes consist of murder and nonnegligent manslaughter, forcible rape, robbery, aggravated assault, burglary, larceny-theft, motor vehicle theft, and arson. Part II crimes include simple assault, forgery and counterfeiting, fraud, embezzlement, vandalism, prostitution and commercial vice, drug abuse violations, gambling, driving under the influence, disorderly conduct, vagrancy, and several other crimes. Table 3.1 contains a brief definition for each of the Part I crimes.

The number and rate of criminal incidents for these crimes are reported annually in *Crime in the United States* (FBI). This publication reports several indices of crime. The crime index is a simple sum of all Part I crimes except arson. This index is broken down into a violent crime index (murder and

TABLE 3.1   OFFENSES IN UNIFORM CRIME REPORTING

Part I Offenses

Criminal homicide: Murder and nonnegligent manslaughter: the willful (nonnegligent) killing of one human being by another. Deaths caused by negligence and justifiable homicides are excluded.

Forcible rape: The carnal knowledge of a female forcibly and against her will. Included are rapes by force and attempts or assaults to rape. Statutory offenses (no force used and victim under age of consent) are excluded.

Robbery: The taking or attempting to take anything of value from the care, custody, or control of a person or persons by force or threat of force or violence or by putting the victim in fear.

Aggravated assault: An unlawful attack by one person on another for the purpose of inflicting severe or aggravated bodily injury. This type of assault is usually accompanied by the use of a weapon or by means likely to produce death or great bodily harm. Simple assaults are excluded.

Burglary-breaking or entering: The unlawful entry of a structure to commit a felony or a theft. Attempted forcible entry is included.

Larceny-theft (except motor vehicle theft): The unlawful taking, carrying, leading, or riding away of property from the possession or constructive possession of another. Attempted larcenies are included. Embezzlement, con games, forgery, worthless checks, etc., are excluded.

Motor vehicle theft: The theft or attempted theft of a motor vehicle. A motor vehicle is self-propelled and runs on the surface and not on rails. Specifically excluded from this category are motorboats, construction equipment, airplanes, and farming equipment.

Arson: Any willful or malicious burning or attempt to burn, with or without intent to defraud, a dwelling house, public building, motor vehicle or aircraft, personal property of another, etc.

---

nonnegligent homicide, forcible rape, robbery, and aggravated assault) and a property crime index (burglary, larceny-theft, and motor vehicle theft). These crime indices can be misleading since they weigh crimes equally regardless of their type. Thus, in the crime index an increase of 2,000 incidents in the murder and nonnegligent manslaughter category would be overwhelmed by a decrease in the number of larceny thefts of 4,000. For this reason, it is best to examine the Part I crimes separately rather than in index form.

Table 3.2 uses data drawn from *Crime in the United States* (FBI, 1992). Here it is aggregated at the national level. The first column, labeled offense, designates the crime index, the two subindices of violent and property crimes, and each of the crimes that make up those crime indices. The next column lists the estimated number of crimes known to the police, the third column reports

TABLE 3.2   **PART I CRIMES AND INDEXES OF CRIME FOR THE UNITED STATES, 1991**

Offense	Number	Rate per 100,000 Inhabitants	Percent Change from 1982 to 1991 in Rate per 100,000
Crime index total	14,872,900	5,897.8	+5.3
Violent crime index	1,911,770	758.1	+32.7
Murder	24,700	9.8	+7.6
Forcible rape	106,590	42.3	+24.4
Robbery	687,730	272.7	+14.1
Aggravated assault	1,092,740	433.3	+49.8
Property crime index	12,961,100	5,139.7	+2.1
Burglary	3,157,200	1,252.0	−15.9
Larceny-theft	8,142,200	3,228.8	+4.7
Motor vehicle theft	1,661,700	659.0	+43.6

SOURCE: Adapted from *Crime in the United States—1991* (FBI, 1992: Table 1).

crime rates per 100,000 inhabitants, and the final column lists the percent change in the crime rate between 1982 and 1991. For example, in 1991 there were 24,700 murders in the United States, a rate of 9.8 per 100,000 persons. This rate represented a 7.6 percent increase over 1982.

In addition to crimes known to the police, which are reported for Part I crimes, the UCR includes data such as arrests for both Part I and Part II offenses, crimes that have been "cleared" by arrests or other means, the number of law enforcement officers killed or assaulted, and crimes that have occurred on college campuses.

The FBI annual publication, *Crime in the United States*, provides data in highly aggregated form with little or no information concerning the victims and little concerning the demographic characteristics of offenders. The general exception to this rule pertains to data regarding homicide. For murders, the UCR provides information on the age, sex, race, and ethnic origin of victims as well as the race, sex, and ethnic origin of the offenders. The race and ethnic origin of victims and offenders are cross-classified, and the types of weapons (for example, firearm, knife, poison, explosives, fire, or fists) used in the offense are tabulated. The relationship between the offender and the victim (for example, wife, husband, son, daughter, boyfriend, girlfriend, neighbor, or stranger) is described. These data help policymakers and researchers since they provide a more detailed view of crime. In the future, we can expect more data like these, and even greater detail concerning criminal incidents, since the FBI is moving to a "National Incident-Based Reporting System," which we discuss further later. This system will provide details about criminal incidents like those currently available for homicide.

TABLE 3.3

PERCENTAGE OF VICTIMIZATIONS REPORTED TO THE POLICE AND TYPE OF REASONS GIVEN FOR NOT REPORTING, 1991

	Rape and Attempted Rape	Personal Robbery	Household Burglary	Motor Vehicle Theft
Percent reported	59	55	50	74
Reasons for not reporting (in %):				
Police inefficient, ineffective, or biased	2*	11	5	4
Police would not want to be bothered	2*	10	9	12
Too inconvenient or time consuming	6*	6	3	7
Private or personal matter	25*	7	6	6
Fear of reprisal	11*	5	1	0*

SOURCE: Data are from *Criminal Victimization in the United States — 1991* (U.S. Department of Justice, 1992a: Tables 101 and 112).

*Estimate is based on about ten or fewer sample cases.

GENERATING UCR CRIME INCIDENTS

A key to understanding and evaluating data on crime rates is to examine how they are produced. Two major stages in the production of official crime statistics involve the reporting of crimes by citizens and the recording of crimes by law enforcement personnel.

Part I and Part II crimes usually come to the attention of the police through citizens' complaints; thus, the reporting behavior of citizens plays a major role in determining the number of crimes known to the police. Whether crimes are reported to the police depends on a number of factors: the seriousness of the crime, the relationship of the victim to the offender, embarrassment, self-incrimination, perceptions about whether the police could do anything about the crime, and fear of reprisals. Table 3.3 displays some of the reasons for not reporting crimes to the police that are given by respondents in the National Crime Victimization Surveys (NCVS), which we describe in detail later in this chapter. Note that NCVS respondents claim to have reported only 59 percent of rape incidents to the police. Twenty-five percent of the respondents who did not report a rape incident to the police said that it was a private or personal matter, and 11 percent said they feared reprisal.

Once an incident has come to the attention of the police, the recording of the act in police records as a "crime known to the police" depends on factors such as the technical qualification of the incident as criminal, organizational pressures to get the crime rate up or down, police officer and offender interactions, and the professional style of particular police departments. Before incidents are recorded as crimes known to the police, they must go through a procedure to determine whether police think that a crime has occurred. If they are unfounded or determined not to be Part I crimes, they are eliminated from the count. There is also a special "counting rule," whereby only the most serious crime that occurred during a single criminal incident is counted. For this purpose, the seriousness of a crime corresponds to the order of the index offenses in Table 3.2. For example, if a person enters a house, steals a camera, then encounters and threatens the owner with a gun and steals his or her car, that person has committed a number of index crimes, but the UCR would record only the most serious — robbery. The reporting of arson serves as an exception; it is reported even if other index crimes have occurred.

Law enforcement agencies exist in a sociopolitical environment in which their performances and needs are often evaluated on the basis of crime statistics. Their detection of crimes may be interpreted as a sign of effectiveness in dealing with the crime problem or as a sign that they do not have the crime problem under control. Their requests for funding and expansion may be based on perceptions of the extent of the crime problem (Chambliss, 1984; Selke and Pepinsky, 1982). Under political pressures, law enforcement agencies may "crack down" on certain crimes such as gambling, prostitution, or drugs (Defleur, 1975; Sheley and Hanlon, 1978). This results in an increase in the detection or recording of these crimes that is not based on an increase in offending behavior. By the same token, Seidman and Couzens (1974) noted an abrupt drop in one city's percentage of larcenies of $50 or more in response to the installation of a new police chief who threatened to replace police commanders who were unable to reduce crime in their jurisdictions. The importance of the more or less than $50 criterion was that larcenies of less than $50 were not reported in the FBI crime index.

In addition to differences in state laws and certain differences in city and county ordinances, individual law enforcement agencies differ in degree of professionalism, style of enforcement, number of police per citizen, and so on. In a study involving eight cities, Wilson (1978) argued that there are at least three distinctive styles or strategies defining the role of patrol officers. The *watchman* style emphasizes an order maintenance function rather than the enforcement function for crimes that are not "serious." This allows patrol officers to ignore many common minor violations that are not a direct threat to public order. The *legalistic* style may induce patrol officers to handle commonplace situations as if they were matters of law enforcement rather than order maintenance. The *service* style demands that police take seriously all requests for either law enforcement or order maintenance; however, departments with this orientation are less likely to make an arrest than police with a legalistic style.

Whether an incident is recorded by the police as a crime involves a great deal of discretion by individual police officers. Several criminologists have examined the factors that contribute to an incident being written-up in an official report. One such study involved a research team of observers who rode with police patrols in Boston, Chicago, and Washington, D.C. In this study, Black (1970) reported that the seriousness of the alleged offense, the complainant's manifest preference for police action, the relational distance between the complainant and the offender (the greater the distance, the more likely a report will be filed), and the more differential the complainant, the more likely an official report will be made. Smith and Visher (1982) and Visher (1983) replicated many of the findings from Black's study. They found that the presence of a bystander, the preference of the complainant for formal or informal action, the demeanor of the suspect (antagonistic or not), whether the suspect is a stranger or not, whether the offense was a felony, and the complainant's race were all significantly related to whether police decide to arrest a suspect.

UCR data require victims who are motivated to report incidents to the police, and then these incidents must pass through the filter of police recording procedures. An alternative strategy for estimating the amount of crime is to survey the victims of crime. We turn now to this form of data.

NATIONAL CRIME VICTIMIZATION SURVEY: VICTIM REPORTS

Problems with the data presented in official reports served to motivate the National Crime Victimization Survey (NCVS; prior to 1990, this was referred to as the National Crime Survey). It was expected that this ongoing survey would provide more reliable measures of the absolute rates of serious crime and more reliable data on crime trends. In addition, the survey would supply more detailed information on a number of situational factors, such as the locations at which crimes occur (home, office, or school), the time of day at which they occur, whether a weapon was used, and how many victims were involved. Finally, data from victimization surveys would provide a wealth of information on victims that was not available for most crimes recorded in the UCR: data describing their sex, race, age, educational background, marital status, whether they were injured, the amount of medical expenses incurred, and whether the property lost was insured.

The NCVS can be divided into two separate major programs. The first of these programs involved surveys of cities conducted between 1972 and 1975, and the second is an ongoing national survey that has been conducted continuously since July of 1972. The city surveys were conducted in twenty-six large central cities. Thirteen of the cities were surveyed twice and thirteen only once. Eight of the cities were surveyed in 1972, five in 1973, thirteen in 1974, and then the thirteen cities surveyed in 1972–1973 were resurveyed in 1975. These studies involved probability samples of both households and businesses and made it possible to compare survey-generated victimization rates for cities with city-level data on offenses reported from the UCR. The city surveys were discontinued in 1975 and have not been resumed.

The national sample, like the city sample, was originally based on both businesses and households. (Businesses were included in the national program from 1972 to 1976.) The household surveys began in July of 1972. They involve a panel of households (addresses) in which interviews are conducted at six-month intervals. The interviewer inquires about criminal incidents that may have occurred during the preceding six months. In 1991, the sample contained about 42,000 housing units with about 83,000 people age 12 or older. The United States Census Bureau, which draws the sample and conducts the interviews, has achieved a very high rate of response. (Ninety-seven percent of the households selected to participate did so in 1991.)

COVERAGE

The classification of crimes in the NCVS publications follows closely the definitions used in the *Uniform Crime Reporting Handbook* (FBI, 1985). Two types of crime counts are made from the survey data: a count of victims of criminality and another of criminal incidents. Victim counts tally the number of people who have had crimes committed against them. Incident counts tally the number of criminal episodes that have occurred. They correspond to UCR crime counts; that is, only one incident is counted for a continuous sequence of criminal behavior: "If a robber enters a bar and robs the cash register receipts and a wallet from the bartender and personal property from five patrons, the UCR counts only one robbery; there was a single incident of robbery in which there were six victimizations" (Garofalo and Hindelang, 1977: 22). For crimes involving households (household burglary, household larceny, and motor vehicle theft) there is no distinction between victimizations and incidents since in these cases the household is considered the victim. For personal crimes, however (rape, assault, robbery, and personal larceny), the distinction between the number of incidents and the number of persons victimized must be carefully observed.

The types of crimes included in the NCVS are more limited than those covered in the UCR. The NCVS "screen" questions concern only Part I crimes (with the exclusion of homicide and arson) as well as questions that elicit information on simple assaults. Table 3.4 contains NCVS estimates of the number of incidents and the number of victimizations in the United States in 1991. The number of incidents is less than the number of victimizations for personal crimes since a single incident may involve more than one victim. For household crimes, the household is considered the victim so that the number of incidents and the number of victimizations are the same.

Several other NCVS breakdowns of victimizations are presented annually in *Criminal Victimization in the United States* (U.S. Department of Justice, 1992a), for example, the percentage of victimizations involving strangers and nonstrangers; victimization rates by sex, age, race, and annual personal income; household victimizations by race, age of head of household, and annual family income; the percentage of victimizations that were reported to the police and the reasons for not reporting; the amount of money lost due to theft; and the number of days of hospitalization resulting from injuries received in victimizations.

The FBI plans to supply similar sorts of data on all Part I and Part II offenses through a vehicle called the National Incident-Based Reporting System (NIBRS). Instead of having most data reported in aggregate-level form (for example, 10,000 homicides, 4,000 completed rapes, and 3,000 attempted rapes in a particular police jurisdiction), the incident would serve as the unit of analysis. The NIBRS would collect data on each incident and arrest within twenty-two crime categories. For each offense known to the police, information on the incident, the victim, the offender, and the arrestee would be gathered. This system would provide details about many types of criminal incidents that now are known only regarding homicide and through the NCVS.

TABLE 3.4   **INCIDENTS AND VICTIMIZATIONS BY TYPE OF CRIME**

Type of Crime	Victimization		Incidents	
	Number	*Rate per 10,000*	*Number*	*Rate per 10,000*
All personal crimes	18,956,060	923.13	18,357,790	894.00
Crimes of violence	6,423,510	312.82	5,836,160	284.21
Rape	173,310	8.44	171,420	8.35
Robbery	1,145,020	55.76	1,064,750	51.85
Aggravated assault	1,608,580	78.34	1,371,610	66.80
Simple assault	3,496,580	170.28	3,228,370	157.22
Personal larceny with contact	482,110	23.48	476,460	23.20
Personal larceny without contact	12,050,430	586.84	12,045,160	586.58
Household sector	15,774,310	768.19	15,774,310	768.19
Burglary	5,138,310	250.23	5,138,310	250.23
Household larceny	8,523,660	415.09	8,523,660	415.09
Motor vehicle theft	2,122,330	103.35	2,122,330	103.35

SOURCE: Data are from *Criminal Victimization in the United States — 1991* (U.S. Department of Justice, 1992a: Tables 1 and 56).

The coverage of the NCVS is limited by its sample design. Because it is a sample of households, no data are included on commercial crimes, such as commercial burglaries and shoplifting. Although the sample is large enough to provide reliable estimates of crime rates for the United States as a whole, or even for males and females in the United States for most commonly reported crimes, the sample is not large enough to provide reliable estimates of rates for crimes that are not often reported (for example, rapes) or to estimate crime rates for states or cities. The UCR is the only database that provides detailed geographic coverage.

GENERATING NCVS CRIME INCIDENTS

Like the UCR data, it is helpful to consider how NCVS crime rates are produced. These estimates are based on sample surveys in which respondents answer a series of questions that are posed by an interviewer. These interviews are social interactions in which the interviewer is asking the respondents for their time and effort, while the interviewer has little or nothing to offer respondents in return. The data that result from these interviews share many of the weaknesses of data gathered in other sample survey interviews (respondent fatigue, sampling errors, social desirability responses, forgetting about past events, and the like).

The form of the NCVS interviews has changed over time. Currently, the first interview is conducted face to face, and follow-up interviews are conducted by phone. (Originally, an attempt was made to conduct the bulk of the interviews face to face.) One part of the interview schedule contains a series of screen questions designed to elicit information about whether a victimization of any kind occurred. These screen questions are followed by more detailed questions concerning any incidents that are reported by the respondent. Examples of some household screen questions are as follows (U.S. Department of Justice, 1992a: 122):

> Now I'd like to ask some questions about crime. They refer to the last 6 months — between _____ 1, 19___ and _____, 19___. During the last six months, did anyone break into or somehow illegally get into your (apartment/home), garage, or another building on your property?

> (Other than the incident(s) just mentioned) Did you find a door jimmied, a lock forced, or any other signs of an ATTEMPTED break in?

> Was anything at all stolen that is kept outside your home, or happened to be left out, such as a bicycle, a garden hose or lawn furniture? (other than the incidents already mentioned)

> What was the TOTAL number of motor vehicles (cars, trucks, motorcycles, etc.) owned by you or any other member of this household during the last 6 months? Include those you no longer own.

> Did anyone steal, TRY to steal, or use (it/any of them) without permission?

These questions and others are answered by a knowledgeable adult responding for the entire household. Individual screen questions concerning personal victimizations also are asked of all household members over the age of eleven. A knowledgeable household member may serve as a proxy interviewee for a household member in some circumstances (for example, a household member is mentally or physically unable to be interviewed or the parents do not want a child of twelve or thirteen to be interviewed). After the screen questions, interviewers ask a series of questions designed to obtain detailed information about any incidents noted in the screen questions.

Several of the procedures in the NCVS are based on extensive pretesting. For example, the panel design "bounds" all interviews after the initial one. After the first interview, the interviewer asks about incidents that have occurred during the six months since the last interview. This is an important design feature. An early study (Woltman and Bushery, 1975) found that unbounded interviews result in estimated victimization rates that are 30 to 40 percent higher than bounded interviews. The reference period of six months was chosen to balance the forgetting of incidents that might occur if a longer reference period were used with the costs of more frequent interviews (Turner, 1972). Finally, using screen questions before asking details about each incident generates more reported incidents. Pretests showed that respondents who had to go immediately through a long series of questions about each incident were more likely not to report that they had been victimized on later screen questions.

To determine whether respondents would report crimes to NCVS interviewers that they had reported to the police, Turner (1972) investigated 206 cases of robbery, assault, and rape from police records that had occurred in the past year. The victims of these reported crimes were then interviewed using a standard survey instrument that asked about criminal victimizations they had experienced during the past year. He found that only 63.1 percent of the incidents found in police records were reported in the interview. Not surprisingly, the percentage reporting these incidents to the interviewers was strongly related to the relationship of the victim and offender. When the offender was a stranger (N = 99), 76.3 percent of the incidents were reported to the interviewer; when the offender was known to the victim (N = 78), 56.9 percent of the incidents were reported; and when the offender was a relative (N = 18), only 22.2 percent of the incidents were reported. A similar study in Baltimore (Murphy and Dodge, 1981) found a relationship between the type of crime and reporting the incidents to the NCVS interviewer: Only 37 percent of the assaults, 75 percent of the larcenies, 76 percent of the robberies, and 86 percent of the burglaries were reported.

Some of this nonreporting of crimes to interviewers can be attributed to respondent embarrassment about the incident, to the seriousness of the incidents, and to other factors. Part of it, however, is due to memory decay or forgetting. In the San Jose study, Turner (1972) found a relationship between the number of months between the reported incident and the interview and the percentage of incidents that were reported to the interviewer. For those incidents occurring one to three months before the interview, 69 percent were reported to the interviewer (N = 101); for those occurring four to six months before, 50 percent were reported (N = 100); for those occurring seven to nine months before, 46 percent were reported (N = 103); and for those occurring ten to twelve months before, only 30 percent of the victimizations were reported to the interviewer (N = 90). This sort of evidence was one of the reasons the NCVS instituted interviews every six months rather than yearly.

Sampling errors are a problem in all sample surveys, but they pose a special problem in victimization surveys because victimizations are a relatively rare phenomenon. For example, in any given year, over 90 percent of the respondents in the NCVS report having not been the victim of any crime, whether attempted, minor, or major. The sampling error is greater for rare events. For example, in any given year, respondents are likely to report about 100 rape incidents to NCVS interviewers. If a researcher wants to study rapes involving white offenders and black victims, there are likely to be far too few incidents to make any reasonable statistical generalizations (for example, what is the typical relationship between the victim and the offender or in what locations are such incidents most likely to occur). In such cases, researchers often combine data from a number of years.

Although the NCVS provide data on the victims of crime and some information on the location of crimes, they provide little data on offenders. For criminologists interested in the causes of criminal behavior, this is a serious shortcoming.

SELF-REPORT SURVEYS: OFFENDER REPORTS

Self-report (SR) surveys constitute the third major method used to gather data on crime. They do not involve examination of police records or asking the victims of crimes about criminal incidents; instead, they involve asking the offenders themselves, or at least samples of respondents, about behavior that might lead to their classification as offenders.

Unlike the UCR and the NCVS, there is no single set of offenses investigated or single design by which SR data are gathered. Different researchers have used diverse sets of questions and sampled different populations. We will focus on three well-known studies: Short and Nye (1958) because of its historical interest and its influence on the studies that followed; the National Youth Survey (NYS) (Elliott et al., 1983) since it is based on a national panel and is the most comprehensive SR study to date; and the Seattle Methods Study (Hindelang et al., 1981) because of the answers it provides concerning some of the strengths and weaknesses of the SR method.

SR studies differ on a number of dimensions. Short and Nye's original studies used questionnaires to ascertain the level of delinquency. They presented a checklist of behaviors to respondents and collected other relevant data such as the sex of the respondent, whether the respondent was from a broken home, and the socioeconomic status (SES) of the home from which the respondent came. The National Youth Survey (NYS) uses face-to-face interviews. Arguments favoring the use of interviews over questionnaires can be made, and bringing empirical data to bear on this question was one of the purposes of the Seattle Methods Study.

Another dimension on which SR studies differ is sampling design. A typical design involves the sampling of a school population and of an institutionalized population or a population with known police records. For example, Short and Nye (1958) sampled high school students in three western high schools, three midwestern high schools, and a western training school. The Seattle Methods Study (Hindelang et al., 1981) sampled three separate groups in order to maximize the variance regarding delinquency and to represent the general adolescent population of Seattle. One sample drew from students enrolled in Seattle public schools for the 1977–1978 academic year; another from those with a record of contact with the Seattle police, but with no official juvenile court record; and the third from the population of adolescents referred to the juvenile court serving Seattle. These samples were drawn to contrast different populations and not to generalize to larger populations of cities or regions of the country. The NYS uses a probability sample of households in the continental United States and is more representative of the population of the entire country.

COVERAGE

The SR method is the dominant method in criminology for studying the etiology of crime. It allows researchers to collect detailed information about individual "offenders." This is in marked contrast to both the UCR and NCVS data. Victimization surveys provide little information about offenders, and UCR data include data on offender characteristics only for those arrested and then only for a few demographic variables. The new incident-based approach, which is being instituted in the UCR, will provide better data on offenders but will not be as detailed as that made possible by surveying offenders.

The type of information on offenders (family background, demographic characteristics, personality measures, and so on) that is included in SR studies varies from study to study, depending on the interests of the researcher. Almost all SR studies, however, have included basic demographic information: the respondent's sex, age, race, and family SES. Then, depending on the researcher's interests, a series of questions concerning various other independent variables are included. For example, Short and Nye (1957) were interested in whether respondents who came from broken homes were more likely to report delinquent activities. Hirschi (1969), who wanted to test social control theory, included questions on interest in school and achievement motivation. The NYS (Elliott et al., 1983) contains measures of the family structure, work status of the respondent, whether the respondent is in or out of school, perceptions of neighborhood crime and environmental problems, and religious attendance.

Most recent SR studies carefully differentiate the prevalence of reported behavior from the incidence of reported behavior. Prevalence refers to the number of persons reporting one or more behaviors of a given type within a specified reference period; whereas, incidence refers to the number of behaviors that occur in the reference period. Thus, "the prevalence rate is typically expressed as the proportion of persons in the population who have reported some involvement in a particular offense or set of offenses" (Elliott et al., 1983: 18). Incidence rates are often expressed as the "average number of offenses per person, or as the number of offenses per some population base (e.g., 100, 1000, or 100,000 persons)" (Elliott et al., 1983: 19). Incidence rates are more comparable to UCR data on crimes known to police since they are based on the number of incidents known to the police. Table 3.5 presents both prevalence and incidence rates for the NYS in 1980 when the respondents were age 15 to 21.

The prevalence rate indicates the percentage of respondents reporting one or more offenses in a particular category. Thus, 62 percent of the respondents claimed to have been involved in a status offense during 1980, whereas only 2 percent claimed to have been involved in a robbery. The incidence rates are

TABLE 3.5 **PREVALENCE AND INCIDENCE RATES FOR
15- TO 21-YEAR-OLDS IN THE 1980 NYS**

	Prevalence	Incidence
Offense-Specific Scales		
Felony assault	9	.29
Minor assault	21	1.20
Robbery	2	.10
Felony theft	9	.44
Minor theft	15	1.09
Damaged property	15	.64
Hard drug use	17	5.79
Offense-Category Scales		
Illegal services	11	4.50
Public disorder	48	10.33
Status offense	62	18.07
Crimes against persons	24	1.60
General theft	18	1.53
Summary Scales		
School delinquency	56	8.89
Home delinquency	14	.70
Index offenses	12	.62
Fraud	5	.65

SOURCE: Elliott et al. (1983, adapted from Tables 4.29 and 4.40).
Note: Prevalence represents the percentage admitting to one or more acts in that category during the past year. The incidence rates represent the average number of reported delinquent acts per respondent in that category during the past year.

reported as the average number of incidents per respondent. The average number of status offenses per respondent is 18.07, whereas the average number of robberies is only .10. Involvement in delinquencies of some sort is widespread among youth; involvement in more serious crime is relatively rare.

GENERATING SR CRIME INCIDENTS

Since SR data are gathered using survey methods, they share many of the strengths and weaknesses of other data gathered by these methods. SR studies allow researchers to ask offenders and nonoffenders a variety of questions concerning their behaviors, perceptions, and attitudes; there is no standard set of SR offense questions. For this and other reasons, the method has great potential for studying the etiology of criminal behavior. By way of example, the seven questions employed by Short and Nye (1958) are much like those that traditionally have appeared on self-report surveys:

Recent research has found that everyone breaks rules and regulations during his lifetime. Some break them regularly, others less often. Below are some frequently broken rules. Check those that you have broken since the beginning of grade school.

1. Driven a car without a driver's license or permit? (Do not include driver training.)
2. Skipped school without a legitimate excuse?
3. Defied your parents' authority (to their face)?
4. Taken little things (worth less than $2) that did not belong to you?
5. Bought or drank beer, wine, or liquor? (Include drinking at home.)
6. Purposely damaged or destroyed public or private property that did not belong to you?
7. Had sex relations with a person of the opposite sex?

More recent studies now tend to include questions concerning more serious crimes. The NYS (Elliott et al., 1983) asks about a wide range of delinquencies and crimes from the trivial "lied about age" to "strong armed robbery" and "physical threat for sex." This range of crimes is much wider than that in the original Short and Nye items. Additionally, the response categories allow for the recording of more specific frequencies for respondents who engage in a great deal of criminal behavior.

When asking about serious crimes, a problem similar to that encountered in the NCVS occurs; that is, for rare events a large sample is necessary to provide reliable measures. Since respondents report far fewer incidents in which they beat someone up so badly that they required hospitalization than incidents in which they defied their parents, rates for these more serious incidents are more difficult to measure reliably.

Information concerning the geographic distribution of crime based on SR studies is even more limited than that obtained from the NCVS. The most extensive study to date is the NYS, which is based on approximately 1,500 respondents. This sample size is sufficient to generate reliable prevalence and incidence rates for the nation as a whole for most of the delinquent behaviors included in the interviews but is not large enough to allow detailed breakdowns by geographic area (for example, rates for states or cities).

Response rates in SR studies have been low. In the methodological study by Hindelang et al. (1981), only about 50 percent of the original sample agreed to participate. Importantly, the rates of participation differed for different groups of potential respondents. For example, only 48.5 percent of the African-American females who were drawn from official court cases in the original sample were located, and only 55.7 percent of those located agreed to participate. For African-American males who were drawn from official court cases, 70.4 percent of the original sample were located, and 66 percent of those located agreed to participate (Hindelang et al., 1981: Table 22). Even in the best financed surveys, there are substantial problems with response rates. For the NYS (Elliott et al., 1983), a sample of 2,360 eligible youths was selected. Of these, 73 percent agreed to participate in 1976. By 1980, the sample size was down to 1,494, or 63 percent of the original sample.

Until Short and Nye (1957), many social researchers believed that the SR method would not work because people would not admit to negative behaviors. After all, the social desirability effect had been well documented in survey research; for example, people overestimate their contributions to charities and their frequency of voting in elections. It would seem unlikely, therefore, that they would admit to criminal or delinquent behaviors. The results were surprising to many social scientists; respondents admit to a great deal of delinquent behavior (see Table 3.5). This does not mean, however, that respondents report their delinquent behaviors accurately, but a large number of respondents are not too embarrassed to admit to some delinquent behavior. Many studies have attempted to assess the validity of respondents' reported behavior.

The most rigorous approach to testing the validity of respondents' reports is to compare self-reports of official delinquency (admission of official contact) with official police and court records. Although Short and Nye did not use this validation technique, it was used in the early 1960s by Erickson and Empey (1963). Of 130 respondents who had been to court, every one mentioned this in their interviews. Hardt and Peterson-Hardt (1977) found no police record for 95 percent of their respondents reporting no record. Hindelang et al. (1981) found moderate to strong correlations between official records and each of the following: respondents' self-reported number of times picked up by the police, self-reported number of times referred to the courts by the police, and an index of self-reported official contacts for both males and females.

SR studies provide yet another picture of the volume and distribution of crime and delinquency. This picture is not based on the law enforcement perspective (police data) or on the perspective of the victims of crime but on data from the offenders. In the next section, we compare results from these three data sources to see if they paint the same picture.

UCR, NCVS, AND SR DATA: CONVERGENCE AND DIVERGENCE

The first sections of this chapter examined three major techniques of gathering crime data. The coverage of these data sources and the methods used to produce them differ. Now we examine the data produced by these methods to see how they compare in terms of the absolute amount of crime recorded, the ecological distribution of crimes, and the demographic characteristics of offenders.

These comparisons are important since they indicate the extent to which the results of studies of criminal behavior depend on the method by which the data are gathered. If the rape rate is increasing according to the UCR, but according to the NCVS it has remained stable over a period of years, we say that the results are method dependent; that is, our conclusions depend on the method used to collect the data.

The comparisons also bear on the issue of the validity of the data gathered using these three techniques since they may be used to examine the convergent validity of the data. It is important to distinguish between convergence and validity. The former is an indicator of validity, since measures of the same underlying phenomenon ought to yield similar results, if the measures are valid. Thus, if both the UCR and SR methods are measuring the same phenomenon, for example, the relative rates of female and male assaults, they ought to agree with each other concerning estimates of the sex ratio for those involved in aggravated assault. If they do agree, this supports the validity of both measures; if they do not, it brings into question the validity of one or both of these measures of the ratio of male offenders to female offenders. Thus, convergence is relatively simple to establish. Validity, however, is more elusive. Before making even tentative statements about the validity of a measure, an investigator should consider several types of evidence besides convergence — potential data collection bias, the content of the measure, the theoretical definitions of the phenomenon.

Note that measures may be valid for one purpose and not for another. The UCR may be invalid as a measure of the absolute amount of aggravated assault but may be a more valid indicator of the sex ratio for aggravated assault offenders. Furthermore, the measurement of some crime rates (for example, motor vehicle theft) may show more convergence than others (for example, aggravated assault).

CONVERGENCE OF ABSOLUTE RATES

Table 3.6 presents data from the NCVS and the UCR on the number of criminal incidents for the year 1991. For the NCVS, this table presents both the number of estimated incidents and the number of incidents that are estimated to have been reported to the police. Comparing these estimates must be done with caution. For rape, the definitions and coverage in the UCR and NCVS are quite similar, except that the NCVS allows for the victim of a rape to be a man. The NCVS shows a much larger number of rapes than the UCR: a ratio of 1.61. Thus the NCVS indicates that there are 61 percent more rapes than does the UCR. Note, however, that the number of those reporting rapes (generally a large underestimate; see O'Brien, 1991) to the NCVS interviewer who say they reported them to the police is less than the number of rapes "known to the police": a ratio of .92.

Robberies, burglaries, and motor vehicle thefts are defined similarly in the NCVS and UCR, but commercial burglaries, robberies, and motor vehicle thefts are not covered in the NCVS since commercial establishments are no longer included in the sample. The data in Table 3.6 include only estimated noncommercial burglaries and robberies from the UCR for 1991. In each case, the number of incidents recorded in the NCVS exceeds the number recorded in the UCR. The number of incidents that respondents claim to have reported to the police is much closer to the number that the police have recorded.

TABLE 3.6   NATIONAL CRIME RATE ESTIMATES FOR RATE, AGGRAVATED ASSAULT, ROBBERY, BURGLARY, AND MOTOR VEHICLE THEFT BASED ON THE UNIFORM CRIME REPORTS AND THE NATIONAL CRIME VICTIMIZATION SURVEYS (1991)

	NCVS		UCR	Ratio of NCVS to UCR	
	Number of Incidents	*Number of Incidents Reported*	*Crimes Known to the Police*	*Total Incidents*	*Reported Incidents*
Rape	171,420	98,210	106,590	1.61	.92
Personal robbery	1,064,750	553,480	420,105	2.12	1.10
Aggravated assault	1,371,610	745,730	1,092,740	1.26	.68
Residential burglary	5,138,310	2,514,560	1,828,151	2.51	1.23
Motor vehicle theft	2,122,330	1,503,650	1,661,700	1.28	.90

SOURCE: NCVS data are from *Criminal Victimization in the United States — 1991* (U.S. Department of Justice, 1992a: Tables 1, 56, and 119). UCR data are from *Crime in the United States — 1991* (1992): Table 1 for rape, aggravated assault, and motor vehicle theft; and Table 23 for residential burglary and personal robbery (street-highway plus residential robbery).

Although the NYS is based on a national sample, it is difficult to compare the incident rates derived from it with the national rates from the NCVS and the UCR. A major problem is the limited age range found in the NYS (always a seven-year range). Any such comparison, however, shows that far more crime is reported in SR studies than in the UCR or the NCVS. In 1980, for example, the rate of aggravated assault in the NYS (for youth age 15 to 21) was 1,400 per 10,000 (U.S. Department of Justice, 1989: Table 3.104). This contrasts with rates of 90.3 and 29.9 for the NCVS and the UCR for the same year. Clearly, the NCVS and UCR rates would be much higher if they were based only on those aged 15 to 21, but they would not be fifteen to sixteen times higher (1,400/90.3).

Most criminologists are not optimistic about estimating the "absolute crime rate." Whether a given behavior is a crime or not depends in part on the perspective that one brings to the situation. Imagine, for example, the situation of an aggravated assault. The "offender" may feel that no crime has been committed because the "victim" was the first one to push. The victim may (or may not) think that the offender's use of increased force was justified given the situation and, therefore, was (or was not) a crime. The police officer investigating the incident may feel that the settlement of the pushing match is better handled informally or that this "criminal incident" is a matter for arrest. In the legal system, lawyers will dispute whether the act was a crime (if the incident gets that far) and a judge's decision may be appealed. Even if the offender loses, he or she may not define the act as a crime. Thus, it is not surprising that the volume of crimes estimated to have occurred during a given year differs depending on whether victims or offenders are asked or whether estimates are based on official police records.

CONVERGENCE OF RELATIVE RATES
ACROSS GEOGRAPHIC AREAS

Whether or not the UCR, NCVS, and SR studies yield divergent or similar results in terms of the absolute amount of crime, they could show similar or dissimilar results when used as measures of the relative amount of crime across geographic areas (for example, SMSAs or states). That is, victims may report to interviewers far more crimes than come to the attention of the police, police might record only some of the crimes that come to their attention, and so on, but these biases could be fairly constant across geographic locations. Then even though noncommercial burglary is reported 151 percent more often to NCVS interviewers than it appears as a "crime known to the police" in the UCRs (see Table 3.6), the relative rate of noncommercial burglary (between, for example, Los Angeles and Chicago) still could be ascertained using either method. This would support the use of both NCVS and UCR crime data in ecological studies of crime. Such studies might investigate the relationship of crime rates to population density, age structure, income inequality, racial composition, and region. Note that crime rates may converge (or be valid) for some purposes (comparing relative rates of crime) even if they do not converge for others (estimating the absolute rate of crime).

A number of researchers have investigated the convergence of NCVS- and UCR-based crime rates for the twenty-six cities included in the NCVS city-level surveys (Booth et al., 1977; Cohen and Lichbach, 1982; Decker, 1977; Nelson, 1978, 1979; O'Brien et al., 1980). Table 3.7 contains Pearson's product moment correlations (r signifies the strength of association) between the NCVS- and the UCR-derived crime rates for these twenty-six cities for each of seven crimes. Correlations have been computed both for all NCVS incidents and for only those incidents that victims said they reported to the police. Examining the columns based on all victims, the strong positive correlation (r = .91) between NCVS and UCR motor vehicle theft rates can be interpreted as indicating that those cities with a relatively high motor vehicle theft rate according to the NCVS data tend to have a relatively high rate according to the UCR data. The squared correlation for motor vehicle theft (multiplied by 100) indicates that the UCR and NCVS measures share 82 percent of their variance in common for this crime across these twenty-six cities.

There is surprisingly strong convergence for the rates of motor vehicle theft (r = .91) and for robbery with a weapon (r = .81). Less convergence is noted for burglary (r = .69) and robbery without a weapon (r = .56), and there is essentially no agreement for simple assault and rape. We find divergence for aggravated assault. (That is, for this crime, there is a tendency for those cities with relatively high rates according to the NCVS to have relatively low rates according to the UCR.) Interestingly, the degree of convergence is greater for each of the seven crimes when correlating UCR rates and NCVS rates for

TABLE 3.7   PERCENTAGE OF VARIANCE EXPLAINED AND ZERO-ORDER CORRELATIONS BETWEEN UCR AND NCVS CRIME RATES

| | Variance Explained and Zero-Order Correlations | | | |
| | All NCVS Victims | | NCVS Victims Who Said They Reported the Victimization to the Police | |
Crime	%	$r =$	%	$r =$
Motor vehicle theft	82	(.91)	85	(.92)
Robbery with a weapon	65	(.81)	72	(.85)
Burglary	47	(.69)	53	(.73)
Robbery without a weapon	31	(.56)	48	(.69)
Simple assault	0	(.05)	4	(.20)
Rape	0	(.04)	0	(.07)
Aggravated assault	13	(-.36)	7	(-.26)

SOURCE: Nelson (1978, Table E).
Note: These UCR and NCVS rates are based on the population at risk. That is, NCVS rates are based on the city's residential population, whereas UCR rates are based on an estimate of the number of persons who used each city on a daily basis (see Nelson, 1978, for further details).

crimes that victims say they reported to the police. The degree of convergence depends on the type of crime under investigation. It is perhaps not surprising that motor vehicle theft shows the highest degree of convergence. Motor vehicle thefts must be reported to the police in order for victims to collect insurance, and there is little embarrassment in reporting this crime to the police or to an interviewer.

An additional question remains: What are the effects of this lack of convergence on the conclusions researchers reach when using either UCR- or NCVS-based crime rates? The answer again depends on the type of crime involved. A number of researchers have addressed this topic (for example, Booth et al., 1977; Nelson, 1979; and O'Brien et al., 1980). A partial replication of a study by Blau and Blau (1982) using not only UCR data but also NCVS city-level crime rates found a lack of convergence in the findings based on these two different measures for the crimes of assault and rape (O'Brien, 1983). Table 3.8 presents the correlations between the crime rates for aggravated assault, robbery, and rape based on both UCR and NCVS data and the percentage of the population who are African-American and the percentage below the Social Security Administration's poverty line. Only in the case of robbery rates do the correlations based on UCR and NCVS data have the same sign

TABLE 3.8 **ZERO-ORDER CORRELATIONS OF UCR AND NCVS CRIME RATES WITH THE PERCENTAGE AFRICAN-AMERICAN AND POVERTY FOR TWENTY-SIX CITIES**

	% African-American		Poverty	
	NCVS	*UCR*	*NCVS*	*UCR*
Assault	-.45	.47	-.42	.50
Robbery	.32	.64	.22	.49
Rape	-.26	.43	-.13	.14

Note: The log to the base 10 of all crime rates was used to make the results comparable to those in Blau and Blau (1982). However, the results are substantially the same whether or not this transformation is made.

(both are positive). For aggravated assault, there is a strong positive correlation with poverty and the percentage of African-Americans for the UCR aggravated assault rate measure and a strong negative correlation for the NCVS measure. Conflicting results also occur for the UCR and NCVS measures of rape. Thus, the degree of convergence between the results based on UCR and NCVS crime rates depends on the type of crime under consideration. For at least some crimes, the findings from studies investigating the structural correlates of crime rates appear to be method dependent.

Zedlewski (1983: 262) drew a similar conclusion with regard to deterrence findings. Using 1977 UCR and NCVS data on 137 SMSAs, he found that "UCR-based measures of apprehension risk and criminal activity uncover no relationship between apprehension risk and crime rates while comparable NCVS-based measures find a strong deterrent effect."

CONVERGENCE OF DEMOGRAPHIC CHARACTERISTICS OF OFFENDERS

It is common knowledge that in the United States the rate at which males commit street crime is higher than the rate for females; the rate for African-Americans is higher than for whites; and the rate for fifteen- to twenty-five-year-olds is higher than for those older than twenty-five (see Chapters 4 and 5). Some of the early SR studies found that the rates of delinquency were surprisingly similar for African-Americans and whites and for males and females. However, later studies found that official and SR measures converge if steps are taken to make the data comparable. The most important steps for ensuring comparability are that the crimes compared are of the same type and level of seriousness

TABLE 3.9   COMPARISON OF ARRESTEES IN THE UCR AND THE ESTIMATED NUMBER OF OFFENDERS IN THE NCVS DATA BY RACE AND SEX, 1989–1991

		% White	% African-American	% Male	% Female
Rape*	NCVS	69.8	30.2	96.6	3.4
	UCR	54.9	45.1	98.8	1.2
Robbery	NCVS	39.6	60.4	93.5	6.5
	UCR	37.0	63.0	91.5	8.5
Aggravated assault	NCVS	72.6	27.4	88.0	12.0
	UCR	60.4	39.6	86.5	13.5
Simple assault	NCVS	76.9	23.1	84.5	15.5
	UCR	64.9	35.1	83.9	16.1

SOURCES: *Crime in the United States—1989* (1990; 1991) and *Criminal Victimization in the United States—1989* (1990; 1991). NCVS data are from Tables 43 and 45 for single offender victimizations, and the UCR data are from Tables 37 and 38 in 1989 and 1990 and Tables 42 and 43 in 1991 for sex and race of those arrested.

*The number of rapes reported to NCVS interviewers is fewer than 100 each year. These rape rates are not highly reliable.

(Hindelang et al., 1979) and that the response sets employed in SR measures allow for differentiation of offenders with high frequencies of offense from those with other levels (Elliott and Ageton, 1980).

Table 3.9 presents data from the NCVS and the UCR comparing the percentage of NCVS victimizations in which the perceived race of the offender was African-American or white and male or female with the percentage of arrestees who were in those categories. UCR arrest data are used rather than crimes known to the police since data by race and sex are available for arrests. Data for 1989, 1990, and 1991 have been aggregated since relatively few rapes were reported to NCVS interviewers. Finally, the choice of crimes is not arbitrary. The NCVS crimes in Table 3.9 all involve contact between the victim and offender, and thus NCVS victims are more likely to be able to report the race and sex of the offender.

For all four crimes, the percentage of offenders who are male (or female) is very similar whether UCR or NCVS data are used. The greatest difference is 3.5 percent in the case of aggravated assault. In each case, male offenders show up slightly more frequently in the NCVS than in the UCR. In the comparison for race, there is not a great difference between the UCR and NCVS estimates of the percentage of robberies that are committed by African-Americans: The difference is only 2.6 percent. For the other three crimes, however, there is a 12- to 15-percentage-point difference between the NCVS and UCR estimates. In each case, the NCVS estimates a higher percentage of white offenders than the percentage found in the UCR estimate. Whether these results indicate a bias in the criminal justice system is not clear since factors such as the differential reporting behavior of victims and the seriousness of the crimes have not been controlled, but they are in a direction consistent with a bias prediction. In either case, both data sets indicate that males and African-Americans are offenders in street crimes at a much higher rate than one would expect given their percentages in the population.

Further evidence comes from SR studies, which find the seriousness dimension to be important when comparing the relative rates of offending for males and females and African-Americans and whites. For example, in the Seattle Methods Study, Hindelang et al. (1981) found that the ratio of the percentage of males divided by the percentage of females having ever committed a theft depends on the seriousness of the theft. For whites, the sex ratio (males to females) is 1.21 for thefts under $2 and 9.60 for thefts greater than $50. The sex ratios for African-Americans are in the same direction but smaller: 1.39 for thefts under $2 and 2.63 for thefts greater than $50. Elliott and Ageton (1980) found that for illegal services, public disorder, hard drug use, and status offenses, the ratio of African-American to white offenders is either less than one or close to one (with no statistically significant differences). For the mean number of predatory crimes against property, however, the ratio is 2.30 (p < .001), and for predatory crimes against persons the ratio is 1.65 (though it is not quite statistically significant).

Crime rate data from the UCR, NCVS, and SR studies converge for some types of comparisons and not for others and for some types of crimes and not for others. For serious crimes, all three data sources indicate that, in relation to their proportions in the population, males offend substantially more than do females, and African-Americans offend more than do whites. All three measures indicate a far greater rate of street crime committed by youth than by middle-age or elderly persons. This convergence is encouraging given early indications that the SR and official records diverged substantially with regard to the demographic characteristics of offenders. Examinations of the ecological distribution of crimes indicate that the UCR and NCVS crime rates (for twenty-six cities) are in substantial agreement with respect to relative rates of crime across large central cities for motor vehicle theft and robbery with a weapon; moderate agreement for burglary and robbery without a weapon; and show essentially no agreement for simple assault, rape, and aggravated assault. The comparison of the number of crimes known to the police and the number of crimes reported to NCVS interviewers shows a substantial difference for noncommercial burglaries and robberies and for rapes. Fewer than one-half of the noncommercial burglaries and robberies reported in the NCVS are recorded in the UCR.

CONCLUSION

UCR, NCVS, and SR studies provide the majority of the data that criminologists use to describe and explain serious street crime. Therefore, it is important to have an understanding of how these data are generated, the extent of their coverage, and their strengths and weaknesses. It is also important to know how well these information sources converge. The message from this chapter with regard to the uses of crime data based on the three types of sources we have examined is neither wholly optimistic nor wholly pessimistic. Care is necessary when using such data, and the appropriateness of any given use depends on the type of comparison being made (absolute rates, relative rates across geographic areas, demographic characteristics of offenders) and the types of crimes being compared.

It is virtually impossible to assess the absolute rate of most crimes (for example, rape, aggravated assault, larceny, and vandalism). This is reflected in a lack of convergence involving crime rates from the UCR, NCVS, and SR data sets, and is consistent with many studies cited throughout this chapter on the underreporting of criminal incidents. For example, UCR crime rates depend on the direct detection of crimes by police or the reporting of crimes by citizens as well as other processes involved in the official recording of crimes. Survey-generated rates (NCVS and SR) depend on such factors as respondent recall, willingness to report, and meaningful bounding points for interviews. There are, however, some exceptions. For example, the homicide rate as measured by the UCR is probably accurate as are statistics on commercial robberies (especially bank robberies). There is also fair agreement between UCR and NCVS regarding estimates of motor vehicle theft.

The yearly warning in *Crime in the United States* that the UCR rates should not be compared across jurisdictions is ignored by many researchers. Although there are good reasons for this advisory, the comparison of UCR and NCVS crime rates in this chapter indicates that some comparisons across geographic areas may be legitimate. UCR arrest data and NCVS data also indicate similar patterns of involvement in crime by racial and gender categories. However, caution is still advised. Convergence is more likely for some crimes (motor vehicle theft and robbery, for instance) than for others (rape and aggravated assault). Ultimately, any crime statistic is only as useful as the reader's understanding of the processes that generated it.

DISCUSSION QUESTIONS

1. How valid and reliable are most forms of official crime statistics? By what methods did you reach your conclusion?

2. Discuss the various ways by which we come to know how much and what types of crime characterize our society. In what ways are the *Uniform Crime Reports* and the National Crime Victimization Survey different? What are the major strengths and weaknesses of each?

3. How did the self-reported criminality survey evolve? What are the advantages and disadvantages of such survey data? What have we learned from these data concerning how much crime we have in society and who commits it?

4. NCVS and self-reported criminality studies both encounter a similar problem regarding the reporting of more serious crimes. What is that problem, and what is its influence on the utility of such statistics?

CHAPTER 4

CRIMINAL BEHAVIOR: GENDER AND AGE

Darrell Steffensmeier
Pennsylvania State University

Emilie Allan
St. Francis College

TWO OF THE OLDEST and most widely accepted conclusions in criminology are (1) that involvement in crime diminishes with age and (2) that males are more likely than females to offend at every age. Because gender and age are far and away the two most robust predictors of criminal involvement, this chapter focuses on how these two variables affect the level and character of criminal offending.

GENDER AND CRIME

The criminological literature has concentrated more on the criminal man than the criminal woman, perhaps because crime has been (and still is) a predominantly male behavior. The prototypical criminal is a young male, and it is his behavior that most theories have tried to explain. Because of the universality of gender differences in crime, examining female crime and the manner in which it differs from male crime can contribute to greater understanding of both criminal behavior and gender differences.

Many sources of information are available on gender differences in crime. We concentrate on FBI arrest statistics, the largest source of data on crime in contemporary America, and the one that has been available for the longest time. To examine the validity of the official data, and to understand better the meaning of arrest patterns for particular crimes and the dynamics of women's roles in crime, however, we make frequent comparison to findings from other sources and from more detailed studies.

Table 4.1 (columns 1–6) displays male and female arrest rates per 100,000 for the years 1960, 1975, and 1990 for all the offense categories in the *Uniform Crime Reports* except forcible rape (a male crime) and runaways/curfew (juvenile

TABLE 4.1

MALE AND FEMALE ARREST RATES PER 100,000, FEMALE PERCENTAGE OF ARRESTS, AND MALE AND FEMALE ARREST PROFILES

Offenses	Male Rates			Female Rates			Female Percentage (of Arrests)			Profiles (in Percents) Males		Females	
	1960	1975	1990	1960	1975	1990	1960	1975	1990	1960	1990	1960	1990
	(1)	(2)	(3)	(4)	(5)	(6)	(7)	(8)	(9)	(10)	(11)	(12)	(13)
Against Persons													
Homicide	9	16	16	2	3	2	17	14	11	.1	.2	.2	.1
Aggravated assault	101	200	317	16	28	50	14	13	13	1	3	2	2
Weapons	69	137	165	4	11	14	4	8	7	1	2	.5	.7
Simple assault	265	354	662	29	54	129	10	13	15	4	6	4	5
Major Property													
Robbery	65	131	124	4	10	12	5	7	8	1	1	.5	.5
Burglary	274	477	319	9	27	32	3	5	8	4	3	1	1
Stolen property	21	103	121	2	12	17	8	10	11	.3	1	.2	.5
Minor Property													
Larceny-theft	391	749	859	74	321	402	17	30	30	6	10	9	20
Fraud	70	114	157	12	59	133	15	34	43	1	2	2	7
Forgery	44	46	51	8	18	28	16	28	34	.5	.5	1	1
Embezzlement	—	7	8	—	3	5	—	28	37	—	.2	—	.1
Malicious Mischief													
Auto theft	121	128	158	5	9	18	4	7	9	2	1	1	1
Vandalism	—	187	224	—	16	28	—	8	10	—	2	—	1
Arson	—	15	13	—	2	2	—	11	14	—	.3	—	.1
Drinking and Drugs													
Public drunkenness	2573	1201	624	212	87	71	8	7	9	36	8	25	4
DUI	344	971	1193	21	81	176	6	5	11	5	15	3	9
Liquor laws	183	276	428	28	43	102	13	14	17	3	5	4	5
Drug abuse	49	523	815	8	79	166	15	13	14	1	7	1	6
Sex and Sex Related													
Prostitution	15	18	30	37	45	62	73	73	65	.2	.4	4	3
Sex offenses	81	55	78	17	5	7	17	8	8	1	1	2	.3
Disorderly conduct	749	597	499	115	116	119	13	17	18	11	5	14	6
Vagrancy	265	45	26	23	7	4	8	14	12	4	.3	3	.2
Suspicion	222	31	13	28	5	3	11	13	15	3	.1	3	.1
Miscellaneous													
Against family	90	57	51	8	7	12	8	10	16	1	.5	1	.5
Gambling	202	60	14	19	6	2	8	9	15	3	.2	2	.2
Other exc. traffic	871	1139	2109	150	197	430	15	15	15	13	23	19	20
Total	7070	7850	9211	831	1383	2122	11	15	19				

SOURCE: *Uniform Crime Reports, 1960–1990.*

offenses). Since few crimes are committed either by those under the age of 10 or over the age of 65, the rates are calculated for persons aged 10 through 64, that is, on the population at risk. Table 4.1 also displays the female percentage of arrests and the profiles of male and female offenders, which we discuss shortly.

For both males and females, arrest rates increased in some categories, decreased in others, and did not change in still others. Overall, the pattern of change was similar for both sexes, with large increases occurring only for larceny, fraud, driving under the influence, drug violations, and assault; and with decreases in arrest rates actually occurring in the categories of public drunkenness, sex offenses, vagrancy, suspicion, and gambling. This suggests that the rates of both sexes are influenced by similar social and legal forces, independent of any condition unique to women.

The similarities in male and female offending patterns outnumber the differences. This is quite evident in the third set of columns (10–13), which provides profiles of male and female arrest patterns by showing the percentage of total male and total female arrests represented by each crime category for 1960 and 1990. The homicide figures of .2 for men in 1990 and .1 for women mean, respectively, that only two-tenths of 1 percent of all male arrests were for homicide, and only one-tenth of 1 percent of all female arrests were for homicide.

The similarities between the male and the female profiles and their arrest trends are considerable. For both males and females, the three most common arrest categories in 1990 are driving under the influence (DUI), larceny-theft, and "other except traffic"—a residual category that includes mostly criminal mischief, public disorder, local ordinance violations, and assorted minor crimes. Together, these three offenses account for 48 percent of all male arrests and 49 percent of all female arrests. (But note that 20 percent and 9 percent of all female arrests are for larceny and DUI, respectively, as compared to 10 percent and 15 percent among males.) Similarly, arrests for murder, arson, and embezzlement are relatively rare for males and females alike, whereas arrests for offenses such as liquor law violations (mostly underage drinking), simple assault, and disorderly conduct represent "middling ranks" for both sexes.

The most important gender differences in arrest profiles involve the proportionately greater involvement of women in minor property crimes such as larceny and fraud (about 28 percent of all female arrests versus 12 percent of male arrests) and in prostitution-type offenses (3 percent of all female arrests, versus only 4 tenths of 1 percent of male arrests), and the relatively greater involvement of males in crimes against persons and major property crimes (17 percent of all male arrests versus 11 percent of all female arrests). The relatively high involvement of females in minor property crimes (larceny, fraud, forgery), coupled with their low involvement in the more "masculine" or serious kinds of violent and property crime (homicide, aggravated assault, robbery, burglary), is found in most comparisons of gender differences in crime.

The same pattern can be seen in columns 7–9 in Table 4.1, which show the female percentage of arrests for three different periods: 1960, 1975, and 1990. (In all cases, the female percentage adjusts for the sex composition of the population at large.) Looking first at the 1990 data, except for prostitution (the only offense category in the table for which the female arrest rate exceeds that of males), the female percentage of arrests is highest for the minor property crimes (about 35 percent) and lowest for masculine crimes like robbery and burglary (about 8 percent each).

We will return to the issue of trends in female offending later; for now, we will simply note that, over the previous three decades, the female percentage of arrests has increased substantially for minor property crimes (from an average of 17 percent for 1960 to 27 percent for 1975 to 35 percent for 1990), whereas the percentages for most other crimes have increased slightly (by 1–3 percent for each period). For a number of categories, the female percentage of arrests has held steady or declined slightly, including arrests for homicide, aggravated assault, public drunkenness, drugs, and a few of the sex-related crimes. For all three periods, percentages for females have been highest for minor property and for public order offenses—both of which appear to reflect traditional female gender roles.

Because the gender-related patterns of criminal behavior observed in official arrest data may reflect selection and processing practices of the authorities rather than actual behavior differences in male and female criminality (Chesney-Lind, 1973; Smart, 1976), it is important to compare the results with nonofficial data sources. In fact, the patterns found in the *Uniform Crime Reports* (UCR) data tend to be corroborated by data from victimization surveys like the National Crime Victimization Survey (NCVS). In NCVS interviews, victims are asked both whether their assailant was male and whether they reported the crime to the police.

The NCVS numbers are very close to those for the UCR. For example, according to NCVS data, women offenders account for about 7 percent of robberies, 8 percent of aggravated assaults, 15 percent of simple assaults, 5 percent of burglaries, and 5 percent of all motor vehicle thefts reported by victims. Hindelang's (1979) comparison of the NCVS and UCR data substantiates the low female involvement in masculine types of crime. Hindelang also found no clear gender differences in reporting to the police, once crime seriousness was taken into account. In other words, no evidence suggested that male chivalry—that is, males' reluctance to report crimes against them by women—reduced the number of victimizations by female offenders that were reported to the police.

The gender-crime patterns we have seen in the UCR data also reappear in data from self-report studies. Self-report studies that concentrate mainly on nonserious classes of behavior often show patterns that are somewhat different from those of the UCR, such as higher female-to-male ratios of offending but lower ratios for sexual misconduct. However, when data are collected on a wide variety of both serious and nonserious misconduct, and on frequency as well as prevalence of offending, studies confirm the UCR patterns of relatively low female involvement in serious offenses, particularly at higher frequencies, and greater involvement in the less serious categories (Elliott et al., forthcoming; Smith and Visher, 1980).

Drawing on these and other data, it is possible to provide a summary portrait of female crime. Relative to males, female involvement in crime, past and present, is greatest in prostitution and sex-related public order offenses like vagrancy, disorderly conduct, and—for juveniles—runaways (often used as legal euphemisms for prostitution and similar offenses); in popular forms of substance abuse (alcohol and marijuana); and—increasingly important in recent years—in petty thefts and hustles (shoplifting, theft of services, falsification of identification, passing bad checks, credit card forgery, welfare fraud, employee pilferage, and street-level drug dealing). Volumes of arrest for larceny in particular have become so great in recent decades as to have an impact on total arrest rates.

In comparison to male offenders, females are far less likely to be involved in serious offenses, and the monetary value of female thefts, property damage, drugs, and injuries is typically smaller than that for similar offenses committed by males. Females are also more likely than males to be solo perpetrators or to be part of small, relatively nonpermanent crime groups. When female offenders are involved with others, particularly in more lucrative thefts or other criminal enterprises, they typically act as accomplices to males who both organize the crime and are the central figures in its execution (see Steffensmeier, 1983, for a review). Perhaps the most significant gender difference is the overwhelming dominance of males in more organized and highly lucrative crimes, whether based in the underworld or the "upperworld."

EXPLAINING FEMALE CRIME

Research indicates that the factors contributing to criminality are generally the same for females as for males. For example, Crites's (1976) review of the literature on gender and crime establishes that female offenders are typically of low socioeconomic status, poorly educated, under- or unemployed, and disproportionately from minority groups. They also often have dependents who rely on them for economic support. Except for the greater presence of dependent children, female offenders appear to have a social profile similar to that of their male counterparts. As is true for male crime and delinquency, moreover, female criminality is attributable to normal learning processes, desire for peer acceptance, search for excitement, weak stakes in conformity, and so on.

Additional evidence that female crime responds to the same sorts of societal conditions that affect male crime is found in the fact that male crime rates are strong predictors of female crime rates (Steffensmeier and Allan, 1988; Steffensmeier et al., 1989). Groups or societies that have high male rates of crime also have high female rates, whereas groups or societies that have low male rates also have low female rates. Over time, when the male rate rises, declines, or holds steady across a specific historical period, the female rate behaves in a similar fashion. This suggests that the rates of both sexes are influenced by similar social and legal forces, independent of any condition unique to women (Steffensmeier, 1980; Steffensmeier and Streifel, 1992).

Because their social situations typically include greater constraints on delinquent behavior, women may need a higher level of provocation before turning to crime—especially serious crime. Females who choose criminality must traverse a greater moral and psychological distance than males making the same choice because (as we discuss later) society views female lawbreaking as much more illegitimate. Thus, in comparison to males, the background of delinquent females is even more likely to be characterized by psychological disturbances (for example, low self-esteem, mental illness), extreme social deprivation or hardships (for example, poverty, broken home, abusive parents), and situational pressures (for example, threatened loss of valued relationships). In this last vein, although the saying "she did it all for love" is sometimes exaggerated as it applies to female involvement in crime, the role of men in initiating women into crime, especially serious crime, is a consistent finding across research (Gold, 1970; Gilfus, 1988; Steffensmeier, 1983; Pettiway, 1987; Miller, 1986). It has been argued that the majority of women in prison would not be there if they had not gotten romantically involved.

DEVELOPING A FRAMEWORK FOR EXPLAINING GENDER DIFFERENCES

Theories developed to account for male criminality seem equally adept at explaining female criminality (see review in Smith and Paternoster, 1987), but can they also account for gender differences in crime? In the discussion that follows, we single out several sets of factors—gender norms, moral development, social control, physical strength and aggression, crime opportunities, and sexuality—that affect men and women differentially in terms of willingness and ability to commit crime.

◆ **GENDER NORMS** ◆ The greater taboos against female crime and deviance that have pervaded most societies throughout history seem rooted in two powerful focal concerns: (1) female beauty and sexual virtue and (2) nurturant role obligations. The nurturant role obligations of women demand more consistent conformity than do male gender roles, and behaviors that could result in sexual disinhibitions or in the inability to fend off sexual advances are disapproved more strongly for women. The gender norms attendant on these very different goals in life do much to explain gender differences not only in conventional roles for men and women, but also in criminal roles. We examine a few such roles here.

Women as caregivers. Marriage and parenthood as major life goals have traditionally been more crucial in the socialization of females than males, and there seems to be little evidence of substantial change (Schur, 1984) despite an increasing career orientation among many women. Women are rewarded for their ability to establish and maintain relationships and to accept family and nurturing roles. The fact that female identity traditionally derives from that of the men in their lives helps explain female restraint from crime when those men conform to conventional norms. It also helps explain the large proportion of female offenders who become accomplices to crimes of their husbands or boyfriends. Further, the arrangements and norms through which women have virtually exclusive responsibility for child-rearing place constraints on their time and mobility that would handicap a would-be criminal career. They also render women less free psychologically to imitate the immaturity, insensitivity, and irresponsibility that historically have characterized the male criminal in relational matters.

Sexual/physical attractiveness. Expectations regarding sexuality and appearance support female dependency and dictate greater surveillance of females by fathers and husbands. They also shape the kinds of labels applied to deviant female behavior and the kinds of deviant roles most available to women (for example, sexual media or service roles). The threat of sexual victimization serves to constrain women's mobility and to keep them away from nighttime streets, rough bars, and other crime-likely locations and situations in a manner that reduces their criminal opportunity. Law enforcement officials, moreover, tend to "sexualize" female delinquency and to charge female delinquents with status offenses such as running away from home, "incorrigibility," and "waywardness." Apparently, juvenile males are expected to "sow their wild oats," whereas juvenile females are more closely monitored.

"Femininity." Traditional feminine qualities include warmth, nurturance, supportiveness, weakness, gentility, talking and acting "like a lady," self-effacement, and deference to the wants and needs of others. Femininity stereotypes are basically incompatible with the qualities valued in the criminal underworld. Patriarchal society requires women to conform more strictly to their assigned roles as wives and mothers; it produces no acceptable deviant roles for women comparable to those for romanticized "rogue" males; and it makes deviant labels for women—witch, whore, kleptomaniac—more stigmatizing than the labels typically applied to deviant men. Although crime is almost always stigmatizing for females, for males—especially young males—crime may serve to enhance status and verify masculinity. The cleavage between what is feminine and what is criminal is sharp, whereas the dividing line between what is masculine and what is criminal is often a thin one.

◆ **MORAL DEVELOPMENT** ◆ Gilligan (1982) suggests that men and women differ significantly in their moral development and that women's moral choices are more likely to constrain them from criminal behavior that could be injurious to others. Because women are bound more intimately into a network of interpersonal ties, their moral decisions are more influenced by empathy and compassion. Compared with men, women are more concerned lest they fail to respond to others' needs, and the threat of separation from loved ones causes them greater anxiety. Such complex concerns inhibit women from undertaking criminal activities that might cause hurt to others.

This "ethic of care" presupposes nonviolence and suggests that serious predatory crime is outside women's moral boundaries. In contrast, men who are conditioned toward status-seeking, yet marginalized from the world of work, are more likely to develop a perception of the world as consisting of givers and takers, with superior status accorded to the takers. Such a moral stance obviously increases the likelihood of aggressive criminal behavior by those who become "convinced that people are at each other's throats increasingly in a game of life that has no moral rules" (Messerschmidt, 1986: 66).

◆ SOCIAL CONTROL ◆   The concept of social control cuts across the issue of women's relative willingness and ability to commit crime. To the extent that females are more subject to parental supervision and control, they have less objective freedom to engage in delinquent behavior. Both early and contemporary studies show that parents exert more control over girls than boys (Thrasher, 1927; Simmons and Blyth, 1987; Morash, 1986). Compared to females in their early teens, boys more often are allowed to go places without parental permission or supervision, to go out after dark, and to be left home alone (Simmons and Blyth, 1987). This contributes to greater risk-taking behavior, including delinquency, among males. In contrast, flirting with or flouting the boundaries of acceptable behavior is not expected—and often not valued when it does occur—for females. Males whose behavior is seen as controlled are even subject to being called names such as "wimp" and "pussy."

Greater supervision and control also leads to greater female attachment to parents, teachers, and conventional friends, which in turn reduces the likelihood of influence by delinquent peers. Because they are socialized by conventional adults rather than by delinquent peers, females also are unlikely to perceive delinquency as being "fun," "exciting," or status-enhancing. Among males, peer groups are a much stronger source of delinquent influence, particularly in the case of male adolescents with weak social bonds or low stakes in conformity (Giordano et al., 1986). Further, adulthood brings little increase in freedom of movement for women. Adult women find themselves encapsulated within the family and the private sphere, and therefore continue to experience less freedom than do men to explore and cope with the temptations and tensions of the world beyond the family boundaries (Sokoloff, 1988).

◆ PHYSICAL STRENGTH AND AGGRESSION ◆   Real or perceived female weakness and lack of aggressiveness and risk-taking in comparison to males serve to limit female ability to engage in certain types of criminal behavior, particularly with respect to access to criminal subcultures. Research indicates that aggressiveness has been found to covary consistently with male crime, and this trait is stronger among males than among females for reasons that are not altogether explained by culture. More important, perhaps, the universal observation that males are naturally stronger and more aggressive, coupled with a strong cultural emphasis on male violence in this country, generates both expectations and rewards that increase the likelihood both of male involvement in aggressive behavior and of defining male behavior as aggressive. This facilitates male criminal involvement in at least two ways. First, physical prowess, strength, and speed obviously are useful for committing crimes that are frequently categorized as traditionally male, such as robbery, burglary, and cargo theft. Second, physical prowess and muscle are useful for protection, for enforcing contracts, and for recruiting and managing reliable associates.

The demands of the crime environment for physical power and violence help account for the less serious and less frequent nature of female relative to male criminality. Females may lack the power, or may be perceived by themselves or by others as lacking the capacity for violence, for successful completion of certain types of crime, or for protection of the "score." Hustling small amounts of money or property protects female criminals against predators who might be attracted by larger amounts. Real or perceived vulnerability can also help account for female restriction to solo roles or to roles as subordinate partners or accomplices in crime groups. This can be seen in a variety of criminal activities, including the exigencies of the dependent prostitute–pimp relationship (James, 1976).

◆ **ACCESS TO CRIMINAL OPPORTUNITY** ◆   Restricted access to crime opportunities and skills both limits and shapes female participation in crime. In part because of the gender norms just described, not only are women limited by greater supervision but also they are less likely than men to have access to crime opportunities as a spin-off of legitimate roles and activities. Women are less likely to hold jobs, such as truck driver, dockworker, or carpenter, that would provide opportunities for theft, drug dealing, fencing, and other illegitimate activities.

Women's involvement in underworld crime groups, ranging from syndicates to loosely structured groups, also is limited (Steffensmeier, 1983). Potential female offenders are at a clear disadvantage in selection and recruitment into criminal groups, in the range of career paths and access to them, and in opportunities for tutelage, increased skills, and rewards. Thus, the dominance of males (and the relative absence of females) is especially evident when we look at more organized and more lucrative kinds of criminal enterprise, from burglary rings, gambling operations, and drug cartels to arson-for-profit mobs, fencing networks, racketeering, pornography, and black-market smuggling of weapons, liquor, and cigarettes. Incidentally, women also participate very little in more organized and lucrative kinds of corporate and upperworld crimes (Daly, 1989; Steffensmeier, 1989).

◆ **SEXUALITY** ◆   Ironically, when female offenders exploit male stereotypes by using their sexuality as a means of entry into criminal organizations, they are likely to find their crime roles restricted in several ways. They may be stereotyped and placed in role traps organized around female attributes, particularly sexual ones that limit the range of opportunities. The sexual role may also introduce an element of sexual tension or conflict in crime groups so that, to reduce the conflict, the female is pushed to align herself with one man sexually, to become "his woman." Even prostitution — often thought to be a female crime — is essentially a male-dominated or male-controlled criminal enterprise (Heyl, 1979: 208). Police, pimps, businessmen who employ prostitutes, and clients—virtually all of whom are male—control, in various ways, the conditions under which the prostitute works (Schur, 1984).

APPLYING THE FRAMEWORK TO PATTERNS OF FEMALE CRIME

To this point, we have described how gender differences in crime generally are influenced by differences in gender roles, moral development, social control, physical strength and aggression, crime opportunities, and sexuality. That female crime is strongly tied to the nature of the female gender role, the types of skills women learn as they grow up, and the network of social relations in which women are involved helps explain *patterns* of female criminality by crime type. We find, as expected, that female participation is highest for those crimes most consistent with traditional norms and for which females have the most opportunity and lowest for those crimes that diverge the most from traditional gender norms and for which females have little opportunity.

In the area of property crime, the percentage of female arrests is highest for the minor property crimes of larceny (comprising the largest volume of female arrests), fraud, and forgery, all of which are compatible with traditional female roles. For example, shoplifting (the charge in most larceny arrests) is compatible with women's traditional involvement in family purchases (Grosser, 1952; Cameron, 1964). Similarly, passing "bad checks" (forgery) and welfare and credit card fraud may also be seen as extensions of female consumer or domestic roles. The percentage of female arrests is also high for embezzlement, ostensibly a white collar crime. However, females arrested for embezzlement are typically lower-level bookkeepers or bank tellers, occupational categories in which women hold over 90 percent of the jobs. (In contrast, women constitute slightly less than half of all accountants or auditors.) Further, women tend to embezzle to protect their families or valued relationships, whereas men tend to embezzle to protect their status (Zeitz, 1981). Female involvement is almost nonexistent in more serious occupational or business crimes, like insider trading, price-fixing, restraint of trade, toxic waste dumping, fraudulent product production, bribery, and official corruption, as well as large-scale governmental crimes (for example, the Iran–Contra affair and the Greylord scandal). Even when similar on-the-job opportunities for theft exist, women are still less likely to commit crime.

The lowest percentage of female involvement is found for serious property crimes like burglary and robbery, offense categories that are very much at odds with traditional feminine stereotypes, and to which women have very limited access. When women act as solo perpetrators, the typical robbery is a "wallet-sized" theft by a prostitute or addict (James, 1977; see also Covington, 1985; Pettiway, 1987). However, female involvement in such crimes is generally as accomplices to males, particularly in roles that at once exploit women's sexuality and reinforce their traditional subordination to men (Steffensmeier and Terry, 1986; American Correctional Association, 1983; Miller, 1986). This is also true for female violence, which although apparently at odds with female gender norms of gentleness and passivity, is nevertheless closely tied to the female role. Unlike males, females rarely kill or assault strangers or acquaintances; instead, the female's victim tends to be a male intimate (husband or lover) or a child, the offense generally takes place within the home, the victim frequently is drunk, and self-defense often is a motive (Jones, 1981; Mann, 1984). For women to kill, they generally must see their situation as life-threatening, as affecting the physical or emotional well-being of themselves or their children.

The linkage between female criminality and gender stereotyping is probably most evident in the case of certain public order offenses for which the percentage of female involvement is high, particularly the sex-related categories of prostitution and runaway or curfew violations, the only offense categories where female arrest rates exceed those of males. The high percentage of female arrests in these two categories reflects both gender differences in marketability of sexual services and continuing stereotypes and double standards with respect to female sexuality. Although customers obviously must outnumber prostitutes, they are less likely to be sanctioned. Similarly, although self-report studies show male rates of runaways to be as high as female rates, female runaways are more likely to be arrested.

Female involvement also is quite high in various kinds of substance abuse, especially of "popular" substances such as alcohol and marijuana, and often begins in the context of teenage dating. Although women are about as likely as men to have ever used alcohol or to be "social drinkers," men are much more likely to be classified as heavy drinkers (Department of Health and Human Services, 1984). Female participation is much lower for drugs that are tied to drug subcultures and to the underworld more generally—that is, for those drugs that are the most stigmatized and bear the greatest risks. Further, a wide range of addiction studies report that women generally are introduced to hard drug use (such as heroin or cocaine) by a lover, spouse, or boyfriend (Rosenbaum, 1981; Waldorf, 1983). In contrast to males, who typically have had substantial criminal involvement prior to addiction, criminal involvement of female addicts, especially in more serious crimes like burglary and robbery, is much more likely to occur after addiction and is more likely to be abandoned when drug use ceases. Drug addiction amplifies income-generating crime for members of both sexes but more so for female drug users (Covington, 1985).

VARIATION IN GENDER ROLES AND IN FEMALE PERCENTAGE OF ARRESTS

Differences in gender norms and arrangements help explain why women commit less crime overall than do men and why the percentage of female offenders varies by type of crime. Thus, we might legitimately inquire whether differences in crime are less when male and female social roles are more similar. Following this line of reasoning, a number of commentators have argued that rates of female offending relative to male offending are higher in social settings where women are assumed to experience greater "emancipation."

In cross-national comparisons, we find fairly large gender differences between developing and developed nations in involvement in minor property crimes, but virtually no gender differences in involvement in homicide and in major property crimes like robbery and burglary. Instead of greater gender equality, developed nations report a higher percentage of female arrests for minor property crimes, apparently because developed nations afford more opportunities for female-based consumer crimes such as shoplifting and welfare fraud and because their more formalized enforcement apparatus increases the visibility and sanction risk of would-be female offenders (Steffensmeier et al., 1989). These findings at the cross-national level parallel those describing recent trends in female arrests in the United States.

An issue that has attracted a good deal of attention in the media is the suggestion that the women's movement has resulted in a reduction in gender differences in crime; indeed, in the early 1970s, women's crime almost overnight came to be viewed as "the shady side of liberation." However, although official data show some increases over time in female rates relative to male rates, they are mainly for minor offenses (as shown in Table 4.1). For both males and females, arrest rates began to increase for most offense categories in the early 1960s, though rates have remained relatively stable since the mid-1970s. Overall, the pattern of change has been similar for both sexes, with large increases in arrest rates for offenses like larceny, fraud, driving under the influence, and drug use, and actual decreases in some categories like gambling, public drunkenness, and vagrancy. In 1990, as in 1960, most arrests of males and females were for minor property crimes and for drug or alcohol violations and other public order offenses. Further, the profiles of typical female and male offenders have not changed over this period: Then, as now, higher proportions of all female arrestees were involved in minor property and sex-related offenses, whereas higher proportions of male arrestees were involved in serious property crimes and crimes against persons.

In terms of female crime relative to male crime, the most dramatic increases since 1960 for females have been for the minor property offenses of larceny, fraud, and forgery. The female percentage of arrests for these offenses now ranges from 30 to 40 percent, as compared to 1960, when women made up about 15 percent of arrests for these crimes (again see Table 4.1). As we noted previously, such offenses are consistent with the female consumer role and fit into the everyday round of activities in which women engage. In contrast, the female percentage of arrests for the more masculine categories of major property crimes increased by only 3 to 4 percent: robbery from 5 to 8 percent, burglary from 3 to 8 percent, stolen property from 8 to 11 percent. Among crimes against persons, whereas the female percentage increased from 10 to 16 percent for simple assault, the percentage has held relatively constant for the more serious category of aggravated assault, and for homicide, it has actually declined from 17 to 12 percent. (See Steffensmeier, forthcoming, for an in-depth treatment of recent trends in female-to-male crime.)

Self-report data provide even less support for the notion of increased levels of female crime. Data from the National Youth Survey and from the

Monitoring the Future survey, by far the best sources of trend data on self-reported delinquency, indicate increases over the past two decades in certain delinquent behaviors (for example, alcohol and drug use) among both male and female adolescents and decreases in other delinquent behaviors (for example, theft and assault), but stable gender differences in delinquency. After reviewing the data from the National Youth Survey, as well as a number of other self-report studies, Elliott et al. (1983) conclude that from roughly the mid-1960s to 1980, the self-report data "show no significant declines in the [male-to-female] sex ratios on eight specific offenses." Further, several researchers have reported that female gang activity is neither much different nor more violent now in comparison to the past (see Miller, 1973; Jankowski, 1991).

Statistics on males and females incarcerated in state and federal prisons provide additional information on female crime trends. From roughly the mid-1920s to the present, the female percentage of the total prison population has held between 3 and 6 percent. The female percentage was about 5 percent in the 1920s, about 3 percent in the 1960s, and is about 6 percent today. As with male incarceration rates, female rates rose very sharply — more than doubled — during the 1980s. Most women in prison today were convicted for homicide or assault (usually against spouse, lover, or child), for property crimes such as theft and fraud that partly reflects escalating penalties for repeat shoplifting and check forgery offenders, and for drug-related offenses. During the 1980s, a larger percentage of female new court commitments than of male new court commitments entered prison each year for drug offenses. Furthermore, a higher percentage of female prison inmates than male inmates were under the influence of drugs or alcohol at the time of their current offense.

Finally, female involvement in professional and organized crime has not been rising and continues to lag far behind male involvement. Women continue to be hugely underrepresented in traditionally male-dominated associations that involve safecracking, fencing operations, gambling operations, and racketeering. In 1991, the Commonwealth of Pennsylvania released its report on organized crime and racketeering activities in the state during the 1980–1990 period (Pennsylvania Crime Commission, 1991). That report identified only a handful of women who were major players in large-scale gambling and racketeering activities, and their involvement was a direct spinoff of association with a male figure (father, spouse, or brother). What's more, the extent and character of women's involvement in the 1980s was comparable to their involvement during the 1970s.

Despite some gains in the occupational realm, some observers argue that the economic and social position of women really has not changed that much in the past couple of decades so that today's female has not yet achieved a "liberated" position. Though increasingly represented in the labor force, women continue to be concentrated in traditional "pink collar" jobs — teaching, clerical and retail sales work, nursing, and other subordinate and "help-mate" roles — that reflect a persistence of traditional gender roles. In fact, the number of occupations that are filled largely or exclusively by women — nearly always at lower salary levels than "male" occupations—has actually increased in recent decades. The ratio of female-to-male median incomes remained essentially unchanged from 1960 to 1985, and has inched upward in more recent years. Women are still virtually excluded from the highest white collar and blue collar occupations, with only negligible representation in top management or in those industrial and service occupations requiring the highest levels of technical or mechanical skills.

Outside the world of work, the traditional gender roles of wife-mother and sex object have remained remarkably stable. Although attitudes apparently have shifted somewhat toward greater acceptance of women working and combining career and family, other research shows little change over the past several decades: in gender-typing in children's play activities and play groups (Fagot and Leinbach, 1983; Stoneman et al., 1984; Maccoby, 1985); in the kinds of personality characteristics that both men and women associate with each sex (Carter, 1987; Simmons and Blyth, 1987); in the importance placed on the physical attractiveness of women and their pressures to conform to an ideal of beauty or "femininity" (Leuptow, 1980; Mazur, 1986). The two major focal concerns of women, beauty and sexual virtue and nurturant role obligations, persist.

If changes in gender roles do not explain the higher rates of female property crime in recent decades and in developed nations, then what does? In many industrialized nations, the economic marginality of women is aggravated by rising rates of divorce, illegitimacy, labor market segmentation, and occupational segregation of women into jobs with low status and income. In other words, for many women, the greater freedoms associated with changing gender roles have not been accompanied by improved economic status. Economic insecurity in turn increases the pressures for women to commit traditional female consumer-based crimes such as shoplifting and welfare fraud (Hartnagel, 1982).

Opportunities for such consumer-based crime have expanded greatly in recent decades in developed nations. Increased supplies of goods, self-service marketing, a credit-based currency, and government-sponsored social services have all resulted in more opportunities for traditionally "female" forms of theft and fraud. Opportunities for such minor property crimes, involving higher proportions of females, have been expanding much more rapidly than have opportunities for more typically masculine types of crime. Ironically, females playing the traditional role of primary consumer may actually have greater access to crime-likely situations than do those women engaged in less traditional roles.

The female share of offending for ordinary property crimes also may in part reflect the increase in drug usage over the past couple of decades, which while affecting the criminality of both sexes, appears to have had a greater impact on female than on male involvement (Steffensmeier and Streifel, 1992; Anglin et al., 1987). Given our prior assertion that females face stronger constraints against crime, illicit drug use and addiction provide a comparatively greater motivational "push" for female than male involvement in crime. In addition, drug use is more likely to initiate females into the underworld and criminal subcultures, particularly by connecting them to drug-dependent males who utilize them as crime accomplices or exploit them as "old ladies" who support the man's addiction (Steffensmeier and Terry, 1986; Covington, 1985; Miller, 1986).

Despite the lack of support for the gender equality hypothesis, the supposed link between the women's movement and female crime patterns is intuitively appealing and is an instant attention-getter so that we can expect it to be a recurring theme in the decades ahead, both in the media and among some criminologists. However, at the very least, any attempt to account for the variation in the female percentage of offending should incorporate a variety of explanatory factors. Any approach emphasizing only one factor or theory at the expense of others is likely to be seriously misleading.

AGE AND CRIME

We turn now from the link between gender and crime to that between age and crime. Of all the factors associated with crime, the impact of age on criminal involvement is one of the strongest. The view that involvement in crime diminishes with age is one of the oldest and most widely accepted in criminology. For most forms of crime, but especially for what in most societies are designated "serious" crimes (murder, rape, assault, robbery), the proportion of the population involved in crime tends to peak in adolescence or early adulthood and then decline with age. This pattern is common to most age–crime distributions across historical periods, geographic locations, and crime types. This relative consistency has led Hirschi and Gottfredson (1983) to make the controversial claim that the age–crime relationship is universal and invariant. Of course, the teenage to young adult years (from early teens to about age 30) encompass a substantial segment of the life span, and as we will show, there is in fact considerable variation among offenses and across historical periods in the parameters of the age–crime curve (for example, peak age, median age, rate of decline from peak age) across this fifteen- to twenty-year age span. A claim of "invariancy" in the age–crime relationship therefore overstates the case (Steffensmeier et al., 1989).

Investigators of the age–crime relationship have tended to focus on crimes against persons and property that are included in the FBI Crime Index (Hirschi and Gottfredson, 1983; Steffensmeier et al., 1989). There is general agreement that involvement in Index crimes—that is, conventional or "garden variety" offenses—is most widespread among teenage and young adult males, and that most of these persons disengage from lawbreaking after a relatively short "career" in crime. However, although the populationwide age–crime curves conform generally to the pattern just described, certain crimes have somewhat older peak ages and a more gradual decline in rates for older age groups—particularly for a number of crime categories not included in the Crime Index. Variations in the age–crime pattern are also found for different population groups, cultures, and historical periods.

To a large extent, variations in societal age–crime patterns reflect patterns of age-stratified inequality. Age is a potent mediator of inequality in both the legitimate and illegitimate opportunity structures of society. Just as the low-wage, dead-end jobs of the legitimate economy are disproportionately held by the young, so too are high-risk, low-yield crimes committed disproportionately by the young. At the opposite end of the opportunity scale, because it is rare to find them in positions of power and influence in business or politics, young people are unlikely to score big in the world of white collar crime or in the lucrative rackets of organized crime.

We begin our discussion of age and crime by looking at the most common societal pattern, whereby conventional crimes are dominated by casual youth offenders, and we discuss factors associated with early entrance and exit. Next we examine ways in which societal age–crime patterns vary by crime type, by race, and across cultures and over time. Then we turn to the issue of individual age–crime patterns, with a consideration of criminal career patterns of more serious offenders, factors associated with their longer persistence in crime and eventual exit, and patterns and trends in both offending and victimization among older age groups in the population. This is followed by a consideration of the impact of age structure and cohort size on societal crime rates. We conclude the chapter with a brief look at the intersection of age and sex differences in crime.

AGE–CRIME STATISTICS FOR THE COUNTRY AS A WHOLE

The peak age (the age group with the highest age-specific arrest rate) is younger than 25 for all crimes except gambling reported in the FBI's UCR program, and rates begin to decline in the teenage years for more than half. In fact, even the median age (50 percent of all arrests occurring among younger persons) is younger than 30 for most crimes. In general, the "younger" age distributions (median ages in the teens or early twenties) are found for ordinary property crimes like burglary, larceny, arson, and vandalism and for liquor and drug violations. Personal crimes like aggravated assault and homicide tend to have somewhat "older" age distributions (median ages in the late twenties), as do some of the public order offenses, public drunkenness, driving under the influence, and certain of the property crimes that juveniles have less opportunity to commit, like embezzlement, fraud, and gambling (median ages in late twenties or thirties). Contrasts in the shape of the age distribution for different property crimes are depicted in Figure 4.1.

Although young people obviously account for a disproportionate share of arrests, official statistics may not provide a completely accurate picture of the participation in crime by different age groups. Because a relatively small proportion of crimes result in an arrest, it is possible that arrest statistics either overrepresent the young (young offenders may be easier to apprehend) or underrepresent them (law enforcement may be more lenient in the handling of youths). Other data sources can supplement our picture of the age–crime relationship.

Using data supplied by victims of crime as reported by the NCVS for the years 1973–1977, Hindelang (1981) examined the perceived age of offenders

FIGURE 4.1
1990 AGE CURVES FOR BURGLARY, FRAUD, AND GAMBLING*

SOURCE: *Adapted from Uniform Crime Reports arrest data.*

*Data averaged over 1989–1991.

†Percentage of arrests adjusted for population size of each group.

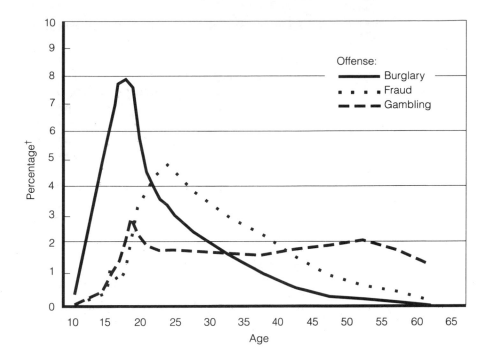

for crimes such as rape, robbery, and assault, and for certain property crimes, such as purse snatching, in which the offender was seen. Taking into account some uncertainty in victims' estimates of the age of an offender, the NCVS data paralleled the UCR arrest data fairly closely. The highest rates of offending were for those age 18–20, followed by those age 12–17. The lowest rates were for those over the age of 20.

On the other hand, according to Hindelang, although juveniles were responsible for a large proportion of the total number of crimes, they were relatively less involved than adults in serious crime, as measured by weapons use, by completion of theft, and by the size of financial loss. Nevertheless, victims were more likely to be injured by juvenile felons than by adult felons, probably because juveniles' reduced access to weapons necessitated greater use of force. Juveniles were also more likely than adults to commit their crimes in groups (thereby inflating juvenile arrest statistics); further, judging from the small monetary gains, juveniles appear to be motivated by peer pressure or sheer adventurousness more than by financial considerations. Except for crimes like purse snatching, where juveniles may select older persons as "easy targets," victims are generally from the same age group as offenders.

Self-report studies of delinquency and of adult criminality also show a general decline in rates of offending following a peak in midadolescence to young adulthood, corroborating the results reported from official data such as the UCR (Rowe and Tittle, 1977; Elliott et al., 1983).

EXPLAINING THE YOUTHFUL PEAK IN OFFENDING

Rates of offending rise rapidly from preteen to teenage years, as, barred from integrating themselves into the world of adulthood, teens suddenly are faced with major sources of reinforcement for offending: money, status, power, autonomy, identity claims, strong sensate experiences stemming from sex, natural adrenaline highs or highs from illegal substances, and peers who similarly value independence or even defiance of conventional morality. Further, their dependent status as juveniles insulates teens from many of the social and legal costs of illegitimate activities, and their stage of cognitive development limits prudence concerning the consequences of their behavior. At the same time, they possess the physical prowess required to commit crimes.

◆ **SOCIAL FACTORS** ◆ Those adolescents most at risk are those whose occupational or "life" goals are least well developed, or whose poor social or intellectual skills place them at a disadvantage. Differences in the availability of employment help explain cross-sectional variation in juvenile arrest rates for property crimes, suggesting that jobs and petty theft constitute alternative sources of status, cash, consumer goods, and other needs of juveniles (Allan and Steffensmeier, 1989). Involvement with drinking and kindred deviance may combine with economic and social "disadvantages" to facilitate the drift into delinquency. Nevertheless, a certain amount of misbehavior seems to be natural to youth; as Jolin and Gibbons (1987: 238) point out, much youthful lawbreaking is simply a stage of "growing up."

As young people move into adulthood, or anticipate entering it, most find their bonds to society strengthening, with expanded access to work or further education and increased interest in establishing permanent relationships and "settling down." Sampson and Laub (1990) report that job stability and strong marital attachment have important social control effects in reducing adult criminal behavior among both those with and those without official records of juvenile delinquency. Improved access to legal means of satisfying needs, along with greater maturity in setting personal goals, coincides with the more severe criminal penalties confronting those just entering adulthood. All these factors help account for the rapid drop-off in age-specific arrest rates during the transition to adulthood.

The transition also involves changes in behavioral expectations as well as in peer associations and lifestyle routines that diminish the opportunities for committing many common street offenses. Warr (1993), using panel data from the National Youth Survey, demonstrates how changes in peer associations during the late teens and the early twenties parallel the sharp decline in self-reported delinquent activity that occurs during this period of life. In fact, Warr reports that age effects on self-reported delinquency are reduced to nonsignificance once controls on peer influences are introduced.

However, for a relatively small proportion of young adults, the "American dream" of a good job and stable family life may be (or may seem to be) unattainable, and for them the rejection of illegitimate activities may be delayed. This is especially likely for those with minority status or with extensive official records of juvenile crime, for whom social bonds will have been weakened and deviant identities confirmed by repeated exposure to the justice system. Deviance amplification for those carrying a legal stigma—especially if they are also low income or from minority backgrounds—will be heightened in regions with weak labor markets, where jobs (if any) available to those with "records" are mainly low-wage or part-time (Allan and Steffensmeier, 1989), providing only limited alternatives to continued criminal involvement (Sullivan, 1989).

Hagan (1991: 579) reports class differences in subculture adaptations that have important implications for whether youths desist from crime and move into normal adult roles. Specifically, middle-class youths are more likely to participate in a "party" subculture than an outright "delinquent" subculture, and even though this may entail a certain amount of illegal drinking, substance abuse, sex, and the like, this party subculture serves to "socialize non-working-class males to participate in the kinds of pursuits that are later a part of male-bounded social networks." Working-class males, on the other hand, show higher rates of participation in a delinquent subculture that has "negative effects on trajectories of early adult occupational attainment," although middle-class participants in the delinquent subculture seem to be "shielded from deleterious effects."

◆ **COGNITIVE DEVELOPMENT** ◆   Cognitive development theory can complement our understanding of youthful lawbreaking and subsequent withdrawal from criminality. Youthful delinquency may be seen as growing out of the egocentrism, hedonism, and sense of invincibility that characterize the early phases of formal thinking during adolescence (Piaget, 1932). As analytical and cognitive skills develop, the adolescent becomes aware not only of the differences between what juveniles and adults are allowed to do (for example, drink alcohol, have sex) and to have (for example, automobiles and money) but also of the different sets of rules that adults apply to their children and to themselves. When awareness of this "double standard" and the conspicuous nature of adult freedoms is combined with youthful egocentrism, a feeling of "oppression" at the hands of adults is virtually inevitable, providing a convenient rationale for misbehavior and rebellion.

Subsequent cognitive development leads to a gradual decline in egocentrism, and late adolescence is marked by movement away from self-absorption to a concern for others. Individuals become more accepting of social values, more comfortable in social relations, and more concerned with the meaning of life and their place in the scheme of things (Gove, 1985). The more mature adult personality thus comes to see the casual delinquencies of youth as childish or foolish.

◆ **BIOLOGICAL AND PHYSIOLOGICAL FACTORS** ◆   The contribution of biological or physiological variables also has been acknowledged explicitly in sociological theorizing about the age–crime relationship (Parmelee, 1918; Reckless, 1950). In a general sense, physical abilities, such as strength, speed, prowess, stamina, aggression, and muscle, are useful for successful commission of many crimes, for protection, for enforcing contracts, and for recruiting and managing reliable associates (for a review, see Steffensmeier, 1983). Although some crimes are more physically demanding than others, persistent involvement in crime, regardless of crime type, is likely to entail a lifestyle that is physically demanding and dangerous. Thus, with age, declining physical strength and energy may make crime too dangerous or unsuccessful, especially where there are younger or stronger criminal competitors who will not be cowed (Wilson and Herrnstein, 1985).

Nonetheless, although declining physical abilities help explain the lower rates of street crime among the middle-aged and elderly in comparison to young adults, the more important issue is whether changes in physical abilities help explain the *abrupt* decline in the age curve during the late teens that occurs in many of the ordinary crimes. Gove (1985) contends that males in their late twenties experience a relatively sharp decline in physical abilities, which is largely responsible for the rapid decline in what he calls "substantial risk and/or physically demanding crimes" (for example, burglary, robbery) among persons in that age group. According to Gove (1985: 138), physical variables like strength and energy peak at the same time these kinds of crime peak and "suggest that their rapid decline is a major contribution to the rapid decline in deviant behavior. If this argument is correct, it would help to explain why the age–deviance relationship seems to be universal across societies and historic time."

However, the available evidence on "fitness" or biological aging is strongly at odds with this intriguing hypothesis. Specifically, the peak age for the high-risk and physically demanding crimes is much younger than the peak age for physical abilities. Further, physically undemanding crimes like larceny-theft and drug violations have the high peaks and rapid declines predicted by Gove for riskier endeavors.

The research literature on biological aging (see especially Shock, 1984) suggests that peak functioning is typically reached between the ages of 25 and 30 for those physical variables—strength, stamina, aerobic capacity, motor control, sensory perception, and speed of movement—plausibly assumed to affect one's ability to commit crimes. Although decline sets in shortly thereafter, it is not abrupt. Rather, the decline is gradual, almost imperceptible, until the mid-fifties or so, when there begins a steady decline throughout the final period of life (Shock, 1984). Other commonly mentioned physical variables like testosterone levels peak in early adulthood but then remain at peak level until at least the age of 50. In contrast, the age curves for crimes like robbery and burglary that presuppose the need for physical abilities do not peak in the mid-twenties as Gove implies; instead, they peak in midadolescence and then decline very rapidly. In short, although biological and physiological factors may contribute toward an understanding of the rapid increase in delinquent behavior during adolescence, neither can explain the abrupt decline in the age–crime curve following the peak age.

◆ **SOCIAL STATUS AND ROLES** ◆   Only in the sphere of social statuses and roles do changes of corresponding abruptness occur. If young people may be thought of as a minority, it is a minority that suddenly moves into the majority on reaching adulthood. (It is pertinent to observe that the law refers to children as "minors," whereas the age at which young people become adults is referred to as the "age of majority.") For those in late adolescence or early adulthood (roughly age 17–22, the age group showing the sharpest decline in arrest rates for Index crimes), important changes occur in at least five major spheres of life:

1. Greater access to legitimate sources of material goods and excitement: jobs, credit, alcohol, sex, and so forth.

2. Age-graded norms: externally, increased expectation of maturity and responsibility; internally, anticipation of assuming adult roles, coupled with reduced subjective acceptance of deviant roles and the threat they pose to entering adult status.

3. Peer associations and lifestyle: reduced orientation to same-age–same-sex peers and increased orientation toward persons of the opposite sex or persons who are older or more mature.

4. Increased legal and social costs for deviant behavior.

5. Patterns of illegitimate opportunities: with the assumption of adult roles, opportunities increasing for crimes (for example, gambling, fraud, and employee theft) that are less risky, more lucrative, or less likely to be reflected in official statistics.

Over a three- to five-year period, starting around age 17, young people make the transition from relative dependence and discredited status to relative independence and higher status, from relative uselessness to taking on most of the rights and responsibilities of adulthood, and from not being taken seriously to confronting the strong social expectation that they will "settle down." Late adolescence is a time when young people take significant charge of their lives and make choices (often stressful ones) that will to a large extent shape the rest of the life course. Leaving school, finding employment, going to college, enlisting in the military, and getting married not only increase social integration, informal social control, and social expectations oriented to the standards of conventional society but also involve a change in peer associations and lifestyle routines that diminish the opportunities for committing these offenses. With the accumulation of material goods and the taking on of social statuses that depend on favorable reactions from others, the potential costs of legal and social sanctions increase—at the same time that the legal sanctions increase substantially. In brief, the motives and opportunities for low-yield or exploratory types of crime decline with the movement (real or anticipated) out of adolescence. (The parsimony of sociological theories in explaining the age–crime relationship is detailed in Tittle, 1988; Steffensmeier et al., 1989).

To complete this maturation process successfully, the availability of adequate employment at adequate wages is crucial. When the labor market for young adults is dominated by marginal jobs with low hours, low pay, high turnover, and limited benefits and opportunities for advancement, all the other goals of a conventional life—marriage, family, community involvement—

become more difficult to attain, and the proportion of the population still attracted to illegitimate alternatives will be greater (Allan and Steffensmeier, 1989; McGahey, 1986).

VARIATIONS IN THE AGE CURVE BY CRIME TYPE

The factors that help account for the sharply peaked age curves for the more common crimes also help explain the flatter age curves found for other types of crimes. The offenses that show the youngest peaks and sharpest declines are crimes that fit the low-yield, criminal mischief, "hell-raising" category: vandalism, petty theft, robbery, arson, auto theft, burglary, and liquor law and drug violations. The high risks or low yields of such crimes reduce their attraction to maturing young adults with strengthening bonds to society and fewer sources of peer reinforcement for such behavior. However, some turn to offense categories that carry lower risks (or higher yields, greater opportunities, less public censure) for adults, such as gambling, alcohol consumption, certain types of fraud, and some types of violence.

Those offenses with flatter age curves are often those for which the structure of illegitimate opportunities changes rather than disappears with age. For example, some opportunities for fraud, such as falsification of identification to purchase alcohol or gain entry to "adult" establishments, exist for young people; but being too young to obtain credit, they lack the opportunities for common frauds such as passing bad checks, defrauding an innkeeper, or credit card forgery. Similarly, young people have more opportunities than do older people for some kinds of violence (for example, playground fights or gang violence) but less opportunity for other kinds of violence that stem from primary group conflicts (for example, spousal violence).

Older people may shift to less visible criminal roles such as bookie or fence. Or as a spinoff of legitimate roles, they may commit surreptitious crimes or crimes that, if discovered, are unlikely to be reported to the authorities, such as embezzlement, stock fraud, bribery, or price-fixing. Unfortunately, we know relatively little about the age distribution of persons who commit these and related lucrative crimes, but the fragmentary evidence that does exist suggests that they are likely to be middle age or older (Shapiro, 1984; Pennsylvania Crime Commission, 1991). An analysis of the age distribution of persons identified as major gambling and loansharking racketeers in the state of Pennsylvania for the 1980–1990 period provides partial confirmation that the age curves for lucrative crimes like racketeering or business crimes not only peak much later but tend to decline more slowly with age (Steffensmeier and Allan, 1993). Most gambling and loanshark kingpins are between their mid-forties and mid-sixties, with some continuing to practice their trade well into their seventies. Evidence suggests that other lucrative rackets in the underworld are also largely populated by older persons. Fences of stolen goods, for example, are typically middle-aged or older (Steffensmeier, 1986).

Still less is known of the age distribution of "respectable" or upperworld offenders who commit lucrative business crimes such as fraud, price-fixing, and bribery. Although data on the age distribution of such crimes are not plentiful, media reports typically include information on age of offenders in business crime cases that attract public attention. An analysis of data extracted from *New York Times* articles on profitable business crimes (defined here as those involving gains of $25,000 or more) during the 1987–1990 period reveals a preponderance of middle-aged or older offenders (Steffensmeier and Allan, 1993). The modal age falls between ages 40 and 50. In contrast, recall that juveniles constitute well over half of those arrested for conventional crimes like burglary or larceny. Of course, one would not expect youths to hold the types of legitimate positions that provide access to such criminal opportunities. But that is the point: The age-stratification of illegitimate opportunities parallels that for legitimate opportunities.

MINORITY DIFFERENCES IN THE AGE–CRIME CURVE

For black inner-city youths, the high level of youth inequality that characterizes modern societies is compounded by problems of racial discrimination that persist in our nation. They are less able to leave behind the inequality of youth status (Wilson, 1987). As they move into young adulthood, they continue to experience limited access to the adult labor market. An inequality perspective would predict that adult offending levels among blacks would therefore continue at higher levels than among whites, and that the proportion of total black crime that is committed by black adults will be greater than the proportion of total white crime that is committed by white adults.

This hypothesis is supported by a comparison of the adult percent of property crime arrests (controlling for differences in juvenile and adult populations) for blacks and whites (Steffensmeier and Allan, 1993). Across all crime categories, the adult percent of arrests (APA) is greater for blacks than for whites, in some cases strongly so. Black APA exceeds 50 percent for nine of ten property crime categories, whereas white APA exceeds 50 percent for only four categories. Significantly, those property crime categories for which the black APA is closest to the white APA are precisely those categories for which blacks might be assumed to have less access to criminal opportunity: fraud, forgery, and embezzlement.

The greater probability of criminal careers continuing into adulthood for members of minorities is substantiated by Sullivan's (1989) case study research with New York street gangs. He reports that white, black, and Hispanic youth gangs all engage in property crime during their teens. But white gang members begin to drift away from the group and from delinquent activities during their late teens as they begin to move into jobs, often secured through family contacts. With black and Hispanic youth, however, the greater dearth of job opportunities delays desistance from delinquency.

CROSS-CULTURAL AND HISTORICAL
DIFFERENCES IN THE AGE–CRIME CURVE

The relationship between age-stratification and the steep rise and fall in the age curve for ordinary property crime is also supported by cross-cultural and historical differences in the age–crime curve. If age inequality is indeed a major determinant of the skewed shape of that curve in contemporary society, then a "flatter" shape would be predicted for societies and for historical periods in which the culture provides for a smoother transition between the periods of youth and adulthood.

For example, in small preindustrial societies, the passage to adult status is relatively simple and continuous. Formal "rites of passage" at relatively early ages avoid much of the status ambiguity and role conflict that torment American adolescents. Youths often begin to assume responsible and economically productive roles well before they reach full physical maturity. It is not surprising, therefore, to find that such societies have significantly flatter and less skewed age–crime patterns (for a review, see Steffensmeier et al., 1989).

Much the same is true for earlier periods in the history of the United States and other industrial nations. The traditional school calendar, with its long summer vacations, testifies to the integral economic roles of youths when agriculture was the dominant economic activity of the nation and the help of young people was crucial to the harvesting of many crops. Youth economic productivity continued through the early years of industrialization when wages were so low that working-class children were expected to leave school at an early age and do their part in helping to support their families (Horan and Hargis, 1991). The responsible roles assumed by many youths in earlier periods forestalled the feelings of rebellion seen among contemporary teens who are isolated from truly productive roles within their families.

Although the stresses of adolescence have been noted since ancient times, it is also widely believed that social processes associated with the coming of industrialization and the postindustrial age have aggravated those stresses, resulting in increased levels of juvenile criminality in recent decades. The structure of modern societies, therefore, encourages crime and delinquency among the young because these societies "lack institutional procedures for moving people smoothly from protected childhood to autonomous adulthood" (Nettler, 1978: 241).

Because reliable age statistics on criminal involvement are not available over extended historical periods, we are limited largely to comparisons that cover only the past fifty years or so. An examination of UCR arrest data clearly shows that changes in the shape of the age curves across the 1940–1980 period are generally significant for nearly all offenses, whereas changes for the 1940–1960 period or the 1960–1980 period are significant mainly for the more youth-oriented offenses, such as ordinary property crimes and drinking and drug violations (Steffensmeier et al., 1989). Moreover, research comparing the criminality of recent birth cohorts with earlier ones finds that juveniles are more violent now than in the past. When a cohort of juveniles born in 1945 was compared with one born in 1958, Tracey et al. (1985) discovered a 300 percent increase in violent crime over the cohorts (see also Shannon, 1988).

The shift toward a greater concentration of offending among the young may be due partly to changes in law enforcement procedures and data collection. Nevertheless, the likelihood that real changes have in fact occurred is supported by the consistency of the changes from 1940 to 1960 and from 1960 to 1980 and over nearly all offense types. Support for the conclusion that real change has taken place over the past century also is found in the age breakdown of U.S. prisoner statistics covering the years 1890 to 1980 (Steffensmeier et al., 1989). As with the UCR statistics, the prison statistics show that age curves are more peaked today than a century ago and that changes in the age–crime curve are gradual and can be detected only when a sufficiently large time frame is used.

Findings showing a general decline in peak age and a greater concentration of offending among adolescents today are consistent with the view that contemporary teenagers in industrialized nations are subject to greater status anxiety than in previous periods of history and that the transition from adolescence to adulthood is more turbulent now than in the past (Friday and Hage, 1976; Greenberg, 1977a, Glaser, 1978). In the post–World War II period, there have been major changes in the family, in education, in the labor force, in the military, and in adolescence more generally (Clausen, 1986). In comparison to earlier eras, youths have had less access to responsible family roles, productive economic activity, and participation in community affairs. In response to this generational isolation, they have formed adolescent subcultures oriented toward consumption and hedonistic pursuits. The weakened social bonds and the reduced access to valued adult roles, along with accentuated subcultural influences, all combine to increase situationally induced pressures to obtain valued goods; display strength, daring, or loyalty to peers; or simply to "get kicks" (Gold, 1970; Briar and Piliavin, 1965).

CRIMINAL CAREERS

The youthful peak and rapid drop-off in offending that constitutes the most common societal pattern for conventional crimes is but one of a number of patterns identified when criminal careers are tracked for individual offenders. With respect to individual lawbreakers, Jolin and Gibbons (1987) describe four different age–crime patterns:

1. Early entry into lawbreaking, followed usually (but not always) by desistance from crime at a relatively early age, the common pattern described previously.
2. "Career criminality," characterized by entry into lawbreaking during the teens or early twenties but with no withdrawal from crime until middle age.
3. "Career criminals," who also begin offending at an early age and continue during adulthood but who do not cease offending at middle age.

4. "Old first timers," whose initial involvement in crime does not occur until middle age or later.

In large cities, as many as half of all males will experience police contacts for nontraffic offenses at some time during their lives. Although this is most likely to occur during adolescence, about half of all adult arrestees have had no juvenile arrests. Most individuals, particularly those with no juvenile police contacts, have very brief criminal "careers," with only one or two police contacts over the life span. On the other hand, a small proportion have numerous police contacts over an extended period of their lives (Tracey et al., 1990).

These career delinquents and career criminals account for a large proportion of all serious crime. In reference to sex differences, the research also shows that the female "chronic" offender is responsible for a larger proportion of all serious crime committed by females than is the case for her male counterpart (see Chapter 23). For now, it is important to note that the research on individual career criminals (for example, the juvenile chronic offender) shows that their age patterns differ in important ways from the age distribution for criminal conduct in the population at large (Blumstein et al., 1986). Rather than a pattern of declining involvement following a high frequency of criminal acts in late adolescence and young adulthood, the career criminal has a relatively constant high rate of involvement from adolescence through adulthood, often not terminating until the late thirties or early forties, or older.

Generally, after the rise in criminal involvement during the teenage years, there is a high termination rate and relatively little recruitment into crime after age 20. Because large numbers of offenders terminate their careers quickly during the early "break-in" period, adult criminal careers are reasonably short, averaging under six years for serious offenses. Relatively few offenders avoid these early high termination rates and remain active in criminal careers into their thirties, but those who do are the ones with the most enduring careers. Termination rates do begin to rise again at older ages, but not until after age 40 (Blumstein and Cohen, 1987).

Among the factors identified by cohort research as predictive of adult criminal careers are labor market difficulties and severity of juvenile disposition. As we noted, most juveniles "mature out" of youthful delinquency when they are faced by age-graded expectations oriented toward more "adult" behavior and as they acquire greater stakes in conformity in the form of work, education, marriage, family, community involvement, and other adult responsibilities. However, those juveniles who have been stigmatized and perhaps alienated by severe juvenile dispositions will be handicapped in entering the job market, particularly if they are additionally handicapped by poor education or minority status. If jobs are available to them at all, they are likely to be low-status, low-paying jobs that will not be adequate to support a family or to develop the stakes in conformity that can offset the attractions of illegal alternatives. Those who have been confined in institutions may be able to offset their limited legitimate opportunities with expanded criminal opportunities in the form of skills and contacts that can be developed in such settings. As individuals become more committed to a criminal lifestyle, legitimate attachments become more remote. Thus, the age–crime curves of individual career criminals are much flatter, with a fairly constant high rate of offending until much later in life.

RETIRING FROM A LIFE OF CRIME

What accounts for the fact that, ultimately, most persistent lawbreakers "burn out," often in spite of what correctional agencies do or do not do to them? Of course, some offenders simply die, and assuming that active criminals are more prone to injury and death, at older ages the population will increasingly consist of persons who are less willing or able to be criminally involved. The available evidence, however, indicates that withdrawal from crime usually occurs well before the offenders in question have become infirm or enfeebled. Thus, exiting from crime cannot be attributed simply to physical deterioration.

Empirical research suggests that exiting from a criminal career requires the acquisition of meaningful bonds to conventional people or institutions. Thieves leave a life of crime as they form attachments to a life of conformity and develop a reluctance to give up those new bonds by risking further imprisonment. One important tie to the conventional order is a job that seems to have the potential for advancement and that is seen as meaningful and economically rewarding. A good job shifts a criminal's attention from the present to the future and provides a solid basis for the construction of a noncriminal identity. It also alters an individual's daily routine in ways that make crime less likely (Meisenhelder, 1977; Shover, 1983).

Good personal relationships with conventional people such as a spouse, lover, children, or friends also create bonds to the social order that an individual wants to protect. These people may be "psychologically present" if the individual faces situations that offer a temptation to engage in criminal activity. Family members and lovers also provide a place of residence, food, and help in the development of everyday skills such as paying bills and scheduling time. Other bonds that may lead people away from crime include involvement in religion, sports, hobbies, or other activities (Irwin, 1970).

The development of social bonds may be coupled with cognitive factors that are triggered by a sort of burnout or belated deterrent effect as offenders grow tired of the hassles of repeated involvement with the criminal justice system. Offenders may come to regard the frequent traveling and other features of theft as overly burdensome. They may have violated the code of the underworld and be excluded from opportunities to work with "good" thieves. They may have experienced a long prison sentence that jolts them into quitting or that entails the loss of contacts that make the continuation of a criminal career difficult, if not impossible. Or inmates may develop a fear of dying in prison, especially since repeated convictions yield longer sentences. Still other offenders may quit or "slow down" as they find their abilities and efficiency declining with increasing age, loss of "nerve," or sustained narcotics or alcohol use (Prus and Sharper, 1977; Adler and Adler, 1983; Steffensmeier, 1986).

OLDER CRIMINALS

Although crime rates among older persons are relatively low, two patterns of offending can still be found: (1) those whose first criminal involvement occurs relatively late in life and (2) those who started crime at an early age and continue their involvement beyond the forties and fifties. Interestingly, a fair number of previously law-abiding persons become involved in crime at an older age, particularly in shoplifting, homicide, and alcohol-related offenses. What evidence is available on first-time older offenders suggests that situational stress and lack of alternative opportunities play a primary role. The unanticipated loss of one's job or other disruptions of social ties can push some individuals into their first law violation at any age (Jolin and Gibbons, 1987; Alston, 1986).

Older offenders who persist in crime are more likely to belong to the criminal underworld. These are individuals who are relatively successful in their criminal activities or who are extensively integrated into subcultural or family criminal enterprises. They seem to receive relational and psychic rewards (for example, pride in their expertise) as well as monetary rewards from lawbreaking and, as a result, see no need to withdraw from lawbreaking (Reynolds, 1953; Klockars, 1974; Steffensmeier, 1986). These older offenders are also unlikely to see many meaningful opportunities for themselves in the conventional or law-abiding world. Consequently, "the straight life" may have little to offer successful criminals, who will be more likely to persist in their criminality for an extended period. But they, too, eventually slow down as they grow tired of the cumulative aggravations and risks of criminal involvement or as they encounter the diminishing capacities associated with the aging process.

Finally, contrary to the assertion in some articles in the popular and social science press about a "geriatric crime wave," there has not been an increase in the frequency or severity of elderly crime per capita in recent decades (Steffensmeier, 1987). The proportionate involvement of the elderly in crime is about the same now as it was twenty-five to thirty years ago. When the elderly do break the law, moreover, their lawbreaking involves minor alcohol-related or theft offenses rather than serious crimes.

EFFECTS OF AGE STRUCTURE ON A NATION'S CRIME RATE

Because involvement in crime diminishes with age, it follows that fluctuations in the age composition of a population can have a significant impact on the crime rates of the population. In the United States, for example, both the dramatic increases in the overall crime rate in the 1960s and early 1970s and the decrease in the rate in the 1980s are linked to the post–World War II "baby boom" and the post-1960s "baby bust" (Steffensmeier and Harer, 1987).

The impact of age structure fluctuations on crime has been investigated extensively over the past twenty years. In an analysis of national crime statistics in the United States, Ferdinand (1970) found that about 50 percent of the increase in the Index crime rate during the 1960s could be attributed to various population shifts, particularly the movement of the baby-boom generation into the crime-prone teenaged years. More recently, Steffensmeier and Harer (1989) analyzed U.S. statistics from the mid-1970s to the late 1980s, using statistics on Index crimes from both the UCR and the NCVS. They note that virtually all the reported decrease in the Index crime rate during the 1980s could be attributed to the declining proportion of teenagers in the population — that is, to a baby-bust effect. In fact, once age effects are purged, the UCR statistics actually show a 7 percent rise in the nation's crime rate during the Reagan years, from 1980 to 1988. Thus, both the rise of crime in the 1960s and the subsequent decline in the 1980s are attributable in large part to shifts in the age composition of the U.S. population.

Interestingly, imprisonment rates doubled and rose far more sharply in the 1980s than in any previous decade in the nation's history — yet there was no discernible drop in the nation's crime rate (Steffensmeier, 1992). In fact, as a group, and once age effects are purged, the UCR violent and really "serious" crimes of homicide, forcible rape, aggravated assault, and robbery increased about 20 percent since 1980. At face value, this suggests the criminal justice system does not contain the solution to the nation's crime problem and that no law enforcement strategy can confidently be recommended to remedy it (see Chapters 16 and 23).

EFFECTS OF COHORT SIZE

A related issue concerns the question of "cohort size" on a nation's crime rate. That is, are higher age-specific crime rates for large age cohorts reaching adolescence from roughly 1960 to 1975 a result of the post–World War II baby boom? A number of demographers (Easterlin, 1978; Ryder, 1965) have proposed that a nation's crime rate may fluctuate not only in response to changes in the age structure of the population but also according to the relative size of particular age cohorts. They argue that social constraints and life opportunities will differ for abnormally large or small youth cohorts. In large cohorts, too many young people compete for jobs and education, and they believe they are comparatively worse off economically than members of other cohorts even though they have been socialized to want the same sorts of material goods. The growth of large juvenile cohorts also can complicate adult society's attempt to reorient the self-interests of youth to the adult community interests and encourage development of youth subcultures and generational conflict.

The idea that large youth cohorts will exhibit a relatively higher crime rate than small youth cohorts is an intriguing one, and a number of studies have sought to test the hypothesis. Some studies report "significant" cohort size effects (Maxim, 1985; Smith, 1986), whereas others do not find any such effects (Steffensmeier and Harer, 1987). However, whether or not significant effects are reported, the more important finding is that all the studies are in agreement that cohort size accounts for very little of the variation in the nation's crime rate over an extended period. The levels of criminality are more similar than different between large and small youth cohorts. In some respects, this is hardly surprising because a nation's crime rate is obviously influenced by other well-established correlates of crime (such as income inequality and access to crime opportunities), which are likely to nullify the small effects of cohort size on crime rates.

AGE-BY-GENDER DIFFERENCES IN CRIME

A final issue concerns the combined effects of age and gender on crime. The age–gender–crime relationship is, of course, two-sided. On the one hand, one can consider gender differences in the age distribution of offending and ask whether males and females have similar or different age–crime curves. Conversely, one can consider age differences in the sex ratio of crime and ask whether different age groups are similar in the female-to-male percentage of offending. A related issue in light of our discussion of changes in the age–crime relationship since World War II is whether the age–gender–offending relationship is constant over time and across crime categories.

If we study UCR arrest statistics to investigate the age–gender–crime relationship in each of three periods—1935, 1960, and 1985—we find, first, that the age curves of male and female offenders are very similar within any given period and across all offenses, with the exception of prostitution. That is, although male levels of offending are always higher than female levels at every age and for virtually all offenses, the female-to-male ratio remains fairly constant across the life span (Steffensmeier and Streifel, 1991).

Second, the age–crime curves of both sexes have shifted since World War II toward younger and more peaked distributions. Moreover, the magnitude and direction of the shift is virtually identical for both sexes and for most offenses. This finding is consistent with the view discussed earlier that youths today are subject to greater status anxiety than in previous periods of history.

Third, the single major difference in the age curves of males and females is for prostitution (and to some extent vagrancy, often a euphemism for prostitution in the case of female arrestees), with females having a much greater concentration of arrests among the young. Although this difference may be due in part to more stringent enforcement of prostitution statutes when young females are involved (Chesney-Lind, 1986), the younger and more peaked female age curve is also a function of the extent to which opportunity structures for sexual misbehaviors differ between males and females. Clearly, sexual attractiveness and the marketability of sexual services are strongly linked to both age and gender: Older women become less able to market sexual services, whereas older men can continue to purchase sexual services from young females or from young males (Steffensmeier and Streifel, 1991).

Finally, when the age–gender–crime relationship is examined in terms of the sex ratio or the female-to-male percentage of crime at different ages, the ratio is remarkably similar across age groups for any given crime at any given period. Over time, if the female percentage of arrests for a particular crime increases, remains stable, or decreases for one age group, comparable changes are found for all age groups.

CONCLUSION

Criminologists have long recognized that both age and gender are very robust predictors of crime rates. Although it is beyond the scope of our purposes here to develop an integrated theory of age and gender differences in crime, it is important ultimately to develop fuller explanations for lower rates of offending among females (of all ages) relative to males and among older persons (both male and female) relative to younger persons. We expect such explanations to center on the data and the theoretical constructs that we have noted in this chapter. Namely, the lower rates of females and older persons can be seen as consequences of gender and age differences in goals and the means to achieve them, in social control, in socialization, and in access to criminal opportunities (including those that dovetail with biological and physiological variables). Moreover, articulating the etiology of the higher levels of criminality among males and among the young should contribute toward greater understanding of crime in general and of other behavioral differences between males and females, young and old.

DISCUSSION QUESTIONS

1. Both gender and age seem related to involvement in criminal activity. In what ways is this so, and how do gender and age interact with each other to influence criminality?

2. We often hear about the "new female" criminal. To what extent does this term have any validity? How has women's involvement in crime changed over the past forty years?

3. Part of the puzzle regarding gender and age differences in criminality involves the opportunity to commit crime. Discuss how our society is structured regarding criminal opportunity.

4. Crime rates in this country began to rise in the 1960s, about the time that baby-boom kids entered high school. Explain the connection between these two phenomena, and link them to the concept of criminal "career."

CHAPTER 5

CRIMINAL BEHAVIOR: RACE AND CLASS

Anthony R. Harris and Lisa R. Meidlinger
University of Massachusetts

COMPARED TO THEIR PROPORTION in the general U.S. population, blacks are consistently overrepresented in arrest data. In 1990, a little over 12 percent of the U.S. population was counted as black. In the same year, of all *Uniform Crime Reports* (UCR) arrests for Index crimes (see Chapter 3), those of blacks totaled just over 34 percent.

Figure 5.1 presents data for blacks and whites on Index crimes against property. Blacks accounted for about 23 percent of the arson arrest total (14,564), 39 percent of the motor vehicle theft arrest total (164,347), 31 percent of the burglary arrest total (332,165), and 31 percent of the larceny–theft arrest total (1,202,828). These simple arrest comparisons are shown in the left half of Figure 5.1. Since they represent only one of about eight Americans, blacks are clearly overrepresented in arrests for serious, common law property crimes. When population size is held constant and arrest rates per 100,000 of particular population groups are calculated, the group comparison is more striking: The rate-adjusted ratio of blacks to whites arrested is 2.0 for arson, 4.3 for motor vehicle theft, 2.9 for burglary, and 3.0 for larceny-theft. These rate-based comparisons are shown in the right half of Figure 5.1.

Figure 5.2 displays data for blacks and whites on Index crimes against the person. For this set of crimes, black overrepresentation is even greater, by a factor of about 2. Blacks accounted for 45 percent of all Index arrests for crimes against the person in 1990: about 56 percent of the homicide arrest total (17,894), 44 percent of the forcible rape arrest total (30,282), 62 percent of the armed robbery arrest total (134,394), and 39 percent of the aggravated assault arrest total (367,492). These simple arrest comparisons are seen in the left half of Figure 5.2. When population size is adjusted for, the group comparison for

FIGURE 5.1
1990 INDEX CRIMES
AGAINST PROPERTY

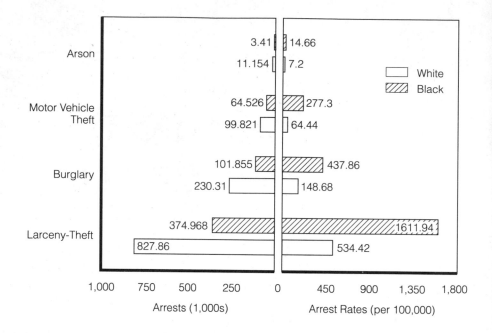

this set of very serious common law crimes is quite striking. The rate-adjusted ratio of blacks to whites arrested for homicide is 8.3, 5.2 for forcible rape, 10.8 for armed robbery, and 4.3 for aggravated assault. These rate-based comparisons are seen in the right half of Figure 5.2.

Race differences in UCR data are striking regardless of whether one looks at rates of arrest or at absolute numbers of arrests. They are so strong, in fact, that basic changes in crime rates for a geographic unit may reflect no more than changes in its racial composition. Chilton (1986), for example, argues effectively that 57 percent of the increase in combined arrests for twelve of the largest cities in the United States, between 1960 and 1980, can be linked to an increase of the proportion of the black population in these cities — even though the black arrest *rate* remained quite stable during this time.

BIAS IN THE UCR CRIME INDEX

Striking as these findings seem, several nagging questions remain. Index crimes focus primarily on what might be called blue collar, or street, crimes. Because a strong relationship still exists between race and occupation, Index crimes by their very nature focus us away from white collar and "silk collar" crimes, and thus away from white offenders. If white collar and silk collar offenses are included, does the race–crime link change? That is, do Index crimes really provide a race-blind Index from the start? Second, suppose we answer yes to the first question and assume that Index crimes are a fair, representative, and race-blind subset of all possible crimes in contemporary America. If we do, it

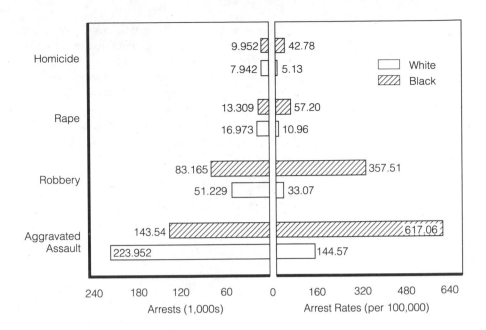

FIGURE 5.2
1990 INDEX CRIMES
AGAINST THE PERSON

Homicide
9.952 / 42.78
7.942 / 5.13

White
Black

Rape
13.309 / 57.20
16.973 / 10.96

Robbery
83.165 / 357.51
51.229 / 33.07

Aggravated Assault
143.54 / 617.06
223.952 / 144.57

240 180 120 60 0 160 320 480 640
Arrests (1,000s)   Arrest Rates (per 100,000)

soon becomes obvious that letting an a priori set of crimes be used as a fair index is one thing, but operationally measuring that Index is quite another. To begin, even if the a priori Index is fair, in real life it is given meaning only by arrests. Suppose that racial prejudice causes a victim to "see" a black burglar when, in fact, the burglar was white? Or suppose that the same sort of prejudice leads the police to arrest a black for armed robbery when, in fact, the robber was white? As Wilson and Herrnstein (1985: 460) note, even under the best of circumstances

> the racial or ethnic identity of a person is far less certain than his sex or age. The ancestors of many blacks and Orientals include some, perhaps many, Caucasians, and vice-versa; when parentage is mixed, a decision that someone is "really" black, Oriental, or Caucasian is a bit arbitrary. At times it is even ludicrous, as when custom dictates that a person who has only one black grandparent is a black, whereas a person who has three white grandparents may not be white.

In short, suppose that however race-blind the Crime Index before the fact, it is subverted by the prejudice and bias of everyday life into a "disfavored-race" index. Are the arrests comprising Index crimes race-biased?

Third, the strong relationship between race and occupation is critical, for it involves a link between race and social class. But race in contemporary America has other important correlates besides social class, including living area, years of education, life expectancy, family structure, IQ scores, and historical experience.

These correlates, along with class, form a generally tight package or bundle of factors. To a large extent, this bundle of relationships reflects our nation's entire social history, including the grim decades of slavery, times of enormous wealth and freedom for some, but appalling poverty and bondage for others. To at least the same extent, this bundle reflects our nation's present social structure, with income inequality and occupational immobility for some but new levels of well-being and material success for others.

Thus, when we ask the third basic question — if there is a relation between race and crime, what causes it? — we realize that because these correlates are so tightly bundled, there is no simple answer. In the center of the often-told American tale of social advantage and disadvantage, these correlates of race form an extremely tight and, to a large extent, virtually inseparable tangle.

A Priori Race Bias

It is important to realize from the start that the Crime Index is not a priori blind to race. This view is based on an understanding of race-related opportunities in contemporary America. The present UCR Index opens a certain kind of window onto crime, a window onto "the streets." Undoubtedly, this crime window is of great importance to all Americans. However, the window is defined not just by what it allows us to see; it is at least as much defined by what it *excludes* from our sight, namely, much white collar and probably most silk collar crime.

Because blacks are underrepresented and whites overrepresented in white and silk collar occupations, we must conclude that the set of crimes called Index crimes is skewed *away* from criminal opportunities where whites are overrepresented. This does not imply that the Index is biased *against* lower-class black street crime per se but rather that it is biased *away from* middle class and elite whites' "suite" crime. No matter what we do, it seems that UCR data do not adequately measure upper-level white collar and silk collar, or suite, crime. This type of crime includes such crimes as stock market fraud, price-fixing and product misrepresentation, corporate tax evasion, industrial pollution, maintenance of unsafe working conditions, and illegal intervention in the political process (Sheley, 1985: 127). Because race is strongly correlated with occupation, and because the conventional UCR Crime Index is intrinsically biased away from silk collar crime, the UCR Crime Index is intrinsically biased away from white, silk collar criminals and toward black, blue collar criminals.

Empirical Race Bias

Is the Crime Index empirically race-biased because it represents arrests, not crimes? Given our answer to the first question, the reader might expect us to conclude that it is. But our answer to the second question is no: The Crime Index is not empirically race-biased because it measures arrests, not crimes.

The reasoning behind this position is quite complicated. It does not have to do with a priori race biases in the choice of which crimes are included in, and excluded from, the Crime Index (that is, with issues raised in our first question). Instead, the reasoning is based on the empirical relationship between arrests for the Index crimes and the "true" distribution of Index crimes as estimated by data other than UCR (or arrest) data.

◆ **SELF-REPORT DATA** ◆   In the 1960s, it became fashionable in many academic circles to deplore the use of UCR data as a fair measure of crime in the United States (see Kitsuse and Cicourel, 1963). To a large degree, this disdain was based on the assumption that police as a group were racially prejudiced and tended to arrest blacks in preference to whites. As a solution, many criminologists advocated the use of the "offender source"—that is, self-report studies (see Chapter 3). These purported to bypass inherent problems in the arrest-based UCR Index by "going directly to the horse's mouth"—to offenders themselves. Typically, such studies offered respondents checklists of mostly minor crimes, such as petty larceny and vandalism. Self-report questionnaires were administered almost exclusively to juvenile populations, particularly students in high school, a limitation that has proven to be quite serious (see Conklin, 1992; Harris and Hill, 1982; Sheley, 1985).

A major conclusion from this research was that UCR ("official/arrest") data overrepresented males from disadvantaged population groups, particularly black and lower-socioeconomic-status (SES) groups. For example, Hirschi's (1969) study found that if self-reports were used as the guide, the prevalence of black delinquent acts exceeded the prevalence of white delinquent acts by only 10 percent (the ratio of self-reported black delinquency prevalence to white delinquency prevalence was 1.1 to 1), but if official police contacts were the guide, the prevalence of black contact exceeded the prevalence of white contact by 100 percent (the ratio of black official contact to white official contact was 2.0 to 1). These findings, and others like them, implied that virtually all differences between disadvantaged and advantaged groups at point of arrest could be attributed to police bias.

◆ **VICTIM-REPORT DATA** ◆   For two decades, opponents of UCR data insisted that these data were mirrors of police racism, not criminal behavior. Opponents of self-report data argued that these data generally measured not-so-serious crimes such as vandalism and status offenses such as truancy and were provided by mostly "good kids"—youths who had *not* dropped out of high school, who had *not* been shot to death, who were *not*, at present, "doing time." In the mid-1970s, a third source of crime data was tapped. It cast the deciding vote: National Crime Victimization Survey (NCVS) data strongly supported the view that the offender characteristics seen in UCR data, and not those found in self-reports, were correct.

Figure 5.3 is based on averaged annual NCVS data from 1973 to 1977. Crimes included are common law personal crimes where face-to-face contact occurs, such as armed robbery or assault. In these cases, victims are asked to

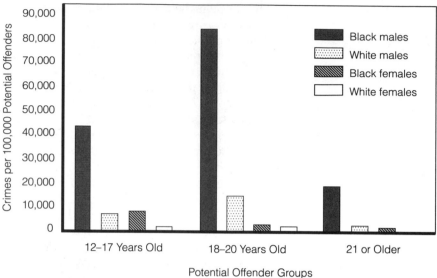

report perceived demographic characteristics of offenders, including gender, race, and age. Estimated offender rates can thus be computed (rates = offenses reported by victims, adjusted per 100,000 potential offenders in each population group). The victim reports used in Figure 5.3 graphically corroborate UCR data on the race–street-crime relationship: Blacks, particularly black males, are substantially overrepresented in the reports. If male and female rates are summed within race and across age categories, the aggregated rate-adjusted race ratio for the entire data set stands at about five black offenses per one white offense.

The "average" year for this observation is 1975. Just two years later, for the four UCR personal crimes of assault, aggravated assault, rape, and robbery, the rate-adjusted race ratios stood at 4.6, 5.6, 7.5, and 13.6, respectively (Hill and Harris, 1982). But the offender rates in Figure 5.3 combine these UCR crimes. If UCR and NCVS data really do correspond (see Biderman and Lynch, 1991, on the general issue of UCR and NCVS correspondence), we would expect the NCVS aggregated race ratio (5.3) to resemble most closely the race ratio for the highest-volume offenses of the four UCR crimes, and it does. These high-volume offenses are assault and aggravated assault (where the race ratios for 1977 are 4.6 and 5.6, respectively). For rape during the same period, a similar UCR–NCVS match has been noted by Hindelang (1978). In addition, Hindelang observes a close UCR–NCVS match on race effects for armed robbery (see also Conklin, 1972; Silberman, 1978; Pruitt and Wilson, 1983).

Victims appear to be telling us that arrests are probably a reasonable indicator of real race-based differences in the commission of street crime (see McNeely and Pope, 1981, for a different view). Equally important, NCVS data suggest that the self-report findings were correct for less serious crime but that unless one were to equate petty theft with armed robbery, the findings were largely useless. One major key to reconciling discrepancies between the offender and the state (UCR) estimates obviously lay in limitations in self-report sampling techniques: Self-report studies typically *undersampled* seriously delinquent offenses (Wilbanks, 1987) and seriously delinquent youths (Hindelang et al., 1979).

In probably the single best self-report study to date, Elliott and Ageton (1980) analyzed data from a national sample of over 1,700 juveniles regarding their delinquencies in 1976. They note a link between race and self-reported delinquency, not particularly noteworthy for less serious delinquencies, like status offenses, but significant for serious or predatory delinquencies. In a parallel and rare look at adult self-report data, the Rand Inmate Survey finds that black overrepresentation in arrest data really does reflect black overrepresentation in serious criminal activities (Petersilia, 1985).

Once revealed, these UCR and self-report discrepancies suggest that at least three major misunderstandings of crime in America occurred among criminologists in the 1960s and the 1970s. The first was the most critical because it reflected so clearly on social policy. It involved a serious underestimation of the nature of institutional racism. In truth, could not racism in America be so far-reaching that it strongly affected people's willingness to choose criminal behavior, as well as which type of criminal behavior to choose? The second misunderstanding involved the intellectually and morally vacuous equating, by some criminologists, of delinquencies like petty theft, where $2 worth of candy might be pilfered, with crimes like aggravated assault, where the injured victim might require hospitalization, endure months of lost income, and suffer years of trauma. The third misunderstanding, somewhat more technical, involved a woefully incorrect reading of the nature of police behavior: Police were incorrectly perceived as being in the business of looking for people, particularly blacks, to arrest. A very important unasked question was: Could not racism in America be so severe that the demographically overrepresented victims of street crime were, in fact, the demographically overrepresented perpetrators of street crime and not the white middle class?

◆ **REEVALUATING UCR DATA: CRIME SERIOUSNESS AND THE REACTIVE POLICE MODEL** ◆ Surely, the UCR Crime Index offers a narrow window through which to see certain types and patterns of crime. As we noted, the Index in this sense is biased away from white collar and silk collar crimes; in addition, the Index observes these patterns by counting arrests (see Chapter 3). However, arrests represent only one kind of data-gathering operation, and one that rests heavily on police practices. Evidence gathered the past twenty years gives us reason to be suspicious of police attitudes toward minorities (Chevigny, 1969; Sheley and Harris, 1976). But it is equally clear that the data produced by arrests are a complex function of actual offenses, the victim's or bystander's behavior, and police practices themselves.

The role of the police in most arrests in the United States is reactive rather than proactive (Reiss, 1971; Conklin, 1972). That is, in most arrests, police react to reports of crime called in by victims or bystanders; they do not initiate arrests based on what they see from patrol cars or on the beat. This has important implications. If the proactive model were operating, and operating fairly, the police would have difficulty in deciding between making an arrest for a serious versus a not-so-serious crime. Under the reactive model, police "take what they get . . . what is reported to them," and as we know, victims and observers are likely to report more, rather than less, serious crimes (Block and Block, 1980; Bureau of Justice Statistics, 1991b). Consequently, the police re-act to and follow through on reported offenses that are relatively serious and tend to produce race-skewed arrests that reflect race differences in actual street crimes committed (see Black, 1980; Blumstein et al., 1993). Thus, to the degree that the reactive police model accurately describes reality, then victims, and other observers, are more likely than police to be the primary source of race bias in incorrectly identifying street-crime offenders (see the discussion in Smith et al., 1984).

◆ **WHO IS THE VICTIM?** ◆ Like their liberal counterparts, conservative stereotypes die hard. The dominant image of the overrepresented victim of street crime in America—supposedly a person who is both middle class and white—is largely incorrect. NCVS data from 1991 indicate that, with one exception, blacks report being victimized at a higher rate than do whites. Moreover, in the past decade, there appears to have been a dramatic increase in victimization reported by blacks, thus further widening the black–white vic-timization gap. For the most serious or violent crimes, including rape, aggravated assault, and armed robbery, black victimization rates in 1991 were 50 percent higher than white rates (versus 32 percent in 1985). For robbery alone, the black victimization rate exceeds the white rate by 207 percent (ver-sus 163 percent in 1985). Personal theft, with and without offender contact, is the only property crime for which black victimization rates have consistently run lower than those of whites. But the gap has narrowed from about 8 percent in 1985 to less than 1 percent in 1991 (61.1 versus 61.4 per 1,000). For house-hold victimizations, however, black rates are again higher. Blacks are about 48 percent more likely to be burglarized than are whites (versus 38 percent in 1985), 11 percent more likely to suffer a household larceny than are whites (versus 28 percent in 1985), and about 90 percent more likely to report a motor vehicle theft (versus 70 percent in 1985).

Even when additional factors such as income are taken into account, the statistically overrepresented victim of street crime clearly resembles the statis-tically overrepresented offender: male, young, poor, and black (see Chapter 6). There is thus good reason to think that if there is race bias in the system, it occurs long before arrest occurs.

CAUSES OF THE RACE–STREET-CRIME RELATIONSHIP

There seems little doubt that in America at present, blacks' overrepresentation in arrests is based mainly on their overrepresentation in criminal behavior "on the streets." In answering our second question, we must conclude that the be-havior–arrest relation is not the major area in which to find racism. Such concerns are more wisely focused on the third, and final, question: If there is a real relation between race and street crime, why does it exist?

Judging the usefulness of theories about the causes of the race–street-crime relationship is equivalent to evaluating the explanatory power of the key contemporary correlates of race. Chief among these is social class. Other key correlates include factors in the areas of constitution, family structure, subculture, and historical caste (see Wilson and Herrnstein, 1985).

SOCIAL CLASS

> Though economic-class divisions are rapidly producing a nation of haves and have nots, for blacks, race still tends to overshadow all else. It doesn't matter whether you are rich man, poor man, beggar or thief, if you are black, there's an artificial ceiling on your ambition. (*Newsweek*, 1987: 57)

The correlation between race and class in America is so strong that any relation observed between race and crime might be nothing more than a cloaked relation between class and crime. If this were true, we could say that the race–street-crime relation was "explained" by social class, a position that has been frequently argued.

◆ **THE USE AND MISUSE OF SELF-REPORT DATA** ◆   We will not attempt a rigorous definition of social class here. Various measures of social class include income, years of education, and occupational status. In the case of juveniles, the best index is probably parents' occupational status (see Sampson and Rossi, 1975). By whatever measure, we need data to evaluate the possibility that social class explains the race–street-crime relation. As it turns out, UCR data do not even try to include information relevant to the arrestee's social class; neither do NCVS data. With one major exception, to which we will return, this leaves us with self-reports.

We noted earlier that one of the problems with self-report data had been the tendency to undersample seriously delinquent offenses. A related problem involved the tendency to truncate delinquency: Respondents were often classified as "delinquent" if they admitted to ever having committed *any one* of a broad range of infractions, from truancy to burglary. At best, this procedure was not a good idea. By this standard, most American teenage males, if not females, would fall into the same delinquent category as a budding Charles Manson. As clearly noted by Wilson and Herrnstein (1985: 37), this procedure "obscures differences between persons who break the law once or twice (many males have done that) and those who break it twenty, thirty, or fifty times per year."

A third problem with self-report data had been the tendency to undersample seriously delinquent youth, at the least youth who were truant from school the day of the self-report survey, or worse, youth who were doing time in a juvenile detention facility. It should come as no surprise, then, that these problems led to some profoundly counter-productive conclusions about delinquency and crime in America. One extraordinarily senseless conclusion was that once self-reports, not arrests, were made the yardstick, there was virtually no relationship between social class and "true" delinquent behavior. A related conclusion, not limited to mere delinquency and, incredibly enough, based primarily on self-report data from high school students, went even further: There was virtually *no* relation between class and crime in America (see Tittle et al., 1978).

Countering this claim, Hindelang et al. (1979) effectively argued that the discrepancy between self-report and arrest findings is mostly an illusion based on the measurement of different "behavioral domains"—a polite way of distinguishing between trivial delinquencies, occasionally engaged in by virtually all teenagers, and serious delinquencies, very frequently engaged in by a small number of youth, probably drop-outs, who are well on their way to a career in crime. For our purposes, Hindelang et al. do not go far enough. In a review of ninety empirical studies of the class–crime link, Braithwaite (1981) fails to find support for the link in only 23 percent (twenty-one) of the studies. And Braithwaite's research omits ecological studies of crime (comparison of crime rates by geographic sector) though these studies consistently report a class–crime association (Sheley, 1985: 154). In a very important theoretical and empirical clarification, Axenroth (1983) argues that social class is related to serious, but not to trivial, forms of delinquency in America and that the strength of this class–delinquency link varies inversely by societal development—the link being weaker in more industrialized societies. But even Axenroth does not go far enough. As long as crime is operationally limited to mean delinquency or street crime, white collar and silk collar crime are necessarily ruled out of the class–crime window. This, in turn, means that the relation between social class and crime is necessarily theoretically restricted.

◆ **JUVENILES** ◆ Elliott and Ageton's major (1980) self-report study of a national probability sample of juveniles helps explicate the race–class relation to street crime. Though this study does not allow us to see the effect on delinquency of race, holding class effects constant (or, for that matter, class, holding race effects constant), it does allow us to see, very clearly, the relative magnitude of race and class effects on delinquency in a national sample *and* the important interaction of these effects with *type* of delinquency (predatory versus nonpredatory). To measure class, Elliott and Ageton basically rely on the occupational status of the primary breadwinner in the juvenile's immediate family. Their results are depicted in Figure 5.4.

Figure 5.4 graphically underscores two basic points. One is that class and race differences are trivial for nonpredatory or "victimless" delinquencies, including public disorder crimes such as drunkenness, status crimes such as truancy, and drug violations such as barbiturate use. For nonpredatory crimes, the maximum class ratio observed is thus 1.05 to 1.00 (working class to lower class), a trivial 5 percent difference at most, whereas the race ratio is 1.06 to 1.00 (blacks to whites), a trivial 6 percent difference at most. These findings are consistent with those of Hagan and Parker (1985) and Hagan et al., (1987).

FIGURE 5.4
DELINQUENCY BY RACE
AND CLASS, BASED ON
SELF-REPORT ESTIMATES
FROM 1976 NATIONAL
YOUTH SURVEY

SOURCE: *Adapted from Elliott and Ageton, 1980.*

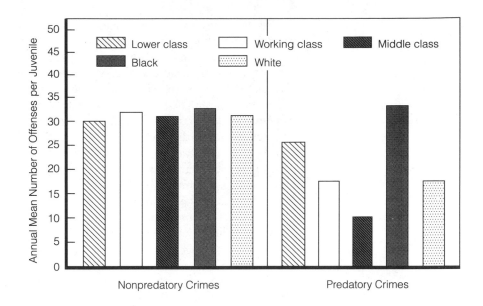

Class and race differences are unmistakable for the more serious predatory delinquencies, including crimes against persons (for example, aggravated assault and robbery) and crimes against property (for example, burglary and auto theft). For this set, annual self-reported delinquent acts vary by class from a low mean of 10.6 for middle-class youth to a high mean of 25.5 for lower-class youth, with working-class youth standing at a mean of 17.4. Mean annual delinquent acts reported by whites stand at 16.8, and by blacks at 33.3. For predatory crimes, the maximum class ratio observed is thus 2.41 to 1.00 (lower class to middle class), a nontrivial 141 percent difference, whereas the race ratio is 1.99 to 1.00 (blacks to whites), a nontrivial 99 percent difference. Additional analysis by Elliott and Ageton (1980: 106), which cannot be observed from Figure 5.4, "suggests a relatively high involvement of lower-class black youth in serious offenses against the person"—that is, in that particular subset of street crimes most likely to lead to arrest.

Elliott and Ageton's data strongly indicate that in modern America, real race and real class differences exist in serious delinquency. Like victim data, these data cross-validate the reasonable use of arrest data as a basis for race comparisons. Unfortunately, these data do not really disentangle race from class. To do this, we need to look at what is probably the best empirical study of street crime ever done in America: the Wolfgang et al. (1972) study of the criminal histories of the birth cohort of white and black males born in 1945 and living in Philadelphia between 1955 and 1962, that is, between their tenth and seventeenth birthdays. Some serious questions arise concerning the researchers' final measure of social class, or better, SES, and once again, we are limited to juveniles; nevertheless, their work has withstood scrutiny extremely well.

In reviewing the findings from the 1972 study, we immediately run into the race–class tangle. If we use general prevalence (percentage having police contact for any offense) as our guide, SES has a more powerful effect than does race. If, however, we use serious incidence (police contact rate per 1,000 for serious offenses) as our guide, the reverse is true: Race has a more powerful effect than does SES. Though the effects of SES and race are in the theoretically expected direction, the findings are contradictory with respect to the relative importance of the two.

As it turns out, these contrary findings are related to the problematic correlation between race and class. Some of the observed race effect is "really" a class effect, and some of the observed class effect is "really" a race effect. In the birth cohort, are there *independent* effects of race, controlling for the effects of class, and class, controlling for the effects of race? And if so, which effects are stronger? The answers are clear: Both effects exist though the independent race effect is stronger. Although the impact of class on general prevalence still exists after the effects of race have been accounted for, the independent effects of race are somewhat stronger. And on the basis of serious incidence, net class effects again exist, but independent race effects are substantially stronger (see Harris, 1989, for details).

Some additional observations may be made. First, as in the case of the Elliott and Ageton (1980) findings, race and class effects are stronger for more serious offenses. Second, in a particularly striking comparison, the serious incidence rate for upper-SES blacks in the cohort is substantially *higher* than the serious incidence rate for lower-SES whites in the cohort. In itself, this finding puts enormous pressure on any simple attempt to reduce race to the economic dimensions of class. Third, it turns out that, although the factors of race and class have clear, independent effects on the chances of being a "one-time" offender in the study, these factors have an even greater impact on the chances of continued involvement in delinquency, that is, on being a recidivist (repeat offender). Among one-time offenders, holding race effects constant, lower-SES youth have a 41 percent higher rate of serious incidence than do upper-SES youth. Among recidivists, however, this difference increases to 119 percent. Among one-time offenders, holding class effects constant, black youth have a 72 percent higher rate of serious incidence than do white youth. Among recidivists, however, this difference increases dramatically to 274 percent. Independent race effects are thus far greater for juveniles who are repeatedly in trouble with the law than for juveniles who appear to be "deterred" after the first police contact.

Finally, it is worth noting that the clear "race-net-of-class" findings for this birth cohort—including the strikingly higher serious incidence rate for upper-SES blacks than for lower-SES whites—are replicated in a second birth cohort study in Philadelphia by Tracy et al. (1990). Exactly how much of this race disproportionality in police contact is due to genuine race differences in street crime, and exactly how much of the disproportionality is due to discriminatory police practices, remains a general question (see Krisberg et al., 1987;

Huizinga and Elliott, 1987; Blumstein et al., 1993). But for juveniles, at least, there seems little doubt that currently in the United States there are significant and real race differences in street crime net of class *and* police discrimination.

◆ **ADULTS** ◆   Though they allow us to help sort out net race effects from net class effects on street crime, observations from the Philadelphia birth cohort are limited to juveniles. What about adults? In a follow-up study of a subset of the first Philadelphia cohort, Thornberry and Farnworth (1982) report still greater SES differences (controlling for the effects of race) once the 1945 cohort reaches adulthood. In addition, they note that this class–street-crime link is greater for blacks than for whites. In related terms, half of the ninety studies reviewed in Braithwaite's (1981) omnibus review of the class–crime link allow arrest-based comparisons for adults; in these studies consistent, inverse relationships are found between SES and street crime though it is not clear whether these relationships are generally net of race.

Unfortunately, at present, no data allow a direct assessment of the race–street-crime relation for adults after the effects of social class have been accounted for. But there are many good reasons to expect it is at least as strong, if not stronger, than the comparable relation for juveniles. First, for juveniles, race and class clearly make a greater difference as we move to more serious offenses and greater risk of contact with law. If race and class make the largest difference where the stakes are highest, should we not expect race and class to make a still greater difference as we move from the protected status of juveniles to the unprotected status of adults?

Second, studies that look at the relationship of any demographic factor to crime, particularly street crime, face a higher than usual risk of what sociolgists call "selection bias" (see Berk and Ray, 1982; Zatz and Hagan, 1985). This bias involves the theoretical impact of lost, unseen, or drop-out portions of the sample under scrutiny. The disappearance of serious offenders from any sample would result in the severe underestimation of the effects of race or class. And this problem literally would multiply in looking at groups that faced repeated arrest and incarceration. Thus, if selection bias presents a serious problem for estimates of street crime by juveniles, it presents an extraordinary problem for estimates of race differences in street crimes by adults. For example, current estimates indicate that whereas 14 percent of white males in large cities will be arrested at least once for an Index offense, the comparable figure is 51 percent for black males (Blumstein and Graddy, 1982), and that whereas 3 percent of adult white males will have served time in prison or jail, the comparable figure is about 20 percent for adult black males (Greenfeld, 1981; Bureau of Justice Statistics, 1985). Finally, the severity of this attrition problem among adults is dramatically underscored by the recent finding (Mauer, 1990) that whereas about one in sixteen of all twenty- to twenty-nine-year-old white males in the United States was currently under the "watch" of the criminal justice system (on probation, in prison, or on parole) the comparable figure for all twenty- to twenty-nine-year-old black males was about one in four.

CONSTITUTIONAL DIFFERENCES

Our review has indicated that one of the strongest theoretical correlates of race, class or SES, cannot alone account for the race–street-crime link. Some of the race–crime link is explained, but a substantial amount remains unexplained. Is it possible that a major portion of the remaining net race difference can be accounted for by constitutional differences between blacks and whites?

What is meant by the term *constitutional differences*? Clearly, we might mean inherited differences that existed prior to socialization and to the acquisition of culture. But this does not go far enough. Differences in skin color are inherited and exist prior to socialization and acculturation, but no one believes that skin color represents a constitutional difference. By "constitutional," we must mean something deeper than surface difference, something predisposing an individual to think or behave in one way as opposed to another, a racially correlated set of inherited differences in cognitive or behavioral style or content.

On this basis, one common domain of difference might involve temperament, such as the predisposition to be aggressive or to be passive. Another domain might involve general intelligence, such as the predisposition to be good at solving problems in spatial relations or to be slow in seeing the potentially negative consequences of one's own behavior. Yet another domain might include somatotype—that is, a blend of body build and temperament (Sheldon, 1949)—such as the combined predisposition to be muscular, energetic, and aggressive or to be pear-shaped, lethargic, and passive.

In contemporary America, some of these predispositions appear to be correlated with race. It is well known, for example, that race and IQ are correlated (Shuey, 1966; Osborne, 1980; Gordon, 1980; Bailey, 1989) (see Chapter 12 for a discussion of IQ tests and criminal behavior). It also appears that, at least among males, race and body build are correlated (Damon et al., 1962, 1966; Malina, 1973). Can such findings make sense of the race–street-crime link? They have a tough time trying to do so. Let us look at some of the specifics.

◆ **IQ** ◆　Because known empirical relationships exist between race and street crime and class and street crime, and between race and IQ and class and IQ, we might expect to find a relationship between IQ and street crime. And indeed, we can. One question is whether this relationship holds true net of race and class. A theoretically more important question is whether the race–street-crime relationship holds true net of IQ *and* class. The answer to both questions is yes, at least as far as the research, heavily skewed by juvenile samples, allows us to see.

The first Philadelphia birth cohort again proves useful. Data from this study make it clear that race, class, and delinquency are correlated with IQ, but they also reveal that IQ has very little impact on delinquency. Other research findings on the IQ–delinquency relationship show similar or somewhat stronger patterns (see Reiss and Rhodes, 1961). In England, West (1982) finds IQ differences between delinquent and nondelinquent boys of close to 6 points on average. And after reviewing a number of studies, Hirschi and Hindelang

(1977) find a general difference of close to 9 points, net of class and race. To some extent, the magnitude of mean IQ differences between delinquent and nondelinquent groups varies according to how delinquency is measured. As might be expected, the difference is greater when arrests, rather than self-reports, are the guide. We see, then, no reason to dispute the empirical IQ–delinquency link per se—the link appears clear. The questions are: (1) Does the link statistically account for the race–street-crime relationship? and (2) If so, how does it explain the relationship?

In answer to the first question, we note that in the first Philadelphia cohort data, net of class and race, mean IQ scores between delinquent and nondelinquent boys differ by about 3–5 points. In these same data, and by about the same quantity, IQ also varies separately by class, net of race and delinquency status. More important, net of class and delinquency status, race differences in IQ of about 8–11 points are seen. The relationship between race and IQ is, in fact, so consistent that in one very revealing comparison, it inverts and trivializes the IQ–delinquency relationship: Nondelinquent, upper-SES blacks, with a 0 percent prevalence rate, show a lower mean IQ score (100.3) than the most delinquent, lower-SES, whites (101.9)! Obviously, if among juveniles there is a relationship between IQ and crime, IQ does a far better job of accounting for differences within race as opposed to those across race, and even then, differences within race accounted for are small.

These studies of the IQ–delinquency relationship typically compare males only, but what happens if gender is brought into the picture? Though we know that race is a powerful correlate of crime, we know that gender is an even more powerful correlate (Harris, 1977; Hindelang, 1979). Thus, if it is to provide a forceful general explanation of street crime, IQ must be able to deal with the gender variable. But can it?

Wilson and Herrnstein (1985: 470) point out that "black IQ scores are, on the average, about twelve to fifteen points lower than those of whites." Because gender differences in IQ are not significant, black female IQ must be about 12–15 points lower at the mean than white male IQ. In the first Philadelphia cohort, which only included males, differences of 3–4 points in mean IQ are associated with General Prevalence gaps of from 0 to 26 percent (upper-SES whites) to 0 to 53 percent (lower-SES blacks). Imagine, then, what an impact 12–15 points would make in the comparison between black females and white males. If, that is, IQ represented a powerful general explanation of criminal involvement, we would expect black female prevalence to run four to five times the comparable white male rate. Obviously, it does not. We are left to conclude that, although IQ might help explain delinquency rates among white males and among black males, there are so many implicit paradoxes involved that it cannot explain the white–black difference in juvenile, let alone adult, street crime.

◆ **OTHER CONSTITUTIONAL FACTORS** ◆ Other constitutional correlates of race besides IQ have been identified. At least among young males, somato-type is one. About forty years ago, Sheldon (1949) found that mesomorphy—

that is, heavy-boned muscularity often paired with high energy and aggressiveness—was empirically linked to delinquency among young white males. Since then, according to a number of researchers (Damon et al., 1962, 1966; Malina, 1973; Malina and Rarick, 1973), young black males have shown higher rates of mesomorphy than comparable whites.

Like the findings on IQ, the findings on somatotype indicate a significant difference by race. Unlike the findings on IQ, however, the findings on somatotype do not show consistent variation *within* race: Although among juvenile white males mesomorphy has a credibly documented relationship to delinquency, among juvenile black males there appears to be no relationship between mesomorphy and delinquency (McCandless et al., 1972). Moreover, like the studies that produce the IQ findings, studies that produce the inconsistent somatotype findings are almost entirely restricted to the juvenile male population.

Generally, constitutional explanations of the race–street-crime relationship are, at best, not very useful, and in the wrong hands, such explanations can become ludicrous. For example, the black homicide rate currently is over eight times the white homicide rate (see Figure 5.2). In the nineteenth century, however, the ratio was closer to 3 to 1 (Lane, 1979). One way of playing the constitutional difference game would be to conclude that black–white differences in constitutional factors have therefore changed significantly in the last hundred or so years. Alternatively, the crime *rates* of American whites currently far exceed those of African blacks (see Bohannan, 1960; Nettler, 1984). Another way of playing the constitutional difference game would be to conclude that the addition of white "genes" to black "genes" over the centuries in America has caused the "naturally" low baseline of black crime to rise. Obviously, such conclusions are foolish.

FAMILY STRUCTURE

> The amount of drunkenness, immorality, and criminality among the parents of many boys, as brought out by local and individual studies, makes the home in many cases as unfavorable . . . as does the loss of a parent or both parents. (Shideler, 1918: 725)

In looking at the impact of family structure on crime, mainstream criminology has focused almost exclusively on the impact of broken families, particularly father-absent families, on the delinquencies of juveniles. In doing so, the tendency has been to assume mistakenly (1) that juveniles in the home are always better off with any father at all, rather than with none at all, and (2) that families and family structure play a role in the production of juvenile, but not adult, crime. These assumptions have caused considerable confusion in the search to establish the impact of family structure on crime. This conclusion becomes painfully clear in the context of the race–street-crime relationship.

Shinn's (1978) omnibus review of the effects of father absence on IQ and school achievement found that in 57 percent of the studies of black homes, father absence was associated either with no negative consequences or with positive consequences (such as better school performance). To some extent, these unexpected findings may reflect the fact that "paternal absence . . . is sometimes the norm rather than the exception in low-income, minority communities" (Farnworth, 1984).

The comparatively high rate of father-absent households among lower-income blacks, particularly among the black underclass, is well documented. Estimates of female-headed households in this "underclass" range from 55 to 70 percent (Wilson and Herrnstein, 1985; Urban Institute, 1988). Rather than ask about the effects of the father's absence in the ghetto, perhaps it might make more sense to ask about the effects of the father's *presence*.

In the United States today, black males fortunate enough to be working full time will, at the median, earn about 74¢ for every $1 earned by comparable white males (Bureau of Labor Statistics, 1989), a rather unbalanced picture in its own right. But such grim comparisons are based on weekly earnings by full-time wage earners and are even more unbalanced for underclass black males. One major reason for this is that almost 60 percent of the employable males among the ghetto poor at some point during the year will be unemployed (Urban Institute, 1988). In addition, out of every 10,000 such males, at least 1,700, and probably over 2,000, have served or will serve time in jail or prison, while at least another 130 or so are currently serving time (Chilton and Galvin, 1985; Mauer, 1990), and more than 500 will die from homicide (LaFree et al., 1992).

With these images in tow, it really should not come as much of a surprise that findings on the impact of father absence on ghetto delinquency are mixed at best. Farnworth's excellent (1984) review of a variety of father-absent studies notes some major anomalies. Among these are Robins and Hill's (1966) finding that the father's presence is more likely than his absence to promote early delinquency among black males; Rosen's (1969) finding that the father's presence increased the violent delinquency of black males; and Austin's (1978) finding that, although the father's presence decreased the delinquency of white juveniles, especially white females, his presence did not lower the delinquency of black juveniles, and actually increased it for black females. In a related study, Montare and Boone (1980) find that, although the father's presence decreased aggressive play in young white males, for young black males it promoted aggressive play. To these may be added Farnworth's own 1984 study in which she, like Rosen, linked the father's presence in lower-income black families to the increased likelihood of violent delinquency for males, and this time, for females as well.

Recent studies find related patterns of black–white differences in the impact of family structure on street crime. Using a nationwide sample of metropolitan areas, Smith (1992) finds that although there is a significant impact of the rate of "family disruption" on homicide among whites, there is no such observable impact among blacks. More inclusive and dramatic in its findings, the work of LaFree et al. (1992) — which relies on nationwide UCR data from 1957–1988 — suggests that although increases in the rate of female-headed households during this period were associated with increases in robbery and burglary arrest rates among whites, the same increases were associated with significant decreases in robbery and burglary arrest rates for blacks.

There seems reason, then, to doubt the simple assertion that "father knows best," at least as far as the modeling of delinquency goes (but see Kellam et al., 1982; Matsueda and Heimer, 1987). One way of looking at this type of finding is through the lens of social psychology. From this perspective, we recognize the key is not the quantity of parents but the quality of parenting (this is very convincingly argued by Wilson and Herrnstein, 1985). Another way of looking at this finding is through the lens of the race–street-crime relationship. From this perspective, one of the sorry correlates of race in America, not surprisingly, is the comparatively high rate of lower-class black fathers locked into a viciously self-perpetuating cycle of unemployment and street crime (see Thornberry and Christenson, 1984), particularly among the extremely poor. As amply documented by Sampson (1987), these phenomena correlate with rates of female-headed homes.

Though the theme is virtually undeveloped in mainstream criminology, there is more than ample reason to expect that family structure affects adult as well as juvenile criminality, especially in the margins of extreme poverty. The presence of a chronically unemployed or underemployed father at home produces major stresses. We know from the huge Federal Income Tax Maintenance studies of the 1970s that direct cash subsidies to poor families have a significant impact on the breakup of these families: Subsidized white families broke up 36 percent more frequently than did control groups, and subsidized black families 42 percent more frequently (SRI International, 1983). Apparently, in many cases, mothers with subsidies simply were "better off" without their husbands than with them. Many husbands in such situations are thoroughly aware of this and of their economic marginality in the legitimate labor market. In short, we can bet that they know a family structure conducive to adult crime when they see one.

To some extent, the current American welfare system produces family structures conducive to crime, and is itself the culprit. So too, the current American criminal justice system, in league with that same welfare system, is also culpable. As some data suggest (see Liker, 1982), a prisoner's wife and children may well lead a materially better life while he is in prison than when he returns home, an ex-con, with no job, and few prospects—an extra tally in the denominator of a now reduced welfare check.

In summary, as long as its impact is not reduced to delinquency, and the meaning of an "intact" home is not trivialized to mean the co-appearance of *any* father and *any* mother, family structure is undoubtedly a powerful antecedent to street crime and may provide the best current explanation of the race–street-crime relationship. It is entirely plausible that the intact underclass black family is as prone as, if not more prone than, the broken middle-class home to produce delinquency. It is also possible that the intact underclass black family places even more pressure to commit street crime on its adult members, especially male, than on its juvenile members, also male.

SUBCULTURE

Americans of all races share a broad variety of cultural values and beliefs. Some of these are shared with respect to the collectivity, including faith in the value of democracy and the belief that it can be realistically attained. Some of these are shared with respect to the individual, including faith in the value of personal material success and the belief that it can be realistically attained. Although blacks and whites may share values and beliefs, however, in the margins of poverty group differences in values and preferences may be important enough to produce group differences in behavior, including street crime. Two such potentially important areas of difference are (1) group members' stress on the value of delayed gratification and (2) their approval of the use of violence.

◆ **DELAYED GRATIFICATION** ◆   Willingness to delay gratification refers to a person's general ability to behave in ways that "see" beyond the short-run pleasures and pains of everyday life, and to consider, equally, that some of today's pleasures may well lead to a great deal of tomorrow's grief. Many substance-related behaviors, from heroin use to alcohol consumption to cigarette smoking, provide good examples of the frequently seen preference for short-run "gains" over long-term costs (see Ainslie and Herrnstein's related discussion, 1981; see also Wilson and Herrnstein, 1985). Some groups have a greater ability to delay gratification than others.

As might be expected, the value of delayed gratification does seem to vary by social class (see Wells and Smith, 1970): Lower-income groups do not appear to see as much value in delaying gratification as do middle-income groups. This type of finding has played a key role in supporting the idea that there is a "culture of poverty" that keeps the poor poor (see Lewis, 1968). No research indicates that the value of delayed gratification varies by race independently of class, but let us suppose that this difference exists. The critical question is: Can the delayed gratification hypothesis really explain, as it is supposed to do, the race–street-crime relationship?

The delayed gratification hypothesis suggests that the ghetto poor genuinely value or prefer short-term over long-term pleasures, that this preference is not tied to realistic assessments of getting on in life, and that the preference lasts for life. It seems to produce impulsiveness and to get the poor into trouble generally. In these terms, the preference for short-term over long-term pleasures seems highly irrational, perhaps even somewhat immature.

One clear way of restating the delayed gratification hypothesis is in terms of what economists call a "discount rate." From this perspective, the poor have a high discount rate, meaning they generally prefer a smaller amount of money in hand today over the promise of a larger amount of money tomorrow. If, in this fashion, you preferred $95 today over the promise of $100 a year from today, you would have the very low discount rate of 5 percent ($100 minus $95, divided by $100); if, on the other hand, you preferred $50 in hand today over the promise of $100 a year from today, you would have the very high discount of 50 percent ($100 minus $50, divided by $100).

Note that once the delayed gratification hypothesis is recast into a hypothesis of discount rates, all those who have ever been poor for even a week, such as college students, recognize that the preference for immediate gains is entirely rational and thoroughly attuned to getting on in life—that is, is quite reasonably aligned with one's present resources, capital, savings, and so on, as well as with one's immediate demands. Note also that you were offered $50 today versus the *promise* of $100 next year. As any ghetto youth knows, promises in the ghetto are often difficult to keep; as any ghetto adult knows, life insurance premiums in the ghetto are very high. This element of uncertainty is theoretically very important in assessing the usefulness of the delayed gratification hypothesis. To the extent that the preference for short-term over long-term gains involves an adult's realistic assessment of the chances that he or she will actually be around to receive $100 next year, the delayed gratification hypothesis states little more than that the poor are needy. If so, this means that the ghetto poor do not really have short-time horizons and are not permanently "impulsive." It also strongly suggests that if they were to experience a major situational improvement, the ghetto poor's discount rate would drop, and the appearance of the preference for short-term over long-term gains would disappear.

◆ **APPROVAL OF VIOLENCE** ◆   What of the second value-based explanation involving group differences in the approval of violence? As initially formulated by Wolfgang and Ferracuti (1967), the so-called subculture of violence hypothesis tried to explain group differences in homicide rates. This theory relied on the idea that people in groups with high rates of violence tend to grow up and live in subcultures that seem to define violence as an *acceptable* form of behavior. The usefulness of this value hypothesis is necessarily restricted to crimes that are exclusively violent or to those with a violent component.

Much research has been done on the subculture of violence hypothesis (see Erlanger, 1975; O'Connor and Lizzotte, 1978; Blau and Blau, 1982; Sampson, 1987; Parker, 1989). One recent variation recasts the subculture of violence as a "subculture of angry aggression" (Bernard, 1990). More in line with the explosion of crack-cocaine in the inner cities in the past decade—a potent and violent "alternative economy" that seemed to evolve in tandem with the devastating loss of less-skilled manufacturing jobs in American cities in the past few decades—along with the growth of an urban "underclass" (see Wilson, 1987), Rose and McClain's (1990) recent formulation points to the role of a "subculture of materialistic aggression" in the joint production of "big and easy money" *and* increased homicide in urban areas.

But as with the research on the role of father absence, little empirical support has yet been provided for the subculture of violence hypothesis (see Chapter 7). There are, however, good reasons to think that the hypothesis fails prior to the gathering of any data. Critical differences exist between people's motivation to commit crime and their motivation *not* to commit crime. Hirschi

(1969), among others, has stressed that the latter issue—what stops people from committing crime?—is more important than the former.

In terms of psychological theory, if Hirschi is right (and there is good reason to suspect he is), this means that in looking for differences between individuals who do and who do not commit crime, we should not be looking for the presence or absence of "green lights" to commit crime; instead, we should be looking for the presence or absence of "red lights" to stop people from committing crime. In terms of sociological theory—if, again, Hirschi is right—this means that in looking for differences between groups of people who commit crime at varying rates, we should not be looking for the presence or absence of values that positively prescribe the commission of crime; rather, we should be looking for the presence or absence of values that *proscribe* it.

The injunction to search for proscriptive norms in the case of economically motivated crime is apt. Crime is often the shortest distance between two points; in modern America, the question frequently concerns what stops people from taking the shorter route to economic gain. If this red-light question is fitting for economically motivated crimes, it is even more fitting for crimes of violence, particularly those that involve no obvious economic gain. Researchers who look for subcultures that are committed to violence (see Erlanger, 1974) are doomed to find little of interest; research in which proscription against violence is measured is far more likely to succeed. In their classic work on delinquency, Short and Strodtbeck (1965), for example, found that lower-class black delinquents and middle-class white nondelinquents in Chicago differed far more on proscriptions concerning what they should not do than on prescriptions concerning what they should.

Based on Hirschi's admonition, we conclude that if we were to look for race differences in the presence or absence of red lights that rule out the use of violence (that is, proscriptive norms), we might find a viable contender in the explanation of the race–violent-street-crime relationship. As we shall see shortly, there are still broader gains to be made in understanding the race–street-crime relationship if we search for red lights instead of green ones.

INEQUALITY AND CASTE

> All [the "brothers"] had dreams—variants, usually, on the American Dream of home, family and material well-being. Some became outlaws. Some zigzagged between the margins of the economy and the street. A few succeeded in the mainstream. The majority would not; the world they were born to, like the projects they lived in, was too heavy with the expectation of their defeat. From ("Brothers," *Newsweek*, 1987)

Earlier, we noted that race differences in the commission of street crime remain after social class is accounted for. This probably is less true for middle-class communities than for lower-class communities. But since street crime is disproportionately a lower-class phenomenon, stronger race differences occur precisely where more street crime occurs. We have thus far examined four competing hypotheses to explain race difference in street crime — class, constitutional factors, family structure, and subculture — and we have found all four wanting. While we do not really expect any one hypothesis to carry the full burden of explanation, we would still like to identify one that is particularly satisfying. Perhaps something important has been left out, or perhaps we have to look for new evidence in unusual places. Are there key correlates of race that we have missed, key correlates other than social class that make one race more advantaged overall than the other? The answer is yes. These key correlates include two related pairs of "old" concepts: (1) inequality and relative deprivation and (2) historical experience and caste.

INEQUALITY AND RELATIVE DEPRIVATION

> When I was a young boy [I listened to] my Mississippi-born grandfather and uncles talking about the limits on black ambition, black hope. "They ain't never gonna let a black man be this or that," they'd say. "If he gets too big, they'll kill him" . . . the men of my family were right: race is an inescapable burden for every black man. (From "Brothers," *Newsweek*, 1987)

In themselves, absolute levels of poverty, or wealth, are not particularly useful predictors of crime. The primary yardstick citizens of different times and places use to measure their success, and their frustration, is not absolute but is, instead, *relative* to local levels of success, and frustration. Though few among the billion or so adults in China in 1993 would kill, or dream of killing, because they could not afford a car, we are to the point in America where such deprivation — such relative inequality — could well be viewed as painful and unfair, an understandable, though perhaps not yet excusable, basis for crime.

In trying to understand the motivation to commit crime across time and place, it is much more useful to focus on the subjective pains of relative deprivation — including the bitter feelings of injustice and inequality — than the objective pains of absolute poverty. This means that it would be important for any powerful theory of crime to identify the major social correlates of perceived deprivation. Unfortunately, in America today, race would still need to be identified as such a correlate, quite possibly the most important. Despite a century of legal effort, racial inequality remains a prominent feature of American life, producing the most socially visible form of injustice and deprivation.

There can be no doubt that the experience of this deprivation, *net* of class, is likely to provide a strong motive for crime. However, although there can also be no doubt that the primary reference groups — the yardsticks of success and failure — of whites in America largely remain *other* groups of whites, there are doubts about the most likely primary reference group for blacks, or, for that matter, any large minority group (see Balkwell, 1990). Depending on the context of comparison, and the historical era, and the specific subset of the minority group in question, this reference group might vary dramatically.

Theories based on the frustrations of inequality are not new. In Henry and Short's landmark (1954) work, *Suicide and Homicide*, trends in economic inequality are used to help explain white and black differences in violence toward the self versus violence toward others. Since Blau and Blau's important piece on racial inequality and violence (1982), a major research effort has been underway to locate the causes of street crime, particularly violent street crime, in the matrix of social inequality (see Simpson, 1991, for a discussion of gender, caste, and violent crime). Thus, the key questions have been raised: What specific kinds of social inequalities produce crime? and What specific kinds of crimes do these inequalities produce?

Blau and Blau's key (1982) finding was that economic inequality in general, and racial inequality in particular, were clearly tied to overall criminal violence. More recent findings tend to distinguish violence both by race of offender and by type of inequality. In an intriguing study of 1980 data, Harer and Steffensmeier (1992) find that although intrarace (white versus white) inequality is a strong predictor of violent crime among whites — supporting the general idea that the socially dominant group, whites, will use their own race as a reference group — intrarace (black versus black) inequality is not associated with violent crime by blacks. This might well lead to the conclusion that the main yardstick of relative deprivation for a disadvantaged minority, such as blacks, would remain inequality vis-à-vis the majority group, whites (that is, interrace inequality). But paradoxically, in the same study, interrace inequality predicted neither white nor — more important — black violent crime! Similar research on black arrests in 1980 (Corzine and Huff-Corzine, 1992) suggests that this puzzling finding might have been different for homicide, at least if Harrer and Steffensmeier had made a distinction between felony homicide (killings connected to another offense, often economic, such as armed robbery) and nonfelony homicide (killings not connected to another offense). In the Corzine and Huff-Corzine study, it was found that though interrace inequality is not associated with felony homicide, higher levels of interrace inequality are significantly associated with higher rates of nonfelony homicide.

In trying to account for related, surprising findings on homicide, Smith (1992) observes that blacks and whites "may be subject to different social forces." In truth, this may be as profound a statement on the race–street-crime relationship as has appeared in the literature in the past fifty years: Similar puzzles characterize the history of research on the relationship (see also Hill and Crawford, 1990). The recent, important, and controversial research by LaFree et al. (1992) on the determinants of black and white crime rates in America from 1957 to 1988 may be the best such example. Among other surprising findings, LaFree and his associates report that measures of economic well-being and opportunity have expected effects on white crime rates but very unexpected effects on black crime rates. For example, whereas fluctuations upward in measures of white economic well-being and opportunity over the three decades are, as expected, associated with drops in robbery and burglary rates among whites, upward fluctuations in separate measures of black well-being and opportunity are associated with *increases* in robbery and burglary rates among blacks!

LaFree et al. are sensitive to the possibility that these findings may reflect the "swamping" effects of a growing arrest rate of urban underclass males and do not reflect increases in crime among lower- ("working poor") and middle-class blacks generally. This view likely is correct; the trend may be due to a growing sense of "double-deprivation" among the urban underclass: That is, during the past twenty years, and accelerating during the 1980s, the expanding black middle class has become an increasingly problematic reference group for the black underclass. As the gap between these two groups has grown (see Wilson, 1987), so too has the burden of the relative deprivation experienced by the black underclass, in effect doubling from what was previously simply an interrace inequality to both an interrace *and* intrarace inequality. This double-barreled combination would seem to be deadly and, with the growth of an alternative crack-cocaine economy in the inner cities, an increasingly plausible alternative explanation of black–white differences in street crime among the poor.

HISTORICAL EXPERIENCE AND CASTE

Wilson and Herrnstein (1985: 474) set the stage for introducing the second alternative pair of "old" concepts — historical experience and caste — by pointing to a very basic paradox: "The [historical] experience of the Chinese and the Japanese [in America] suggests that social isolation, substandard living conditions, and general poverty are not invariably associated with high rates of crime among racially distinct groups."

African- and Asian-Americans have, in common, faced difficult social conditions in America's past, yet, at present, show widely disparate levels of involvement in street crime. Apparently, by itself, caste cannot explain the black-white difference in street crime. But there is still a missing element in the equation, one involving core differences in the historical experiences of these different groups — most critically the deplorable experience of slavery. Although references to slavery are rarely drawn out in contemporary discussions of race, the practice of slavery was abolished in America only some 120 years ago, well within historical earshot of the present generation. There is good reason to expect that at a bare minimum, the emotional tone of slavery, and reconstruction, is still communicated in contemporary, oral family histories among American blacks.

In related terms, a number of very important differences separated early Oriental from early black arrivals to America. One was that the earliest Chinese arrivals were relatively well-to-do. More critical, and often overlooked, the Chinese (and Japanese) came to seek their fortune *voluntarily*. Many were abused, but were still free to negotiate their own labor rate. In contrast, most of the first black Americans, not so long ago, came to America against their will, as slaves; they were told what to do, and there was no labor rate to negotiate.

What is common to Asian- and African-Americans in U.S. history is caste and the accompanying negative experiences, including visible discrimination, imputations of differences that arrive at birth and continue to death, residential segregation, and the hostility of many whites. What is *uncommon* to Asian- and African-Americans in U.S. history is the recent experience of slavery and the meaning of caste to people who realize, according to *Newsweek* (1987), that "the world they were born to [is] heavy with the expectation of their defeat."

These analyses are all too well known to most blacks, particularly those in the underclass. For them, the history of class in America is largely the history of race, the history of social mobility little more than the history of a huge, white, back-slapping, fraternity. For them, in short, there is by virtue of caste a recent link to a real historical process in which they, the black underclass, have been cast as outsiders, as people who have been promised full membership in the fraternity but who have been functionally *disqualified* from it from the start.

If one appears to have been disqualified from full-membership because one is black, and if, in addition, one is poor, the analytic question becomes: Are there any further disqualifications to be suffered if one is caught committing a crime? Exactly what else is there to lose? The answer is, very little. Where are the red lights? The answer is, there are very few:

> In all his years on the street, prison had been less a deterrent than a constantly pending due bill. . . . Doing time was not a troubling event in his world, or even terribly newsworthy. A brother would disappear from the street, and people would say, "Aw, the ole boy's in jail," as matter-of-factly as if he were away visiting a maiden aunt in Mississippi. . . . Doing time didn't scare him; the joint was like the projects, except they fed you free. (From "Brothers," *Newsweek*, 1987)

For this underclass male's *white* counterpart, also poor, also uneducated, in a less obvious way also residentially segregated, there is a major difference: He can regale himself with tales of Horatio Alger and Abraham Lincoln—white folks, members of the fraternity. With a little effort, the right way of dressing, and so on, he could even pass for a full-fledged member of the fraternity. For him, the same analytic question can be asked: Is there any further tax to be paid if he is caught committing a crime? The answer is yes—membership in the fraternity is lost. His black counterpart has already paid his taxes by virtue of being black, not by virtue of being poor.

A surprisingly large number of studies over two decades lend support to these arguments. Unexpectedly, these studies look mostly at the potential aftermath of committing crime: What is the impact of getting caught on one's sense of identity and self-worth? They strongly suggest that being a member of the caste-disadvantaged underclass provides, as it were, an insulator against the ego losses of being caught (Harris, 1976). Alternatively, they strongly imply that being caste-advantaged or white, even if you are poor, acts as a red light in deterring street crime. For example, at the start of Ageton and Elliott's (1974) longitudinal study of high school youth, blacks with *no* police contact show more strongly delinquent self-conceptions than do comparable whites (see also Short and Strodtbeck, 1965; Schwartz and Stryker, 1970; Jensen, 1972a). But with increased police contact over the years, and net of class, whites' sense of themselves as delinquent increased substantially more than blacks'; such contact appeared to lower whites' self-esteem but not that of blacks. Similarly, among an almost exclusively lower-class sample of young adult offenders in a New Jersey correctional facility (Harris, 1976), time spent in prison appeared to affect whites far more than blacks, with white inmates maintaining significantly stronger delinquent self-conceptions *and* significantly lower self-esteem than black inmates (replicated in the Rand Inmate Survey of adult prisoners in California; see Peterson et al., 1981; Harris, 1988). In short, we must conclude that the advantages of race are not equivalent to those of class, and that these advantages exist over and above class, in the form of historical caste—quite possibly the most powerful explanation of the *overall* race–street-crime relationship.

RACE, WHITE COLLAR CRIME, AND SUITE CRIME

We have pursued in detail the question of the race–street-crime relationship, both empirically and theoretically. But what would happen if the UCR Index were to include traditional white collar arrests? Would the race–crime relationship in fact change directions, such that whites were now overrepresented? A superficial look at the data, surprisingly, suggests that the relationship does not change. Blacks accounted for about 34 percent of all UCR "white collar crime" arrests in 1990, including 34 percent of forgery arrests, 33 percent of fraud arrests, and 33 percent of embezzlement arrests. The rate-adjusted ratios of blacks to whites arrested for these crimes thus run at about the same level as they did for Index crimes against property (see Figure 5.1). Paradoxically, even if the UCR Crime Index included traditional white collar crimes, the same 3 to 1 black-to-white weighting would be seen as that observed for 1990 Index crimes against property! This finding appears to put a great deal of pressure on theories that stress situational disadvantages in trying to explain the race–crime relationship. The finding also appears to support Hirschi and Gottfredson's theoretical attempts (1987, 1989) to search for the causes of white collar crime in the demographic correlates of such UCR white collar crimes as fraud and embezzlement.

As it turns out, such theoretical efforts are probably wasted (see Steffensmeier, 1989). It is highly unlikely that these UCR data actually represent arrests for what is commonly understood as white collar crime, that is, the phenomena to be explained. Although the individuals arrested for these crimes may have worn white shirts at the time of the crime or the arrest, the criminal events involved are generally *not* occupationally related, that is, are neither committed by individuals in the course of work in a legitimate occupation nor committed by individuals working as legitimate employees in legitimate firms.

We need to distinguish far more carefully race differences in the offenses of isolated entrepreneurs who work "on the fly" or of relatively low-level bureaucrats who work in cubicles from race differences in the offenses of middle- and upper-level managers and executives who work in offices and suites. There are at present very few detailed data on the demographics of white collar offenders, but a few that exist (Wheeler et al., 1988; Daly, 1989)

FIGURE 5.5
BLACK–WHITE
INVOLVEMENT IN CRIME
BY CRIME TYPE AND SES

allow us to distinguish between lower- and middle-level offenders. These findings show that blacks are overrepresented among lower-level offenders by a factor of about 2.5 to 1, that middle-level offenders are more than twice as likely to be college educated as lower-level offenders, and that whites are overrepresented among middle-level offenders by a factor of about 2.7 to 1 (Harris, 1989).

Thus, as we try to focus on higher levels of white collar crime, we begin to see traces emerging of the photographic negative of the race–street-crime relationship: an image in which whites are overrepresented by a factor approximating blacks' overrepresentation in street crime! If this "inverted" race–crime relationship holds for middle-level white collar crime, whites are undoubtedly overrepresented in corporate, silk collar, or suite crime, to an extent equal to, if not greater than, blacks' overrepresentation in street crime. This observation underscores our theoretical need to examine the relationship of race to crime *in general*, not just to street crime, in the United States.

In looking at street crime, one question we asked was whether or not race could be reduced to social class. It could not be, and we concluded that the disadvantages of race existed over and above those of class. The same question may be raised vis-à-vis suite crime: Can the association between race and suite crime be reduced to that between class and suite crime? Our answer here is a somewhat tentative, no; the advantages of race exist *over and above* those of class. The opportunity to commit suite crime is still greater for a class-advantaged white than a class-advantaged black. Paradoxically, we must conclude that, although caste disadvantage net of class is a cause of street crime, caste advantage net of class is a cause of suite crime.

This conclusion reflects an attempt to think about the relationship between race and crime in modern America in a unified way and to challenge the ways in which we have tended to see crime in the past—as essentially a phenomenon occurring on the streets. Perhaps a view in which white criminal figures are in the foreground and black criminal figures in the background is a tough picture for the public to accept, a "bad gestalt." But this need not be the case for criminology.

The schematic diagram in Figure 5.5 suggests that in fact there is only *one* basic race–crime relationship in America, and it is parabolic, not linear. Figure 5.5 also illustrates the point that race, or caste, is first and foremost aligned with social class in shaping the adult opportunity to commit one type of crime, street crime, versus the opportunity to commit another type of crime, suite crime. The parabolic relationship graphically suggests that race or caste differences net of class have the greatest impact at the extreme edges of the class spectrum. Ironically, upper-class whites and underclass blacks may well have something rare but theoretically very important in common: a pronounced, and perhaps highly rational, lack of fear when it comes to committing crime. On the one hand, elite whites are likely to believe that their chances of being caught or severely punished for crime are very low. On the other hand, if as an underclass black, you feel that "the joint is like the projects, except they feed you free," then you are likely to believe that, in getting caught for crime, you do not have very much left to lose.

CONCLUSION

The key criminological issues to resolve about race must reduce to other, more manageable issues: general questions involving the pressures to commit crime, the constraints against committing crime, the opportunities to commit crime, and the relative attractiveness of one type of crime versus another type of crime. Mostly, these are the classical questions in criminology. The issue of race's relationship to crime ought not to signal the question, Which racial group is more likely to commit crime? Rather, it ought to signal the question, Which type of crime is this disadvantaged group, or this advantaged group, more likely to commit? America's longstanding history of the caste segregation of blacks and whites has created a parallel caste segregation in the commission of street and suite crime.

DISCUSSION QUESTIONS

1. Some criminologists have argued that there is no systematic proof that socioeconomic status is linked to serious criminality. Are they correct? What is the quality of the evidence bearing on this question?

2. Official arrest statistics point to an overrepresentation of African-Americans in certain types of crime. What are those types? To what extent do other sources of information about criminality support the conclusion suggested by the official arrest statistics?

3. Turn the typical question around. What types of crime are white Americans more likely to be involved in? What does the answer suggest about the interrelationship among race, class, and criminal opportunity?

4. We hear much today about crime resulting from the breakdown of the American family. To what extent does this phenomenon influence racial differences in criminal involvement?

CHAPTER 6

◆

CRIME VICTIMS

Andrew A. Karmen
John Jay College of Criminal Justice, City University of New York

REDISCOVERING VICTIMS AND STUDYING THEIR PLIGHT

FOR CENTURIES, the real flesh-and-blood individuals harmed bodily, mentally, and economically by criminals were largely ignored by the public as uninteresting people, while their pressing needs were routinely overlooked within the legal system. But in recent decades, crime victims finally have been "discovered" by the police, prosecutors, judges, lawmakers, political activists, journalists, authors, businesses selling products and services, and social scientists studying the crime problem.

Starting in the 1960s, several social movements began to call attention to the plight of crime victims. The emerging women's movement challenged the traditional indifference shown toward female victims of male violence by initiating self-help projects like rape crisis centers and shelters for battered women. The civil rights and civil liberties movements demanded equal protection under the law for all in order to quell police brutality against members of minority groups, as well as terrorist violence (lynchings, bombings, assassinations) unleashed by segregationist hate groups. The law and order movement criticized landmark decisions handed down by the Supreme Court that changed the operations of the justice system in ways that seemed to favor "criminals" (suspects, defendants, prisoners) at the expense of the innocent people they injured. By the 1980s, a broad-based victims' rights movement coalesced to empower individuals trying to exert some influence over how officials handled "their" cases.

Today, the suffering of crime victims is receiving attention. Progress has been made, but serious problems persist. Although the news media regularly depict the experiences of street-crime victims, much of the coverage is highly sensationalized and crudely insensitive (see Chapter 1). A whole industry marketing security products (like guns, locks, and alarms) and services (such as insurance, guards, and self-defense courses) promises it can help prevent victimization or at least minimize its aftershocks, but the sales pitches often exploit fears and foster illusions. Highly trained professionals along with dedicated volunteers attend to the casualties of street crimes, but the depth and scope of the needs and misery they encounter usually overwhelm the limited resources set aside for victim assistance. Police chiefs, district attorneys, judges, corrections officials, and parole board members acknowledge the legitimacy of victims' demands for progress reports and input into decision-making, but these criminal justice officials are reluctant to alter their own priorities and standard operating procedures.

Victims also have been "discovered" by social scientists. The first scholars in the 1940s, 1950s, and 1960s to consider themselves victimologists were criminologists. But they were more interested in treating victims as causal agents of their misfortunes than in helping them return to the conditions they were in before the crimes occurred. This initial bias—that victims might unwittingly or even intentionally contribute to the crimes they suffered—was counteracted in the 1970s and 1980s when the fledgling discipline attracted academics and practitioners whose primary concern was aiding people in distress. Now, victimology has become a recognized area of specialization within criminology, with its own journals, conferences, courses, and textbooks. It is an interdisciplinary field, drawing heavily on sociology, psychology, social work, medicine, and law. Its knowledge base expands exponentially as special populations of victims with specific problems requiring innovative solutions are studied. For example, victims of sexual assaults, of domestic violence, of crashes caused by drunk drivers, and of bias crimes motivated by blind hatred now demand and attract attention. Victimologists are systematically examining how familiar groups face threats that were previously unanalyzed, such as children physically and sexually abused by their parents or kidnapped by strangers, tourists preyed on while on vacation, college students victimized on and off campus, police officers injured or killed in the line of duty.

Victimologists carry out research to gather data revealing rates, trends, and patterns of risk; investigate the way the criminal justice system handles victims; evaluate the effectiveness of programs intended to aid recovery; and analyze the social and political reaction to the growing threat and reality of victimization. A major issue that currently divides victimologists is whether the scope of the field should be confined to just those who are harmed by illegal acts (mostly "street crimes" of violence and against property) or whether it should be broadened to embrace the suffering brought about by accidents, diseases, natural disasters, and political oppression. (For an overview of the discipline, see Viano, 1976; Schafer, 1977; Parsonage, 1979; Galaway and Hudson, 1979; Schneider, 1982; Elias, 1986; and Karmen, 1990.)

This chapter highlights some of the key concerns in victimology: what categories of people are harmed by street criminals the most frequently and the least often—and why; whether some victims are partly to blame; how individuals are trying to avoid victimization; what methods are available for reimbursing losses; which new legal rights victims have secured; and what informal means victims are turning to in order to resolve their conflicts with offenders.

EXPLORING THE RISKS OF BECOMING A VICTIM

MEASURING VICTIMIZATION: SOURCES OF DATA

Victimologists need accurate statistics about crimes and victims in order to estimate losses, calculate rates, test theories that explain why some people fall into high-risk groups, and evaluate prevention strategies and recovery programs. Unfortunately, many of the figures generated by official record-keeping agencies are collected in ways that undermine their credibility and usefulness. The two most widely cited sources of data are the Federal Bureau of Investigation's (FBI) *Uniform Crime Reports* (UCR) and the Department of Justice's National Crime Victimization Survey (NCVS) (see Chapter 3).

From a victimologist's point of view, the FBI's annual report has two serious shortcomings. First, it does not provide any information about the characteristics of crime victims except for those who were murdered. Second, the UCR is strictly a compilation of crimes known to the police. Because crimes that were not reported to the authorities are excluded from the calculations, UCR rates unavoidably underestimate the actual (but unknown) rates of rape, robbery, aggravated assault, burglary, larceny, and motor vehicle theft.

The NCVS represents an improvement over the UCR. The questionnaire used during interviews with about 83,000 people collects data about the victims' backgrounds (age, sex, race or ethnicity, household size, family income, marital status, and area of residence), their relationships to offenders (strangers or nonstrangers), details about the crimes, and the extent to which they were harmed (financial losses and physical injuries). Survey interviewers gather information about incidents that were not reported to the police and the reasons victims did or did not report the crimes.

Although victimologists find the NCVS a more valuable and accurate source of data than the UCR, NCVS annual reports suffer from some problems too. As noted in Chapter 3, even though the NCVS probes the "dark figure" of unreported crime, underestimates of the actual rates still can result if respondents do not confide in the interviewers about incidents that they never revealed to the police as well. There is also the possibility of "memory decay," when some people forget to discuss (presumably minor) crimes committed against them during the preceding six months, since they were last telephoned or visited by the NCVS staff. Overreporting can arise from "forward telescoping," when a respondent believes an incident occurred within the six-month interval, but it actually took place further back in time and should not be counted. Some people might mistakenly assume that a possession actually lost through carelessness was stolen by a criminal. And finally, as in all surveys, the credibility of what people tell pollsters is always subject to doubt. Despite the wealth of detail gathered by the NCVS, its scope is limited to street crimes of violence and theft; the survey excludes kidnapping and commercial burglaries and robberies, as well as other harmful acts like swindles and instances of blackmail. (For more detailed methodological critiques, see Garofalo, 1981; Levine, 1976; O'Brien, 1985; Reiss, 1986; and Skogan, 1986.)

The key statistics derived from the annual surveys are the rates of rape, robbery, assault, and personal larceny for every 1,000 individuals in a year; and of burglary, larceny, and vehicle theft per 1,000 households per year. (Chapters 7 and 8 discuss victimization rates for acts of violence and theft.)

In 1991, NCVS findings indicated that about 6.4 million crimes of violence (rapes, robberies, and assaults), 12.5 million personal thefts, and 15.7 million thefts of household property (including burglaries and motor vehicle thefts) were committed across the country. The robbery rate was estimated to be 5.6 victims for every 1,000 persons twelve years old and older that year. The rape rate was computed to be about 1.4 per 1,000 females twelve years old and over. For every 1,000 households, over 53 were burglarized, and nearly 22 suffered a car theft. (When interpreting all these rates, note that unsuccessful attempted crimes are combined with completed acts.) The most common kind of victimization disclosed by survey respondents was "household larceny," which was defined to include all thefts and attempted thefts of property and cash from a residence by persons invited in (such as maids, repairpeople, or party guests, as opposed to burglars) or thefts of possessions from a home's immediate vicinity (such as lawn furniture) by trespassers. About 88 out of every 1,000 households experienced losses of this kind (Bastion, 1992a).

ESTIMATING THE PROPORTION OF HOUSEHOLDS TOUCHED BY CRIME

The NCVS also informs a composite statistic called "households touched by crime in a year." The rationale for treating an entire family as the unit of analysis is that all members suffer hardships and share a sense of violation and outrage whenever someone in the living arrangement is victimized. A household is touched by crime if anyone in it is raped, robbed, or assaulted, or if a possession is stolen by a thief, burglar, or someone invited into the home, or if a motor vehicle is taken (again, attempts are counted as well as completed acts). This indicator of the extent of the crime problem produces higher victimization rates because it records any misfortune that strikes any one of several people who live together. It can be used to estimate the relative frequency of occurrence of various kinds of crimes (see Figure 6.1). In 1991, the most common crime (experienced by 10.4 percent of all households), was a theft of some member's unguarded possession (away from home, without any contact by the offender).

Another way that this statistic can be used is to highlight changes in victimization rates over time. Contrary to widespread impressions, the level of criminal activity throughout the country has not been rising rapidly. In 1975 (when this calculation was carried out for the first time), as many as one-third of the nation's households were touched by at least one crime of theft or violence. By the early 1990s, that fraction had dropped to about one-fourth of all households, a decline of 26 percent. (See the downward trend in the line

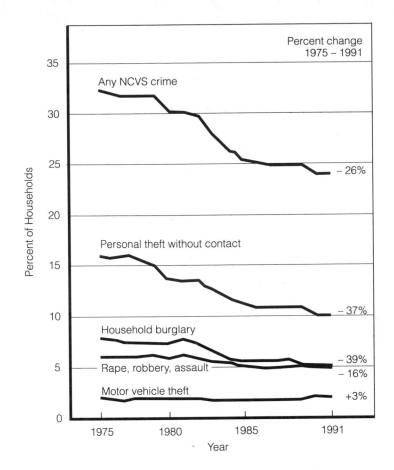

**FIGURE 6.1
HOUSEHOLDS
EXPERIENCING SELECTED
CRIMES OF VIOLENCE
AND THEFT, 1975–1991**

SOURCE: *Bastion, L.* Crime and the Nation's Households. *Washington, D.C.: Bureau of Justice Statistics, 1992b.*

labeled "Any NCVS crime.") The percent of households touched by burglaries, thefts of property owned in common, and thefts of unguarded personal possessions dropped significantly during this period, along with lesser declines in the rates of robbery and assault (Bastion, 1992b).

INFORMING AUTHORITIES: REPORTING RATES

Victimologists study NCVS findings to discover what proportion of crimes are reported to the police and to find out the reasons why people do or do not inform the authorities. In 1991, victims told the police about 38 percent of the incidents that they disclosed to survey interviewers. Reporting rates vary by type of crime and characteristics of the victim (for example, age, social class). Several patterns are worth noting: Crimes are more likely to be reported if they involve violence rather than just theft, if they are completed rather than merely attempted, and if victims sustain physical injuries or suffer financial losses they consider to be substantial. Teenagers are less inclined to call for help than older

TABLE 6.1   **REPORTING VICTIMIZATIONS TO THE POLICE, 1973–1991**

	Percent of Victimizations Reported to the Police							
	1973	*1974*	*1975*	*1976*	*1977*	*1978*	*1979*	*1980*
All crimes	32%	33%	35%	35%	34%	33%	33%	36%
Personal Crimes	28%	30%	32%	32%	30%	30%	30%	33%
Crimes of violence	46	47	47	49	46	44	45	47
Rape	49	52	56	53	58	49	51	41
Robbery	52	54	53	53	56	51	55	57
Assault	44	45	45	48	44	43	42	45
Aggravated	52	53	55	58	51	53	51	54
Simple	38	39	39	41	39	37	37	40
Crimes of theft	22	25	26	27	25	25	24	27
Personal larceny								
With contact	33	34	35	36	37	34	36	36
Without contact	22	24	26	26	24	24	24	27
Household Crimes	38%	37%	39%	38%	38%	36%	36%	39%
Household burglary	47	48	49	48	49	47	48	51
Household larceny	25	25	27	27	25	24	25	28
Motor vehicle theft	68	67	71	69	68	66	68	69

SOURCE: Bastion, L. *Criminal Victimization in the United States, 1991.* Washington, D.C.: Bureau of Justice Statistics, 1992a.

people, and members of higher-income families complain to the authorities about thefts more often than those from lower-income households.

Of all the crimes asked about on the survey, the highest reporting rates are registered for completed auto thefts. (Failed attempts to steal vehicles are reported much less often.) Victims inform the police in over 90 percent of completed vehicle thefts for several reasons: They hope their stolen cars, trucks, and vans will be recovered; their insurance policies require filing a complaint to receive reimbursement; and they do not want the police to assume they were behind the wheel if the vehicle is involved in an accident or is used as a getaway car in a crime. The lowest reporting rates are noted for minor thefts, such as personal or household larcenies of items worth less than $50. As for the more serious crimes, rapes, robberies, and aggravated assaults were reported between 55 and 59 percent of the time in 1991 (Bastion, 1992a).

Victims report crimes to the police for a variety of reasons: to recover stolen property, to become eligible for insurance reimbursement, to fulfill a sense of civic duty, to prevent the offender from striking again against someone else, and to get an offender into legal trouble. Relatively few victims tell NCVS interviewers that they failed to notify the authorities because they were intimidated and feared reprisals (however, frightened victims might not reveal

				Percent of Victimizations Reported to the Police						
1981	1982	1983	1984	1985	1986	1987	1988	1989	1990	1991
35%	36%	35%	35%	36%	37%	37%	36%	37%	38%	38%
33%	33%	32%	33%	34%	34%	34%	34%	34%	35%	35%
47	48	47	47	48	50	48	48	45	48	49
56	53	47	56	61	48	52	45	51	54	59
56	56	53	54	54	58	55	57	51	50	55
44	46	46	45	46	48	46	46	43	47	47
52	58	56	55	58	59	60	54	52	59	58
39	40	41	40	40	41	38	41	38	42	42
27	27	26	26	27	28	28	27	29	29	29
40	33	36	31	33	38	36	35	30	37	38
26	27	26	26	27	28	27	27	29	28	28
39%	39%	37%	38%	39%	41%	40%	40%	41%	41%	41%
51	49	49	49	50	52	52	51	50	51	50
26	27	25	27	27	28	27	26	28	27	28
67	72	69	69	71	73	75	73	76	75	74

their fears) or because they did not want to invest the time and effort to get involved in the criminal justice process. Victims do not report crimes when they believe the incidents are not serious enough; the conflicts are personal matters; nothing can be done; or the police do not want to be bothered or are inefficient, ineffective, or insensitive (Sparks et al., 1977; Harlow, 1985; Gottfredson and Gottfredson, 1988).

Despite campaigns by police officials to encourage victims to file complaints, no dramatic increases in reporting rates can be detected although the composite rate for all reported crimes has improved from 32 percent when the first survey was carried out to 38 percent during the most recent surveys. Yet, for specific crimes, the reporting rate may fluctuate considerably. For example, the reporting rate for forcible rapes (by strangers as well as acquaintances) has dipped to as low as 41 percent and has risen to as high as 61 percent (Bastion, 1992a). These yearly changes in reporting rates for the crimes covered in the NCVS appear in Table 6.1.

Victimologists suspect that the most underreported crimes are offenses committed by nonstrangers, especially intimates like family members (Pagelow, 1989) and lovers. Acts that are not well detected by either the NCVS or the UCR—because victims are as reluctant to reveal their plight to interviewers as they are to police officers—include wife-beating (Frieze and Browne, 1989), acquaintance rape (Koss, 1992) and incidents in which children are physically (Mash and Wolfe, 1991) or sexually abused, especially incestuously (Garbarino, 1989). The incidence (number of victimizations occurring) and the prevalence (percent of people victimized) of underreported crimes like these must be estimated by researchers from other sources and surveys.

UNCOVERING PATTERNS: DIFFERENTIAL RISKS

The basic statistics derived from the annual NCVS findings estimate the risks faced by "typical Americans" and "average households." But NCVS data can also be used to provide a sense of the odds of being victimized for specific groups within the population. When these national figures are broken down into their constituent parts, distinct patterns emerge revealing that different categories of people face widely varying risks (see Harlow, 1987). This notion of differential rates and varying risks can be illustrated by an analysis of robberies committed during 1991.

The burden of robbery victimization falls unevenly, striking certain kinds of people much more than others. For 1991, the overall rate for all categories of persons was estimated to be 5.6 per 1,000 individuals (see Table 6.2). But NCVS calculations indicate that males were robbed at more than twice the rate as females. Black people faced more than three times the risk that white people did. Teenagers and young adults were robbed many times more often than were middle-aged and elderly people. Single persons who were never married plus those who were separated or divorced experienced far greater risks than married people. Persons from lower-income families were more likely to be robbed than were persons from higher-income families. Similarly (but not shown in Table 6.2), less educated people were robbed more often than better educated people. Residents of urban areas were robbed at a higher rate than their rural counterparts, with suburbanites somewhere in-between. The highest robbery rate suffered by any NCVS grouping was for black people between the ages of 20 and 24, with nearly 30 attempted and completed muggings and holdups per 1,000 persons that year (Bureau of Justice Statistics, 1992b).

The recognition of such differential rates can help correct widely held stereotypes derived from the news media's coverage or from the campaigns of politicians about who suffers most from street crime. For example, the data indicate that although females and the elderly may be easier to rob, young males, especially from minority groups, are victimized much more often.

ESTIMATING LIFETIME LIKELIHOODS: CUMULATIVE RISKS

Annual rates yield the impression that victimization is an unusual event since only a few people out of every 1,000 are unfortunate enough to be targeted by offenders during a given year. But when the chances of becoming a victim

TABLE 6.2 **DIFFERENTIAL ROBBERY RATES, 1991**

Victim Characteristics	Robbery Victimizations
	Rate per 1,000
All persons	5.7
Sex	
Male	7.8
Female	3.5
Race	
White	4.4
Black	13.5
Other	7.4
Ethnicity	
Hispanic	10.0
Non-Hispanic	5.2
Age	
12–15	10.0
16–19	8.3
20–24	13.9
25–34	7.2
35–49	4.0
50–64	1.8
65 and older	1.9
Marital Status	
Married	2.6
Widowed	2.0
Divorced or separated	8.6
Never married	10.7
Family Income	
Less than $7,500	9.6
$7,500–14,999	7.8
$15,000–24,999	5.0
$25,000–49,999	4.9
$50,000 and above	3.3

SOURCE: Bureau of Justice Statistics. *Criminal Victimization in the United States, 1991.* Washington, D.C.: Department of Justice, 1992b.

TABLE 6.3   LIFETIME CHANCES OF BEING VICTIMIZED

Type of Crime and Kind of Person	Percentage of Persons Currently 12 Years Old Who Will Be Victimized at Least Once During Their Lifetimes
Rape	
White females	8
Black females	11
Robbery	
Males	37
Females	22
Whites	27
Blacks	51
Assault	
Males	82
Females	62
Personal Thefts	
All persons	99
Persons now 60 years old	43

SOURCE: Adapted from Koppel, 1987.

are estimated for an entire lifetime, what seems highly unlikely during any *single* year appears to be much more possible over a span of sixty years or so. According to projections based on NCVS findings (see Table 6.3), just about all persons (99 percent) currently twelve years old will someday become victims of a theft (a personal larceny with or without contact). Lifetime likelihoods are correspondingly lower for persons who are well past the age of twelve. For example, of people who are now sixty years old, 43 percent (as opposed to 99 percent) will experience a theft of personal property in their remaining years. Taking differential risks into account, it is predicted that most males will be assaulted at some point in their lifetimes. More than half of all black youths eventually will suffer a completed or attempted robbery, and one out of every nine black females now twelve years old will become a victim of an attempted or completed rape (Koppel, 1987).

The methodological and sociological premises underlying these anticipated victimization rates are complex and subject to challenge. Basically, if the crime rate rises in future decades, these estimated percentages will be far too low. But if the rates in the twenty-first century decline substantially from current levels, then these odds of eventually being victimized will turn out to be too high.

FIXING BLAME: THE CONTROVERSY OVER SHARED RESPONSIBILITY

The possibility that victims did or said something that in some manner contributed to their being harmed is what inspired criminologists to become victimologists from the 1940s through the 1960s (see Von Hentig, 1941, 1948; Ellenberger, 1955; Wolfgang, 1958; Schafer, 1968; Amir, 1967). The concepts of victim *facilitation, precipitation,* and *provocation* were formulated to specify the actions taken by victims right before and during the incidents that contributed to their losses and injuries.

Facilitation is said to occur when victims fail to take conventional precautions and thus through negligence make the criminals' task easier. Classic examples include facilitating burglary by leaving a window open and making auto theft easier by leaving keys dangling from a car's ignition lock. Precipitation suggests an even more active role by the victim. In cases of murder, for example, victim precipitation is said to occur whenever the person who was slain was the first to resort to physical force (including brandishing a deadly weapon) during a conflict. According to several studies, between 20 and 40 percent of all homicides could be considered victim precipitated (Wolfgang, 1958; Voss and Hepburn, 1968; National Commission on the Causes and Prevention of Violence, 1969).

Surely the most controversial application of the concept of shared responsibility was the definition of a victim-precipitated rape as an incident culminating in forced intercourse in which the female first agreed to sexual relations, or clearly encouraged the male verbally or through gestures, but then retracted the invitation (Amir, 1967; National Commission on the Causes and Prevention of Violence, 1969).

The concepts of precipitation and provocation have been used interchangeably, perhaps obscuring an important difference between singling oneself out for attack by attracting a motivated offender (precipitation) and instigating an otherwise law-abiding person to launch a counterattack (provocation). For example, supporters of clemency drives for battered women who finally slay their tormentors argue that the dead "victims" provoked the violent acts of self-defense in their otherwise law-abiding wives (Browne, 1987).

Some victimologists seek to determine the proportion of murders, rapes, robberies, assaults, and car thefts that were victim facilitated, precipitated, or provoked, but others reject such endeavors as encouraging an unfair tendency to blame victims for their own plights. Victim-blaming has been denounced as a form of scapegoating, in which people are held responsible for situations beyond their control. Victim-blaming shifts the burden of accountability away from offenders and away from the social conditions that generate criminal behavior. For example, finding fault with the words and deeds of battered women and rape victims diverts attention from the institutionalized sexism within a society's culture and legal system (Brownmiller, 1975; Browne, 1987). Similarly, blaming auto theft on careless motorists relieves manufacturers of any responsibility for designing cars that are so easy to steal that vehicle security must be a low priority of top executives (Karmen, 1979, 1980, 1981).

Indeed, the attempt to establish the degree of shared responsibility, if any, on the victims' part raises a host of theoretical problems. Critics contend that victim-blaming arguments merely restate self-serving rationalizations originating with offenders and that such arguments are plagued by the fallacy of circular reasoning, picturing offenders as reactive, with the victims' actions as the necessary and sufficient conditions for crimes to occur (Weis and Borges, 1973; Franklin and Franklin, 1976; Sheley, 1979; Reiff, 1979; Karmen, 1991).

While the experts debate these theories, the issue of fixing responsibility retains great practical importance within the criminal justice system and arises routinely at every stage of case processing (McDonald, 1976; Williams, 1978). For example, judgments about the degree of shared responsibility for a brawl can influence the decision of a police officer about whether to arrest just the victor or the injured party as well. Concerns about the appearance of shared responsibility for causing the brawl might convince a prosecutor to engage in plea negotiations rather than press for a conviction for assault and risk acquittal by a trial jury. The sentencing judge might consider aggressive acts by the wounded victim to be provocations that mitigate the severity of punishment deserved by the assailant.

AVOIDING CRIME AND ACCOUNTING FOR VICTIMIZATION

Victimologists and criminologists share a common interest in developing theories to explain why some categories of people are more likely to be preyed on by criminals than others (differential risks) and why certain individuals lead more dangerous lives (perhaps they share responsibility through facilitation, precipitation, or provocation) than others (who are crime conscious and take precautions). Concepts that are useful to account for who becomes a victim and who escapes harm are crime prevention, victimization prevention, avoidance and minimization strategies, lifestyles and routine activities, and displacement and deflection.

In the past, the term *crime prevention* conjured up images of major governmental campaigns designed to get at the social roots of street crime by tackling problems like poverty, unemployment, racial discrimination, failing school systems, and lack of teenage recreational facilities. But today, the term refers to measures taken to anticipate, recognize, and appraise risks, along with actions designed to reduce or eliminate these threats (National Crime Prevention Institute, 1978). Clearly, this redefinition reflects a shift away from large-scale social programs and toward a reliance on individual or small-group strategies to protect persons and property. These preemptive moves and defensive tactics might better be termed "victimization prevention" rather than "crime prevention" because their intent is really much more modest: simply to deter or deflect would-be offenders from their intended targets (Cohn et al., 1978).

"Avoidance strategies" (such as staying home after dark) are devised to limit the exposure of individuals to dangerous persons and potentially threatening situations. "Risk management tactics" (such as traveling in groups rather than alone) aim to minimize the chances of being harmed when exposure to risk is unavoidable. "Crime prevention through environmental design" relies on the establishment of "defensible space" through surveillance (guarding) and "target hardening" (such as using alarms, locks, and fences) to make the offenders' tasks more difficult (see Newman, 1972; Skogan and Maxfield, 1981).

The effectiveness of victimization prevention strategies is extremely difficult to evaluate, given the problems involved in trying to measure how many potential offenders are discouraged from committing crimes. Some evidence supports the "valve theory" (National Commission on the Causes and Prevention of Violence, 1969) that if one avenue of illegal opportunities is shut off (for example, protecting bus drivers from robbery by requiring passengers to have exact change), then criminally inclined persons will shift their attention to more vulnerable targets (perhaps cab drivers). The growing proliferation of burglar alarms may not have had any appreciable impact on the overall rate of attempted or completed forcible entries, but such security hardware might cause a social redistribution of the burden of victimization. Would-be burglars might be avoiding homes with visible alarm systems, especially in communities with neighborhood patrols, and increasingly striking unprotected homes in unguarded areas. If so, the victimization prevention measures some people are taking are deflecting predatory street criminals onto others (Rand, 1985; Barr and Pease, 1990). To the extent that purchasing security equipment is a function of income, the privileged are enhancing their safety at the expense of the underprivileged.

The tradeoff between security and risk ultimately hinges on personal decisions. In principle, more security requires greater expenditures of money, time, and effort, up to a point of diminishing returns. Individuals decide — often on the basis of irrational, emotional, or vague impressionistic factors — what sacrifices to limit exposure to danger are reasonable, how safe is safe enough, and what constitutes an acceptable risk (see Lynn, 1981).

Both criminologists and victimologists have tried to account for the differential risks various categories of people face of becoming a victim of theft, robbery, rape, assault, and even murder. According to recent research, the variables that account for differences in risk levels include lifestyles (how people spend their time and money), routine activities (whether or not engaged in by choice), role expectations (the way people are supposed to behave), exposure to motivated offenders (dangerous persons) and threatening situations, the availability of suitable targets (such as electronic goods), the presence or absence of capable guardians (police, private security, alarm systems), and proximity to high-crime "hot spots" (Cohen et al., 1981; Messner and Tardiff, 1985; Garofalo, 1986; Sherman et al., 1989; Miethe et al., 1990). (See Chapters 7 and 8 for further discussions of these factors.)

SEEKING REIMBURSEMENT FOR VICTIMIZATION

Victims can recover their financial losses in a number of ways: (1) by receiving restitution from the offender, (2) by winning a civil court judgment against the offender or some responsible third party, and (3) by collecting reimbursement from a private insurance policy or a governmental compensation fund.

RESTITUTION BY OFFENDERS

In many states, victims are now entitled to receive restitution in the form of payments or services from the offenders who harmed them. This ancient practice was specified in the Code of Hammurabi, the laws of Moses, Roman law, and the original legal codes of the thirteen colonies before the American Revolution. It was revived by legislation passed by Congress and many states during the 1980s although restitution by juvenile offenders always has been an option in family court. Today, a growing number of judges are handing down "alternative," "constructive," or "creative" sentences in order to tailor the punishment to fit the crime. The renewed interest in restitution reflects a number of pressures, including the demands of the victims' movement, the crisis of overcrowding in jails and prisons, and a growing disenchantment with traditional forms of rehabilitation and punishment.

Advocates of restitution argue that many opportunities arise for arranging reimbursement: as a settlement of a conflict in lieu of arrest; as a condition for dropping charges; as a term of a negotiated plea; or as a condition of a suspended sentence, probation, or parole. However, advocates of a greater reliance on restitution are split over priorities and goals. Some view restitution as an additional penalty and contend that offenders must first "pay their debts to society" by being punished through confinement before they can repay their financial debts to their actual victims. For others, the primary consideration is that restitution serve as a means of rehabilitation, by developing in offenders a sense of responsibility for wrongdoing, by cultivating good work habits and marketable skills, and by building self-confidence through tangible accomplishments. Still others see restitution as a vehicle for reparation and then reconciliation, whereby the offenders make amends, repair damage, and thus restore balance and harmony (see Galaway and Hudson, 1979; Hudson and Galaway, 1977; McGillis, 1986; McDonald, 1987; Hillenbrand, 1990).

Major obstacles stand in the way of any expanded dependence on restitution as a routine sanction. First, suitable jobs for offenders are difficult to find. Second, judges remain reluctant to impose restitution unless agreements are likely to be enforced. Third, probation and parole officials resent being relegated to the status of "bill collection" agencies. Finally, many appropriate cases slip through the cracks in the system, through a process called "shrinkage" or "funneling," because of unreported crimes, unsolved cases, dropped counts, and dismissed charges.

CIVIL LAWSUITS AGAINST OFFENDERS AND THIRD PARTIES

Victims who do not receive court-ordered restitution can launch civil lawsuits against their offenders. If the lawsuit is successful, the victim not only can feel vindicated but also can collect judgments reflecting actual out-of-pocket expenses (for medical bills and lost earnings), plus compensation for the mental anguish of pain and suffering, and even punitive damages. To prevail, the plaintiff must convince a judge or a jury by a preponderance of the evidence (a somewhat easier criterion to meet than guilt beyond a reasonable doubt) that the defendant caused economic, physical, and mental harm. However, victims contemplating civil litigation confront several obstacles: the substantial contingency fees charged by lawyers (ranging up to 50 percent of the victorious victim's judgment); incidental expenses that must be paid, even in defeat (filing fees, expert witness fees, deposition costs); the ordeal of another round of protracted legal proceedings, including testifying, jury deliberations, or negotiations leading to an out-of-court settlement; and the difficulty of actually collecting money awarded by a civil court jury or judge (see Stark and Goldstein, 1985).

When offenders are not apprehended, or appear to be "judgment proof"—that is, without substantial income or assets—victims might launch third-party lawsuits against persons or entities who, they contend, share responsibility with the offenders for their plight. The victim must prove in court that a special relationship existed with the third party, whose gross incompetence or negligence was a proximate cause of a failure to prevent a foreseeable crime from being committed. Third parties can be private individuals, institutions, and corporations. In these cases, suits can pit students against school systems, tenants against landlords, customers against store owners, and employees against employers. Charges may involve failure to maintain conventional security safeguards, or negligently putting dangerous persons in positions of trust.

Another set of third parties can be government officials and agencies. For instance, the police can be sued for negligence, either malfeasance (improper acts) or nonfeasance (failure to act). Criminal justice officials can be sued for wrongful release of dangerous persons known to pose a foreseeable risk to specific potential targets. Correctional authorities can be sued for gross negligence leading to the escape of prisoners or for failure to warn intended victims about the lawful release of former prisoners or mental patients. One result of successful third-party lawsuits is that criminal justice officials who exercise professional judgment when deciding whom to let out on probation, parole, work release, educational release, or furlough now must pay more attention to the potential threat to public safety posed by the release from confinement of a prisoner in their care (see Carrington, 1977, 1978a; Stark and Goldstein, 1985; Austern, 1987).

COMPENSATION FROM INSURANCE POLICIES AND GOVERNMENT FUNDS

Victims can be compensated for their financial losses by insurance companies or by governmental boards. Private companies sell policies that provide coverage to offset expenses arising from medical bills (health insurance), lost earnings (income maintenance), loss of future support (life insurance), and stolen or damaged property (homeowners, automobile owners, and boat owners insurance).

By purchasing policies beforehand, victims and their dependents can be financially secure in the face of crimes like murder, robbery, assault, theft, burglary, and vandalism.

Several patterns of loss and recovery stand out. More families are insured against medical costs than against property losses. Large losses are more likely to be the subject of claims than small ones because of deductible clauses that force victims to absorb the first $100 or more of outlays. Higher-income households are more likely to purchase protection in advance than are other families. And those who face the greatest risks and need insurance the most are the least likely to be offered policies and to be able to afford coverage. Only victims of motor vehicle theft are likely to receive significant reimbursements from private insurance; most burglary losses are not reimbursed (Harland, 1981).

As a response to the inadequacy of private insurance underwriting, the ancient practice of governmental assistance to crime victims has been revived by the federal government and by nearly all the fifty states, a trend that started in the 1960s. Advocates of government-financed and government-administered compensation funds developed several different arguments to justify the establishment of public insurance coverage: to fill a glaring hole in the existing safety net of social welfare programs; to routinize acts of compassion and charity to deserving persons suffering needlessly from unforeseen tragedies; to fulfill the social obligations incurred by governments that take responsibility for maintaining order by disarming law-abiding citizens and then fail to protect them from harm; and to provide an incentive to victims to report crimes, assist police investigations, press charges, and testify for the prosecution.

Those who were against the establishment of these state funds, or who opposed their growth and expansion into new areas of coverage, countered that the tendency to bail out people in financial distress smacked of governmental paternalism at the expense of self-reliance, that taxpayers already were burdened by the costs of running the criminal justice system, and that "welfare state tax-and-spend" social insurance programs encroached on the preserve of private enterprise (see Geis, 1976; Meiners, 1978; Carrow, 1980).

The existing state compensation programs across the country have a great deal in common. All of them restrict eligibility to innocent victims of violent crimes who were physically wounded and as a result suffered out-of-pocket expenses, or to their families or dependents who incurred funeral expenses and lost support of a breadwinner. The various state boards have different rules concerning reporting procedures and filing deadlines, hiring attorneys, proving financial need, limiting the amount of awards, and excluding acts of intrafamily violence (Austern et al., 1979; McGillis and Smith, 1983).

In many states, compensation programs are now funded in part or entirely from penalty assessments levied on traffic law violators, misdemeanants, and felons, and in some places from bail forfeitures, community service work by offenders, and gun license fees. But the compensation boards do not give money away freely. Many eligible victims are never informed about the opportunity for reimbursement, and of those who do apply, many have their claims rejected because of stringent requirements. And in some states, the boards run out of money before the year is over. Of those who do receive awards, many must wait years to collect, and then feel demeaned by the process. To some extent, the establishment of compensation funds was an exercise by lawmakers in "symbolic politics" intended to mollify the humanitarian concerns of the public about the plight of victims (Elias, 1983).

CAMPAIGNING FOR GREATER VICTIMS' RIGHTS

Just like other groups, most notably minorities, women, gays, students, and prisoners, victims have been struggling to secure rights and guarantees of fair treatment since the late 1960s. Unlike the rights of suspects, defendants, convicts, and even crime reporters, however, victims' rights are not derived from any of the amendments to the U.S. Constitution. In the American "adversarial" justice system, only two parties participate in criminal proceedings: the state (representing the victim only to a degree) and the accused. Because victims lacked "standing" in legal terms, their role until recently has been limited to signing the complaints that set the criminal justice process into motion and serving as "walking pieces of evidence" brought into courtrooms to testify for the prosecution. What the victims' rights movement seeks is aptly summed up by a model amendment for state constitutions that reads, "The victim of crime or his or her representative shall have the right to be informed of, to be present at, and to be heard at all criminal justice proceedings at which the defendant has such rights, subject to the same rules which govern defendants rights" (National Victim Center, 1988).

In 1982, Congress enacted a law setting forth standards for the fair treatment of victims and witnesses. Throughout the 1980s, many states have granted victims opportunities to participate in decision-making within the criminal justice process. These legislative packages, known as "Victim's Bills of Rights," empower victims at the expense of criminal justice agencies and officials (including the police, prosecutors, judges, corrections administrators, and parole boards) as well as defendants and convicts (see President's Task Force, 1982).

Ideally, the police can serve victims in a number of crucial ways. They can respond promptly when called, administer first aid, apprehend the suspect, gather evidence sufficient for conviction in court, recover any property that was stolen, and protect the complainant as a key prosecution witness from any intimidation or reprisals for cooperating with the authorities. In practice, the police might respond slowly, deliver a "second wound" by being insensitive, fail to solve the crime or recover stolen property, and close the investigation without telling the victim (see Brandl and Horvath, 1991; Karmen, 1990). To address these problems, some states have passed statutes requiring that victims "be read their rights"—that is, be informed of all of their obligations (to cooperate and testify), their opportunities (to participate and to apply for compensation), and services available to them (counseling and protection from harassment). In some jurisdictions, victims also have gained the right to be kept posted about any progress in their cases (arrests, bail, prosecutions, plea negotiations, convictions, sentences, parole hearings).

In theory, the prosecutor's office is a public law firm that vigorously represents the best interests of victims at no cost to them. Prosecutors can serve victims by securing indictments and convictions, and by recommending sentences that reflect the seriousness of the harm done to their "clients." In reality, prosecutors' offices often are large bureaucracies that sacrifice the interests of victims to what are perceived to be the best interests of the government, the entire society, the prosecutor's reputation, or the personal careers of the attorneys working there. In response, the victims' movement in some states has secured guarantees of fair treatment that include advance notification of changes in the dates of court appearances; secure waiting facilities in courthouses; reasonable witness fees for testifying; intercession by government attorneys in behalf of the victim with landlords, employers, and creditors who might be unaware of the victim's plight; expedited return of stolen property recovered by the police and held as evidence; and information about negotiated pleas. To regain the confidence and cooperation of the public, many district attorneys have set up victim–witness assistance programs to deliver these services (Kelly, 1990).

Ideally, judges are impartial arbiters who exercise professional discretion as they preside over fair trials and hand down appropriate sentences. In practice, victims might feel neglected or even endangered by the decisions and rulings of judges. To ensure equitable treatment, the victims' movement in some states has secured guarantees that judges will consider the victim's safety when setting bail, take the victim's needs into account when scheduling court appearances, and weigh seriously the victim's views as set forth in a written impact statement (detailing the physical, emotional, and financial consequences of the crime) or as stated in person (allocution) before handing down sentences (Villmoare and Neto, 1987; Stark and Goldstein, 1985; National Organization for Victim Assistance, 1988; Elias, 1990).

SEARCHING FOR JUSTICE INFORMALLY

Victims who don't want to turn over their cases to criminal justice officials for formal processing have two informal options: to seek peaceful resolutions of their conflicts as part of an emerging trend toward "restorative justice" or to try to inflict retaliatory violence, do-it-yourself style, in the vigilante tradition.

RESTORATIVE JUSTICE

Restorative justice refers to a bold, new, experimental paradigm whose goal is not punishment but reconciliation between the offender and the victim, to the advantage of the entire community. Unlike the traditional "retributive model" of justice, in which the police and prosecution respond punitively to lawbreaking as offenses against the state and threats to the social order, restorative justice treats criminally inflicted injuries and losses as social damage that must be repaired. For this nonpunitive alternative to adjudication and incarceration to work effectively, offenders have to acknowledge their responsibilities, express remorse, undergo rehabilitation, and make amends to all those they harmed through creative restitution. Restorative justice through dispute resolution started out as a way of handling misdemeanors (like acts of vandalism, minor thefts, and simple assaults), but even felonies (such as burglaries and serious assaults) are sometimes diverted by the courts to victim–offender reconciliation programs (VORPs) (Alper and Nichols, 1981; McGillis, 1982; Wright and Galaway, 1989; Galaway and Hudson, 1990; Pepinsky and Quinney, 1991; Wright, 1991).

The primary method for determining appropriate ways of resolving cases is through alternative dispute resolution (ADR), a mediation-oriented process offered at "neighborhood justice centers." ADR substitutes an informal "moot model" of far-reaching inquiry, unfettered dialogue, and flexible negotiation as a replacement for the strictly limited testimony and evidence that can be introduced within the winner-take-all adversary model that guides formal case processing. In this method of problem-solving, a neutral third party, preferably a mediator, but if necessary an arbitrator, replaces the prosecutor, defense attorney, judge, and jury. Because the goal is to resolve an ongoing conflict before it escalates by hammering out a mutually acceptable settlement, the most appropriate kinds of cases involve quarreling parties who had a prior relationship (such as family members, neighbors, co-workers, and fellow students) that must be repaired and incidents in which both parties shared responsibility for the violations of law. (The clear-cut labels "victim" and "offender" did not fit the facts of the case.) Compromise settlements usually involve apologies, pledges to alter behavior or to stay away from each other, promises to enter treatment programs, and restitution agreements.

VIGILANTISM

Whereas restorative justice embodies an informal approach whose aim is to achieve reconciliation between the two estranged parties, return them to a condition of well-being, and bring back harmony to their community, vigilantism embodies an informal approach in which retaliation and subjugation is the goal. Punishment of the offender directly by the victim (or family members or supporters) is considered a prerequisite for "justice." Vigilantism's roots go back to the time of the frontier and pioneers, when the total absence of a formal criminal justice system compelled upright citizens to "take the law into their own hands." Today, the impulse toward vigilantism arises within those who have completely lost confidence in the ability of the police, prosecution, courts, and prisons to mete out to predatory street criminals their "just deserts."

Vigilantism occurs when victims (and their allies) intentionally use excessive force to inflict on-the-spot summary punishments to suspects. By definition, vigilante violence is illegal because those who impose "street justice" appoint themselves as judge, jury, and even executioner. Their retaliatory violence exceeds the legal limits on the justifiable use of force in self-defense and disregards provisions in the law about "proportional responses" and "imminent danger." Vigilantes cast aside the constitutional guarantees of due process safeguards for the accused and run the risk of physically harming innocent persons they mistakenly assume are guilty of heinous crimes. An outbreak of vigilantism brings about a transformation of relationships: Offenders become victims and victims turn into victimizers (see Brown, 1975; Burrows, 1976; Rosenbaum and Sederberg, 1976).

CONCLUSION

Clearly, victimology helps counteract the tendency of criminology to reduce itself to "offenderology." Until criminologists developed an interest in victims, they tended to be preoccupied with lawbreakers: their characteristics, the causes of their illegal behaviors, their handling by the criminal justice system, and their potential for rehabilitation. Now, criminology is better balanced because it also studies the characteristics and situations of people harmed by criminals: how the police, prosecutors, judges, and other officials and agencies handle them and how they might be restored to the conditions they were in before criminals harmed them.

DISCUSSION QUESTIONS

1. Victimology is a relatively recent field of study. What are its roots, and why has its popularity risen in recent years?

2. Some categories of people seem to have higher victimization rates than do others. Discuss some of these patterns and, especially, the reasons for them.

3. How much crime is reported to the police? What factors influence whether or not the victim of a crime will report it to the police? What have been the effects of campaigns to increase the percentage of crimes reported?

4. The notion of victim precipitation suggests that some victims do things to encourage their victimization. Are there problems with this notion? Are there better ways to conceptualize victim involvement in crime commission?

TYPES OF CRIME

In Part Two, we reviewed crime statistics and presented profiles of offenders and victims. In Part Three, we examine various types of crime: violent offenses, property crime, vice offenses, organized crime, and "respectable" (that is, white collar) crime. Our purpose again is to gain a fuller sense of the inaccuracies of most people's ideas about various forms of offense behavior and, thus, to allow readers to assess more accurately the "crime problem" and to propose solutions to it.

Robert Nash Parker opens Part Three with a detailed examination of violent crime—the offenses that bother the public most, though they occur less frequently than do the other types of crime reviewed in this section. In Chapter 7, "Violent Crime," Parker begins by outlining recent crime rate trends and noting that by most indicators, violent crime generally is declining. He then challenges the traditional view that the South has the highest rate of violent crime; in fact, the West now seems to lead in this category. Two related theories are explored as explanations of violent crime rates and situations. The first is the routine activities approach, which locates violent crime levels in the extent to which everyday lifestyle activities place people in varying risk situations. The second is the situational transaction model, by which we come to understand that much violent crime results from interactions whereby perceived insults are not amicably negotiated by the parties involved. The remainder of the chapter is devoted to what the research findings tell us about homicide, rape, robbery, and assault.

The routine activities approach to understanding crime patterns is carried over to Chapter 8, "The Distribution and Dynamics of Property Crime," in which Robert Bursik examines property crime characteristics and trends using both police statistics and victimization survey results. His review suggests that rates stabilized or even declined somewhat in recent years. He then turns his attention to the variable so often linked in the public's mind to property crime: unemployment. He concludes that the unemployment–crime relationship remains viable and is clearly more complex than has been previously thought. Shifting to the notion of criminal opportunity, Bursik locates property crime levels in differential exposure of property to crime risk. The primary determinant of the likelihood of a successful burglary, for example, is the behavior of the residents of the potential target home. Bursik closes with a reminder that we err too often in thinking that property crime is easily understood and, thus, controlled. This misperception underlies the many seemingly contradictory anticrime policies that confront us.

In Chapter 9, "Vice Crimes: Individual Choices and Social Controls," Henry Lesieur and Michael Welch explore an entirely different form of crime from the violent and property offenses just discussed. They introduce us to the thorny issue of offenses without victims—that is, behaviors that occur between consenting adults. In most senses, the outlawing of these behaviors represents the imposition of one group's definition of proper personal morality on another group. Further, as the authors note, there has been a marked tendency to view the "outlaws" as mentally, emotionally, and in some cases, physically ill; thus, the rise of what is called the medical model of deviance. This backdrop informs their discussions of prostitution, pornography, homosexuality, gambling, and drugs. Lesieur and Welch close by discussing how vice peddlers remain in business only because there is a substantial demand for their services. Indeed, much vice activity is intimately intertwined with legitimate activity.

The discussion of vice crimes leads naturally into an examination of the organized interests seemingly behind them. Jay Albanese introduces us to these interests in Chapter 10, "Organized Crime: The Mafia Mystique." His study of organized crime centers on what he considers an empirically groundless conception of the Mafia in America. He argues persuasively that our preoccupation with the Mafia has hindered any meaningful understanding of organized crime's dynamics. Recent research indicates that the notion of a national syndicate should be replaced by a sense of flexible, informal networks of associations at a local level. More important, Albanese ties organized crime's success or failure to prevailing market conditions. Thus, if the local configuration of suppliers, customers, regulators, and competitors is favorable, organized crime will flourish. Paradoxically, to the extent government intrudes into private decisions—for example, those involving sexual behaviors—market conditions for organized crime are enhanced. Albanese concludes with a discussion of the effects of prosecution efforts against mob figures in recent years, noting that although these law enforcement activities have had short-term disruptive effects on organized crime, they also have caused organized crime to shift into safer, more sophisticated criminal markets.

James Coleman directs our attention to yet another aspect of crime in Chapter 11, "Respectable Crime." This form of crime is probably our most costly economically, but it is also our most ignored. "Respectable" crime refers to law violations by persons or groups in the course of otherwise respected and legitimate occupational or financial activities. In short, Coleman is discussing crimes by middle-class and upper-class persons—people who wear white collars. These offenses include employee theft, drug violations by physicians, bribery and corruption of public officials, fraud and deception by legitimate businesses, monopolies and business conspiracies, governmental civil liberties violations, and maintenance of unsafe work conditions. Coleman examines the key to most forms of such crime, opportunity, but also notes that some form of motivation must encourage white collar crime. It is not enough simply to point to greed—though this is sometimes a sufficient causal element. Instead, we must pay attention to the manner in which industries and government agencies encourage their subordinates to violate the law, not for personal gain but for organizational purposes. Coleman closes with a discussion of the potential for controlling respectable crime.

CHAPTER 7

◆

VIOLENT CRIME

Robert Nash Parker
Prevention Research Center, Berkeley, California

VIOLENT CRIME is probably the most problematic and anxiety provoking of all the behaviors discussed in this book. It is more personal than any other type of crime: Victims of violent crime often are injured physically, or at least are threatened with physical injury, and they can even lose their lives. In addition, victims of violent crimes often suffer psychological trauma that can last for months or years after their physical injuries have healed. How much violent crime is there in our society, and why does it happen? What do we know about the causes of violent crime? These will be the major topics in this chapter. This discussion will focus on four particular crimes: homicide, rape, robbery, and aggravated assault.

Our definitions of these four crimes are drawn from the *Uniform Crime Reports* (UCR) (FBI, 1992), the standard source for much of the crime data available in this country. Homicide is defined as including the willful or non-negligent killing of one human being by another individual or group of individuals. Acts not included in this definition are deaths caused by negligence, attempts to kill, assaults that lead to the victim's death, and accidental deaths. Also not included is justifiable homicide, defined as occurring when the victim was engaged in the commission of a serious crime, or when the victim was known to be a felon wanted by law enforcement agencies. Rape is defined as the carnal knowledge of a female forcibly and against her will. Included in this definition are attempted rapes and assaults directed toward rape; however, statutory rape, which usually occurs without force but involves a victim under the legal age of adult responsibility, is excluded. Robbery is defined as the taking or attempt to take anything of value from the care, custody, or control of a person or persons by force or threat of force or violence or by putting the victim in fear. Finally, aggravated assault, which will be referred to here simply as

TABLE 7.1   **LEVELS AND RATES OF VIOLENT CRIME IN THE UNITED STATES, 1991**

Type of Crime	Uniform Crime Reports (UCR)		National Crime Victimization Survey (NCVS)	
	Level	*Rate**	*Level*	*Rate**
Homicide	24,700	9.8	—	—
Rape	106,590	42.3	130,000	80.0
Robbery	687,730	272.7	1,145,000	560.0
Assault	1,092,740	433.3	1,609,000	780.0

*Rate per 100,000 population.

assault, is defined as an unlawful attack by one person on another for the purpose of inflicting serious bodily injury. This crime involves the use of a weapon or other means likely to produce death or great bodily harm; simple assaults, a much larger category of crimes, are excluded.

VIOLENT CRIME IN THE UNITED STATES: LEVELS AND TRENDS

The first two columns of Table 7.1 list the levels and rates of violent crime as reported in the UCR, in this case for the year 1991. The second two columns list levels and rates of rape, robbery, and assault based on data collected in the National Crime Victimization Survey (NCVS) (Bureau of Justice Statistics, 1992b). Clearly, the NCVS data reveal violent crime to be a much greater and more serious problem than do the data from the UCR, with the NCVS data yielding estimates of from two to three times greater rates for rape, robbery, and assault. (For a discussion of why people do not report crimes to the police, see Chapter 6.)

In the abstract, numbers like those in Table 7.1 are difficult to evaluate. For example, is 9.8 per 100,000 a high or low rate of homicide? Most people — criminologists, students, and the general public — want to know whether or not the crime rate is increasing, decreasing, or staying the same over time. The only way to answer such a question is to examine trends over time to help us place a particular crime rate within the context of recent experience.

Figure 7.1 shows the trend in homicide rates from the UCR over the period 1975–1991. Although the graph reveals that homicide rates have fluctuated over this period, from a high of 10.2 in 1980 to a low of 7.9 in 1985, notice how the range of 8 to 10 per 100,000 forms the lower and upper bounds within which homicide rates have varied. During the late 1970s, affected officials and concerned citizens were disturbed over what was perceived as a great increase in homicides; during the early to mid-1980s, some of the same leaders

FIGURE 7.1
UCR HOMOCIDE RATES,
1975–1991

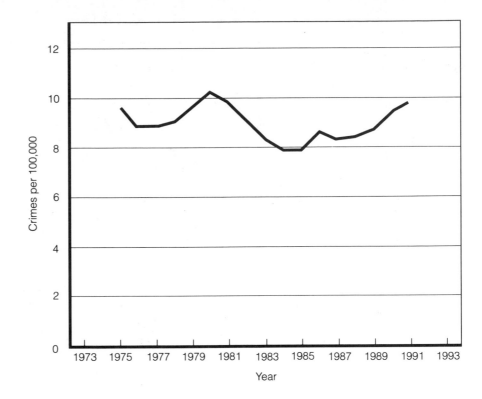

were claiming credit for falling rates of violence. During the latter part of the 1980s and into the 1990s, concern over increasing rates of violence was once again the subject of newspaper articles and television news programs. But a consideration of the data shown in Figure 7.1 suggests the danger of overinterpreting each annual fluctuation. In fact, homicide rates exhibited remarkable stability over the last decade and a half.

In Table 7.1, as noted, the NCVS data revealed substantially higher rates and levels of violence than did the UCR data. Figures 7.2, 7.3, and 7.4 compare the trends during the last decade and a half as reported in these two sources. In Figure 7.2, in which rape rates are compared, both sources show a sharp increase in the late 1970s although the peak rates in that period are found for different years—1979 for the NCVS and 1980 for the UCR. Both trend lines begin to decline in the early 1980s although rape rates as reported to the police began to climb in the mid-1980s and have continued to do so into the 1990s. This trend reflects the change in police and prosecuter behavior toward rape cases and rape victims, as well as new legislation in many states that has made it more difficult for those defending people accused of rape to cast at least partial blame on the victim. The NCVS rate is still substantially higher than that of rapes reported to the police though the two sources may be converging in the long run.

**FIGURE 7.2
UCR AND NCVS RAPE
RATES, 1975–1991**

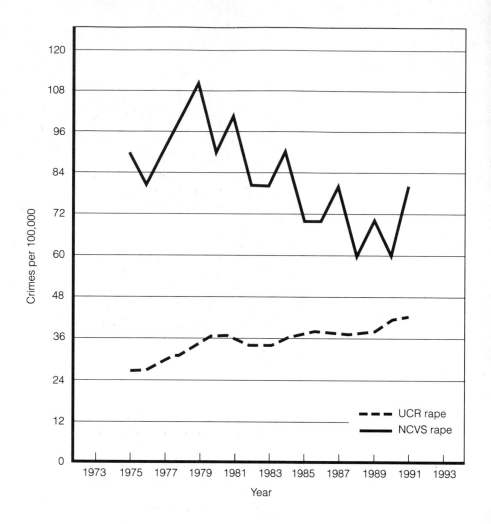

Figure 7.3, which presents trends in robbery rates, is striking for the similarity between the trends in the two sources. Both sources show that robbery rates declined in the mid-1970s and increased sharply in the late 1970s. Both sources indicate peaks in 1981, with rates of 258.7 and 740.0, respectively, for the UCR and the NCVS. In the early 1980s, robbery rates were on a general decline, but during the last five years, rates in both sources have begun to increase; with UCR robbery rates being the highest in 1991, at 272.7 robberies per 100,000.

Finally, NCVS and UCR assault rates, presented in Figure 7.4, show a trend toward the convergence just discussed since 1980. Both sources display an initial increase in the mid-1970s, but this trend continues quite sharply in the UCR, with a peak of 298.5 assaults per 100,000 population in 1980. In addition, after reaching a plateau in the early 1980s, UCR assault rates began

FIGURE 7.3
UCR AND NCVS ROBBERY
RATES, 1975–1991

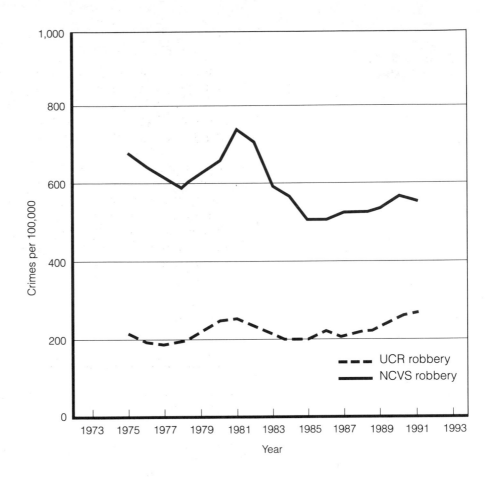

to increase again beginning in 1983, and by 1991, the rate for this violent crime reached a decade-and-a-half high of 433.3. On the other hand, by 1991, NCVS assault rates were at their lowest since 1975, 780 per 100,000 population. In both the cases of rape and assault, one must ask if the nation's police departments are getting better at detecting crime, or perhaps receiving reports on a higher proportion of crimes, as suggested by a comparison of 1988 and 1991 NCVS results (Bureau of Justice Statistics, 1992b: 102; Bureau of Justice Statistics, 1990: 80).

On the other hand, it may be that the NCVS is suffering from greater underreporting than in the past. Whatever the reasons, this divergence in trends between the two sources means that the overall trend in violence in the United States is unclear at the present. Whether or not this lack of clarity continues is for some as interesting as the trends in violent crimes themselves. However, the available evidence does not suggest that violence is on the decline, and as such, violent crime is likely to remain an important topic on the national agenda during the 1990s.

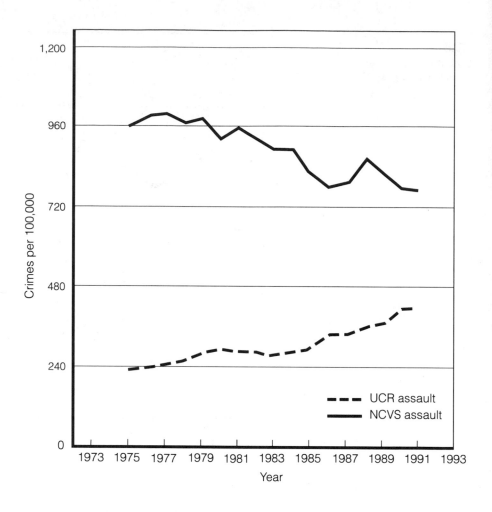

FIGURE 7.4
UCR AND NCVS ASSAULT RATES, 1975–1991

VIOLENCE, WEAPONS, RELATIONSHIPS, AND REGIONAL VARIATION

Three additional important issues in assessing how much violence there is in the United States need to be addressed. Violent crime, unlike hair or eye color, is not uniformly distributed across people, places, and alternative means or methods. Indeed, if we examine the distribution of homicide, rape, robbery, and assault rates for the four U.S. Census Bureau-defined regions of the United States, we find that the West has the highest rates of violent crime, followed by the South, the Midwest, and the Northeast, respectively. The fact that the western region currently has the highest rates of violence is quite interesting in light of the number of theoretical and research studies that have attempted to explain why the South dominated rates of violent crime in the 1950s through the mid-1970s. However, as we will discuss later in this chapter, theories have been advanced recently to explain violence that do not depend on the unique history and culture of the South. Regardless, the fact remains that rates of violence vary substantially by region of the country.

Rates of violence also vary in terms of the people involved as victim and offender and the nature of their prior relationship. In 1991, the majority of homicide victims had some prior relationship with their murderer. Of those cases in which a relationship can be determined, the clear majority occur between those who have some kind of personal relationship, for example, friend, neighbor, or co-worker. Although family members, especially spouses and those involved in sexually intimate relationships, represent about a fifth of the total, less intimate relationships between the victim and the offender are more typical in the case of homicide. Although still less common, homicides committed by strangers have increased dramatically over the past twenty years. The significance of this is heightened by the fact that for over one-third of the total homicides in 1991, the police were unable to determine whether or not a prior relationship existed between victim and killer, either because they did not discover who the offender was or because the lack of evidence made it impossible to determine prior relationship. No conclusive evidence suggests that in all or even most of these cases, the victim and the offender were strangers, but this certainly was true in some cases.

How are violent crimes carried out? Homicides most often are committed with firearms, with the largest subcategory being handguns. Knives and other cutting or stabbing instruments rank a distant second, followed by personal weapons such as hands and feet, blunt objects like lamps or clubs, and finally other weapons, a category that includes poison, murder by drowning, arson, and explosives. Personal attacks on victims without any weapon other than the human body account for about 40 percent of robberies. Firearms are used in about the same percentage of cases, and knives and other weapons in about a fifth of robberies.

Unlike homicide or robbery, in which firearms play a major role, firearms are used in just over 20 percent of assaults. This may be explained by the fact that firearms are more deadly than are other weapons, and therefore, the use of a firearm may lead to an upgrading of an assault to a homicide. In fact, some researchers have argued that most homicides are gun assaults in which the victim ended up dead (Zimring, 1972; Reed, 1971; Doerner, 1983; Doerner and Speir, 1986). However, the truth may lie in the opposite direction—that is, most gun assaults are homicides in which the victim did not die. Regardless, clubs, blunt objects, tire irons, lead pipes, and the like are the most common weapons used in assault, followed by hands and feet, with knives accounting for the remaining assaults. Violent crimes, therefore, differ with regard to the methods offenders use to inflict violence on their victims.

RECENT DEVELOPMENTS IN THE THEORY OF VIOLENT CRIME

For much of the past thirty years, economic deprivation, subculture of violence, and deterrence theories (see Chapters 13 and 14) framed thought and research on the causes of violent crime. However, in the previous decade, two new approaches—the lifestyle or routine activity approach and the situational approach—were developed to answer one simple question: Why does crime occur?

THE LIFESTYLE–ROUTINE ACTIVITY APPROACH

The lifestyle–routine activity approach was developed under each of these labels by two different groups of scholars — the former by the criminologists Hindelang, Gottfredson, and Garofalo (1978), and the latter by Cohen and Felson (1979). Although these two approaches were developed separately, they are virtually the same, and have been merged in the work of most researchers and theorists (see Maxfield, 1987). For Hindelang et al., the central question was: Why are some people much more likely to be victims of violent crime? For Cohen and Felson, the question of interest was: Why have crime rates gone up to such an extent since World War II when the social conditions that are supposed to cause violent crime (for example, poverty) have improved so dramatically during the same period? For both, the answer lay in the nature of everyday life in this country and the changes that have occurred during the past forty years.

Cohen and Felson in particular draw their inspiration from the work of Hawley (1950), whose theory of human ecology has been widely applied to other areas of social science such as demography, family studies, and geography. In particular, Cohen and Felson argue that Hawley's concepts of the rhythm, tempo, and timing of daily movements and activities of individuals and families as they go about the business of obtaining the necessities of life — food, shelter, companionship, entertainment — are the keys to understanding rates of crime in our society. They argue that certain changes in these aspects of daily life have created the conditions for increased violent crime: more couples in which both persons work outside the home; more people living by themselves in independent households; the proliferation of outside-the-home recreational activities; the extension of shopping hours into the night; more persons eating outside the home; and so on. Cohen and Felson suggest that the effect of these social trends has been to bring together, in time and space, more suitable targets for violence and more motivated offenders; at the same time, fewer capable guardians have been present. Thus, the normal everyday activities that people engage in — working, going out for a movie, shopping at a store open late — place them at higher risk of being a victim of violent crime.

For Hindelang et al., this notion of risk is of primary concern. Certain lifestyles either require or tend to lead to increased movement of people and associated goods across time and space, thereby exposing individuals to more human contact in general and to more contact with potential offenders in particular. Why are certain lifestyles so risky? Hindelang et al. argue that at least three factors help determine the level of risk of any particular lifestyle. First, certain people occupy statuses with role expectations that are more or less risky. For example, most young single people are actively involved in dating, which raises their risk of victimization by increasing their exposure to potential offenders. Dating brings people out at night to attend parties or to go to bars and clubs; it means accepting the occasional blind date; and so on. Second, one's position in the social structure places certain limits or constraints on behavior. For example, a retail sales clerk often will be required to work in the evening, when targets, offenders, and the lack of guardians converge. Or one's race might constrain one to live in certain areas because of housing discrimination, which would make the journey to school or work riskier. Finally, individuals or groups make choices or adapt to the potential risks that role expectations and structural constraints place on them, thereby lowering or raising their risk. For example, individuals may decide not to go to bars but only to date people they meet through their church or synagogue, not to work for a retail company that stays open late, or always to be inside their homes or apartments by a certain hour. In short, lifestyle–routine activity theory suggests that violent crime rates are a consequence of the fact that people, sometimes willingly and sometimes unwillingly and unknowingly, engage in risky behavior that exposes them to the potential for violent crime. The more people engage in such risky behavior, the higher violent crime rates will be.

THE SITUATIONAL APPROACH

One of the advantages of the lifestyle–routine activity theory is that it places the source of violent crime, at least in part, in the normal activities of individuals. The situational approach to violence further develops this idea by arguing that violence results, in Luckenbill's (1977) terms, from a "situated transaction" between the victim and the offender.

Luckenbill suggests that homicides result from a specific, six-stage set of dynamic interactions. In stage 1, the victim typically makes a move, usually verbal but sometimes behavioral, that is seen by the offender as an affront to his (or her) self-esteem, authority, or overall character. Although the intent of the victim's opening move may not necessarily have been to provoke the offender, Luckenbill argues that in most cases the intent was clear. In stage 2, the offender verifies the meaning of the victim's opening action, often by consulting bystanders or observers. (Seventy percent of the cases examined in Luckenbill's study occurred in the presence of observers, strong evidence of the social nature of homicide.) The offender's initial reaction constitutes stage 3, during which the vast majority of offenders respond with a verbal challenge to the victim, typically requesting a halt in the behavior or remarks that initiated the transaction in the first place. Often, this challenge is coupled with a threat about what will happen if the victim does not comply. In stage 4, the victim continues the transaction, explicitly agreeing to the escalation of the situation toward violence by refusing to comply with the offender's request in stage 3. Thus, in stage 5, the actual violence occurs in short order. At this point, weapons may be secured from the environment or from the usual equipment carried by each participant. (Luckenbill found that in 36 percent of the cases he examined, offenders carried the weapon they used in the homicide as a part of their daily routine.) Stage 6, the final aspect of the transaction, involves the offender's actions after the crime: Does the offender flee or call the police, or is the offender restrained by the bystanders (as happened in 35 percent of Luckenbill's cases)?

Luckenbill's situational theory argues that violence is a dynamic, social, and interactional phenomenon that can be understood fully by examining the way in which the victim and the offender act and react at each stage in the interaction process, as well as by considering the role that others play in the transaction. Although this approach is not inconsistent with the lifestyle–routine activity approach discussed previously, notice how much more fine-grained it is in explaining why violence occurred. Carrying weapons is part of a risky lifestyle, as is seeking leisure with others in public settings. (Forty-two percent of the cases Luckenbill examined occurred in "public" places like bars, taverns, and street corners.) However, this theoretical approach points out that in order for the risk to be actuated, the victim must be an active social participant, play certain roles at certain times, and engage in concrete and direct action. The same is true for the offender; notice that at any time during the first four stages, either the offender or the victim could have decided to pursue another course. Clearly, in our society, people argue a lot and insult one another a great deal without ultimately resorting to violence.

Other researchers have applied this approach to national studies of homicide (Parker and Smith, 1979; Loftin and Parker, 1985; Williams and Flewelling, 1987, 1988; Parker, 1989). The theoretical arguments advanced in these studies place the prior relationship (or the lack thereof) between the victim and the offender in an intermediate position between violent outcomes and their social, economic, and cultural origins.

RESEARCH ON THE CORRELATES OF HOMICIDE

Perhaps because it is the crime with the most serious consequences, studies of homicide have dominated much of the research on violence. Further, data on homicide often are the best and most complete of all data on violent crime. Specifically, research has focused on one of several factors as a correlate to homicide: economic deprivation, subculture of violence, lifestyle–routine activities, situational factors, and victim–offender relationships.

ECONOMIC DEPRIVATION

Research on economic deprivation as a correlate of homicide has utilized two major indicators of deprivation: poverty and inequality. Poverty is defined as absolute deprivation, an absence of economic resources; inequality is defined as relative deprivation, in which one has fewer economic resources than others in society. The findings of most studies are consistent for both of these concepts although in the opposite direction. For example, in a study of the relationship between homicide rates and poverty in America's largest cities, poverty was found to be consistently and positively related to various types of homicide rates, independent of such variables as racial composition, the region in which the city was located, and population size and density (Loftin and Parker, 1985). However, with regard to inequality, Golden and Messner (1987) found that measures of inequality of various kinds had no impact on homicide rates, again independent of such variables as racial composition, region, and population density. These studies present findings that are typical of this research area (see Messner and Tardiff, 1986; Bailey, 1984; Sampson, 1987).

SUBCULTURE OF VIOLENCE

Research on the subculture of violence and homicide has also been extensive, with many studies contrasting economic deprivation explanations with those of the subculture of violence. This concept, originally advanced by Wolfgang and Ferracuti (1967), is based on the existence of a subculture in which violence is part of normative expectations governing everyday behavior. In a pioneering study, Loftin and Hill (1974) criticized earlier subculture-of-violence studies of the high rates of homicide then found in the South for ignoring the potentially important effects of poverty on homicide rates. Loftin and Hill created an index called "structural poverty," and found that when poverty was held independent, regional indicators were no longer significant correlates of the homicide rate.

These findings have been replicated a number of times with different units of analysis (Bailey, 1984; Williams, 1984), and with data from different periods (Bailey, 1984; Loftin and Parker, 1985; Williams and Flewelling, 1987). One recent study at the state level, by Huff-Corzine et al. (1986), suggested that both the subculture-of-violence and economic deprivation theories might be supportable, particularly when homicide was broken down by the race of the victim. These researchers found that poverty and regional indicators affected white homicide rates but not nonwhite rates. The most recent studies, however, do not find a great deal of evidence for the southern subculture-of-violence thesis (Williams and Flewelling, 1987; Parker, 1989). Recall, too, that the data concerning region mentioned previously in this chapter shed further doubt on this thesis by showing that the West, not the South, currently has the highest homicide rates in the United States. Thus, we must ask: Did the West become more "southern"? Did the South become less "southern"? The southern subculture-of-violence thesis may simply have been an artifact of the time when criminologists and others began to study it, and if the vast majority of the evidence is to be believed, may never have existed anyway.

With regard to a racially based subculture of violence, the picture has been less clear. Messner (1983a, 1983b) finds several important effects of the percentage of the population that is black on homicide rates, as do Bailey (1984), Huff-Corzine et al. (1986), Williams and Flewelling (1987), and Parker (1989). However, Sampson (1987) provides convincing evidence that the position of blacks in the socioeconomic structure is the root cause of homicide. Once the effects of economic deprivation and its outcomes, namely, family disruption, are properly specified, Sampson finds that racial composition, the usual indicator of the black subculture of violence, has no impact on homicide rates. In fact, Sampson finds that similar processes explain white and black violence, again undermining the existence of a unique black cultural effect. Thus, the vast majority of the empirical evidence suggests that regional and racial subcultures of violence either do not exist or, if they do, have little impact on homicide rates.

LIFESTYLE–ROUTINE ACTIVITIES

A number of researchers have studied the relationship between homicide and lifestyle–routine activities. Cohen and Felson (1979), in analyzing the United States as a whole from 1947 through 1974, derived a measure referred to as the "household activity ratio," consisting of number of households with married women in the labor force plus the number of households headed by a single adult with children, divided by the total number of households of all kinds. Cohen and Felson argued that these two types of households were most vulnerable to crime because their lifestyles either required or allowed increased absence from home, more time outside the home in labor force participation, and more leisure activities outside the home. The household activity ratio was found to be a positive correlate of the homicide rate.

Carroll and Jackson (1983) have attempted to gain additional understanding of the role of routine activities in producing violent crime. They argue that the household activity ratio, because of its differential impact on various types of individuals in the economy, produces greater economic inequality, which in turn, leads to increased rates of violence. On the one hand, routine activities of dual-income, intact households, not surprisingly, permit more out-of-home leisure, but also increase their potential exposure to violent crime. On the other hand, the difficulties of being a single parent, often with little labor force experience, cause the socioeconomic status of women heads of households to decline and consign many of their children to a life of poverty, alienation, and victimization. In an analysis of ninety-three large, nonsouthern cities, Carroll and Jackson do, indeed, find that the household activities ratio has a positive impact on economic inequality, which in turn, has a positive impact not only on homicide but on rape and assault as well. These results are interesting in light of the lack of importance most studies of homicide and economic deprivation have assigned to various indicators of inequality.

Finally, Messner and Tardiff (1985) present a fairly unique analysis of the impact of routine activities on homicide, in that they analyze individual homicides rather than rates of large aggregate units like cities or states. Using data gathered in New York City, Messner and Tardiff find support for several hypotheses derived from the routine activities theory: Males are more likely than females to be victims of homicides away from home; whites are more often victims than are persons of other races of homicides involving strangers; those who are employed are more likely to be victims farther away from home than are those who are unemployed. In each case, lifestyle–routine activities theory suggests that victims more likely had lifestyles that subjected them to greater exposure to potential homicide offenders. Thus, the routine activities approach has shown great promise empirically as an important correlate of homicide, although a great deal more research is necessary before its impact can be understood fully.

SITUATIONAL FACTORS

Recent research on the situational factors involved in homicide has produced some modifications of the correlates found through tests of the other theoretical perspectives. Studies in this vein have highlighted two themes: the importance of victim action in the events leading up to a homicide and the importance of considering the victim–offender relationship when attempting to determine the correlates of homicide rates. Luckenbill (1977) and Felson and Steadman (1983) have focused on the sequence of events that terminates in the death of one of the actors involved. In both of these studies, victim actions prior to the actual killing were important in determining the outcome. For example, Felson and Steadman found that persons in disputes who were aggressive and who used weapons were more likely to be killed than were those who did not act in this manner. Luckenbill found that most victims were unwilling to allow the offenders to "save face" in a dispute, thus making murder seem the best way for the offender to resolve the situation.

VICTIM–OFFENDER RELATIONSHIP

Results from studies of homicide rates suggest that the nature of the prior victim–offender relationship leads to the identification of different factors as important correlates of homicide rates. For example, Williams and Flewelling (1988), in a study of 168 large cities for the period 1980 through 1984, find that, although poverty and divorce rates had impacts on all the types of homicide they considered, the magnitude of those effects varied widely depending on the victim–offender relationship and the circumstances. For other factors, however, the determination of the correlates of homicide rates depended on the victim–offender relationship so that southern regional indicators were important correlates for only one type of homicide, "family other" (homicides involving family members as victim and offender, but where circumstances did not directly involve family-based conflicts or arguments). Racial composition was most important in predicting acquaintance homicide rates and less important for other types. Similarly, Parker (1989) found that southern regional indicators had no positive impact on any type of homicide, whereas poverty affects all types except those involving robbery. With regard to racial composition, the percentage of the population that is black is an important correlate of robbery and acquaintance-related homicide, but not familial homicide and those involving other crimes.

RESEARCH ON THE CORRELATES OF RAPE, ROBBERY, AND ASSAULT

Smith and Bennett (1985) published one of the few studies focusing on rape. In their study of 250 standard metropolitan statistical areas (SMSAs) for the period 1979 through 1981, they included measures of poverty, inequality, racial composition, the southern region, and family structure. They found that the most important correlates of the rape rate were poverty, percentage black, and percentage divorced, thus paralleling much of the research discussed previously on the correlates of homicide rates. Similarly, Golden and Messner (1987) found that various measures of inequality had little or no impact on rape rates in their sample of SMSAs.

Cohen and Felson (1979) examined the relationship between rape rates over time (1947–1974) and the household activity ratio, and found that the latter was an important correlate of the former. Maxfield (1987), in a study that treated rape, assault, and robbery as a single measure of personal crime, also found that several measures derived from lifestyle–routine activity theory were important correlates of violence. These included employment status, household composition (with households in which one adult lives with children being particularly likely to report victimizations), and routine leisure activities away from home. Thus, the research reviewed here on rape suggests that the important correlates of this crime parallel those for homicide.

A number of studies have examined the relationship between economic deprivation and robbery, assumed to be the most clearly economic of the four violent crimes considered here. Using data from neighborhoods in three SMSAs, Smith and Jarjoura (1988) found that poverty and residential mobility together were important correlates of robbery and assault (combined into a single category). Sampson (1987) found that per capita income had consistently negative effects on white and black robbery rates, and Carroll and Jackson (1983) found that income inequality in ninety-three nonsouthern cities was an important correlate of robbery rates. However, Golden and Messner (1987), in a broader sample of SMSAs, found that various measures of inequality were not important predictors of robbery rates, controlling for other important correlates such as racial composition and percentage divorced.

A relationship between subcultural indicators such as racial composition or the southern region and robbery rates seems nonexistent. Sampson (1987), for example, found no impact of these variables on robbery rates, and Smith and Jarjoura (1988) also failed to find an effect for percentage black or the regional indicator. The picture has been significantly brighter in terms of evidence for a relationship between lifestyle–routine activity variables and robbery, however. For example, Miethe et al. (1987) found that pursuing leisure activities outside the home one night or more per week was an important correlate of robbery and assault rates, with other important factors such as poverty and age structure controlled. In an analysis of British data, Sampson and Wooldredge (1987) also found that the number of nights spent outside the home per week was an important correlate of robbery victimizations. Both Cohen and Felson (1979) and Smith and Jarjoura (1988) found that household structure was an important correlate of robbery rates and victimizations. Thus, a great deal of support has been found for routine activities and lifestyle indicators as major correlates of robbery.

As was the case for robbery, lifestyle–routine activity measures are more successful than are subcultural measures in showing relationships with assault. Cohen and Felson (1979) and Smith and Jarjoura (1988) once again found important effects for household structure as a correlate of this type of violence. Both Miethe et al. (1987) and Maxfield (1987) found that pursuit of leisure activities outside the home is an important correlate of measures of violence that include assault.

To summarize, what do we know about the correlates of rape, robbery, and assault? Although the empirical evidence on the correlates of these crimes of violence is neither as extensive nor as definitive as that concerning homicide, the conclusions to be drawn from the research reviewed here are very similar. Economic deprivation, perhaps both inequality and poverty (rather than just the latter, as is the case with homicide), seem to be the most consistent correlates. However, even more so than for homicide, routine activities–lifestyle measures are strong and consistent correlates of these types of violence and, over time, may prove to be more important than deprivation-related measures. The case against subcultures as a correlate, although not as extensive as it was for homicide, is equally negative.

A RESEARCH AGENDA FOR VIOLENT CRIME

It would be easy to conclude from what has been presented in this chapter that the empirical knowledge base for homicide, although not perfect, is substantially more extensive than that for the other three violent crimes discussed here. Why have there been so few studies of nonlethal violence? First, homicide has a kind of mystique about it, which attracts both scholarly and public attention. It is the most final of crimes in its consequences and is therefore perceived as the most serious crime; yet the data presented at the beginning of this chapter suggest that the other three crimes are much more important in their numerical impact on society. Perhaps because of this mystique, studies of homicide have been stimulated by the availability of substantially better data than those available for nonhomicidal violence. We are not able to analyze victim–offender relationships for cities, SMSAs, and states for the crimes of robbery, assault, and rape. We have not had the kind of detailed data on weapon or circumstance. We also have not asked for better data on these other crimes, perhaps because, in the case of rape, most criminologists are male and most rape victims are female, or because, in the case of assault, we have assumed that assaults are just uncompleted homicides. Whatever the reason, more and better data and research quite likely will reveal substantial differences between the correlates of homicide and the correlates of rape, robbery, and assault.

Violence within the family was, until recently, a seeming contradiction in terms; after all, the family is supposed to be a haven of love and concern in a world of strife and turmoil. However, in recent decades, the pioneering research of Straus and Gelles (1986), Steinmetz and Straus (1974), Dutton and Browning (1984), and Browne (1987) has revealed the family to be one of our most violent institutions. Although researchers favoring the situational approach have begun to study family relationships, among others, in the context of homicide, additional research on the correlates of violence of all types is needed; the family may be an arena where intervention to prevent violence has some chance of success, but our knowledge base first must be substantially increased.

We must also examine the level of analysis at which research on violent crime is conducted. We read about studies done with individual cases, neighborhoods, central cities, SMSAs, states, and the United States as a whole, and a detailed examination of the findings from some of these studies shows that data from different levels of aggregation yield different evidence concerning the correlates of homicide. For example, in one study that specifically examined this problem (Parker, 1985), contradictions were found between the state and county levels of analysis concerning the impact of racial composition and poverty on homicide rates, two of the major areas of focus in the research literature. Do anomalies like this exist simply because of counting and aggregation procedures, or are they due to some more fundamental feature of the way individuals react in different contexts?

The research by Sampson and Wooldredge (1987) cited previously provides an example of the potential for multilevel analysis that exists in the study of crime in general and violence in particular. In addition to studying the likelihood of victimization as determined by individual lifestyle–routine activity measures such as marital status and nights spent outside the home per week, Sampson and Wooldredge were able to examine simultaneously the impact of the neighborhood context in which respondents lived: Percentage of family disruption in the geographic area around the respondent's residence, level of street activity, and degree of social cohesion extant in the area all had independent effects on victimization. We might ask as well: What is the impact on victimization if one is richer or poorer than is typical for a given neighborhood? What would homicide rates be like in a city that almost never hands out a death penalty in a state that uses such punishment frequently? These and many other interesting hypotheses and relationships await discovery if we can concentrate our efforts in obtaining multilevel data and constructing multilevel theories.

A recent paper by Land et al. (1990) suggests an additional direction for research that may prove to be very important in gaining increased understanding of the causes of violence. Land et al. examine the large body of research reviewed previously with regard to homicide and point out that a number of inconsistencies exist across studies about the factors considered to be the most important or even significant predictors of homicide. In addition to problems of inconsistent measurement of indicators and the use of different levels of aggregation (for example, cities, metropolitan areas, or states) across studies, Land et al. argue that a major unresolved issue is whether or not findings in the homicide literature are period specific. That is, is the reason that one study concludes that variable x predicts homicide and another study concludes that variable x does not predict homicide to be found in the fact that the first study used 1960 data and the second used 1980 data? More generally, Land et al. pose the question of structural change or stability in the causes of homicide over time, and after examining data for 1950, 1960, 1970, and 1980, they find that resource deprivation, population density and size, and family structure are consistent predictors of homicide in each of the four decades they examine. Studies like this clearly expand the scope of research on violent crime.

CONCLUSION

Although following the recommendations made thus far may require direct action from scholars and citizens, a final recommendation may occur eventually because of the regular progress of scientific knowledge. Many of the studies cited here in the deprivation and subculture areas were specifically designed to compare these two theories. However, with the development of two new perspectives, the lifestyle or routine activity approach and the situational approach, as well as renewed interest in deterrence theory, a number of studies exist side by side in the literature that do not attempt to compare these perspectives simultaneously. Yet, some of the most interesting results come from studies that attempt to bring together disparate perspectives for comparison; for example, Sampson's (1987) attempt to examine subculture, deprivation, and routine–lifestyle activities; Carroll and Jackson's (1983) study of inequality and routine–lifestyle activities; Parker's (1989) examination of deprivation and subculture in the context of a situational approach; Land and associates' (1990) study of structural stability and change across four decades. Bringing additional theoretical perspectives into the research makes it more complicated and difficult, but these examples suggest that the benefits outweigh the costs. This is not to say that better studies within these perspectives or some new ones that may develop are not valuable, but simply to urge more research in which explanations and measures successful in previous research be brought face to face in a single model of the correlates of violent crime; increased knowledge surely will result from such studies.

DISCUSSION QUESTIONS

1. Discuss recent trends in violent crime in terms of the sources of data indicating those trends. Do UCR and NCVS figures differ regarding the pictures they show over time? If so, regarding what specific types of violent crime? Why?

2. We hear much about firearms and crime in this country. In what percent of homicides are firearms used? How about in other forms of violent crime? What are the implications of these findings for anticrime policy?

3. Describe the lifestyle and routine activities approaches to the explanation of crime. What kinds of activities seem associated with violent victimization? In what ways is this issue related to the discussion of victim precipitation in Chapter 6?

4. Having read the chapter, what factors seem most linked to homicide in this country? Poverty? Economic inequality? Population characteristics? Or is homicide simply governed by situational factors that are impossible to measure?

CHAPTER 8

THE DISTRIBUTION AND DYNAMICS OF PROPERTY CRIME

Robert J. Bursik, Jr.
University of Oklahoma

ONE OF the most deceptively simple concepts in criminology is that of property crime. Although there are differences of opinion concerning the particular illegal behaviors that should constitute such crimes, most widely accepted images of property crime are consistent with that of Hepburn (1984: 73): "any criminal behavior by which property is damaged or by which possession of property is transferred."

With the development of capitalist market societies in the eighteenth century, the concept of property generally has become equated with guaranteed, legal assurances that an individual can exclude others from the use or benefit of some material resource (MacPherson, 1978: 9–10). As a result, the kinds of illegal behaviors that are most immediately identified as being property crimes represent transgressions against private property. Thus, a motor vehicle theft involves the illicit use of a means of transportation by someone to whom full access rights to that vehicle have not been granted.

In this chapter, we seek a better sense of the notion of property crime through examination of a number of issues. Of major importance is the definition of property crime. We begin with Part I UCR offenses and then focus on a crime that only recently has joined the list of major offenses—arson. Next, we examine a number of lesser property crimes and explore recent trends in property crime. Finally, two themes that merit much criminological attention are reviewed: (1) the relationship of unemployment to property crime and (2) the extent to which property crime rates reflect the opportunities for crime provided by potential victims.

The classification of particular behaviors as property crime is not a completely straightforward process. Consider, for example, the crime of robbery. Robbery is defined in the *Uniform Crime Reports* (UCR) as "the taking or attempting to take anything of value from the care, custody, or control of a person or persons by force or threat of force or violence and/or by putting the victim in fear" (FBI, 1992: 383). Although such a definition makes it clear that robberies involve the violation of property rights, such behaviors are classified as personal rather than property crimes by the UCR because of the nature of the interaction between the offender and the victim. However, Hepburn (1984) convincingly argues that robbery is primarily a property offense because of the illegal transfer of a material resource from the victim to the offender. The decision to categorize robbery as a property crime might therefore affect the conclusions that can be drawn concerning the distribution and causes of property crime overall. Considerable attention should be given to the offenses that are included in overall indices of property crime before unwarranted comparisons among various studies are made.

UCR PART I OFFENSES

The index of property crime provided by the UCR is computed on the basis of four different offenses (FBI, 1992: 383):

> **Burglary — breaking or entering.** The unlawful entry of a structure to commit a felony or theft. Attempted forcible entry is included.
>
> **Larceny-theft (except motor vehicle theft).** The unlawful taking, carrying, leading or riding away of property from the possession or constructive possession of another. Examples are thefts of bicycles or automobile accessories, shoplifting, pocket-picking or the stealing of any property or article which is not taken by force and violence or by fraud. Attempted larcenies are included. Embezzlement, "con" games, forgery, worthless checks, etc. are excluded.
>
> **Motor vehicle theft.** The theft or attempted theft of a motor vehicle. A motor vehicle is self-propelled and runs on the surface and not on rails. Specifically excluded from this category are motorboats, construction equipment, airplanes, and farming equipment.
>
> **Arson.** Any willful or malicious burning or attempt to burn with or without intent to defraud, a dwelling house, public building, motor vehicle or aircraft, personal property of another, etc.

Most studies of property crime focus only on these Part I offenses. Although these classifications are very general, much greater detail is available from the UCR concerning the rates of particular crimes within each category. For example, the larceny–theft rates can be further broken down in terms of purse snatching, pickpocketing, shoplifting, theft from motor vehicles, bicycle theft, theft from buildings, theft from coin-operated machines, and other miscellaneous thefts.

Although the UCR statistics for Part I offenses are the most common source of data used in the study of property crime, they still are somewhat problematic in that information is available only for those crimes that come to the attention of the police (see Chapter 3). We must recognize that a large percentage of property crimes never are reported to the police and, therefore, are not reflected in these data; the most recent estimates indicate that although 74 percent of motor vehicle thefts came to the attention of law enforcement agencies in 1991, the proportion was much lower for other property offenses: robbery, 55 percent; larceny with contact, 38 percent; larceny without contact, 28 percent; household burglary, 50 percent; household larceny, 28 percent (Bureau of Justice Statistics, 1992b: 8).

THE SPECIAL CASE OF ARSON

Crimes of arson have a unique history as UCR Part I offenses. Although arson for economic profit always has been considered an extremely serious offense, the designers of the initial reporting system believed that relevant statistics could not be gathered in "a uniform manner" because the crime is so frequently and easily concealed (International Association of Chiefs of Police, 1929: 180). Therefore, arson originally was classified as a Class 21 (all other offenses) crime, along with such activities as criminal anarchism and the desecration of graves. However, the number of arsons reported to the National Fire Protection Association increased by over *3,100 percent* between 1951 and 1977, and the Law Enforcement Assistance Administration estimated that arson losses accounted for almost 40 percent of all total fire damages in 1977 (reported in Brady, 1983). As a result, in October 1978, arson was reclassified as a Part I offense by congressional mandate. This has been the only significant revision of the UCR classification system in its sixty-year history.

However, an interpretation of the UCR arson statistics is somewhat problematic. For example, although 11,706 law enforcement agencies reported such offenses during 1991, only 8,963 of them (representing 71 percent of the U.S. population) submitted reports for all twelve months of the year (FBI, 1992: 54); this is far below the population coverage for the other Index offenses. Jackson (1988) has presented evidence suggesting that the volume of 1985 arson figures represented only 59 percent of the reported arsons in the United States, and that the rate per 100,000 persons reported in the UCR may be less than half the actual rate. Thus, the validity and reliability of the arson figures are highly questionable.

In part, this may be due to confusion concerning reporting responsibilities. Battle and Weston (1978), for example, note that many police officials believe arson is the primary responsibility of fire departments, whereas many fire departments believe the responsibility lies with the police departments. In addition to such state and local agencies, at least eleven federal agencies, ranging from the FBI to the U.S. Department of Forestry, also have programs geared toward detecting and investigating arson (Incove et al., 1979: 5). Thus, unlike the other property crime recorded in the UCR, arson typically does not fall solely within a police jurisdiction (Jackson, 1988: 183). Although the UCR has attempted to create liaisons with the law enforcement, fire service, and insurance communities to upgrade the quality of reporting practices (FBI, 1980), the collection of accurate data involves a complicated coordination of the efforts of various agencies, not only public and private but also local and national.

The arson statistics differ from those of the rest of the Part I offenses in two other important ways. A fire is recorded as arson only after an investigation has determined it to have been "willfully or maliciously set"; fires of "suspicious or unknown origin are excluded" (FBI, 1992: 53). As Jackson (1988: 123) notes, the reports of the other offense types need not be substantiated by an investigation before being reflected in the crime rate. In addition, *all* reported cases of arson are reflected in the UCR statistics. This differs from the hierarchical rule that applies to all the other Index crimes; that is, when a series of offenses occurs within a single incident, only the most serious of those crimes is reflected in the UCR. For these reasons, extreme caution must be used when evaluating trends over time in the extent of arson and when comparing such trends with those characterizing the other Index property offenses.

UCR Part II Offenses

Property crime also may be studied in terms of the following Part II offenses reported by the UCR (FBI, 1992: 383):

Forgery and counterfeiting: Making, altering, uttering, or possessing with intent to defraud, anything false in the semblance of that which is true. Attempts are included.

Fraud: Fraudulent conversion and obtaining money or property by false pretenses. Included are confidence games and bad checks, except forgeries and counterfeiting.

Embezzlement: Misappropriation or misapplication of money or property entrusted to one's care, custody or control.

Stolen property; buying, receiving, possessing: Buying, receiving and possessing stolen property, including attempts.

Vandalism: Willful or malicious destruction, injury, disfigurement, or defacement of any public or private property, real or personal, without consent of the owner or persons having custody or control.

Although the UCR contains data pertaining to the number of crimes reported to the police, as well as to the percentage of these crimes that have been cleared through an arrest, for Part I offenses, only arrest statistics are available for Part II offenses. Many researchers believe that the gatekeeping processes of the criminal justice system make such arrest data fairly unrepresentative of the overall patterns of property crime. For example, in 1991, only 17.8 percent of all property crime reported to the police were cleared by an arrest; the offense-specific clearance rates range from a low of 13.5 percent for burglary, to 13.9 percent for motor vehicle theft, to a high of 20.3 percent for larceny-theft; similarly, only 24.3 percent of all reported robberies are cleared by an arrest (FBI, 1992: 204). Therefore, the data pertaining to Part II offenses rarely are analyzed.

CURRENT TRENDS IN PROPERTY CRIME IN THE UNITED STATES

Table 8.1 lists the UCR estimates of recent patterns of Part I property crimes reported to the police in the United States. We can note several trends in these data. For example, the rates tended to increase until the mid-1970s, when they stabilized somewhat. However, they again began to increase, reaching a peak in 1980, followed by several years of general decline. Modest increases in the rates of all offenses except burglary have been apparent since 1984.

The various alternative sources of crime data sometimes provide very different pictures of the existing patterns of criminal behavior. This is apparent when we compare Table 8.1 with Table 8.2, which lists the trends in property crime between 1973 and 1991 as reflected in the data collected by the National Crime Victimization Survey (NCVS). According to the NCVS report, there has been a general decline since 1973 in the rate of each of the six reported property crimes. However, as O'Brien (1985: 82–87) has noted, extreme caution must be used in making direct comparisons between the rates provided by the UCR and the NCVS. First, the different definitions of property crime used by the two sources of data make such comparisons problematic. In addition, as Biderman et al. (1991) have pointed out, many of the activities reflected in the UCR rate are not used in the creation of the NCVS rate (and vice versa). For example, whereas the UCR rates include commercial crime, the NCVS rates do not. This has an especially large effect on estimates of property crimes such as larceny. In addition, different population estimates are used in the computation of the crime rates. Biderman et al. show that the estimates used by the UCR tend to result in increasingly inflated estimates in the years directly preceding the collection of updated U.S. Census Bureau population estimates. In general, Biderman et al. conclude that we need to know much more concerning the behavior of these components over time before a valid comparison of such trends can be made.

Finally, generalizations concerning overall trends in property crime should be made with extreme caution given the important changes in the age structure that have characterized the United States (Steffensmeier and Harer, 1991; see Chapter 4). Note that the rates in Table 8.1 are calculated on the basis of the entire U.S. population, whereas those in Table 8.2 are calculated on the basis of residents age 12 and older. One of the few well-established facts of criminology concerns the important differences that exist in the age-specific rates of crime: After a peak in mid adolescence to late adolescence, crime rates tend to decline with age (see Hirschi and Gottfredson, 1983). If the relative size of a high-risk age grouping increases over time, the crime rate would reflect this demographic shift in an increased rate of illegal behavior. However, such increases would not necessarily reflect an increase in the rate of criminal activity within any particular age group (see Sagi and Wellford, 1968; Chilton and Spielberger, 1971; Steffensmeier and Harer, 1991). Rather, it might imply simply

TABLE 8.1 UCR ESTIMATED RATE OF PART I PROPERTY OFFENSES KNOWN TO POLICE, 1960–1991*

Year	Property Crime				Total
	Robbery	*Burglary*	*Larceny-Theft*	*Motor Vehicle Theft*	
1960	60.1	508.6	1,034.7	183.0	1,726.3
1961	58.3	518.9	1,045.4	183.6	1,747.9
1962	59.7	535.2	1,124.8	197.4	1,857.5
1963	61.8	576.4	1,219.1	216.6	2,012.1
1964	68.2	634.7	1,315.5	247.4	2,197.5
1965	71.7	662.7	1,329.3	256.8	2,248.8
1966	80.8	721.0	1,442.9	286.9	2,450.9
1967	102.8	826.6	1,575.8	334.1	2,736.5
1968	131.8	932.3	1,746.6	393.0	3,071.8
1969	148.4	984.1	1,930.9	436.2	3,351.3
1970	172.1	1,084.9	2,079.3	456.8	3,621.0
1971	188.0	1,163.5	2,145.5	459.8	3,768.8
1972	180.7	1,140.8	1,993.6	426.1	3,560.4
1973	183.1	1,222.5	2,071.9	442.6	3,737.0
1974	209.3	1,437.7	2,489.5	462.2	4,389.3
1975	218.2	1,525.9	2,804.8	469.4	4,800.2
1976	199.3	1,448.2	2,921.3	450.0	4,819.5
1977	190.7	1,419.8	2,729.9	451.9	4,601.7
1978	195.8	1,434.6	2,747.4	460.5	4,642.5
1979	218.4	1,511.9	2,999.1	505.6	5,016.6
1980	251.1	1,684.1	3,167.0	502.2	5,353.3
1981	258.7	1,649.5	3,139.7	474.4	5,263.9
1982	238.9	1,488.8	3,084.8	458.8	5,032.5
1983	216.5	1,337.7	2,868.9	430.8	4,637.4
1984	205.4	1,263.7	2,791.3	437.1	4,492.1
1985	208.5	1,287.3	2,901.2	462.0	4,650.5
1986	225.1	1,344.6	3,010.3	507.8	4,862.7
1987	212.7	1,329.6	3,081.3	529.4	4,940.3
1988	220.9	1,309.2	3,134.9	582.9	5,027.1
1989	233.0	1,276.3	3,171.3	630.4	5,077.9
1990	257.0	1,235.9	3,194.8	657.8	5,088.5
1991	272.7	1,252.0	3,228.8	659.0	5,139.7

SOURCE: Data for 1960–1990 drawn from Flanagan and Maguire (1992: 372); data for 1991 based on estimates for each particular offense by the Federal Bureau of Investigation (1992).

*The overall property crime rate reflects the sum of the robbery, burglary, larceny–theft, and motor vehicle theft rates. Because data concerning arson were collected for the first time in 1979, those rates are not reflected in this table. Rates per 100,000 U.S. inhabitants.

TABLE 8.2 **NCVS ESTIMATED RATES OF PROPERTY VICTIMIZATIONS, 1973–1991***

Year	Robbery	Personal Larceny (Contact)	Personal Larceny (No Contact)	Crimes of Theft	Household Burglary	Household Larceny	Motor Vehicle Theft
1973	6.7	3.1	88.0	91.1	91.7	107.0	19.1
1974	7.2	3.1	92.0	95.1	93.1	123.8	18.8
1975	6.8	3.1	92.9	96.0	91.7	125.4	19.5
1976	6.5	2.9	93.2	96.1	88.9	124.1	16.5
1977	6.2	2.7	94.6	97.3	88.5	123.3	17.0
1978	5.9	3.1	93.6	96.8	86.0	119.9	17.5
1979	6.3	2.9	89.0	91.9	84.1	133.7	17.5
1980	6.6	3.0	80.0	83.0	84.3	126.5	16.7
1981	7.4	3.3	81.9	85.1	87.9	121.0	17.1
1982	7.1	3.1	79.5	82.5	78.2	113.9	16.2
1983	6.0	3.0	74.0	76.9	70.0	105.2	14.6
1984	5.7	2.8	69.1	71.8	64.1	99.4	15.2
1985	5.1	2.7	66.7	69.4	62.7	97.5	14.2
1986	5.1	2.7	64.7	67.5	61.5	93.5	15.0
1987	5.3	2.6	66.1	68.7	62.1	95.7	16.0
1988	5.3	2.5	68.0	70.5	61.9	90.2	17.5
1989	5.4	2.7	66.0	68.7	56.4	94.4	19.2
1990	5.7	3.1	60.7	63.8	53.8	86.7	20.5
1991	5.6	2.3	58.7	61.0	53.1	88.0	21.8

SOURCE: Adapted from Bureau of Justice Statistics (1992b: 6).

*See note on the overall property crime rate under Table 8.1.

that an increasingly greater proportion of the age groups in the population is most likely to be involved in criminal behavior.

Overall, although it is relatively easy to account for the differences in the UCR and NCVS profiles over time, it remains extremely difficult to provide a definitive presentation of the *actual* trends in property crime (see Blumstein et al., 1991; McDowall and Loftin, 1992; Menard, 1992).

UNEMPLOYMENT AND PROPERTY CRIME

Given the different assumptions that underlie the many causal theories of criminal behavior (see Part Four), a wide variety of factors have been examined in relation to the distribution of property crime. However, whether these theories assume that society generally is characterized by processes of cooperation and consensus or by processes of conflict and diversity, nearly all the dominant frameworks predict that a strong positive relationship should exist between rates of unemployment and property crime (see Bursik and Grasmick, 1993; Cantor and Land, 1985; Devine et al., 1988; Hughes and Carter, 1981; Long and Witte, 1981; Thornberry and Christenson, 1984; Wilson, 1987).

Given this relative consensus concerning the expected form of the relationship, one would assume that the empirical relationship would be fairly strong, regardless of its interpretation. Surprisingly, three extensive reviews of existing research (Gillespie, 1978; Freeman, 1983; Long and Witte, 1981) fail to find consistent results. Some studies present evidence of the expected relationship; some fail to document any such association; and some even find a *negative* association between unemployment and property crime rates (see Cantor and Land, 1985: 217). There are several possible explanations for the prevalence of such contradictory evidence. Wilson and Herrnstein (1985: 315) note that *both* crime and unemployment may represent outcomes of some third common cause. If the effects of this common cause were taken into account, then the association between crime and unemployment should disappear. That is, despite all the predictions to the contrary, there may not actually be a relationship between these two rates. On the other hand, Devine et al. (1988) provide evidence that the failure to specify fully the processes related to property crime (such as the distribution of opportunities) may actually *suppress* the relationship between unemployment and property crime. In particular, specification issues can have a great effect on the conclusions that are drawn from time-series analyses (see the exchange between Hale and Sabbagh, 1991, and Cantor and Land, 1991).

In addition, Chiricos (1987) argues that the different levels of aggregation used in these studies may account for some of the inconsistencies. He notes that studies using statistics for the nation as a whole generally have produced results less consistent with the hypothesized unemployment–crime-rate association than have studies that have analyzed data at lower levels of aggregation, such as the state, county, standard metropolitan statistical area (SMSA), or census tract. He argues that the results from these lower levels of aggregation may in fact be the most valid because smaller aggregates tend to have much more homogenous compositions. Analyses at this level also may provide a better sense of the noneconomic aspects of unemployment that can filter through a community (such as widespread demoralization) and that may be related to crime.

Finally, a growing body of research suggests that the effects of unemployment on crime are conditional on certain social contexts. Allan and Steffensmeier (1989) present evidence that this relationship varies by age, the type of property crime, and the way in which unemployment has been measured. For example, although unemployment is related to the rates of property crime committed by juveniles age 14–17, this is not the case for crimes committed by those age 18–24. Likewise, LaFree et al. (1992) conclude that unemployment is related to white but not black rates of property crime.

Such considerations have two basic implications. First, many criminologists may have rejected prematurely the unemployment–crime hypothesis. Second, if it in fact exists, the relationship is much more complex than has been generally recognized. This complexity is well illustrated in the paper of Cantor and Land (1985), who argue that although rises in the unemployment rate may increase the criminal motivation of potential property offenders, such increases in unemployment may influence property crime rates negatively; that is, the higher the unemployment rate, the lower the rate of property crime. This counterintuitive prediction reflects two different processes. First, as some individuals are removed from employment outside the home, there may be a greater concentration of activities in or near the home. This increased ability to guard one's property may decrease the number of situations in which the successful commission of a property offense may occur. Second, higher unemployment reflects a general slowdown in production and consumption activities for all persons. Therefore, property circulates at a lower rate, which also decreases the opportunity for property crime.

CRIMINAL OPPORTUNITIES AND PROPERTY CRIME

As noted in Chapter 7, theories of criminal opportunities emphasize the processes by which potential victims and offenders converge in space and time (see Gottfredson, 1981: 715). Such orientations have a long history in criminology. In fact, Shaw (1929), who had a major impact on the development of one of the most traditional offender-based theories in American criminology (social disorganization), also noted that a prominent feature of areas with high delinquency rates was the presence of large amounts of commercial or industrial property, which provided the opportunities for property crime. Three decades later, Morris (1957: 20–21) argued that it was necessary to differentiate between the background characteristics that may predispose an individual to crime and the situations in which these potentialities become actualized.

More recently, Boggs (1965) examined the question of why potential targets of crime were exploited more in certain areas than others. She concluded that targets differ in kind and amount over space, and that the selection of a target reflected the familiarity that existed between offenders and their targets and the potential profitability of the criminal act. Several years later, Gould (1969) took a similar position, noting that in addition to the value of certain property and the ease with which it can be stolen, the abundance of particular targets was related to variation in rates of property crime.

In the late 1970s, two more developed theoretical approaches to criminal opportunity appeared nearly simultaneously. Two reasons may be suggested for the appearance of these models. The first was the publication of two books that strongly influenced the development of the opportunity perspective. The first, *Defensible Space*, by Oscar Newman (1972), was ostensibly concerned with architectural design. However, Newman's primary emphasis was on "the real and symbolic barriers, strongly defined areas of influence and improved opportunities for surveillance . . . that combine to bring an environment under the control of its residents" (p. 3). That is, Newman's thesis is grounded in the assumption that particular designs could decrease the opportunity for criminal victimization. Similarly, *Residential Crime*, by Thomas Reppetto (1974), emphasized the relationships among the ease of access, the degree of local surveillance, and rates of property crime. In addition, through his consideration of an enormous body of data, Reppetto stressed the importance of physical design, the visibility of potential crime sites, and the travel and work patterns of potential victims.

The second likely reason for the historical timing of opportunity theories was the increasing attention being paid to the development of victimization research (see Chapter 6). As Gould (1969: 50) argued, an understanding of the role of victims in the etiology of property crime is essential to the development of an opportunity theory because victims are the actual targets of crime. Unfortunately, as he noted, such studies were only sporadically conducted prior to the publication of his research.

The growing emphasis on victimization research culminated in the publication of *Victims of Personal Crime*, by Hindelang et al. (1978), which presented a theory of victimization called the lifestyle model. This model assumes that the manner in which individuals allocate their time to vocational and leisure activities is related to the probability of being in a particular place at a particular time. These lifestyle differences are associated with differential exposure to situations in which a person (or that person's property) has a high risk of victimization (Gottfredson, 1981: 720; Hindelang et al., 1978; Garofalo, 1987). Such differences are assumed to be determined by individual and group adaptations to structural constraints and role expectations reflected in the demographic characteristics of potential victims (Hindelang et al., 1978: 243; Garofalo, 1987: 26). In turn, lifestyle differences affect one's exposure to the risks of victimization inherent in particular places and times, as well as one's potential association with others who are more or less likely to commit crime. Victimization is assumed to reflect the direct effects of such exposure and association.

As Parker pointed out in Chapter 7, a very similar perspective called the routine activities approach was presented by Cohen and Felson (1979). In addition to assuming that crime represents a convergence in time and space of motivated offenders and suitable targets, Cohen and Felson introduced the central dimension of the guardianship (that is, surveillance and protection) of persons and property by fellow citizens as they go about their routine activities. In a later paper, Cohen et al. (1981) provided more detail concerning the dynamics that underlie the convergence of potential victims and offenders, incorporating the dimensions of exposure (the physical visibility and accessibility of persons or objects to potential offenders at any given time or space), proximity (the physical distance between areas where potential targets of crime reside and areas where relatively large populations of potential offenders are found), and target attractiveness (the material or symbolic desirability of personal or property targets, the physical size of those targets, and the ease of transportability) into their model.

The widespread interest in these two models is not solely a reflection of the desire for theoretical refinement. Rather, the lifestyle and routine activities models make certain predictions concerning victimization that have important implications for the development and implementation of crime control policies. In the broadest sense, Garofalo (1987: 40) notes that any social policy that affects the routine activities of a population may be reflected in changes in the distribution of criminal opportunities. However, the opportunity model also suggests much more immediate strategies for the control of property crime, such as reducing the physical opportunities of offending or increasing the chances that an offender will be caught. Both Newman and Reppetto, for example, noted that apartment buildings provided with doormen were less vulnerable to burglary.

A voluminous body of research focusing on the role of the guardianship factor has been produced by Cohen, Felson, and their colleagues using the UCR statistics (see Cohen et al., 1980; Felson and Cohen, 1980; and Cohen, 1981; Cantor and Land, 1985, is also related). A particularly interesting question that has been raised in this research concerns the relative abilities of the guardianship factor and the unemployment rate to explain recent trends in property crime. Although a large body of evidence has been presented in support of the routine activities perspective (for related analyses, see also Lynch and Cantor, 1992; Sampson, 1985a; Smith and Jarjoura, 1988), some studies have concluded that the relationship with property crime is fairly weak. Unfortunately, the inability to measure more directly the central dynamics of the model, and the general failure to separate individual and contextual effects, makes such a conclusion only tentative. Nevertheless, the perspective is an extremely promising one that should continue to generate exciting future research as more detailed data become available.

CRIMINAL OPPORTUNITIES AND POTENTIAL PROPERTY OFFENDERS

Just as potential victims of property crimes are characterized by lifestyles and routine activities that determine their movement in space and time, potential offenders also exhibit differential patterns of behavior that affect the number of criminal opportunities with which they come in contact. Criminology has a long tradition of research that has described the background characteristics of property offenders (see, for example, Shover, 1973; Pope, 1980) as well as the relationship between police operations and the geographic distribution of such activity (see McIver, 1981). More recently, a great deal of attention has focused on the decision-making processes that lead to the commission of an illegal act (see Bennett and Wright, 1984; Brantingham and Brantingham, 1984; Cromwell et al., 1991; Cornish and Clarke, 1986; Rengert and Wasilchick, 1985; Rengert, 1989).

Unfortunately, there are no large data sets comparable to the UCR and NCVS that easily facilitate such studies; likewise, self-reports based on large samples of respondents have yet to be widely used for the study of adult criminal motivation. However, a group of studies has used alternative forms of data collection to provide some insight into these decision-making processes (see Bennett and Wright, 1984; Carter, 1974; Cornish and Clarke, 1986; Cromwell et al., 1991; Rengert and Wasilchick, 1985; Tunnell, 1992). Because they generally have been limited to the study of relatively small samples of property offenders (particularly burglars), the representativeness of the ensuing findings is not entirely clear. Nevertheless, these studies suggest that the dynamics that shape the convergence of potential offenders and victims in space and time also are strongly influenced by the lifestyles and routine activities of those offenders.

This is most apparent in the processes that have been described concerning the selection of a geographic area in which to commit a property offense. Carter (1974: 126) notes that potential offenders have only a vague environmental image of the entire geographic space available for victimization. Likewise, Rengert and Wasilchick (1985: 72) argue that property offenders "are not aware of all the area around them and do not give equal consideration to all of the area they are aware of." Rather, they select potential areas of victimization on the basis of information they have gathered primarily through their noncrime-related recreational and work travel patterns (although this information may be supplemented by information supplied by other offenders). That is, such decisions are made, to a large extent, on the basis of observations made in the course of their routine activities.

Once the general target area has been determined, the particular household to be victimized must be chosen. The findings of Bennett and Wright (1984: 194–196) indicate that two primary factors underlie this decision. The first, which they call "surveillability," reflects the likelihood that the offender will be detected by others in the area. For example, offenders often prefer to victimize households located on the corners of an intersection, because the potential number of neighbors that may observe an illegal entry is minimized (Rengert and Wasilchick, 1985: 84). In addition, such considerations as the degree of cover provided by the target and the ease of access to that cover also shape the possibility of being observed.

The second factor, noted in most studies, concerns the occupancy of the household. Over 90 percent of the offenders interviewed by Bennett and Wright (1984: 196) indicate that they would never attempt a burglary in a house that they suspected was occupied. Therefore, property offenders may use a series of cues to determine the occupancy status of the targeted household, such as the presence of uncollected mail and newspapers, the absence of lights, and so forth. Some of these techniques are fairly ingenious, such as noting funeral announcements or an air conditioner that is turned off on a very hot day (Rengert and Wasilchick, 1985: 81).

However, Rengert and Wasilchick also note that potential offenders attempt to maximize the probability of a successful burglary by restricting their activities to those times in which the vacancy of a household is most likely. Sometimes, the probability of a vacancy can be manipulated by the potential burglar. For example, a technique that reportedly has been used in Chicago to ensure that a household is vacant is to provide the victim with tickets to a sold-out athletic event with a note attached, apparently signed by a good friend of the victim, indicating that the owner of the tickets has to go out of town and could not use them. The potential offender can then be fairly sure that the household will be unoccupied for the course of that event. Such an approach obviously necessitates a degree of research by the potential offender concerning the tastes and personal networks of the victim. Yet, this technique and other variants of it apparently have been very successful.

Nonetheless, the primary determinant of the likelihood of a successful burglary is the behavior of the residents themselves. Rengert and Wasilchick present evidence that when the typical routine of a resident, such as that of the traditional housewife, necessitates extended periods of activity in or near the household, the periods of vacancy are very unpredictable and sporadic. On the other hand, households in which all the members have schedules that necessitate long periods of absence (for example, through employment or school) have large predictable periods of vacancy. According to Rengert and Wasilchick (pp. 21–24), these are the targets preferred by successful burglars. Other factors related to the selection of targets are also noted in these studies, such as the expected profitability of the theft, familiarity with the area, and the presence of alarm systems (see Carter, 1974: 133).

Property crime has very immediate and costly consequences for our society; the FBI has estimated that the economic costs of property crime during 1991 were $16.1 billion (FBI, 1992). The risks of such victimization are very widespread: 11 percent of the households in the United States were affected by personal theft and 7.5 percent by household theft during 1990 (Flanagan and Maguire, 1992: 294). Therefore, property crime is an issue in which all citizens have a vested interest.

However, the societal processes reflected in property crime are extremely complex, and the control of such behavior is very difficult, for several reasons. For one thing, there is nothing inherently "natural" in the laws that define property crime. For example, Michalowski (1985) has argued that the development of property rights in the nineteenth-century United States reflected the view that thefts and burglaries represented "attacks upon the very basis of the emerging capitalist order" (p. 108). Therefore, the definition of property crime itself is subject to an ongoing process of reevaluation and development. In addition, the general public often assumes that criminologists know much more than we actually do concerning the causes of such crime. The most central limitation of the current state of knowledge is that all the sources of data that are used to examine the distribution and causes of property crime so that social control programs can be developed suffer from certain deficiencies. Therefore, programs that have been developed have had to assume that these deficiencies are not serious enough to result in a misunderstanding of the phenomenon.

This chapter has attempted to introduce the reader to the basic definitional, data-related, and theoretical issues involved in the study of property crime. The emphasis on the *basic* has been intentional, for the goal here has been to provide the reader with a sufficient familiarity with the issues involved in property crime so as to make informed evaluations of the sometimes contradictory conclusions and proposals concerning the control of property crime that appear in the popular and professional literature.

DISCUSSION QUESTIONS

1. What crimes traditionally have been counted as Index property crimes? What do these offenses have in common? Arson now is on the list of such crimes, but we rarely see statistics about arson. Why?

2. As with violent crime trends, trends in property crime are calculated using both UCR and NCVS data. Do the same pictures emerge when we examine these data?

3. Bursik discusses criminal opportunities as they relate to property crime. Review the core of this discussion, and identify the key elements of opportunity. How do property offenders select their targets? What can be done to change the opportunity for property crime?

4. Many believe that property crime rates will rise as unemployment rates rise. Is this assumption borne out in the research that has been done on the subject? Does the picture change when we look at certain age or race categories? If so, why?

CHAPTER 9

VICE CRIMES: INDIVIDUAL CHOICES AND SOCIAL CONTROLS

Henry R. Lesieur
Illinois State University

Michael Welch
Rutgers University

CRIMES AGAINST MORALITY, also called *vices*, "are activities thought by many to be immoral and liable to bring spiritual and even bodily harm to those engaging in them" (Sheley, 1985: 115–116). These activities, including public drunkenness, possession of illegal substances like cocaine and marijuana, illegal gambling, consensual sex crimes (for example, oral and anal intercourse, adultery, and prostitution), and pornography, are said to offend morality. As of the early 1990s, if we count related offenses like drunk driving, disorderly conduct, and vagrancy, over five million people are arrested yearly for vice crimes — 37 percent of all arrests (see Table 9.1).

The large numbers of persons arrested yearly for vice crimes signal the importance of these crimes for our society and its criminal justice system. In this chapter, we examine the debate over whether or not vice activities should be treated as crimes. We look as well at the recent trend toward defining vice activities as illnesses and addressing them as we would any medical problem. Against this backdrop, we focus on several types of vice crimes: prostitution, pornography, homosexual activity, gambling, and drugs. We close by looking at the overlapping social worlds of persons who, directly or indirectly, both engage in and condemn various activities labeled "vice crimes" in this society.

THE DEBATE OVER VICE CRIMES

Moralists and civil libertarians have taken different positions concerning whether private morality should be controlled through the criminal justice system. For example, Mill (1892), Hart (1963), Geis (1979), and others have

TABLE 9.1   TOTAL NUMBER OF ARRESTS FOR VICE CRIMES AS A PERCENTAGE OF ALL ARRESTS*

Vice Crime	1960		1970	
	Number	*Percentage*	*Number*	*Percentage*
Prostitution	26,482	0.67	51,700	0.64
Other sex offenses†	50,101	1.27	59,700	0.74
Drug abuse violations	27,735	0.70	415,600	5.12
Liquor laws	106,347	2.69	309,000	3.81
Driving under the influence	183,943	4.65	555,700	6.85
Drunkenness	1,412,167	35.66	1,825,500	22.49
Disorderly conduct	475,502	12.00	710,000	8.75
Vagrancy	153,201	3.87	113,400	1.40
Gambling	122,946	3.10	91,700	1.13
Totals	2,558,424	64.6	4,132,300	50.9

SOURCE: Adapted from UCR data.

*Arrests for 1960 are for reporting agencies; those for 1970, 1980, and 1991 are FBI estimates of both reported and unreported arrests.

†Sex offenses include some offenses with victims.

advocated that crime and sin should not necessarily be equated; in other words, there should be a realm of activity that is "not the law's business." Countering this, Lord Devlin (1965: 23) has advocated state intervention in private morality because "society cannot ignore the morality of the individual any more than it can his loyalty; it flourishes on both and without either it dies."

Why criminalize vice? Homosexual activity and prostitution are called abominations that not only corrupt youth but undermine the ideals of family and morality, and both are blamed for spreading AIDS and venereal diseases. Pornography, claim its opponents, is a cause of rape and other sexual violence. Alcohol, drugs, and gambling create havoc and personal ruin for both the users and their families; drugs in particular are said to lead to more serious forms of criminal behavior. Proponents of laws outlawing alcohol consumption, drug use, and gambling argue that such "vices" create poverty and are part of the cycle of social and economic inequality. Further promotion of these behaviors, they assert, could lead to a disintegration of society.

On the other hand, the criminalization of private morality produces what Schur (1965; see also Bedeau, 1974) has termed "victimless crime." Schur refers to "the willing exchange, among adults, of strongly demanded but legally proscribed goods or services" (p. 169). One feature of victimless crimes is a lack of agreement in the general population about what laws should be

TOTAL NUMBER OF ARRESTS FOR VICE CRIMES AS A PERCENTAGE OF ALL ARRESTS*

Vice Crime	1980		1991	
	Number	*Percentage*	*Number*	*Percentage*
Prostitution	88,900	0.85	98,900	0.70
Other sex offenses†	67,400	0.65	108,000	0.76
Drug abuse violations	580,800	5.56	1,010,000	7.11
Liquor laws	463,500	4.44	624,100	4.39
Driving under the influence	1,426,700	13.66	1,771,400	12.46
Drunkenness	1,125,800	10.78	881,100	6.20
Disorderly conduct	769,700	7.37	757,700	5.33
Vagrancy	30,700	0.29	38,500	0.27
Gambling	87,000	0.83	16,600	0.12
Totals	4,640,500	44.4	5,306,000	37.34

passed, how those laws should be enforced, and how violators should be punished. A second feature is the element of exchange: A product (like drugs or pornography) or service (like gambling or sex) is exchanged for money, sex, and so on. The third feature, Schur suggests, is the lack of apparent harm associated with the offense—with the exception of possible harm to the offenders themselves. Schur also notes that victimless crime laws lack enforceability because of the lack of a complainant.

One associated trait of some but not all victimless crimes is the development of a deviant subculture based on the need of persons to have contact with others who are also involved in the illegal acts. A deviant subculture exists when people come together to solve common problems surrounding their deviant status. Drug addicts, for example, share values, attitudes, rationalizations, skills, and knowledge about illicit drug use and sales. In addition, because of the illegal nature of the activity, black markets arise that drive up the price. A consequence of the high cost is that drug addicts resort to crimes like shoplifting, prostitution, and robbery to pay for drugs; Schur refers to this as "secondary crime" (p. 174). Aside from secondary crime, the net result of victimless crimes is to create a class of criminals whose only "crime" may be to engage in an activity that certain segments of a society have deemed deviant.

Kadish (1967), in a classic article concerning the "crisis of overcriminalization," commented on problems that arise as a result of attempts to enforce public standards of private morality. According to Kadish, the moral message of the law is contradicted by the lack of total enforcement. Only some activities are enforced, while others are ignored. For example, activities that are engaged in by youths are more likely to be sanctioned than are those engaged in by adults, which tends to breed cynicism toward the law. Similarly, when laws are not enforced, widespread disrespect for the law may result, as in the case of marijuana laws (see Kaplan, 1970).

Further, when public campaigns or media activities raise the specter of unenforced laws, law enforcement agencies become more active, resulting in discriminatory enforcement of the law (see Sheley and Hanlon, 1978). Therefore, anticrime drives are launched for reasons unrelated to the purpose of the law. This activity is most likely to be directed toward the most vulnerable groups of society, most notably the poor. According to Kadish (1967), vice laws also waste resources because police personnel who could be used to combat street crime are instead diverted to vice squads, and then driven to excessive behavior in pursuit of violators. Civil liberties issues arise as wiretapping and bugging are used in attempts to fight offenses like gambling and narcotics trafficking. In addition, police must engage in demeaning and degrading behavior, such as undercover operations in men's rooms and the use of police decoys to arrest prostitutes. Some of this police behavior is even illegal (for example, entrapment). Finally, like Schur, Kadish notes that the illegal nature of a vice activity gives rise to black markets, which in turn, create large-scale organized systems of crime that engage, among other activities, in bribery and corruption of officials.

Similar approaches have been taken by Packer (1968), Skolnick (1968), Kaplan (1970), and Morris and Hawkins (1970), whose critiques fueled legislative efforts in some states that decriminalized consensual sodomy, marijuana consumption (in eleven states), and public drunkenness. Weppner and Inciardi (1978), in writing about marijuana, have noted that those states that do not decriminalize such behaviors incur serious human, social, and financial costs, including a heavier burden on the criminal justice system because of increased demands on enforcement and corrections agencies. Finally, Nettler (1982: 126) notes the potential link between totalitarianism and vice laws:

> Totalitarian regimes are strengthened by an ideology that includes moral conceptions of how people should behave. Modern tyrants therefore have no hesitation about punishing activities they define as immoral, activities ranging from homosexuality and prostitution to drunkenness, absenteeism from work, the use of narcotics and the expression of "wrong" ideas. There is no freedom in Cuba or in the People's Republic of China to be a "drag queen," a whore, an addict, or a dissident. Moreover, there is no public debate [about these issues].

THE MEDICALIZATION OF VICE CRIME

Many (by no means all) of the customers, dealers, prostitutes, and other victimless crime offenders are classified by one authority or another as "addicts" who have a "disease." Programs like Alcoholics Anonymous, Narcotics Anonymous, and Gamblers Anonymous promote the disease conception of alcoholism, narcotics addiction, and compulsive gambling (see Sagarin, 1969). Such programs are, in turn, supported to a greater or lesser extent by the psychiatric establishment. The designation by the American Psychiatric Association of homosexuality as a mental disorder was challenged and eventually overturned in 1973 when that organization decided by vote that only "ego-dystonic" homosexuality should be classified as a disorder. The *Diagnostic and Statistical Manual* of the American Psychiatric Association classifies "vices" as behavioral disorders: psychoactive substance dependence (for alcohol and other drug problems) and pathological gambling (American Psychiatric Association, 1987). The primary characteristics of psychoactive substance dependence represent the paradigm or model of addiction, and deserve mention. According to the American Psychiatric Association (1987: 167–168), the criteria for diagnosis include:

1. Taking the substance more often or over a longer period than intended.
2. Failed attempts to cut down or stop using the substance.
3. Spending much time in activities to get the substance or recovering from its use.
4. Frequent interference with work, school, or home as a result of use or use when it is hazardous to do so (for example, driving while intoxicated).
5. Giving up important social, occupational or recreational activities in order to use.
6. Persistent use of the substance in spite of problems.
7. Development of physical tolerance.
8. Withdrawal symptoms.

These symptoms have to last at least a month or persist over a long time. In other words, use without interference does not qualify as dependence.

BENEFITS OF THE MEDICALIZATION APPROACH

The medicalization of deviant behavior has both brighter and darker sides (Conrad and Schneider, 1992). In their ideal form, medical definitions increase tolerance and compassion for human problems. The alcoholic, for example, is no longer "weak willed," but instead is "sick." Consequently, the individual cannot be blamed for what she or he did while sick. The ill person is "treated" rather than "punished" as the prestige and power of the medical profession is brought to bear on the problem. Medical controls are, by their very nature, more flexible and efficient than judicial controls because they can be easily adjusted to the needs of the individual patient and can be applied without formal proceedings. In drunk-driving programs, for example, the offender can be required to attend education sessions that concentrate on the disease conception of alcoholism. Many of these programs assess each client for alcoholism and have the power to mandate further treatment where alcoholism is detected.

Drawbacks to the Medicalization Approach

The virtues of medicalization also can be viewed as drawbacks, however, because the altered label (from badness to sickness) creates confusion over issues of responsibility. For example, if compulsive gamblers are sick, how culpable are they for crimes engaged in while they gambled? Should they be provided with treatment and offered an opportunity to make restitution rather than be sentenced to prison? This very issue is currently being debated in the courts (Lorenz and Rose, 1988), where two systems of justice result, one for those who can hire expert witnesses to testify in court and one for those who cannot.

When medical control is applied, it is based on the assumption that it is more effective at altering (controlling) behavior than no treatment at all. However, this assumption frequently is not justified. For example, little evidence suggests that individual, group, or milieu therapy works in the prison environment (Lipton et al., 1975). In addition, the assumption that medical control is more humane than the criminal justice system is not always warranted. Although medical control can entail greater leniency, it can also lead to harsher treatment of the offender: psychosurgery, electroshock "therapy," implanted electrodes, and the like.

The dominance of a medical model also implies an individualistic approach to the offender (Conrad and Schnieder, 1992). For example, drug treatment plans commonly focus on personality disorders, education about genetic inheritance of the disease, deficiencies in self-esteem, and personal traumatic experiences. However, treatment professionals rarely enter the communities their clients come from, and individual and group therapy takes place in hospitals or outpatient settings with little, if any, attention paid to the outside world.

Social science research widely acknowledges that treatment for alcohol and other drug dependencies is more effective with middle-income than with lower-income individuals (Armor et al., 1976). When treatment fails, as individual causes are given paramount importance, individuals are blamed for failing. Rather than reorienting rehabilitation to fit the conditions, the failures are rationalized on individualistic grounds, or the treatment center refocuses its efforts on treating those clients who can be influenced by the methods used (that is, middle-income individuals). For the most part, social conditions are overlooked because they are not amenable to medical intervention. Doctors do not treat inequality, racism, and urban blight but do participate in alcohol detoxification and methadone maintenance programs designed to return individuals to those very conditions. The medical approach fails to recognize that rates of street crime and heroin and crack use are highest in the inner-city areas characterized by severe social problems.

Activities that we commonly call vice represent probably the clearest intersection of the worlds of crime, medicine, and religion. Illegal drugs have been and still are used for medical purposes: Heroin is prescribed for cancer patients in the United Kingdom, and THC (the psychoactive ingredient in marijuana) is dispensed to glaucoma patients in the United States. Wine is still used in religious services in the West; hallucinogens have been known as the flesh of the gods and treated with reverence among South and Central American

Indian tribes (Furst, 1972). Finally, house prostitutes were once part of early Near-Eastern religions.

In some instances, the intersection between crime and medicine leads to some misleading metaphors (such as the use of the word *sick*) regarding vice crimes, particularly those involving sex. For example, a porn queen may be considered "sick" only in the sense that she is extremely offensive to the opponents of pornography. Such metaphors should not be taken literally since medical techniques usually are not applied to alter these behaviors.

PROSTITUTION

The controversy surrounding prostitution cannot be fully understood apart from its social and historical context, especially as it relates to the regulation of women's sexuality. Generally, such regulation has two major sources. The first is puritanical. That is, women who exhibit promiscuous tendencies are often punished on grounds that their conduct is immoral; hence, a puritanical approach to prostitution leads to forms of repression. The second source involves capitalistic motives by which men profit from the prostitution. Whereas women sell their labor by engaging in prostitution, most of the profit is absorbed by men who control the enterprise (pimps). Regarding both the puritanical and the capitalistic sources, each is structured within a patriarchal framework insofar as men dictate the terms of regulating women's sexuality.

Some observers argue that prostitution is not a crime; rather, it is a consensual contract between adults. In either case, its practice is widespread. There are an estimated quarter of a million full-time prostitutes in the United States who claim to be servicing a total 1.5 million customers a week. Overall, gross annual revenues are estimated between seven and nine billion dollars (Pateman, 1988; also see Rhode, 1989).

A BRIEF HISTORY

Often regarded as the "world's oldest profession," prostitution dates back to ancient societies. Bullogh (1980) points to ancient Mesopotamia as having the earliest record of prostitution. There, priests engaged in sexual activities for procreation, and women were expected to contribute by giving themselves to "temple duty." A similar system was developed in Greece, where licensed brothels financed the temple of Aphrodite in 550 B.C. (Rathus, 1983). During the Middle Ages, prostitution also was part of the economic structure insofar as the church imposed taxes on it (Hagan, 1986). A cross-cultural and historical approach to prostitution demonstrates that prostitutes have earned a respectable social status in some societies. For example, Davis (1961) notes that the Greek *hetaerae*, the Roman *lupanaria*, the Indian *devadasis*, and the Japanese *geishas* all enjoyed elevated social status and prestige.

History also shows that prostitution has not been exclusively heterosexual. During the 1700s, for example, Molly Houses served as places for homosexual prostitution, where the men often dressed in drag and threw parties for their customers (Karlen, 1971). Karlen points to a famous Molly House in an

English resort managed by Margaret Clap, whose surname became the popular term for a venereal disease.

In early American history, tightknit communities worked against prostitution. However, as America underwent industrialization and urbanization (along with immigration), prostitution became widespread. Indeed, in most growing urban centers, prostitution was not only visible but also viewed as part of metropolitan life. Prostitutes worked in nearly every neighborhood of the city, and solicited bakeries, cigar stores, delicatessens, barber shops, hotels, saloons, theaters, and fine restaurants. Their clients were men of every ethnic group, social class, and occupation (Gilfoyle, 1992; also see Roberts, 1992). The notion of prostitutes as *hookers* derives from the label given women who provided sexual services for Union General "Fighting Joe" Hooker and his army. In the early twentieth century, "redlight districts" earned their name from railroad workers who hung red lamps outside their tents during visits to prostitutes—the red light helped the dispatcher locate these men for railroad duty (Winick and Kinsie, 1971).

The contemporary history of prostitution is highlighted by some sensational portrayals of famous houses of ill repute: for example, the notorious Texas brothel that inspired the play and film *The Best Little Whorehouse in Texas*, as well as New Orleans' Storyville and Nevada's Mustang Ranch, Pink Pussycat, and Miss Kitty's. In the 1980s, the socially prominent former debutante Sydney Biddle Barrows glamorized prostitution by managing a bordello on the upper West Side of Manhattan in New York City. Ms. Barrows, a descendant of the Mayflower settlers, became known as the Mayflower Madam, and her prostitutes earned between $125 and $400 an hour.

Taking care not to glamorize prostitution as a promising road to financial independence, we note that, as has been the case throughout much of history, women continue to turn to prostitution because of the low value of female labor in society. As George Bernard Shaw noted: "Prostitution is caused not by female depravity and male licentiousness but simply by underpaying, undervaluing, and overworking women. If, on the large scale, we get vice instead of what we call virtue, it is because we are paying more for it" (1905: preface). As we shall see in this section, prostitution also invites other forms of exploitation and victimization.

In tracking the popularity of prostitution over time, Kinsey et al. (1948, 1953) and Hunt (1974) surveyed the frequency with which men visited prostitutes. Kinsey and associates revealed that before World War II, about 50 percent of white men had sought the services of a prostitute. More recently, Hunt found that 45 percent of noncollege-educated and 35 percent of college-educated males had visited prostitutes. Whether this represents a true decline is unclear because survey methods in the two studies are not directly comparable. Nonetheless, with the wave of health concerns in the 1990s (AIDS, herpes, and so forth), observers speculate that visits to prostitutes are becoming less common or, at the very least, clients are becoming more cautious by using condoms.

Health concerns have been addressed by both opponents and advocates of legalized prostitution. Opponents argue that prostitution should remain illegal to minimize public health risks, whereas advocates assert that it is precisely through legalization that health risks can be monitored better (for example, through regular AIDS and venereal disease screening).

THE LEGAL STATUS OF PROSTITUTION

The history of prostitution suggests that one may view it as an extension of social life rather than as a social problem. Yet, nations vary in their views of prostitution. For example, in the Netherlands, prostitution is legal and carefully regulated to minimize the risk of disease. On the other hand, in some Mid-Eastern nations and third-world countries, prostitution is not tolerated. In fact, in Somalia, prostitution is punishable by death. Clearly, with respect to prostitution, the United States is neither as liberal as the Netherlands nor as draconian as Somalia. Nevertheless, federal, state, and local governments traditionally have attempted to control prostitution socially through legal reform, in which prostitution is commonly defined "as the practice of having sexual relations with emotional indifference on a promiscuous and mercenary basis" (Hagan, 1986: 243).

At the federal level, prostitution is controlled by the Mann Act of 1925 (also known as the "white slave" act), which prohibits the transportation of women across state lines (or bringing them into the country) for the purposes of prostitution. The penalty is a $5,000 fine or a five-year sentence, or both. With the exception of Nevada, which has legalized brothels in some counties, states enforce their own statutes on prostitution. Prostitutes can be arrested for such violations as accosting, soliciting, or being a "common prostitute"; in addition, they may be cited for violating disorderly conduct or vagrancy statutes. Prostitutes also have been arrested and detained for health regulation violations.

Prostitution is a misdemeanor, and convicted prostitutes usually are fined or serve a sentence of less than one year. Between 1960 and 1991, prostitution arrest rates almost doubled (see Table 9.2). Whether this is a product of increased willingness by police to arrest women, the heightened extent of prostitution itself as a result of drug-related activity, or some other factors is not known precisely. We do know that police generally are tolerant of prostitution except when instructed or pressured to launch temporary enforcement campaigns. These enforcement campaigns, also known as "social sanitation," are initiated when prostitution becomes overly visible, especially in commercial or residential areas (Welch, forthcoming). Therefore, the street prostitute is the most common target of police activity. Most major cities informally designate a district, commonly referred to as an adult entertainment district or "combat zone," where prostitutes can market their trade without much police interference.

TYPES OF PROSTITUTES

Streetwalkers are the most visible prostitutes and are commonly found in the combat zones of major cities as well as those districts identified as drug areas. Consequently, streetwalkers face the worst occupational hazards: They remain

TABLE 9.2   **ARREST RATES FOR VICE CRIMES***

Vice Crime	Year			
	1960	*1970*	*1980*	*1991*
Prostitution	24.3	32.5	41.2	42.9
Other sex offenses†	46.1	32.5	30.5	43.3
Drug abuse violations	25.5	228.5	256.0	411.3
Liquor laws	97.8	146.7	205.5	238.9
Driving under the influence	169.1	279.4	626.3	678.5
Drunkenness	1,298.2	997.8	504.2	345.9
Disorderly conduct	437.1	484.8	347.9	299.7
Vagrancy	140.8	85.1	14.1	16.5
Gambling	113.0	55.9	22.4	6.8

Source: Adapted from UCR data.

*Rates per 100,000 population.

†Sex offenses include some offenses with victims.

vulnerable to diseases, arrests, and mistreatment by pimps and customers. The financial rewards of this form of prostitution are relatively low, and the working conditions (streets, alleys, stairwells, cars, cheap hotels) are markedly inferior. Streetwalkers often are members of poverty-stricken minority groups. Moreover, many pursue prostitution to finance their chemical dependency (Inciardi et al., 1991; Inciardi, 1989).

Another type of prostitute is the bar girl (b-girl), who works in cooperation with the management of a tavern, ordering diluted drinks for herself and allowing the client to pick up the tab before the actual act of prostitution. Bars near military bases have traditionally served as popular settings for bar girls (see Winick and Kinsie, 1971). Yet another type of prostitute is the house girl, who works in a brothel and is directly managed by the madam. Today, most brothels have been replaced by massage parlors and escort services, from which comparable services are purchased.

Male prostitutes are similarly categorized as street hustlers, bar hustlers, and escort service employees (Luckenbill, 1986). However, unlike their female counterparts, their form of prostitution is generally homosexual in nature. Very little research attention has been paid to male prostitution though a third of the arrestees for "prostitution and commercialized vice" (which would include pimps) are male (FBI, 1991: 191).

At a higher level of professionalism is the call girl, who reportedly charges as much as $500 per client and may earn as much as $100,000 annually (Siegel, 1986). Call girls often have had middle-class upbringings and claim to provide more than just sexual services. For example, they purport to enhance the self-esteem of their clients as well as sexually satisfy them. Although call girls may also be vulnerable to abuse by their customers, they have been known to conduct "background checks" on their customers before their "date." The working conditions for the call girls are much better than those for other prostitutes insofar as they work in expensive hotels or their own apartments. Compared to other types of prostitutes, the call girl assumes high occupational status and prestige.

THE SOCIALIZATION OF PROSTITUTES

The role of the prostitute is not always fully embraced by a person who is identified as a prostitute. In fact, the socialization of a prostitute is best understood by tracking the various stages that reflect the gradual transformation of a prostitute's identity. Davis (1978) describes a process known as being "turned out." During the first stage, the woman learns that it is exciting and profitable to sell sex instead of "giving it away." Then the woman enters a stage of transitional deviance: Her self-definition is conventional, yet she uses prostitution as a part-time occupation. In the final stage, she accepts the deviant identity of a prostitute. Traditionally, the socialization process involves group interaction insofar as argot, social support, and apprenticeships are generated by other prostitutes.

Occupational mobility also exists within prostitution, and apparently resembles conventional occupational paths. As with conventional occupations, the following qualities enhance mobility for male and female prostitutes: race, mental acumen, personal contacts, self-presentation, and ambition (Goldstein, 1983; Luckenbill, 1986).

Recently, investigations have focused on the "pseudo-families" of streetwalkers that underscore the relationship between women prostitutes and their "men" (or pimps). Whereas the initial attraction to a pseudo-family lies in its glitter and economic opportunity, Romenesko and Miller (1989) report that, in such overwhelmingly heteropatriarchal arrangements, prostitutes soon find themselves trapped and their life chances dramatically reduced instead of enhanced. This downward mobility becomes clearer as younger, more attractive and obedient women join the "family," thereby marginalizing the older prostitutes.

Finally, attempts have been made to formalize prostitution as a legitimate profession. In the United States, COYOTE ("Call Off Your Old Tired Ethics") emerged as a social movement that set out to challenge traditional beliefs about prostitution. COYOTE launched several campaigns in the 1970s and 1980s to sever prostitution from its historical association with sin and crime. Organizers of COYOTE emphasized that prostitution should be viewed in light of civil and labor rights, which also include promoting freedom for women who wish to use their bodies as they see fit (Weitzer, 1991; Jenness, 1990).

THE VICTIMIZATION OF PROSTITUTES

Prostitution clearly has a less than glamorous side. It is often interpreted as an extension of women's inferior social status (Millett, 1973). A closer look at the stereotypical "independent" working girl reveals a woman who is greatly exploited by her customers and management (Sheehy, 1973). These women are dominated by men who wish to fulfill their sexual fantasies, and suffer abuse from the pimps who control their income and their work lives (Conklin, 1986). Additionally, Heyl (1979) identifies other ways in which men profit from female prostitution: as landlords, as owners of massage parlors, and as politicians who base their campaigns on "cleaning up vice."

The criminal justice system also is accused of contributing to the victimization of the prostitute. For example, more women are arrested for providing illegal services than are men who also work as prostitutes. During enforcement campaigns, the prostitute, not the client, is usually arrested and prosecuted. Prostitutes often are beaten and abused, and sometimes are murdered, yet these abuses are passively viewed by the public as "occupational hazards." For example, during the 1978 "Hillside Strangler" mass murders in Los Angeles, the community initially was unconcerned because the victims were presumed to be prostitutes. Public anger was aroused only when this perception proved to be inaccurate (Balkan et al., 1980).

Another form of victimization associated with prostitution is the contraction of illnesses, especially venereal diseases and AIDS. Although rates of contraction likely are exaggerated in the public's mind—prostitutes generally are quite careful to protect themselves—increased levels of exposure surely accompany persistent impersonal sex. However, it is important to emphasize that though prostitutes (in particular, streetwalkers) have exceedingly high rates of AIDS contraction, this is due primarily to high-risk intravenous drug use (such as sharing hypodermic needles) (Cohen et al., 1988).

Of current public concern is the emergence of the underage prostitute (under the age of 18), which remains common in large cities. For example, Hagan (1986) notes that 10,000 underaged male prostitutes (mostly homosexual prostitutes who are also called "chicken-hawks") work in New York City alone, and half of Portland's prostitution workforce are underaged girls. Underaged prostitution has also been identified in New Orleans, where eighteen Boy Scouts age 8–15 operated as a sex ring.

Unlike adult prostitution, commonly viewed as a more victimless crime, child and adolescent prostitution is more closely monitored by state and federal law enforcement officials. The general view is that the youth is, indeed, the victim in underage prostitution, so additional efforts are made to "rescue" youths from this form of exploitation. The most common characteristic of male and female adolescent prostitutes is their status as runaways from physically or sexually abusive homes. While attempting to survive on the streets of large cities, these youth turn to substance abuse and prostitution to alleviate the burdens of transient living arrangements and homelessness (Simons and Whitbeck, 1991; Cates, 1989; Campagna and Poffenberger, 1988; Robertson, 1990; Seng, 1989).

PORNOGRAPHY

Pornography often is as controversial as prostitution largely because it shares many of the same issues: degradation, exploitation, and capitalistic patriarchy. However, at times pornography is *more* controversial than prostitution, especially when issues of censorship and potential harm are introduced. Concerns surrounding censorship and First Amendment protections of reading and pictorial materials run deep among many citizens, even if such materials are deemed offensive. But what motivates many attempts to censor pornography is the claim that such materials are potentially harmful insofar as they may inspire some men to commit acts of sexual violence.

In this section, we shall explore historical considerations, the politicization process, and issues of harm as they relate to pornography. Yet, the focus of this section will remain on adult pornography, not child pornography ("kiddie porn"). Since child pornography is routinely prosecuted as a crime (via the federal Child Protection Act of 1984), it does not meet the definition of a vice (or victimless) crime.

HISTORICAL CONSIDERATIONS

Pornography shares more common historical and theoretical linkages with prostitution than is often acknowledged. In fact, the term *pornography* is traced to the graphic sexual writings or pictures (graphos) of prostitutes (pornos). Over the course of history, the term became synonymous with sexually explicit material intended to promote sexual arousal. Recently, attempts have been made by some feminists to return to the original definition of the term. "From their perspective, it was important to distinguish between pornography, which involved scenes of degradation and dominance, and other forms of erotic material premised on equality and mutual respect" (Rhode, 1989: 263; also see Dworkin, 1981).

Pornography existed in ancient Greek and Roman societies, as well as during the rise of Christianity, but there was little attempt to suppress or censor such images. In the early years of the printing press (in the mid-sixteenth century), English law required printers to receive licenses from the church and the state. Yet, at the time, there was little interest in censoring sexual material since church and state officials were more concerned about subversive political literature (Rhode, 1989; Donnerstein et al., 1987; Barber, 1972).

In Colonial America, and through the early 1800s, pornography was not widespread; consequently, there was little legal interest in banning sexual materials. Eventually the same social forces that promoted prostitution (secularization, industrialization, migration, and urbanization) also affected the growth of pornography. Accordingly, a legal interest to control the distribution of sexual materials also grew. In 1873, the federal Act for the Suppression of Trade and Circulation of Obscene Literature and Immoral Use was passed, primarily under the leadership of Anthony Comstock. The implications of this statute were far-reaching. Since it was designed to suppress materials that would corrupt those minds that were open to immoral influences, such a law was broad, vague, and equipped with unlimited discretionary power. Indeed, under the forty-year reign of Postal Inspector Comstock, approximately 160 tons of material (ranging from classical art to indecent playing cards) were destroyed (Rhode, 1989; Boyer, 1968).

Although the courts after World War I began to take into account the merits of the work as a whole in determining whether material was obscene, existing definitions of pornography remained expansive. Decades later, the Supreme Court (in *Roth* v. *United States*, 1956) declared that obscene material was not within the zone of constitutionally protected speech; however, it was still not clear what constituted obscene material. Indeed, the famous phrase by Supreme Court Justice Potter Stewart best characterized the controversy over the definition of obscenity when he quipped: "I know it when I see it."

Finally, in *Miller* v. *California* (1973), the high court formulated a three-part test in determining whether material met the definition of obscene. Material that met these qualifications was subject to prohibition:

1. Whether an average person applying contemporary community standards would find the work as a whole appealed to the "prurient interest."
2. Whether the work depicted sexual conduct in a "patently offensive way."
3. Whether the work taken as a whole lacked "serious literary, artistic, political, or scientific value."

THE POLITICIZATION OF PORNOGRAPHY

The history of pornography cannot be understood apart from its political context. Pornography is controversial not only because many people consider it morally and aesthetically offensive but also because they believe that it degrades women. Moreover, it also has been suggested that pornography (especially violent pornography) directly (or indirectly) leads to sexual assaults against women. In light of this controversy, an unusual political alliance has formed between right-wing conservatives and some left-wing feminists who favor banning pornography. Indeed, one of the most controversial ordinances enacted to curb pornography had strong support from both conservatives and some feminists.

This controversial ordinance, drafted by Andrea Dworkin and Catherine MacKinnon in 1983, was first proposed in Minneapolis and later adopted in Indianapolis (though here it ultimately was declared unconstitutional by the courts). The ordinance defined pornography as the "sexually explicit subordination of women, graphically depicted in words or pictures," which debases women in several contexts: enjoying pain, rape, or humiliation; serving as sexual objects for domination, conquest, exploitation, and possession; or appearing in positions of "servility or submission or display." The ordinance declared that "trafficking" in pornography (or coercing one to participate in the making of the material) would be a civil offense. Consequently, "any aggrieved individual could claim injunctive relief and monetary damages under judicial or special administrative proceedings" (Rhode, 1989: 266–267).

Civil libertarians harshly criticized Dworkin and MacKinnon for drafting and advocating this antipornography legislation, arguing that it undermined individuals' rights to freedom of expression and to privacy. In fact, the American Civil Liberties Union (ACLU) selected Dworkin and MacKinnon as two of their 1992 recipients of the Arts Censors of the Year Awards. This dubious distinction is intended to recognize individuals "who have tried to impose their personal ideological, moral or religious standards on all Americans" (*Civil Liberties*, 1992–1993: 7). Dworkin and MacKinnon were selected "for drafting and advocating legislation that would allow lawsuits aimed at banning sexually oriented entertainment, and allow victims of sexual crimes to collect damages from the producers and distributors of such entertainment" (*Civil Liberties*, 1992–1993: 7).

IS PORNOGRAPHY HARMFUL?

The cornerstone of the Indianapolis ordinance is its presumption of harm stemming from pornography. Recently, the debate over the harmful effects of pornography has been renewed. Baron and Straus's (1987, 1989) research found pornography consumption to be related to rape rates. But in a similar study, Gentry (1991) failed to find support for such a conclusion. She found no relationship between the circulation of sexually oriented magazines (*Chic, Club, Gallery, Genesis, Hustler, Oui, Penthouse*, and *Playboy*) and rape rates. In sum, Gentry emphasizes: "If subsequent research confirms the findings reported here, we may conclude that efforts to control the consumption of sexually oriented magazines in an effort to reduce violence against women are misdirected" (1991: 285).

To date, three major government-sponsored commissions have found that exposure to nonviolent pornography does not cause sexual violence against women (Commission on Obscenity and Pornography, 1970; Attorney General's Commission on Pornography, 1986; and Special Committee on Pornography and Prostitution in Canada, 1985).The 1970 Commission on Obscenity and Pornography "found no evidence that explicit sexual material plays a significant role in the causation of delinquency or criminal behavior." Accordingly, the Commission recommended the repeal of local, state, and federal laws against the sale, exhibition, and distribution of sexual materials to consenting adults.

Other studies reveal a cathartic effect, meaning that there is a reduction in aggression by subjects exposed to nonviolent pornography (Donnerstein, 1984; Donnerstein et al., 1987; Malamuth and Donnerstein, 1983; Nelson, 1982). In a cross-national study, Kutchinsky (1991; also see 1973) examined criminal justice statistics in Denmark, West Germany, Sweden, and the United States (1964–1984) and found support for the hypothesis that the legalization of pornography reduced sex crimes in these nations. Some studies actually identify positive aspects of pornography, especially in the form of education. Nicholson and Duncan (1991) included 388 U.S. university students in their study and found: "Men generally report gaining a greater amount of their sex knowledge from pornography than do women, but substantial numbers of women report that pornography was a source of information regarding certain topics, especially oral–anal sex and foreplay" (1991: 802).

Additional research focuses on exposure to *violence* rather than exposure to pornography per se as a possible cause of sexual assaults since some sex offenders have reported that violent pornography fosters erotic notions of rape (Fishbach and Malamuth, 1978). In experiments comparing violent and nonviolent pornography, Sullivan (1980) found that pornography that incorporated violence promoted aggression among male subjects. Conversely, the nonviolent erotic material failed to promote aggression toward females. These findings are consistent with other research (Malamuth and Donnerstein, 1983), and more researchers are concluding that it is exposure to *violence* (whether or not presented in a sexual context) that leads to sexual aggression (Donnerstein and Linz, 1986; Gray, 1982; Baron and Straus, 1987).

The Attorney General's Commission on Pornography (the Meese Report) (1986) also examined the relationship between pornography and violence. However, its recommendations are not consistent with its findings. Although the commission conceded that there lacks a causal connection between pornography and violent sex offenses, it nevertheless recommended strict enforcement of obscenity laws and an increase in penalties for their violation. This created a controversy that was further compounded by the problem in which two of the commission members refused to sign the document (Turkington, 1986; Nobile and Nadler, 1986). Nonetheless, Attorney General Meese mounted an ambitious campaign against distributors of pornography by expanding the use of the RICO (the Racketeer Influenced and Corrupt Organizations) statute (see Chapter 10) and establishing the National Obscenity Enforcement Unit (Snow, 1990; Welch, 1988). Ironically, this enforcement campaign occurred amid generally liberal sentiments toward pornography. A 1985 Gallup poll of 1,020 Americans revealed the following: 60 percent favored being able to go to X-rated movies; 53 percent favored being able to buy magazines that show sexual relations; 68 percent favored being able to buy or rent X-rated videotapes; and 76 percent believed depictions of scenes of sexual violence led some people to commit sexual violence and thus should be outlawed (*Newsweek*, 1985).

Yet, despite the publication of empirical investigations that state that there is *no conclusive evidence* that pornography poses a violent threat to women, many feminists challenge such findings (see Dworkin, 1981, 1985; MacKinnon, 1984; Morgan, 1980; Ratterman, 1982; McCarthy, 1982). It is important to emphasize that adjectives such as "harmful" and "dangerous," which are common descriptors of pornographic material, are actually metaphors to describe material regarded as "offensive." Yet feminist scholars argue that it is precisely this offense that harms women as a group.

> The harm resulting from pornography is not confined to discrete acts of aggression against individual women. It also extends to women as a group, by eroticizing inequality, by linking female sexuality with female subordination, and by making

that subordination a powerful source of male pleasure. Pornography that objectifies and brutalizes women in order to entertain men cannot help but affect the social construction of gender (Rhode, 1989: 269).

It is also argued that pornography degrades men as well as women. Brod (1988) notes that "pornography's image of male sexuality works to the detriment of men personally even as its image of female sexuality enhances the powers of patriarchy" (p. 265). In other words, the view of male sexuality is also distorted by pornographic scenes, and this may lead to a form of alienation among men.

In sum, feminists point to the political aspects of inequality, arguing that pornography perpetuates and eroticizes society's male-dominated hierarchy. Traditional conservatives also focus not on the political aspects of pornography, but rather as it deals with morality. Conservatives are concerned with prohibiting materials that they view as "smut," and believe that ordinances against pornography "not only protect women, but would restore them to what ladies used to be" (Rhode, 1989: 269). Considering the traditional views of women among conservatives, many feminists are understandably hesitant to form political alliances with right-wing antipornography crusaders.

HOMOSEXUAL ACTIVITY

Considering the large number of adults who are gay or lesbian, it is suggested that homosexuality be regarded as variant instead of deviant. The Kinsey Institute for Sex Research reported that in the 1960s, 4 percent of the total male population were gay, and 1–2 percent were lesbian. Applying these figures to the 1990 census, the gay population may consist of 12 to 15 million individuals; however, these are considered by some to be conservative estimates. Indeed, the National Gay and Lesbian Task Force (the nation's largest gay and lesbian organization) estimates that homosexuals make up 10 percent of the general population, or approximately twenty-five million Americans.

Regardless of the size of the homosexual population, as well as growing social tolerance toward gays and lesbians, there still remain numerous religious, moral, medical, political, and legal sanctions against them. Indeed, today there is considerable public support for laws banning homosexual relations. In a 1991 Gallup poll, 54 percent of the adults surveyed believed that homosexual relations between consenting adults should *not* be legal (36 percent favored legal homosexual relations, and 10 percent had no opinion) (Gallup, 1991). In this section, a discussion of homosexuality (in the context of vice crimes) will include a brief history and recent legal and law enforcement activities.

A BRIEF HISTORY

Homosexual activity was common among ancient Babylonians and Egyptians. Similarly, the ancient Greeks considered homosexuality (as compared to heterosexuality) to be a more genuine expression of love (Karlen, 1971). Among ancient Greeks, however, most homosexuality often took the form of pederasty—that is, sexual activity between men and boys.

The criminalization of homosexual activity actually began during the Middle Ages and the Renaissance in Europe; sodomy (both homosexual and heterosexual) became a crime punishable by death (Karlen, 1971). In 1533, Henry VIII enacted the buggery statute, which outlawed homosexual anal intercourse (Barlow, 1987). These laws remained active until 1861 in England and 1889 in Scotland, where anal intercourse was still punishable by death. Many homosexuals were burnt at the stake along with alleged witches. In fact, the pejorative term *faggot* derives from the practice of using kindling wood, known as faggots, to burn homosexuals (Katz, 1976). In early America, some colonies also imposed the death penalty on homosexuals though these laws were "reformed" by Thomas Jefferson in 1776 when death was replaced by castration (Katz, 1976). More recently, Hitler's armed forces persecuted and exterminated homosexuals along with Jews and other political, ethnic, and religious outcasts, and homosexuals have been persecuted by the Castro regime in Cuba.

Finally, as technology in science and medicine advanced so did interest in applying such technology to reorient homosexuals toward becoming heterosexual through clinical experiments. Through the 1940s and 1950s, this unsuccessful practice persisted among some American psychiatrists who believed that homosexuality was a "curable disease." Today, such experiments are rare in the United States although similar experiments continue in China and Russia.

RECENT LEGAL AND LAW ENFORCEMENT ACTIVITIES

Modern statutes prohibiting oral–genital and anal sex are based on the notion that these acts are unnatural and, therefore, should be unlawful for heterosexuals and homosexuals alike. Although such statutes are infrequently enforced, male homosexuals are occasionally the targets of enforcement campaigns. In fact, a recent Supreme Court decision upheld state laws that forbid consensual sodomy. In *Bowers* v. *Hardwick* (1986), the U.S. Supreme Court ruled that the state of Georgia, as well as other states, could constitutionally prohibit sodomy as long as the state offered a rational base for such a law. In that case, the Supreme Court interpreted the Constitution as not guaranteeing any fundamental right to engage in consensual sodomy.

Attempts to decriminalize homosexual acts generally arose in the late 1960s when homosexuals began "coming out of the closet" to fight society's repression of their sexual preference. Some homosexuals stress that they choose their lifestyle, whereas others assert that their sexuality is biologically determined: Either way, homosexuals do not want to be viewed as pathological, sinful, or criminal. One of the goals of this movement was the repeal of state statutes prohibiting sodomy (for both homosexual and heterosexual couples). Such legal reforms occurred in Illinois, Connecticut, and Nebraska, with each state adopting the American Law Institute's Model Penal Code policy (Section 207.5), which legalizes consensual sexual relationships. Today, seven states have sodomy laws prohibiting sexual acts between people of the same sex. Sixteen states and the District of Columbia have sodomy laws applying to people of the opposite sex as well as to homosexuals.

Forty states currently have laws that ban discrimination based on sexual preference, yet some of the policies that were intended to protect homosexual rights have changed recently. For example, in 1977, Miami struck down its gay rights ordinance, and in 1985, Houston gays failed to gain legal protection for their municipal jobs. Today, homosexuals continue to fight discrimination. Among other things, they are prohibited from living together in public housing projects and may be discriminated against by private employers (as well as some government agencies that consider homosexuals a security risk).

Law enforcement campaigns to control consensual homosexual activities have targeted public places such as parks, theaters, bathhouses, and men's restrooms (tearooms). In a classic sociological study, Humphreys (1970) explored these interactions while engaging in participant observation as the "watch-queen" in a tearoom. One of Humphreys's most revealing findings in this controversial research was that many of the participants were seemingly conventional men stopping at the tearoom on their way home from work. These participants did not fit the stereotype of gay men. Rather, many were married, some had children, and most followed "straight" lifestyles without a gay identity. Among the motivating forces for the tearoom trade were invisibility, anonymity, variety, and intense excitement.

Law enforcement campaigns against gays in public places reflect homophobic hatred for what are perceived as deviant groups. Fleming (1983), who conducted a case study of raids on bawdy houses from 1979 to 1981 (before the AIDS epidemic was recognized), noted that social distance developed as gays were subjected to the enforcement of laws regulating sexual conduct. Fleming commented on how the regular functions and routines of police were complicated because the bawdy house raids drew police resources away from other criminal activities. As a consequence of law enforcement campaigns against homosexuals, socially harmless people were branded as criminals.

GAMBLING

Like pornography, prostitution, and homosexual activity, gambling has long been identified as a vice. Opposition to it, however, typically has been along social class lines, the assumption being that the poor were less able to control themselves and therefore required control by the law.

A Brief History

The first recorded gambling law was in ancient Egypt, where the masses were forbidden to gamble under the penalty of slavery in the mines. Such a system, Wykes (1964) notes, benefited the wealthy, who could thereby depend on having a pool of workers not sitting idly by engaging in leisurely pursuits. Lest we think such class-biased legislation was restricted to the ancient Egyptians,

Wykes uncovered legislation enacted in 1190 by Richard of England and Philip of France restricting betting to the nobility, who themselves could not wager any more than 20 shillings in a twenty-four-hour period. (The kings, of course, were exempt from the law.) Sociologists who have researched vagrancy laws also find a class bias. Vagrancy statutes, initiated in England in 1349, were modified in 1743 to include illegal betting, and offenders could be branded, enslaved, or executed with repeat offenses (Chambliss, 1964). More recently, the "Street Betting Act" in Britain made working-class wagering on the streets (off-track betting) illegal and kept it that way from 1906 until 1960, when the British approach to gambling was modified (Dixon, 1980).

Although such laws have existed for centuries, no evidence suggests that outlawing gambling has eliminated the practice. Steinmetz (1969), Wykes (1964), and others have documented the numerous failures in this respect throughout the world. Quite obviously, too, not all cultures have condemned or outlawed gambling. The cultural ambivalence of numerous societies toward gambling and the creation of gambling laws is illustrated in the checkerboard history of U.S. statutes (Commission on the Review of the National Policy Towards Gambling, 1976; Rosecrance, 1988a). Most recently, of all the victimless crimes, gambling has been legalized at the most rapid pace: As of 1992, forty-eight states had legalized some form of gambling (LaFleur and Hevener, 1992). Lotteries in particular have become legitimized. In 1975, thirteen states had legalized lotteries (*Time*, 1976); by 1992, this number had risen to thirty-three (LaFleur and Hevener, 1992). The growth of gambling has been in the billions of dollars. The gross dollar volume went from $17.3 billion in 1974 (Commission on the Review of the National Policy Towards Gambling, 1976) to $183.8 billion in 1987 (Christiansen, 1988) and $304.1 billion by 1991 (Christiansen and McQueen, 1992). California's lottery alone is a $2-billion-a-year operation (Mathews, 1986). In addition to this, some form of gambling is available on Indian reservations in twenty-one states with casino style gambling in nine of these states (National Indian Gaming Association, 1992). The primary reason for the increase in legalized gambling has been budgetary, and this has removed much of the moral stigma from gambling (Rosecrance, 1988a). Coincidentally, there has been a dramatic decline in gambling arrests, from 122,946 in 1960 to 16,600 in 1991 (see Tables 9.1 and 9.2).

COMPULSIVE GAMBLERS

Although the moral stigma has been removed from gambling itself, it remains for individuals who gamble to excess. Compulsive (pathological) gamblers experience difficulties in personal, family, financial, vocational, and legal realms as a consequence of their gambling. They become outcasts as a result of neglecting their families, failing to repay loans, taking time out from work to gamble, and engaging in crimes to support an increasingly expensive addiction (Lesieur, 1984).

Studies have uncovered a wide variety of illegal behaviors among compulsive gamblers. Livingston (1974) found compulsive gamblers involved in check forgery, embezzlement and employee theft, larceny, armed robbery, bookmaking, hustling, running con games, and fencing stolen goods. Lesieur (1984) uncovered these patterns as well and found gamblers engaged in systematic loan fraud; tax evasion; burglary; pimping; prostitution; drug dealing; and hustling at pool, golf, bowling, cards, and dice. He found that compulsive gamblers first employ legal avenues for funding. As involvement in gambling intensifies, legal options for funding dwindle, and gamblers seek money through increasingly serious illegal activity. For some, the amount of money runs into the millions of dollars. Larceny, embezzlement, forgery, and fraud are the most common offenses among pathological gamblers (Blaszczynski and McConaghy, 1992; Brown, 1987; Lesieur, 1984; Lesieur and Blume, 1991; Meyer and Fabian, 1992).

A study of pathological gambling among prisoners at Yardville and Clinton prisons in New Jersey found that 30 percent of the inmates showed clear signs of pathological gambling (Lesieur and Klein, 1985), and another done in Western Australia uncovered 22 percent as "probable problem gamblers" (Jones, 1990). Pathological gamblers in hospitals, Gamblers Anonymous programs, and prisons admit involvement in a wide range of illegal behaviors in order to finance their gambling activities or to pay gambling debts, but they vary in the types of crimes they committed. This difference appears to be based on socioeconomic variations among the samples. Whereas prisoners are more likely to have been unemployed, Gamblers Anonymous members and hospital inpatients are more likely to be involved in embezzlement, employee theft, tax evasion, and tax fraud — that is, white collar crimes. An exception to this pattern is the greater likelihood of forgery among female prisoners with no significant difference among other samples (Blaszczynski and McConaghy, 1992; Brown, 1987; Lesieur et al., 1985; Lesieur, 1987; Nora, 1984). By contrast, prisoners are more likely to commit commonplace crimes. With the exception of larceny, all the financially motivated commonplace crimes — including burglary, robbery, pimping, selling drugs, and fencing stolen goods — are engaged in much more frequently by prisoners. In addition, the female prisoners engage in prostitution at a greater rate than do female Gamblers Anonymous members. Selling drugs is more popular among the prisoners and hospital inpatients than among the Gamblers Anonymous. Virtually all the pathological gamblers who sell drugs to finance their gambling habit are either drug addicts or abusers (Lesieur and Klein, 1985).

A third cluster of crimes is engaged in by compulsive gamblers — gambling-system-related crimes such as bookmaking, writing numbers, and working in an illegal gambling setting — in much the same way that drug sales are related to drug addiction (Lesieur, 1984). Compulsive gamblers are also heavily involved in gambling-related hustles and cons. Pool, bowling, and golf hustling, as well as card and dice cheating (also called hustling), is more likely to occur earlier in their careers. While engaging in these activities, compulsive gamblers become embroiled in heavy wagering and losses at other forms of gambling (most frequently, betting on athletic events and horse races). Compulsive gambling hustlers move on to other crimes like bookmaking and con games because of increasing indebtedness.

It appears that many con men would classify as pathological gamblers. Other categories of thieves, hustlers, and streetwise persons also have recognized that they were addicted to gambling (Joey, 1974; Theresa and Renner, 1973; Prus and Irini, 1980; Lesieur, 1984). In his study of the American confidence man, Maurer (1974: 150–155) recognized that most con men are gamblers who make a lot of money illegally but spend the bulk of it gambling. Indeed, they showed signs of addiction. Maurer notes that most con men recognize that they are hooked but feel unable to stop: "This indulgence of the gambling instincts becomes more than relaxation; their gratification is the only motive which many con men have for grifting [stealing]. . . . They win and lose, win and lose, always losing more than they win, until they come away broke and full of reasons why their *systems* didn't work that time" (p. 155).

DRUGS

What is a drug? When this question was asked in 1973, 80 percent of both juveniles and adults perceived heroin, cocaine, barbiturates, marijuana, and amphetamines as drugs (National Commission on Marijuana and Drug Abuse, 1973). In the same survey, only 39 percent of adults and 34 percent of juveniles considered alcohol to be a drug, and only 27 percent of adults and 16 percent of juveniles viewed tobacco as a drug. In another study, selling heroin and LSD were ranked as more serious than forcible rape and assassination of a public official (Rossi et al., 1974a). Using heroin was perceived to be more serious than armed robbery and assault on a police officer. Public drunkenness was ranked as the least serious of 140 offenses surveyed. This public sentiment existed even though alcohol is more toxic to the body than most illegal drugs — including heroin (Goode, 1984). The average penalty in some states for possession and sale of illegal drugs is harsher than for all offenses except rape, murder, and kidnapping (Bradley, 1984).

In annual surveys between 1975 and 1991, Johnston et al. (1992a) found similar results among high school students. In each of those years, regular use of cigarettes and alcohol was perceived to be less dangerous than regular use of any illegal drug, in spite of overwhelming evidence that alcohol and tobacco are correlated with more deaths than are all illegal drugs combined. The results are mirrored in research on college students as well (Johnston et al., 1992b; Globetti et al., 1992).

In 1991, 6,601 fatal drug overdose cases were reported to the Drug Abuse Warning Network (DAWN) (National Institute on Drug Abuse, 1992); 36.9 percent of these fatal overdoses involved alcohol, and another drug in combination. However, this is an underestimation of the dangers of alcohol because overdose cases involving alcohol alone are specifically excluded from the DAWN reporting system. Further, alcohol is associated with 40–60 percent of all auto accident fatalities (Haberman, 1987; National Highway Traffic Safety Administration, 1991), as well as being linked with cirrhosis of the liver, pancreatitis, gout, several forms of cancer, neurological disorders including dementia, brain abnormalities, and general tissue damage (Secretary of Health and Human Services, 1983; 1990). Tobacco, like alcohol an addictive drug, is associated with diseases of the lungs (including cancer and emphysema) and heart disease; smokers are one-and-a-half times as likely to die in any one given year as nonsmokers (Grawunder and Steinmann, 1980). Both alcohol and tobacco are associated with low birth weight in infants (and consequent higher risk of mental retardation) (Duncan and Gold, 1982).

Ironically, in spite of their popularity and current legal status, alcohol and tobacco, as well as caffeine, have been outlawed in the past. The general public is familiar with Prohibition and the movement to ban "demon rum," but the history of attempts to control tobacco and caffeine is less well known. The American Indians brought tobacco with them when they were taken to the Spanish court by early explorers (Brecher et al., 1972). After their introduction into Europe, even though tobacco and snuff were seen by many as ungodly and unclean, people squandered away fortunes on the drug, which had to be shipped over from the New World. In 1642, Pope Urban VIII issued a bull (that is, an edict) of excommunication against those who used tobacco. Some European states outlawed it, and Sultan Murad IV of the Ottoman Empire even decreed the death penalty for smoking tobacco. Nevertheless, according to Brecher et al. (1972), no country that has taken up tobacco has been successful in outlawing it regardless of the penalty. Similar attempts at the suppression of coffee, tea, and cocoa (all containing caffeine) have failed. In sixteenth-century Egypt, for example, coffee was under controls similar to those pertaining to marijuana in the United States today. Sale was a crime, and stocks of coffee were burned. In Europe, medical opinion was used to back up opposition to the drug. Antagonism continued there even into the twentieth century as actual cases of overuse, including coffee psychosis and deliriums, were cited.

Public views of different drugs are in all probability a product of the legislation of morality (Duster, 1970). Some evidence suggests that laws themselves create a moral sentiment in opposition to the behavior being regulated. We forget that caffeine and nicotine are drugs (both have stimulant properties) because they are legal. Because of the impact on present laws of historical attempts to regulate various substances, it is important for readers to obtain a knowledge of the history of specific drug laws.

OPIATES AND COCAINE

Evidence that coca, a leaf with stimulant properties similar to caffeine, was used about 2,300 years ago in Peru and Ecuador comes from the discovery in graves of statues with puffed-out cheeks indicating coca leaf chewing (Grinspoon and Bakalar, 1985). At the time of the Spanish conquest, the Incas used coca leaves in divination, and the leaves were scattered by priests before religious rites. In 1551 and 1567, Catholic bishops called coca use idolatry and obtained a royal decree denouncing it. However, the Spaniards encouraged the use of coca by workers in gold and silver mines for its stimulant properties. Today, the coca leaf appears on the Peruvian coat of arms and is used as a folk medicine in Peru and Colombia and in religious ceremonies by some Colombian Indians. Cocaine, an alkaloid, was first extracted from coca in 1860 (Grinspoon and Bakalar, 1985). It is a short-acting stimulant that can be used as a local anesthetic. Consequently, it rapidly became popular for its medicinal qualities, as well as for recreational purposes. In 1863, Angelo Mariani patented *Vin Mariani*, a combination of coca extract and wine that was endorsed by numerous individuals, including the pope. By 1886, Coca-Cola was also being produced using coca extract. (It was later removed, and caffeine substituted.) Both Coca-Cola and Vin Mariani were seen as elixirs and stimulants. By the latter part of the nineteenth century, cocaine was recommended as a treatment for timidity and depression, and as a cure for morphine addiction.

Eventually, when people began exhibiting signs of cocaine dependence and psychosis after extended use, cocaine came to be touted as a "dangerous drug," associated with "Jew peddlers," "Negro users," and crime. By 1914, when the Harrison Act taxed and prohibited its use for all but medical purposes, more states controlled cocaine sales than sales of opiates. In 1922, Congress prohibited most importation of coca leaves and cocaine and defined cocaine as a narcotic (it is not). In 1951, Congress passed the Boggs amendment, which called for mandatory prison terms for possession or failure to register for importation of cocaine; penalties were increased in 1956.

Opium has a different but interconnected history. In the nineteenth century, opium (usually in the form of morphine) was as accessible as aspirin is today (Brecher et al., 1972; Duster, 1970; Inciardi, 1986; Lindesmith, 1965). It was sold in grocery stores in various forms as an over-the-counter medication. Patent medicines like Dover's Powder, Ayer's Cherry Pectoral, Mrs. Winslow's Soothing Syrup, and Godfrey's Cordial were easily obtainable—even by mail. Like many patent medicines, morphine was promoted as a cure for a wide variety of diseases, and in the late nineteenth century, it was thought to be the lesser of two evils when compared with alcohol. It was argued that morphine was cheaper, was less likely to be associated with criminal activity, contributed to general family happiness, and entailed no physical degeneration. Most users in the nineteenth century were white women, and the average user was about forty years old. Morphine was also used across all social classes.

The first antiopium laws in the United States were passed in response to Chinese immigration (Brecher et al., 1972). In the 1850s and 1860s, opium smoking was introduced to the United States by thousands of Chinese who came to America to construct the Western railroads. Many of these workers stayed in West Coast cities, which produced an anti-Chinese sentiment that was vented when, in 1875, San Francisco passed an ordinance prohibiting opium smoking in smoking-houses or "dens." Other cities and states followed suit by passing progressively more stringent laws against the drug. Opium was dealt a further blow by the Food and Drug Act of 1906, which led to product labeling. By this time, the general public had become aware of the addictive qualities of the drug, and the patent medicine industry declined. Its death blow came with the passage of the Harrison Act of 1914, a law designed to provide for the registration and taxation of opium and coca leaves and their derivatives. The act, in part, read: "Nothing contained in this section shall apply . . . to the dispensing or distribution of any of the aforesaid drugs to a patient by a physician, dentist, or veterinary surgeon registered under this Act in the course of his professional practice only" (Lindesmith, 1965: 4).

Despite this wording, physicians were arrested for dispensing opiates (including morphine and heroin) to addicts. The last eight words were eventually interpreted by the Supreme Court to mean that maintenance of opiate addicts (many of whom had been addicted by these same physicians) was not "professional practice" because it was not directed toward a cure (Lindesmith, 1965). Over 25,000 physicians were arrested in the years following passage of the act, and some 3,000 went to prison (New York Academy of Medicine, 1963; Goode, 1984). As a result of the attack on physicians, the composition of the addict population changed. By the 1920s, the vast majority of narcotics addicts were young, lower-class males, a pattern that continued into the 1990s (Goode, 1993; Kandel and Maloff, 1983).

Currently, at the federal level, drugs are regulated through the Comprehensive Drug Abuse Prevention and Control Act of 1970, which classifies drugs into five schedules according to their "abuse" potential (Drug Enforcement Administration, 1985). Trafficking in schedule I and II drugs (including heroin, benzodiazepines, hallucinogens, cocaine, marijuana, and some barbiturates and amphetamines) can be punished by up to fifteen to twenty years in prison and $125,000–$250,000 in fines, depending on the amount sold. The sale of marijuana (in amounts under one kilogram) and schedule III drugs (weak narcotic solutions like codeine and paregoric, some barbiturates, and widely prescribed amphetamines) can result in a maximum of five years in prison and up to $50,000 in fines.

Drug arrests rose dramatically between 1960 and 1991, primarily due to the widespread use of illegal drugs in the 1960s and an increasingly antidrug mood in the country (see Tables 9.1 and 9.2). Periodic "epidemics," like that recently involving crack (a smokable form of cocaine), increase enforcement efforts and create a class of criminals whose only offense is experimentation with drugs. In spite of sensational cases involving crack homicides (due primarily to the drug trade), the vast majority of crack users are nonviolent (see Chapter 20).

Marijuana

Between 1973 and 1978, eleven states decriminalized marijuana (Murphy, 1986). This change was primarily a product of the alteration in the population that was using the substance. From the 1930s to the 1950s, marijuana use was associated with blacks, Mexican-Americans, jazz musicians, and other low-status or culturally deviant groups (Polsky, 1969: 144–182). Penalties for possession were particularly draconian: "Typically, simple possession was a felony that carried penalties of two years for the first offense, five for the second, and ten for the third" (Himmelstein, 1986: 4). During the turbulent 1960s, middle-class individuals experimented with the drug, and it became popular across all social strata. Arrests for possession reached the middle class with increasing frequency, and pressure emerged from this quarter to alter the laws. All states except Nevada eventually reduced possession of small amounts of marijuana to a misdemeanor. Marijuana was decriminalized (reduced to the equivalent of a traffic offense for possession of small amounts—usually an ounce or less) in eleven states (Himmelstein, 1986; Jamieson and Flanagan, 1987: 62–65; Galliher and Cross, 1982). More recently, Alaska has recriminalized marijuana though that decision is under appeal and the law is not enforced.

PUBLIC DRUNKENNESS

The drug that precipitated the decriminalization movement is alcohol. A public health rather than a criminal justice approach to the problem of drunkenness was advocated by the 1967 President's Commission on Law Enforcement and Administration of Justice in reaction to the medicalization of alcoholism and the overcrowding of the courts and jails by chronic inebriates. When the commission advocated the elimination of penalties for public drunkenness, thirty-seven states removed public drunkenness from the criminal law (Whitford, 1983). Whereas in 1960, public drunkenness accounted for almost 36 percent of all arrests, by 1991, arrests dropped to about 6.2 percent; arrests for other public-inebriety-related offenses (notably disorderly conduct and vagrancy) also declined in this period. Despite this trend, however, there were 1,677,300 arrests for public drunkenness, disorderly conduct, and vagrancy combined in 1991 (see Table 9.2).

Ample evidence suggests that public drunks are arrested primarily because shopkeepers and store owners in central cities pressure police to do so, claiming the presence of drunks hurts their business (Speigelman and Wittman, 1983). For these businesses, detoxification facilities serve a similar purpose—they get the inebriate off the street. However, detoxification facilities' personnel prefer to work only with voluntary patients and hence try to avoid (and may refuse entry to) the most troublesome of the skid row types (Aarronson et al., 1978). Short-term detoxification also tends to be ineffective with chronic public inebriates (Daggett and Rolde, 1980) and represents a more expensive alternative than jail primarily because of the need for medical professionals. Thus, localities continue to rely on understaffed alternatives to jail while maintaining the jail as a backup.

DRUNKEN DRIVING

In 1960, drunken driving arrests represented fewer than 5 percent of all arrests; by 1991, they accounted for over 12.5 percent of all arrests. In actual numbers, they increased from slightly less than 200,000 to just under

1,800,000 during those years. According to some estimates, alcohol is a factor in 50–60 percent of single-vehicle auto fatalities (Haberman, 1987; National Highway Traffic Safety Administration, 1983), and involves other serious costs to society, estimated at $21–$24 billion per year by the President's Commission on Drunk Driving (1983). Despite a recent decline in the number of alcohol-related fatalities on the highway, the highway safety movement has taken on the "killer drunk" as a major target (Ball and Lilly, 1986).

The attack on the drunk driver has been two-pronged: mandatory minimum sentencing and mandatory alcohol education and treatment programs. Forty-three states have mandatory prison sentences for drunk driving, seventeen for the first offense (however, mandatory treatment is an option in some states) (Flanagan and Maguire, 1992: 166–167). In actual practice, however, police and the courts are reluctant to enforce these laws, and charges are frequently reduced to reckless driving (Ball and Lilly, 1986). Where they have not been reduced, legal challenges have been mounted, courts have become backlogged with these cases, and jail overcrowding has been exacerbated (Nienstedt, 1986). For example, cases of driving under the influence in Massachusetts in 1983 accounted for 25 percent of all county jail commitments (Forcier et al., 1986). Nationwide, DUI offenders account for 10 percent of jail inmates (Cohen, 1989) and 22.6 percent of all individuals on probation (Bureau of Justice Statistics, 1991a). The increasing use of criminal sanctions is occurring in spite of little evidence that jail terms reduce recidivism and accidents, whereas license suspensions and revocations do (Hingson and Howland, 1990).

An estimated 50–75 percent of first offenders and 75–98 percent of second offenders are alcoholic (Forcier et al., 1986). In recognition of this fact, alcohol and drug education or treatment programs are provided by statute in all but three states (Flanagan and Maguire, 1992: 662–665). This coincides with the emergence of the medical model as a supplement to legal action.

OVERLAPPING SOCIAL WORLDS

Americans have a love–hate relationship with vice. Various forms of vice are simultaneously practiced and condemned by an overwhelming proportion of the population. As a result, there is substantial overlap between the conventional and the deviant. People fluctuate between one and the other, flirting with the deviant while maintaining respectability. Matza (1964: 63–64) uses the term *subterranean values* to denote those elements in American culture that support some deviance. This overlap and movement back and forth between the conventional and the deviant receives considerable support through conventional social institutions.

One example of the expression of subterranean values is widespread support for illegal sports gambling. Newspapers publish point spreads for gambling purposes and sports commentators help gamblers make their picks for the day. Sports bettors also rely on legal information services like the *Gold Sheet* and an estimated 600–700 telephone call-in and "sports sheet" services (Frey and Rose, 1987). Similarly, racetrack bettors consult newspapers, including the likes of the *Washington Post*, the *Miami Herald*, and the *Chicago Tribune*, to obtain betting lines on the day's races (D'Angelo, 1987).

In a study of illegal gambling occurring in connection with legal bingo games, Lesieur and Sheley (1987) used the concept of *illegal appended enterprise* to denote a situation in which illegal activities depend on as well as support legitimate enterprises. In this case, illegal gambling benefits charities that run bingo games because the illegal activity attracts customers; at the same time, the illegal games need to have the customers of the legal operation in order to stay in business. Other illegal appended enterprises with symbiotic relationships in the world of vice include hotel prostitution (Prus and Irini, 1980); independent bookmaking businesses run out of the neighborhood bar (Perrucci, 1969); and drug sales from pizza shops, video gamerooms, and hotel lobbies (Henry, 1978; Valentine, 1978). In addition, there is at least tacit support for illegal behavior in "head shops," which sell pipes, cigarette papers, and other accoutrements of the drug world. Some businesses make it obvious that they combine both legal and illegal enterprises; others operate more secretly.

Not only do legitimate and illegitimate worlds overlap, but illegitimate worlds overlap as well. For example, in *Black Mafia*, Ianni (1974) discusses the Harlem network where prostitution, drugs, gambling houses, and boosting (professional shoplifting) intersect with boutiques and dry cleaning establishments that act as fronts for the illegal operations. In a different fashion, Prus and Irini (1980) discuss the intersecting worlds of hookers, strippers, rounders (professional thieves), the hotel and barroom staff, and desk clerks (involved in many varieties of illegal hustling in connection with their occupation), who all operate in one way or another in the hotel community.

Those who engage in illegal activity and work part time in that world (they are far more numerous than full-time workers) *straddle* both the legitimate and illegitimate worlds (D'Angelo, 1984). Because the vast majority of Americans engage in one form of illegal activity or another, we are actually a nation of straddlers. Some of us rail against the immorality of others while engaging in what others would call immoral conduct. As straddlers, we conceal our own immorality and avoid self-indictment by cleverly giving our offenses another name.

CONCLUSION

We have explored a number of themes in this chapter. Clearly, vice crime is not limited to a small number of people in this society; indeed, many people engage in behaviors that, technically, violate the law, and many more engage in activities that others want to outlaw. Few people realize the extent to which the economies of their communities rely in part on the delivery of products and services deemed illegal by the same communities. The decision to outlaw vices necessitates the allocation of large amounts of criminal justice resources to enforce laws against acts that have no complaining victim. Some would argue that governments produce even more crime by the very act of legislating against vices. For example, laws against drugs produce black markets that drive up drug prices and foster property crimes by people seeking to pay for drug habits. Ultimately, the lack of a complaining victim is the crux of the vice crime issue. To what extent should governments be permitted to enter the private worlds of consenting adults, to tell them what they may or may not do as long as they do not directly interfere with the rights of others not wishing to engage in the same behaviors?

<table>
<tr><td>

**DISCUSSION
QUESTIONS**

</td><td>

1. Why criminalize the vices? What is gained by making drug possession a crime, for example? Once criminalized, why is it so difficult to change the legal status of the vices?

2. The medical model of vice crime has become increasingly popular in recent years. Discuss the key elements and assumptions of the model. Why is it popular? What problems are associated with the model?

3. What is the process by which persons enter into the occupation of prostitution? How do prostitutes move up the income ladder in their occupation? In this sense, is prostitution different from most conventional occupations?

4. The rather vocal movement to outlaw pornography rests with the assumption that pornography influences behaviors ranging from violence toward women to the treatment of women as sex objects. What does the research literature tell us in this regard? What constitutional issues also enter the debate?

</td></tr>
</table>

◆ The authors thank Mark Evangelista and Thomas Payne for their research assistance.

CHAPTER 10

ORGANIZED CRIME: THE MAFIA MYSTIQUE

Jay S. Albanese
Niagara University

ORGANIZED CRIME always has conveyed a mystique that has made it appear larger than life. This image was fostered by a widespread belief that some mysterious organization was behind certain crimes, and it was pumped up by popular fiction and by Hollywood. Today, it is difficult to distinguish where the reality ends and the fiction begins. Many people have no clear conception of what the "Mafia" actually is, what it does, and whether or not it is a large or small part of all organized crime. For nearly a century, the nature and origins of organized crime have been obscure, preventing a clear sense of what should be done about it.

This chapter will outline the nature and history of organized crime in North America and demonstrate how the Mafia came to dominate most discussions of organized crime. A review of important events and research, focusing on the past twenty-five years, will demonstrate how the characterization of organized crime as dominated by the Mafia is a gross oversimplification. New models, or paradigms, to explain organized crime have now emerged that challenge some historical beliefs and shed more light on how organized crime develops and carries out its illicit activities. As this chapter will suggest, a model of organized crime as an illicit business "enterprise" is superior to other existing models that portray it as an ethnically based form of deviant behavior.

THE NATURE OF ORGANIZED CRIME

The various popular images of organized crime often make it difficult to define the phenomenon properly. Like any form of criminal behavior, however, it is best defined by the nature of the conduct involved, rather than by who commits it, because many different types of groups engage in organized crime. Historically, the government has chosen to define organized crime in terms of the ethnic derivation of those who engage in it. For example, in its final report, the President's Commission on Organized Crime (1987) defined "organized crime today" by describing known organized crime groups, distinguishing them according to their membership; included were Italian, Mexican, black, Chinese, Canadian, Vietnamese, Japanese, Cuban, Colombian, Irish, and Russian groups, in addition to motorcycle and prison gangs. As this chapter will show, however, organized crime is explained most satisfactorily in terms of the behaviors involved rather than in terms of its continually changing participants.

Three types of activities characterize organized crime: the provision of illicit goods, the provision of illicit services, and the infiltration of legitimate business. Provision of illicit goods involves the manufacture, sale, or distribution of illegal drugs, untaxed cigarettes, stolen property, and other goods that are either illegal or sold without proper government approval. Provision of illicit services includes running gambling operations, lending money, and offering sex outside the control of the law; illegal lotteries, lending money in excess of legal interest rates (loansharking), and prostitution are examples of illicit services. Common to the provision of both illicit goods and services is the crime of *conspiracy*. Conspiracy occurs when two or more people agree to commit an unlawful act, or to commit a lawful act by unlawful means. The distinction between organized crime and an individual prostitute, gambler, loanshark, or drug possessor has to do with conspiracy. Only when individuals *organize* (through a conspiracy) to provide illicit goods or services do the crimes of individuals become organized crime.

The third type of organized crime, the infiltration of legitimate business, occurs when a company (or government agency) is coerced through the use of force, threats, or intimidation to sell out to criminal interests, hire someone against its will, or engage in undesirable business or labor agreements. Whereas conspiracy characterizes the provision of illicit goods and services, *extortion* characterizes the infiltration of legitimate business. Extortion occurs when anything of value is taken and the owner is placed under duress due to threats of future force or violence. For example, legitimate businesspersons sometimes are forced to pay "protection money" to organized criminals in order to prevent vandalism on company property or to ensure labor peace. The nature of organized crime can be defined, therefore, as the provision of illicit goods and services (conspiracy) and the infiltration of legitimate business (extortion).

The precise extent of organized crime is unknown, as is its cost to society. Its extent is difficult to determine because most organized crime activity is never detected. Its costs to society were acknowledged by the 1967 President's Crime Commission Task Force on Organized Crime and the 1987 President's Commission on Organized Crime, but both these investigations observed that reliable estimates of the costs of organized crime were not available. It has been recognized, however, that the costs of organized crime in terms of illicit profits, unpaid taxes, disruption of legitimate business, and political and commercial corruption far exceed the costs to society incurred from street crimes (President's Commission, 1967a; President's Commission on Organized Crime, 1987).

THE ORIGINS OF THE MAFIA MYSTIQUE

Most historians have traced the alleged roots of organized crime in North America to a rather ambiguous event. The superintendent of police of New Orleans, Louisiana, David Hennessey, was shot by a group of unknown assassins in 1890. On his deathbed, the superintendent is said to have uttered either "Sicilians have done for me" or "Dagoes." This was interpreted at the time as indicating that Italians were responsible for his murder. Based on Hennessey's statement, seventeen Italian immigrants were arrested and accused of belonging to a Sicilian assassination league (Nelli, 1981; Smith, 1990). Although none of the suspects was convicted (due to a lack of evidence), an angry mob broke into the jail and killed eleven of the defendants.

Several separate historical inquiries into the Hennessey murder have since been conducted in both the United States and Canada. Each has concluded that his murder resulted from a business rivalry between two Italian families that controlled the dock area of New Orleans: the Matrangas and the Provenzanos. Hennessey supported the Provenzanos and his partiality apparently provoked the Matrangas into having him killed (Albini, 1971; Dubro, 1986; Nelli, 1981; Smith, 1990).

Of course, no Sicilian assassination league existed. Popular belief held that more than 1,000 Italian criminals had emigrated to the area in the late 1800s. During an investigation into the murders of the Italian defendants, however, authorities discovered that only about 300 Italian immigrants had criminal records, most of these were petty offenders, and this total of 300 was less than 1 percent of the Italian population of the city. The strong community hostility toward the suspects in Hennessey's murder reflected anti-immigrant sentiments associated with the large Italian immigration into North America during this period.

The anti-Italian sentiment did not die easily. The language barrier and apparent secretive nature of Sicilian immigrants (see Servadio, 1978: 3) fueled the belief in a "secret society" of Italians that engaged in criminal activity. Since the New Orleans incident, a continuous debate has raged over whether organized crime in North America evolved, was imported, or was modeled after an Italian Mafia—even though numerous historical investigations have been unable to document a central Mafia organization that existed beyond the local level in Italy (Albini, 1971; Hess, 1973; Blok, 1974; Servadio, 1978; Arlacchi, 1986).

THE KEFAUVER HEARINGS OF THE 1950s

After Superintendent Hennessey's death in 1890, the notion of the Mafia as a fundamental source of organized crime quickly faded. In the twenty-five years from 1918 to 1943, the word *mafia* appeared in *The New York Times* only four times, with most public attention during this period focused on Chicago's gangsters. The Illinois Crime Survey of 1929 produced what may be the first objective investigation of organized crime in the United States. After the murder of a Chicago prosecutor and the subsequent grand jury investigations, authorities concluded that "an underworld system of control" existed in Chicago that "has no formal organization" but is "held together by powerful leaders" who control criminal gangs (Landesco, 1929: 278). From the early 1900s to the late 1920s, the "overlordship of the underworld" in Chicago was said to be controlled by Big Jim Colosimo, John Torrio, Scarface Al Capone, and Mont Tennes. These men engaged primarily in gambling and bootlegging activities, but there was no clear Mafia connection. In addition, Chicago had thirteen different chiefs of police from 1900 to 1925, only one of whom served for as long as four years. This high turnover resulted, "almost without exception," from charges of graft or incompetence (p. 278). The Illinois Crime Survey found that the "huge revenues from bootlegging have given gangsters enormous funds with which to buy political protection and immunity from prosecution" (p. 279). It was also reported that these "gangsters" had recently begun to expand their activities into the infiltration of legitimate business.

This study of organized crime in Chicago during the early 1900s was not imitated in other cities. Recent investigations of organized gambling activities and political corruption, however, have revealed that continuing criminal enterprises often maintain themselves through co-optation or coercion of law enforcement or elected officials (see Brady, 1984; Chambliss, 1971, 1988). As the Illinois Crime Survey reported in 1929, a "mutuality of services" exists between organized crime and the political system: "The politician affords protection or immunity from prosecution, the gangster rallies his friends for legal as well as fraudulent voting" (Landesco, 1929: 280). Chambliss (1988) reported a similar finding in his study of illegal gambling in Seattle. He noted that the gambling activities were protected from prosecution by corrupt police officers who, in turn, were protected by corrupt politicians. Likewise, Brady (1984) found that instances of arson in some abandoned buildings in Boston occurred in which alleged racketeers bought properties at inflated prices with equally high mortgages and insurance coverage. Buildings were then intentionally torched and paid for by the insurance consortium, which spreads out the losses within the industry. In this way, legitimate businesses (for example, real estate companies, banks, and insurance companies) tacitly conspired with organized criminals (Brady, 1984: 216).

In 1950, organized crime and the Mafia became synonymous in the public's mind. A United States senator, Estes Kefauver, held televised hearings across the country throughout 1950 at which law enforcement officials and criminals testified. The officials claimed that a centralized criminal organization called the Mafia controlled much of organized crime in North America, but the criminals denied knowledge of the existence of such an organization. Kefauver's investigation concluded, however, that the Mafia exists: a "sinister criminal organization" that operates in several nations and is a "direct descendant" of a Mafia in Sicily.

Perhaps the most disappointing aspect of the Kefauver hearings was the fact that no actual investigation of organized crime ever took place. The televised hearings produced only *opinions* about the nature of organized crime. Police and public officials offered their opinions about organized crime, and Kefauver added his, but no one bothered to gather any evidence to substantiate these views. The most comprehensive analysis of the Kefauver hearings was conducted by the historian William Moore. He concluded that the committee's statements were "overblown and unfounded," largely ignored "the economic, legal, and social conditions giving rise to organized crime," and implied that it "originated outside of American society" and was continued here by "immoral men, bound together by a mysterious ethnic conspiracy" (Moore, 1974: 134, 237; see also Bell, 1953; Turkus and Feder, 1951).

Despite its flawed attempt to shed light on organized crime, the Kefauver committee solidified the view that most organized crime was at least controlled, if not operated, by a Mafia comprised exclusively of men of Italian origin. This apparently unshakeable belief was reinforced in 1957 when sixty-five men of Italian origin who had gathered in Apalachin, New York, were arrested. Theirs was termed a "meeting of the Mafia" because some of the men had criminal records (Smith, 1990). Several government investigations were conducted into this "Mafia meeting," and a trial was held in which those who refused to testify were charged with contempt, but no objective evidence was ever produced to connect these men with criminal activity. The U.S. Court of Appeals reversed the decisions brought against the men who had been convicted for obstructing justice by refusing to answer questions about the Apalachin incident. The court labeled the case no more than "pervasive innuendo" that "this was a gathering of bad people for an evil purpose." The judges concluded that "a prosecution framed on such a doubtful basis should never have been allowed to proceed so far" (*U.S.* v. *Buffalino*, 285 F.2d 408, 1960). Despite this conclusion, the Apalachin incident continued to be cited by many as "proof" of the existence of a Mafia that controlled most of organized crime in North America.

THE PAST THIRTY YEARS: THE GENERATION OF THE INFORMANT

Since 1963, we have seen a barrage of information about organized crime. Some is fact, much is fiction, and the largest portion never has been examined critically to determine the difference. The bulk of this information came from government informants, most of whom were criminals who agreed to provide the government with evidence in exchange for immunity from prosecution.

The first government informant who revised public thinking about organized crime was Joseph Valachi, the first "insider" to claim that there was, in fact, a centralized organization of Italian criminals in North America. Valachi claimed to be a member of a crime "family" in New York City. He testified about a confederacy of criminal groups in North America called Cosa Nostra, and alleged never to have heard of the Mafia. Interestingly, the President's Crime Commission in 1967 resolved this discrepancy by suggesting the Mafia had changed its name to Cosa Nostra even though no extrinsic evidence proved the existence either of a particular name or of a name change. Rather, the name Mafia or Cosa Nostra apparently was merely a popular way to describe organized crime in general.

According to Valachi, this federation of criminals of Italian origin arose from a 1930s gangland war called the Castellammarese War. The war resulted in the current organization of the Cosa Nostra into families that controlled organized crime in various cities in North America. In general, a single family, or group, directed activities in a given city, except for New York City, where five groups divided the territory. Though little effort was made to corroborate much of what Valachi said, his testimony resulted in the now familiar charts and "family trees" of organized crime groups, consisting of "bosses," "lieutenants," and "soldiers," that have been reproduced in various government reports on organized crime (President's Commission, 1967a; President's Commission on Organized Crime, 1987).

Valachi's claim of a national gangland war in which up to sixty people reportedly died has not found support among objective investigators. Several independent evaluations have been able to confirm only a handful of deaths during this period, and no evidence of a gangland "war" (Block, 1978; Nelli, 1981). Valachi's description of the organization of the Costa Nostra was also accepted uncritically. Although this description suggested a militarylike structure, Valachi testified to a looser confederation. He agreed that the function of the family is "mutual protection," but "otherwise, everybody operates by himself. They may take partners but that is their option" (U.S. Senate, 1963: 116, 194). Thus, Valachi indicated that organized crime may not have been as "organized" as was commonly believed at the time.

In any event, no one (including police officials) could provide supporting information regarding the existence of the Cosa Nostra or of the Castellammarese War independent of Valachi (U.S. Senate, 1963). Further, objective indications of Valachi's veracity, such as convictions in criminal trials, never were presented. Hawkins (1969: 46) has observed that Valachi "contradicted himself and was contradicted by others," and that his testimony "produced nothing in the way of tangible results." Yet, Valachi's testimony gave the Senate committee what it "wanted to hear . . . , and once [Valachi] had satisfied that desire there was little need to be skeptical or press for additional, independent information" (Smith, 1990: 234).

Valachi's version of organized crime was taken by the government to indicate that "organized crime is a society that seeks to operate outside the control of the American people and their governments." Further, "the core of organized crime consists of 24 groups" operating as "criminal cartels" in large cities—although Valachi was able to identify only sixteen organized crime groups (President's Commission, 1967a: 1, 6). The cartels allegedly controlled the bulk of illegal gambling, loansharking, narcotics trafficking, and prostitution in North America.

EMPIRICAL INVESTIGATIONS OF THE 1970s

In the 1970s, for the first time, organized crime groups drew the attention of independent researchers. The result was a growing collection of empirical investigations conducted by nongovernment officials into the nature of organized criminal activity.

LOCAL ETHNIC GROUP MODELS

The pioneering study was conducted by Albini (1971), who focused his investigation in both Italy and the United States. He relied on historical data, as well as on the accounts of informants on the streets and local police officials. He found that those involved in organized crime "do not belong to an organization." Instead, organized crime is a network of patron–client relationships wherein a person's "connections" provide him with access to a particular illicit activity. Rather than a "criminal secret society, a criminal syndicate consists of a system of loosely structured relationships" that exists so each participant can further his own welfare (p. 288). Albini's conclusions about the nature of organized crime represented the first empirically based effort drawing conclusions that differed radically from the government's perception of organized crime as a "nationwide conspiracy."

Albini's findings received support from the anthropologists Ianni and Reuss-Ianni (1973), who conducted a study of an organized crime family in New York City. Ianni lived with the family for two years as a participant-observer and became part of its social milieu. Like Albini, the Iannis found that criminal groups "have no structure apart from their functioning" (p. 20). Based on their observations of this family, and several other criminal groups, they concluded that such groups are *not*, as depicted by criminal justice officials, a "private government of organized crime" or a "cartel with national oversight" (U.S. Senate, 1965: 117; President's Commission, 1987: 42). Instead, they are loosely organized local groups, often consisting of members of the same ethnic derivation.

Another investigation that arrived at a similar conclusion was conducted by Anderson (1979). Using federal law enforcement data concerning a family suspected of being part of the Cosa Nostra, Anderson performed an economic analysis of the group's activity. Like the Iannis, she found that the use of violence was minimal and that no evidence linked the group to any national cartel. Interestingly, she also found that the family was "neither of major significance in the economy of the city where it operates nor a serious threat to its legitimate business competitors" (p. 140). Organized crime groups were less financially successful than the government had claimed they were in amassing "huge profits" (President's Commission, 1967a: 1).

In yet another investigation, Abadinsky (1981) constructed a life history of a former organized criminal (now in the witness protection program). The respondent, "Vito," described the structure of organized crime as neither complex nor bureaucratic. Abadinsky agreed with Anderson that "successful prosecution of a few leaders ('headhunting') does not have a significant impact on the organization; clients will shift to other patrons and continue their operations" (p. 126).

Clearly, though these various investigations each employed somewhat different approaches, their findings are remarkably consistent. They found organized crime to be characterized by informal networks of associations existing at the local level and often comprised of individuals of similar ethnic origin.

ENTERPRISE MODELS

A second group of objective investigations of organized crime was conducted from the mid-1970s into the 1980s. Once again, each researcher employed slightly different investigative techniques, making the consistency of their findings still more impressive. In his comprehensive history of organized crime in the United States, Smith (1990) found that organized crime and legitimate business are engaged in the same activities but do so at different ends of the "spectrum of legitimacy." He developed this notion into a "spectrum-based theory of enterprise" in subsequent publications (Smith, 1978, 1980). According to Smith, organized crime arises in the same way as do legitimate businesses. Loansharking, for example, exists for the same reason that banks do: Many potential customers wish to borrow money for various purposes; the supply of money to lend is assured through an interest rate charged on all loans; there are few enough competitors in the marketplace to assure a profit; and government regulators place certain restrictions on the market but nevertheless make it possible to survive and make a profit.

This configuration of suppliers, customers, regulators, and competitors forms the basis for both the legal and the illegal enterprise of lending. The only difference between the two, according to Smith, is the interest rate charged. As the legal interest rate changes, or as the legal lending market is opened up to more customers, the market for loansharking is affected proportionately. A similar analogy could be drawn for legal and illegal gambling, narcotics trafficking, and prostitution. The provision of illicit services, the source of much of the income generated by organized crime, is made possible, according to this view, by arbitrary distinctions between licit and illicit enterprise.

Block's (1979) historical investigation into the illicit cocaine market in New York during the early part of the twentieth century supported Smith's characterization of organized crime as a form of enterprise. Using archival data, Block discovered that the cocaine trade was not run by a single ethnic group or conspiracy but instead was characterized "by criminal entrepreneurs who formed, re-formed, split and came together again as the opportunity arose" (p. 94). He found, based on a review of the records of over 2,000 criminals, that these individuals "were in reality criminal justice entrepreneurs" organized through a "web of small but efficient organizations" (p. 95). Block's findings also indicated that ethnic ties did not appear to govern the organization of these activities, as the Iannis' study suggested. He discovered evidence "of interethnic cooperation which clearly suggests that at times parochialism was overcome by New York's criminals" (p. 95). Likewise, an account of the Irish "Westies" gang in Manhattan's Hell's Kitchen described efforts to cooperate with Cosa Nostra groups in New York City (English, 1991: 136–178).

Additional support for the enterprise model of organized crime appeared in a study of the solid waste collection and vending machine industries by Reuter et al. (1983). Using law enforcement files and street informants, they found that racketeer infiltration in these industries "may be a problem of small and declining importance" (p. 14). Improving technology has produced "market forces which simply prevent old-time muscle tactics and coercion from being effective." As a result, the racketeer is forced to "act like any other member of the industry, making decisions based on economic factors and shaped by market demand" (p. 33). In fact, continued assertions of racketeer involvement in these industries was found to make it more difficult for legitimate entrepreneurs to survive and make a profit.

A separate investigation by Reuter (1983) into loansharking and illegal gambling in New York City reached a similar conclusion. He found these markets populated by "small and ephemeral enterprises" that survive or fail based on market factors. In addition, no centralization of the illicit markets was established because "economic forces arising from the illegality of the product tend to fragment the market" (p. 176). In 1985, Adler similarly found the illicit narcotics market in "Southwest County" to be "largely competitive . . . rather than visibly structured." The smugglers themselves often referred to their activities as "one of the last arenas of free enterprise in existence" (p. 80). Individual entrepreneurs and small organizations, rather than centralized bureaucracies, characterized the market. Finally, Arlacchi (1986) ascertained through his own investigation that organized criminals in Italy have been "radically transformed by [their] identification with market forces" (p. 119). Rather than the pursuit of honor, as Arlacchi claims was the objective years ago, organized criminals now seek wealth and power through enterprises that keep costs and competition to a minimum, while maintaining access to financial resources.

COMPARING THE VARIOUS MODELS

The three different models, or paradigms, of organized crime discussed to this point are presented in Table 10.1. The traditional view, established through criminals turned informants and in government reports, describes organized crime as a national conspiracy controlled largely by one group. Based on this view, the logical prevention strategy has been to neutralize the leaders of the group. Once they are incarcerated or otherwise neutralized, the conspiracy will collapse.

The second model, established through several different empirical investigations, depicts organized crime as a collection of locally organized ethnic groups. This model suggests that prosecution of organized crime leaders will lead only to their being replaced by others because the culture and the patron–client relationships that permit the existence of organized crime will still exist. Control of organized crime, according to this model, will be effected only through increased awareness of its costs to the community and through legalization of those consensual behaviors that are now in high public demand but are illegal.

Finally, the enterprise model is similar to the local ethnic groups model in that organized crime is characterized by an informal, decentralized structure that rarely employs violence to achieve its goals. Rather than focus on the unity within ethnic groups, however, the enterprise model sees market conditions as the controlling factor in the establishment and maintenance of organized crime. If the configuration of suppliers, customers, regulators, and competitors is favorable, then organized crime will flourish (Albanese, 1987a). The control of organized crime, according to this view, will be achieved only when the market conditions that breed it are better understood. Arbitrary distinctions between

TABLE 10.1 **PARADIGMS OF ORGANIZED CRIME**

View of Organized Crime	Source of Data	Implications for Control
Nationwide Conspiracy		
25 + "families" and a "commission" Members of Italian descent Controls virtually all gambling, loansharking, prostitution, and narcotics Murder and violence part of organization policy	Government reports (e.g., 1967 and 1986 presidential investigations) and informants (e.g., Valachi and Fratianno)	Dismantle the nationwide conspiracy through prosecution and incarceration of its leaders
Local Ethnic Groups		
Organized crime groups not formal organizations Organized crime groups not significant to local economy Use of violence minimal No evidence of nationwide conspiracy	Albini, 1971 (police and informants) Ianni, 1973 (participant observation) Anderson, 1979 (FBI records) Abadinsky, 1981 (protected witness)	Prosecution of leaders will never be successful; they will only be replaced by others Need changed community awareness to understand social costs of organized crime Legalization of consensual behaviors
Enterprise		
Both organized crime and normal business involve similar activity on different ends of "spectrum of legitimacy" Not limited to operations within certain ethnic groups Use of violence minimal No evidence of nationwide conspiracy	Smith 1978, 1990 (organizational theory) Block, 1979 (historical records) Reuter, 1983 (police and informants) Adler, 1985 (participant observation) Arlacchi, 1986 (records and interviews)	Assertions of "racketeer involvement" in certain industries hurts legitimate business Improve understanding of market forces conducive to organized crime Eliminate arbitrary distinctions between legal and illegal gambling, lending, narcotics, and sexual behavior

legal and illegal lending, narcotics trade, gambling, and sexual services are examples of market conditions, created by government, that favor the establishment of organized crime groups (see Albanese, 1993; Haller, 1992).

RECENT PROSECUTION TOOLS

Joseph Valachi's testimony, echoed in the 1967 President's Crime Commission report, resulted in several important new laws designed to combat organized crime in the 1970s and 1980s. These laws created powerful prosecution tools for the government.

THE OMNIBUS CRIME CONTROL AND SAFE STREETS ACT OF 1968: TITLE III

The first law passed in response to the concern about organized crime was Title III of the Omnibus Crime Control and Safe Streets Act of 1968. The provisions of this statute permitted federal law enforcement officials to use wiretaps or electronic microphones to eavesdrop on the conversations of suspected organized criminals, provided they first obtained a warrant. This enabled electronic surveillance information to be admitted as evidence in federal court for the first time. Subsequent decisions by the U.S. Supreme Court have further broadened the scope of wiretap authority so that prosecutors may introduce as evidence information overheard regarding third parties not the subject of the warrant, warrantless pen register recording (that is, lists of telephone numbers dialed), and warrantless electronic "beeper" surveillance, among other things (for a summary, see Albanese, 1984a).

The desirability of electronic surveillance as an investigative tool has been widely debated. Proponents argue that it is an efficient means of infiltration of criminal organizations. The use of undercover agents, as an alternative, is seen as time consuming, dangerous, and not always feasible in organized crime cases. Likewise, it is argued that the warrant requirements and procedural restrictions prevent unnecessary invasions of privacy. A large number of convictions also have resulted from wiretaps—from 1976 to 1986, convictions arising from electronic surveillance doubled to 761.

Critics of electronic surveillance point both to its prohibitive cost and to its violation of basic rights to privacy. In 1986, wiretaps and bugs averaged $35,508 per tap, due to the intensive personnel requirements in monitoring and analyzing conversations. From 1969 to 1986, the number of wiretaps installed more than doubled to 670, but the proportion of incriminating conversations overheard dropped from 49 to 19 percent of all intercepted conversations. This has led critics to argue that electronic surveillance is not being used scrupulously. Further, arrests have resulted in convictions only about half the time. The disputable ability of electronic surveillance to investigate criminal conspiracies effectively, its high costs, the fear of violations of privacy rights, and scandals regarding illegal electronic surveillance by police in at least twenty states since 1969 are certain to keep the debate over its desirability alive (Katz, 1983; Krajick, 1983; National Wiretap Commission, 1976; Schlegel, 1988). As a reflection of uncertainty about electronic surveillance, twenty-one states still prohibit its use.

THE ORGANIZED CRIME CONTROL ACT OF 1970

The second legislative outcome of Valachi's testimony and the 1967 President's Crime Commission was the Organized Crime Control Act of 1970. Witness immunity, the witness protection program, investigative grand juries, and new racketeering provisions were among the significant components of the act.

◆ **WITNESS IMMUNITY** ◆   The witness immunity provisions allow federal prosecutors to grant reluctant witnesses immunity from prosecution in exchange for their testimony. Witnesses who fail to testify under a grant of immunity are held in contempt of court and can be jailed indefinitely until they testify. The rationale is to permit prosecution of higher-level organized crime figures from the testimony of less important offenders. The lack of objective evidence of the utility of this provision, however, has led critics to point to several significant organized crime trials in which the defendants were acquitted because of the jury's unwillingness to believe the government's immunized witness (Dershowitz, 1987). In addition, "use" immunity provided under this law allows incriminating evidence to be used against the witness if it is obtained independently of his or her testimony. As Block and Chambliss (1981: 205) have observed, "proving evidence was tainted" would be difficult. The intuitive credibility problems of immunized testimony and its potential misuses have not yet been addressed through an objective cost–benefit examination of witness immunity in organized crime cases.

◆ **WITNESS PROTECTION** ◆   The witness protection program, also established as part of the Organized Crime Control Act, provides a mechanism for the government to protect witnesses whose lives are in danger from persons against whom they have testified. The program, administered by the U.S. Marshals Service, gives protected witnesses new identities and moves them to a different location to begin a new life. The U.S. General Accounting Office evaluated the program in 1984 and found that federal organized crime cases utilizing protected witnesses resulted in a high proportion of convictions (75 percent), and of those convicted, 70 percent were sentenced to two years or more in prison. This was twice the rate of federal organized crime cases not involving protected witnesses. On the other hand, protected witnesses had been arrested an average of 7.2 times prior to their admission to the program, and 21 percent were arrested again within two years of gaining entrance to the program. In addition, the program's size and cost have far exceeded projections: More than 4,400 witnesses and 8,000 family members have now been relocated at an annual cost of $25 million. Clearly, therefore, the benefits of the program (high conviction rate and longer sentences) must be weighed against its costs (crimes by protected witnesses and the program's $25 million annual expenditure).

◆ **SPECIAL GRAND JURIES** ◆   Title I of the Organized Crime Control Act established special grand juries designed to investigate more effectively organized crime activities that cross state lines. Like traditional grand juries, special grand juries hear evidence from prosecutors to determine if probable cause exists for indictment. In addition, special grand juries can issue a public report on organized crime or corruption in an area at the end of their term. They also can conduct continuing investigations along with police. Some states have established statewide grand juries that perform an analogous function across county lines. Supporters of these investigative juries argue that such broad authority is needed to investigate organized crime, which often is multijurisdictional. In addition, such juries may be better insulated from local political pressures that can prevent investigations into organized crime at the local level. Critics argue that special grand juries have been used to harass individuals based on their political leanings, and to "invent" cases rather than determine whether one already exists (Rhodes, 1984). As might be expected, both proponents and detractors can cite examples to support their positions, but no objective cost–benefit evaluation has yet been undertaken to determine the actual worth of such grand juries over a large number of cases.

◆ **RACKETEERING PROVISIONS** ◆   Perhaps the most controversial prosecution tool established as part of the Organized Crime Control Act is the section on Racketeer Influenced and Corrupt Organizations (RICO). This section prohibits acquisition, operation, or income from an "enterprise" through a "pattern" of "racketeering activity." Enterprise has been defined as any individual or group, a pattern is two or more offenses within a ten-year period, and racketeering activity is any offense punishable by a year or more in prison. Persons violating this law are subject to extended penalties of up to twenty years imprisonment, fines up to $25,000, forfeiture of any interest in the enterprise, and treble civil damages and dissolution of the enterprise itself.

Although RICO was established to fight organized crime, it has been used to prosecute illegal activities in a county sheriff's department, a state tax bureau, the Philadelphia traffic court, the Tennessee governor's office, and several corporations (Poklemba and Crusco, 1982). This broad application of RICO has made it perhaps the most controversial part of the Organized Crime Control Act.

The disagreement over the proper scope of RICO was ultimately resolved in 1985 in a U.S. Supreme Court case involving two corporations (*Sedima* v. *Imrex Co.*). The case arose from a civil suit between two companies involved in a joint venture where one company thought it was being defrauded by the other in an overbilling scheme. A RICO suit was filed against the other corporation, charging it with mail and wire fraud (to establish the pattern), and claiming $175,000 in overbilling. Treble damages and attorney's fees were sought under RICO.

The U.S. Supreme Court had to determine whether preexisting criminal convictions were required to establish a pattern under RICO, and whether simple monetary loss constitutes a racketeering injury sufficient for a RICO suit. In a 5–4 decision, the Court held that "no such requirement exists" for prior criminal convictions to initiate a RICO suit, as long as at least two offenses are charged in the suit to establish the pattern. The Court also held that no more harm is required under RICO "separate from the harm from the predicate acts." The RICO suit between the corporations was upheld, thereby permitting the broad application of RICO to all forms of organized crime, whether committed by professional criminals or by corporations. This broad application of the RICO provisions will undoubtedly expand the law's use in the future, and it formed the basis for many of the cases of "insider trading" among Wall Street firms during the 1980s. State RICO laws that apply to patterns of state law violations now exist in twenty-four states.

Clearly, all five investigative tools discussed here involve tradeoffs. It is more than a simple empirical issue to determine whether the socioeconomic costs versus benefits of electronic surveillance, witness immunity, the witness protection program, special grand juries, and the RICO provisions make them desirable law enforcement tools. Value judgments must be made, inasmuch as powerful investigative and prosecution tools are likely to be abused at one time or another. Whether sufficient safeguards are in place and the abuses are few enough, compared to the results gained in combating organized crime, remains arguable. In order to make educated judgments, however, it is necessary to gather more information regarding the effective uses, and abuses, of these tools in practice.

THE MOB TRIALS OF THE 1980s AND 1990s

Despite the research findings of the past twenty-five years, the government's approach to organized crime has favored prosecution of alleged leaders rather than alteration of market conditions. The government has experienced a great deal of success in recent years, however, beginning with the testimony of a number of criminals turned informant. Unlike Joseph Valachi, some of these informants, such as Jimmy Fratianno, appeared to be high-ranking members of organized crime. Although Fratianno's testimony had inconsistencies, it resulted in the conviction of a number of high-ranking organized criminals in recent years (Albanese, 1983). Other insiders have been granted immunity or placed in the witness protection program. The result has been an unprecedented effort to prosecute organized crime out of existence.

The alleged leaders of sixteen of the twenty-four "Mafia" groups identified by the government were indicted between 1983 and 1986. Nearly 5,000 federal organized crime indictments were issued by grand juries in 1985 alone (Powell et al., 1986). This increase in prosecutions was not due to new laws but rather to the utilization of existing laws and the application of more investigative resources to the problem. On the federal level, the Reagan administration authorized more than 700 federal wiretaps in its first four years, more than double that of the previous four years. Many of the prosecutions of the 1980s took place in New York City and relied on the investigative efforts of a reorganized New York State Organized Crime Task Force. In addition, the RICO provisions came to be utilized more frequently once the U.S. Supreme Court had upheld its broad application in both civil and criminal cases.

These efforts resulted in numerous trials of high-level organized crime figures and in the conviction of well over 200 individuals (for a list of these trials and outcomes, see Albanese, 1989). Six facts become apparent when one examines the defendants, their roles, their alleged offenses, and the sentences handed down in these cases.

First, many of the cases clearly were significant. Most involved racketeering convictions that entailed the infiltration of legitimate business through bribery or extortion. The sentences imposed on the principals, excluding the life sentences, average more than twenty-five years per offender.

Second, many of the cases involved organized crime in New York City although many other parts of the United States were affected as well. Convictions involving organized crime operations in New England, Chicago, Las Vegas, and Philadelphia attest to the national scope of the prosecution results.

Third, the prosecution's focus remains on organized crime of Italian-Americans. The overwhelming majority of cases involved Mafia groups although conviction of members of the United Bamboo Chinese gang and various Jamaican groups on narcotics distribution and murder conspiracy charges indicates a change in enforcement focus and perhaps a shift in the types of groups participating in organized crime activity.

Fourth, the debate over the existence of a Mafia was finally rendered moot in a 1986 trial, when the defendants (the alleged bosses of the New York City crime families) in the "Commission" trial conceded that the "Mafia exists and has members." Further, the defense confirmed the existence of the commission that was mentioned in wiretapped conversations of the defendants. Sicilian informer Tommaso Buscetta stated that he was told by Joseph Bonanno in 1957 that "it was very advisable" to set up a commission in Sicily "to resolve disputes" among criminal groups (Lubash, 1985). In his autobiography, Bonanno (1984: 127–188) claims to have set up such a commission in America though he refused to testify in the Commission trial and was jailed for contempt. The role of the commission, according to the defendants in the Commission trial, is only to approve new members and to mediate conflicts among the groups. The prosecution argued, however, that four of the defendants participated in "the ruling council of La Cosa Nostra, or the 'Mafia' which directed criminal activity" (Lubash, 1986; Smothers, 1986).

The defense in the Commission trial argued that the Mafia represented a loose social and business association of individuals with similar backgrounds, but without a criminal purpose, that could be likened to a businessmen's professional association whose goal is the *avoidance* of conflict (Magnuson, 1986). Thus, the purpose of the defense's admissions was to challenge the government "to prove it has actually engaged in the crimes of which it has been accused" (Oreskes, 1986). The charges included bid-rigging of concrete prices, extortion, and in the case of one defendant, murder. The charges ultimately were proved, and each defendant was sentenced to a hundred years in prison.

Fifth, at least five significant mob trials resulted in acquittals and mistrials. Some observers have argued that the government's heavy reliance on former criminals as paid government witnesses is a questionable practice. Juries are not always willing to convict a defendant when the case is based largely on the testimony of a criminal turned informant (Dershowitz, 1987).

Finally, many of those convicted during the 1980s and 1990s were senior citizens: The average age of the principals was 62, and some were over 70. Given an average sentence of twenty-five years, even counting parole eligibility, an entirely new leadership likely will emerge among Italian-American organized crime groups.

THE FUTURE OF ORGANIZED CRIME

What impact the outcomes of the mob trials of the 1980s and 1990s will have on organized crime is not yet clear. The combination of convictions of older leaders of criminal groups, convictions for serious crimes, long prison sentences, involvement of a number of cities, and emerging organized crime groups does, however, suggest some interesting projections. Certainly, the mob trials will have some immediate impact on organized crime although modification of public policy will be required for longer-term changes. The future of organized crime can be characterized by probable changes in the nature of its operations, in its level of violence, and in its primary activities.

The mob trials already have resulted in increased violence within and among organized crime groups. The murders of Paul Castellano and Frank DeCiccio, among others, have demonstrated that the threatened incapacitation of a high-level organized crime figure can result in a power struggle for control of the illicit enterprise. The car-bombing murder of Frank DeCiccio in New York City, soon after Castellano's murder, was viewed by some police officials as a retaliatory act (O'Brien and Kurins, 1991). This violence likely will continue in the struggle for leadership of organized crime groups and in the effort to avoid prosecution by "protecting" illicit enterprises and "eliminating" suspected informants. As we noted, observers have found that successful prosecution of organized crime leaders will bring to power younger, more aggressive leaders who will use violence more freely to protect their interests and to avoid prosecution (Anderson, 1979: 144).

A second projection has organized criminals shifting to "safer" activities that are better insulated from street-level investigation and prosecution. Increasing organized crime involvement in credit card and airline ticket counterfeiting and in illicit toxic waste disposal have been cited as examples of this trend (Powell et al., 1986). As a result, the infiltration of legitimate business, rather than the more visible activities necessary in catering to the vices of narcotics, gambling, and prostitution, may prove to be an area of greater interest to organized crime.

A third projection involves the sophistication of organized crime. The general success of the mob trials in prosecuting traditional organized crime may result in changes in the operation of illicit enterprises. As McIntosh (1975) has suggested, the "technology" or sophistication of organized crime responds to law enforcement effectiveness. Once law enforcement strategy becomes more effective, as the mob trials indicate, "we can expect the criminal technology to reach rapidly the same level of efficiency in order to maintain acceptable levels of success" (Albanese, 1987b: 73). This sophistication may take the form of increased interest in the *financing* of criminal activities and decreased involvement in the *operation* of criminal enterprises. Gambling and narcotics sales have been cited as the two largest sources of organized crime revenue. It is possible that traditional racketeers who wish to remain in the gambling and narcotics businesses will cease operating these higher-risk enterprises and rather be content to finance other illicit entrepreneurs for a percentage of the profits. Illegal profits can then be laundered through legally owned businesses, such as restaurants and nightclubs. In order to accomplish this, organized criminals may make a greater effort in the future to infiltrate legitimate businesses to obtain access to money for financing and to have the means to launder illicitly obtained cash. Labor union funds and the construction industry have been favorite targets in the past.

As a result, the successful prosecution of organized crime leaders in recent years may be a mixed blessing. Although it may disrupt operations for a short period, it also will shift organized crime activities to "safer," but more complex, scams and possibly encourage further organized crime infiltration into legitimate business to finance illicit enterprise and to launder illegally obtained profits.

Without more attention to the market conditions under which organized crime operations emerge and flourish, however, we must resign ourselves to the short-term satisfaction of periodically incapacitating a relatively small number of organized criminals. A longer-term remedy will result only when the economic opportunities for organized crime are better understood and the large market for illicit products is reduced.

CONCLUSION

The goal of this chapter was to challenge the reader's everyday assumptions about organized crime. Most people's notion of organized criminals relies on and perpetuates the Mafia mystique—organized crime conducted by a national band of interlocked families of Italian descent. As our review of the issue indicates, the evidence challenges this notion. Indeed, if we compare it with other models of organized crime based on serious empirical investigation, we find that organized crime is far more local than national in character, that family is of little consequence, and that members of many ethnic groups engage in organized crime. More important, organized crime is driven by local economic and business conditions—just as any legitimate local enterprise is driven. This means, of course, that if the criminal justice system pursues only the leaders of organized criminal groups, little control can be exerted over organized crime. To the extent that the government has been successful in prosecuting leaders of local organized crime groups, these groups have been moving to other, more subtle forms of criminal activity, as market conditions would dictate, or they have been replaced by new organized criminal groups who cater to the demands of the illicit marketplace. Ultimately, control of organized crime will occur only when we fully understand and can disrupt the market conditions that shape it.

DISCUSSION QUESTIONS

1. Criminal justice professionals often caution that organized crime is a serious problem for this society. Is it? Why are the extent and cost of organized crime so difficult to determine?

2. Albanese discusses three models of organized crime. What are they? How different are these models in terms of their assumptions and their implications for control?

3. Is there really a nationally linked Mafia or Cosa Nostra? Discuss the evidence for both sides of this question.

4. What strategies have federal and state governments developed to combat organized crime? Have they been successful? Discuss the projections for the future of organized crime.

CHAPTER 11

◆

RESPECTABLE CRIME

James W. Coleman
California Polytechnic State University, San Luis Obispo

ALTHOUGH "STREET CRIMES" such as robbery and murder may spark the greatest fear in the public, and gain the most attention from the media, the damage they do is dwarfed by that of "respectable" criminals who wear white collars and work for our most powerful organizations. In 1985, the average robbery netted about $628 and the average burglary about $953 (Jamieson and Flanagan, 1987: 270). The next year, a single respectable criminal, Ivan F. Boesky, agreed to pay $100 *million* in fines and penalties for his illegal stock market dealings (Hiltzik, 1987)—far more money than 150,000 average robberies would net. Still, that huge sum was only about half of Boesky's net worth, and in all likelihood was far less than he actually made from his crimes. Moreover, the crimes of major corporations cost the public a far greater amount. For example, the A. H. Robins Company's "ongoing fraud," in which it knowingly misrepresented "the nature, quality, safety and efficacy of the Dalkon Shield" (a widely used but very dangerous birth control device), is expected to cost the company between $1.7 and $5 *billion* to compensate the hundreds of thousands of women who were injured (Siegel, 1985). And the asbestos producers' cover-up of their product's deadly hazards may cost as many lives as all the murders in the United States in an entire decade—over 150,000 (Cooper and Steiger, 1976).

These examples indicate that respectable, or white collar, crime is more than a bit of embezzlement or tax evasion by people who seem not to need more money than they have. In the coming pages, we will define and look more closely at respectable crime committed by individuals and by corporations. We will see that it takes many forms, most of which cost the public enormous amounts of money, some of which cost the public precious civil liberties, and some of which even cost lives. Opportunity and motivation are examined as crucial variables in understanding respectable crime. Finally, we investigate the reasons for government's relative inactivity in seeking to control these costly law violations.

DEFINING RESPECTABLE CRIME

In the early days of criminology, the crimes of the rich and powerful were hardly given a thought. Most crime and violence was seen as the product of a "social pathology" among the poor and the immigrants who lived in our rapidly growing industrial cities. Although others had tried to focus attention on the respectable criminal, it was Sutherland (1949) who introduced a term that soon became part of the American vocabulary and was translated into numerous other languages around the world. The term was, of course, *white collar crime*.

Sutherland's definition of white collar crime was simple and straightforward: "a crime committed by a person of respectability and high social status in the course of his [her] occupation" (Sutherland, 1983: 7). To be a white collar criminal, therefore, someone must have a reasonably high social status and commit a crime as a part of an occupation. A top executive who poisoned her husband would not be a white collar criminal; nor would a janitor who stole from his boss. At first, Sutherland's definition raised a storm of controversy. Critics charged that white collar offenders were not real criminals because they did not consider themselves to be criminals and were not usually prosecuted by the law. But over the years, criminologists have come to accept Sutherland's thesis that widespread criminality indeed exists among the rich and powerful, even if they are seldom punished for their crimes.

Though practically all criminologists now recognize the importance of the problem of white collar crime, many still object to the way Sutherland formulated his definition. Some would include any nonviolent economic crime as a white collar offense (Edelhertz, 1970: 4; Webster, 1980)—an approach that shifts attention away from the respectable criminals that the term was intended to describe. Such a definition would, for example, include a welfare mother who kept secret an outside job, while excluding a business executive convicted of reckless homicide for causing the death of an employee. Most criminologists therefore stick closer to Sutherland's original definition, but that does not mean it cannot be improved. Persons in the middle ranks of the status hierarchy are commonly included along with the high-status offenders Sutherland mentioned; it is also useful to recognize explicitly that entire organizations may be considered offenders independently of the guilt of any one of their members. For the purposes of this chapter, a white collar crime will be defined as "a violation of the law committed by a person or group of persons in the course of an otherwise respected and legitimate occupation or financial activity" (Coleman, 1985b: 5).

CRIMES OF THE RESPECTED

The definition given has the virtue of being broad and encompassing, but it includes so many different types of crime that it is difficult to grasp them all. To understand the crimes of the respectable, it is necessary to divide them up into

TABLE 11.1   COMMON WHITE COLLAR CRIMES

Type of Crime	Common Subtypes	Social Impact
Occupational Crimes		
Employee theft	—	May add 2–4 percent to the cost of typical retail merchandise
Embezzlement	—	Individual crimes may run into hundreds of millions of dollars; typical embezzlement much smaller
Crimes in the professions	Unnecessary services Fraud	Over 10,000 lives and tens of billions of dollars lost per year
Bribery* and corruption	Commercial bribery Political bribery	Annual cost is $3–$15 billion, but worst impact is the subversion of democratic government.
Organizational Crimes		
Fraud and deception	False advertising Tax fraud Commercial fraud	Yearly losses in the hundreds of billions, loss of confidence in business and tax system
Antitrust violations	Illegal mergers and acquisitions Price fixing and collusion Unfair competition	Probably the most costly of all white collar crimes — over $350 billion per year
Violations of civil liberties	Discrimination in employment Surveillance Political harassment Political violence	Represses freedom of expression, denies basic human rights, undermines democratic rule
Violent corporate crimes	Unsafe products Unsafe techniques of production	Death toll exceeds 100,000 per year, many more injuries

SOURCE: Data drawn from Coleman, 1985b.

* Bribery is often committed by organizational offenders as well.

smaller, more discrete units. Although white collar offenses may be classified in many ways, one of the most useful distinctions is between organizational and occupational crimes. *Organizational crimes* are offenses committed by an organization as a whole or by individual members with the help, encouragement, and support of the organization. *Occupational crimes* are carried out by individuals or groups without such organizational encouragement and support. We can safely assume that most white collar criminals are seeking to advance their own personal interests, but individuals involved in organizational crimes are also seeking to promote the goals of their organizations, whereas occupational criminals are not.

This section will focus on eight major white collar crimes. Three of them (employee theft, embezzlement, and crimes in the professions) usually are occupational crimes, and four of them (occupationally related fraud and deception, antitrust offenses, violations of civil liberties, and violent offenses) typically are organizational crimes (see Table 11.1). Bribery and corruption are unique in that they often are both occupational and organizational crimes. For example, if an elected official takes a bribe to help a corporation land a lucrative government contract, the official is committing an occupational crime, while the representative of the corporation is committing an organizational crime. The reader who compares the descriptions in the following pages will see that organizational crimes generally are far more harmful to the public than are occupational offenses, whether the criterion for comparison is financial loss or the injuries and deaths they cause.

RIPPING OFF THE BOSS: EMPLOYEE THEFT AND EMBEZZLEMENT

Employee theft is one of the most common of all crimes. One-third of the people interviewed in a large study by Hollinger and Clark (1983) admitted stealing from their employer in the previous year. Considering that some thieves probably denied it, it seems reasonable to assume that most people will commit an employee theft sometime during their life. In fact, employee theft is so common and widely accepted that many types are barely considered criminal. Studies of the subcultures that develop in different organizations indicate that workers develop a clear-cut set of rules about what kinds of property employees can and cannot take. For example, the workers in one midwestern television plant saw nothing wrong with taking such things as light tools, electrical tape, screws, nails, and scraps, but drew the line at the theft of large items such as heavy machines and large power tools (Horning, 1970). However, the relationship between workers and management at some firms is so bad that most of the employees consider virtually anything fair game. Indeed, in many cases, groups of employees together have practically stripped their employers bare. It is estimated that about a thousand firms go bankrupt every year because of employee theft (McCaghy, 1987: 178). Many of the biggest employee thefts are committed against stockbrokers and securities dealers—police raids have uncovered stashes of stolen stock valued at as much as $10 million.

Embezzlement also involves taking something that belongs to one's employers, but whereas embezzlers violate a financial trust that was placed in them, other thieving employees do not. Because only a few employees are placed in such positions of trust, the opportunities for embezzlement are far more restricted than for employee theft. Yet, the embezzler's take is likely to be far greater than the thief's. Embezzlements by top corporate executives have been known to run into hundreds of millions of dollars although most embezzlers must content themselves with a far smaller profit.

Current data suggest significant changes in the profile of the typical embezzler in recent years. Embezzlement, like most other crimes, was traditionally a man's business. But data from the Bureau of Justice Statistics (1987c) indicate that 41 percent of persons arrested for embezzlement in 1984–1985 were female—one of the highest percentages for any type of crime. This significant increase probably reflects the growing number of women employed in positions of financial trust such as bookkeepers and accountants. However, female criminals still suffer from the same sexual discrimination as other women. Daly's (1989) analysis of the presentence reports from a large sample of white collar offenders indicates that male embezzlers are more likely to hold managerial positions, whereas female embezzlers are more likely to be tellers and clerical workers. Men, moreover, made far more from their white collar crimes than did women.

The use of the computer to commit embezzlement and other white collar crimes has captured the public's imagination in a way that few other crimes have. The computer criminal sometimes is seen as a kind of Robin Hood who outsmarts a faceless bureaucracy by turning its own tools against it, sometimes as a new threat to the very stability of the financial system. But all the attention computer crime receives hardly seems justified on the basis of its cost to the public. Most estimates of the yearly losses from computer crime range from $100 million to $300 million (*Business Week*, 1981; Sloan, 1984: V); by contrast, far greater losses commonly result from a single corporate crime. Perhaps computer crime should be considered the "crime of the future," for given the fact that electronic fund transfers handle over $173 *trillion* a year, the potential for much more serious problems certainly exists (Bureau of Justice Statistics, 1986b).

CRIMES IN THE PROFESSIONS

Of all white collar crimes, offenses committed by doctors, lawyers, accountants, and other professionals tend most often to be ignored. One reason, of course, is the great prestige of these professional groups and the assumption that their members therefore must be law-abiding citizens. But equally important are their political influence and determined opposition to "outside interference" in their professional activities. All the major professions have established organizations for professional self-regulation that serve, to one degree or another, to restrict outside scrutiny of their affairs. And they all share a strong sense of solidarity that provides a shield behind which the incompetent and the unethical can hide.

For example, because almost all medical procedures pose some small hazard to the patient, and some are quite dangerous, the problem of "overdoctoring" is probably the most serious conflict of interest in the professions. One study concluded that 22 percent of all the antibiotics prescribed in American hospitals are unnecessary and that they cause about 10,000 potentially fatal adverse reactions a year (Rensberger, 1976). Another study found that one-third of the patients who visited the general medical service of a major university hospital were actually harmed by the treatment they received (usually an adverse reaction to a medication) (Steel et al., 1981). But the most serious problem of overdoctoring is unnecessary surgery. A subcommittee of the House of Representatives in the 1970s estimated that 2.4 million unnecessary operations were performed in the United States every year and that they annually cost the public about $4 billion and kill about 11,900 people (Brody, 1976). And many professional activities tread a similar fine line between the ethical and the unethical, to say nothing of the illegal.

Although members of prestigious professions rarely are criminally prosecuted for such activities, a professional who knowingly misleads a client about the kinds of services he or she needs in order to make more money is committing fraud. The difficulty is proving that the deception was intentional, rather than a legitimate exercise of "professional judgment." Fortunately, not all cases of professional abuse are so difficult to prove. It is estimated that fraud in Medicaid and Medicare, the two biggest government health care programs, cost the public over $1 billion a year. Apparently, it is common practice for medical laboratories to charge the government for tests that were never conducted and to pay kickbacks to physicians who order a large number of tests for their patients. In addition to the often rushed and haphazard care given to welfare patients, numerous physicians have been caught submitting phoney bills for government reimbursement (Pontell et al., 1982).

BRIBERY AND CORRUPTION

The history of bribery and corruption seems to date back almost as far as the creation of the first officials who had something to offer in exchange for a bribe. A prohibition on bribery was included in the Code of Hammurabi, one of the first known legal documents, and was mentioned in the laws of most other ancient civilizations as well. Although many Americans see bribery and corruption as a kind of third-world disease that seldom infects our own citizens, this view has little basis in fact. As far back as 1918, a Federal Trade Commission report to the Congress concluded that "commercial bribery of employees is a prevalent and common practice in many industries," and most authorities believe that is still true today. But it is difficult to say exactly how common bribery is or how much money is involved. Estimates of the annual cost range from $3 billion to $15 billion (Coleman, 1985b: 47), but those figures are little more than educated guesses.

The international bribery scandal of the 1970s was certainly the most publicized case in recent times. The scandal originally was touched off by allegations that the Lockheed Aircraft Corporation was involved in a widespread system of bribes and payoffs that included such dignitaries as the prime minister of Japan and the prince married to the queen of Holland. In its defense, Lockheed claimed that such activities were a common practice among all American corporations doing business abroad, and indeed, in the course of the investigation, ninety-four other firms admitted making overseas payoffs. The bribes were paid not only to such third-world countries as Brazil and Malaysia, but to such oil-rich nations as Saudi Arabia and Iran, and to such major industrial powers as Japan, West Germany, and France (Sobel, 1977: 106–112; Kugel and Gruenberg, 1977: 12).

At the time, many business leaders made statements implying that bribes are simply an expected part of doing business in corrupt nations. But similar cases have occurred involving domestic bribes to promote the sales of virtually every conceivable product from phonograph records to bicycle speedometers. Another common defense of such activities is that the total amount of money involved in the bribery is small and that it really does not do very much harm. Although the amount of a typical bribe may be fairly small compared to the size of the sales involved, the damage bribes do often is quite significant. A $5,000 bribe paid to a purchasing agent, for example, may easily cost the agent's employer half a million dollars in expenses otherwise avoided through legitimate bidding mechanisms. Moreover, small firms that lack financial resources or the connections to match the payoffs made by their larger competitors literally may be driven out of business.

But of all such offenses, government corruption has the most serious consequences because it threatens the foundations of democracy itself. This corruption is probably more common among police officers than among any other large group of government employees. As far back as the 1890s, state and federal investigating committees have uncovered police corruption virtually every time they looked for it. The best known of the recent investigations was carried on by the Knapp Commission (1972) in New York City. According to their report, honest cops were more the exception than the rule. The commission found the acceptance of small favors and gratuities virtually universal among New York City police officers. Although large payoffs were restricted mainly to the vice and narcotics details, the subculture of the NYPD clearly placed the financial interests of the officers above the interests of honesty and justice. Officers who attempted to report the corruption they encountered were shunned and rejected by their co-workers. Moreover, studies of other police departments reveal much the same attitudes (see Coleman, 1985b: 92–100). Although some may argue that most police corruption is only petty misconduct of little real importance, it is hard to imagine anything more corrosive to the legitimacy of a society than these symbols of justice so openly on the take.

Despite the devastating symbolic impact of police corruption, political corruption is undoubtedly far more important in the long run. The current system of campaign financing provides many legal channels for wealthy individuals and groups to purchase political influence through campaign contributions. But political influence seekers in search of ways to control government policy often step over the boundary from the unethical to the illegal. For example, a legal donation to a politician's campaign fund becomes a bribe when it is given directly to the politician for personal use. Similarly, trading general goodwill for campaign contributions may slide over into the direct purchase of a particular vote or other specific "favors." About 40 percent of all the criminal charges brought against congressional officeholders between 1940 and 1981 involved some kind of bribery. The most commonly sought-after favor was the introduction of a special bill or the right vote on a particular issue. Help in winning a government contract was second, and the use of congressional influence on the federal bureaucracy third.

Such official indictments of federal officeholders are relatively rare, and it is difficult to determine how common the bribery of public officials actually is. In its famous ABSCAM operation, the FBI had little trouble finding state and federal legislators who would accept money from an agent posing as an Arab oil sheik (*U.S. News & World Report*, 1980; *Time*, 1981; *Newsweek*, 1982). The same thing apparently could be said of the Korean government as well. The investigation of the case that came to be known as "Koreagate" revealed that aside from the usual forms of lobbying and persuasion, agents of the Korean government had made direct payments to thirty-one different members of Congress (*Los Angeles Times*, 1979).

FRAUD AND DECEPTION

Fraud and deception are common tools of both professional criminals and "legitimate" businesses. But even though new enforcement policies and improved technology have sharply reduced the number of professional "con men" (Hagan, 1987: 385–386), the government has shown far less interest in punishing powerful corporate offenders. For instance, when corporate advertisers are caught telling specific lies (for example, claiming that a mouthwash prevents the flu when it does not), there is little or no punishment. The worst likely consequence is that the offender will be required to run corrective advertising that tells the truth about the product. Similarly, not only are the tax laws written to favor big business over small business, but the Internal Revenue Service focuses most of its enforcement effort on individual taxpayers instead of the major corporations. A recent estimate by the General Accounting Office held that the government loses about $7 billion a year from one of the most obvious and easily detected corporate tax frauds—the failure to report taxable income. Yet, in testimony before a House subcommittee in 1987, the IRS said it was not interested in using the sophisticated computer system that tracks the income of private citizens to catch corporate offenders (*Corporate Crime Reporter*, 1987).

Although the fraudulent practices of major corporations tend to be complex and difficult to prove, crimes of small and medium-sized firms that make up what Schrag (1972) calls the "commercial underworld" are much more blatant. Typical of these firms are door-to-door sales organizations that use outright lies to sell low-quality merchandise. Customers are often low-income people with little education who are persuaded to buy something because of the "easy credit terms." As soon as the loan papers are signed, they are sold to finance companies at a discount, and according to the law, the "holder in due course" of a note is entitled to collect on it whether or not the original holder lived up to the deal. Land fraud and development schemes use the same tactics on more affluent victims. Salespeople use high-pressure tactics, lavish brochures, and false claims to sell lots in "planned communities" that often turn out to be in a swamp or a desert.

Sociologists have found that certain structural conditions promote fraudulent business practices. For example, both Farberman (1975) and Leonard and Weber (1970) concluded that the economic organization of the automobile industry virtually forces some dealers to engage in shady business practices. They argue that the oligopolistic firms that control the supply of new automobiles pressure their franchises to sell cars at an extremely low price, and dealers therefore are forced to make up their losses through repair and service rackets and other fraudulent activities. Juth (1987) drew similar conclusions about the multilevel marketing system used by many door-to-door sales companies, such as the Amway Corporation and Nutrilite. Because distributors are independent contractors who are encouraged to recruit other independent distributors, the parent firm often exercises only limited control over a constantly changing sales force whose entire income depends on its ability to persuade the public to buy the product.

MONOPOLIES AND CONSPIRACIES

Although critics try to portray antitrust legislation as some kind of radical economic experiment, government opposition to monopolies actually dates back at least to twelfth-century England (Jones, 1926). But whereas common law was more than adequate for traditional feudal economies, the realities of industrialization and the growth of big business required stiffer measures. The Sherman Antitrust Act of 1890 was the first and most important piece of antitrust legislation, and it has been supplemented by several newer laws over the years.

The goal of antitrust legislation is to prevent one firm or group of firms from choking off competition, thus allowing them to charge exorbitant prices for their products. Although estimates of the cost of any kind of illegal behavior are always unreliable, the bill for these anticompetitive activities undoubtedly runs into hundreds of billions of dollars a year, making them the most expensive of all types of crime.

The objectives of antitrust legislation have always been popular with the public, but getting the government to enforce such legislation has proved to be much more difficult than winning its enactment. The Celler-Kefauver Act of 1950, for example, explicitly forbids acquisitions and mergers that may tend to restrict competition or restrain trade, yet one wave of mergers after another has occurred since its enactment. In 1983, for example, 2,533 corporate mergers were reported to the government, but they investigated only 30 of them, and sought a total of just six injunctions (Hiltzik, 1984). More recently, the government has allowed many corporate giants to buy up their competition, as General Electric did when it purchased RCA, or as Texas Air did when it acquired Eastern and Continental Airlines, again raising the issue of government commitment to antitrust enforcement.

The government's response to corporate price-fixing has been similarly indifferent. This classic technique of market control involves a conspiracy among the corporations that produce a particular product to raise prices, cut production, or otherwise restrain competition; and numerous studies have shown it to be a common practice in American business (Green et al., 1972: 149–150; Clinard et al., 1979: 184). Yet, once again, the government agencies charged with enforcing antitrust legislation (principally the Antitrust Division of the Justice Department and the Federal Trade Commission) seem to prefer to go after small-time offenders instead of the corporate giants that have the greatest impact on the public.

One of the classic examples of the failure of antitrust enforcement was the oil cartel case, which in all likelihood was the most costly crime ever committed. This conspiracy began in a Scottish castle in 1928 with a meeting between the heads of the companies now known as Exxon, Shell, and British Petroleum. These men hammered out a complex agreement that explicitly required their companies to fix prices and carry on other illegal restraints of trade. The other major petroleum corporations soon signed on, and the oil cartel agreement allowed them all to reap huge illegal profits for decades after its signing. The text of the agreements was first uncovered and published in the 1950s. Following the public outcry these revelations created, President Truman ordered the Justice Department to begin a complete investigation of the oil cartel case and to prosecute the wrongdoers. The investigation and prosecution of the case against these influential corporate giants took an unbelievable fifteen years, and the final outcome was that most of them were required to sign consent decrees agreeing not to break the law again. No punishment was given to any company, and considerable evidence indicates that their antitrust activities continued unabated (Coleman, 1985a).

ATTACKING CIVIL LIBERTIES

There is no greater challenge for a democratic society than protecting the liberty of its people—the right to free political expression is an essential democratic right. Although the record of the American government is far better than most countries in the world, it still has a long tradition of responding to legal dissent with illegal political repression. Numerous campaigns of repression have been aimed against different dissident groups since the end of World War II. First were the anticommunist witch hunts led by Senator Joseph McCarthy in the 1950s, then the coordinated campaign by the FBI and other law enforcement agencies against the civil rights and black power movements, and the attack on the peace movement opposing the Vietnam War. Though the repression decreased as these political issues cooled down, the recent campaign against groups opposing American involvement in Central America follows much the same pattern (Jacoby, 1988; Kunstler and Ratner, 1988).

Although there have been occasional attacks on right-wing groups, the government's principal domestic target since the time of FBI director J. Edgar Hoover has been the American left (Marx, 1974). These illegal government activities generally fall into one of two categories: illegal surveillance or direct harassment and repression. Among the most common offenses in the first category are illegal wiretaps. Although the laws concerning wiretapping have changed from time to time, the FBI and other police agencies frequently have conducted illegal wiretaps when they felt the need to do so. The evidence shows that those agencies also conducted numerous burglaries to plant listening devices and copy records and membership lists. A freedom of information suit brought by the Socialist Worker's Party led to the discovery that the FBI had burglarized the party's headquarters once every three weeks for over six years (Chomsky, 1975). A more recent series of unexplained burglaries at the offices of groups opposing the Reagan administration's Central American policy has led some to believe that the same illegal activities are still occurring (Jacoby, 1988).

Character assassination has been one of the government's most popular weapons to harass political dissidents. The evidence indicates that the FBI ran a concerted campaign to discredit Martin Luther King, a Nobel Peace Prize winner and the leader of the Civil Rights Movement (Wise, 1976). The FBI also leaked false stories to the press to discredit other left-wing political activists, and sent fraudulent letters to leaders of the Civil Rights and antiwar movements making false charges against their colleagues. The FBI even sent fake letters to the husbands and wives of political activists accusing them of extramarital affairs (Chomsky, 1975; Nicodemus, 1979; Blackstock, 1975). Agent provocateurs were another widely used tool against left-wing groups; these agents would infiltrate a group, urge them to violence, provide weapons and bombs, and then inform the police, who would step in and make large-scale arrests when the violence occurred (Marx, 1974).

But attacks on the opponents of the American government's policies went far beyond harassment to direct violence and outright murder. For example, the CIA instigated conspiracies that resulted in the murder of numerous foreign leaders, including Patrice Lumumba in the Congo, Rafael Trujillo in the Dominican Republic, Ngo Dinh Diem and his brother Nhu in South Vietnam, and General Rene Schneider in Chile (Select Committee, 1975: 12). The CIA also has organized and run numerous secret wars that not only violated international law but in some cases violated explicitly worded American statutes as well (Branfman, 1978). Domestically, the FBI has been linked by some observers to assaults on antiwar activists, fire bombings, and the assassination of militant black leaders (Horrock, 1976; Kifner, 1974; Chomsky, 1975: 12–13).

VIOLENT CRIMES

Opinion polls have shown that the public is growing increasingly aware of the problems caused by respectable criminals in good jobs. But when we think of these white collar crimes, some kind of nonviolent financial manipulation, such as embezzlement or fraud, usually comes to mind. The average citizen still is unaware of the number of deaths and injuries caused by organizational criminals. Although some industrial corporations that have shown a consistent pattern of irresponsible behavior have avoided violating any specific criminal or civil codes, they are likely to run afoul of the law for their dangerous activities in one of two ways: (1) by violating government regulations and standards or (2) by making fraudulent statements to cover up their activities and avoid the financial liability they often bring. (On the reasons why both criminal and civil offenses must be included in the definition of corporate crime, see Blum-West and Carter, 1983.)

Because the regulatory agencies charged with enforcing worker safety and environmental legislation often are extremely lax in their enforcement efforts, many businesses have made the rational decision that it is cheaper to violate the law and risk getting caught than it is to pay the cost of meeting government standards. The Wisconsin study of the legal actions against America's 477 largest corporations, which is the best study done on this issue, found that over three-fourths of the "sanctions" handed out by government agencies were merely warnings or orders not to commit any more offenses (Clinard et al., 1979: 291). Moreover, the fines that were assessed seldom even equaled the profits gained from the offenses and thus often were considered justifiable business expenses from an accounting standpoint. Individual employees occasionally do suffer direct sanctions, but such cases are rare. The toughest such action taken to date probably was the murder conviction of three executives of a small Illinois firm, Film Recovery Systems, for the death of a worker exposed to extremely unsafe working conditions (Coleman, 1989: 174). No executives from the major corporations who carry on most of the industrial production in the United States ever have faced similar charges, however, and occupational and environmental violations still seem a rational choice for many corporate decisionmakers.

In carrying on dangerous activities not explicitly forbidden by government regulations, many corporations eventually cross the line between irresponsible and criminal behavior when they try to cover up the consequences of their actions. A typical example is the case of vinyl chloride, which is a fundamental ingredient in the widely used plastics known as PVCs. Exposure to vinyl chloride not only produces a soreness of the hands and fingers but also leads to an otherwise rare form of cancer known as angiosarcoma of the liver. When complaints concerning these problems were voiced to company physicians, they repeatedly told the workers that their symptoms had nothing to do with their job. As the incidence of this rare cancer soared, the trade association of the American chemical industry joined with a European firm to conceal one of its researcher's findings that vinyl chloride caused cancer in rats, even while the firms continued to deny the hazards of their product (Brodeur, 1974: 253–254). Clearly, these companies participated in an act of fraud, trying to avoid liability and keep their workers on the job by intentionally making false and misleading statements about the hazards of the substances they were producing.

The story of asbestos is practically the same, except that the number of victims was far greater and the companies went to greater and more obviously illegal extremes to cover it up. Even though records of the dangers of asbestos date back to the ancient Romans, and conclusive scientific studies were published generations ago, the asbestos companies repeatedly tried to conceal the problem from their workers, covered up unfavorable evidence, and funded research to prove no danger existed. It is estimated that exposure to asbestos will cause 100,000 workers to die from lung cancer, another 35,000 from asbestosis, and 35,000 more from a rare cancer of the linings of the lungs and stomach (Berman, 1978: 85; Coyners, 1980; Weinstein, 1978; Cooper and Steiger, 1976).

Although the victims are consumers rather than workers, the general pattern of cases involving unsafe products is very similar. A company designs an unsafe product and fails to test it adequately before putting it on the market. This is not a violation of the law, but as the number of injuries and deaths mounts, many companies succumb to the temptation to issue fraudulent denials that their product is dangerous and try to cover up any evidence of a serious problem. The government typically does little more than ask for a recall or a redesign of the product; however, victims who can prove the cause of their difficulties may win large judgments in civil court. A short list of some of the most famous cases of unsafe products would include the following: the Firestone 500 tire whose tendency to lose its tread is believed to have caused the deaths of 41 people (*Time*, 1979); a brake problem in the General Motors line of "X cars," which is estimated to have killed 13 persons; the dangerous gas tank of the Ford Pinto and Mercury Bobcat credited with the deaths of more than 50 persons (Dowie, 1979); Oraflex, the arthritis drug marketed by Eli Lilly that is believed to have killed at least 49 elderly patients (Mokhiber, 1986); and the Dalkon Shield contraceptive that is estimated to have killed 17 women and injured as many as 200,000 more. Although these companies had to pay substantial civil judgments to some of their victims (A. H. Robins, the maker of the Dalkon Shield, was forced into bankruptcy by the multibillion dollar costs of compensating the women it had injured), the government launched only one prosecution, and no one served any prison time despite the loss of life (Coleman, 1989: 45, 46).

UNDERSTANDING RESPECTABLE CRIME

Respectable crime is both one of the easiest and one of the most difficult crimes for the average citizen to understand. Easy, because respectable crimes do not arise out of some isolated underworld subculture, but out of the everyday working world with which almost everyone is familiar. Difficult, because the offenders seem already to have so much that it is hard to comprehend why they need to turn to crime to obtain even more. Yet, whether difficult or easy, a clear understanding of the causes of this pressing problem is necessary in order to formulate a realistic response.

No matter who the criminal or what the offense, two conditions must be satisfied for a crime to occur: (1) Potential offenders must have the opportunity to commit a crime, and (2) they must have the motivation. We begin by examining how the opportunities for white collar crime are distributed among different groups and individuals. Then we turn our attention to the reasons those criminal opportunities are so attractive to some people and the role society's ethical standards play in the decision to commit a white collar crime.

OPPORTUNITY

Everyone has had the opportunity to commit some kind of crime, and almost everyone who holds "a respected and legitimate" occupation has had the opportunity to commit a white collar crime. Yet, most of the time we pass those opportunities by. In some cases, it may be that we lack sufficient motivation, perhaps because we are inhibited by our ethical standards. But all opportunities are not equal. Individual actors evaluate the potential dangers and rewards of each opportunity in terms of their view of the world and how it operates. Each opportunity is judged in comparison to the other available options. The fewer legitimate opportunities an actor has, the more attractive a particular crime is likely to appear.

An individual's menu of opportunities obviously is determined in large part by the jobs he or she may hold. The opportunities associated with a particular job are in turn shaped by such factors as the legal system that determines which behaviors are criminal, the industry and the organization in which the job is located, and the type of occupation involved. In addition, a number of other factors exert an indirect influence by pushing certain individuals toward one job and away from another. For example, one reason women are less likely to commit white collar crimes than men is that a higher percentage of women are not employed and therefore have no opportunity to commit such offenses. As noted previously, crimes committed by women are less profitable than those committed by men, apparently because women are likely to work in lower-level jobs with less lucrative criminal opportunities.

In a sense, the law is the most basic of all forces shaping the distribution of illicit opportunity, for it is the law that ultimately determines what is and is not a crime. But what determines which actions the law will forbid? One obvious factor is the harm those actions cause. But many extremely harmful activities are perfectly legal, whereas the law prohibits others that are far less destructive. The reason for this anomaly is that even though those activities harm some people, they benefit others. As a result, new legislative proposals seldom win the support of all the different groups with an interest in the issue. Our system of laws is a product of the struggle among these competing groups, and the outcome of that struggle must inevitably reflect the structure of power of our society (see Chapter 2).

The high degree of economic concentration in modern capitalist societies has given the corporate elite far more power than any other segment of society, but it is not unlimited power. Under the right circumstances, the abuses of elite groups may spur strong popular discontent. When large numbers of people join into a mass movement demanding social reforms, it places great pressure on the government to make some sort of legislative response in order to maintain the legitimacy of the system. Many of the laws defining white collar crime are the result of the efforts of legislators to respond to the demands of these social reformers without threatening the interests of the corporate elite. On the other hand, the laws designed to protect the interests of the elite, such as the prohibitions on embezzlement and insider trading, generally have been far easier to enact and have not involved widespread social movements or run into intense opposition (see Coleman, 1985b: 123–190).

Both the distribution of opportunities and their relative attractiveness vary significantly from one industry to another. There is a sharp cleavage in the structure of opportunity between profit-seeking private organizations that are frequently involved in organizational crimes and government organizations in which such offenses are significantly less common. Government employees are seldom involved in such organizational offenses as price-fixing, consumer fraud, false advertising, stock manipulation, and deceptive sales practices because their employer is not pursuing the profits those crimes are intended to produce.

Among the most important influences on corporate crime rates are the government regulations under which an industry operates. Industries whose products and processes of production cause serious and clearly identifiable harm to the public tend to be subject to the most stringent regulation and to have the most crime. According to one study of corporate crime, the highest crime rates are found in the pharmaceutical, automobile, and petroleum industries (Clinard and Yeager, 1980), all of which produce dangerous products or use highly polluting techniques of production and all of which are tightly regulated.

Researchers also have examined a number of other variables that influence the crime rates in an industry. There is, for example, considerable evidence that illegal practices diffuse from one organization in an industry to another (Sutherland, 1983: 246–250; Clinard and Yeager, 1980: 60–63; Cressey, 1976). For one thing, knowledge about the availability of criminal opportunities and the techniques necessary to carry them out is inevitably transmitted by the social contacts and the movement of employees among firms producing the same kinds of products (Barnett, 1984). The illegal activities of a corporation also have a direct economic impact on its competitors. If a firm's competitors are using illegal means to reduce their costs, the firm may be forced to follow suit to protect its own profits. And even if no direct threat is involved, seeing one's competitors earn lucrative illegal profits is likely to enhance the psychological attractiveness of such behavior. A great deal of research on the effects of economic concentration on an industry's crime rate also has been conducted, but the results have been too inconsistent to draw any firm conclusions (Burton, 1966; Pfeffer and Salancik, 1978; Riedel, 1986; Posner, 1970; Simpson, 1986).

Many internal forces within an organization also play an important part in promoting criminal behavior. Considerable research indicates that firms experiencing economic difficulties are more likely to become involved in organizational crimes than are firms that are highly profitable (Barnett, 1984; Lane, 1954; Staw and Szwajkowski, 1975). An organization's system of social control is also an important factor. Most corporations maintain some official policy condemning illegal activities by their employees. Yet, the literature on white collar crime is full of examples of top corporate officials who not only were unconcerned about the organizational crimes of their subordinates but intentionally tried to avoid knowledge of their activities.

Employees involved in such crimes are commonly rewarded for the benefits their illegal behavior brings (specifically, higher profits), while suffering no penalties as long as they avoid detection by outside authorities. Some organizations, such as the notorious Equity Funding Corporation, go even further, explicitly requiring illegal activities of employees in certain positions (Blundell, 1978). Of course, those who commit occupational crimes against their employer receive no such support, yet there are significant differences in the way organizations respond to this problem as well. Some take strong measures to prevent, uncover, and punish employee thefts and embezzlements, whereas others show far less interest. Some employers even look at minor employee thefts as a kind of fringe benefit that need not be viewed too seriously, as long as it stays within reasonable limits (Horning, 1970).

Each occupation also has its own special array of illegal opportunities. The opportunities for bribery, for instance, depend on the services the holder of a particular job can offer in exchange for corrupt payments. Research shows that police corruption is most common among officers working in vice and narcotics details because they are in constant contact with criminals willing to pay large sums of money to gain their cooperation (Knapp Commission, 1972). Other occupations with rich opportunities for corruption include purchasing agents, government inspectors, and politicians. The opportunities for embezzlement vary with the degree of financial trust placed in a particular job. Accountants, bookkeepers, and some clerks have many opportunities for embezzlement, whereas other employees in the same organizations may have none. Criminal opportunities also vary among workers in the same job, when their pay is determined in different ways. Physicians who work on a fee-for-service basis, for example, perform more unnecessary procedures than those who work on a fixed salary (Brody, 1976) because the salaried physician has no financial incentive for "overdoctoring."

MOTIVATION

An understanding of the opportunity structure, no matter how complete, can never provide more than half the answer to the riddle of white collar crime. Once we know the opportunities available to an individual, we must still explain the motivation that spurs that person to pursue one opportunity and ignore the others. To many people, this isn't really much of an issue — respectable criminals break the law because they want to make a fast buck, and they will pursue whatever opportunity offers the biggest payoff with the fewest hazards (see Hirschi and Gottfredson, 1987; Steffensmeier, 1989). Although this is undoubtedly true of most white collar criminals, it still does not explain why they are so driven to make that fast buck. For one thing, many respectable criminals are already extremely wealthy, and would seem to have little to gain from criminal behavior. But the more fundamental question is why they are so attracted to material accumulation in the first place, unlike the people in many cultures around the world who simply have no interest in accumulating a horde of money or possessions (for examples see Dentan, 1968; Lee, 1979).

The answer lies in the culture of competition that is found in one degree or another in all industrial societies. From this perspective, the struggle for wealth and status is the central goal of human endeavor, a struggle that not only builds individual character, but ultimately provides the greatest economic benefits for society as a whole. The desire to best one's fellows in the competitive economic struggle, and the pervasive fear that one may come out a loser, provides a powerful motivation to take advantage of whatever legitimate or illegitimate opportunities are available. A complete explanation of this cultural orientation is beyond the scope of this chapter, but its origins can be traced to the fundamental structural characteristics of industrial society. The production of great surplus wealth, and the complex hierarchy of specialized roles on which that production depends, provide the objects of competition. The relatively high degree of social mobility and the accompanying economic uncertainty not only promote individualistic competition but provide the wellsprings of the pervasive fear of failure (Coleman, 1987).

The culture of competition is, of course, only one strand of the complex cultural fabric that makes up modern industrial society. There are also strong ethical standards that hold the values of cooperation and mutual support over those of competitive individualism, as well as "rules of the game" under which the competitive struggle is supposed to be carried out. Such norms certainly prevent many white collar crimes. But interviews with convicted white collar offenders show that those standards can be undermined by a variety of "techniques of neutralization" used to justify illegal activities and maintain the offender's self-respect (Sykes and Matza, 1957). In his pioneering work on convicted embezzlers, Cressey (1971) found that they justified their crimes by telling themselves they were "just borrowing" the money and would soon pay it back. Other common rationalizations include the claim that the crime didn't really hurt anyone, that the laws themselves are wrong, that the crime was necessary to the survival of one's business or one's family, that everybody else is doing it, and that the offender deserved the money (Chibnall and Saunders, 1977; Geis, 1967; Benson, 1985). The subcultures that develop in large organizations are another powerful force in neutralizing ethical restrictions on white collar crime. These subcultures not only reinforce the kinds of rationalizations just described but often define criminal acts in such a way that an employee carries them out without realizing they are illegal or even unethical (see Geis, 1967).

FIGHTING RESPECTABLE CRIME

Given the serious dimensions of respectable crime, we can legitimately ask: What can be done about it? We begin with a look at what has (or has not) been done to date. We then shift to an examination of the obstacles in the way of eliminating or, at least, better controlling respectable crime.

THE FAILURE OF ENFORCEMENT

Although the data are far from perfect, convincing evidence suggests that our justice system fails to deliver on its promise to provide equal treatment under the law for all citizens. The simple fact is that white collar crime continues to take such an economic and social toll because the government often does little or nothing to punish white collar criminals, especially those involved in the most serious organizational crimes. The evidence clearly shows that the more wealth and power the offenders have, the less punishment they receive. Numerous studies indicate that in terms of both the percentage of convicted offenders given jail terms and the length of those terms, street crimes (non–white collar crimes) are punished more severely than are occupational crimes, and occupational crimes are punished more severely than are organizational crimes (Seymour, 1973; Bureau of National Affairs, 1976; Clinard and Yeager, 1980: 296).

According to the Bureau of Justice Statistics (1987c), 40 percent of convicted street criminals received jail sentences in 1985, whereas the rates of incarceration for those convicted of the two occupational crimes they list, tax fraud and embezzlement, were only 18 and 9 percent, respectively. Those convicted of regulatory offenses (the only type of crime reported that was predominantly organizational in nature) had only one chance in twenty of going to prison. It is also possible to direct sanctions for organizational offenses against an entire corporation, but the penalties in such cases are even more lenient than those given to individual offenders. The average fine levied against the largest corporations in the United States in 1975 and 1976 was only about $1,000 — obviously not a serious penalty for firms that commonly make billions of dollars a year in profits (Clinard et al., 1979: 291).

Because we have no reliable way of determining how many white collar crimes actually occur, it is difficult to compare the percentage of street crimes and white collar crimes that escape the attention of enforcement agencies. However, the minuscule number of persons charged with white collar offenses provides strong evidence that they not only receive less punishment if they are convicted, but are far less likely even to be accused of a crime. Take, for example, the case of the Occupational Safety and Health Administration. In its sixteen-year history under four different presidents, it has issued only eighteen health and twenty-three safety standards, despite a clear legal mandate to promulgate rules that will ensure the safety of all American workers (Bock, 1987). An estimated 128,000 people were killed on the job during that time, yet not a single person has been sent to prison as a result of federal action in any of those cases (Weinstein, 1978).

An examination of all the reported legal actions involving America's 477 largest corporations during a two-year period found only fifty-six cases in which corporate executives were charged with criminal offenses for their involvement in organizational crimes (Clinard and Yeager, 1980: 291). Similarly, McCormick (1977) found that less than 700 criminal charges had been brought against antitrust violators in the eighty-year period from 1890 to 1969 and that most of the early cases were brought against labor unions, not against big business as the framers of the law originally intended.

A thorough explanation of the reasons for the failure of enforcement would take far more space than we have here, but at least for organizational crimes, those reasons can be summarized in a single word: power. Corporate criminals have teams of the highest-paid and most skilled attorneys in the nation, whereas the government must make do with a smaller number of low-paid, often young and inexperienced lawyers. Attorneys for the major corporations have virtually unlimited time and ample funding to pursue endless appeals and delays, whereas the enforcement agencies are plagued by chronic shortages of all kinds of resources. Corporate criminals often command an enormously complex bureaucracy with the power to conceal their activities from the view of the public and the government. The corporations make huge campaign contributions to the politicians who write the laws and set the budgets of the enforcement agencies, and they often dangle the prospect of lucrative future employment before low-paid enforcement agents. Corporations also have powerful weapons to coerce the government, such as the threat to wreak economic chaos by closing plants and offices and moving them to a more "cooperative" jurisdiction (see Coleman, 1985b: 172–188).

REFORMING THE SYSTEM

Criminologists long have argued that a certain amount of crime is inevitable and that we must learn to accept it. Undoubtedly, the kinds of respectable crime we have been discussing will always be with us in one form or another, but that does not mean that the number of those crimes could not be sharply reduced. The very fact that our current efforts to stop respectable crime are so weak suggests that a serious campaign against such crime is likely to produce far greater results. White collar crimes tend to be rational crimes, not crimes of passion or compulsion, and are therefore far more easily deterred than such crimes as murder or the use of illicit drugs. The essence of the problem is not that we do not know what kinds of programs can stop respectable crime but that we lack the political will to put such programs into effect.

The first step toward controlling white collar crime should therefore be an indirect one: reforming the political process so that mighty corporate offenders are no longer able to block effective measures to deal with the problem. Many steps might be taken, but a good place to start would be reforming campaign financing practices. Providing federal funding for campaign expenses and forbidding politicians from accepting money from special interest groups would be a major step toward making our society a truly democratic one.

Once a political consensus to really do something about white collar crime is achieved, the next steps are fairly obvious. The federal and state agencies assigned the task of punishing white collar offenders need much larger budgets and bigger staffs to do the job. To insulate those agencies from outside influence, their employees might also be required to sign an agreement that they would never accept employment or other rewards from any of the firms they are expected to monitor, investigate, or prosecute.

The laws themselves also need to be changed. The fines and penalties handed out to corporate offenders usually do not even equal the profits from their crimes, much less act as a credible deterrent. A law requiring that white collar criminals automatically forfeit all profits gained from their illegal activities, and empowering judges to impose substantial punitive fines on top of that, would seem sensible. The existing laws should also be rewritten to make them easier to enforce. For example, instead of forbidding mergers that would tend to restrain trade or create a monopoly as the current law does, it would make more sense simply to forbid all mergers and takeovers among giant corporations, unless they could prove to a court that their actions were in the public interest.

For some white collar crimes, the focus might usefully be shifted from punishment to prevention. A law might be passed, for example, requiring corporations with several convictions to pay for enough full-time government inspectors to monitor constantly such things as environmental pollution and the safety of working conditions, and to give those inspectors the power to shut the plant down as soon as violations were detected. A different approach would be to nationalize firms with long criminal records. The government could then replace the top managers, restructure the corporation, and either sell it back to private owners or run it as a government business.

Another tactic would be to make structural reforms that eliminate the opportunities for white collar crime. If, for example, physicians were paid a salary, rather than working on a fee-for-service basis, the incentives for overdoctoring would be removed. Many changes in corporate structure also have been suggested to promote public responsibility and reduce corporate crime. For example, Ralph Nader and his associates have proposed the federal chartering of corporations so that they would no longer be able to play one state off against another to get a better deal. Under Nader's proposal, a high standard of social responsibility would be required in order for a corporation to keep its operating charter (Nader et al., 1976). Braithwaite (1984) argues for an internal corporate restructuring to reduce illegal activities. He proposes the creation of a single "compliance group," within each corporation, charged with ensuring conformity with all state and federal laws and given real power within the firm. Many also believe that the addition of public and employee representatives to corporate boards of directors could be a major deterrent to corporate crime if they were given specific responsibility to search out and report illegalities.

There is, of course, no guarantee that all these proposals would actually help or that they would not have undesirable side effects. The point here is that many promising options exist, and what is now needed is some pragmatic experimentation: trying out a few proposals at a time, keeping the ones that work, and changing the ones that do not.

CONCLUSION

We conclude by noting that, as the public misunderstands organized crime, so too it misunderstands respectable crime. Much of the latter misconception is due to the average citizen's failure to perceive just how much damage is done by respectable criminals. Indeed, most people have little conception of the types of offenses committed by respectable citizens, much less their number and consequences. In large part, this translates to little in the way of pressure to control white collar crime. Even were the public educated in this regard, we still would face the enormous task of ferreting out offenders and offense situations from a vast web of corporate and government interests and ties. Comparatively speaking, combatting street crime seems almost an easy task.

DISCUSSION QUESTIONS

1. Though many people use the term *white collar crime*, the concept is not well defined. What is white collar or respectable crime generally, and what specific types of offenses are considered respectable?

2. Discuss the differences between occupational and organizational crime. Why are crimes committed by professionals so often ignored? By way of example, discuss crimes within the medical profession.

3. Coleman locates the possibility of respectable crime in the nexus of two factors. Discuss each and supply examples.

4. How successfully has our government combated respectable crime? What factors have influenced that success rate? Will we ever view respectable crime in the same manner that we now view street crime?

PART FOUR

EXPLAINING CRIMINAL BEHAVIOR

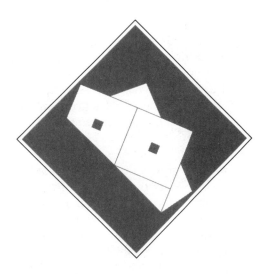

Attempting to explain criminal behavior is probably the most complex of criminological endeavors. The search for the causes of crime traditionally has taken two forms. In the first, criminal behavior is viewed as an inherent or acquired individual trait with genetic, biological, or psychological roots. In the second, criminality is explained mainly by sociological variables; crime is believed to originate in problems inherent in the structural or cultural makeup of society. Some sociological explanations treat the individual criminal passively. That is, they do not attempt to explain how societal factors induce the individual to commit crimes. Instead, they deal simply with the relationship between variations in societal crime levels and variations in other societal conditions. Others try to account for criminal behavior by establishing a link between societal conditions and individual perceptions of them.

Despite considerable traditional weaknesses of method, biogenetic causal research remains popular, especially in attempts to explain violent crime. More often than not, reviewers of the findings of such research fall into one of two camps: those strongly favoring biological explanation and those strongly opposing it. Janet Katz and William Chambliss fall in the latter group. In Chapter 12, "Biology and Crime," they critically examine research linking criminality to heredity, problems with the autonomic nervous system, chromosomal abnormalities and hormonal imbalances, and IQ. They conclude that the evidence for espoused links is weak, but more important, that the theoretical assumptions underlying the search for such causes are flawed.

Robert Agnew reviews more traditionally sociological explanations of criminal behavior in Chapter 13, "Strain and Subcultural Theories of Criminality." Strain theory essentially locates crime in the individual's inability to achieve socially promoted goals through legitimate means. Blocked from conventional channels of goal achievement, individuals turn to property offenses to compensate. Frustrated and angry, some engage in violent crime. Agnew examines both classic and revised renditions of this approach, and then offers his own general revision of both. He turns next to an evaluation of subcultural crime theory. This brand of explanation links criminal behavior to individuals' interaction with groups that possess values conducive to crime. He examines the evidence, first, for the existence of social subgroups who hold criminal values and, second, for whether individuals exposed to such groups are more criminal. In each instance, Agnew offers a qualified yes.

In Chapter 14, "Control and Deterrence Theories of Criminality," by Marvin Krohn, the focus shifts from the basic question informing the previous two chapters. Rather than trying to understand why people violate the law, control theorists study the factors that constrain people from violating the law. They assume at base that most people are motivated toward crime, and ask, Why don't they do it? Why do people obey the law? Krohn locates the answer in the amount of freedom individuals possess, the extent to which they perceive themselves at risk of losing what they value: relationships, investments, possessions. Krohn also examines the deterrence doctrine, with roots traced to the same assumptions as control models generally. Deterrence research investigates the inhibitory power of threatened legal punishments on offense behavior. He concludes that the findings of such research are weak and ambiguous, and that we should resist the temptation to build anticrime policy around the deterrence doctrine.

Part Four concludes with Chapter 15, "Alternative Approaches: Labeling and Critical Perspectives," in which Gray Cavender discusses alternative ways of structuring our questions about criminal behavior. More specifically, he examines the labeling and critical perspectives. Both, he argues, have gained prominence precisely because the etiological approaches described in the previous three chapters have produced little in the way of satisfactory answers. For advocates of the labeling perspective, criminality is less a matter of law-violating activity than a status negotiated between individual and society. Power generally determines the upper hand in such negotiations. The resultant stigma attached to the labeled individual may have any number of consequences, not the least of which is the individual's movement into deviant activity as he or she adjusts conceptions of self and role in response to the label. Critical criminology more broadly examines the issue of social order with the underlying assumption that social relations reflect the many dimensions of the economic structure of society. Criminal activity in Western societies must be viewed as a direct or indirect response to contradictions inherent in capitalist economic structure. Ultimately, critical criminologists have attacked traditional criminology itself for asking the wrong questions—for chasing etiological problems and, thus, distracting attention from the conflicts that are the real basis of law and law violation.

- Heredity Studies
- Twins Studies
- Adoption Studies
- Heredity and Crime: Meta-Analysis
- Biological Bases of Conditioning (Autonomic Nervous System)
- Abnormal EEGs and Violent Behavior

  Causal Order

  Epilepsy

  Psychosurgery

- Stereotypic, Biology-Based Research Hypotheses

  The XYY Hypothesis

  The PMS Hypothesis

  Testosterone-Related Hypotheses

  Additional Hypotheses

- Studies of Intelligence and Crime
- The Current Status of Biological Theory

  The Biological Predisposition Model

  The Constitutional–Developmental Model

- Politically Sensitive Debate
- Conclusion

CHAPTER 12

BIOLOGY AND CRIME

Janet Katz
Old Dominion University

William J. Chambliss
George Washington University

ARE SOME PEOPLE predisposed toward antisocial behavior? The answer to this deceptively simple question has eluded researchers since the beginning of the scientific study of crime. Researchers currently studying the genetic, biochemical, and hormonal characteristics of criminals believe that, to some degree, the question can be answered and the relationship between biological factors and crime discovered. Critics argue that the issue may never be resolved and that the question itself distorts our understanding both of crime and human nature.

During its long and sometimes controversial history, the biological approach to crime has ebbed and waned in popularity, in its presumed predictive abilities, and in its effects on public policy. Recently, biological explanations have generated renewed interest among the public, press, politicians, and certain criminologists. This chapter examines some of the more popular of such explanations and addresses the critical issues they raise.

Although this chapter focuses on the more current biological explanations, the search for the "born criminal" is more than 200 years old. From bumps on the head (Gall) to stigmata and degeneration (Lombroso) to moral anomalies (Garofalo) to mental inferiority (Goring) to criminal stock (Hooton) to mesomorphic physique and aggressive temperaments (Sheldon, Glueck and Glueck, Cortes and Gatti), earlier researchers claimed that criminals were not simply distinct from noncriminals but, on the whole, inferior to them as well. And because the majority of those studies focused on lower class or minority offenders (those most likely to be officially labeled and processed and, therefore, the most accessible subjects of study), these theories also were used to support racist and classist ideologies. The history of these approaches shows the continuing interconnection between theory and policy. These "criminal anthropologists," as Nicole Rafter calls our "founding founders," left a legacy that continues to confront the discipline, whether criminology's ultimate goal should be crime control or the production of knowledge (Rafter, 1992).

HEREDITY STUDIES

The theory that antisocial behavior could be inherited was very popular in the late nineteenth century though theorists were never very clear about exactly *what* is inherited (Katz and Abel, 1984). At the most extreme, hereditarians, or eugenicists, believed in the existence of "germ-plasm," an immutable inherited substance that predetermined all mental, moral, and physical characteristics. If a person committed crimes, the propensity toward that behavior would be passed on in the germ-plasm of his or her offspring, who would manifest similar antisocial behavior. To demonstrate this position empirically, researchers turned to the study of family lineages, and from 1874 to 1926, fifteen family studies were published, each of which claimed to trace the descent of a particular family to demonstrate the genetic base of antisocial behavior.

The first of these studies—*The Jukes*, allegedly an account of six generations of this fictitiously named family—was written by Richard Dugdale (1970 [1877]). Of the 709 members he found, Dugdale claimed that 76 were criminals, 128 were prostitutes, and 206 were on public welfare. Clearly, antisocial behavior was concentrated in this family and, in Dugdale's view, was partially inherited.

An equally famous family study was *The Kallikak Family*. Its author, Henry H. Goddard (1923), traced the descendants of Martin Kallikak, who had an illicit encounter with a feeble-minded barmaid during the Revolutionary War before returning home to marry an upstanding Quaker woman. In following the offspring of both unions, Goddard found numerous paupers, criminals, alcoholics, and mentally deficient persons from the illegitimate union, but few, if any, from the legitimate one. Ignoring all the differences in social and economic circumstances experienced by the children of these two unions (and, some charge, altering some of the photographs of the "deficient" Kallikaks to make them appear moronic and shifty [Gould, 1981]), Goddard concluded that the genetic cause of antisocial behavior had been established.

Not surprisingly, Goddard was one of the most avid supporters of a relatively new "science" in the early twentieth century—eugenics, the science of the improvement of the human race through better breeding. According to this science, individual worth and potential were genetically determined; to improve the quality of life in the United States, one needed to improve the quality of the individuals in it. This inner quality could be determined easily by one's present station in life. Individuals, classes, races, and countries in power obviously were superior to those who, on the bottom of the status hierarchy, had only their defective genes to blame. Eugenicists were fairly successful in translating their theories into public policy. To keep inferior people from immigrating, eugenicists argued for the passage of the 1922 and 1924 federal laws, which severely curtailed the entry of southern and eastern Europeans into the United States. Efforts were made to reduce the numbers of the "low-quality" persons already here (for example, the poor, the disabled, and the deviant), through institutionalization, marriage restrictions, and involuntary sterilization. Because heredity, not environment, was the cause of social ills, heredity needed altering (see, for example, Haller, 1963; Beckwith, 1976).

Today, one can see the weaknesses of both the family studies and the eugenics philosophy. The fact that family members have similar environments as well as similar genes makes it impossible to conclude that similar behavior is the product of genetics and not environment. But the history and impact of the eugenics movement — 64,000 persons involuntarily sterilized, the increased number of miscegenation laws, the barring of thousands from this country even as the Nazi horrors threatened their lives — make it clear that theories need not be accurate to affect many innocent victims. Even when these theories have been discredited, practices based on them may continue to exist. For example, based on the perception of potential savings in welfare payments and vague standards like "fitness for parenthood," improperly coerced sterilizations were aimed at the same group at risk from the earlier eugenicists — low-income, black, and other minority women (Petchesky, 1979). Only if we believe that children of the poor are destined (or predestined) to poverty and public welfare does this practice make any sense. Both past and present abusive practices locate the cause of poverty in its victims. The solution to poverty, then, is simply to reduce the procreative abilities of the present poor rather than examine or change the complex social conditions that deny children of the poor the opportunity to succeed.

TWINS STUDIES

Even though family studies have been abandoned, the effort to identify the genetic influences on crime has not (see Ellis, 1982). One of the major problems with the study of genetic influence on behavior is the inability to control genetic variation. If one could create an experiment in which genetically identical persons were placed in different controlled environments, one might be able to distinguish genetically and environmentally produced similarities and differences in behavior. Nature provides researchers with part of these experimental conditions in the form of identical twins. Monozygotic (identical) twins are the product of a single egg and sperm, and therefore are 100 percent genetically similar. Dizygotic (fraternal) twins, on the other hand, are the product of two eggs and two sperm, and have the same genetic similarity as any two siblings (approximately 50 percent).

This biological fact led researchers to compare the similarity (or concordance) of behavior manifested by identical versus fraternal twins. Because both types of twins are raised together and exposed to similar environments, greater similarity in behavior among identical twins could be the result of greater similarity in genetic makeup. Lange (1929) identified prisoners who were twins and then located and determined whether the remaining twin was also in trouble with the law. Of the thirteen pairs of identical twins he found, ten were concordant (77 percent); that is, both twins were criminals. Of the seventeen pairs of fraternal twins found, only two were concordant (12 percent). He concluded

TABLE 12.1　　　　SUMMARY OF TWIN-CRIMINALITY STUDIES

	Monozygotic		Dizygotic	
	Numbers of Pairs	*Pairwise Concordance Percent*	*Number of Pairs*	*Pairwise Concordance Percent*
Lange (1929) (Germany)	13	76.9	17	11.8
Legras (1932) (Holland)	4	100.0	5	0.0
Rosanoff et al. (1948) (U.S.A.)				
Adult criminality	45	77.8	27	22.2
Juvenile delinquency	41	97.6	26	80.8
Stumpfl (1936)* (Germany)	18	64.5	19	36.8
Kranz (1936) (Germany)	32	65.6	43	53.5
Borgström (1939) (Finland)	4	75.0	5	40.0
Yoshimasu (1962)†(Japan)	28	60.6	18	11.1
Dalgard and Kringlen (1976)				
‡(Norway)	31	25.8	54	14.9

SOURCE: Christiansen, 1977b; reprinted in Wilson and Herrnstein, 1985.

* The same monozygotic concordant pair is found in both Stumpfl's and Kranz's samples.

† The figures from Yoshimasu (1962) stem from two investigations in 1941 and 1947.

‡ Crime in the strict sense.

that the significantly higher level of concordance for identical twins was due to heredity rather than to environment. Until the 1960s, the majority of twins studies followed this methodology of identifying incarcerated twins and then locating their siblings. In a more recent study, Christiansen (1977a, 1977b) used the *Twin Register* in Denmark to locate all the same-sex twins born between 1881 and 1910. By then examining the Danish Penal Register for the names of any of the 6,000 pairs of twins he had identified, he was able to locate any twins with a criminal conviction. For the 67 cases in which an identical male twin had a criminal record, 24 had twin brothers who were also listed in the Penal Register (36 percent concordance). But of the 114 cases of fraternal male twins with criminal records, only 14 had twin brothers with records (12 percent concordance). For the female twins, the numbers were smaller, but the trend remained the same.

In the United States, Rowe (1985) studied twins in grades 8–12 in Ohio during the 1978–1980 academic years. Fifty percent of the questionnaires were returned (168 identical twins and 97 same-sex fraternal twins). The twins were asked about their delinquency as well as the delinquency of their twin and friends. The identical twins were more similar in their self-reported delinquency than were the fraternal twins. The substantial correlation between the delinquency of a twin and his or her friends was explained, in Rowe's view, by the presence of genetic traits that led some twins both to delinquency and to friendship with delinquent friends. In addition, Rowe concluded that the underlying genetic traits determining delinquency are temperamental traits: empathy, anger, and impulsiveness.

The majority of twins studies have reported greater similarity in criminal behavior for identical twins than for fraternal twins. A recent book (Wilson and Herrnstein, 1985) reviewing the twins research pooled the twins studies conducted between 1929 and 1976 (see Table 12.1) and concluded that, with a pooled concordance of 69 percent for identical twins and 33 percent for non-identical same-sex twins, the genetic component of delinquency had been demonstrated.

Yet, if there are methodological weaknesses in these studies, in particular the six pre-1940 studies conducted primarily in Germany and with a number suffering from extremely small samples, pooling the results only reiterates the initial weaknesses; it does not provide added support (Rose, 1986). Even Christiansen (1977a) warned that his findings could not be used as proof that heredity explains the higher concordance among identical twins. The reason for this caution is the continued inability to control, and therefore remove as a possible factor, the environmental impacts on two individuals who look to the outside world like the same person. Although generally all siblings grow up in the same family and have generally comparable environmental and social backgrounds, identical twins have unique experiences. Often dressed alike, treated alike, and able to confuse friends and teachers, identical twins may experience an environment significantly more similar than same-sex fraternal twins. The similarity in behavior may be explained by this fact rather than by genes. Until that possibility is disproved, twins studies cannot be used with assurance to further the genetic argument.

ADOPTION STUDIES

Another method used to examine the impact of heredity on criminal behavior is the comparison of adopted children with both their genetic and their rearing parents. If adopted children are more similar in behavior to their genetic (though absent) parents than to their adopted parents, it would provide support for the genetic argument.

Mednick et al. (1984) conducted a large adoption study in Copenhagen, where males born between 1927 and 1941 and adopted by nonfamily members were identified and compared with both biological and adoptive parents. The records of 4,000 adoptees contained sufficient information about both sets of parents to be usable. The researchers concluded that the criminality of the biological parents was more predictive than the criminality of the adoptive parents, but that the effects were interactive. That is, the impact on the subject of both parents having criminal records was greater than the simple sum of the effects of each parent (see Table 12.2). In addition, they reported that chronically criminal biological parents (those with three or more convictions) were three times more likely to produce chronically criminal sons than were biological parents with no convictions (Wilson and Herrnstein, 1985: 97). In most

TABLE 12.2
"CROSS FOSTERING" ANALYSIS: PERCENT OF ADOPTIVE SONS WHO HAVE BEEN CONVICTED OF CRIMINAL LAW OFFENSES

	Are Biological Parents Criminal?	
	Yes	*No*
Are Adoptive Parents Criminal?		
Yes	24.5% (of 143)*	14.7% (of 204)
No	20.0% (of 1,226)	13.5% (of 2,492)

SOURCE: Mednick et al., 1984: 244; reprinted in Wilson and Herrnstein, 1985.

* The numbers in parentheses are the numbers of cases in each cell, for a total of sample of 4,065 adopted males.

cases, there was no contact between the adoptee and the biological parent (Mednick and Volavka, 1980: 99).

In the United States, Crowe (1974, 1975) matched fifty-two adopted children of natural mothers with conviction records with fifty-two adopted children of noncriminal natural mothers. Of the adoptees of convicted women, three had been convicted of felonies, six had been incarcerated, four had multiple arrests, and seven had been hospitalized for psychiatric reasons (these individuals overlap). By contrast, only one adoptee from the control group had been hospitalized, and none had criminal records. When the "antisocial" adoptees of the criminal mothers are compared with the nonantisocial adoptees of criminal mothers and with the control group, one finds that the age at placement for adoption is quite different for the first group (18.8 months versus 7.7 months versus 7.1 months). It is difficult to know how this might have affected the findings. Others report that the results of prior studies may be incomplete because of their failure to examine alcohol abuse. Bohman (1978) reports in his study of adoptees that it is alcohol abuse rather than criminality alone that is genetically transmitted. Criminality may appear inherited only because it is a possible consequence of alcohol abuse (Bohman et al., 1982).

Although adoption studies in general are more successful in separating environmental and genetic influences than are twins studies, they too suffer some potentially serious problems. Children are not placed in adopted homes in ways best suited for experimentation (that is, randomly) but in ways best suited for the child. The attempt by adoption agencies to match adoptive parents with genetic parents may result in fewer environmental differences between these two sets of parents than we might expect (Kamin, 1985). Further, although adoption agencies may try to match sets of parents, they also screen prospective adoptive parents. (The biological families are not "selected" by the adoption agencies.) The result of this selection process (for example, in the Danish study, adoptive parents could not have a criminal record for the preceding five years) is to reduce the variation in the environment provided by the adoptive parents. This makes it difficult to find a high correlation between the adopted children's criminality and any environmental measure, including adoptive parents' criminality (Lewontin et al., 1984: 111). In addition, in the Danish study, a number of adoptive parents were informed of the criminal records of their children's biological parents.

HEREDITY AND CRIME: META-ANALYSIS

More recent reviews of the heredity–crime relationship recognize multiple methodological problems. Many still conclude that the biological relationship with crime exists though that relationship need not be direct or the only significant cause of crime (Walters and White, 1989; Fishbein, 1990). Walters (1992) reports in his review of thirty-eight family, twin, and adoption studies that the more recently published and better designed studies share less support for the gene–crime hypothesis than the more poorly designed and older studies. But while acknowledging that both year of publication and quality of research design explain outcome differences, Walters speculates that the date of publication impact "may indicate an important shift in the etiological foundation of crime over time, with heredity playing a more significant role in the criminal behavior of subjects raised during the early part of this century than is the case with more contemporary samples of subjects" (p. 607). How the effects of genetics are so significantly altered within a time span of fifty-nine years (the time span of the studies reviewed) is not discussed.

BIOLOGICAL BASES OF CONDITIONING (AUTONOMIC NERVOUS SYSTEM)

Although the previous studies were predicated on the assumption that criminal behavior may be inherited, the inherited trait that would predispose a person to this behavior was left undefined. Except for the early eugenicists, who believed every trait imaginable (from seafaringness to promiscuity to the ability to accumulate wealth) was inherited, most researchers have left unspecified the actual genetic characteristic passed on to future generations. A few, though, have attempted to identify the trait inherited.

In *Crime and Personality*, the psychologist Hans Eysenck (1964) argues that particular aspects of personality have a biological base and that a strong causative relationship exists between particular personality types and behavior. The two personality types of most interest are extroversion (characterized by people who are sociable, impulsive, outgoing, and assertive) and introversion (characterized by people who are shy, quiet, inward-looking, and controlled). Psychological tests allow subjects to be located on an introversion–extroversion scale. Differences in placement on the scale are determined, according to Eysenck, by the genetically affected central nervous system (CNS), which determines reactions to external stimulation. The CNS of extroverts works to lessen stimuli before they reach the cerebral cortex; the CNS of introverts works to magnify stimuli. Consequently, introverts will feel "overloaded" by outside stimuli, and therefore attempt to avoid stimulus-producing situations.

Punishment (a form of stimulus) will be seen as threatening by introverts, and they will strive to avoid it (via conforming behavior). Extroverts, with a poorly aroused cerebral cortex, will have a more difficult time establishing the connection between behavior and negative consequences (stimuli) and be more likely to perform illegal acts.

This, according to Eysenck, explains a phenomenon all parents have experienced—that whereas a single reprimand is sufficient to curb one child's behavior, repeated punishments seem to have little effect on another. The two children simply are born with differing levels of conditionability; some learn quickly, others more slowly.

Mednick (1979) examines the way in which we teach children to behave in socially acceptable ways. If a child has been punished previously for aggressive behavior, contemplating further aggression should produce fear about the subsequent punishment. Children learn that if they inhibit aggressive thought, the fear is reduced. Therefore, they are rewarded (by reduction of fear) for inhibiting aggression. Mednick believes that people differ in the speed and efficiency with which their bodies respond to the inhibition and consequent reduction of fear. Therefore, people differ in the extent to which they are reinforced or rewarded for inhibiting antisocial behavior. That fear response is controlled in part by the autonomic nervous system (ANS). Mednick hypothesizes that individuals with an ANS that recovers quickly from fear will receive immediate rewards for inhibiting antisocial behavior and will therefore learn acceptable behavior quickly. Those with a slow ANS will receive less reward for inhibiting antisocial behavior and will learn acceptable behavior more slowly. Mednick claims that his preliminary research supports this hypothesis because he found that those who get in trouble with the law possess an ANS with slower responses than do law-abiding individuals.

The empirical evidence to date does not demonstrate conclusively that extroversion occurs at a significantly higher rate among criminals, nor that it has a genetic base. In addition, there is insufficient evidence to conclude that a person's susceptibility or predisposition to conditioning is a biologically determined, unchanging characteristic. Instead, a person's conditionability is a product of both biology and earlier environmental factors. If an individual's ANS, for example, could be modified by the environment or by an individual's personality that is itself externally produced, then the causal order assumed by this approach could be questioned. On a more general level, this theory reduces antisocial behavior to uncontrolled responses to insufficient conditioning. It deemphasizes the initial societal choices about which behaviors are to be extinguished by punishment, as well as the fact that those who do violate this conditioning could be making rational choices (Taylor et al., 1973).

One place this research has been applied is in the study of psychopathy. The term itself raises concerns. Some have argued that it is impossible to define psychopathy and that research has succumbed to the tautological error of defining the disorder by the behavior the disorder is to explain. Seymour Halleck's query about whether psychopathy is "a form of mental illness, a form of evil or a form of fiction" (Kittrie, 1971: 170) has yet to be answered fully. Currently, typical definitions include the following:

The psychopath is a socially dominant low anxiety individual who engages in frequent but relatively nonviolent antisocial behavior. (Prentky, 1985: 36)

The psychopath has "at least average intelligence, lack of neurotic or psychotic symptomatology, irresponsibility, untruthfulness, lack of guilt associated with antisocial behavior, inability to learn from experience, poverty of affect, lack of insight, lack of responsibility in personal relationships, poorly integrated and impersonal sex life and failure to follow any life plan." (Cleckley, 1976)

Although these characteristics may indeed describe certain criminals, they also seem to describe a number of successful politicians, businesspersons, and television evangelists. Admittedly, many psychopaths are not criminals, and most criminals are not psychopaths; unfortunately, the definition of psychopathy is so broad that any or all criminals could be labeled as psychopaths. Regardless of those definitional concerns, some have concluded that "to understand psychopathy better is to understand more about the individual traits that foster criminal behavior in the typical offender" (Wilson and Herrnstein, 1985: 199). In the meantime, some legal reformers have moved to eliminate psychopathy from the list of mental disorders that justify an insanity acquittal in the criminal courts.

The biological basis of psychopathy is premised on the assumption that psychopaths possess a nervous system that dampens stimulation; suffering from "stimulation hunger," they either seek out stimulation or fail to learn from aversive conditioning, or both. The next step is to identify and measure those physiological reactions presumed effected by this diminished autonomic nervous system (Mednick's study is one such example). Using heart rate, blood pressure, respiration, muscle tension, or electrical activity of the skin, researchers have attempted to differentiate the psychopathic offender from the nonpsychopathic offender or the nonoffender; this should then explain the personality traits—such as impulsiveness, poor socialization, stimulation seeking, low anxiety, lack of affect—attributed to psychopaths (Prentky, 1985). The research findings have been inconclusive. Some have even questioned whether some of the physiological measures (for example, peripheral sweat gland activity) reflect the relevant internal system (Mednick and Volavka, 1980: 121).

Regardless of these inconsistent findings, until there is evidence that psychopathy is more prevalent in criminal populations than in any other "career" group, it seems premature to conclude that psychopathy is an important tool for our understanding of criminal behavior.

ABNORMAL EEGs AND VIOLENT BEHAVIOR

Some recent criminological research assumes that abnormal behavior (that is, violent behavior) is a product of an abnormal central nervous system identified through the EEG, or electroencephalogram. Given this assumption, the majority of studies, predictably, have concentrated on institutionalized populations of violent offenders. Researchers disagree on whether violent offenders have a greater likelihood of brain wave abnormalities. Some have reported that

50 percent of incarcerated psychopaths have abnormal EEGs; others report that less than 6 percent of violent offenders tested had abnormal EEGs. By comparison, estimates of abnormal EEGs in the general population range from 5 to 20 percent (Shah and Roth, 1974; Mednick et al., 1981; Wilson and Herrnstein, 1985). Still other researchers claim that EEG abnormalities are greater among violent recidivists than among offenders guilty of a single violent crime. Ostrow and Ostrow, on the other hand, found a higher incidence of EEG abnormalities among conscientious objectors than among psychopaths (Nassi and Abramowitz, 1976).

CAUSAL ORDER

These contradictory results are in some part a product of methodological problems endemic to these studies. EEG interpretations depend in part on the judgment of the particular reader. This is particularly problematic since many of these studies did not utilize double-blind procedures (Nassi and Abramowitz, 1976). In addition, both the use of already incarcerated violent offenders and the variety of ways these individuals are selected for testing leave open the question of whether these results are generalizable and whether one can assume a causal order.

To address the question of causal order, two longitudinal studies have been conducted in Scandinavia. In one study, Swedish researchers obtained EEG readings from 1967 on 571 schoolchildren under the age of 15. An examination of official records in 1980 uncovered 54 who had committed at least one criminal act, and an analysis of the 22 recidivists among the 54 revealed distinctive childhood EEG readings (see Mednick et al., 1982). In a second study, 265 children in Denmark were tested in 1972, and in 1978 were matched for delinquency using the official Danish *Police Register*. Based only on the 129 males in the sample, the researchers concluded that criminal activity was predicted by abnormal EEG readings, specifically slow alpha frequencies (see Mednick et al., 1981). In both studies, the offenses committed were theft or traffic violations, not violent crime. Both studies concluded that abnormal EEG readings (and therefore, abnormal brain function) precede delinquent behavior; however, it is possible that the children had been delinquent prior to the tests, and therefore, the causal order may still be in question. In addition, although the EEG readings were taken prior to the recording of official delinquency, the readings apparently were interpreted *after* the children were identified as delinquent or nondelinquent.

Mednick argues that slow alpha frequency readings are the most common abnormality distinguishing criminal and noncriminal populations. Because slower EEG frequencies are typical of childhood (alpha activity increases as a function of age between 5 and 20), slow alpha readings could reflect a developmental lag or brain immaturity. Mednick believes instead that the data are more consistent with a theory of low cortical stimulation, consistent with his belief that a poorly aroused ANS is causally linked to delinquency.

EPILEPSY

Epilepsy is a condition characterized by excessive electrical discharges in the central nervous system, which produces abnormal EEG readings. Historically, the relationship between crime and epilepsy rested on the assumption that an individual with uncontrollable seizures might be unable to control his or her antisocial impulses, especially during a seizure. However, research established that the incidence of criminal acts, including violence, during a clinical seizure is extremely rare, if not nonexistent (Delgardo et al., 1981; Shah and Roth, 1974; Gilgi et al., 1981). Those still convinced of a relationship between epilepsy and criminality then began to focus on criminal activity between seizures, and on one type of epilepsy in particular, temporal lobe (or psychosomatic) epilepsy. Most research indicates that the incidence of criminal activity by noninstitutionalized epileptics is comparable to that of the general population; only those studies that focus on psychiatric or institutionalized populations conclude that psychosomatic epileptics are responsible for more antisocial behavior than the general population (Coleman, 1974; Gilgi et al., 1981; Gunn, 1977; Mark and Ervin, 1970). For example, Mark and Ervin report that the incidence of temporal lobe epilepsy was ten times higher in a sample of 400 violent prisoners than would be predicted for the general population. In the past fifteen years, there has even been a suggestion that some individuals, without the presence of clinical seizures, may have undiagnosed epilepsy — that is, may be so-called epileptoids (Coleman, 1974). The conclusion that epilepsy is related to crime, especially violent crime, has been criticized by those who question the use of institutionalized populations, the failure to examine the social or psychological problems epileptics face independent of their clinical disorder, and the anecdotal and retrospective nature of many of the studies (Oliver, 1980: 436).

PSYCHOSURGERY

Even with these inconclusive findings, the assumption of a link between epilepsy and violence has led some to support the most radical and intrusive physical intervention, psychosurgery. Psychosurgery is defined by the National Commission for the Protection of Human Subjects of Biomedical and Behavioral Research (1977: 57) as "brain surgery performed either (1) on normal brain tissue of a person, for the purpose of changing or controlling the behavior or emotions of such person or (2) on diseased brain tissue of a person, if the primary purpose of performing the procedure is to control, change or affect any behavioral or emotional disturbance of such person."

Although lobotomies were first performed on chronically hospitalized mental patients, and are still predominantly reserved for those suffering from severe emotional distress, a more sophisticated procedure, called an amygdalotomy, has recently been used as a treatment for aggressive epileptics. In *Violence and the Brain*, Vernon Mark and Frank Ervin (1970) have argued, as have others, that violent behavior often results from brain damage, particularly to the amygdala in the temporal lobe. These researchers claim that abnormal brain function in the amygdala can trigger both epileptic seizures and violent behavior. They also claim that they have a successful technique for locating and destroying those triggers of violence and that they have a success rate of close to 75 percent.

A leading critic of their work challenges their assertion that epilepsy is related to aggression and that they have successfully treated it. According to Breggin (1975, 1979), psychosurgery (even the early crude prefrontal lobotomies) tends to pacify individuals, regardless of the presence or absence of any brain disease and regardless of the cause of the violence. The fact that the epilepsy of individuals operated on was unaffected demonstrates that psychosurgery can reduce violence, not that the violence was caused by the epilepsy.

On a broader plane, Chorover (1980), a neuropsychologist, labels the use of psychosurgery to control violence a classic example of "neuropsychological reductionism." He notes that, building on the unsatisfactory idea that human problems of social interaction (which include violence) can be reduced to specific acts by particular people, neuropsychological reductionism views behavior as an "expression of or as traceable to particular or localizable brain states (or processes)" (p. 268). Not only is this incorrect, he claims, "but so long as we pursue this approach, we will never come close to solving the problems of violence and aggression or any other serious human problem that threatens our survival. The individual localizationist perspective is then more than merely mistaken. It is also a barrier to meaningful social change" (p. 268). One need only refer to a 1967 letter to the *Journal of the American Medical Association* by Mark, Sweet, and Ervin, which suggested that some of the violence and looting accompanying the urban race riots of the 1960s might be a product of ongoing brain dysfunction, to appreciate that potential.

Given psychosurgery's success in pacification, it should not be surprising that the procedure has been recommended not simply for violent individuals, but for violent inmates as well. In the early 1970s, it was suggested that California prisons might deal with the problem of aggressive males through "psychosurgical pacification" (Chorover, 1980). In 1973, in *Kaimowitz* v. *Department of Mental Hygiene*, the court ruled that involuntarily confined patients could not give adequate informed consent to experimental psychosurgery. But the 1977 National Commission on the Protection of Human Subjects of Biomedical and Behavioral Research did not exclude prisoners and involuntarily confined patients as possible subjects, arguing that prisoners and involuntarily confined patients should have the opportunity to seek benefits from new therapies.

STEREOTYPIC, BIOLOGY-BASED RESEARCH HYPOTHESES

XYY refers to a chromosomal abnormality found in a minute number of men and hypothesized to be associated with criminal behavior. PMS (premenstrual syndrome) is a hormonal imbalance found in differing degrees in women and also supposedly related to criminal activity. Although the groups under investigation (men versus women) and the biological abnormalities (chromosomal versus hormonal) differ, the underlying explanation for the alleged relationship between these biological oddities and crime is based on stereotypic and unsupported views of men and women. For example, the XYY theory is predicated on the assumption that men are innately (chromosomally) more aggressive than women. Only if one assumes that the single Y chromosome of the normal male causes aggression (and the absence of a Y chromosome explains the lack of aggression in women), could one predict that an extra Y chromosome would make a man extra malelike, that is, extra aggressive. And the PMS theory rests on the unproven assumption that women are naturally and inevitably the pawns of their hormones. Only if one assumes that female behavior is normally under the control of hormones, could hormonal imbalance be a satisfying explanation for female crime. Similar theories purporting to explain the link between aggression and crime on the one hand, and testosterone levels, vitamin deficiencies, food allergies, or diet on the other, have been advanced.

THE XYY HYPOTHESIS

The average person possesses twenty-three pairs of chromosomes, one of which determines that person's sex. Two X chromosomes produce a female; an X and a Y produce a male. Occasionally, a person is born with an excess or a deficiency in the number of chromosomes, and this variation can occur in any of the twenty-three pairs. Down syndrome, for example, is a relatively common cause of mild retardation caused by an extra nonsex-related chromosome, resulting in a total of forty-seven. Variations also occur with the sex-linked chromosomes. Klinefelter's syndrome is a condition of certain males who possess an extra X chromosome (XXY) and appears to be related to some mild retardation and degeneration of certain sex characteristics. Another, seemingly rare variation is the possession of an extra Y chromosome—the XYY chromosomal abnormality, a noninherited but genetic characteristic.

In 1965, Jacobs et al. published an article, "Aggressive Behavior, Mental Subnormality and the XYY Male," which summarized their research at a Scottish maximum-security institution for mentally disturbed patients with violent or criminal histories. Though the expected number of XYY men in the general population is .15 percent, their examination of 315 male patients revealed 9 with the extra Y variation—3 percent of the total. The response to this finding was immediate. Hundreds of studies in prisons and mental hospitals followed, in which researchers often claimed that they too had found a larger than expected percentage of XYY men. The mass media focused on these reports, and the publicity that resulted had tangible results. Richard Speck, the 1968 murderer of eight Chicago nursing students, was falsely reported as having the XYY variation. The California Center for the Study and Reduction of Violence—founded in 1972 and jointly funded by the state and federal government—set up a program to screen junior high school boys for the XYY chromosome. A few states passed laws to screen delinquent boys for use in sentencing decisions, and in 1968, a group of doctors started a massive screening of newborn male infants at the Boston Hospital for Women.

The potential impact of such programs is obvious. Boys with XYY configurations might be seen as greater threats and in greater need of confinement than XY boys convicted of identical offenses. The impact on newborns identified as XYY might have been even greater. Thus, when the doctors in Boston announced plans to follow the development of the XYY infants, serious ethical and moral questions were raised immediately (and were partially responsible for ending this study). Do researchers tell parents that their son has an extra Y chromosome and potentially affect how they raise their child? Or do researchers withhold information from parents who want to know why they find their son so interesting?

Some people believed that, at last, a simple, single cause of serious criminal behavior had been found. Something in the chromosomal makeup of these men caused violent, aggressive behavior. If we could locate these men, we would pinpoint the serious offenders. One hundred and sixty studies later, however, research does not support the thesis that XYY men are more aggressive and violent than XY men (Craft, 1978; Fox, 1971; Hastings Center, 1980; Hook, 1973; Pyeritz et al., 1977; Theilgaard, 1983).

Though inconclusive, these studies found a limited number of traits characteristic of XYY men:

1. XYY men tend to be taller than comparable XY men.

2. XYY men convicted of crimes are more likely to be guilty of property offenses and *less* likely than convicted XY men to have committed violent offenses.

3. The families of XYY inmates tend to have less history of crime or mental illness than do the families of XY inmates.

4. The prevalence of XYY men appears to be higher in mental and penal institutions than in the general population.

Even these findings are inconclusive, given methodological problems that include small sample sizes, inadequate control groups, and lack of double-blind studies. But the problems are more fundamental than weak methods. The research claims to establish a slight relationship between an extra Y chromosome and institutionalization in mental and penal institutions. The explanation for this finding is what is most troubling. Because men are more aggressive (in our society), and men alone possess the Y chromosome, XYY men must be "extra men," or extra aggressive. This unquestioned assumption meant that researchers failed to consider other explanations. For example, XYY men have an increased probability for mild retardation, a characteristic of other chromosomal abnormalities as well (for example, the XXY configuration associated with Klinefelter's syndrome). The increased institutionalization or increased likelihood of detection for antisocial behavior may have more to do with intelligence than with "criminal-like tendencies" or aggressiveness. What's more, if XYY men tend to be taller as well as mildly retarded, they may make more visible targets for, and poorer respondents to, police questioning. But the extra X chromosome found in males with Klinefelter's syndrome does not fit our stereotypic explanation of male behavior. The similarities between XYY and other disorders are then ignored, and the press and the public are impressed with the "unique" qualities of the XYY male. It is also interesting to note the absence of research on XXX syndrome in women.

In addition, there is reason to question whether any actual syndrome is related to an extra Y chromosome. Certainly, the significant number of XYY men leading perfectly normal and uneventful lives (an estimated quarter million in the United States alone) does not support the existence of certain behavioral characteristics endemic to these men (Shah and Roth, 1974). Moreover, the importance of the XYY variation in explaining crime is seriously in question when we consider the rarity of the phenomenon. In 1976, Witkins and others examined all men born in Copenhagen between 1944 and 1947 who were over six feet tall; of the 4,139 men examined, they identified only 12 XYY men (and 16 XXY men). (Given that Witkins's sample is taken from the general population, the comparison of his finding of 2.9 percent XYY with Jacobs's finding of 3 percent for institutionalized men makes one question whether XYY men are at greater risk of institutionalization, at least when one controls for height.) Although they reported that XYY men were more likely to have criminal convictions than either XY or XXY men (XYY = 43 percent, XXY = 19 percent, XY = 9 percent), they concluded that the differences were due to lesser intelligence, not greater aggression. In addition, do these very few men have any significant impact on the total crime rate? Even if these men were somehow controlled or confined, the problem of crime would be virtually untouched. The popularity of the XYY myth, now on the decline, can be explained more by its support of stereotypic views of men than by its scientific evidence (Sarbin and Miller, 1971; Fox, 1971; Pyeritz, 1977).

THE PMS HYPOTHESIS

Another biological theory of crime — related to PMS — rests on equally stereotypic views but, nevertheless, is gaining popularity with the public. Whereas the XYY theory rests on the assumption that crime and aggression reside in the genetic code of men, PMS theory relies on a view of women as helpless victims of raging hormonal imbalances.

While even the nineteenth-century criminologist and physician Lombroso mentioned menstruation, the scientific study of its relationship to crime is credited to Dalton's (1961) research in an English women's prison. There she interviewed 156 newly convicted women whose crimes had occurred within the previous twenty-eight days. After obtaining information on their menstrual cycles, she calculated where in the cycle the women were at the time of the crime. Dividing the twenty-eight-day cycle into seven four-day segments, she reported that 49 percent of the women either were in the premenstrual phase (four days before the onset of menstruation) or were menstruating at the time of their crime (first four days of menstruation). If crime was unrelated to the menstrual cycle, only 29 percent of the crimes should have been committed during these eight days. Dalton concluded that the hormonal changes either caused women to commit crimes (through feelings of aggression, irritability, or emotionality), or increased the likelihood of detection (through increased lethargy and carelessness), or both.

Horney (1978), in a reanalysis of Dalton's data, offered an alternative explanation for these findings. Instead of concluding that this higher incidence of crime during the premenstrual and menstrual phases proved that hormonal changes cause an increase in crime, Horney argued that crime and subsequent arrest could produce these hormonal changes. The trauma of arrest and imprisonment could trigger early menstruation; later calculations would then indicate that the woman was in the premenstrual phase at the time of the crime when, in fact, she was not.

Evidence exists that a variety of events—such as surgery, divorce, and even travel—can affect a woman's menstrual cycle; arrest is certainly traumatic enough to be included in that list. To support her thesis, Horney reviewed Dalton's claim that approximately 50 percent of female drivers involved in accidents that led to hospitalization were in the eight-day premenstrual–menstrual phase. This might support the notion that women are more lethargic and clumsy during this time. Horney found, however, that 50 percent of the female passengers involved in accidents were also in that same eight-day phase. Unless we wish to argue that the passenger's lethargy somehow caused the accident, it would appear that the trauma of the accident triggered menstruation, not vice versa.

The assertion that these hormonal changes cause crime through heightened aggression or tension contradicts Dalton's own findings that 155 of the 156 women examined were convicted of nonviolent crimes (in particular, theft and prostitution). In addition, claiming that the hormonal changes that occur to some degree in all menstruating women explain violent crime is at odds with the enormous differences in the violent crime rate for men and women.

As with the XYY theory, the popularity of the PMS theory far exceeds the empirical evidence. Articles on PMS have appeared in popular magazines, and in at least two cases in England, PMS was used successfully by the defense to reduce murder charges to manslaughter. However, popularity with the public and success in the courts is not evidence of its validity. Instead, its popularity may be attributed more to its support of the traditional view of women as pawns of their biology than to the amassing of empirical data. Even though modern science is identifying certain physiological problems associated with menstruation, we need not conclude that these problems increase the probability of crime or mean that a woman is less responsible for her behavior. The evidence does not support the conclusion that women are irresponsible during menstruation; the stereotypic view of women prevents the exploration of other explanations for Dalton's findings.

The assumption that women are controlled by their emotions but men are not has resulted in an absence of studies on emotional cycles in men (Bowker, 1978). Preliminary evidence from these extremely rare studies indicates that men do indeed appear to have regularly occurring emotional cycles. Unless we wish to argue that both sexes are irresponsible at least part of the time, and that *mens rea* (criminal intent) is a figment of the legal imagination, it is illogical to conclude that hormonal menstrual changes make women more criminal or less capable of making rational decisions.

TESTOSTERONE-RELATED HYPOTHESES

PMS theory is not the only approach that looks to the body's production of hormones and the effects of glandular functioning on crime. The research concerning the relationship between hormones and crime, in particular the male hormone testosterone and aggressiveness, to date has produced no consistent findings (Olweus et al., 1980; Ellis, 1986; Mednick and Volavka, 1980; Shah and Roth, 1974; Prentky, 1985; Wilson and Herrnstein, 1985; Buikhuisen and Mednick, 1988). In addition, the research has been plagued with a number of serious methodological problems. First, generalizing from the numerous studies on primates is questionable scholarship. Second, research on humans often has concentrated on institutionalized prison populations, a group already demonstrating antisocial behavior and not even representative of criminals. In addition, prison conditions of limited diet and exercise may alter the physical condition of prisoners (Nassi and Abramowitz, 1976). Third, single testing of testosterone is suspect because testosterone levels fluctuate daily and seasonally. As a rule, men produce far more testosterone than needed for sexual activity, but this "excess doesn't necessarily mean more, better or specific kinds of sex" (Hales and Hales, 1982). Fourth, studies that have reported a positive relationship often are examining aggressive attitudes or self-reported physical and verbal aggression (Olweus, 1988), and it is possible that testosterone may be more related to the feeling of anger than to the expression of it (Prentky, 1985).

The research on testosterone levels and crime rests on a presumed causal order: that men with high levels of testosterone are more aggressive, domineering, or assaultive than are men with lower levels. The data do not support such an assumption, however. Studies have found that males experience a drop in testosterone following a variety of stressful situations. Research on primates reports that monkeys who become dominant in new social groups subsequently experience an increase in testosterone levels, whereas subordinate monkeys show a subsequent decrease in testosterone levels. Therefore, although a correlation has been reported between testosterone levels and aggression in young men (though not in older men), no proof exists that aggression causes a rise in testosterone or that increased testosterone causes aggression, or both (Hoyenga and Hoyenga, 1979). Contrary to widely held beliefs, no simple conclusion regarding the relationship of sexual hormones to aggressive behavior can be drawn. Though aggressive behavior normally does involve the presence of hormones, the absence of hormones does not prevent aggressive behavior. Indeed, the evidence would suggest that hormones are necessary for normal productive psychological development quite apart from sexual or aggressive behavior. Regardless, modern science is able to regulate normal balances (or imbalances) artificially, and sex offenders have been treated by reducing the level of testosterone or increasing the level of the female hormones estrogen and progesterone (Berlin and Schaef, 1985).

ADDITIONAL HYPOTHESES

It is not just substances produced naturally by the body that have been studied. The roles of vitamin deficiencies, food allergies, and diet have also been examined, particularly in relation to juvenile delinquents. Hippchen's (1978) study of delinquents points to the lack of sufficient quantities of certain vitamins, especially vitamin B, as a cause of a number of youth-related problems, including truancy, running away, and a general "restlessness." Others argue that excessive levels of sugar or caffeine are common in institutionalized delinquents (Schauss and Simonsin, 1979). Hypoglycemia (a low-blood-sugar disorder) (Shah and Roth, 1974; Yaryura-Tobias and Neziroglu, 1975) or allergies to particular foods (Newman, 1979) and additives also are suggested as causes of hyperactivity and violence among children. Other researchers, however, have found no differences between delinquent and nondelinquent populations on these nutritional components; certainly, it is too soon to conclude that these factors are known to contribute to delinquent behavior.

There may also be a link between nutritional deficiencies and social class. Poorer children may have greater vitamin deficiencies because of the expense of buying the varieties of food necessary for a well-balanced diet. In addition, the availability and relative low cost of fast foods could lead to excessive chemical additives and sugar in the diets of lower-class children. But the policy implications for research on diet and crime are significantly different from those of the previous discussions. The use of vitamin supplements and the reduction of refined sugar are not intrusive therapies in the same way that the use of artificial estrogen or XYY screening would be.

On the other hand, the type of antisocial behavior being examined in these studies — uncontrolled and seemingly irrational outbursts or drastic mood swings and restlessness — is extremely narrow. To impose this model on crime in general is to describe crime as some spontaneous and irrational action beyond the control of the individual. It defines crime as nonrational maladaptive behavior when, in reality, most criminal actions are quite rational and extremely adaptive for the individual. Truly irrational antisocial behavior, behavior that is unpredictable and inexplicable to both society and the individual actor, is rare and often treated from its onset outside the criminal justice system.

STUDIES OF INTELLIGENCE AND CRIME

In 1904, Alfred Binet (1857–1911) was commissioned by the French minister of public education to devise a method of identifying children whose poor school performance suggested the need for special education. Binet accomplished this by developing numerous tests of varying levels of difficulty, to each of which he assigned an age level. The difference between the child's mental age (the age associated with the last tasks performed successfully) and the child's chronological age was the subject's intelligence quotient (IQ). Binet never claimed that this score represented "inborn intelligence"—the number was simply an average of many scores. It represented neither a scalable entity nor a permanent feature but merely served as a pedagogical guide for helping the mildly retarded.

By the time IQ tests were introduced into the United States by people like Lewis Terman—who revised and popularized the test under its new name, Stanford-Binet—the meaning of IQ scores had changed. The score came to represent intelligence—a single quantifiable entity that was both fixed and inherited. Because smart and successful people seemed to produce equally successful children, the assumption went, intelligence must be inherited; because IQ scores were predictive of this same success, IQ scores must then represent intelligence. IQ tests are still administered to thousands of American schoolchildren. The test scores correlate highly with school performance (not surprisingly, in that Binet wrote and standardized these tests using scholastic achievement) and often are predictive of occupational success. What has not been demonstrated, however, is that intelligence tests measure *intelligence*. Instead of being proof that intelligence exists, high IQ scores and success may both be the product of high socioeconomic status. Upper-class children are more likely to be successful in the adult world and are also more likely to have the academic background that increases IQ scores. The same is true for differences in IQ scores between white and black children. The difference in scores proves neither that one group is innately more intelligent nor that the differences are inherited or unchangeable.

How does this apply to crime? Among the first groups to be given IQ tests were incarcerated populations—prostitutes, delinquents, adult felons. Reports claimed that 30–70 percent of these people scored below the mental age of 13 (the score that purportedly indicated feeble-mindedness), which led to the conclusion that low intelligence was a cause of crime. But prisoners are not representative of all criminals; they are only the select few who are caught, convicted, and imprisoned. Further, these scores and conclusions were reported before the scores of prisoners could be compared with the test scores of the general public. When this comparison was done, it raised serious doubt about the earlier results. For example, tests administered to 1.75 million army recruits during World War I showed that close to one-half of these recruits also scored below the mental age of 13. And when one looks at the actual questions from the standard Binet IQ test, it is easy to understand why so many people score low and why they tend to be concentrated among the lower classes or among newly arrived immigrants. To illustrate, consider the following excerpt from the test:

Underline the correct answer.

1. Five-hundred is played with rackets/pins/cards/dice.
2. The Percheron is a kind of goat/horse/cow/sheep.

3. The most prominent industry of Gloucester is fishing/packing/brewing/automobiles.
4. Christie Matthewson is famous as a writer/artist/baseball player/comedian.
5. Chard is a fish/lizard/vegetable/snake.
6. Alfred Noyes is famous as a painter/poet/musician/sculptor.
7. Becky Sharp appears in *Vanity Fair/Romola/The Christmas Carol/Henry IV*.
8. Habeas corpus is a term used in medicine/law/theology/pedagogy.

The relationship between intelligence test scores and crime has continued to be examined by some criminologists. Wilson and Herrnstein (1985) claim that research has consistently revealed a ten-point difference in test scores between officially defined offenders and nonoffenders in Great Britain and the United States. There are further differences, they claim, by type of tests and type of offender. They report that delinquents are more likely to be deficient on verbal IQ tests than on performance on spatial tests. According to some studies, recidivists have poorer school records than nonrecidivists. Wilson and Herrnstein report that offenders' IQ test scores vary according to offense, with forgers, bribers, embezzlers, and security violators having higher scores than burglars, auto thieves, and drug and alcohol offenders, who in turn have higher scores than assaulters, murderers, and rapists. In a longitudinal study using both self-reported and official delinquency rates, Farrington (1988) reported that boys who were identified as having low intelligence before the age of 10 were more likely to become delinquent later on. The many measures of intelligence all correlated closely with primary school performance.

For those who believe that a relationship exists between low intelligence and criminal behavior, the next question is how these two variables are related. Hirschi and Hindelang (1977) reviewed past research on IQ and delinquency, using both official and self-reported data. Even when controlling for social class and race, they conclude that "IQ is an important determinant of delinquency." Specifically, they assert that IQ affects delinquency indirectly through its effects on school performance. Others (Wilson and Herrnstein, 1985; Buikhuisen, 1987) suggest that the relationship may be more direct: Those with low intelligence may be more impulsive or lacking in moral reasoning or social competence. Wilson and Herrnstein suggest that one explanation for the low intelligence scores of prisoners is that low intelligence may be related to impulsive, unplanned crimes with immediate payoffs but with a higher risk of detection.

Certain questions remain unanswered. Hindelang and Hirschi never established whether IQ tests measure anything innate, or whether they simply represent another measure of school performance. Nor did they address the questions of where intelligence comes from, whether it is impervious to change, and what factors might produce that change. Though never explicitly stating that IQ tests measure some innate ability, a causal model of the three relevant variables precedes in one direction:

$$\text{IQ} \longrightarrow \text{School Performance} \longrightarrow \text{Delinquency}$$

Without the assumption that IQ is an *a priori*, innate quality, independent but predictive of school performance, the theory falls apart. Delinquency may lead to poor school performance and subsequent low test scores. Or delinquency and school performance may affect each other so that delinquency leads to less time in school, which produces poor grades and makes delinquency more attractive, and so on. The questions of whether intelligence is an inherited trait with fixed parameters, whether or not IQ tests measure intelligence or are simply another measure of school performance, and whether intelligence relates to criminal behavior, are all still open to debate (Eysenck and Kamin, 1981; Gordon, 1980; Karmin, 1980; Lewontin et al., 1984). But the assumption that criminals are mentally inferior narrows considerably the type of crime one considers. No one would seriously explain corporate crime, state crime, political crime, or organized crime by reference to mental inferiority, whether or not one believes the relationship is direct or indirect.

The Current Status of Biological Theory

Although the previous sections make clear that the search for biological causes of crime has continued unabated, the renewed interest it now enjoys appears to coincide with the 1975 publication of a book entitled *Sociobiology*, by E. O. Wilson. Wilson proposed that the biological, and in particular the genetic, base for behavior needs to be emphasized in order to understand human behavior. Trained as an entomologist, Wilson asserted that the techniques and knowledge acquired from the study of animal behavior can be applied directly to humans. The social behaviors of interest include (but are not limited to) religion, ethics, warfare, genocide, cooperation, competition, conformity, spite, patriarchy, homosexuality, and xenophobia. Wilson did not simply state that biology or our genes have something to do with our behavior. He postulated a direct genetic link to specific social behaviors and argued that human nature itself is a direct result of genetic adaptation to the physical environment. Wilson, using Darwinian theory, concluded that these social characteristics were the result of natural selection and reflected the optimal adaptation to our physical world. He was not saying that patriarchy, xenophobia, or genocide are good, but that they are natural in some evolutionary manner. According to Wilson, we may be able to change our behavior, but we will have to fight against our "nature" to do so.

THE BIOLOGICAL PREDISPOSITION MODEL

This assumption that individuals enter the world with some preestablished disposition is the underlying premise of Jeffery's recent work. According to Jeffery (1978), behavior is the result of learning, and learning is the product of an interaction between the physical environment and the brain. He depicts this model of behavior in the following way:

Genetic Code × Environment = Brain Code × Environment = Behavior

Therefore, although the external environment certainly plays a role in behavior, Jeffery maintains that its role is limited by the unique and inherited capacities of the individual's brain and nervous system. We are not all the same and we will not respond to the world in similar ways. "We do not inherit behavior any more than we inherit height and intelligence. We do inherit a capacity for interaction with the environment" (p. 162).

Once we recognize that behavior is controlled by the brain, our response to deviant behavior must also change. Specifically, Jeffery believes that we must abandon our current practices of responding to criminal behavior after it has occurred and turn instead to crime-prevention programs. If the predisposition to crime exists in the brain prior to criminal behavior, then the discovery of individuals who possess that predisposition could prevent crime.

> This means experimentation and research. It will mean brain scans and blood tests. It will mean tests for learning disabilities and hypoglycemia. All of this involves medical experimentation, intrusion into the privacy of the individual, and controversial and experimental surgeries and/or drug therapies. (p. 164)

Recognizing the political dangers and public opposition if the government were to operate such a system, Jeffery suggests a private treatment system to parallel or even replace the current criminal justice system. This, he believes, would remove the treatment of behavioral disorders, including crime, from the *political arena* (his emphasis).

THE CONSTITUTIONAL–DEVELOPMENTAL MODEL

More recently, two Harvard professors, one an economist–political scientist and the other a biology-trained psychologist, have set forth what they claim is the "definitive study of the causes of crime." In *Crime and Human Nature*, James Q. Wilson and Richard Herrnstein (1985) suggest that biological predispositions in combination with certain unspecified environmental experiences explain why some people commit crimes and others do not. In other words, they argue that constitutional and developmental factors predispose some individuals to criminality. These constitutional predispositions include age and gender (for example, young males), mesomorphic body types, low intelligence, and aggressive personalities. Even when we control for inadequate family life and poor school performance, they conclude, "individuals differ at birth in the degree to which they are at risk for criminality" (p. 70).

A central thesis of the Wilson and Herrnstein theory is that biological traits such as impulsiveness, aggressiveness, and intelligence are inherited. They argue that research shows criminals share these traits disproportionately, compared to noncriminals, and that as a result of these inherited tendencies, some societies have more people with a propensity toward crime than do others. As evidence for their theory, they cite research they claim demonstrates that criminals are less likely to be willing to "defer gratification" than are noncriminals. They believe this research indicates that young people growing up in the 1960s were more willing to defer gratification than were young people growing up in the 1970s, and that this explains why the crime rate of juveniles was higher in the 1970s than in the 1960s. As Kamin (1986) notes in his review of *Crime and Human Nature*, the study they cite as evidence compares fifty juvenile delinquents institutionalized in Rhode Island in 1974 with fifty-seven delinquents institutionalized in the same state in 1959. This study revealed that 16 percent of the 1974 delinquents said they would save rather than spend a dollar if it were given to them, whereas in the 1959 sample of delinquents, 30 percent said they would save it. When the amount to be given to the delinquents was raised to $100, 48 percent of the 1974 subjects, compared to 58 percent of the 1959 subjects, asserted that they would save the money.

Wilson and Herrnstein interpret these findings as evidence of the causal relationship between deferred gratification and delinquency rates in the two periods. However, the difference between the responses of the two groups of delinquents may, in fact, be no more than the result of sampling error or chance. Further, even if the difference were statistically significant, it may indicate only that the delinquents are better economists than are Wilson and Herrnstein, for the value of a dollar in 1974 was 41 percent less than it was in 1959. It should come as no surprise, and it certainly does not indicate any difference in a willingness to defer gratification, that intelligent juveniles (or adults) were less likely to save a dollar in 1974 than they were in 1959 (Kamin, 1986).

Another study cited in support of their theory compared the responses of delinquents and high school students in Anglo, Chicano, and Mexican cultures. Wilson and Herrnstein report that when these students were asked whether or not they would save or spend money, the delinquents were less likely than the nondelinquents to report that they would save the money. What Wilson and Herrnstein failed to point out is that this was only true when the sums were 25¢ and $2. When the sums were $20 and $200, the proportions of delinquents and nondelinquents reporting that they would save their money did not differ. In addition, many of the studies they cite do not measure actual behavior, but only what respondents claim they would do in response to a question on a questionnaire. We should never assume that what people say and what people do are always the same.

Wilson and Herrnstein also claim support for their theory from the fact that Japan has a much lower crime rate than does the United States. Although admitting that the two cultures differ significantly, they assert that these cultural differences are a product of biological differences, in particular, greater introversion among the Japanese. As evidence, they cite a single study that used a paper-and-pencil test to attempt to measure personality traits of people in Japan and the United States. The study did, in fact, show that the Japanese are more introverted than the Americans. Wilson and Herrnstein fail to mention that this sort of personality testing has also shown that the people of Uganda and Ghana score as high on introversion scales as the Japanese. They also fail to advise readers of the fact that the same personality test provides a score for an individual's tendency toward "psychoticism." The paper cited by Wilson and Herrnstein points out that the Japanese have the highest scores of any culture on this trait. The countries scoring the lowest on this trait are Canada, the United Kingdom, and the United States, all countries with higher official crime rates than Japan. Psychoticism, according to the study, is associated with brutality, insensitivity to the feelings of others, and self-centeredness (Kamin, 1986).

The overall goal of Wilson and Herrnstein's book is to provide a comprehensive explanation of why certain individuals commit crimes and others do not. But, as they admit, they examine only the traditional street crimes of murder, rape, and theft, while reluctantly ignoring embezzlement, political corruption, and fraud (due to a paucity of research). Murder, rape, and theft are certainly serious crimes that warrant investigation, but they are not representative of all serious crimes. Wilson and Herrnstein's individualistic approach to criminology is therefore limited to a select few individuals. This is not to imply that people of all classes are not capable of committing traditional street crimes but rather to suggest that class position does affect the type of crime chosen through its effects on opportunity, profit, ease, and so forth. For example, an executive vice president "can" commit burglary, but the opportunity for, profit from, and ease of embezzlement will make the latter type of theft more desirable. Conversely, the out-of-work laborer cannot choose embezzlement. The end result is that traditional street crime is predominantly a lower-class behavior.

Wilson and Herrnstein accept the possibility that persons of one class or one ethnic background are born with constitutional and genetic criminogenic factors significantly different from those of other classes and backgrounds. This genetic link surfaces when they hypothesize that Japan's low crime rate may be the product of constitutional traits inherent in the psychological makeup of the Japanese. In particular, they suggest that the high intelligence and introverted personality traits of the Japanese produced both the low crime rate and the specific cultural characteristics usually associated with that low rate. To accept this explanation for low crime rates, it seems logical to accept biological explanations for high crime rates. And, if one limits, as Wilson and Herrnstein do, the definition of crime to traditional lower-class street crime (so that only members of the lower class could cause high crime rates), one is left with a theory of crime that could be accused of being racist or classist.

POLITICALLY SENSITIVE DEBATE

The most recent public debate over biological theories of crime centers on a conference scheduled for October 9–11, 1992, at the University of Maryland, and canceled when the National Institutes of Health (NIH) withdrew its funding. Originally entitled "Genetic Factors in Crime: Findings, Uses, and

Implications," the conference organizers found themselves amid the controversy over the role of genetics in crime and the potential racial implications of such research. Arguing that the university had "grotesquely distorted" the conference in a way that could heighten racial concerns and damage the reputation of NIH, the Institute froze and then withdrew $78,000 originally earmarked for the conference (*Washington Post*, 1992a).

NIH officials pointed to the original brochure prepared for the conference, which stated that "genetic research holds out the prospect of identifying individuals who may be predisposed to certain kinds of criminal conduct, of isolating environmental factors which trigger those predispositions, and of treating some predispositions with drugs and unintrusive therapies" to argue that the proposed conference went beyond a discussion of the issues to suggest that genetic research was the "wave of the future" (*Washington Post*, 1992b). Criticism by a number of black organizations, international researchers, and others helped bring the issue into the public arena and officials of the University of Maryland have argued that the NIH's withdrawal of support was a political response and a violation of academic freedom. But whether or not the conference promoted a genetic link to crime, the initial support and its subsequent withdrawal by the NIH were both "political" decisions, in the sense that choices about funding are fundamentally choices about the relevance and value of particular approaches to understanding and controlling crime.

The conference on genetics was not the only arena where the issues of biology and crime were discussed. A proposed Public Health Service plan to study the causes of youth violence includes environmental and biological factors and suggests programs to combat youth violence that could include pharmacological treatments (*Washington Post*, 1992b). One of the agencies that would be included in the study would be the Alcohol, Drug Abuse and Mental Health Administration, that until recently was headed by Frederick K. Godwin, who compared the behavior of inner-city males to monkeys in the jungle and who expressed hope that biological research might yield clues to violent behavior. Political and community organizations have asked for a clarification of the proposed research.

There is no connection between the violence initiative proposal and the genetics and crime conference. But the continued interest in the study of biology and crime runs through both proposals. What may be new is greater public and political awareness and concern over the direction and implications of those approaches.

CONCLUSION

Biological theory offers a seemingly simple and straightforward solution to the problems of understanding and preventing crime: Some people are biologically predisposed to crime. Find these individuals, cure or isolate them (depending on their condition), and crime will be reduced. It is not an issue of politics, fairness, opportunity, or class. It is a scientific problem, best handled by the scientific community, not politicians or lawyers.

But the definition of crime is a product of a particular political and social milieu. To ignore this leads to a fatal misunderstanding of the nature of crime. Specific behaviors may be good or bad, but this often has little to do with their designation as crime. To aim a gun at a stranger and demand money is bad, and it is also a crime. To expose knowingly a half million schoolchildren to asbestos while in search of profit is also bad, but it is not a crime. To deny that crime is a social construct does not make the study of crime apolitical. It simply attempts to provide "scientific" support for the existing definitions of crime without recognizing that alternative definitions exist.

A half century ago, Garofalo recognized the political nature of crime. He attempted to deal with this fact by making an artificial and arbitrary distinction between "natural crimes" and all other crimes, claiming that only the former were universal and biologically explained. Today, we can see that his solution was without empirical justification. He demonstrated neither that natural crimes are of a biological origin nor that they are more objectively real and universal than the excluded crimes.

Jeffery (1971) repeats this argument when he claims that biosocial criminology is best reserved for street crimes, the traditional personal and property crimes committed disproportionately by the lower classes (which look suspiciously like Garofalo's natural crimes): "Perhaps organized and white-collar crime should be regarded not as problems in criminology but as problems of politics and economics" (p. 231). Jeffery argues that there are different causes and solutions for crimes committed by members of different social classes. Nearly fifty years ago, Sutherland criticized criminology for its failure to include white collar crime under its umbrella. Jeffery advocates its removal once again. Wilson and Herrnstein (1985) fall victim to the same class bias by limiting their analysis to traditional lower-class crime. Although they allude to the possibility that upper-class and middle-class criminals may also share genetic traits with lower-class criminals, the weakness of their approach becomes clear when those excluded upper-class crimes are reentered into the analysis. Do the corporate executives of the Manville Corporation have low intelligence? Are embezzlers suffering from psychopathic personalities?

Some biological theorists limit the applicability of their explanation to "irrational" crime, but the very definition of rational and irrational reflects value judgments. For example, whereas the machine smashing of the nineteenth century was seen by property owners as typically senseless vandalism, to the rioters themselves, their actions were very rational (Pearson, 1978). For agricultural laborers and workers in cottage industries, these were the acts of persons whose very livelihood was threatened by industrialization. For the factory workers, these were the acts of a new industrialized work force protesting and rioting for (and sometimes achieving) improved working conditions. In 1967, three physicians and leading advocates of psychosurgery suggested that some of the violence and looting accompanying the urban riots of the mid-1960s might be the product of organic brain dysfunction (Mark et al., 1967). During the Revolutionary War, only a minority actually fought against the British although everyone suffered under the same laws. Could the difference be related to organic brain dysfunction? What is rational and irrational depends on our perspective and our social class.

Biological theory reduces criminal behavior to uncontrolled but predetermined responses by a human organism. Not only is this an inaccurate depiction of crime in general, but it also distorts the relationship of biology to human behavior. We are biological creatures, but that does not mean we are ruled by our biology or that biology and environment compete for control of our actions.

For the biological theorist, the method of analysis is reductionist, and the starting point for the study of crime is the individual. He or she becomes the basic unit of analysis, and his or her physical or genetic codes become the ultimate components. The characteristics of society are seen simply as the sum total of the characteristics of its individual members, and the individuals, in turn, the product of their genetic codes. Societies are aggressive because the individuals in these societies are aggressive. Crime and even war, the most organized form of aggression, thus are seen as the products of clusters of hostile, aggressive individuals. Economics, politics, culture, and social relations are all reduced to the sum total of individuals and their biological makeup. Human history is studied by reducing every event to the behavior of its parts (people), as if these parts exist separate from, and unaffected by, the whole.

An assumption of many of the biological theorists is that "biological" (and in particular, genetic) means innate and permanent. It is this premise that allows us to discuss criminal potential or assume we can detect it prior to the onset of crime. This is true for the sociobiologists who argue that certain human traits (for example, aggression) are universal and the natural product of evolution, as well as for those who argue that the genetic code of specific individuals predisposes them to maladaptive behavior. Both approaches assume that certain behaviors are more natural, and therefore more expected, than other behaviors, either for specific individuals or for the species as a whole.

In his book *Understanding Violence*, Graeme Newman (1979) concluded that because the brain mediates aggressive behavior (being the mediator of all behavior), aggression may be caused by an internal mechanism: specific neural systems that are inherited and organized to evoke violent behavior. Thus, there is such a person as a "born killer," to use Newman's own phrase. The idea that some brains are innately organized to be aggressive, simply waiting for the appropriate trigger from the environment, has not been proved. A leading anthropologist, Montague (1980), points out that there is no such thing as an innate basic aggressive circuitry. Although neural systems can be organized by experience to function as aggression, an individual learns to be aggressive in the same manner that he or she learns to inhibit aggression. One is not a natural state and the other culturally imposed; both are within our biological potential.

In a similar fashion, there is no persuasive evidence to support Wilson's (1975) contention that we are genetically programmed for aggression simply because we are often aggressive. Genetic potentials do not lead to inevitable outcomes. Violence, sexism, and racism are biological only in the sense that they are within the range of possible human attitudes and behaviors. But nonviolence, equality, and justice are also biologically possible. What predominates in a particular society, historical period, or individual is not determined by biological predispositions, nor is the presence or absence of these qualities explained by theories deriving from the biological paradigm (Gould, 1976).

Although current exponents of biological explanations of crime often recognize the dialectic relation between the organism and the environment, this relationship seems forgotten when solutions are proposed. In particular, the suggestion that we treat the predelinquent through physical intervention is predicated on the following assumptions:

1. That a condition exists in the individual prior to the onset of the behavior
2. That we have the ability to identify that condition independent of the behavior
3. That left unaltered the condition will produce unwanted behavior
4. That we have the right, both morally and medically, to intervene to change or eradicate that condition

These were certainly the assumptions that justified eugenic sterilizations and more recent suggestions of psychosurgery and screening of infants, small children, or high school students (Nelkin and Swazey, 1982; Hastings Center, 1980). This is not to argue that preventive measures are impossible, impractical, or even undesirable but rather that a public health model cannot simply be transplanted onto the crime problem (Jeffery, 1985). One cannot have a disease model of crime in the absence of an identifiable disease. The majority of the abnormalities identified are defined by their association with unwanted behavior. The goal of the "therapy" then becomes control or elimination of the behavior rather than the cure of an identifiable disease (Bedeau, 1975).

One can see the potential for abuse. Crime is removed from its social, legal, ethical, and political context, and defined solely as a medical problem requiring medical expertise, not process protection. A danger unique to biological theories is their ability to invoke the traditional prestige of science as objective, value neutral, and free of political motives. But the history of biological intervention in the control of crime is a history of political decisions. The choice of crimes and criminals to be researched is a political decision; the definition of crime is a political decision.

DISCUSSION QUESTIONS

1. Discuss the various types of studies that have tried to establish whether or not criminality is an inherited trait. What does the evidence suggest? What are the limitations of those studies?

2. Scientists have sought answers to the criminality puzzle through studies of abnormal EEGs, extra Y chromosomes, PMS, and testosterone levels. What have they found? What are the limitations of these types of studies?

3. Are criminals less intelligent than noncriminals? Discuss the possibility in terms of general research findings and in terms of difficulties in measuring intelligence.

4. Discuss the social and political dangers of research aimed at linking criminality with biology. Is there any way in which to make this topic less sensitive?

♦   An earlier version of this chapter appeared in William J. Chambliss, *Exploring Crime* (New York: Macmillan, 1988).

CHAPTER 13

STRAIN AND SUBCULTURAL THEORIES OF CRIMINALITY

Robert Agnew
Emory University

THIS CHAPTER examines two major sociological theories of criminal behavior: strain theory and subcultural crime theory. Although these theories are conceptually distinct from each other and thus are treated separately, there is good reason for placing them both in the same chapter: Strain and subcultural theories often have been combined into more comprehensive theories (Elliott et al., 1979; Sheley, 1983). Certain of the theorists we will discuss, in fact, can be classified as both strain and subcultural theorists.

Numerous versions of both strain and subcultural theory have been advanced, and it is not possible to describe all these versions in their full complexity. The focus, rather, will be on describing the essential features of strain and subcultural crime theories and the major variations in these theories. Both theories have been used to explain juvenile delinquency and virtually every type of adult crime. In particular, they have been applied to explanations of why some *groups* have higher crime and delinquency rates than do other groups, and why some *individuals* are more likely to engage in crime and delinquency than are other individuals (see Cressey, 1960; Agnew, 1987b). These theories differ from the individual-level theories described in the previous chapter in that they explain crime in terms of the individual's social environment rather than biogenetic characteristics.

STRAIN THEORY

Strain theory argues that crime results when individuals are unable to get what they want through legitimate channels. In such cases, individuals become frustrated, and they may try to satisfy their wants through illegitimate channels or they may strike out at others in their anger. The several versions of strain theory differ from one another in specifying (1) the wants that individuals in our society pursue, (2) the factors that prevent individuals from satisfying their wants, and (3) the factors that influence whether the resulting frustration results in crime. (All strain theories acknowledge that only *some* strained individuals turn to crime.)

We will focus on three major versions of strain theory. First, we will review the classic strain theories of Merton (1938), Cohen (1955), and Cloward and Ohlin (1960). Second, we will review a set of revisions in these classic strain theories, represented most prominently in the work of Elliott et al. (see Elliott and Voss, 1974; Elliott et al., 1979, 1985). And third, we will review Agnew's (1992) General Strain Theory of Delinquency.

CLASSIC STRAIN THEORY

Merton's (1938) is the most influential of all strain theories — not only has it inspired much research, but most revisions in strain theory trace their origins to Merton (Clinard, 1964; Cole, 1975). Merton's theory seeks to explain a wide range of deviance in both adults and juveniles. The strain theories of Cohen (1955) and Cloward and Ohlin (1960), however, focus on the explanation of juvenile delinquency — particularly, the gang delinquency of lower-class urban males. All three theories are treated together although relevant differences between the theories are noted.

◆ **THE WANTS THAT INDIVIDUALS PURSUE** ◆ Classic strain theory argues that *everyone* in the United States, poor as well as rich, is encouraged to strive for success. This encouragement comes from parents, school and government officials, religious figures, and the mass media. Whereas Merton argues that the primary measure of success in the United States is monetary, however, Cohen asserts that individuals are encouraged to pursue the somewhat broader goal of middle-class status. That is, individuals are urged to seek the financial success, reputation, and lifestyle associated with the middle class. Cloward and Ohlin present something of a compromise, suggesting that the definition of success varies somewhat among and within social classes. Some people seek to become a part of the middle class, whereas others simply desire monetary success. Most lower-class individuals, however, are said to desire only monetary success. These theories recognize that not all individuals adopt this cultural emphasis on success but argue that a "substantial" or "significant" number of people in all social classes develop high aspirations for success (Merton, 1968).

◆ **THE BARRIERS TO THE SATISFACTION OF THESE WANTS** ◆ Although everyone is encouraged to strive for success, large segments of the population are prevented from achieving such success through legitimate channels. In the United States, one is supposed to achieve success through hard work, careful planning, self-denial, and honesty. Through these means, one first obtains a good education and then a good job. Classic strain theory, however, argues that large segments of the lower class are prevented from achieving success through these channels. In particular, lower-class individuals are socialized in families that do not place a high value on such qualities as hard work, careful planning, and self-denial, as well as other traits necessary for successful goal achievement. Lower-class families do not provide the adolescent with the instruction and support necessary to do well in school. Lower-class individuals often encounter discrimination in the school system and other middle-class environments. Lower-class families lack the money to finance an advanced education for their children. And lower-class families lack the finances and connections to set up their children in business or a profession. As a result, lower-class individuals often are unable to achieve success through legitimate channels. And this creates much strain or frustration in them.

◆ **THE LINKS BETWEEN STRAIN AND CRIME** ◆ The frustration engendered by goal blockage does not necessarily lead to crime. In fact, Merton states that most strained individuals remain *conformists*, continuing to accept the cultural emphasis on monetary success and trying to achieve such success through legitimate channels. Other individuals, however, try to reduce their frustration by employing one of four possible adaptations to strain (goal blockage)—several of which may involve crime. According to Merton, individuals may adapt to strain by rejecting either the cultural emphasis on success or the legitimate means by which success is supposed to be achieved. In some cases, new goals and means may be substituted for the old ones.

Innovation. According to Merton and to Cloward and Ohlin, the adaptation most closely linked to crime is innovation. Here, the individual continues to accept the cultural goal of monetary success but rejects the legitimate means to obtaining such success. Rather, the individual resorts to such illegitimate means as theft, prostitution, and drug selling. Crime in this view is utilitarian—it is a means to achieve a goal.

Cohen, however, does not employ this adaptation in his explanation of delinquency. According to Cohen (1955: 36), the adaptation of innovation may explain "adult professional crime and the property delinquency of some older and semi-professional juvenile thieves," but it does not explain most juvenile delinquency. Most juvenile delinquency, Cohen states, is nonutilitarian in nature. Delinquents, for example, do not steal because they need the money; rather, they steal for "the hell of it." Stolen items often are "discarded, destroyed, or casually given away" (p. 26). Even though Cohen's description of most delinquency as nonutilitarian appears to be exaggerated (see Cloward and Ohlin, 1960, especially Chapter 7), the point that at least some delinquency is nonutilitarian is well taken. At best, the adaptation of innovation explains only some delinquency.

Ritualism.　A second adaptation to strain is ritualism. Here, the individual continues to accept institutional means (for example, hard work and honesty) but lowers success goals to the point where they can be satisfied or abandons the goal of success altogether. The behavior associated with ritualism may be viewed as deviant but is seldom criminal. This adaptation, according to Merton, is expressed in such cultural cliches as "I'm not sticking my neck out," "I'm playing it safe," "I'm satisfied with what I got," and "Don't aim high and you won't be disappointed."

Retreatism.　A third adaptation to strain is retreatism, in which the individual rejects both institutional means and the cultural emphasis on monetary success and middle-class status. Merton argues that the individual withdraws or retreats from society, becoming, for example, an alcoholic, a drug addict, or a vagrant. Cloward and Ohlin provide an example of this adaptation in their description of a retreatist subculture made up of adolescents who have oriented their lives around drug use.

Rebellion.　A final adaptation, rebellion, involves (1) the rejection of both goals and legitimate means and (2) the substitution of new goals and means in their place. Rebellion often manifests itself in political action. Cohen, however, uses the adaptation of rebellion to explain the origins of lower-class juvenile gangs.

Cohen argues that lower-class adolescents often are unable to achieve middle-class status through legitimate channels. One solution to this problem involves setting up an alternative status system in which they can compete successfully. In particular, Cohen suggests that they set up a status system that values everything the middle-class condemns. The middle class, for example, opposes physical violence and the theft and destruction of property. The delinquent subculture set up by lower-class boys, however, accords high status to individuals who engage in violence, theft, and vandalism. The oppositional nature of the delinquent subculture is partly explained by the fact that lower-class boys feel hostile toward the middle-class world that so often frustrates and humiliates them. The delinquent subculture legitimizes the expression of such hostility by placing a positive value on violence and property crime.

◆ **FACTORS DETERMINING THE REACTION TO STRAIN** ◆　Thus, individuals may adapt to strain in a number of ways, only some of which involve crime. A major question, then, is what factors determine how one adapts to strain. Why, for example, does one strained individual become a ritualist while another becomes an innovator?

Commitment to Legitimate Means.　According to Merton and to Cloward and Ohlin, strain or goal blockage is more likely to result in crime when the individual is not strongly committed to legitimate means. Merton goes on to argue that there are class-related differences in the commitment to means.

Lower-class individuals are "imperfectly socialized" and do not place a high value on means such as honesty and hard work. As a result, these individuals are more likely to turn to crime when faced with goal blockage. Cloward and Ohlin argue that even individuals who are committed to legitimate means may come to reject them. In particular, individuals who fail to achieve success by following legitimate means may come to reject these means, especially if they blame the social system (rather than themselves) for their failure.

Interaction with Other Strained or Delinquent Individuals. Cohen and Cloward and Ohlin also argue that the likelihood of delinquency is strongly influenced by whether the individual interacts with other strained or delinquent individuals, who may provide the adolescent with social support for delinquency. Because delinquency may be sanctioned by others, and may arouse some guilt in the adolescent, the support of other adolescents is quite important in overcoming these barriers. Further, other adolescents may foster delinquency by (1) teaching the adolescent how to engage in delinquency and (2) providing opportunities to engage in delinquency.

Cohen and Cloward and Ohlin go on to discuss certain of the factors that influence whether strained individuals will interact with other strained or delinquent individuals. The adolescent's family plays an important role in this area. If adolescents are closely supervised by parents and feel a strong attachment to them, they are less likely to come under the influence of delinquent peers (see Elliott et al., 1985, for an expanded discussion of this point). Also important is the nature of the adolescent's neighborhood. In particular, Cloward and Ohlin argue that different types of neighborhoods provide different opportunities for delinquency.

◆ **EVALUATION OF CLASSIC STRAIN THEORY** ◆ Classic strain theory, in sum, argues that everyone in the United States is encouraged to pursue success, but lower-class people often are prevented from achieving such success through legitimate channels. This creates much frustration, which may, in turn, lead to crime. The individuals who engage in such crime are not biologically or psychologically disturbed, nor are they evil individuals. Rather, they are simply "responding normally to the social situation in which they find themselves" (Merton, 1968: 186).

The first proposition of classic strain theory—that the universal emphasis on success is internalized by significant numbers of people in all social classes—has been challenged by a number of researchers claiming that lower-class individuals have low aspirations for success and therefore are not under any strain. Hyman (1953) was the first to raise this argument, and most subsequent research has shown that lower-class individuals have lower absolute levels of aspiration than do middle-class individuals (see Agnew and Jones, 1988, for a review). That is, lower-class individuals on average desire less education, less money, and less prestigious occupations than do middle-class individuals. However, a large number of lower-class individuals—a majority in some studies—have absolute levels of aspiration as high as the middle class

(Agnew and Jones, 1988). Further, limited evidence suggests that, *relative to what they have*, lower-class individuals desire as much, if not more, success than do middle-class individuals (see Empey, 1956; Cloward and Ohlin, 1960).

The second proposition of classic strain theory—that, relative to middle-class individuals, lower-class individuals are less able to achieve their goals through legitimate channels—has usually been tested by examining the relationship between aspirations and expectations. Aspirations refer to "ideal goals": what one would *ideally* like to achieve. Expectations refer to "expected goals": what one *realistically* expects to achieve. The gap between aspirations and expectations is sometimes taken as an indicator of strain. If strain theory were correct, we would expect lower-class individuals to experience a greater gap between aspirations and expectations. That is, lower-class individuals should be more likely to report that they do not expect to achieve their aspirations. Research has focused on educational, occupational, and to a lesser extent, monetary goals, and the evidence does suggest that the percentage of people who do not expect to achieve their goals is somewhat higher in the lower class (Agnew, 1987a).

The final proposition of classic strain theory—that strained individuals are more likely to engage in crime—has been the most heavily criticized. This proposition usually has been tested by examining the relationship between delinquency and aspirations and expectations. If strain theory were correct, we would expect delinquency to be highest among those with high aspirations and low expectations. Delinquency, however, typically is highest among those with both low aspirations and low expectations. Based largely on these studies, several prominent criminologists have called for the abandonment of classic strain theory (Hirschi, 1969; Kornhauser, 1978).

These studies, however, suffer from certain problems. First, as Bernard (1984) points out, they have focused on the desire for a high education or a prestigious job, not on the desire for monetary success. This is surprising, in that Merton and Cloward and Ohlin specifically focus on this goal. Cloward and Ohlin, in fact, state that most lower-class adolescents are concerned about money and little else. They are not interested in education or occupational advancement, and their inability to achieve educational or occupational goals would probably not strain or frustrate them. In their recent study of Seattle youths, Farnworth and Leiber (1989) provide support for Bernard's argument. They found that while the failure to achieve educational goals bore little relationship to delinquency, the failure to achieve monetary success was positively related to delinquency. Indirect support for this argument is also provided in a series of studies indicating that the crime rate is higher in areas where there is much income inequality or a large gap between the poor and wealthy (Blau and Blau, 1982; Sampson, 1985b; Krahn et al., 1986; Messner, 1989). It has been suggested that the poor in such areas are frustrated over their inability to achieve the wealth that surrounds them.

Second, those studies that fail to support strain theory usually are based on samples of high school students. They do not examine adults, and they do not include a high portion of the hard-core poor living in urban slums. Classic strain theory may be more relevant to adults, to whom the pursuit of money is a more serious matter, and to the hard-core poor, who face the greatest barriers to goal achievement.

Finally, most studies do not examine those factors that influence the relationship between strain and delinquency, factors such as the commitment to legitimate means and degree of interaction with other strained individuals. For these reasons, the previous studies do not prove that classic strain theory is wrong. They do, however, raise some doubts about the theory.

One final criticism of classic strain theory should be noted. Classic strain theory tries to explain why the poor in the United States are more likely to engage in crime than are others. Recent data, however, suggest that crime among the middle-class is much more extensive than previously believed. The precise relationship between class and crime is still a matter of debate (see Hagan, 1992; Tittle and Meier, 1990). It is fairly certain, however, that little or no relationship exists between class and minor crime, and that middle-class individuals engage in a significant amount of serious crime — although perhaps not as much as poor individuals. If we take into account white collar crime (see Chapter 11), the extent of middle-class crime is even greater. Strain theory is unable to explain the extensive nature of middle-class crime. This point is important because many of the revisions in classic strain theory attempt to extend the generalizability of the theory to the middle class.

REVISIONS IN CLASSIC STRAIN THEORY

Most of the revisions in classic strain theory focus on the explanation of juvenile delinquency although they could easily be applied to adult crime as well. The revisions were developed in response to the criticisms of classic strain theory, and they deal with (1) the goals that individuals pursue, (2) the barriers to goal achievement, and (3) the links between strain and delinquency.

◆ **THE GOALS THAT INDIVIDUALS PURSUE** ◆ Classic strain theory argues that the dominant goal in our society is monetary success and middle-class status. The revisions, however, assert that adolescents pursue a variety of different goals that vary from adolescent to adolescent and from group to group. These revisions, then, treat goal commitment as a variable, and do not assume in advance that adolescents are pursuing a particular goal (Elliott and Voss, 1974; Greenberg, 1977a; Elliott et al., 1979; Agnew, 1984a; Elliott et al., 1985).

Although goal commitment is treated as a variable, many theorists also state that adolescents are concerned more with the achievement of immediate goals than with long-range goals such as monetary success or middle-class status (Quicker, 1974; Elliott and Voss, 1974; Greenberg, 1977a; Empey and Stafford, 1992; Agnew, 1984a; Elliott et al., 1985). In particular, they point to research suggesting that most adolescents are not overly concerned about their future educational or occupational status. Rather, they are more concerned with the present—with achieving such immediate goals as popularity with peers and the opposite sex, good grades, athletic success, owning a car, and getting along well with parents.

This focus on immediate goals allows these revisions to overcome certain of the problems of classic strain theory. The revisions can explain middle-class delinquency by arguing that the achievement of many immediate goals is largely independent of social class (Elliott and Voss, 1974). Middle-class adolescents, for example, may have as much trouble achieving popularity with peers as do lower-class adolescents. Moreover, middle-class adolescents may pursue goals that are more difficult to achieve, and this may offset whatever advantage their class affords them (Elliott and Voss, 1974). The revisions also can explain why those studies focusing on the disjunction between aspirations and expectations fail to support strain theory. As indicated, these studies emphasize future goals like occupational success. If such goals are unimportant to the adolescent, we would not expect the disjunction between aspirations and expectations to be related to delinquency. The failure to achieve an unimportant goal is not likely to promote much strain. Further, adolescents often pursue several goals at once so that the failure to achieve one goal may be offset by the achievement of other goals.

◆ **THE BARRIERS TO GOAL ACHIEVEMENT** ◆ The revisions also differ from classic strain theory in arguing that goal achievement is a function of several factors in addition to social class. Goal achievement, for example, may be influenced by one's intelligence, creativity, physical attractiveness, athletic ability, personality characteristics, and other factors. Popularity with the opposite sex, for example, may be just as much (if not more) a function of appearance and personality as it is of social class. Recognizing these additional determinants of goal achievement also helps the revisions explain middle-class delinquency. Although many of these additional factors are related to social class, the relationship often is far from perfect. Middle-class individuals, as well as their lower-class counterparts, may lack the skills or traits necessary to achieve their goals through legitimate channels.

◆ **THE LINKS BETWEEN STRAIN AND DELINQUENCY** ◆ According to the revisions in classic strain theory, the failure to achieve most or all of one's important goals increases the likelihood of delinquency. Adolescents may turn to delinquency in order to (1) achieve their goals through illegitimate channels or (2) vent their frustration or anger. To test these revisions, we would first have to determine what goals the adolescent considered important. Then we would determine the extent to which the adolescent was achieving (or expected to achieve) these goals. Adolescents unable to achieve all or most of their important goals should have the highest levels of delinquency.

These revisions recognize that not all strained individuals turn to delinquency. And the revisions have drawn heavily from classic theory in specifying those factors that influence the relationship between strain and delinquency. In particular, it is argued that strain is more likely to result in delinquency when the adolescent (1) rejects legitimate means and (2) associates with other delinquents (see Elliott and Voss, 1974).

◆ **EVALUATION OF THE REVISIONS IN CLASSIC STRAIN THEORY** ◆ The first proposition of the revised strain theories—that adolescents pursue a variety of goals—has a fair degree of support. Studies indicate that adolescents and even adults pursue a variety of different goals (Clark and Wenninger, 1963; Christenson and Yang, 1976; Agnew, 1984b, 1987a). Rokeach (1973), for example, found that the adults in his sample possessed an average of 12.5 "terminal values" (or goals). Classic strain theorists might react to these studies by arguing that, although individuals consider a number of goals important, they attach greatest importance to the goal of monetary success. Studies that ask respondents to rank the relative importance of goals, however, do not support this argument. Goals such as material comfort, prestige, and advancement often are ranked toward the middle to bottom of goal hierarchies (Rokeach, 1973; Christenson and Yang, 1976).

The second proposition of the revised strain theories—that goal achievement is a function of several factors in addition to social class—also is quite reasonable. A number of studies suggest that the achievement of various goals—ranging from educational and occupational advancement to popularity—depends on factors like intelligence, creativity, and appearance (Hauser et al., 1976; Barron and Harrington, 1981; Agnew, 1984a), though this is not to say that social class is unimportant.

The final proposition of the revised theories—that goal blockage increases the likelihood of delinquency—has been more difficult to support. Only a limited number of studies have tested the revised theories, and the studies that have been done suffer from a number of problems. For example, they frequently examine only a small number of adolescent goals, and assume that these goals are important to the adolescents being studied. Nevertheless, these studies tend to find that goal blockage is unrelated or only weakly related to delinquency (Reiss and Rhodes, 1963; Elliott and Voss, 1974; Greenberg's, 1979, reanalysis of Quicker, 1974; Elliott et al., 1985). One study (Agnew, 1984c), for example, asked adolescents to rate the importance of seven goals and then determined the extent to which adolescents were achieving those goals they had rated as important. The measure of goal achievement was largely unrelated to delinquency. Virtually all the adolescents in the sample, however, were able to achieve at least some of their important goals. This partial goal achievement may have been enough to prevent the type of severe strain and frustration that might lead to delinquency. Agnew (1984c) has speculated that adolescents may avoid strain by pursuing several goals at once so that, although they might not be able to achieve all of their goals, they probably will be able to achieve at least some. And this may be enough to prevent serious strain and frustration. Further, Agnew and Jones (1988) argue that individuals often exaggerate actual and expected levels of goal achievement. Adolescents who are doing poorly in school, for example, will often report that they are good students and expect to attend college. This too serves to prevent serious strain.

We must conclude our evaluation of modern strain theory in much the same way we concluded our evaluation of classic strain theory. The theory has not been tested adequately although the limited studies that have been done tend to cast some doubt on it.

CONTEMPORARY GENERAL STRAIN THEORY

Several additional revisions in strain theory have been suggested (see, for example, Merton, 1964; Mizruchi, 1964). One revision that appears to have some potential for explaining crime is the author's own General Strain Theory (Agnew, 1992).

Classic and revised strain theories assume that strain results from the inability to achieve positively valued goals. These goals may be monetary success, middle-class status, popularity with peers, good grades, and so forth. And strain is measured in terms of the disjunction between aspirations (ideal goals) and expectations or actual achievements. The General Strain Theory (GST) argues that there are several types of strain. According to the GST, strain theory focuses on *negative relations* with others, that is, relations where individuals are not treated as they want to be treated. There are three major types of strain or negative relations with others. In particular, strain occurs when others (1) prevent or threaten to prevent you from achieving positively valued goals, (2) remove or threaten to remove positively valued stimuli that you possess, or (3) present or threaten to present you with noxious or negatively valued stimuli.

The classic and revised strain theories consider only the first type of strain, involving the failure to achieve positively valued goals. And they measure this type of strain by asking individuals whether they have achieved or expect to achieve their *ideal* goals. The author argues that this is not the best way to measure this type of strain since many individuals may not take their *ideal* goals seriously. This type of strain would be better measured by asking individuals if they have achieved their *expected* goals or if they have gotten what they feel they *deserve* from others. So, for example, we might measure strain among college students by asking them if they got the grades they expected or deserved (versus the grades they ideally desired).

The second type of strain, involving the loss of positive stimuli, includes such things as the loss of a boyfriend or girlfriend, moving from one's neighborhood, or the death of a parent. The individual loses something that is valued. The third type of strain, involving the presentation of noxious or negative stimuli, includes criminal victimization of various types, a wide assortment of stressful life events, and negative relations — marked by insults, verbal threats, and the like — with parents, teachers, and others.

These types of strain increase the likelihood that individuals will experience such negative emotions as disappointment, depression, and fear; anger and frustration, however, are especially important in the GST. These negative emotions create pressure for corrective action, and crime is one possible response. Crime may be a method for reducing strain, that is, for achieving positively valued goals, for protecting or retrieving positive stimuli, or for terminating or escaping from negative stimuli. Crime may be used to seek revenge against those who have mistreated us. And crime may occur as individuals try to manage their negative emotions through illicit drug use. Whether individuals respond to strain with delinquency is said to depend on a number of factors, including the individual's temperament, problem-solving skills, level of conventional social support, level of social control, self-efficacy, and association with delinquent peers.

At heart, the GST is very simple. It argues that if we treat people badly, they may get mad and engage in crime. The theory has not been tested in its entirety, but preliminary tests are encouraging (Agnew, 1985a, 1989). Agnew and White (1992), for example, constructed a measure of strain that focused on the loss of positive stimuli and the presentation of negative stimuli. Adolescents who scored high on this measure reported that they had lost a close friend through death, that their parents had divorced, that they did not get along with their classmates, that their parents and teachers mistreated them in a variety of ways, that their neighborhood had numerous problems, and so forth. These adolescents were more likely to be delinquent, especially if they were low in self-efficacy (perceived control over the environment) and had delinquent friends. The GST, then, is much broader than the classic and revised strain theories discussed earlier, and the data are more supportive of this theory.

Although the evidence concerning strain theory is mixed, that is not the case for the next theory we will discuss: subcultural crime theory. Subcultural crime theory, in fact, is perhaps the dominant theory of crime in the current literature.

SUBCULTURAL CRIME THEORY

Subcultural crime theory argues that certain groups or subcultures in our society approve of crime or at least hold values conducive to crime. For that reason, individuals who interact with the members of these groups may eventually adopt the criminal values of the group and engage in crime. Individuals who engage in theft, for example, may do so because they learned from others that theft is good or at least permissible. Such individuals are not necessarily strained (although strain theory is often used to explain the origin of criminal groups or subcultures). Subcultural theory, then, states that criminal behavior is learned in interaction with others who approve of crime or hold values conducive to crime. Sutherland provides the leading statement of this position (Sutherland and Cressey, 1978; also see Matsueda, 1988).

Numerous versions of subcultural theory exist, and these versions differ from one another in specifying (1) the groups that have criminal values and the nature of these values, (2) the origins of these groups, and (3) the ways in which these groups affect the individual.

CRIMINAL GROUPS AND CRIMINAL VALUES

Subcultural theorists have argued that there are four types of criminal groups or subcultures: (1) groups that unconditionally approve of all or most crime and condemn all conventional behavior, (2) groups that justify or approve of crime under certain conditions but otherwise have some commitment to conventional behavior, (3) groups that do not explicitly approve of crime but have values that are *conducive* to crime, and (4) groups that unconditionally approve of select forms of crime (usually minor crimes) but otherwise are committed to conventional behavior.

◆ **UNCONDITIONAL APPROVAL OF CRIME** ◆ This position represents the most extreme form of subcultural deviance theory and is best expressed in the work of Cohen (1955). As we noted in the previous section, Cohen uses strain theory to explain the origin of delinquent gangs among lower-class urban males. He argues that such males are unable to achieve middle-class status through legitimate channels, so they adapt by setting up an alternative status system in which they can compete successfully. Their hostility toward the middle class, among other things, leads them to create an oppositional subculture; that is, they come to value everything the middle-class condemns. In particular, they come to value the property and violent crimes so strongly opposed by the middle class. They also come to condemn everything the middle class values, including conventional forms of behavior such as studying and hard work. The delinquent subculture is initially made up of the strained males described earlier, but after it comes into existence, it may recruit nonstrained individuals.

Cohen is careful to note that members of the delinquent subculture continue to have a lingering attachment to the conventional values they violate. This attachment, however, is repressed, and if anything, is dealt with by *overreacting against* these conventional values or, in Cohen's terms, "reaction formation."

◆ **APPROVAL OF CRIME UNDER CERTAIN CONDITIONS** ◆ Most subcultural crime theorists are less extreme than Cohen. They do not believe that certain groups unconditionally approve of all crime and condemn all conventional behavior. A more common position is that some groups generally approve of conventional behavior but believe that criminal behavior is justified, even required, *under certain conditions.* For example, the youths about whom Cloward and Ohlin (1960) write cannot achieve monetary success through conventional channels. Rather than set up an alternative status system, they try to achieve monetary success through illegitimate channels, such as theft. They soon come to justify their criminal behavior by arguing that the social system has unfairly prevented them from achieving success through legitimate channels. Given this fact, they believe they are justified in trying to achieve success through illegitimate channels. They do not, however, believe that criminal behavior is morally superior to conventional behavior, but simply that it is necessary and justified *given their situation.* Further, they continue to engage in conventional behavior in other areas of their lives (Cloward and Ohlin, 1960: 19).

Wolfgang and Ferracuti (1967) developed a similar theory in order to explain the high rate of homicide among young males in urban slums, particularly among black males. They point out, for example, that the homicide rate among nonwhite males age 20–24 in their Philadelphia study is 92 per 100,000. This compares to a rate of 3.4 for white males of the same ages. According to Wolfgang and Ferracuti, this difference is explained by the value system of the young black males. Although they accept many conventional values, they differ from the larger society in that they believe violence is justified in certain situations. "A male is usually expected to defend the name and honor of his mother, the virtue of womanhood . . . and to accept no derogation about his race (even from a member of his own race), his age, or his masculinity" (1967, p. 153). So individuals in this group believe that one should retaliate with violence in response to certain types of insults and threats. They develop what Wolfgang and Ferracuti refer to as a "subculture of violence." A similar argument has been used to explain the higher rate of homicide in the South (see Hawley and Messner, 1989; Messner, 1988; Parker, 1989).

Finally, Sykes and Matza (1957) have attempted to categorize the justifications that delinquents employ for their behavior. According to Sykes and Matza, most delinquents believe that crime is bad and conventional behavior is good. These delinquents, however, are taught that crime is justifiable and even good in certain situations. In particular, they learn certain "techniques of neutralization." These techniques are justifications or rationalizations, and they specify those situations in which crime is justified. These techniques are used before the commission of a delinquent act, and they make the act possible by neutralizing one's belief that crime is bad (for an alternative view, see Sheley, 1980). Sykes and Matza list five techniques of neutralization:

1. Denial of responsibility. Delinquents using this technique claim that their acts are due to forces beyond their control, such as unloving parents or drug use.

2. Denial of injury. Here delinquents claim that their acts are harmless; that shoplifting, for example, does not hurt stores because their insurance will cover the loss.

3. Denial of the victim. Delinquents claim that their victims got what they deserved. They claim, for example, that they stole from a dishonest storeowner or they beat someone up in self-defense.

4. Condemnation of the condemners. Here delinquents claim that those who condemn them also engage in questionable behavior. Adolescents who use marijuana, for example, may point to the drinking behavior of their parents, or thieves may point to the corruption among police and politicians.

5. Appeal to higher loyalties. Delinquents state that loyalty to friends and others may sometimes necessitate delinquent behavior. Delinquents may steal, for example, to help their family.

Sykes and Matza capture the sentiments underlying these techniques, in order, with the following phrases: "I didn't mean it," "I didn't really hurt anybody," "They had it coming," "Everybody's picking on me," and "I didn't do it for myself." Sykes and Matza, then, go beyond Cloward and Ohlin and Wolfgang and Ferracuti in stating that there are a wide range of justifications for criminal behavior. Still other justifications, thought to be common among delinquents and others, have been listed by additional theorists (see Minor, 1981; Conklin, 1992).

◆ **VALUES CONDUCIVE TO CRIME** ◆   A number of theorists have argued that certain groups have values that are conducive to crime but do not explicitly approve of or justify crime. That is, they hold values that make crime appear a more attractive alternative than might otherwise be the case. Matza and Sykes (1961) provide the most explicit description of these values in their paper on subterranean values (also see Curtis, 1975). They draw on numerous accounts of delinquent values and state that certain common themes emerge in these accounts. In particular, they state that delinquents in all social classes tend to pursue certain values that are conducive to delinquency.

First, Matza and Sykes (1961: 713) state that delinquents are "deeply immersed in a restless search for excitement, 'thrills,' or 'kicks.'" Many other theorists have made the same argument. Miller (1958), for example, states that lower-class individuals in general and lower-class gang members in particular place great value on "excitement" and "thrills." And the same desire for excitement and thrills has been said to characterize middle-class delinquents (Vaz, 1967). This search for excitement can, of course, be satisfied through legitimate as well as illegitimate means. Criminal activities, however, hold a special appeal since they have the added element of danger — of "experimenting with the forbidden." Individuals who value excitement, then, are likely to view crime as a more attractive alternative in a given situation than are others.

Second, delinquents are said to have a disdain for hard work and a desire for quick, easy success. Again, this theme is emphasized by several researchers. In his theory of middle-class delinquency, for example, England (1960) states that delinquents reject such values as "hard work, thrift, study, and self-denial." Miller (1958) makes the same point in his discussion of lower-class culture. At the same time, however, delinquents have "grandiose dreams of quick success." They desire much money and all the luxuries money can buy. Crime, of course, would have an obvious appeal to someone who places a low value on hard work and a high value on money and pleasure.

Third, delinquents are said to place much value on toughness — on being "macho." In particular, much emphasis is placed on being physically strong, on being able to defend oneself, on not letting others "push you around," and on showing bravery in the face of physical threat. According to Miller, the hero for this delinquent is the "tough guy," represented "by the movie gangster of the thirties, the private eye, and the movie cowboy." Clearly, individuals who place a high value on toughness will view delinquent acts like fighting as more attractive than do others.

◆ **APPROVAL OF SELECT FORMS OF CRIME** ◆ Finally, certain subcultural crime theorists argue that some groups have some commitment to conventional values but approve of select forms of crime. Various theorists have argued, for example, that all young people, or at least certain segments of the youth population, approve of such activities as underage drinking, underage driving, sexual intercourse, gambling, truancy, and curfew violations (Matza, 1964; Vaz, 1967). A similar argument has been made with respect to the lower class. And finally, it has been argued that white collar executives in certain corporations approve of or justify certain forms of corporate crime, such as restriction of competition and consumer fraud (see Conklin, 1977).

THE ORIGINS OF CRIMINAL SUBCULTURES

Subcultural crime theorists have explained the origins of criminal subcultures in several ways. In the early part of this century, the United States had just experienced a massive influx of new immigrant groups, and many observers claimed that some of these groups approved of certain forms of criminal behavior or held values conducive to crime. According to Sellin (1938), for example, it was commonly asserted that many of the new immigrant groups approved of or condoned such activities as gambling, prostitution, the manufacture and consumption of alcohol (during Prohibition), and the use of narcotics. Further, certain of these groups were said to justify the use of violence in a much broader range of situations than was permitted by the law. Sellin, for example, describes a Sicilian father who felt justified in killing the 16-year-old seducer of his daughter. Immigration into the United States dropped dramatically in the 1930s, however, and migration is no longer one of the major explanations of criminal subcultures in the United States. Today, subcultural crime theorists explain the origins of criminal subcultures primarily in terms of strain theory and, to a lesser extent, in terms of the tendency of certain groups to focus selectively on and distort certain values in the dominant culture.

Strain theory is used to explain the origins of criminal subcultures in two ways, both of which have already been illustrated. The first way involves the process of innovation as an adaptation to strain. Theoretically, when individuals cannot achieve their goals through legitimate channels, they may try to achieve their goals through illegitimate channels like theft. And in doing so, they may come to justify their illegal behavior (see Minor, 1984). Cloward and Ohlin (1960) provide the best illustration of this approach: Such individuals justify their crime by claiming that the social system unfairly prevents them from achieving monetary success through legal channels.

This argument also has been used to explain why adolescents (1) value excitement, pleasure-seeking, and toughness and (2) approve of such minor misdeeds as drinking, sexual intercourse, and truancy. Several theorists have pointed out that adolescents occupy a very special position in our society. On the one hand, they are physically adults and often are told to "behave like adults." On the other hand, they often are treated like children and denied many of the privileges of adulthood—like the right to drink, vote, and marry. Adolescents find this situation frustrating, and they often respond by engaging in the "symbolic equivalents of the adult behavior denied them" (Bloch and Neiderhoffer, 1958: 29). According to Bloch and Neiderhoffer, they engage in such behaviors as "drinking, sexual escapades, wild automobile rides, immature assertiveness, violent reactions to parental restraints, protests against authority, and other forms of intransigence" (p. 30). They soon come to approve of such behaviors, as well as the more general values associated with these behaviors.

The second way in which strain may lead to the development of criminal subcultures involves the process of rebellion as an adaptation to strain. Theoretically, if individuals are unable to achieve status through legitimate channels, they may create an alternative status system in which they can successfully compete. Cohen (1955) provides the best illustration of this argument in his discussion of the origin of delinquent gangs: Unable to achieve middle-class status through legitimate means, lower-class adolescents rebel and set up a status system in which they can compete. For reasons discussed previously, this status system values criminal behavior and condemns conventional behavior.

Finally, several theorists have argued that deviant subcultures derive not so much from strain but from the tendency of some individuals and groups to endorse selectively and to distort certain values that are part of the dominant culture. The leading proponents of this position are Matza and Sykes (1961). In their article on subterranean values, they claim that values such as toughness, excitement, and pleasure-seeking are emphasized in the larger culture although they are not as overtly stressed as are other values. The larger culture, for example, does place some value on toughness and violence—a fact quickly confirmed by an examination of any of the mass media. Delinquents, however, come to place more emphasis on this value than do other individuals. Matza (1964) makes a similar argument with respect to the techniques of neutralization. The justifications delinquents employ for their behavior are not invented anew; rather, they are derived from the criminal law and larger culture. To illustrate, the law recognizes that certain conditions excuse or justify misdeeds. Under certain conditions, for example, the law allows individuals to use physical force to defend themselves. Delinquents, according to Matza (1964: 61), duplicate, distort, and extend these conditions. For example, they come to believe that physical force is justified in a much wider variety of situations than the law allows—not only when one is physically threatened but also in response to a wide range of threats and insults.

According to this argument, then, criminal subcultures do not necessarily have their origins in strain. Rather, they reflect the tendency of some groups to selectively focus on and distort certain values in the dominant culture. Matza and Sykes, however, do not clearly indicate *why* some groups and individuals display this tendency and others do not.

The Impact of Criminal Subcultures on the Individual

Why do the individuals in criminal subcultures turn to crime? Most versions of subcultural crime theory give the same answer: The individuals in these subcultures interact with others who hold criminal values, and eventually they come to adopt these values themselves. That is, they come to approve of crime or hold values conducive to crime. They then act in conformity with their values.

Of course, not everyone who interacts with members of a criminal subculture becomes a criminal. Individuals are likely to adopt criminal values and turn to crime to the extent that (1) they are isolated from conventional groups, (2) they interact frequently and over a long period with the members of a criminal subculture, and (3) they like and respect the members of the criminal subculture. So individuals who associate primarily with conventional groups and only occasionally come into contact with criminal subcultures are unlikely to develop criminal values (Sutherland and Cressey, 1978).

Recently, certain theorists have expanded subcultural crime theory and argued that criminal subcultures may also lead individuals to engage in crime without affecting their values. The social learning theory of Akers (1985), in particular, specifies two additional ways in which criminal subcultures may cause individuals to engage in crime.

First, the members of criminal subcultures may reinforce criminal behavior when it occurs, either positively or negatively. In positive reinforcement, the individual is rewarded for his or her criminal behavior. The gang member who wins a fight, for example, may receive much praise from fellow gang members. Rewarding a criminal act increases the probability that the act will be repeated in the future. The criminal act may also result in the removal of something negative—some painful or aversive stimulus. Gang members, for example, may stop accusing an individual of being a coward after the person engages in a fight. The removal of this negative or aversive stimulus also increases the likelihood that the criminal act will be repeated in the future. In general, individuals tend to repeat those acts that result in reinforcement.

The reinforcement for a criminal act does not necessarily have to come from the members of a criminal subculture. The money obtained from a robbery, for example, is likely to be experienced as reinforcing even though it does not come from the criminal subculture. Much of the reinforcement for crime, however, is likely to come from one's friends and associates in the form of social approval.

Second, the members of criminal subcultures may provide models for criminal behavior. Individuals, in particular, may come to imitate the criminal behavior they see other members of the subculture displaying. As Akers points out, such behavior is most likely to be imitated if the observer (1) likes or respects the model, (2) sees the model receive reinforcement or show pleasure, and (3) is in an environment in which imitating the model's behavior is reinforced.

EVALUATION OF SUBCULTURAL CRIME THEORY

Research on subcultural crime theory has focused on several questions. First, are there in fact groups and individuals who approve of crime or hold values conducive to crime? Second, are the individuals in such groups more likely to engage in crime? And third, if such individuals are more likely to engage in crime, is it because they have adopted values conducive to crime? Research, then, has focused on establishing the existence of criminal subcultures and exploring their impact on the individual. Little research has been directed to the origins of criminal subcultures although Cernkovich (1978) and Matsueda et al. (1992) present evidence suggesting that strained individuals are more likely to hold values conducive to delinquency.

◆ **WHO APPROVES OF CRIME?** ◆ A number of studies have tried to determine if certain groups are more likely to approve of crime or hold values conducive to crime than are other groups. Somewhat more common, however, are studies that simply ask whether *any* individuals approve of crime or hold values conducive to crime.

First, these studies suggest that no groups unconditionally approve of crime and condemn conventional behavior. All major groups, and the overwhelming majority of individuals, tend to believe that criminal behavior generally is bad and conventional behavior generally is good (Buffalo and Rodgers, 1971; Siegel et al., 1973; Kornhauser, 1978; Dorn, 1969; Matsueda et al., 1992). In one of the best studies in this area, Short and Strodtbeck (1965) interviewed a sample of adolescent boys in Chicago. Included were gang and nongang boys, white and black boys, and lower-class and middle-class boys. Each boy was asked to evaluate a number of conventional and deviant images. For example, each boy was asked how he would evaluate "someone who works for good grades at school" and "someone who gets his kicks by using drugs." All groups evaluated the conventional images equally highly—black the same as white, lower class the same as middle class, and gang the same as nongang. Further, most of the deviant images were negatively evaluated.

However, although crime generally is condemned and conventional behavior generally is approved, there are differences in the *extent* to which crime is condemned and conventional behavior is approved. Some groups and individuals condemn crime less strongly than do others, with a number of individuals being close to amoral in their view of crime (that is, they neither approve nor disapprove of crime). In Short and Strodtbeck's study, for example, gang members and lower-class boys rated the deviant images less negatively than did the middle-class boys (see also Hirschi, 1969; Sheley, 1980). Likewise, certain studies suggest that some individuals approve of conventional behavior less strongly than do others (Hirschi, 1969). The extent to which one approves of conventional behavior or condemns criminal behavior does have a strong relationship to crime. It is unclear, however, to what extent these results can be explained in terms of subcultural crime theory—they are probably better explained in terms of social control theory (Hirschi, 1969; Kornhauser, 1978; see also Chapter 14 in this volume). In particular, social control theory would argue that some individuals are close to amoral because of a breakdown in the socialization process. That is, these individuals were not effectively socialized by parents and others and so lack a strong commitment to any system of values.

Second, research suggests that many individuals do approve of or believe crime is justified under certain conditions. A number of studies in this area have focused on Sykes and Matza's techniques of neutralization (Minor, 1981; Agnew and Peters, 1985). These studies, in particular, have measured the extent to which adolescents accept the neutralization techniques by asking them whether they believe crime is justified under certain conditions. Hirschi (1969: 208), for example, asks respondents if they agree that "most things that people call delinquency don't really hurt anyone" (denial of injury). These studies generally find that a significant percentage of adolescents regard crime as justified under at least certain conditions. Hirschi, for example, found that 24 percent of the adolescents in his sample agreed that "most things that people call 'delinquency' don't really hurt anyone," and that 13 percent agreed with the statement "I can't seem to stay out of trouble no matter how hard I try" (denial of responsibility).

Although the research tells us that a significant percentage of people believe crime is justified under certain conditions, it does not provide much information on whether some groups are more likely than other groups to feel this way. Studies in this area suffer from a variety of problems, including the following: Many studies employ homogenous samples (college students at an elite university) or unrepresentative samples (high school students in a southern city), which make it difficult to examine group differences. Many studies employ questionable measures of values. For example, they do not directly measure values regarding crime but employ indirect measures like the preference for violent TV shows (see Parker, 1989). There is some question whether such indirect measures accurately reflect values. Further, data from Blumenthal et al. (1972) suggest that we should be very careful in making generalizations about groups. They found that blacks were much more likely to believe that violence is justified in the service of social change, whereas whites were more likely to believe that violence is justified in the service of social control. The conclusions one draws about group differences, then, may depend on the types of justifications one considers. Presently, there is no good evidence concerning what groups, if any, are more likely to accept justifications for crime (although there has been some research and speculation in this area, especially on race and regional differences in values regarding violence — see Blumenthal et al., 1972; Rogers and Buffalo, 1974; Agnew and Peters, 1985; Messner, 1988; Hawley and Messner, 1989; Luckenbill and Doyle, 1989; Parker, 1989; Matsueda et al., 1992).

Third, a number of studies indicate that individuals hold values that are conducive to crime (Silverman and Dinitz, 1974; Agnew, 1984b, 1984c). Lerman (1968), for example, presented a sample of youths from Manhattan's lower East Side in New York City with a list of eight traits having to do with toughness ("ability to be hard and tough"), excitement ("ability to find kicks"), pleasure ("ability to make a fast buck"), and conventional behaviors ("ability to get good grades"). When the youths were asked to pick the trait they admired most, 15 percent of the males and 7 percent of the females picked one of the deviant traits. Cernkovich (1978) likewise found that a significant percentage of adolescents valued such things as toughness, excitement, and pleasure. Again, however, it is difficult to make firm statements about which groups are more likely to hold values conducive to crime. Additional research is needed in this area.

Finally, certain studies indicate that many individuals approve of specific types of crime—particularly minor forms of crime. For example, significant numbers of individuals favor the legalization of such minor forms of crime as marijuana use and gambling (Conklin, 1971; Johnston, 1973; Eve, 1975). A 1985 Gallup poll reported that 23 percent of those surveyed in the United States thought that the use of marijuana should be made legal (Jamieson and Flanagan, 1987). Some evidence also suggests that executives in certain corporations approve of or justify various types of white collar crime (see Conklin, 1977). Group differences do emerge in certain of the studies that have been done in this area although such differences tend to be slight (see, for example, Conklin, 1971; Eve, 1975).

Only a small number of people unconditionally approve of more serious types of crime (Rossi et al., 1974b; Wolfgang et al., 1985). This is true even if we focus on criminals and delinquents themselves. Matza (1964), for example, found that of the institutionalized delinquents in his sample, only 3 percent generally approved of theft, 2 percent approved of auto theft, 1 percent approved of vandalism, and 1 percent approved of fighting with a weapon. Hindelang (1974), by contrast, found that of the institutionalized delinquents in his sample, 18 percent approved of theft, 20 percent approved of auto theft, 15 percent approved of vandalism, and 20 percent approved of fighting with a weapon. Further, when Hindelang limited his focus to those delinquents who had actually engaged in the specific act, the approval levels were even higher. Hindelang's percentages, however, may be on the high side (see Hindelang, 1970, 1974; Siegel et al., 1973; Kornhauser, 1978; Minor, 1981). And even among institutionalized delinquents—the most serious of delinquent offenders—approval levels for serious crime clearly are still low.

The data suggest, then, that many individuals and possibly groups in our society hold values conducive to crime (although few individuals unconditionally approve of crime and condemn conventional behavior). Are people who associate with these individuals more likely to be criminals?

◆ **HOW ARE CRIMINAL SUBCULTURES AND CRIME RELATED?** ◆ Most research on this question has tried to determine whether individuals with delinquent friends are more likely to be delinquent themselves. (It is usually assumed that these delinquent friends have delinquent values.) The data indicate that a strong relationship exists between having delinquent friends and delinquency (Short, 1957; Voss, 1964; Jensen, 1972b; Johnson, 1979). Hirschi (1969), for example, found that among those boys who had four or more friends picked up by the police, 75 percent had committed delinquent acts;

among those boys without any friends picked up by the police, only 27 percent had committed delinquent acts.

Some researchers have raised questions about this relationship. They argue that the association between delinquent friends and delinquency is not necessarily because delinquent friends cause one to engage in delinquency. In fact, it may be the other way around—individuals who engage in delinquency may seek out delinquent friends. A few recent longitudinal studies, however, suggest that adolescents who associate with delinquent friends at one point in time are more likely to be delinquent at a later point in time. These studies, in other words, suggest that associating with delinquent friends does have a causal effect on delinquency (Elliott et al., 1985; Krohn et al., 1985; Massey and Krohn, 1986; Burkett and Warren, 1987; Paternoster and Triplett, 1988; Agnew, 1991).

◆ **WHY DO CRIMINAL SUBCULTURES CAUSE CRIME?** ◆ Finally, researchers have asked why individuals with delinquent associates are more likely to be delinquent themselves. The leading argument in this area is that individuals who interact with delinquent friends develop delinquent values and turn to crime for that reason. Delinquent values, in other words, mediate the relationship between delinquent friends and crime. There is some indirect support for this position. Adolescents with delinquent friends (or friends who have delinquent values) are more likely themselves to have delinquent values (Lerman, 1968; Jensen, 1972b; Jaquith, 1981; Matsueda et al., 1992). And delinquent values are related to delinquency (Lerman, 1968; Jensen, 1972b; Cernkovich, 1978; Johnson, 1979; Minor, 1984; Agnew and Peters, 1985; Matsueda et al., 1992). That is, there is a positive relationship between crime and (1) values that justify or approve of crime under certain conditions; (2) values that are conducive to crime, such as excitement, pleasure-seeking, and toughness; and (3) the approval of select forms of crime, such as marijuana use.

Several studies have focused directly on the relationship between delinquent friends, delinquent values, and delinquency. These studies suggest that while delinquent values may explain part of the effect of delinquent friends on crime, they do not necessarily explain all the effect. In particular, most studies find that when we hold delinquent values constant, delinquent friends still have an effect on crime (Jensen, 1972b; Johnson, 1979; Jaquith, 1981; Johnson et al., 1987; see also Matsueda, 1982). These studies should be interpreted cautiously because researchers have examined only a limited range of delinquent values. Nevertheless, researchers have begun to explore additional ways in which delinquent friends may cause delinquency.

The work of Akers (1985) and his associates is prominent in this area. As indicated, he suggests that other individuals may cause delinquency not only by affecting values but also by reinforcing delinquency and providing models for delinquency. Limited support has been provided for this argument (Krohn et al., 1985). And still other mechanisms by which delinquent friends might cause delinquency have been suggested (see Short and Strodtbeck, 1965; Johnson et al., 1987).

CONCLUSION

Two major theories of crime have been reviewed: strain and subcultural crime theory. Although distinct, these theories often have been joined into more comprehensive theories. Strain theory frequently is used to explain the origin of criminal subcultures, and subcultural crime theory frequently is used to explain why only some strained individuals turn to crime.

Three major versions of strain theory were presented. Classic strain theory dominated criminology during the 1950s and 1960s (Cole, 1975; Bernard, 1984), and had a large impact on public policy as well. Among other things, classic strain theory was one of the inspirations behind the War on Poverty, which tried to reduce crime and other social maladies by providing poor people with the opportunity to succeed through legitimate channels (Empey and Stafford, 1992). Empirical studies of classic strain theory, however, have been mixed, and this theory no longer dominates the field as it once did—although it remains one of the prominent theories of crime.

Several revisions were made in classic theory, with most revisions arguing that individuals may pursue a variety of goals and that goal achievement is a function of a variety of factors. Empirical tests of these revisions, however, have not been encouraging. And so, as with classic strain theory, we have to conclude that the support for these revised theories is mixed. Support for the most recent version of strain theory, Agnew's (1992) General Strain Theory, is more encouraging, however.

Subcultural crime theory argues that individuals engage in crime because they are socialized in groups that approve of crime or at least hold values conducive to crime. The data are more supportive of this theory. Like strain theory, subcultural crime theory has had an impact on public policy. Several major programs have tried to reform criminals by removing them from their criminal subcultures and placing them in conventional groups where they are resocialized. The early years of the Synanon program provide an example. Drug addicts in this program were isolated from their old drug-using friends and associates, and instead interacted primarily with a group of reformed addicts, who attempted to convince them that drug use and the drug lifestyle were bad (Volkman and Cressey, 1963). Organizations like Alcoholics Anonymous and Narcotics Anonymous employ similar procedures, and delinquency control programs like the Silverlake Experiment, Provo Experiment, and St. Louis Experiment have made much use of subcultural crime theory (see Empey and Stafford, 1991; Elliott et al., 1985, Chapter 8). Although these programs have not been uniformly successful, they show some promise. In short, subcultural crime theory appears to have some potential for dealing with the crime problem.

DISCUSSION QUESTIONS

1. Discuss the ways in which sociological theories of criminality differ from biological theories. How would each define "abnormal behavior"?

2. Discuss the concept of social strain. What are the sources of theories that link criminality to strain? How do contemporary versions of strain theory differ from more classical ones?

3. Discuss the basic assumptions underlying subcultural theories of criminality. Agnew discusses various types of criminal groups or subcultures. How do these differ?

4. Choose any theory discussed in this chapter, and determine the extent to which it contains elements of strain and subcultural theories of criminality.

CHAPTER 14

CONTROL AND DETERRENCE THEORIES OF CRIMINALITY

Marvin Krohn
State University of New York at Albany

SOCIAL CONTROL THEORIES reflect diverse notions of the specific social or social psychological factors that constrain criminal behavior. However, they seek an answer to a common question and share common assumptions that distinguish them from other theoretical perspectives on crime. Simply stated, the question addressed by all social control theories relates to why and how people *conform* to the rules of society. The question implies that the critical issue in explaining criminal or delinquent behavior is what *constrains* people from committing such behavior and also that it is not important to account for why people are motivated to commit criminal behavior. Control theorists assume that deviant behavior is either naturally attractive, situationally induced, or rationally chosen. They strive to provide an explanation for conforming behavior: Why do people obey the rules?

The question posed by social control theorists focuses on social integration and social regulation. In his book *Suicide*, Emile Durkheim (1951 [1897]) examined the societal conditions that constrain or prevent people from taking their own lives. He looked first at the concept of social integration. Although Durkheim never explicitly defined social integration, he clearly had in mind the degree to which individuals and groups are attracted to and attached to society and social institutions. For example, Durkheim observed that married people, especially those with children, have lower rates of suicide than do unmarried people. Attachment to these significant others allows individuals to find meaning in social institutions and, as a consequence, to be less likely to pursue purely individual interests. Durkheim stated that "the bond that unites them with the common cause attaches them to life and the lofty goal they envisage prevents their feeling personal troubles so deeply" (p. 210). As integration decreases, people will be less constrained from responding to their personal troubles in a nonconforming manner (for example, suicide).

In addition to integrating individuals into its institutions, society provides norms by which people's behaviors are regulated. Durkheim assumed that people have potentially insatiable desires; thus, cultural norms are necessary to place limits on those desires and to define the proper means to achieve them. Without clearly defined and effective norms, individual variation in behavior in pursuit of desires would increase. For example, norms define appropriate and inappropriate responses to failure and frustration. To the extent such regulation of behavior views suicide as an inappropriate response to personal crisis, suicide rates are held down.

The concepts of social integration and social regulation are intertwined. Social integration is fostered by rules of conduct, making groups and institutions (for example, church and the family) more of a presence in peoples' lives. Durkheim also recognized that social regulation could be effective only where there was a degree of social integration. That is, people would have to feel attached to a collectivity to adhere willingly to its rules. Although a collectivity could still enforce its will on individual members, this would be an ineffective form of control in the long run. Social integration, then, refers to the attraction of people to society, whereas social regulation refers specifically to the power society has to coerce certain forms of behavior. The interplay of these two factors is seen throughout diverse social control theories. Some of these perspectives fail to distinguish clearly between the two; others emphasize the role of either integration or regulation. What characterizes all, however, is a concern for what social and social psychological factors constrain criminal behavior.

Against this backdrop, in this chapter we will examine social disorganization theory and its emphasis on the ecology of crime. We will explore two major types of control theory: social bonding theories and individually oriented theories. Finally, we will discuss the classic deterrence doctrine and its present-day forms.

SOCIAL DISORGANIZATION THEORY

Sociology as a recognized discipline in the United States emerged around the turn of the twentieth century, inspired by the upheavals that had taken place in European society throughout the previous century. In the United States, as in Europe, the ongoing dramatic changes in the production system significantly disrupted social life. The dominant form of economic production was shifting from one based on agriculture to one based on industry. Urbanization in the United States was fueled by a continuing supply of immigrants, as well as by the migration of native workers to the city to seek employment in the growing number of factories.

Perhaps nowhere was this social disruption more evident than in the city of Chicago. With its population rapidly expanding with the influx of immigrants and the general westward movement of the population, Chicago represented a natural laboratory for the sociologists at the University of Chicago to examine an eclectic array of theoretical ideas borrowed from their primarily European mentors. Perhaps because of their willingness to draw on a diverse set of ideas, social disorganization theory contains elements of a number of theoretical perspectives. It has been characterized as a social control theory, a strain theory, and a cultural deviance theory (Finestone, 1976). At its heart, however, it is a social control model (Kornhauser, 1978); therefore, it is treated as such in this chapter.

Park and Burgess (1925) set the research agenda for a continuing investigation of modern urban life. They likened the growth of the city to ecological processes among plant life, emphasizing competition over land use as the population grows and areas of the city expand. The process of competition led to adaptations resulting in eventual cooperation in a continuing dynamic equilibrium. However, in this process, areas of the city would experience changes that would render social institutions ineffective, a condition they labeled "social disorganization" (Burgess, 1925).

Specifically, Burgess suggested that Chicago was growing in a series of concentric circles from the center of the city out to the residential suburbs. These concentric zones were characterized by the dominant activities taking place within them. For example, the central business zone was used primarily for commerce and industry. The second zone, the zone of transition, most clearly illustrated the process of expansion whereby commerce and industry was encroaching on what previously had been residential property. Because the transition was not complete, however, people still lived in this zone. And because the housing was not particularly desirable, it was here that the poor and the people who had recently arrived in the city (immigrants and migrants) lived. From this second zone, the city grew by establishing ever more desirable residence areas as one moved away from the central zone.

By examining behavior patterns within these zones, Park and Burgess (1925) and, later, Shaw and McKay (1931, 1942) established that the second zone, the zone in transition, contained the highest rates of deviant behavior, ranging from mental illness to crime. Based on the nature of this area, several explanations for the observed pattern were advanced. Because the available residences were typically the cheapest housing within a reasonable distance from the factories, a disproportionate number of poor people lived in this zone. Immigrants and migrants coming to Chicago also needed cheap housing, and thus located in disproportionate numbers in this area. As residents became financially established, they would move to better housing outside this zone, and new immigrants and migrants would replace them. Hence, the population of the zone of transition was, itself, ever changing.

Among the likely candidates to explain these high rates of crime were poverty, cultural conflict, and mobility. Instead of focusing on any one of these conditions, however, the Chicago sociologists introduced the term *social disorganization* to describe the intervening mechanism between the social conditions described and the rates of crime. The combined effects of a lack of resources, cultural ambiguity, and a highly transitory population resulted in these areas having inadequate and unstable social institutions, which meant residents were not being socially integrated into these institutions or with one another. Social institutions were therefore unable to control the behavior of the residents through either social integration or normative regulation.

Shaw and McKay were able to discount the possibility that the values of a particular ethnic or racial group resulted in a high rate of crime. By examining patterns of crime and population distribution over time, they observed that even though the dominant ethnic and racial composition of an area was constantly shifting, the high crime rates persisted. In their study of changes over time, they also observed that high rates of crime persisted even when the growth rate was stable. To explain the persistence of crime, Shaw and McKay developed what Kornhauser (1978) has characterized as a mixed model of delinquency. In this model, they emphasized the lack of opportunities (strain) that people living in these areas experienced and the subcultural traditions (cultural deviance) that were being transmitted from one generation to another.

THE LEGACY OF THE SOCIAL DISORGANIZATION PERSPECTIVE: THE ECOLOGY OF CRIME

The influence of the social disorganization perspective has continued in what has come to be known as the ecological tradition, which focuses on the relationships between social structural characteristics of urban areas and crime or delinquency rates. Although some aspects of the theoretical arguments and methodology of the Chicago School have been abandoned or modified, much of the ecological tradition centers on those variables identified in the School's early work.

Social Structural Characteristics

One of the first studies done using more sophisticated statistical techniques to explore implications of the social disorganization perspective was Lander's (1954) investigation of delinquency rates among 155 Baltimore census tracts. Lander found social structural variables grouped into two types: (1) the social class composition of an area, in terms of overcrowding, substandard housing, rental costs, and level of education, and (2) the level of social disorganization, in terms of percentage of nonwhites and owner-occupied homes. Comparing the contribution of these variables to the explanation of the variance in delinquency rates across the census tracts, Lander concluded that social disorganization variables were more important than the social class characteristics of areas. Interestingly, the percentage of nonwhites was curvilinearly related to delinquency rates. That is, as the number of nonwhites increased from 0 to 50 percent, the rate of delinquency increased, but as the number of nonwhites increased from 50 to 100 percent, the rate of delinquency decreased. Lander interpreted these findings as suggesting that increasing numbers of nonwhites at first reflect a community that is in transition and subject to social disorganization. At some point, the percentage of nonwhites reaches a sufficient level to allow the community to stabilize and, therefore, be better able to regulate its residents.

Two subsequent studies attempted to replicate Lander's findings. Although neither duplicated his results regarding the percentage of nonwhites, both reaffirmed the importance of home ownership (Bordua, 1958; Chilton, 1964). Chilton concluded that there was no clear support for the social disorganization perspective.

One of the difficulties with these studies is how to interpret the findings. For example, Gordon (1967) correctly observed that all the indicators included in the previously mentioned studies could be interpreted as measuring aspects of socioeconomic status (SES). Hence, the results could be interpreted as supporting a strain argument instead of a social disorganization perspective. Kornhauser (1978) countered that assertion by noting that in other studies, SES has not consistently been related to delinquent behavior or rates of delinquency, whereas more pure social disorganization variables (mobility, heterogeneity) have been.

One study that provides partial support for the social disorganization perspective rather than a strain interpretation was done by Maccoby et al. (1958). To remove the possible confounding effects of SES, the researchers selected two low-income communities, one with a high rate of delinquency and the other with a low rate. Based on interviews with samples of adults in the respective communities, they concluded that the two areas were distinguished by the amount of cohesiveness evident in them. In the high-delinquency as opposed to the low-delinquency area, fewer people knew their neighbors by name, fewer had compatible interests with their neighbors, and fewer liked their neighbors. In addition, people in the low-delinquency area apparently were more willing to intervene when their neighbors' children were involved in lawbreaking than were citizens in the high-rate area. Interestingly, people in the high-rate area did not have more tolerant attitudes toward crime than those in the low-rate area. Maccoby et al. attributed part of these differences to a stronger church institution in the low-rate area. In sum, the areas differed in the degree to which residents were integrated with one another and in the church, and in the degree to which they tried to regulate the behavior of children.

COMMUNITY DYNAMICS

Although research on social structural characteristics identified by the early social disorganization perspective continued, the perspective itself fell out of favor for much of the 1960s and 1970s. It was criticized for failing to appreciate the diversity of values that exists within urban areas (Matza, 1969); for not recognizing that communities in urban areas indeed may be organized, but around unconventional values; and for failing to define clearly its main concept, social disorganization, thereby making the identification and operationalization of variables difficult (Liska, 1987; Gibbons and Jones, 1975). Recently, however, the ecological approach has been revived with the publication of two important edited collections (Byrne and Sampson, 1984; Reiss and Tonry, 1986).

Perhaps the most important contribution of the articles contained in these volumes is the recognition that the dynamics of communities change over time and are affected by social and political events that occur around them. This recognition has led researchers to analyze *community* careers of crime (Schuerman and Kobrin, 1986; Reiss, 1986), much like one might analyze individual crime careers. Schuerman and Kobrin investigated the twenty-year histories of the highest crime-rate areas in Los Angeles County using a developmental model. They suggested that these histories could be categorized into three distinct stages reflecting periods (1) when changes in community crime rates are emerging, (2) when crime rates undergo significant transitions, and (3) when crime rates apparently are enduring. The correlates of high crime-rate areas varied depending on the stage of the communities' crime career. For example, changes in land use from single-family to multiple-dwelling houses were important precursors of changes in neighborhood crime levels for those communities that were categorized as emerging. However, in transitional or enduring crime communities, this variable was unimportant, whereas socioeconomic status factors were important.

ROUTINE ACTIVITIES

Another approach that has its roots in the ecological tradition and shares social disorganization theory's focus on factors that control the occurrence of crime is the routine activities approach. While assuming the existence of motivated offenders (and, therefore, not including a measure of this variable in analyses), the approach emphasizes the role that guardianship and the suitability of targets play in generating crime (Cohen and Felson, 1979). Guardianship refers to how well the potential target of a crime (for example, a household) is protected. Such protection could be provided by neighbors looking after the home when residents are not there, the use of locks and other security devices, or merely the presence of someone in the household. Guardianship, combined with whether the target is appealing (target suitability), determines the probability of crime.

Research examining hypotheses derived from the routine activities approach has supported the main implications of the theory (see Chapters 7 and 8). For example, Cohen and Felson (1979) found that crime rates are related to the proportion of households that are female-headed or in which both husband and wife are employed. This finding represents a measure of the absence of guardianship because it assumes that those households would be less likely to have someone at home during the day. Miethe et al. (1987) relied on more direct measures of what individuals did at night, as well as their primary activity during the day. Both indicators were significantly related to the probability of being victimized.

The new directions taken in the ecological tradition have revitalized it. Currently, researchers are working to integrate the social disorganization approach with routine activities (Felson, 1986; Hirschi, 1986). Such an integration not only is justified on the basis of common assumptions but also may well lead to new directions for ecological research.

SOCIAL BONDING THEORIES

Social disorganization theorists were well aware of the importance of social institutions such as the church and social groups such as the family in integrating and regulating individuals. They conceptualized the problem at the community level, viewing the ineffectiveness of specific institutions as reflected in the overall social disorganization of an area. Theoretical perspectives that we will refer to as social bonding theories (in order to distinguish them from the broader categorization of social control) narrow the focus of attention to those specific institutions and groups.

ORIGINS OF SOCIAL BONDING THEORIES

An early version of social bonding theory is that of Nye (1958). Though he recognized that delinquency could be produced by learning, Nye also stated that it could result from the absence of control. For Nye, social control resulted from the socialization process. Through this process, individuals developed their sense of right and wrong (conscience), which Nye saw as a form of internalized control. Behavior is also indirectly controlled through one's affectional ties to significant others (for example, parents) and through the availability of opportunities to satisfy needs. That is, if such opportunities were available, persons would conform in their behavior. Nye also recognized the importance of direct control through restricting people's behavior and punishing them if they fail to conform.

Following Nye, the most prominent social bonding theory is the version presented by Hirschi (1969). Hirschi's answer to the question of why juveniles conform most of the time revolves around his concept of the *social bond*—that is, the ties that people have with the conventional social order. The stronger the tie to the social order, the more constrained individuals will be from behaving in ways that may jeopardize their position in that order. Hence, the stronger the social bond, the lower the probability of delinquent behavior. If those ties are weakened or severed, individuals are free to deviate. Note that a weakening of the social bond does not necessarily mean that a person will deviate; rather, it simply puts that person in a position where it is possible. Hirschi assumes that deviation is likely because such behavior is attractive.

ELEMENTS OF THE SOCIAL BOND

Hirschi identified four elements of the social bond—attachment, commitment, involvement, and belief—which are similar to the types of social control identified by Nye. *Attachment* refers to the affective ties one has with other people. Individuals with good relationships with other people will not want to do anything to threaten those relationships. For example, if parents and their child have a good relationship, the child will not want to do anything to disappoint his or her parents.

Commitment refers to the degree to which people want to pursue conformist lines of conduct. Those people who want to participate in some activity that may entail adherence to rules of conduct (such as an athletic team) or who have aspirations to achieve some conformist goal (such as a college education) will be more likely to conform so as not to jeopardize such participation or goals.

Participation in activities can have another kind of constraining effect. *Involvement* refers to the time spent in conventional activities. According to Hirschi, the more time someone spends in conventional lines of action, the less time there will be for deviant behavior. One of the difficulties with involvement as a separate element of the social bond is that it is often difficult to distinguish empirically from commitment. If one wants to participate in a current activity (commitment), one probably will be spending quite a bit of time doing so (involvement). Hence, the two variables are often so highly intercorrelated that they cannot be applied separately (Krohn and Massey, 1980).

Belief refers to the strength of peoples' attitudes toward conformity. Hirschi is interested in the varying extent to which individuals believe they should obey the rules of society. Beliefs that require or justify crime are not as important as the weakening of beliefs in the moral validity of conventional standards of conduct. Although the element of belief generally has been found to be a good predictor of delinquent behavior (Krohn and Massey, 1980; Sheley, 1980, 1983), the fact that it has been measured in a variety of ways has made it problematic. Some researchers have conceptualized belief primarily in terms of general standards of behavior (as Hirschi suggests), whereas others have interpreted the concept in terms of attitudes that neutralize or justify deviant behavior. Although most of these different measurements have been shown to be related to criminal behavior, the strength of the relationship and the meaning of the findings vary.

The four elements of the social bond may operate in a variety of social arenas. Hence, one could be attached to a member of the family as well as to a teacher or religious leader. However, for adolescents, the most critical social arenas are the family, peer group, school, and religion. For adults, they are family, religion, and work. Though Hirschi implies that attachment should be considered causally prior to the other elements (Massey and Krohn, 1986), he does not specify a causal order among the elements of the social bond. Yet, he does indicate that all four should be interrelated. For example, stronger ties to one's family may make people more likely to be committed and involved in conventional pursuits and to believe in conventional values. Of course, a weakening of commitment or belief might also adversely affect relationships with the family. As we will note in reviewing the research on social bonding theory, the causal order question is a difficult but important one.

RESEARCH ON SOCIAL BONDING

An extensive research literature is devoted to the relationship between variables relevant to social bonding theory and delinquent and drug-using behavior. Given space considerations, we will review those studies that have examined the elements of the social bond in a multivariate analysis rather than those studies that have focused on only one element.

Hirschi provided research evidence when he first presented his theory. He surveyed a large sample of adolescents from Richmond, California, asking them about their relationships with parents, peers, and teachers, their participation and success in school, their educational aspirations, and their attitudes toward the law and their parents' values. He correlated these measures with self-reported delinquent behavior to determine whether hypotheses concerning attachment, commitment, involvement, and belief were supported. The results supported most of his hypotheses though at a weak to moderate level. One finding did call into question the assumption that attachment to others is a barrier to delinquency, even if those others are involved in delinquency. Hirschi found that having friends who were delinquent did increase the probability of delinquent behavior by the respondents. Subsequent research has found a positive, rather than the predicted negative, relationship between attachment to peers and delinquent behavior (Empey and Lubeck, 1971; Hindelang, 1973; Krohn and Massey, 1980).

Two more recent studies examined the viability of Hirschi's theory. Krohn and Massey (1980), using a sample of 3,065 boys and girls in grades 7–12 in six communities (ranging in size from rural to urban), not only examined this issue but did so for delinquent behaviors ranging in their degree of seriousness. They found that some indicators of commitment, attachment, and belief were significantly related to four scales measuring self-reported alcohol and marijuana use, minor delinquent behavior, use of hard drugs, and serious delinquency. Variables intended to measure the commitment element contributed most strongly to the explanation of the variance in these scales. The theory did a better job in explaining the less serious forms of delinquent behavior than more serious delinquency and did slightly better in explaining female delinquency than male delinquency. However, at best, variables in the equation accounted for only a moderate amount of the variance.

Wiatrowski et al. (1981) extended the examination of the elements of the social bond by testing a causal model of Hirschi's theory. Adding a measure of SES and academic ability to Hirschi's basic model, they found that parental attachment was indirectly related to self-reported delinquent behavior through school-related variables and belief. School-related variables and belief were directly related to delinquent behavior. Approximately one-third of the variance in delinquent behavior was explained by the social bonding variables.

An important limitation to the Krohn and Massey and the Wiatrowski et al. studies is that they both use cross-sectional data. The logic of Hirschi's theory suggests that an erosion in the social bond precedes delinquent behavior, and both the aforementioned studies assumed this to be the case. However, with data collected at one point in time, it was not possible to determine if the assumption is correct.

A partial investigation of the causal structure of social bonding theory was done by Liska and Reed (1985). They used the Youth in Transition data of 1,886 tenth-grade boys who were resurveyed at the end of their eleventh-grade year. They focused on the causal order among parental attachment, school attachment, and self-reported delinquent behavior. Using sophisticated simultaneous equation models, they found that instead of the simple causal structure suggested by Hirschi, reciprocal relationships were observed. That is, parental attachment was found to affect delinquency, but delinquency also was found to affect school attachment. Thus, the assumption that the attenuation of school attachment precedes delinquent behavior was called into question. One difficulty with their study was that the boys were already in high school when they were first surveyed — it may be that the causal order suggested by Hirschi would exist for younger school children. Nevertheless, the Liska and Reed study has forced us to reconsider what appeared to be commonsense assumptions of the social bonding perspective. In addition, other longitudinal studies have demonstrated that the elements of the social bond measured at one point in time are not effective predictors of delinquency reported at a subsequent time (Agnew, 1985b).

A frequent observation in the literature on delinquency and adult criminality is that most people who committed delinquent behavior do not go on to become adult criminals. In some way, we "mature out" of criminal behavior. The social bonding perspective may be used to explain, at least partially, this maturation process. As adolescents pass into young adulthood, many acquire more stakes in conformity (Karacki and Toby, 1962) by making investments (time, money, emotions) in a course of action (Becker, 1960). For example, in going to college, students invest more time and money in conventional lines of action than they had when they were teenagers. Hence, they have more to lose by behaving in ways that would jeopardize those investments. Some evidence supporting this position can be found in the literature on drug use (Brown et al., 1974; Henley and Adams, 1973). Henley and Adams, for example, in assessing what factors led to the cessation of marijuana use among a sample of young adults, found that the best predictor of cessation was getting married (attachment). However, more recent research demonstrates that the relationship between drug use and marriage is more complex (Yamaguchi and Kandel, 1985). In fact, the use of marijuana may actually postpone entry into a marital relationship. Again, the causal order hypothesized by social bonding is questioned by these results.

EVALUATION OF SOCIAL BONDING THEORY

Social bonding theory is intuitively appealing because it focuses on the relationship between the individual and social institutions that should have an influence on constraining criminal behavior. It is a flexible theoretical perspective in that it is not class-based as are some other theories (for example, strain). The theory should be as applicable to middle-class crime as it is to that of the lower class. Indeed, Hirschi and Gottfredson (1987) have suggested recently that it could be used to account for white collar criminality. Another advantage to the perspective is that it may, in part, explain why we mature out of crime.

On the other hand, the research evidence presents a more ambiguous picture of social bonding theory. Although cross-sectional studies clearly have established a relationship between variables measuring elements of the social bond and delinquent behavior, when combined in multivariate analysis they are able to explain only a moderate to small amount of the variance. When examined longitudinally, models based on the theory do substantially less well. Longitudinal research also has raised the possibility that the attenuation in the elements of the social bond may be a consequence rather than (or as well as) a cause of delinquent behavior.

Moreover, a more serious problem must be addressed. Hirschi argues that attachment to others would be a constraining influence on delinquent behavior whether or not those others had committed delinquent or criminal behavior. Put another way, an adequate explanation of delinquent or criminal behavior may need to include the motivating influence of delinquent or criminal peers. That is, crime occurs because individuals learn from and are influenced by others to commit crime. If the influence of criminal others is included as an intervening variable between the social bonding variables and criminal behavior, it contradicts the assumption of social control theories that the motivation for criminal behavior need not be explained. Sheley (1983) has stated that the assumption that everyone is motivated to deviate at one time or another limits the theory because, although such a statement may be true, it does not take into account the various factors that may result in one form of deviance rather than another. The strong effect of criminal associations has led some scholars to generate what Kornhauser (1978) called mixed models (see, for example, Elliott et al., 1985; Johnson, 1979; LaGrange and White, 1985; Massey and Krohn, 1986). Hirschi (1979) has rejected this approach, arguing that such "integrative" strategies change the very nature of the theory. If the inclusion of criminal association variables is logically inconsistent with social bonding theory, then scholars will need to determine whether it is more advantageous to abandon the theoretical assumptions of social control theory in favor of a mixed model or to treat criminal associations as an alternative dependent variable.

INDIVIDUALLY ORIENTED THEORIES

Thus far, the critical question posed by all social control theories has been answered by emphasizing the capacity of communities to integrate and regulate their residents (social disorganization) and by focusing on people's relationship with conventional social institutions and groups (social bonding theory). The theories reviewed in this section — self-concept theory and self-rejection theory — locate the source of constraint or containment primarily within the individual. They suggest that the critical factor in constraining people is what they think of themselves.

SELF-CONCEPT THEORY

Reckless (1961, 1973) has been the chief advocate of self-concept or containment theory. When viewed in its entirety, his theoretical statement includes not only inner containments but also outer containments (for example, supervision and opportunity for acceptance), internal pushes (for example, rebellion and hostility), external pressures (for example, poverty and group conflict), and external pulls (for example, deviant companions and criminal subculture). However, for Reckless, inner containment in the form of a prosocial self-concept is the critical factor in insulating people from the various pushes, pulls, and pressures that may lead them to delinquent behavior. His concept of inner containment reflects a grab bag of poorly defined variables such as self-concept, self-control, goal orientation, and normative commitment. The key problem with these concepts is that they are related to delinquency by definition. For example, if a lack of self-control is defined as the inability to control impulses toward deviant behavior (as Reckless defined it), then a relationship must inevitably exist between a lack of self-control and delinquency.

Self-concept is the variable on which Reckless et al. focus their research. Reckless was perplexed by how some boys living in areas of high delinquency managed to remain nondelinquent. He hypothesized that a favorable or prosocial self-concept was the reason that some boys were able to resist criminogenic influences. In a series of research articles (see, for example, Reckless et al., 1956, 1957a, 1957b; Reckless and Dinitz, 1972),Reckless et al. examined this hypothesis. They first requested teachers to identify good boys who were unlikely to get in trouble with the law and bad boys who were likely to do so. They found that items measuring what they labeled as self-concept differentiated the good from the bad boys. Following these boys over the next four years, they found that those with a more positive self-concept were less likely to acquire official records.

The research on self-concept theory has been criticized for a number of methodological problems (Orcutt, 1970; Schrag, 1972; Schwartz and Tangri, 1965; Tangri and Schwartz, 1967). Most important, Reckless et al.'s method of measuring self-concept contained items that probably reflected the boys' prior troublesome behavior rather than being a measure of self-concept. For example, their self-concept scale included the following items:

Have you ever been told that you were headed for trouble?

Have most of your friends been in trouble with the law?

Subsequent research using better measures of self-concept has failed to support Reckless's argument (Jensen, 1973; McCarthy and Hoge, 1984). Jensen correlated measures of self-esteem, self-control, and acceptance of moral beliefs with self-reported delinquent behavior. The weak relationships he found led him to conclude that elements of inner containment may not be as important for delinquency as are variables reflecting the social environment (such as family, class, and neighborhood).

Schrag (1972) has observed that Reckless's formulation contains few testable statements. Further, he concluded that its "logical and empirical defects call for a fundamental reconstruction" (p. 89). Although Schrag was correct in his criticism of the perspective, a reformulation of Reckless's theory would probably not be an efficient means of salvaging any insights one might derive from his work. Rather, it might be more profitable to begin anew in focusing on individual sources of constraint.

SELF-REJECTION THEORY

In some respects, the work of Kaplan and his associates can be seen as just such a new beginning. Kaplan's (1980) self-rejection or self-derogation theory begins with the assumption that people will behave so as to minimize negative self-attitudes while maximizing positive ones. Devaluing experiences may occur in interaction in membership groups. If they do, and if the individual is unable to cope with them, he or she will develop attitudes of self-rejection or self-derogation. These attitudes will, in turn, result in a loss of motivation to conform to the normative patterns represented by the membership group. Up to this point, Kaplan's argument falls well within the assumptive parameters of the social control perspective. However, he then suggests that the individual also will be motivated to deviate from those normative patterns. Hence, Kaplan does not present a pure social control argument; nevertheless, the thrust of the theory suggests that it be reviewed as one.

Self-rejection theory is a much more carefully constructed and researched perspective than self-concept theory (Kaplan, 1972; Kaplan et al., 1982, 1986). The hypotheses are identified clearly, and the arguments are presented logically and do not suffer from the same form of circular reasoning evident in Reckless's work. The key concerns with the perspective that remain to be clarified are the strength of the unique contributions that measures of self-rejection make to the explanation of forms of deviant behavior and, more important, the causal order of the variables in the model. In terms of the latter issue, self-rejection and measures of family and school involvement and deviant behavior have been found to be reciprocally related in a more complex way than originally suggested by Kaplan (Kaplan et al., 1986). More work needs to be done, however, to clarify this issue and to assess the contributions of the theoretical perspective to our understanding of crime and delinquency.

THE DETERRENCE DOCTRINE

The perspectives discussed thus far have been theoretical statements that have implicit or explicit social policy implications. The deterrence doctrine, on the other hand, is essentially a policy orientation that has theoretical implications. In labeling the perspective a doctrine rather than a theory, Gibbs (1975: 5) characterizes it as "a congery of vague ideas with no unifying factor other than their being legacies of two major figures of moral philosophy, Cesare Beccaria and Jeremy Bentham." Nevertheless, the deterrence doctrine has generated hypotheses, and scholars are continuing the process of incorporating research findings into a set of interrelated statements. Unfortunately, that process has proved more difficult than the early statements concerning deterrence would have suggested.

BASIC PRINCIPLES OF DETERRENCE

The deterrence doctrine is similar to other social control perspectives in that it focuses on reasons why people do not commit crimes. However, the other social control perspectives emphasize the role of social integration in constraining people and in allowing for effective regulation, whereas the emphasis in the deterrence doctrine is clearly on the social regulative role of the legal apparatus.

As Gibbs indicates, the deterrence doctrine was first stated systematically by Beccaria (1764) and Bentham (1892), in reaction to a harsh, inequitable, and often capricious criminal justice system. They sought to establish policy guidelines to reform the system based on utilitarian principles and hedonistic psychology. They assumed that social policy should operate to generate the greatest good for the greatest number of people. Further, they argued that people behaved rationally so as to maximize the rewards for their behavior while minimizing the potential costs. Thus, the objective of the criminal justice system should be to deter people from committing crime by having the cost of punishment outweigh the potential reward from the criminal act. Punishment should be severe enough *only* to offset the potential reward.

Formally defined deterrence is "the omission of an act as a response to the perceived risk and fear of punishment for contrary behavior" (Gibbs, 1975: 2). Deterrence can be further subdivided into two types defined by the intended target. *Specific* deterrence occurs when a person is punished with the intention of preventing that person from committing future crimes. *General* deterrence occurs when the intention is to prevent people other than (or in addition to) the criminal actor from committing crimes by setting an example. Clearly, in practice, the two are not mutually exclusive, and typically we try to accomplish both goals. The distinction is necessary, however, in assessing the effectiveness of punishment.

Most of the work on the deterrence doctrine has focused on two of the three variables originally identified by Beccaria and Bentham. They suggested that the effectiveness of punishment varies in terms of its *certainty* (the likelihood that you will be punished), *severity*, and *celerity* (the swiftness with which punishment is meted out). Celerity of punishment is difficult to assess and has not been included in most studies of deterrence.

RESEARCH ON DETERRENCE

The research on deterrence has been concerned primarily with the general deterrent effect of punishment. Specific deterrence often is confounded by other factors involved in punishing individuals, such as rehabilitative efforts, incapacitation, or simply, the passage of time.

Research on general deterrence has been done at the aggregate or ecological level as well as at the individual or perceptual level. The review of research that follows will exclude the work on the deterrent effect of capital punishment that is covered in Chapter 23 of this volume.

◆ **THE AGGREGATE LEVEL** ◆ Aggregate-level research takes an ecological unit, most frequently a state, and examines the correlation between rates of crime and computed measures of certainty and severity of punishment. Certainty is computed as the ratio of the number of arrests, convictions, or prison admissions to the number of crimes reported. Severity is operationalized as the average length of sentence for a particular crime. Tittle (1969) examined the relationship among these variables for all Index offenses. He found that states with a higher probability of punishment (certainty) had lower crime rates. However, severity of punishment was significantly related only to homicide rates. Subsequent studies have confirmed the low to moderate inverse relationship between certainty and crime rates (Logan, 1972; Bailey et al., 1974; Geerken and Gove, 1977). A possible explanation for failing to establish a relationship between severity and most types of crime is that an inverse correlation exists between certainty and severity. That is, in states that have harsh penalties, people are less likely to be convicted (Logan, 1972). When Logan statistically controlled for certainty, a slight inverse relationship was found between severity and crime rates.

Tittle and Rowe (1974), in further examining the relationship between certainty and crime rates, found evidence for what they called a "tipping effect." For cities and counties in the state of Florida, certainty made a difference in crime rates only after a 30 percent certainty rate was reached. This suggests that some threshold of certainty must be reached before it is likely to have a deterrent impact.

Although the research evidence is consistent in finding a relationship between aggregate measures of certainty and crime rates, the meaning of such findings is ambiguous. For example, the observed inverse relationship could be due to system overload. If crime rates exceed the capacity of the system to locate and arrest offenders, then a negative relationship between certainty and crime rates would occur. However, the cause and effect would be reversed and not support a deterrence argument. By using data from ninety-eight cities over a six-year period, Greenberg et al. (1979) were able to examine the past effect of certainty on present crime rates and the past effect of crime rates on certainty. Their results supported neither the deterrence nor the overload hypothesis. Rather, they concluded that the relationship between certainty and crime rates is due to some unknown social conditions that affect both crime and certainty.

A few studies have investigated the possibility of social factors that would serve to explain the observed relationship between certainty and crime rates. When the effect of variables such as poverty, urbanization, and socioeconomic status are controlled, the relationship between certainty and crime rates has been found to be reduced substantially (Pogue, 1986; Parker and Smith, 1979; Tittle and Rowe, 1974).

In extensive reviews of aggregate-level deterrence research, Nagin (1978) stated that although all but one of the studies he reviewed found an inverse correlation between the probability of sanctions and crime rates, the evidence in support of the deterrence argument is actually weak. He based his conclusion on the fact that most studies of this nature used the same or similar data sets to generate similar results. Moreover, these data are problematic in that extraneous factors could be accounting for the levels of crime reported and the probability of sanctioning. Nagin argued that the one study that did not find the expected inverse correlation was the more thorough study in that it incorporated a number of other control variables. Blumstein et al. (1978: 7) provided the following summary evaluation of this literature: "The major challenge for future research is to estimate the magnitude of the effects of different sanctions on various types, an issue on which none of the evidence available thus far provides very useful guidance."

The most problematic feature of aggregate studies on deterrence is the implicit assumption that people are aware of the certainty and severity of punishment, and that these perceptions have an effect on the probability that they will commit crime. However, Erickson and Gibbs (1978) found that juveniles are ignorant of the penalties for crimes and the probabilities of getting caught. Rather, their perceptions of certainty are related to how serious they ranked the offense (Erickson, 1977). Apparently, their perceptions of certainty were related to how they believed the legal system should operate rather than how it does operate (Empey, 1982).

◆ **THE INDIVIDUAL LEVEL** ◆ An alternative method of examining the deterrence doctrine is to ask individuals directly what they perceive the likelihood of arrest and the severity of punishment to be for specific offenses and to acquire self-reported data on whether they had committed any of those offenses. One of the first such studies was done by Waldo and Chiricos (1972) using a sample of college freshmen. They found an inverse relationship between perceived certainty of punishment and criminal behavior, but not between perceived severity and crime. A number of subsequent studies on adolescents and college students have provided support for that same general conclusion (Grasmick and Bryjak, 1980; Silberman, 1976; Jensen et al., 1978; Anderson et al., 1977).

More recently, studies on diverse populations have appeared. Hollinger and Clark (1983b) examined whether employee theft was deterred by perceptions of certainty and severity of sanction. They found both dimensions of deterrence were significantly related to theft but that certainty was more strongly related. These results held across different types of corporations, but age did condition the relationships; that is, older employees, with more to lose, were more affected by their perceptions of certainty and severity. This suggests that commitment may interact with certainty of punishment to deter employee theft.

Piliavin et al. (1986) reported findings that questioned the applicability of the deterrence doctrine to a sample of serious offenders. When they surveyed 3,300 adult offenders and adolescents who had dropped out of school, they found that perception of personal risk was not related to subsequent crime. Although the cost side of the rational choice model was not related to criminal behavior, the reward side was. That is, a measure of whether people perceived greater opportunities to earn money illegally was significantly and substantially related to criminal behavior.

As in the case of aggregate-level research, the possibility exists that the relationship between certainty and self-reported criminal behavior is spurious due to a third variable that is related to and causally prior to both certainty and criminal behavior. For example, Meier and Johnson (1977) found that having criminal associates minimizes the deterrent effect, whereas Erickson et al. (1977) concluded that moral condemnation of behaviors explains the relationship between certainty and criminal behavior.

Specifying the appropriate causal order is also of paramount importance in individually based research on deterrence. Saltzman et al. (1982) raised the possibility that the observed inverse correlation between certainty and delinquent behavior may be due to what they called an experiential effect. This term refers to the possibility that individuals who had already committed delinquent behavior would have lower levels of perceived certainty based on that experience. By acquiring data at two points in time, Saltzman et al. were able to compare the experiential hypothesis to the deterrence hypothesis. They found that the experiential effect was stronger than the deterrent effect, suggesting that if people commit criminal behavior, they will think that they are not likely to get caught for doing so in the future. Unfortunately, even their own research has not consistently supported the experiential effect in favor of the deterrent effect (Paternoster et al., 1985). Therefore, they concluded rather pessimistically that "even after a decade of intensified perceptual deterrence research, very little is known about the relationship between perceptions and behavior" (Paternoster et al., 1985: 430).

EVALUATION OF THE DETERRENCE DOCTRINE

As suggested at the outset of the discussion of deterrence, the perspective was not generated as a theory of behavior but rather as a doctrine concerning the proper role of punishment. To date, a formal theory of deterrence has yet to be achieved. Indeed, Gibbs (1975) has suggested that because of the difficulties in identifying a unique effect of punishment due to deterrence, we might be better served by generating a theory about the general preventive consequences of punishment. This type of theory, incorporating such outcomes as incapacitation, would be more inclusive than deterrence.

The research on deterrence has illustrated quite well the problems with the perspective. The aggregate-level research requires assumptions about a citizen's knowledge of sanctions, assumptions that appear to be incorrect. Results at both the aggregate and individual level have suggested that the observed relationship between certainty of punishment and crime may be spurious. Finally, there remains the problem of determining whether punishment is affecting crime or crime is affecting the level of real or perceived punishment. Although the research results clearly indicate a relationship between certainty of punishment and crime, until these issues are resolved, it will not be possible to determine whether even this most basic assumption of the deterrence perspective is viable. Gibbs (1975: 1) noted that his book represented "a continuous denial of immediate prospects for satisfactory answers to questions about crime, punishment and deterrence." Over a decade later, we find that statement still summarizes the state of the deterrence doctrine.

Research aside, the deterrence doctrine developed as a recommendation of appropriate objectives for the criminal justice system. Therefore, not surprisingly, one of its appeals is its clear policy implications (Wilson, 1975) — clear, that is, if one does not take into account the weak or ambiguous research results described here.

The doctrine suggests that the most appropriate strategy to deter crime would be to increase the probability of punishment. To do so, however, would be very difficult and might engender other social and economic costs that may not make the effort worthwhile. For example, increasing the probability of arrest would require more police and possibly a greater infringement on civil liberties. More court and correctional personnel would be needed if the strategy included increasing the probability of conviction and incarceration. The economic costs of such a strategy would be great. Given the unclear message from deterrence research, it may not be prudent to invest in such policies if their only purpose is to deter crime.

CONCLUSION

The social control perspectives reviewed in this chapter all share an emphasis on identifying those social or social psychological factors that constrain people from committing delinquent or criminal behavior. They differ in the level (community to individual) of their analysis and, to some extent, in their relative emphasis on social integration and social regulation.

Clearly, the social control perspectives have served to reorient criminologists to the study of factors that inhibit crime. Hirschi (1987) has suggested that this emphasis can be seen as a revitalization of the classical image of man as a rational actor who is constrained from deviating only by those social forces that make coexistence possible. This emphasis has highlighted the role of primary social institutions such as the family, schools, the church, and the legal system. By focusing research efforts on these institutions, we have learned much about how and why they generate conformity.

The research effort also has raised a number of questions about the viability of some of the assumptions contained in these perspectives and about their ability to explain criminal behavior. Two problems appear to be generic to social control perspectives. The assumption that a motivation for criminal behavior need not be included in the theory limits the ability of these perspectives to explain that behavior. Hirschi (1987) has asserted that theories work best in opposition to one another — that is, when integrated across assumptive parameters. At some point, however, evidence concerning the role of delinquent peers and the role of definitions favorable to the violation of the law seemingly would need to be taken into account. This could be done through theoretical elaboration (Elliott et al., 1985; Thornberry, 1987) or, possibly, through raising the level of abstraction of assumptions (Krohn, 1986).

The other generic problem for social control perspectives is to determine the appropriate causal order among the variables in the respective models. For example, does a weak commitment to school lead to delinquency, or does engaging in delinquent behavior result in juveniles becoming less committed to school and getting an education? Does more effective enforcement lead to lower crime rates, or do higher crime rates result in law enforcement being less effective? These types of questions are critical not only for evaluating the theoretical perspectives but also for using them to generate any policy recommendations.

It is in the area of policy that social control perspectives are most appealing. They identify arenas that can be manipulated to some extent (the law, schools). Moreover, the logic of the arguments would suggest preventive approaches rather than dealing with crime after people are already engaging in it or interacting with others who are doing so. Not unimportant, the perspective is consistent with the current political ideology regarding the need to return to more traditional methods of socialization and control.

Gibbons (1975) has suggested that social control theory apparently will be an enduring contribution to the discipline. He was correct in his assessment. What is not yet known is just what the nature of that enduring contribution will be. These perspectives may simply have served to reemphasize arenas of social integration and regulation within integrated models of criminal behavior. Or more elaborate social control models incorporating both social structural and social psychological factors may be developed. How social control theorists and researchers deal with some of the concerns raised here will determine just what its contribution will be.

DISCUSSION QUESTIONS

1. Discuss the manner in which social control theory differs from strain and subcultural theories of criminality. With this in mind, describe the essential question each theory asks.

2. What is social disorganization theory? In what ways is it linked to research on crime and routine activities? Discuss how social disorganization theory might be applied to our crime situation today.

3. Discuss Hirschi's notion of social bonding as it relates to juvenile delinquency. How much support exists in the research literature for the social bonding approach? In what ways does it differ from self-concept and self-rejection approaches?

4. Discuss the deterrence doctrine, and distinguish between general and specific deterrence. What variables are necessary to an understanding of the doctrine? How well has the doctrine fared when subjected to empirical testing?

CHAPTER 15

◆

ALTERNATIVE APPROACHES: LABELING AND CRITICAL PERSPECTIVES

Gray Cavender
Arizona State University

DURING ALMOST a century of criminological research in the United States, two explanations for what "causes" crime have dominated. One of these is the Chicago tradition; the other is the anomie tradition. For now, let us note simply that each tradition presented not only a theory of criminal behavior but also ideas about how research should be conducted and even basic assumptions about the nature of crime and criminality in society.

Over the past twenty-five years or so, two new approaches have emerged—the labeling perspective and critical criminology—both of which have sought to shake up criminology and shift it away from the dominant traditions. The labeling perspective is less interested in what causes people to commit crimes than in why we react to some people as criminals and what happens when we do. Critical criminology addresses the socioeconomic structure of society and its relationship to the law and criminal behavior. Each of these two approaches has several versions, as well as several different names. In this chapter, studies and theorists are cited as representatives of the labeling perspective or critical criminology because their themes generally are consistent with those of the approach in question. They do not necessarily refer to themselves as advocates of the labeling perspective or of critical criminology.

THE CHICAGO TRADITION

The *Chicago School* dates back to the beginning of this century. However, its roots lie in positivism, an intellectual paradigm that emerged in Europe in the late 1800s. The central tenets of positivism include the following ideas: (1) Human behavior is caused by forces or factors that are beyond the control of the individual; (2) knowledgeable experts, using the appropriate methodology or technique, can discover these causes; and (3) the experts can then correct problematic behavior by remedying the factors that cause it.

Positivism involved biological, psychological, and sociological explanations of behavior. For sociological positivists, criminal behavior was a matter of social pathology; the cause was viewed as social rather than biological or psychological. With respect to crime, the ideas of causation, scientific expertise, and correction became the basis of the so-called *medical model*, which ultimately informed our correctional system, including prison treatment programs, parole, and juvenile training schools (Bean, 1976).

Sociologists at the University of Chicago offered the first major analysis of criminal behavior in the United States, framed in terms of sociological positivism. Early in this century, Chicago experienced massive population growth, the result of the Industrial Revolution, urbanization, and large-scale immigration from Europe. Increases in crime accompanied this growth. According to the Chicago sociologists, the usual vehicles of socialization such as the family were overwhelmed by the size and the diversity of the population influx so that social control essentially broke down. That is, crime was caused by social disorganization. They "verified" this observation empirically by demonstrating that transitional neighborhoods — those experiencing growth especially from ethnic and minority populations — had the highest crime rate (see Chapter 14).

The Chicago School dominated sociology and criminology throughout the first three decades of the century. However, that dominance began to wane in the 1930s because of criticisms of social disorganization theory, the Depression, and some resentment against the University of Chicago (Lengermann, 1979). The result was the emergence of the second tradition that would dominate criminological thought — anomie theory.

ANOMIE THEORY

Anomie theory emerged in the 1930s in the United States and became the dominant explanation for criminal behavior until the 1960s. Like the Chicago School, anomie theory relates to the European sociology of the 1800s. Its intellectual heritage lies with an offshoot of positivism — functionalism. Whereas positivism was a paradigm of social action, functionalism was one of theory construction (Martindale, 1960: 465–466).

For functionalists, the central issue was how social stability was maintained (Davis, 1980: 87). Emile Durkheim, a French sociologist from the late 1800s who analyzed the necessary or normal features of a healthy society, exemplifies the functionalist approach. For Durkheim, a particular aspect of society was "functional" if it had positive consequences, if it contributed to social stability; by contrast, an aspect with negative consequences was "dysfunctional" (Pfohl, 1985: 178). Interestingly, even crime might be a normal feature of society.

Durkheim actually described several functions that crime (and punishment) serve in society (see Chapter 2).

Despite the link to positivistic sociology, many functionalists trace their intellectual origin to anthropology (Martindale, 1960: 454). However, functionalism received a theoretical boost through the writings of Talcott Parsons, a Harvard sociologist. When the influence of the Chicago School waned in the 1930s, Robert Merton, one of Parson's students, revitalized functionalism in a way that was especially relevant for criminology.

In developing an "anomie explanation" for crime, Merton drew on Durkheim's concept of "anomie," or state of normlessness in which social regulation is weakened. Many forms of deviance might occur in such a situation (Pfohl, 1985: 203). Merton (1938) reworked Durkheim's concept of anomie into an explanation for criminal behavior in this country. According to Merton, the primary goal of nearly all citizens is economic success, the "American Dream," but the opportunities for achieving it are not equally available to everyone. The malintegration between the goal of success and the opportunity to achieve it produces anomie. People respond or adapt to this situation in several ways, including criminal behavior (see Chapter 13).

In sum, the Chicago tradition saw criminal behavior as a matter of social pathology, something to be explained and then corrected, whereas the anomie tradition saw crime as a normal adaptation to an anomic society. Despite this and other differences, there were similarities between the two traditions. For both, crime reflected a breakdown of social control: social disorganization for the Chicago School; social deregulation for anomie theory. Both traditions generally accepted the legal definition of what constitutes crime, which meant that crime was essentially a working-class phenomenon. Both provided the major theoretical explanations for criminal behavior from the turn of the century to the 1960s. Early in the 1960s, however, things changed, in criminology and in the larger society. Amid these changes, the labeling perspective emerged.

THE LABELING PERSPECTIVE

For more than half a century, criminologists in the United States had tried to explain the etiology of criminal behavior—that is, what causes people to commit crimes. Labeling theory emerged as an exciting new perspective in criminology in the 1960s. Criminologists writing from the labeling perspective were not interested in the etiological question; instead, they focused on how and why some people come to be defined as deviant and what happens when they are so defined.

Many criminologists of the 1960s were aware of the shortcomings of the Chicago School and anomie theory, and had grown increasingly disenchanted with those traditions (Kotarba, 1980: 86–87). They criticized positivism's fascination with empiricism, functionalism's concern with social stability, and criminology's link to the bureaucracy of crime control (Davis, 1980: 198). Labeling theory emerged in part as a response to those criticisms.

Some of those who pioneered the labeling perspective were trained at the University of Chicago, or in the Chicago tradition (Davis, 1972: 451; Kotarba, 1980: 86–87; Pfohl, 1985: 287). The perspective's theoretical underpinnings drew heavily on George Herbert Mead, a professor at the University of Chicago in the 1930s (Davis, 1972: 455; Kotarba, 1980: 87; Pfohl, 1985: 288). Some labeling theorists incorporated ideas that were grounded in Durkheim's functionalism: Criminal or deviant behavior was not necessarily pathological and did not always constitute a threat to social stability; rather, crime or other deviant behavior might actually help preserve the social order (Erikson, 1962: 309–310). The labeling perspective also drew from other intellectual traditions, like sociological jurisprudence and legal realism, that challenged the conventional wisdom about law (Melossi, 1985: 194–195).

Finally, the 1960s were a time of considerable social upheaval in the United States. The Civil Rights movement, opposition to the Vietnam War, and other protests had raised serious and unavoidable challenges to dominant social institutions, especially on college campuses. The labeling perspective's challenge to mainstream criminology paralleled the attack on dominant social institutions (Kotarba, 1980: 88; Pfohl, 1985: 285–286).

Thus, ongoing criticism of the Chicago School and anomie theory created a possibility for something intellectually new in criminology; new theoretical ideas appear in times of crisis or when old traditions are no longer workable. Not surprisingly, however, new ideas sometimes carry remnants of the ones they replace. The social context of a cultural revolution offered a supportive milieu for a shift in criminology's theoretical stance.

THEORETICAL THEMES

Two of the central theoretical tenets of the labeling perspective were offered in 1962. Erikson (1962: 308) argued that behavior was not deviant in itself; rather, it was *defined* as deviant by a social audience. Kitsuse (1962: 248) argued that we should study the process whereby some people come to be defined as deviant by others.

Such statements established a research agenda for the labeling perspective, an agenda that was rich with implications for criminology. First, the perspective offered a new glossary of terms. Second, by arguing that criminality (or deviance) was not a quality inherent in an act or in a person who commits an act, labeling theorists challenged criminology's etiological focus. These theorists were more concerned with the definitional process wherein an act or a person comes to be defined socially as criminal or deviant. The deviant label resulted from a definitional process wherein some members of society interpret certain behavior as deviant, define as deviant the people who perform that behavior, and then respond to them as deviants (Kitsuse, 1962: 248).

THEORETICAL DETAILS

No act is inherently deviant; it must be defined as such. But, of course, the rules are a product of social interaction. For this reason, labeling theorists often are interested in historical analyses of how and why certain behaviors come to be defined as deviant. Typically, these analyses reject an important assumption held by the Chicago and anomie traditions that rules reflect a social consensus. Labeling analyses suggest, instead, that rules reflect the viewpoint of people with power. Labeling theorists refer to these people as "moral entrepreneurs" (Becker, 1963), whose moral position, or views about right and wrong, becomes the definitional rule. The application of rules follows the same path, with the rules tending to be applied to those with less power, vulnerable populations such as women or minorities.

The process of applying the rules further reveals other significant elements of the labeling perspective. First, rules often are applied in a ceremonial manner. In one of the best-known statements of this point, Garfinkel (1956) referred to "status degradation ceremonies." The rules are applied in such ceremonies, but equally important, the manner of their application contributes to the process wherein individuals are defined by society and by themselves as deviant. Criminal trials are an example of status degradation ceremonies: Not only do courts determine guilt or innocence, their ceremonies are designed to affirm both the majesty of the law and the "wrongness" of those who have violated it. They locate the evil not only in the act but in the person who committed it.

The result of a degraded status is a "spoiled identity," or "stigma" (Goffman, 1963). If persons with spoiled identities or stigmas cannot somehow overcome them, we reject them; we often refuse to associate with stigmatized people like criminals. Moreover, Goffman notes how difficult it is to neutralize the effect of a spoiled identity because, for the rest of us, the stigma, whatever it is, tends to become the dominant trait of the person. Hughes (1945) called deviance a "master status," a concept that was popularized by his student, Howard Becker (1963). We respond to a person's deviance as if it were the defining characteristic of the person. Moreover, once persons are labeled deviant, their deviance becomes undifferentiated; other categories of deviance that go beyond the original charge are imputed to them.

Certainly, all this does not happen instantly—it is not as if someone commits a deviant act and is immediately and irrevocably labeled deviant. Some people who get into trouble may be motivated to forgo acts that are defined as deviant; they may conform to society's rules. Others may continue to commit deviant acts but reject the deviant label even though society may view them as such. However, some people who commit deviant acts and who are viewed as deviant may come to accept that label and actually respond to it by exhibiting a greater commitment to deviant behavior or by engaging in new forms of deviance: "When a person begins to employ his deviant behavior or a role based upon it as a means of defense, attack, or adjustment to the overt and covert problems created by the consequent societal reaction to him, his deviation is secondary" (Lemert, 1951: 75–76).

Labeling theorists who were interested in this third potential outcome focused on "deviant careers." Deviant careers comprise sequential stages. They evidence a process of action, reaction, action, reaction, and ultimately, for some, a reaction to society's reaction—secondary deviance. Of course, secondary deviance moved the labeling perspective closer to an etiological statement: Labeling someone might "cause" secondary deviation.

CRITIQUE OF THE LABELING PERSPECTIVE

Even though the labeling perspective offered a timely critique of traditional criminology, and the turmoil of the 1960s provided a supportive intellectual context for such new ideas, the perspective was not an immediate success. In fact, there were serious criticisms of it. The critiques can be organized into four concerns about or objections to the perspective: (1) rules and their violation, (2) scientific objections, (3) empirical evidence, and (4) structural-level criticisms (for a similar four-point categorization, see Pfohl, 1985: 318–322).

◆ **RULES AND THEIR VIOLATION** ◆   Some criminologists criticized the labeling perspective because it did not address the cause of crime (Davis, 1972). They argued that in accepting the idea of secondary deviance, they still were faced with the question of primary deviance: Where do those original acts that elicit society's reaction come from? Criminology was reluctant to abandon its interest in etiology. On the other hand, some criminologists argued that the labeling perspective had reneged on its intellectual agenda by offering a causal theory—that is, societal reaction *causes* secondary deviance (Davis, 1972: 461; Warren and Johnson, 1972: 80).

Perhaps labeling theorists had reneged in other ways as well. Although the labeling perspective claimed that deviance was not a quality inherent in an act, the perspective still accepted the same categories of criminal and deviant behavior that criminologists and sociologists usually studied, such as drinking or taking drugs (Gibbs, 1966; Davis, 1972: 460; Warren and Johnson, 1972: 80). But the perspective had little to say about why the incidence of behaviors that fell in those existing categories varied among and within societies (Gibbs, 1966). Some voiced the opposite criticism: When the labeling perspective argued that no act was inherently deviant, it overlooked the fact that behaviors like homicide are universally deemed "wrong" (Wellford, 1975: 334–335; for further discussion of this point, see Chapter 2 of this volume).

◆ **SCIENCE** ◆   The labeling perspective rejected the very nature of criminological research. In place of research that was grounded in the empiricist branch of sociological positivism—high-level statistical analyses, for example—the labeling perspective stressed field research and participant observation (Schur, 1971; Warren and Johnson, 1972: 70–71). The goal of such a methodology was to produce "sensitizing observations," to "deal with" deviance, and to consider the perspective of those who were so labeled (Becker, 1967; Schur, 1971: 22–27).

Not surprisingly, criminologists trained in the positivist tradition criticized labeling's research methods. They argued that the goal of criminology, like the goal of science generally, was to develop theoretical propositions about phenomena such as criminal and deviant behavior that could be tested with data. The results would be used to reformulate the original theories, to improve them (Gibbs, 1966: 9; Tittle, 1975: 161). This is the nature of theoretical research, of the scientific method. Some criminologists condemned the labeling perspective because it offered no testable hypotheses, no empirical generalizations; they said it was "mushy" and unscientific (Davis, 1972: 459–460; Tittle, 1975: 159, 175; Hirschi, 1975: 198).

◆ **EMPIRICAL FINDINGS** ◆   Although the labeling theorists tended to reject empiricism, some empirical research "tested" the perspective, or at least the results of some research were interpreted as supporting it (see Schur, 1971: 75–76, 96). The critics argued, however, that the results of most empirical research were not favorable to the labeling perspective.

For example, research in the area of mental illness suggested that hospitalization did not result from the violation of common, everyday rules of behavior, that is, residual deviance. Instead, hospitalization was the result of "serious psychiatric disturbances" (Gove, 1970). Criminological research reached similar conclusions: It was lawbreaking and not other factors that increased the likelihood of being officially labeled a deviant (Wellford, 1975; Tittle, 1975: 163–170). Indeed, both mental health and criminological research concluded that official agencies were extremely cautious about processing people.

◆ **POWER STRUCTURE** ◆   The labeling perspective stressed the importance of power in terms of who does the labeling and who is labeled. Nevertheless, scholars criticized the way the perspective addressed the conception of power. First, the critics claimed that labeling's position — official bureaucracies react and thereby begin the labeling process — not only overlooked the importance of informal social reactions, it also oversimplified the complex relationships and hierarchies that characterized most social control organizations (Mankoff, 1971; Davis, 1980: 214). For instance, when people come into contact with organizations like police or probation departments, they usually interact with lower- or mid-level personnel. The high visibility of these interactions caused labeling researchers to neglect the importance of those at the top of social control organizations (Liazos, 1972). The labeling perspective ended up doing exactly what it had criticized traditional criminology for doing: It studied the powerless and ignored the existing power relations in society.

This point was expanded into the second structural critique: The labeling perspective conceptualized power in pluralistic terms. The rules were created supposedly as a result of competition and compromise among interest groups with relatively equal power; no one group or class had the power to define deviance on its own (Lemert, 1974: 462). Some critics claimed that the labeling perspective's pluralism was wrong: Power was not shared equally by competing interest groups; rather, it could be understood only in terms of the larger institutional structures that characterized contemporary society (Mankoff, 1971: 213–215; Davis, 1972: 462–463).

This line of argument prompted one critic, Alvin Gouldner, to repeat the charge that the labeling perspective had reneged on its intellectual agenda. Gouldner (1968) charged that labeling theorists were essentially "trying to be cool," that they romanticized the deviant. Moreover, the labeling perspective had not changed traditional criminology, it had perpetuated it. Labeling theory maintained the Chicago tradition not just in terms of an interactionist stance but also in terms of a correctional approach that served, not challenged, the powerful institutions in this society (see Melossi, 1985: 196–197). Gouldner (1968: 110) called the labeling perspective "establishment sociology." (Later, we shall see how these structural criticisms contributed to a more critical criminology.)

LABELING THEORY'S RESPONSE

Labeling theorists countered that some of the criticisms were valid but that others were unfair because they were based on misrepresentations and misinterpretations of the perspective (Kitsuse, 1975: 273). For example, labeling theorists were annoyed that they were being criticized for not offering a causal explanation when a central theme of their perspective was to enlarge the scope of deviance theory beyond the etiological issue (Becker, 1974: 42). They also believed that critics had misstated their position about the societal reaction: Although the societal reaction was extremely important, actors and their behavior were also a part of the deviance process (Becker, 1963; Kitsuse, 1975: 280–281). Similarly, labeling theorists responded that their discussion of deviance vis-à-vis norms or rules was just as valid as that offered by their critics (Schur, 1969: 312; Kitsuse, 1975: 276–279; Lemert, 1981: 286–287).

In what was perhaps an overall rebuttal, several scholars argued that "labeling theory" essentially was a straw person created by the critics. The labeling perspective never was offered as a full-blown theory of deviance; instead, it was offered as a perspective, a way of looking at deviance that opened for consideration subjects that had not been addressed, such as the operation of social control organizations (Schur, 1969: 317; Becker, 1974: 42–44).

As to the scientific critique, labeling theorists argued that they were being held to a view of science that was limited to the empiricist branch of positivism (Scheff, 1974: 444). They were not interested in predictive statements about deviance or in hypothesis testing (Schur, 1969: 316; for an exception, see Lemert, 1981: 299). And even if science required such endeavors, they occurred in the later stages of theory development. In the early stages, theories were primarily "sensitizing" endeavors that challenged traditional thinking—the sorts of endeavors labeling theorists stated as their aim (Scheff, 1974: 445).

Labeling theorists rejected the empirical critique as well. They claimed that much of the empirical research was simply not true to the labeling perspective: The evaluations were based either on traditional criminological conceptualizations or on oversimplistic statements of labeling theory (Kitsuse, 1975: 275; Schur, 1975: 285). One commentator noted it was unlikely that empirical research ever would prove or disprove the labeling perspective—the results of such studies often were so inconclusive that the same study might be cited by proponents and opponents alike (Schur, 1975: 286–288).

The response to the structural critique was mixed as well. Some proponents acknowledged that the focus on the interaction between deviants and the lower-level functionaries in social control organizations had diverted attention from the upper echelon in those organizations and in society generally. However, they pointed out that nothing in the perspective prevented a more macro-level or structural analysis (Becker, 1974: 61). Some labeling theorists advocated broadening the labeling perspective to include a consideration of the larger social structure (Becker, 1974: 48–49; Pfohl, 1985: 322; see also Horowitz and Liebowitz, 1968). However, other labeling theorists resisted the idea of analyses that were framed in terms of power elites or a Marxian focus on social class (Lemert, 1974: 462).

IMPLICATIONS OF THE LABELING PERSPECTIVE

Despite the criticisms, once the labeling perspective emerged, it had an impact. It affected social policy by providing theoretical support for decriminalization, diversion, and deinstitutionalization movements. Labeling theory supported the view that we should decriminalize "victimless crimes" because they were not especially hurtful, and defining and then reacting to them as crimes could initiate the labeling process with its adverse consequences (Schur, 1965). Similarly, if the reaction by social control agencies contributed to criminal careers, the logical step would be to divert selected offenders from the justice system and avoid the imposition of the label. The worst stigma was reserved for people who had been institutionalized, so the same logic suggested that we should use prisons and mental hospitals only as a last resort. Some labeling theorists extended this position to a general attitude of "radical non-intervention" (Schur, 1973).

The labeling perspective reaffirmed the importance of interactionism for the study of deviance. Today, criminologists address issues such as the sociology of trouble (Emerson and Messinger, 1977) or how "a complex matrix of interactions" makes deviance happen in collectivities like corporations or the government (Cohen, 1990). Labeling also signaled a willingness to go beyond interactionism to other reaches, such as phenomenology and ethnomethodology (Lemert, 1974; Warren and Johnson, 1972; Melossi, 1985; see also Pfohl, 1985: 292–293).

Social control organizations now are a worthwhile topic of study because of the labeling perspective. Decisionmaking is understood as a holistic process of interpretation, categorization, and affirmation that is structured by the operational norms of a given agency. Official records are seen as accounting procedures that justify the process and its outcomes (McCleary, 1978; Drass and Spencer, 1987; Rosecrance, 1988b).

The study of the media is informed by labeling theory's interactionism. The media are a significant source of information about the world around us; they help define our view of reality on a variety of issues, including deviance (see Altheide, 1978; Fishman, 1978). The labeling perspective has also contributed to the study of social problems. Some forms of deviant behavior come to be regarded as social problems, not because of some inherent feature of the behavior but rather through a process of social contruction (Spector and Kitsuse, 1975). Finally, the labeling perspective sensitized scholars to the importance of social, political, and economic power in the formulation of the rules that regulate our lives.

The labeling perspective had its heyday during the 1960s, generating dozens of studies, essays, and books that analyzed all sorts of issues. Because some of the work was sloppy, theoretically and methodologically, it drew sharp criticism from critics and proponents alike (see Kitsuse, 1975: 273; Regoli et al., 1985: 19). It was downgraded from a theory to a perspective, and by the late 1970s, even as a perspective it had lost much of its appeal. Of course, the perspective did not disappear because of empirical research or because of the criticisms (Schur, 1975; see also Palamara et al., 1986: 102–103). In part, it was displaced by related sociological approaches—phenomenology and ethnomethodology—and by the critical criminology that we will discuss in the following sections. And in part, the labeling perspective survived and informs these approaches.

CRITICAL CRIMINOLOGY

The labeling perspective was a product of the turbulent 1960s, and of dissatisfaction, at least in some camps, with traditional criminology. The appearance in the 1970s of what can be called "critical criminology" was prompted by those same concerns. Indeed, critical criminology represented a deeper, more penetrating elaboration of those concerns.

The 1970s were even more turbulent than the 1960s had been. The drama of the Vietnam War played nightly in our homes, while during the day, college students protested the war on campuses across the United States. There was a seemingly endless cycle of disclosures—about assassination plans, the My Lai massacre, and the invasion of Cambodia—followed by ever larger demonstrations. Ultimately, tragically, the cycle peaked when authorities opened fire on college students at Kent State University in Ohio and at Jackson State University in Mississippi. The very foundations of our society were shaken by these events, as well as by others, including revelations about the CIA, the feminist critique of the United States, and Watergate. If Watergate produced a constitutional crisis, all these events and disclosures taken together produced a crisis of legitimacy for our social order (Friedrichs, 1980). Critical criminology attempted to address this crisis as it related to criminal law and criminal behavior.

Critical criminologists argued that the crisis applied to criminology as well. They denounced scientific positivism (Taylor et al., 1973). As for functionalism, they asked, "functional for whom?" and answered that criminal law was functional for the wealthy (Chambliss, 1976). Like the social order, criminology was under attack as a tool of that order. Even the labeling perspective was condemned as traditional criminology in disguise (Young, 1975).

"Critical criminology" is applied here as a kind of generic term that includes several perspectives: conflict criminology, the new criminology, radical criminology, Marxian criminology, and critical criminology. Most of these perspectives appeared in the 1970s, and many of them carried over into the 1980s. Additionally, the term *critical criminology* suggests challenge or critique, and it is consistent with some of the ideas of the 1970s (Sykes, 1974) and with the trends that criminology will encounter in the 1990s—critical social theory and critical legal studies (Groves and Sampson, 1986; Hunt, 1987).

IN THE BEGINNING: CONFLICT CRIMINOLOGY

Conflict criminology was a product of the same conditions — social and intellectual — that generated the labeling perspective. It shared with that perspective the view that crime represented a social definition made by those with power and applied to those with less power (Becker and Horowitz, 1972; Turk, 1969). The labeling perspective had been sensitive to issues of power (see Becker, 1974), but its primary concern was with the societal reaction and the consequences of being labeled. Conflict theorists, on the other hand, focused almost exclusively on power, specifically on how those with power used criminal definitions to protect their interests.

Quinney (1970) offered an early statement of conflict criminology. Crime for Quinney was a definitional matter — a constructed social reality — but the key was that this definition occurred in a politically organized society. The criminalization of behavior was the end product of competition for political power; the victors in this power contest define as criminal the behaviors that threaten their interests (Quinney, 1970: 16).

Thus, society was characterized by perpetual political conflict, not by a consensus of values. This position drew from earlier criminological works (see Sellin, 1938) and from sociologists who had delineated a conflict perspective (Dahrendorf, 1959; Horton, 1969). The conflict criminologists focused specifically on the role of political power in shaping the definition of certain behaviors as criminal.

Rather quickly, however, conflict criminology, like labeling, was criticized for adhering to a pluralistic view of power. According to the critics, this pluralistic view hovered somewhere between naive and wrong, failing to explain how existing authority or power structures were informed by larger, institutional arrangements in society (Taylor et al., 1973: 249, 256).

Although the conflict perspective has continued (Bernard, 1981), a different, more radical sort of criminology emerged in response to the critique of pluralism. The emergent criminology, which drew on the writings of Karl Marx, exploded onto the scene in the mid-1970s.

RADICAL–MARXIAN CRIMINOLOGY

Karl Marx formulated a social theory that addressed the relationship between the economic structure of a society at any given point in history and the various social relations that corresponded to it — everything from political and legal institutions to the very consciousness that informs our perceptions of our lives. Radical criminologists attempted to use Marx's theory to create a Marxian criminology. They were as strident in their intellectual agenda as the campus activists were in their protests against the Vietnam War and the social order that sponsored it. The radicals criticized the criminal law, the criminal justice apparatus, and criminology.

◆ **THE PROCESS OF LAWMAKING** ◆   Radical criminologists rejected the idea that the state was a democratic institution that enacted laws necessary to ensure social order. This was more than just a restatement of conflict criminology. The radicals adopted a kind of Marxian view and argued that the state essentially served the interests of the ruling class—the capitalists. The legal order protected the power and privilege of the capitalists, and perpetuated their exploitation of the working class (Quinney, 1977). If the behaviors of the working class were more likely to be criminalized, the behaviors of the ruling class, even if socially harmful, were less likely to be criminalized. Or, if criminalized, the laws were less likely to be enforced (Krisberg, 1975: 20–41). The radicals argued that the law's focus on so-called street crime engendered a false consciousness that diverted attention from the inequities of our economic system, from the wrongs committed by the government, like the Vietnam War, and from wrongs committed by capitalists, like violations of antitrust laws (Reiman, 1984: 4–5).

What was needed to overcome this false consciousness, the radicals argued, were historical analyses that revealed how specific criminal laws came into being and how those laws reflected the interests of the ruling class. For example, studies of drug laws went beyond Becker's moral entrepreneur analysis and portrayed drug legislation, enacted earlier in this century, as an effort to control immigrant workers, especially the Chinese, who were being exploited by the railroads and other industries (Tracy, 1980). Other studies suggested that even laws that had supposedly produced social reforms were not what they seemed but rather reflected the interests of the ruling class. For example, legislation in England in the 1700s that reduced the number of capital offenses had more to do with the desires of economic elites than with any humanitarian concerns (Rustigan, 1980). Similarly, antitrust legislation enacted in the United States early in this century was primarily symbolic and was seldom enforced against large corporations. Such legislation shored up the government's legitimacy by making it appear responsive to public concerns about big business (Barnett, 1979). In short, criminal law protected the interests of the rich and powerful, even when it appeared to regulate them.

◆ **THE PROCESS OF LAWBREAKING** ◆   Like labeling theory, radical criminology focused less on etiology, but it still had something to say about what caused crime. The radicals argued that crime, like other social phenomena, had to be understood in terms of capitalism. Capitalism generated extreme egoism, and crime in capitalistic society was the result. The wealthy committed crimes because they always wanted more—because they were greedy. For the poor, economic crime was essential for survival. Poor people lived in a society that stressed materialism, yet they were unable to afford the essentials, much less luxuries, because of the unequal distribution of resources that is a defining characteristic of capitalism. Crime was a rational response for the poor (Gordon, 1973). The often violent nature of crime, even the fact that the poor tend to victimize one another, was due to the miserable living conditions that capitalism produced (Quinney, 1977).

Crime could not be separated from the social conditions produced by capitalism. Following Marx, Spitzer (1975) has argued that capitalism produces an entire population of people who are chronically unemployed as one of its byproducts. These people are on the economic margin, they are problematic for our society, and they have to be controlled. More important, they are an embarrassment because they represent the failure of capitalism. We use the criminal law to control them and thereby depoliticize them; they become common criminals rather than chronically unemployed.

◆ **THE PROCESS OF THE SOCIAL REACTION TO LAWBREAKING** ◆ Radical criminologists view the criminal justice apparatus as a mechanism of social control. Social control is not seen in terms of the necessary enforcement of a set of socially shared values but rather as a form of repression that serves the interests of the ruling class (Michalowski and Bohlander, 1976). Radical criminologists suggested that police departments were created and controlled by commercial elites in the 1800s. The police were a mechanism for repressing the working class through strike-breaking activities or the sometimes violent enforcement of vagrancy statutes (Harring, 1977). More contemporary analyses detailed the tremendous expenditures for policing by the federal government. It was no coincidence, the radicals suggested, that such expenditures on repressive technologies occurred during the late 1960s and early 1970s, when the established power structure was seriously challenged (Quinney, 1977). Even such matters as the size of police departments or the likelihood that police would use deadly force were related to income disparities, and thus, to the degree to which the ruling class was threatened by the working class (D. Jacobs, 1979; Jacobs and Britt, 1979).

As for the courts, radical criminologists concluded that the legal system served the interests of the ruling class. The juvenile court, for example, was created as a mechanism that would ensure more effective social control and transform immigrant children into a disciplined working class (Platt, 1977). Similarly, the creation and operation of public defender offices was portrayed as a system that appeared to protect the legal rights of the poor but actually deprived them of legal representation (Barak, 1980). Radical scholars noted that key legal positions such as federal judgeships were reserved for lawyers whose family background and education reflected their ruling-class heritage (Domhoff, 1967). The prevalence of upper-class judges helped explain why upper-class criminals received preferential treatment (Quinney, 1974), whereas the poor and minorities received unduly severe sentences (Krisberg, 1975: 25).

Updating earlier Marxian theory, radical criminologists argued that even if prisoners could not be credited with truly political crimes, the very presence of a predominantly poor or minority prison population evidenced the political nature of imprisonment and its relationship to economic repression (Wright, 1973; Smith and Fried, 1974). They argued further that the incarceration rate had more to do with the unemployment rate than with the crime rate (Jankovic, 1977).

Repressive social control was the hallmark of the criminal justice apparatus for radical criminology. Innovations and reforms that occurred in the nineteenth and twentieth centuries were simply mechanisms whereby the state expanded its control over vulnerable populations in the interests of the ruling class (American Friends Service Committee, 1971; Dahl, 1977). Yet, the state maintained the illusion of fairness and depoliticized the nature of crime in capitalism. This helped the state maintain its legitimacy and that of the dominant social order (Krisberg, 1975: 53–55).

◆ **ACADEMIC CRIMINOLOGY** ◆   Radical criminologists reserved their harshest criticisms for their own discipline. They condemned criminology's acceptance of the official definition of criminal behavior, which was based on a belief in a shared set of social values. They attacked the tenets of scientific positivism. They debunked the determinism and correctionalism that had been the mainstays of both etiological research and treatment programs. They argued that determinism fostered the view that criminality was a pathology or a sickness resting in the individual, not in the social conditions that accompanied capitalism (Smart, 1976: 29). Correctionalism maintained the illusion that the state was doing something about crime and that it was doing it in a humanitarian fashion (Bean, 1976).

The radicals claimed that criminology hid behind the rhetoric of scientific neutrality and expertise, but in the end, it provided the knowledge and the rationalizations for the state's control over vulnerable populations (Taylor et al., 1973: 35). This charge echoed Gouldner's (1968) critique of the labeling perspective. Indeed, the radicals charged that the labeling perspective was voyeuristic and that both the labeling perspective and traditional criminology, despite their focus on liberal reforms, were nevertheless a tool of the state and therefore of the ruling class (Young, 1975). Even the agenda for criminological research was determined by the availability of federal grants—criminologists had sold out (Platt, 1974).

What was needed, the radicals argued, was a movement beyond the official, class-biased definitions of crime. Instead, criminologists should study war and imperialism, racism, sexism, and poverty (Schwendinger and Schwendinger, 1970). Moreover, if capitalism was the context that generated crime, criminology should pursue a working-class criminology (Young, 1975) or a socialist criminology (Quinney, 1977).

Thus, the radical agenda included a critique of the criminal law, of crime, and of criminology. Radicals sought to demystify and debunk all the assumptions that made repression possible. And they had an agenda for reform: socialism.

◆ **CRITIQUE OF RADICAL–MARXIAN CRIMINOLOGY** ◆   Not surprisingly, traditional criminology responded to these charges. Some critics acknowledged that radical criminologists had actually done criminology some good: They had produced revealing insights about the origin and nature of certain laws and legal institutions (Sykes, 1974) and they had acquired those insights through valuable historical research that had been lacking in the discipline (Sparks,

1980: 195). However, critics noted that radical criminology did little else, providing virtually no ethnographic or quantitative research (Sparks, 1980: 196).

Other criminologists were less excited about those historical insights. They charged that, contrary to the radical view, there was evidence of an underlying consensus in terms of the definitions of criminal behavior (Akers, 1979: 532; Klockars, 1979: 490). Similarly, they noted that laws against such crimes as murder, rape, and armed robbery protected everyone, not just the ruling class. In fact, such laws were especially important for poor people because the poor were usually the victims of violent crimes (Klockars, 1979: 498).

In the same vein, traditional criminologists rejected the claim that class bias existed in the administration of the criminal justice system (Akers, 1979: 538). They even challenged the idea of class distinctions in the contemporary United States (Klockars, 1979: 484–485). They also argued that the link between crime and social class had been overstated (Tittle et al., 1978). And they pressed radicals on the issue of how a transition to socialism would reduce crime; the former Soviet Union, for example, had crime but was a repressive country as well (Klockars, 1979: 499).

Traditional criminologists claimed that radical criminology, like labeling theory, had reneged on its intellectual agenda. It was not a new criminology at all. It represented a restatement of the familiar deterministic model. They argued that it was a rehash of anomie theory's differential opportunity structure plus a heavy dose of labeling theory's emphasis on power and social definitions. It simply relocated the "cause" of crime in the social structure and the evils of capitalism (Meier, 1976). Some critics argued that radical criminology was not a social science as much as a kind of sentimental moralism (Toby, 1979).

In addition, traditional criminologists resented the radicals' condemnation of the discipline as a tool of the state (Akers, 1979), and criticized radical criminology's "intellectual amnesia." Criminologists since Sutherland, they noted, had been concerned about the legal definition of crime and the crimes of the powerful, and they had produced genuine social reform (Sparks, 1980: 184–186, 201).

Labeling theorists and conflict criminologists were critical of the radicals, too. The former resented the cavalier dismissal of labeling theory with little or no mention of symbolic interactionism (Rock, 1979). The conflict criminologists argued that conflict could exist apart from classes. They charged that radical criminology was too ideological and that it did not formulate testable propositions (Turk, 1979; Bernard, 1981).

In short, traditional criminology as well as alternative criminologies acknowledged some contributions, but for the most part, they rejected radical criminology, sometimes angrily. Interestingly, Marxian scholars critiqued radical criminology, too. Some even argued that the very effort to construct a Marxian criminology was misguided. Marx had said little about law and crime, and many of the inferences that had been drawn from his work by the radicals—on class and crime as political struggle, for example—were considered incorrect (Ainlay, 1975; Hirst, 1975). Perhaps this new form of criminology expressed a legitimate outrage about what was happening in society, but it was not true to Marx's social theory; it was more radical than Marxian (Bankowski et al., 1977).

Indeed, many Marxists were as scathing in their critique as traditional criminologists had been. They considered radical criminology shoddy and sloppy, and believed it gave Marxian scholarship a bad name (Mankoff, 1978; Steinert, 1978). And they pointed out inconsistencies. For example, members of the working class had little choice but to commit crimes—that is, their behavior was determined—whereas the ruling class controlled the state and its law—that is, their behavior was voluntary (Mankoff, 1978: 295). What was needed, they suggested, was a more careful reading of Marx, or perhaps an abandonment of the study of crime and deviance altogether, and a return to the analytic categories Marx had used in his social theory of capitalism (Hirst, 1975).

THE EMERGENCE OF CRITICAL CRIMINOLOGY

Spurred on by the critiques, and probably more by those from other Marxists than by those from traditional criminologists, an improved critical criminology emerged in the 1970s. By the 1980s, it was vastly superior to the early efforts of radical criminology.

Critical criminology began to employ a more sophisticated version of Marxian theory, one that was truer to Marx and that incorporated contemporary Marxian scholarship. Informed by this more sophisticated framework, critical criminologists no longer portrayed law as simply a tool of the ruling class. The relationship between law and the social structure is now viewed as quite complex. Studies have addressed various dimensions of this complex relationship, including the nature of the relationship (Stone, 1985); the form of law, transitions in it, and the affect on crime policies (Balbus, 1977; Santos, 1985); the autonomy of the state (Thompson, 1975); legal responsibility (Lilly and Ball, 1982); ideology (Hunt, 1985); legitimacy and property relations (Hay, 1975); and law and community (Santos, 1980). More recently, scholars have moved toward critical legal studies, addressing the deficiencies of law and legal ideologies, how legal ideologies mask those deficiencies, and how we might work to overcome them (Munger and Seron, 1984; Hunt, 1987).

In their discussion of criminal behavior, critical criminologists have renewed the claim that the unemployment rate, one of the byproducts of the expansions and contractions of capitalism, is related to the crime rate (Chiricos, 1987; Devine et al., 1988). Similarly, they have shown that social class is an important factor in the analysis of crime (Braithwaite, 1981). Critical criminologists have added the middle class and "class fractions," or subdivisions, to their analyses of the relationship between crime and class. For example, they address juvenile delinquency in terms of "structures of control" that are grounded in the different workplace experiences of different classes or class fractions, and that are reproduced in the family, in school, and in peer associations. Ultimately, these structures are the context in which delinquency occurs (Colvin and Pauly, 1983). Thus, delinquency is still related to class but through a complex web of linkages (Schwendinger and Schwendinger, 1985).

Critical criminology provides more sophisticated analyses of the criminal justice apparatus. These range from studies of the legal system and the legal profession in contemporary capitalism (Hagan et al., 1988; Abel, 1990) to historical research that links imprisonment and economic conditions in England (Hogg, 1979) and in the United States (Adamson, 1984).

Critical criminology also has generated a number of other theoretical advances. The critique of positivism continues but in a manner that is more conversant with social theory and philosophy. The critique demonstrates that a Marxian alternative need not be deterministic; human beings do indeed make their own history (Groves, 1985). Critical criminologists are also trying to forge links with critical social theory to open up a consideration of crime that can deal with the importance of culture but at a structural level (Groves and Sampson, 1986).

CRITICAL CRIMINOLOGY:
PROBLEMS AND IMPLICATIONS

Critical criminology not only has survived, it has flourished; nevertheless, some problems remain unresolved for the approach. First, there is a methodological problem. Critical criminology now employs quantitative methodologies more so than in the past (Greenberg, 1979). Still, it is difficult to verify empirically all the linkages asserted by critical criminology (Sheley, 1985: 244), especially as the linkages become more complex. The situation becomes even more tangled if scientific inquiry is equated with scientific positivism, the very paradigm that critical criminology has criticized (Groves, 1985).

Second, critics still charge that critical criminology reduces everything to economic determinism. Of course, to the degree that critical criminology draws on Marx, economic issues are significant. However, critical scholars have moved beyond the economic determinism and reductionism of radical criminology, in part by sticking closer to Marx, who explicitly rejected such determinism. Similarly, the acceptance of critical social theory broadens the inquiry into issues of culture that, although informed by economic arrangements, go beyond them (Groves and Sampson, 1986; see also Williams, 1977).

Third, the role of the individual remains unresolved. Why do some people in the working class commit crimes whereas others do not? Why do some capitalists and government leaders commit crimes whereas others do not (Sheley, 1985: 244)? Such issues of individual motivation and behavior long have plagued Marxian theory. Marxism is a *social* theory about *social* relations, about how societies operate. However, critical scholars now address the nature of individual behavior within the larger social structure. They have elaborated theories of human agency that are sensitive to the social dimensions of individual life (Henry, 1985; Groves, 1985). Some advocate a merger of critical criminology with approaches like interactionism or phenomenology that deal with individual-level behavior (Smart, 1976; Melossi, 1985). Others would merge critical criminology with a more cultural approach (Schwendinger and Schwendinger, 1985).

Despite these unresolved matters, however, critical criminology has made significant contributions to criminology as an academic discipline. The historical research on crime, criminal law, and criminal justice organizations has been of unquestionable benefit to criminology. As a result, we have a more accurate and sophisticated view of the legal order and of the nature of social control within it. Perhaps the historical picture will give us more insight into contemporary issues.

Similarly, sensitivity to the social structure has improved the quality of theoretical inquiry in criminology. To be sure, not all the theoretical questions have been answered. There is still debate about Marx's relevance to criminology (O'Malley, 1988). And, of course, there are theoretical innovations in criminology other than critical criminology (see Colvin and Pauly, 1983). In any case, perhaps the questions that criminologists ask have become more sophisticated.

Critical criminology has heightened the awareness of ideological issues in terms of criminal behavior, the criminal law (Hunt, 1985), and even the legitimacy of the social order (Friedrichs, 1980; Sumner, 1979). As was the case with the labeling perspective, one implication of this awareness has been attention to the role of the media as a vehicle for disseminating ideologies (Hall et al., 1978).

CONCLUSION

Criminology, like everything else, is dynamic. It changes with the times, as social conditions change, and as new people come along with new questions and new ideas. In this chapter, we have explored two theoretical innovations that occurred in criminology during the past twenty-five years or so: the labeling perspective and critical criminology.

Both innovations set out to change criminology, and in large part they succeeded. The changes they produced were not just some new statistical techniques, however important that might be; instead, they contributed new conceptualizations and insights that improved criminology theoretically. At the same time, labeling theory and critical criminology maintained some continuity with the past. Labeling theory revitalized the analysis of deviant behavior in terms of social interactionism, and critical criminology reaffirmed the powerful analytic insights of Marx.

As a result, criminology will end the century as it began it—with bright prospects. Perhaps we will still study, with Sutherland, the processes of lawmaking and lawbreaking, and the social reaction to lawbreaking, but we likely will study these processes in a new way. Labeling theory and critical criminology have facilitated the improvement.

DISCUSSION QUESTIONS

1. Discuss the Chicago tradition of sociological theory about crime. In what ways does the labeling perspective derive from that tradition? Describe the major themes underpinning the labeling perspective.

2. Describe the process by which a deviant label is applied to an individual. What is meant by "stigma" and "master status"? What are the various outcomes of the labeling process, and what seems to determine outcome?

3. What precisely is a "Marxian" criminology? What makes it "critical" or "radical"? According to this perspective, what role does the state play in defining crime problems and solutions?

4. Discuss the similarities and dissimilarities between the labeling and critical perspectives. Describe the criticisms aimed at each perspective. Are these related in any way?

◆   I appreciate the comments of Nancy Jurik and Joseph Sheley on earlier versions of this paper.

PART FIVE

CRIMINAL JUSTICE

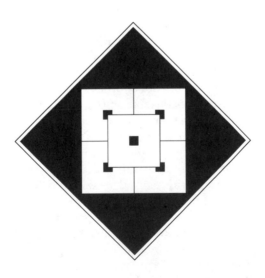

When a society creates rules, it also creates the need for rule enforcers. In larger societies, legal systems generally are complex, and legislative, enforcement, and judicial duties are relatively distinct from one another. Indeed, the public's notion that criminal justice agencies constitute one large, integrated system is misguided. In fact, the criminal justice system in the United States is a collection of somewhat interrelated, semiautonomous bureaucracies. Criminal justice agencies possess considerable discretion, often bounded only by other agencies' abilities to embarrass them in the political arena. At root, however, all agencies face the same dilemma: They have developed missions for themselves that they cannot complete. In one fashion or another, they are charged with reducing crime and dissuading current and potential offenders from violating the law. Their record in this regard is problematic.

Stephen Mastrofski examines policing in America in precisely this manner in Chapter 16, "The Police." In the first of the chapters concerning criminal justice agencies, Mastrofski lends a historical perspective to the issue of policing in America. Though the concept of police as we know them originated in England, our concept differs in that officers here traditionally have been given varingly more personal freedom to accomplish order. This situation has provoked a seemingly perpetual process of police reform designed to eradicate police corruption, define the role that police are to play in this society, and establish the outer limits of police discretion. Mastrofski closes with a discussion of the exceptional difficulty of the crime control mission for contemporary police and cautions that to maintain social legitimacy, the police must develop new mechanisms by which to engage in social control.

In Chapter 17, "The Courts: Prosecution and Sentencing," Martha Myers examines the decision-making behavior of the two most powerful figures in the courthouse, the district attorney and the judge. She notes that although these actors have a considerable amount of autonomy in the exercise of their duties, their great discretion is not unbridled. Instead, it is structured in large part by the types of cases before the court, by decisions made in earlier reviews of the cases, and by largely indirect community pressures. What is clear from Myers' careful analysis of the court is that it represents the operations of people who are concerned with more than simple processing of offenders and the accomplishment of justice and punishment of crime. Courtroom decisions occur in a political arena. Yet, blatant discrimination in sentencing seems to have decreased in American courtrooms. Extralegal factors do influence decisions, but they seem to do so in a subtler way—through reliance by decisionmakers on previous bureaucratic process outcomes and recommendations, for example.

Chapter 18, Neal Shover and James Inverarity's "Adult Segregative Confinement," and Chapter 19, Todd Clear's "Correction Beyond Prison Walls," investigate correction of offenders in America. Shover and Inverarity trace the history of confinement in this country, including reform movements that eventually produced the individualized treatment model. Within this approach, inmates were viewed as persons in need of therapy and counseling by which they could be rehabilitated. This model has given way in recent years to a custody model whereby prisoners are viewed as in need of incapacitation. The result of this shift has been a serious crowding problem in jails and prisons. At the same time, these institutions are taking in greater numbers of poor and minority inmates. Inmate culture has become destabilized, and the tension and danger within prisons has escalated. The authors close with a discussion of the application of various sociological models to what is known about prisons today.

Clear uses the notion of prison overcrowding as the springboard into his discussion of nonincarcerative correction. This is correction by which convicted persons are supervised while remaining in the community. As Clear notes, this is the more common means of dealing with offenders; to abolish it would be to swell the ranks of prisons many times over. Nonincarcerative correction includes probation, work release, treatment programs, parole, and so forth. Some forms seek to change offenders, whereas others wish to control them. Are such programs effective? Clear suggests that, overall, incarceration and nonincarceration seem to produce much the same results when types of prisoners compared are equal. He closes by pointing out how little we still know about the various forms of correction he discusses, including how well or how poorly different types of programs fare relative to one another. Equally important, he calls for a better assessment of public attitudes regarding all forms of correction.

CHAPTER 16

THE POLICE

Stephen D. Mastrofski
The Pennsylvania State University

ORIGINS AND DEVELOPMENT OF MODERN POLICING

AMERICA'S "MODERN" police were modeled after the London Metropolitan Police, formed in 1829 in response to large-scale public disorders, violent crimes, political riots, and common property crimes in a city undergoing industrialization and urbanization. English society had experienced crime waves for over a century, but by the 1820s it was clear that old methods of crime and disorder control (the watch, constables, and sheriffs) were ineffective (Bittner, 1970; Lane, 1992). Yet, there was widespread concern that the formation of an institution with adequate powers to deal with crime and disorder would concentrate too much power in the hands of the executive, leading to tyrannical suppression of precious civil liberties. In this context, the Metropolitan Police, or "Bobbies," emerged and developed. Several features were intended to legitimize the police: (1) a public (not private) enterprise, (2) staffed by full-time, paid employees, (3) focused on crime prevention by maintaining a more-or-less constant presence on patrol beats, (4) uniformed, and therefore clearly identifiable, (5) organized in military fashion, and (6) unarmed (except for a small truncheon) (Klockars, 1985).

By making police work a public responsibility, Parliament strengthened the likelihood that a respected social institution (the national government) would control those who did it, and thus minimize the rampant corruption of the private entrepreneur "thief takers," who were widely despised in English society for entrapping citizens or making false accusations (Klockars, 1985: 34). By making them full-time employees, the government gave the new police something to lose (their jobs), should they perform badly, thereby providing a means of control irrelevant to private and part-time policing.

By restricting the police mission to crime prevention and their principal deployment to patrol, the founders of the Metropolitan Police effectively restricted the scope of police intervention to occasions when citizens summoned them for help or the constable observed from the street something deserving his attention. Patroling on beats also made it easier for supervisors to locate constables to ensure at least that they were on the job. The uniform additionally increased the constable's visibility to the public, provided a ready symbol of authority, and made it impossible for the officer to assume the *agent provocateur* role that had been a frequent resort of private thief takers. By forbidding constables to carry firearms, the founders limited the capacity of the officer to resort to the most powerful coercive tools available, forcing him instead to rely on and nurture other bases for securing the compliance of sometimes reluctant and even rebellious members of the public: the authority of his office, his power to ensure compliance through personal acts or summoning other constables, his persuasive abilities, and his skill in negotiation. The assumption of a military style organization was thought to establish internal accountability through recruitment and assignment practices that severed ties between the police and policed, a chain of command and strictly enforced discipline. Finally, London's Police Commissioners stressed impersonal administration of the law, attention to procedural regularity, and civil liberties. Administrators emphasized that officers should secure the public's voluntary compliance with police and support for their actions by minimizing resort to coercion and relying as much as possible on the impersonal authority they could derive from their image as *legal* actors.

American communities were much influenced by London's new police, but they made several important adaptations to suit the peculiarities of American society, many of which endure to this day (Miller, 1977). American police were creatures of local, not national government, thus fostering a fragmented, decentralized system of urban policing across the nation. Their staffing, organization, and activities were heavily influenced by the ebb and flow of *local* politics and the inclinations of the elected politicians to whom they were accountable. Rather than create a police force that might transcend political and social strife (or at least give the appearance of doing so), American cities placed their police very much in the center of those conflicts (often between different ethnic groups and sometimes between social classes), making little effort to link the authority of officers to higher, impersonal sources (Monkkonen, 1981; Schneider, 1980). Further, the founders of early American police forces shunned some aspects of the London police that were viewed as authoritarian and antidemocratic. Military organization and uniforms were unpopular because they were associated in many Americans' memory with the still recent tyranny of royal governance during the colonial experience.

The new American police were expected to maintain order without much interference from such institutional restraints as the law and were therefore inevitably forced to rely on their *personal* power, such as might derive from physical strength, street savvy, cunning, and contacts. Wielding personal power required considerable freedom to interpret the law or ignore it entirely without fear of being countermanded. Not surprisingly, then, American police were freer to use force against citizens, and although initially forbidden to carry firearms, they quickly moved to reinforce their personal authority with such weapons—in no small part because the population they policed was far more likely than Londoners to be armed as well. American police departments were far less willing and able to impose discipline on how officers exercised their personal authority. To the extent that discipline was imposed, it came largely from loyalty to the local political party in power and in turn involved such things as the ability of an officer to deliver votes and enforce the law as it pleased those in political power (Fogelson, 1977; Walker, 1977).

It was not until the late nineteenth and early twentieth centuries that reform movements in America began to make inroads into the power of the political machines into which the police had become thoroughly integrated. In attempting to break the hold of the machines on the police (and sometimes vice versa), the reformers of the next half century relied at various times on the images of the police as *law* enforcers, soldiers in a war against crime, and "professionals," selected for their skill, honesty, and devotion to service—not to politicians (Klockars, 1988: 241–247). Reform efforts were stoked by scandals of corruption and brutality, and images of police as ineffective and inefficient in the face of growing crime and disorder in urban America as waves of immigrants moved into and through cities that were expanding rapidly (Monkkonen, 1981). By mid-twentieth century, the power of the political machines was broken in most cities. The Federal Bureau of Investigation and the Los Angeles Police Department became for many the models of what police agencies at their best could be: legalistic, militaristic, corruption-free, immune from outside political influence, and dedicated to the eradication of crime (Fogelson, 1977).

However, in all practical senses, adherence of these and other "model" police agencies to these ideals was largely illusionary. Although police departments were more autonomous from political parties, corruption and brutality had not been eliminated. Day-to-day police work was still filled with a wide range of minor disorders; law enforcement and crime fighting were only a small part of a police officer's work. The law and bureaucratic structures still played a peripheral role in shaping the highly discretionary decisions of the individual police officer on his beat. And despite the war-on-crime rhetoric that justified substantial growth in America's police force in the 1960s, crime rates continued to rise. Studies showed that crime-control tactics held in high esteem by police (preventive patrol, rapid response to calls for service, and specialist criminal investigators) demonstrated no substantial impact on the capacity of police to apprehend criminals and reduce crime (Kelling, 1978). At the same time, large-scale urban riots and unrest projected an image of police who were unable to maintain order and who had alienated the poor, racial minorities, and the nation's youths (President's Commission on Law Enforcement and Administration of Justice, 1967b).

Once again calls were made to reform the police—to make them more accessible and more effective against crime and a host of other, related problems plaguing urban areas (Wilson, 1975). By the 1980s, a different vision of what policing could accomplish and how it could be done had emerged and rapidly gained popularity among some of the nation's most visible police leaders and reformers. Going by the name, "community policing," it called for a reformulation of the role of the police, going beyond mere enforcement and crime-fighting to solving a broad array of urban problems (Greene and Mastrofski, 1988). It emphasized various tactics and strategies thought to bring the police and the policed into closer "partnerships" to solve these problems. And it advocated new indicators of police performance to replace the crime, arrest, and clearance statistics that had previously served to legitimate police budgets: citizen satisfaction with police, fear of crime, and numbers of calls for service.

This thumbnail history of American policing suggests three recurring themes that frame the issues central to an understanding of what policing is and how it is done. The first theme is the *role* of police: what their function is and should be. The second is the *control* of police: how much discretion police have and how it is governed. The third is *legitimacy:* how police are made acceptable to society and receive support. These themes are at the core of the most important efforts to define and transform American police, and they serve as the organizing themes of this chapter.

THE ROLE OF THE POLICE

To understand the police, we must first be able to define them, a conceptually difficult task (Manning, 1993). The most widely cited contemporary definition of modern police is Bittner's (1970: 39, 46), who wrote that the police role "is best understood as a mechanism for the distribution of non-negotiable coercive force employed in accordance with the dictates of an intuitive grasp of situational exigencies." In another essay he described this function as doing something about situations in which "something-ought-not-to-be-happening-and-about-which-something-ought-to-be-done-NOW!" (1974: 30).

From Bittner's perspective, the essence of the police role is to handle situations that appear to require decisive intervention to prevent or correct something that is or might be amiss. The two key elements of this role are the capacity to use violent methods ("coercive force") and to do it on short notice — within a time frame that usually precludes the kind of careful investigation, diagnosis, tests, and mulling of evidence available to decisionmakers in courts of law or doctors' offices (Klockars, 1985: 16–17). Bittner presented police work as keeping or restoring the peace. He noted that even though police are uniquely endowed with a general authority to use violence (up to and including lethal force) within their jurisdiction, they actually exercise their authority in its more extreme forms quite infrequently.

As Muir (1977) notes, the police typically use methods falling far short of physical coercion: asking questions; making commands, requests, suggestions, threats and warnings; negotiation; persuasion; various forms of "controlling assistance" (for example, taking a public drunk to a detoxification center); and simply being physically present. Nonetheless, the police capacity and authority to use violence suffuses their work and makes possible their capacity to use nonviolent forms of intervention and control effectively, including their authority to arrest. Finally, in attempting to restore or maintain peace, the police produce only "provisional" solutions to problems — not permanent solutions that alter the forces underlying those problems. Thus, for Bittner, the law and legal institutions have very little influence on the actual exercise of police coercive powers because the *police* were granted authority to coerce, and those institutions responsible for making the laws (legislatures) and monitoring police compliance (for example, the courts) cannot stipulate with much precision when and how those powers should be used.

Countering Bittner, Reiss (1971, 1992, 1993) argues that Bittner's perspective is too restrictive and that it lacks grounding in broader theories of social organization, formal organizations, and interorganizational relations. In attempting to set forth what is unique about police, Reiss contends that Bittner overlooks the many ways in which police and police organizations are like other occupations and organizations. Additionally, Reiss takes issue with the notion that the order maintenance function of police is purely situational, meaning that it occurs exclusively in small-scale encounters between one or a few officers and a small number of the public. Various forms of traffic regulation, crowd management, and regulation of businesses through license revocation are examples where the context of order maintenance is strikingly different, if in some cases, highly problematic (for example, organized terrorism). Reiss argues as well that the domain of police discretion to coerce, enforce the law, or take other actions that intrude into the public's freedom is not fixed but rather responsive to changes in the environment of policing. For example, changes in constitutional law since the 1960s have placed severe restrictions on the use of a wide range of police powers (interrogation, arrest, lethal force, search and seizure). Whether or not police abide by these strictures, there is *some* degree of accountability; police coercive powers are not, at least presently, absolute or "non-negotiable."

Reiss also suggests that environmental change, affecting who is recruited into police work and the values they hold, has implications for the nature of police discretion and how it is exercised. Further, the coercive powers of police (up to and including lethal force) are not sovereign to police. Others have been granted coercive authority in restricted circumstances or for restricted populations (for example, prison guards, mental health workers, bailiffs, private security agents).

Finally, Reiss, along with others, has noted that the *core technology* of policing is the "*production and processing of information*" (Reiss, 1992: 82; Muir, 1977; Manning, 1992a, 1992b). That is, the police decide what to do about their clients by collecting, analyzing, coding, and communicating information about them. This is part of the process of determining their "fate." In this regard, they are not unlike other "street-level bureaucrats" and professionals, such as educators, administrators, social workers, and health care deliverers, who perform key intake functions of diagnosing and categorizing clients so that others in the system have some idea of what to do with them (Lipsky, 1980; Prottas, 1978). The patrol officer who responds to a domestic fight will be expected to determine whether a crime has occurred, who has criminal liability and of what sort, whether further police investigation is required, whether medical and other forms of assistance are warranted, and whether any of a host of other potential forms of intervention may be needed. If, as is often the case, the officer decides not to use any formal intervention options, he or she must still decide whether and how to handle the situation informally, and how to characterize the incident to the departmental hierarchy that monitors performance. The police domain may be broader than those of other street-level bureaucrats, but they share with them the function of achieving some authoritative "disposition" of their problem and, sometimes, person.

THE DISTRIBUTION OF POLICE

In 1990, there were about 800,000 sworn officers and civilians employed in America full or part time in police protection activities at the federal, state, and local levels. Of these, nearly 600,000 were full-time sworn state and local officers, and an additional 35,000 were part-time sworn state and local officers. The national average number of full-time sworn officers per 1,000 inhabitants was 2.2 in 1990 (FBI, 1991, 1992).

In general, American police are concentrated where Americans concentrate: in large cities. Further, the police tend to concentrate where crime and other problems are concentrated, which is also in the large cities. However, small cities, suburban counties, and rural areas enjoy much higher ratios of officers to reported crime than do larger cities. Although some police specialists work out of headquarters and routinely serve the entire jurisdiction, patrol officers, who are the most numerous, are geographically dispersed. That is because patrol officers are "first responders," expected to handle reported problems quickly and otherwise spend their free time watchful for problems. They tend to be concentrated at places and times where the workload (in terms of calls for service) is concentrated (Bieck et al., 1991: 88). Even within the geographic areas or "beats" to which they are assigned, patrol officers tend to focus on the people and places believed most likely to cause and experience problems. A study of Minneapolis found that half of all dispatched calls went to about 3 percent of all addresses and intersections (Sherman et al., 1989: 37). Although it is widely accepted that municipal services, including police, were distributed according to political favoritism during the time of urban political machines, most studies of the distribution of police services suggest that police operate now by a "bureaucratic" standard, concentrating services where the quantity and severity of crime and calls for service are greatest. The race and socioeconomic characteristics of neighborhoods are generally unrelated to levels of service delivery (Worden, 1984) although it may influence the *nature* of the service rendered (Smith, 1986).

WHO THE POLICE ARE

It has long been a tenet of reformers that an important way to influence the way policing is done is through the recruitment and selection of officers (Berman, 1987; Fogelson, 1977; Walker, 1977). For most of its brief history, American policing has been dominated by white males who have modest (at least by professional standards) amounts of formal education and training. Policing traditionally served as a source of employment for immigrants to America, whose involvement in machine politics yielded patronage jobs in the nineteenth century for waves of Irish, German, Italian, Polish, and other immigrant groups (Monkkonen, 1981; Fogelson, 1977). Certain ethnic and racial groups have not been as well represented relative to their presence in the population: Africans, Asians, and Hispanics. Recently, however, some of these groups have become a growing presence in American police departments, due to the implementation of affirmative action standards, employment discrimination litigation, growing minority-group political power in large cities, and supportive administrative leadership (Potts, 1983; Walker, 1985). The proportion of police who are black rose from less than 4 percent in the mid-1960s to about 13 percent by the late 1980s (Walker, 1989: 246). A 1990 national sample survey of local police departments shows that 17 percent of the force was black, Hispanic, or other minority group, and nearly as large a proportion of county sheriffs were also minority (Flanagan and Maguire, 1992: 41). Although the number of minority officers has risen rapidly, they are still underrepresented in most of the nation's largest cities when compared to the number of minority residents in those cities (Walker, 1989).

Women are even more underrepresented on America's police forces although their number is growing. In 1976, the FBI reported that 2.4 percent of sworn officers were female; by 1991, they had grown to 9 percent (FBI, 1977, 1992). Policewomen were traditionally assigned to specialist and administrative duties, but by 1979 they were almost as likely as policemen to receive a general patrol assignment, a trend that appears to be continuing (Martin, 1988).

Very few local police departments require a college education to enter the force or advance (Bureau of Justice Statistics, 1992b), but most recognize college education as an important element in promotion decisions (Carter et al., 1989). One survey of police departments shows that the average educational level of police has increased from 12.4 years in 1967 to 13.6 years in 1988 (Carter et al., 1988). *Some* college education is now common to a large majority of officers although relatively few have acquired four-year degrees (Carter and Sapp, 1991: 8–11).

Training in police work has been a growth industry in recent decades. Since 1967, most states have mandated minimum entry-level training standards, and many departments require much higher levels (Ostrom et al., 1978). The amount of entry-level training varies considerably, the smallest departments averaging about 400 hours and the largest (those serving populations of more than one million) averaging over 1,200 (Bureau of Justice Statistics, 1992a: 6). The amount of specialized training required of police is, of course, substantially less than that required for physicians, lawyers, and teachers, but the current trend toward more formal training and education for police is clear. This aspect of professionalization has long been a key element of police reform and promises to continue to serve as a means of enhancing the professional status of the occupation (Berman, 1987; Carter et al., 1988; Fogelson, 1977; Walker, 1977).

Despite the clear progress in professionalism, policing in America remains an occupation by which its members enter untrained and then advance through the *organization* (Reiss, 1992: 55). Unlike other professions, access to higher ranks within the occupation is not available to those who receive special education and training outside the job (for example, the military officer corps and physicians). Lateral transfers from one police organization to another are still relatively infrequent. Policing is done mostly by people who enter a given force and remain on that force for all or most of their career.

HOW POLICE ARE ORGANIZED

Today, American police remain predominantly creatures of local government. Of the estimated 16,961 state and local law enforcement agencies operating in the United States in 1990, 12,288 were general-purpose local police departments, all but 1 percent of these being municipal. An additional 3,093 were county sheriffs' departments. Although America's municipal police are disproportionately concentrated in large departments serving large cities (about half serve in cities with 100,000 or more residents, and nearly three-fourths serve in cities with populations of 25,000 or more), small departments serving small cities account for the vast majority of municipal agencies (76 percent of the *agencies* serve communities with populations below 10,000 — accounting for only 15 percent of the nation's municipal sworn force) (Reaves, 1992b, 1992c). The structure of American policing remains localized, decentralized, and fragmented (Geller and Morris, 1992; Reiss, 1992: 61–68) although this arrangement may not be as inefficient as many claim (Ostrom et al., 1978).

Police agencies today, especially those that employ the vast majority of officers, are organized bureaucratically. Since the late nineteenth century, American police forces engaged in bureaucratization (Reiss, 1992: 69). Some of the key bureaucratic features of police organizations include hierarchical differentiation (a multilevel formal rank structure from police officer to chief), functional differentiation (job specialties, such as patrol, criminal investigations, communications, training), routinization of procedures and practices that are formalized (written), and centralization of command (ultimate authority rests at the top of the police hierarchy, and decisionmaking within the hierarchy is accountable up the chain of command, while being protected from outside influences).

An example of command centralization is found in the contemporary police communications system, which uses the telephone (to communicate with the public), two-way radio (to communicate with officers), and computer (to enter and retrieve information about the work demands and availability of officers to receive work assignments and to record what the officers did) (Manning, 1992b; Reiss, 1992). Police administrators can structure how officers are deployed and mobilized by establishing dispatch policies carried out by communications personnel. These policies state which kinds of citizen requests for assistance receive priority and outline procedures for assigning officers to respond. Further, the system controls radio communications among officers and enables management to monitor their location and activities. There are, of course, many ways in which the administrator's capacity for "command and control" through this system can be subverted (Manning, 1992a), but it has undeniably enabled a degree of centralized control that would be otherwise unavailable to highly dispersed, low-visibility workers (Reiss, 1993). Other organizational structures that emphasize top-down command and control include personnel systems (hiring, promotion, and discipline of employees), training, and records systems that document police activities.

Numerous forces circumscribe the effects of the bureaucratization of police forces (Manning, 1977; Reiss, 1992: 73–91). Perhaps most important is the desire of police to control, or at least manage, their work environment. Because so much police work requires determining in a short time whether there is a problem and what it is, most police work is infused with a high degree of uncertainty. This uncertainty requires that the organizational representative on scene be granted considerable leeway in determining what the problem is and what should be done about it. Rules and formal procedures to control police discretion, though important, are often cumbersome and counterproductive. Further, given the high dispersion and unpredictability of occasions for police intervention with the public, most police–citizen encounters occur with a low degree of visibility to the rest of the organization, and the officer himself or herself is the principal source of information on what occurred during that encounter. Police supervisors are rarely present at the scene of most encounters with the public, less than 5 percent in one observational study (Allen, 1982).

In addition to the task environment of everyday police work, there are a number of institutions, both formal and informal, intended to influence police practice, and these limit the capacity of the departmental hierarchy to shape police work (Reiss, 1992: 75–91). These include a number of institutions created throughout the history of American police to make them accountable to external authority: mayors and city managers, civil service boards, civilian review boards, police unions, prosecutors, the judiciary, labor relations boards, and a host of other state and federal regulatory agencies. Also included are groups that lobby or pressure police and others in government to shape what police do, for example, victim advocate groups, civil liberties groups, business associations, and neighborhood and civic associations. Although police departments have varied in their ability to withstand pressure from such forces, none has been completely buffered from them.

The creation of specialist job functions is one of the ways that organizations have attempted to become, or at least appear, more efficient and effective, and police agencies have followed this path. In general, the larger the department, the larger the proportion of the force that is given to specialist functions, such as criminal investigations, juvenile, communications, and forensics. However, even the largest police departments, which have the highest proportion of their force devoted to specialist functions, still rely on the generalist patrol officer as the "backbone of policing," typically devoting more officers to this than any other division (Ostrom et al., 1978: 319). These generalists not only constitute the largest group of police "practitioners," their work heavily influences the nature and quantity of work performed by most police specialists and has important implications for success or failure of those specialist units. Specialist crime investigators typically rely heavily on the information reported by the patrol officer who first responded to the scene of a crime, and their capacity to apprehend a suspect and construct successful prosecution is determined largely by the patrol officer's ability to find and interview witnesses on the scene and collect other evidence (Chaiken et al., 1977; Eck, 1983). The enduring commitment of most police officers to the generalist patrol assignment is particularly remarkable when compared to the marked decline in reliance on generalists in other occupations, such as medicine, the military, and education. This is undoubtedly due to the need of police to be flexible in dealing with a more unpredictable, or "turbulent," environment (for example, the threat of riots and other disasters large and small) (Reiss, 1993).

Despite the generalist orientation of police work, increased specialization is a clear trend in the twentieth century. This is especially so in the use of civilians in the organization. In just the period between 1971 and 1991, full-time city police employees who were civilians increased from 13 to 22 percent (FBI, 1972, 1992). In municipal departments with 100 or more officers, civilians are heavily concentrated in technical support functions (communications, crime analysis, maintenance), whereas sworn personnel are overwhelmingly concentrated in field operations (patrol, criminal investigations, juvenile, narcotics) (Reaves, 1992a). Further, "civilianization" has become a hallmark of progressive police reform and is associated with a variety of other contemporary trends, such as increased use of technology (especially information management) and research, planning, and development (Reiss, 1992).

HOW OFFICERS SPEND THEIR TIME

One of the enduring research findings about police work over the last quarter century is that most of the workload is minor disorders and requests for miscellaneous services; relatively little of their work focuses on criminal offenses, and very little of that focuses on felonies and offenses that capture newspaper headlines and television time (Greene and Klockars, 1991; Mastrofski, 1983; Whitaker et al., 1982). It is clear from time–budget studies of patrol behavior that officers undertake actions that visibly demonstrate their coercive powers much less frequently than entertainment media and news accounts imply. Very large portions of their workday are given to general patrol, administrative tasks, meals and breaks (47 percent according to one detailed task analysis study) (Greene and Klockars, 1991: 281). A recent observational study of patrol officers in a medium-sized municipal department showed that only 19 percent of the officers' work time was spent directly engaging citizens in work-related encounters; the remainder was spent on general patrol (24 percent), patrol focused at a particular offender, offense, or location (10 percent), travel enroute to a specific location (15 percent), administrative activities (18 percent), and personal breaks (14 percent) (Mastrofski and Snipes, 1993). Even studies of police who specialize in criminal investigation reveal that large portions of detectives' workdays are committed to administrative and legal-processing tasks, not the kind of "detective work" characterized in popular fiction, such as Kojak and Columbo. The most common forms of authority when police engage citizens are inquiry (in the form of questioning or searching), making a written report, lecturing, and rendering some form of assistance (most often, just providing information) (Bayley, 1986; Whitaker et al., 1982: 71).

Arrest or issuing a citation is the exception, not the rule. One study found that an arrest was made in only 8 percent of the recorded incidents where there was some indication of a criminal offense (Reiss, 1971: 74). Citations, by far the most frequent form of formally entering offenders into the legal process, occurred in only 35 percent of the traffic stops observed in another study (Whitaker et al., 1982: 71). Police use of physical force is very rare, and use of verbal threats to use force, though more frequent, are still uncommon (Mastrofski, 1983: 43). One must be careful not to overinterpret these data since studies of attorneys and physicians would probably reveal similar sorts of diffuse activity, only a small portion of which clearly reflects their "core" function. That police exercise the more dramatic aspects of their authority with relative infrequency does not diminish the importance of that authority.

POLICE DISCRETION AND ITS CONTROL

Until the 1960s, there was little scholarly interest in the exercise of police discretion, due to a widely held belief that police rarely exercised it, but rather were governed by the requirements of law and departmental regulations. However, some legal scholars then argued that the law itself often provided substantial leeway to the officers in deciding whether certain actions, such as arrest or search and seizure, were required or justified (Goldstein, 1960; LaFave, 1965; Davis, 1969). They noted that the occasions for invoking the law were typically low visibility to the public at large and even to most other police, thus providing a protective environment to foster discretion. Further, they noted many competing motivations that might incline an officer *not* to follow the requirements of the law, such as trading leniency for information when finding illicit narcotics on a suspect.

Several researchers also noted that police decisionmaking occurred within a subculture distinctly attributable to the occupation and that the effect of this subcultural influence was to deflect officers from the rule of law and make them resistant to governance by police administrators, as well as institutions outside the department (Brown, 1981; Manning, 1977, 1980; Reuss-Ianni, 1983; Rubinstein, 1973; Skolnick, 1966; Van Maanen, 1974; Westley, 1970). In his review of this body of research, Manning (1989) notes several recurring themes interwoven in the attitudes and beliefs that serve to manage the pressures of their work. One of these is that police work is infused with *uncertainty*; the events they are asked to manage are often not what they appear to be, and the consequences of their actions and those of others involved in these events are also unpredictable, ladened with the potential for danger or disorder. Second, and understandable in light of uncertainty is the theme of *mutual dependency* among officers—to deal with physical, emotional, and career threats from the department hierarchy, the public, and "watchdog" groups. A third theme is *autonomy* from the very sources of threat within and outside the department that make dependency so valued. That is, officers treasure independence in exercising judgment about when and how their authority is to be exercised. Finally, the theme of *authority* permeates the police perspective. Maintaining authority or control of events is seen as essential in the face of uncertainty.

Research on the police subculture has tended to look for commonalities among police, typically what accounts for widespread patterns of behavior. For example, the subcultural explanation was used to understand why police tended *not* to enforce the law or why citizens who showed insufficient deference to police authority were more likely to be sanctioned by police, regardless of the legal evidence. Another line of research, however, has focused on the *diversity* of behavior patterns *among* police. This was stimulated by Wilson's oft-cited research that distinguished styles of policing among *agencies:* watchman, legalistic, and service (1968). Several years later a number of scholars began to differentiate styles of policing exhibited by individual officers (Broderick, 1987; Muir, 1977; White, 1972).

EXPLAINING VARIETIES OF POLICE BEHAVIOR

Noting that the practice of policing varies among officers, and even from situation to situation, scholars have attempted to account for variance in police behavior. Most studies have concentrated on the use of arrest; a few have looked at the use of physical force; and very few have looked at other aspects of police discretion, such as more subtle forms of control, information gathering, or rendering assistance to victims.

Sociological Explanations

Sociological explanations rely on the features of the specific incident that afforded the police the opportunity to make an arrest. Such features include the characteristics and behaviors of the citizens involved (for example, their age, race, and sex), what they asked police to do, how they were related to each other, their degree of deference to police, other indicators of their governability (for example, sobriety), the nature of the presenting offense or problem, and the quality of available evidence. According to this perspective, these "situational" considerations signify to the officer the things that matter in deciding whether to arrest someone, and according to some, comply with general propositions about the impact of social status on legal outcomes (Black, 1980).

Among the most consistent of findings is that a suspect's failure to show deference to police substantially increases the likelihood of arrest, constituting in the officer's eyes, contempt for his or her authority. However, some recent research suggests that when the *illegality* of (some) contemptuous behavior (for example, assault on an officer) is taken into account, the effects of citizen demeanor toward the officer are greatly diminished (Klinger, 1993; Mastrofski et al., 1993). This suggests that, regardless of the officer's motivation for making the arrest, the effects are not "extralegal."

Other situational influences that show effects with some consistency are the preference of the victim, the seriousness of the offense, and the quality of the evidence. When a victim expresses a preference for arrest, the probability of an arrest increases substantially. Generally, the more serious the problem (for example, felony versus misdemeanor), the greater the likelihood of an arrest, although some research finds the effects conditional on the sex of the suspect (Visher, 1983) or the organizational culture of the police department

(Smith and Klein, 1983). The presence of injuries has little effect on arrest likelihood, and weapon use increases the risk of arrest in some cases, but not in others (Riksheim and Chermak, 1993). Finally, evidence quality, a basic indicator of the extent to which officer decisionmaking is governed by legal considerations, generally shows a positive influence on the probability of arrest. The victim's ability to identify a suspect, the rapidity of the crime report, whether the officer directly observed evidence of a crime, the availability of witnesses, corroborating evidence, the availability of a warrant, and other considerations have been shown to be relevant (Black, 1980; Riksheim and Chermak, 1993). In a recent study of patrol officers, the quality of evidence was the most powerful predictor of arrest (Mastrofski et al., 1993).

Findings are inconsistent across studies with regard to the characteristics of citizen–police encounters. The age, race, and sex of the suspect show significant effects in some analyses but little or none in others. For example, the suspect's race, one of the most frequently estimated effects, often fails to show significant influence once other situational factors are controlled (Riksheim and Chermak, 1993). Some studies have found a significant effect for suspect race (Smith and Visher, 1981) although it is conditional on the victim's presence and on the suspect being both black and female (Smith et al., 1984).

At this stage, it is hazardous to accept generalizations about the influence of most of the situational factors that capture greatest public interest, such as the suspect's race. Not only is it difficult to find a coherent pattern in the results of these studies, most of them fail to take into account the race of the victim or complainant, which arguably is more important in shaping the officer's perception of the need for arrest than the race of the suspect (Black, 1980) and has been found to be an important factor in other aspects of the criminal process, such as sentencing and imposition of the death penalty (Aguirre and Baker, 1990). Indeed, one study that took into account the impact of victim race found that the officer was significantly more likely to make an arrest if the victim was white (Smith et al., 1984). Another found no such effect, however (Mastrofski et al., 1993).

PSYCHOLOGICAL EXPLANATIONS

Psychological explanations rest on the assumption that officers develop predispositions to exercise their discretion in certain ways, that they vary among officers, and that they influence officers' behavior. These predispositions are believed to derive from a wide variety of sources: the officer's personal background (race, sex, socioeconomic status, education), formative experiences that shape personality, and the formal and informal socialization acquired as a police officer (training, nature and extent of exposure to the police subculture). These predispositions are variously measured as attitudes, beliefs, and perceptions, or as personal characteristics hypothesized to embody certain attitudes and proclivities. Psychological explanations are sometimes called "individual" explanations, for they represent the proposition that what matters most is what each officer carries with him or her.

Psychological explanations have considerable appeal to reformers and police themselves because they focus responsibility for corrective action on specific individuals, who presumably can be identified by their personalities and "orientations" as well as their behavior. This perspective makes relevant several kinds of correctives that currently enjoy favor among policymakers and reformers: altering recruitment and selection standards, training, counseling, and dismissal. Despite the theoretical elegance and appeal of several treatises that develop psychological typologies of police (Broderick, 1987; Brown, 1981; Muir, 1977; White, 1972), there is little systematic support for the proposition that officers possess workstyle predispositions that generate predictable behavior patterns. Officer attitudes, beliefs, and perceptions show weak to nonexistent effects on arrest behavior (Riksheim and Chermak, 1991; Worden, 1992).

Personal characteristics, on which there has been more research, have demonstrated mixed effects. Studies of officer education indicate no influence on arrest behavior. A few studies indicate that male officers are more proactive and arrest-prone than female officers although most studies find differences between the sexes to be inconsequential. However, most of these are poorly designed to detect sex-related differences of greatest theoretical and practical interest (Mastrofski, 1990). Only a few studies rigorously explore behavioral differences that might be attributable to the officer's race. One study found that black officers are more aggressive on patrol, more arrest-prone, and more likely to adopt a "neutral" demeanor toward citizens (Friedrich, 1977). However, other studies have failed to find a significant officer race impact on the resort to arrest (Mastrofski et al., 1993; Smith and Klein, 1983; Worden, 1989). This absence of individual officer effects has also been found in analyses of officers' use of force, whether deemed "reasonable" or "improper" (Worden, 1992).

Psychological models have not yet shown much power in explaining police behavior, particularly when their effects are compared to those of situational factors. However, most of these studies employed psychological measures that were unable to capture many aspects of officer predisposition that are theoretically most relevant to the behavior in question. One recent study of drunk-driving arrest productivity attempts to rectify this problem by drawing on a set of personal and organization-based motivational factors bearing direct relevance to drunk-driving enforcement. It finds substantial individual-level influence on officer arrest productivity (Mastrofski et al., 1994).

ORGANIZATIONAL EXPLANATIONS

Some studies concentrate on the characteristics of police organizations and their environments to account for variation in the exercise of officer discretion. Most research of this sort focuses on those features of the organization that ostensibly serve to control discretion: policies, rules, and structures. Wilson's (1968) study of eight police departments is probably the most influential. Wilson argued that the degree of bureaucratization (for example, formality of rules and records, differentiation of job assignments, and centralization of rulemaking authority) and professionalism (for example, education and training) in a department shape the patterns of arrest practice. The police leadership plays the central role in shaping these organizational characteristics over time so that the choice of that leadership is critical in determining the style of policing practiced in a community. Wilson presented data in support of the thesis that the type of chief selected is influenced by the type of selection process employed, which is itself a product of local politics and the "political culture," the set of widely held expectations within a community as to "how issues will be raised, governmental objectives determined, and power for their attainment assembled" (p. 233). For example, reformed, "good government" cities were predicted to select chiefs who would develop bureaucratic and professional structures, leading to a "legalistic" style of policing (high arrest rates for a wide range of offenses), whereas old-style, "unreformed" cities would be inclined to select chiefs who were less bureaucratic and professionally minded, thus producing a "watchman" pattern of arrests (lower for many minor offenses and dependent on the offender's race).

Wilson and a number of others have confirmed organizational effects by looking at variations in arrest and use of force patterns aggregated to the *department* level (Crank, 1990; Gardiner, 1969; Langworthy, 1985; Mastrofski, 1981; Slovak, 1986; Wilson and Boland, 1978). These studies find weak-to-moderate relationships between a variety of organizational characteristics (department size, bureaucratization, political and demographic environment) and arrest rates. Generally, larger, more bureaucratized agencies have higher arrest rates (but see Mastrofski et al., 1987). Other studies have focused on specific department policies and, especially in the area of use of lethal force, have found that restrictive policies and intensive review practices have been associated with lower rates of police discharge of firearms at citizens (Fyfe, 1988).

Relatively few studies have explored the impact of organizational characteristics on the behavior of *individual* officers, especially on an encounter-by-encounter basis. Such studies are particularly valuable, for they permit a comparison of the effects of organizational factors with situational and individual-level variables. These studies tend to confirm that situational characteristics account for most of the explanatory power of the statistical models. However, many also find significant organizational effects. For example, Friedrich (1980) found that whether a department's organizational ethos is traditional, professional, or transitional has an effect on the proclivity of officers to use force. Smith and Klein (1984) found that the propensity to arrest in domestic disputes was significantly greater for officers in departments that scored high on both bureaucratization and professionalism. They also found that the impact of some situational factors depended on these two organizational factors, implying that different types of organizations do in fact propagate different decision algorithms for street-level officers (Smith and Klein, 1983). However, one study of situational and attitudinal explanations of various police behaviors (initiating traffic and suspect stops, and the disposition of traffic stops and disputes) found that adding the police chief's priorities as an organizational feature to the model made little difference in officers' behavior (Worden, 1989: 703).

Despite the widespread finding of police ethnographers that the informal police subculture dominates the everyday perspective of the officer, few studies attempting to explain different patterns of discretion have explored the unofficial, or informal, aspects of the police organization. In his review of the literature, Worden (1992) observes that many scholars have emphasized the importance of the informal peer socialization process, but very few have attempted to distinguish ways in which this process can vary within and between police departments. Some studies have suggested that the size of the department influences the nature and strength of the effects of peer pressure to conform street-level practice to informal expectations (Brown, 1981; Mastrofski et al., 1987), but the results are not entirely consistent. One case study of a large urban department indicates that informal pressures from the rank and file can subvert top management's efforts to control the drunk-driving arrest rate (Mastrofski and Ritti, 1992). Different perspectives on drunk-driving enforcement seem to flourish among various cliques, even within the same agency, and that these produce distinctly different arrest patterns between the high-arrest "rate-busters" and the typical officers (Mastrofski et al., 1994).

CONTROLLING DISCRETION

Although research over the last thirty years has emphasized the considerable discretion enjoyed by low-ranking police officers, administrators and reformers have grown even more concerned about how to control it. A wide range of strategies have been proposed and employed to control or at least influence how officers exercise their discretion. Most fall into one or more of four categories: (1) external legal institutions, (2) rulemaking and internal methods controlled by police administrators, (3) professional governance, and (4) arrangements with the private sector.

THE RULE OF LAW

In America, much homage is paid to the notion of a government of laws, not of men and women. Indeed, one of the fundamental features of American government is the check-and-balance system between the various branches: the executive (of which the police are a part), the legislative (which at the state level determines the criminal code and at the local level sets the budget), and the judiciary (which considers the facts, interprets the law, and reviews police actions). In the late nineteenth and much of the twentieth century, it was the fervent hope of many reformers that the police could be more closely and effectively governed by laws passed by legislatures and later by procedural standards set by appellate courts and enforced by lower courts. The "due process" revolution of the Warren Court created tremendous interest among jurists, prosecutors, defense attorneys, and legal scholars about what standards *should* apply to police, resulting in a large increase in appellate cases on matters such as the appropriate basis for making an arrest, stopping and searching a citizen, methods of interrogation, and use of deceptive investigation methods. In the 1980s, as political sentiment shifted, greater interest was shown in shaping police discretion by making changes to the criminal code. Some offenses (public intoxication, mental illness) were decriminalized, removing arrest as a legitimate option (Aarronsen et al., 1984; Murphy, 1986; Teplin, 1986). New offenses were created or made more serious (a variety of actions associated with drugs, spousal rape, various forms of child abuse), and in some cases, the legal basis for police discretion was eliminated (drunk driving, domestic violence).

How effectively have the courts, legislatures, and other legal institutions controlled the police? The answer depends largely on one's expectations. If one adheres to the unrealistic, but still common supposition that police will be *absolutely* governed by these legal institutions, then a great deal of social science clearly indicates that they have failed (Klockars, 1985: ch. 5). First, most laws, even so-called "mandatory arrest" laws, still leave considerable discretionary leeway for officers. For example, new laws mandate that police must make an arrest when evidence is available indicating that a misdemeanor domestic assault has occurred, but the officer must still make judgments about whether the "facts" of the case meet the legal standards, and there is still room for debate about where to draw the lines (Sherman, 1992b). Most offenses observed by and reported to police are misdemeanors, and in many of these cases, the statutes themselves do not require an arrest but simply empower the officer to make an arrest.

Second, and more important, the law fails even to recognize most of the discretionary choices open to police, and therefore provides no guidance on what to do when an arrest cannot be made. For example, suppose an officer is dispatched to respond to a domestic dispute complaint and makes a careful determination that although the parties are engaged in a heated dispute, no law has been violated. Therefore, the officer is legally obliged not to make an arrest. But what is the officer to do as an alternative? Warn or threaten one or both parties that they *could* be arrested if things get out of hand in the future? Order or encourage one of the parties to leave the premises? Try to arbitrate, mediate, or otherwise conciliate the disputants? Encourage the parties to seek family counseling or legal advice? Ask other family members or neighbors to intercede in the matter? Or should the officer just inform all parties that there has been no violation of the law and then depart, risking that the dispute will escalate sometime in the future to more severe consequences? The laws of most states are silent regarding which of these responses is appropriate under what circumstances. Further, whether the officer's actions satisfied legal criteria is seldom the most appropriate question to ask if one seeks a standard that goes beyond "legal minimalism." The standards of the *craft* of policing are often considerably higher than those imposed by the law (Bittner, 1983).

Recent observational studies suggest that, in general, patrol officers make arrests in something like 15 to 20 percent of the nontraffic incidents where a suspect is present (Mastrofski et al., 1993), but the law is virtually mute about what to do with the many cases that simply do not meet the legal standards for an arrest. Some contemporary reformers suggest that criminal laws might be adjusted to cover a wider range of police options or that police could become more involved in using and adapting civil laws to deal with certain kinds of disorderly behavior (Goldstein, 1990), but even these enlargements of the legal penumbra could not conceivably cover the range of police discretionary options in a way that would make most police officers and citizens comfortable that the path to fair and effective policing could be specified *a priori* by lawmakers (Klockars, 1985: 113).

It is particularly important to note how limited are the legal mechanisms for overseeing police compliance with even the narrow range of substantive and procedural criminal law that some believe constitutes the bulwarks of discretion control. The courts are thought to serve a central function in this regard, yet they can review the actions of police only when they are brought before them. With the exception of the rare internal affairs investigation or special blue ribbon study, the street-level police officers themselves play the most important role in determining which of their actions come to the court's attention. Officers who conduct an illegal search or drug seizure run a very low risk that their actions will be reviewed by the courts, unless an officer files charges against an offender. And if an officer does file charges, the closest review the case will receive will be by the supervisor on duty, who often has a vested interest in protecting subordinates from censure or other discipline, often viewed as arbitrary and out of proportion to the seriousness of the officer's error or offense (Van Maanen, 1983). Further, cases with major police procedural errors that make it past the supervisor are usually screened out in the prosecutor's office or taken into account in plea bargaining. They rarely become an issue before the judge, and when they do, it is even rarer that they cause the case to be lost because the exclusionary rule was successfully invoked (Davies, 1983; National Institute of Justice, 1982; Oaks, 1970), and rarer still that those in the chain of command down to the street officer suffer any direct consequence in terms of discipline or corrective action because "constable blundered."

We must be particularly careful not to understate the extent of effects that legal institutions may exert *indirectly*. Over time, police may become more or less inclined to know and be guided by the law in their street-level decisions. Early studies of officers' reactions to changes in procedural law about interrogation indicated that Supreme Court rulings appeared to have little impact on how officers behaved (Medalie et al., 1968; Milner, 1971; Wald et al., 1967). This may have been due in part to ignorance of the new rulings or misperception of what the Court required, but there is also reason to think that over a long time police interrogation practices have changed at least in part because police recruitment, training, and supervision changed in response to Court rulings (Orfield, 1987), thus altering subcultural norms about what is and is not acceptable interrogation practice. Some have suggested that this has resulted only in a switch from routine application of the highly coercive "third degree" to more subtle, but nefarious, psychological techniques that rely on deception and isolation of the defendant (Leo, 1992). Nonetheless, the courts have played an important role in encouraging even this shift, giving far more latitude for these methods in criminal investigations than the application of force (Klockars, 1984).

Legislative changes to the criminal code also show evidence of influencing police street-level practices. For example, the decriminalization of public drunkenness in the late 1960s and early 1970s produced a marked decline in arrests (Aarronsen et al., 1984), and conversely, the get-tough-on-drunk-drivers reform wave in the early 1980s that mandated arresting offenders was followed by a substantial increase in the rate of DUI arrests (Greenfield, 1988). And although it is harder to obtain reliable figures, it is estimated that the widespread shift to mandatory arrest for misdemeanor domestic violence also precipitated a substantial increase in the arrest rate for these cases (Sherman, 1992b: 109). Detailed studies of street-level officers repeatedly show, however, that police discretion may be affected, but not eliminated by legislative mandate, and officers can respond very differently (Aarronsen et al., 1984; Buzawa, 1982; Mastrofski and Ritti, 1992; Mastrofski et al., 1994; Teplin, 1986).

Another avenue of legal influence is filing civil suits for monetary damages and injunctions against the police officer and his or her department. Since the 1970s, changes in case law (especially in the area of federal civil rights) have increased the potential for plaintiffs to receive substantial financial payments from state and local governments for wrongful and negligent performance by police (McCoy, 1984). It does appear that more civil suits are being filed (Mastrofski, 1990: 47), and a few awards against municipalities have exceeded a million dollars, receiving great attention (Skolnick and Fyfe, 1993: 202). There is little systematic analysis available, but one study based on insurance records does suggest that the risks of paying awards over $10,000 are quite small (McCoy, 1987). Ironically, police apprehension about these risks based on sensational news stories may far exceed the reality. The nature and extent of this trend's impact on street-level practices may be profound but remains empirically unexplored.

Another legal mechanism designed to deal with abuse of police powers is the "civilian review board." This is a special agency fully or partially comprised of nonpolice who have oversight responsibility for reviewing complaints against police officers. Civilian review boards vary in their structure and power to investigate complaints and make recommendations about their disposition (Kerstetter, 1985; Muir and Perez, 1992). In many cases, nonlawyers and laypersons serve on the board. However, all boards are governed by rules that set forth criteria for reviewing cases and stipulate procedural rights of officers who are accused of wrongdoing. Although these boards are often characterized as "community" rather than legal institutions, they are clearly expected to apply laws and rules and to be bound by them in their deliberations. The impact of civilian review on police practice — as opposed to the alternative of review performed entirely *within* the police department — has not been submitted to rigorous empirical inquiry. However, one impressionistic, comparative analysis of several types of review systems concluded that purely internal review systems are more effective in shaping street-level police behavior than those involving external civilian review (Muir and Perez, 1992).

RULEMAKING BY POLICE ADMINISTRATORS

Recognizing the limits of legal institutions for governing police discretion, many reformers since the 1960s have advocated "administrative rulemaking" (Walker, 1986: 365). The police executive is expected to see that rules and guidelines are issued that *regulate*, as well as define the limits of police discretion (Davis, 1969). Because criminal laws typically employ broad, general terms, advocates of administrative rulemaking argue that police executives need to see that written departmental guidelines are created to channel discretion in ways that further the law's intent and that are practicable from the officer's point of view. For example, a department might issue a series of guidelines about when to issue a citation or make an arrest when dealing with a type of situation that is very ambiguous, a noise disturbance. Such a guideline might indicate that the officer should take into account the amount of noise, the time of day, the ambient noise typical for that location at that time, the number of people disturbed by the noise, and the prior record of the offender. Or, considering a more serious situation, the department might even specify in some detail the circumstances under which an officer is and is not permitted to use lethal force and then set forth a detailed process for reviewing officers' decisions to resort to such force. Administrative rulemaking such as this is the central feature of the police agency accreditation movement, which was institutionalized in a national organization in the late 1970s (Mastrofski, 1986) and has been advocated by a variety of scholars and blue-ribbon commissions (Goldstein, 1977; Schmidt, 1974; Walker, 1986).

Despite the popularity of administrative rulemaking among contemporary progressive reformers, skepticism and caution have also been expressed (Aarronsen et al., 1984; Klockars, 1985: 112; Mastrofski, 1986: 62; Walker, 1992: 215). Being more forthright about the nature and extent of police discretion and more explicit about their own policies will make it more difficult for police executives to take refuge in the "law" on controversial issues. It is not at all clear that rules can be written that are sufficiently precise to cover the particulars of a given situation and sufficiently numerous to cover the variety of situations — and still be comprehensible and useful to an officer in the field attempting to make decisions with limited time and information. Rules and guidelines also are easily dodged and reports distorted; it is difficult to verify the nature of the circumstances and the particulars of police action without relying heavily on those whose very actions are under review.

Finally, rules and guidelines, as with laws, serve to provide a moral lamp unto the officer's feet, but if they are to be effective according to the logic of the reformers, they must also be linked to consequences that the officer cares about. This requires an effective system of internal accountability, which in American police departments tends to rely heavily on supervision and record keeping (Reiss, 1993). Routine supervision is the responsibility of the line supervisor, but observational studies show that those who have supervisory responsibilities have or take limited opportunities to observe the work of their subordinates directly (Allen, 1982; Manning, 1980), and they are often more sympathetic to the concerns of the street-level officer than the administrators whose rules they are supposed to apply (Van Maanen, 1983, 1984). Consequently, much of the capacity to hold officers accountable for their behavior relies on records of that behavior that they themselves create and can manipulate to serve their ends (Chatterton, 1983).

Independent verification of those records (through follow-up interviews with citizen-participants, for example) is quite rare (Reiss, 1993). When independent follow-up inquiry does occur, it is usually through the department's internal affairs unit. These units do engage in proactive investigations of police misbehavior, but the most common investigation is a reaction to a citizen's complaint (Reiss, 1971; Sherman, 1974). There is little rigorous evidence on the impact of internal affairs units on police behavior. Some have argued that they are most effective when the police chief ensures that investigations are rigorous and that substantiated allegations of misconduct result in meaningful discipline (Goldstein, 1977). However, even with the special resources available to internal affairs units, establishing the facts is often problematic, boiling down to contradictory testimony between the complaining citizen and the accused officer. Many cases are dismissed because there is no independent corroborating evidence, and other officers, who make the most compelling witnesses, are unwilling or unable to offer it. Finally, internal affairs units concentrate exclusively on identifying misbehavior and bad performance; their punitiveness epitomizes much of the entire internal system of police accountability in concentrating on punishable actions, virtually ignoring competent or exemplary performance. Police organizations are by no means unique in this regard, but their focus on the negative makes it difficult to use positive incentives to structure police behavior.

In addition to an effective compliance monitoring system, effective governance by administrative rulemaking requires a system of incentives and disincentives that can be offered and withheld with some degree of certainty. This kind of power is rarely available to contemporary police administrators. Indeed, substantial fragmentation of policy-making power among a number of formal and informal governing bodies inside and outside the department is far more characteristic (Reiss, 1992: 87). Unions, civil service boards, courts and regulatory agencies, local elected and appointed officials, civilian review and advisory boards—all these and others make illusory the notion of a hierarchical, rule-bound infrastructure with the police chief in command at the top.

Relatively few studies of the impact of administrative rulemaking on police discretion have been conducted. Some researchers have found that restrictive use deadly force policies have been followed by substantial reductions in the level of deadly force (Fyfe, 1979, 1988; Sherman, 1983). Research on rulemaking in handling public drunks and making pornography arrests appears to have produced mixed results (Aarronsen et al., 1984: 408–436), and case studies of the implementation of domestic violence arrest policies at three sites suggest that effects of rulemaking can be quite variable (Sherman, 1992b: 112). Finally, rulemaking on criminal investigations procedures had little impact on police compliance with evidence-gathering standards (Krantz et al., 1979).

Although the evidence is impressionistic, it has been suggested that rulemaking is most likely to be effective for behaviors that have high visibility or are easily monitored (Walker, 1992: 216) and when police leaders can use external pressure generated by crises to alter old practices (Sherman, 1983; Skolnick and Fyfe, 1993: 185). It has also been suggested that rule compliance is greater when the police "clientele" knows what the rules require of police and are therefore in a position to point out to the officer when he or she is not conforming (Walker, 1993: 49). The threat of a report to higher authority, particularly when the citizen knows an accessible procedure to file such a grievance—with the prospect that it will be taken seriously—is thought to provide additional reasons for compliance. The extent to which these conditions can be met, especially for the disadvantaged segments of society, remains to be demonstrated. Finally, it might be observed that rules are most likely to be obeyed when they meet the personal needs of the officers, such as reducing ambiguity about how the department will react to a given action (Brown, 1981), whether it will involve less "hassle" (Mastrofski et al., 1994), and whether it is seen to produce desired results (Bayley and Bittner, 1984).

PROFESSIONAL GOVERNANCE

A third system for governing police discretion is police professionalism, which requires that (1) police officers pursue broad societal or client-based interests, not their own; (2) they identify standards of performance based on a special, technically sophisticated body of knowledge that is empirically validated and documented; (3) they be thoroughly educated in achieving these standards; (4) they be given the leeway to exercise their judgment as their professional knowledge and skills dictate; and that (5) other police professionals serve as the principal reviewers of their performance. These features (public-spirited, access to special knowledge and technology, rigorous education and training, discretion, and autonomy from external review) are the classic characteristics of what some call the "true" professions: medicine, law, education (Klockars, 1985: 108; Walker, 1992: 209).

Of all the systems of discretion control, professionalism is the least developed for police. Of the five criteria listed, the police have a secure grasp only on the first, something that was acquired as much by the pursuit of bureaucratic and legalistic objectives as professional ones. Policing as practiced daily is presently most accurately characterized as craft-based (Wilson, 1968: 283). That is, its practitioners obtain their most critical skills on the job—either from others more experienced or by trial and error. The ethnographies described earlier show that very little of what police learn in their formal education and special training is used on the street. Despite the profusion of criminological research in the last three decades, the term *police science* is more wish than fact, and this limits the capacity of police to become true professionals. Most of the research on police effectiveness has, if anything, demolished long-held views about once-cherished police tactics and strategies that presumably deterred crime, apprehended offenders, and solved cases. Although the amount of research that can document what works and what does not is increasing, it is painstakingly slow, even in so narrow a domain as the benefits of arrest in domestic disputes, where more resources have been committed to rigorous, experimental evaluation than any other (Sherman, 1992b: 267).

As mentioned earlier, the amount of education and training that police receive has been growing considerably in recent decades, due in no small part to professionalization efforts. The quality of this training is also undoubtedly improving, and its relevance to and impact on everyday practice may be increasing although there is really insufficient evidence to know at this point (Mastrofski, 1990: 15). At present, it may be doing more to bolster the image of police as professional than reinforcing the reality.

Police professionalism has made the least progress in the fourth and fifth requirements. The rhetoric that has long suffused police "professionalization" movements in America belies the real nature of that movement's thrust: bureaucratization (Klockars, 1988; Reiss, 1992). Indeed, what the legalistic and militaristic reformers most valued, and what they called "professionalism" was officer adherence to the law and the edicts that wended their way down the department hierarchy. This is precisely the opposite of what true professionalism demands, which is the freedom to exercise one's professional judgment as the circumstances and one's knowledge dictate. Police officers enjoy considerable discretionary leeway in reality, but it is neither embraced nor supported by professional standards; it simply exists and is quietly ignored until an officer does something that draws publicity. Finally, there are very few mechanisms for police practitioners to govern discretion by reviewing each other's performance, such as boards of physicians, educators, attorneys, accountants, and engineers use either to certify competence or review malpractice complaints. To the extent that such reviews take place, they occur either within the department hierarchy (a bureaucratic phenomenon), the courts, or on rare occasion, a civilian review board with authority to review evidence.

Although true professional status seems beyond the reach of most police in the foreseeable future, it has, if anything, become an even more important part of the contemporary police progressive's agenda. Bittner (1970) articulated a vision of professionalism, and others have subsequently offered blueprints on how it might be achieved (Bayley and Bittner, 1984; Goldstein, 1977, 1990; Sparrow et al., 1990). At least one state has introduced a peer-review process to revoke or suspend a police officer's license to practice policing (Skolnick and Fyfe, 1993: 197). Finally, police themselves seem to be warming to the idea of a professionalism based on systematic scientific research (Cordner et al., 1991; Klockars and Harver, 1993).

PRIVATE CONTRACTUAL ARRANGEMENTS

One way to influence the discretion of the public police is to exclude them from some situations altogether by hiring a private security force (which may or may not have the peace officer's power of arrest and the right to bear firearms). By entering into a contractual arrangement, the purchaser of services is able to focus the provider's energies on particular problems, offenses, or offenders, and may be able to influence how those problems are handled. The principal mechanism of control is the incentive of continuing the financial arrangement. For example, hiring private security for shopping malls, universities, and housing developments may effectively turn over most of the routine police functions in those "mass private spaces" to the *employees* of those very establishments (Shearing and Stenning, 1983). It is conceivable that a police force would be more inclined to enforce the liquor consumption laws at university sporting events in a manner desired by the university if the police officers in fact received their pay check from that university rather than the city in which it is located. Given that private security employment far exceeds that of public police in America (Cunningham and Taylor, 1985), several analysts have suggested that the public police are being displaced by private agencies in providing a host of order maintenance and crime control services. There is also considerable concern about the extent to which private interests are served at the expense of broader public interests (Shearing and Stenning, 1987; Sherman, 1986; Sparrow et al., 1990: 48).

Another form of contractual arrangement is between a private employer and public police. The purchase of off-duty public police services appears to have grown rapidly in recent years, and as with contracting with private agencies, there is concern about potential conflicts of interest between public and private duties (Reiss, 1988). Public and private interests are often the same, whether the policing occurs in public or private space (Reiss, 1987), and there are legal limits to the kinds of contractual work that public police may do. Further, there is reason to wonder just how much hierarchical control of *any* kind is exerted when police work in the private sector in an off-duty capacity (Reiss, 1988: 5). Who is legally liable for off-duty officers in a contract status is rather a different question from the nature and extent of control actually exerted under these arrangements. Supervision is characteristically *not* performed by the police department, and misconduct on off-duty jobs is seldom handled by the police department's internal affairs division.

Of the four systems of discretion control reviewed, the least is known about this one. For example, there has been no systematic research on the influence of the "brokers" who arrange contracts between public police officers and private employers (for example, unions, department administrators, or police officers and their agents). Where such private employment accounts for a substantial portion of an officer's income, it is conceivable that this special relationship could even influence the way the officer acts while on regular duty.

TRENDS IN DISCRETION CONTROL

Presently, police officers are subjected to all or most of these systems of control to some degree. It is often difficult to assess the separate impact of these forces on officer discretion because in addition to the external, readily observable processes by which they might influence police, they may be internalized, changing officers' values, premises, and ways of perceiving problems. Further, they will not necessarily present police with conflicting objectives; they may, in fact, reinforce each other. For example, administrative rulemaking is often presented as a way to *extend* the influence of the law, and professional education and training curricula are heavily ladened with legal topics. Finally, all of these systems of control are themselves products of larger, diffuse social forces that influence a society's cultural orientations and ways of defining and solving problems. It is difficult to know how much a new law changes the habits of society generally and how much the law is a symptom of broader social changes.

Walker (1993) argues that the *idea* of legal control of police (especially through the courts) reached its apogee in the 1960s and that within a decade reformers had achieved a new consensus that administrative rulemaking was the preferred mechanism of discretion control. He also suggests that professionalism has failed to play a strong part in everyday policing because broader social currents in America continue to run in the direction of increased rulemaking and bureaucratization, even for the profession with the highest status, medicine. And periodic scandals and critical incidents, such as the Rodney King affair, make it difficult for professionalism's advocates to rely more heavily on the standard professional nostrums (recruit screening, training, and peer review) for control of the worst abuses. This view of administrative rulemaking as the dominant control paradigm today more accurately reflects the intentions of reformers; it is not at all clear that this form of rational administration has actually permeated police practice to a great extent (Manning, 1977; Mastrofski et al., 1987).

One of the trends that may well influence the development and interplay of various formal control systems is the rapid growth of communications and computerized information technology. Just as the telephone and radio increased the department hierarchy's capacity for centralized monitoring of street-level officers in the second quarter of the twentieth century, developing technologies may further enhance or complicate management's ability to review and even intervene in officer decisionmaking on the street (Reiss, 1992: 82). Videotaping traffic stops has been advocated as a way to determine after the fact whether an officer's actions met legal standards (Skolnick and Fyfe, 1993). It takes little imagination to go a step further and suppose that police will soon be able to transmit video and audio information live from the scene to headquarters via portable instruments worn by the officers. The extent to which such technological innovations enhance administrators' discretion control remains to be seen (Manning, 1992a).

IN SEARCH OF POLICE LEGITIMACY AND SUPPORT

In the previous section, the focus was the individual officer. However, it is also important to understand policing at a broader, more abstract level. This section looks at an *organizational* rather than individual level. It focuses on the structures and practices in which American police organizations engage to sustain legitimacy and thus accrue support for their continued existence and authority.

SUPPORT FOR POLICE AGENCIES: HOW ARE THEY DOING?

Like all public agencies, police departments are not self-sustaining but rely heavily on their environment to continue and flourish. The support that police departments seek can take a variety of forms. The most obvious is financial: the resources derived from taxes, fines, seizures, fees, grants, and other revenues that pay for the people and material of the department. Support can also be expressed in other, "political" ways: votes for policies and programs important to the organization, such as the effort by some departments to get voters and their elected leaders to pass gun control legislation. Or support for police can be expressed in terms of trust and autonomy granted. For example, to the extent that police departments are able to review and discipline allegations of police misconduct without interference from courts and civilian review boards, they enjoy a substantial degree of autonomy for self-governance. Support for police departments can also take the mundane form of participation or at least acquiescence in some police-sponsored activity. This could be citizens participating in a crime watch group, placing a call to the police to report a crime, or testifying in court. It could even take the form of doing as police command, such as complying with a curfew or ensuring that one's children do.

By most convenient indicators, local police departments have done remarkably well in obtaining support in the last half century. Between 1938 and 1982, police per capita expenditures in America's larger cities quadrupled, adjusting for inflation. Much of this increase, especially in the 1960s and early 1970s, was due to substantial gains in officers' pay and benefits, reflecting in part the growing power of unions but also the enhanced status of the occupation (Fogelson, 1977). The number of sworn officers per capita in these departments increased considerably after World War II until 1973, and has remained fairly stable since then, while civilian employment has continued to grow.

In recent decades, public opinion surveyors have monitored support for police. The pattern of responses shows remarkable stability; positive assessments of the job local police are doing fluctuate within a few points of the 60 percent level since 1967 (Flanagan et al., 1982: 196; Flanagan and Maguire, 1992: 178) although black respondents are consistently less likely to offer positive assessments than white respondents (Albrecht and Green, 1977). When the question is asked somewhat differently, the level of support is even higher. In 1965, 70 percent of a national sample said they had "a great deal of respect" for their police; it rose to 77 percent in 1967, but dropped to 60 percent in the immediate aftermath of the Rodney King incident in 1991 (Flanagan and Maguire, 1992: 179).

What one can infer about public support for police from surveys is hard to say. Even when public opinion takes a precipitous dive, it is exceedingly rare for the department to be disbanded although consolidations sometimes occur in smaller agencies (Mastrofski, 1989). When Americans are unhappy with their police department, they tend to blame it on the top leadership, forcing out the old regime and bringing in a new chief. This accounts for the fairly short tenure of most police executives, especially in larger departments. The forced retirement of former Los Angeles police chief Daryl Gates in the aftermath of the Rodney King incident and the subsequent riot is a dramatic example of what has been termed a ritual of "moral degradation" (Crank and Langworthy, 1992). The commission that criticized Gates's handling of the riot also recommended that more resources be committed to prevent and respond to future civil unrest (Webster and Williams, 1992). The department endures but is exorcised of the leader who is blamed for the crisis.

Short of being replaced, police administrators under fire face the prospect of having their department reorganized or losing control over something. Even during the height of negative publicity for American police in the late 1960s and early 1970s, the most drastic political movements opposed to existing arrangements called, not for abolition of the police, but merely reorganizing them by various methods of "community control" (Skolnick, 1971; Wilson, 1975). Much of the impetus for the current community policing movement can be seen as a response to or anticipation of negativity from the public that was perceived as widespread in the 1960s and early 1970s (Kelling and Moore, 1988; Manning, 1988).

People's opinion about police may be related to the nature of their direct contact with police or exposure to news stories. However, research does not provide a clear indication that these relationships are strong, and it is not entirely clear what the direction of influence is (Surette, 1992; Brandl et al., 1993). A person's general predisposition about police may have more influence on his or her assessment of police performance in a specific incident than the reverse. Regardless of fluctuations over time in what people think of their police, it appears that the public's actual demand for their services is unabated and, if anything, growing continuously. If calls for service are any indication, American police are desired now more than ever, even in the nation's largest cities, where populations are in decline (Mastrofski, 1983). Some have argued, however, that the "market share" of police work has declined since private police have grown substantially, indicating a dilution of faith in police to provide for public and private security in the face of heightened concern about crime and disorder (Sparrow et al., 1990: 48).

Another indicator of support for police organizations is the degree of autonomy their administrators are granted in running the department. Police are and always have been among the most "penetrated" public service organizations in America. Even when the popularity of "good government" autonomy reforms was highest, systems for governing police—both formal and informal—provided ample opportunities for outside control and influence (Manning, 1993; Mastrofski, 1988; Reiss, 1993). Nonetheless, some chiefs have been more successful than others in securing autonomy in their running of the department, some of the more widely known cases being Harold Brier in Milwaukee, Daryl Gates in Los Angeles, and Frank Rizzo in Philadelphia (Skolnick and Fyfe, 1993: 134–136). However, the capacity to sustain a high degree of autonomy seems ephemeral, and often overstated, since maintaining administrative autonomy is accomplished in large part by *anticipating* what powerful external political forces want or will accept from their police (Wilson, 1968). If one attempts to discern broad patterns of autonomy or lack thereof across the wide range of police departments in America, one is likely to see big differences in the *manner* by which external control is exerted rather than the total *amount* of autonomy from it. For example, reformers during the heyday of the political machines bemoaned the lack of bureaucratic autonomy of police agencies and were especially aggrieved that chiefs exerted so little control over departmental hiring, promotion, firing, and operational matters

(Fogelson, 1977; Walker, 1977). But not too long after the power of the machines was broken, scholars and police administrators lamented the many ways in which the chief's capacity to govern had been meted out to other external agencies: courts and affirmative action regulatory agencies, unions, and most recently civilian review boards. External governance of police may be more fragmented today than it was when political machines were powerful, but it cannot be said with confidence that police are generally more autonomous.

POLICE LEGITIMACY AND THE CRIME CONTROL MISSION

Being perceived as legitimate means being perceived as conforming to what people see as "right" or "appropriate" (Scott, 1992: 305). Organizations can also seek support by brute force or threats, or they can secure support by making deals, but as the sociologist Max Weber noted, it takes a lot of effort to sustain an organization for long periods by these methods, and the result is often a high degree of instability both inside and outside the organization. Not surprisingly, then, most major American institutions try to justify themselves by getting society to accept them as legitimate. This affords such institutions a range of discretion in which they can exercise their authority without having to justify it each time or expend precious resources in coercion or negotiation. The importance of maintaining legitimacy is paramount to police because, it will be recalled, of American society's ambivalence about the core element of police authority: the capacity to coerce.

From their very beginnings, American police have been concerned with establishing their legitimacy. The various waves of reform can be interpreted as attempting to establish new bases of police legitimacy (Fogelson, 1977). Efforts to "legalize," "militarize," and "professionalize" police each appeal to somewhat different sets of values about what police should be and do, and these movements responded to values that were growing in popularity in American society at the time. The present reform movements to make police "community-" and "problem-oriented" may also be interpreted as attempting to establish new bases of legitimacy in a changing political climate (Bayley, 1988; Kelling and Moore, 1988; Klockars, 1988; Mastrofski, 1988).

Attaching such missions or "mandates" to the police has been the dominant means by which police departments sustain themselves over their history, altering the vision of the mission to fit the times (Manning, 1977). What is expected or hoped for from police at any given time may not be what they can actually deliver, but police organizations nonetheless adapt their structures and operations to conform—or at least give the appearance of conforming—to those expectations. Because it is difficult to define and measure precisely how well police perform in meeting those expectations, police adopt structures and practices that are widely accepted as constituting such performance, whether or not they in fact do.

There are many ways in which police organizations attempt to enhance their legitimacy (Crank and Langworthy, 1992). The creation of specialist units to deal with new, emerging problems is a convenient way to signify that a department is doing something about those problems. As targets in the "war against crime" change, so do the police specialists. The proliferation of narcotics enforcement units in the last decade is an example of a widespread effort to signify that *something* is being done about drug crime although all indications suggest that neither illicit drug consumption nor drug-related crimes have abated (Reuter and Kleiman, 1986). Legitimacy is also derived from such things as the uniforms and appearance police assume, the civil service systems (signifying that jobs are obtained by merit, not political influence), the training (that "credentials" officers as professional), participation in professional organizations (for example, the International Association of Chiefs of Police), accreditation of the department by a state or national law enforcement accrediting agency (signifying organizational efficiency), an internal affairs unit (signifying internal control), and the conspicuous use of technological gadgetry (computers, weapons, forensics).

Among the most important sources of police legitimacy in the years following World War II have been several strategies thought to be essential to the police mission of crime control: random preventive patrol, rapid response to reports of crime, and follow-up investigations by detectives. When departments engaged in these activities, they were regarded as adhering to the popular vision of an "effective" police department even though there was no rigorous evidence about the effectiveness of these strategies. When research was eventually conducted, it suggested that these strategies appear to contribute little to the deterrence of crime and the apprehension of criminals (Kelling, 1978; Walker, 1989). These "crime control" strategies served to enhance police legitimacy—even though they had no demonstrated relationship to actual accomplishment of those objectives. They had thus become "institutionalized," and they endure even today, some time after the best available evidence suggests that they have no bearing on crime rates. These and other structures persist as important features of police work because they incorporate certain "myths" about crime and policing that remain powerful in American society and useful to police departments (for example, that government can solve large, complex social and economic problems). These structures help police reassure the public that they are doing something about crime and justify budget requests to sustain or enlarge the police resource domain. This view of how police secure legitimacy is referred to in organizational theory as the "institutional" perspective (Crank and Langworthy, 1992).

Championing the crime-fighting mission has been a much-used approach to seek police legitimacy since the Great Depression. Yet, it is not entirely clear that the general public holds police accountable for the level of crime. When asked to volunteer ways to reduce crime, adding more police is mentioned by very few survey respondents (Flanagan and Maguire, 1992: 207); the association between respondents' fear of crime and their evaluations of police performance is very weak (Garofalo, 1977: 30); and only one-fourth or less feel that "our system of law enforcement works to really discourage people from committing crimes" (Flanagan et al., 1982: 201). Yet the public seems to have lenient standards when asked to assess how good a crime control job police are doing. About six in ten surveyed respondents gave positive assessments of the job their police were doing in solving and preventing crime, even in the face of declining crime clearance rates (*Law Enforcement News*, 1992). It may be that, despite the best efforts of advocates of the police crime control mission, the public's support for police derives from something more amorphous: the desire for police *presence* (Walker, 1989: 129; Whitaker et al., 1982: 44).

THE MYTH OF POLICE CRIME CONTROL

If the crime control capacity of police is "mythical," it is nonetheless important to note that the term as used here refers to beliefs that are unverified or unverifiable, not necessarily proven false. Rigorous efforts to validate scientifically the extent of the police's crime control capacity have emerged only in the last couple of decades. Even so, the amount of research in this area is minuscule compared to medicine, dentistry, education, and engineering, for example. Not surprisingly, then, there are differing views among researchers about whether police efforts *can* decrease crime. In general terms, these views fall into two groups (Sherman, 1992a). One group argues that police have little or no impact on the level of crime because they have no control over the powerful forces that cause it (unemployment, age demographics, poverty, family dysfunctions, culture clashes, the value placed on personal liberty, and so on). The second group, though often acknowledging that police can do little to affect the "root causes" of crime, also argues that police *can* contribute significantly to crime reduction.

In a series of essays, Sherman (1986, 1990, 1992a, 1992b) reviews the evidence on the crime control capacity of police. He finds evidence in some cases for a crime control effect (drunk-driving enforcement), in some cases not (burglary stings), and in some cases for a crime-producing effect (arresting spouse abusers). He draws several important conclusions from his analysis of the empirical research. First, it is neither extensive nor rigorous enough to offer definitive judgments about most of the strategies that have been tested. Second, many strategies that appear to be directed at other objectives, such as order maintenance and routine service, may in fact have greater crime control impact than law enforcement and punishment-oriented strategies that comprise the popular vision of "crime fighting." Thus, developing a stronger sense of neighborliness in a community stricken with fear of crime may do more to strengthen its capacity to resist crime than making more arrests and citations. Finally, Sherman (1990) suggests that many innovative police strategies remain to be tried and evaluated, especially those that strategically concentrate police resources on the people, places, and times where crime problems cluster. He is particularly encouraged at the prospects for success of such "crackdowns," while acknowledging that the effects may be only temporary.

It is exceedingly difficult to isolate the contribution that police make to crime control, given the joint responsibility of other criminal justice and government agencies in the process—not to mention taking into account the broader demographic, social, economic, and cultural forces at work. This task is further complicated by a growing sensitivity to the importance of informal institutions of social control, such as the family and neighborhood. The increasing popularity of community policing as a partnership between public police and these informal mechanisms of social control suggests a blurring of the lines of responsibility that were so painstakingly drawn by police reformers of earlier times. Whether such police–citizen partnerships, such as the now-popular community crime prevention programs, will really yield significant crime control dividends is not well established. Some review the limited research and are skeptical (Rosenbaum, 1988), others more optimistic (Skogan, 1990).

It remains to be seen whether a substantial crime control capacity for police can be established on a foundation of solid scientific evidence. Crime control, nonetheless, would appear to have enduring appeal as a basis for legitimacy to those who make policy and administer police agencies. Much of the impetus for community policing, for example, arose from criticism of the failures and excesses of earlier efforts to fit police departments into the crime-fighting mold, popular among police leaders since the Depression. Scholars criticized police agencies for unrealistically defining their mission strictly in terms of law enforcement (Goldstein, 1979) and for failing to attend to the small disorders and disruptions that feed the cycle of social and physical decay in urban neighborhoods (Wilson and Kelling, 1982). Support grew for the notion that police priorities should not come from criminal statutes and court decisions, not even from city hall, but from the very neighborhoods in which the officers worked. When the denizens of these neighborhoods were asked what problems *they* felt needed police attention, the top priorities were indeed the mundane aspects of police work—noisy neighbors, barking dogs, abandoned autos, traffic, street people, and rowdy juveniles (Weisburd et al., 1991; Skogan, 1990). Indeed, the common thread that ties together the diverse tactics and strategies gathered under the tent of community policing is linking the police and their community in closer partnership. Foot patrol, ministations, neighborhood crime prevention, advisory boards, and a host of other programs are all justified by this objective. At the same time, however, these and other community policing programs have been drafted in the war against drugs and violent crime. Highly publicized examples are federally sponsored programs, such as the Bush administration's "Weed and Seed" and the Clinton administration's program to make community policing a centerpiece of its initiative against violent crime. Less visible, but perhaps more telling, is the manner in which local community policing programs have been evaluated. Nearly all evaluations focus on the extent to which crime was reduced or citizens' fears and perceptions of crime were diminished (Rosenbaum, 1988; Sherman, 1986; Skogan, 1990). Whether or not these concerns are uppermost in the minds of the public, and whether or not they pervade the everyday practices of police, crime control is likely to remain a central concern of those who devise, criticize, and administer public policies pertaining to police.

CONCLUSION

This chapter has highlighted three enduring themes: the role, control, and legitimacy of American police. Debate, ambiguity, and unresolved empirical issues swirl about each of these. Much of the debate about the police role derives from differing values about what police *should* be although there are many unresolved questions about what they *could* be. With the realization that police exercise discretion in the practice of their authority to intervene in citizens' private lives, there has been an increasing concern about how to control that discretion. How and how much to control the state's power have always been central issues in America's political history. It will undoubtedly continue to be a matter of central importance in the twenty-first century, even should policing continue the trend of relying on less obtrusive means of surveillance and deception instead of the more obvious forms of coercion. Finally, the bases of police legitimacy shift with the prevailing political and cultural winds. Despite the dubiousness and outright resistance with which Americans greeted the new police organizations that emerged in the nineteenth century, they have long since become "sacred" (Manning, 1991: 357), enduring even in the face of repeated reminders of their limitations to control crime, disorder, corruption, and brutality. The existence of public police seems more secure today than ever, even in the face of tight local budgets and crises of legitimacy. What seems more mutable are their structures and practices, which are the objects of transformation from many groups external to police (Mastrofski and Uchida, 1993). Although it is difficult to say what impact the current efforts to transform police, such as community policing, will achieve, it does appear that the police leadership itself is taking an increasingly consequential role in the process. The emergence of a growing "national" market for top police executives in the "plum" police jobs, instead of the long-time practice of hiring from within the department, is one indication that changes are afoot. America's police leaders are becoming less isolated in other ways as well, through participation in progressive associations, obtaining graduate degrees, and using social science research (Klockars and Harver, 1993). The nationalization of crime and disorder as perpetually potent political issues since the 1960s has meant that presidents, Congress, and federal funding agencies have helped frame and shape local policing issues. To the extent that the selection of local police leadership is more responsive to issues raised in the broader, national arena, and to the extent that police administrators themselves take a more active role in shaping that national agenda, the prospects of greater administrative homogeneity across local departments are enhanced.

The implications of these administrative trends for street-level police work are not obvious, but there are other systemic trends that suggest dramatic consequences for everyday policing. Perhaps none is more compelling today than the resource limits placed on police in using the criminal process for handling problems. The rest of the criminal justice process is already overtaxed in most metropolitan areas: jails are full, court dockets are overflowing, prisons are overcapacity, and community corrections programs cannot keep up with demand. The get-tough, enforcement approach to crime that dominated the criminal justice system in the 1980s has produced more people and paper than the system can handle in the 1990s, and there are no reasonable prospects that sufficient court and correctional resources will be available in the future to keep pace.

Faced with the reality of an overloaded criminal justice system, the police must find ways to engage in social control by other means — or simply "give up" on some problems, people, or geographic areas. Assuming no diminution in the level of crime and disorder confronting them, that means that police must necessarily become even more selective about using criminal sanctions — whether by default or through a managed process. But it is not at all clear that *alternative* systems of social control are sufficiently developed either (Aarronson et al., 1984; Black, 1980). These conditions provide compelling reasons for students of police to refocus their attention on how police respond in the areas of their discretion that thus far have remained darkly shrouded under the "informal" or "no arrest" categories. Whether and how police mobilize other government agencies and the private sector on these occasions, and how effective and efficient these responses are, are yet to be demonstrated. Determining who gets what from police, and the consequences, remains a challenge for future research.

DISCUSSION QUESTIONS

1. Though our notion of police originated in England, it differs from the English version. In what ways? Discuss the role of the police in this society and the problems linked to that role.

2. Discuss the notion of police discretion and provide examples. How easy is it to monitor and control police behavior in the field? What can communities do to constrain discretion? What can departments themselves do?

3. What does it mean to have a "professional" police department? Discuss the aspects of policing that make professionalization difficult.

4. Does the public support its local police? Discuss trends in support for the police. What happens when the public loses confidence in the police?

CHAPTER 17

◆

THE COURTS: PROSECUTION AND SENTENCING

Martha A. Myers
University of Georgia

IN EVERY COUNTY and major city, the courthouse stands as a visible symbol of justice in America—as the place where, without regard for race or creed, the guilty are to be separated from the innocent and punished for their wrongdoing. Yet, we see daily reminders of the painful gap between our ideals of justice and the real processes that occur behind courthouse doors. We read of district attorneys who refuse to pursue strong cases, choosing instead to prosecute cases that will put their offices in the best possible light. Adversaries in theory only, prosecutors and defense counsel negotiate bargains so that the guilty obtain lenience they seemingly do not deserve. Judges appear to punish the undeserving harshly one day, and the deserving mildly the next. Editorials tell us that discretion is unbridled, discrimination is rampant, and the powers of district attorneys and judges must be curbed. Yet, with every attempt to limit the use of plea bargaining or to restrict judicial choices during sentencing, we hear of circumvention or refusals to comply.

In short, the conventional wisdom is that justice comes off a conveyor belt in an assembly line. But does it? This chapter looks at the decision-making behavior of the two most powerful figures in the courthouse: the prosecutor and the judge. It identifies the major decisions these officials make on a daily basis and isolates some of the factors that affect those decisions. As we shall see, the exercise of discretionary power is far from unbridled. Rather, it is constrained by the nature of the cases before decisionmakers, by decisions other officials previously have reached about the case, and by the broader community within which prosecution and sentencing occur. Our look at the major figures of the courts also will permit us to examine the courthouse role of a third important figure, the defense attorney.

**FIGURE 17.1
THE DUAL COURT
SYSTEM OF THE
UNITED STATES***

SOURCE: *Adapted from
Neubauer, 1988.
*Arrows denote routes of
appeal.*

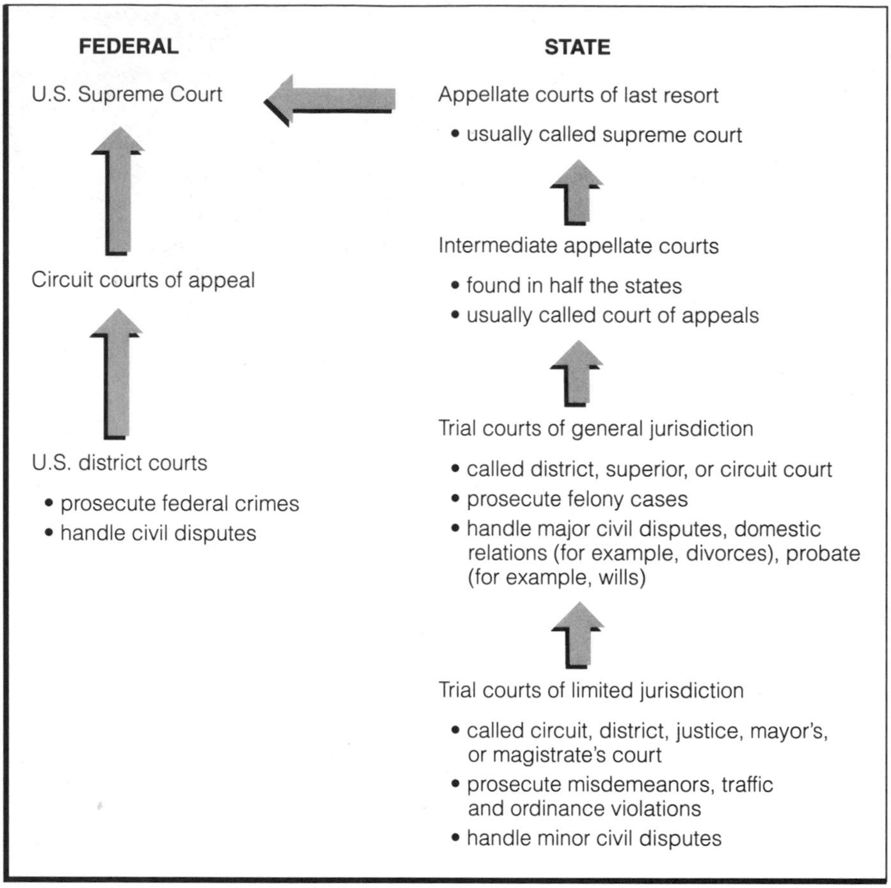

FEDERAL

U.S. Supreme Court

Circuit courts of appeal

U.S. district courts

- prosecute federal crimes
- handle civil disputes

STATE

Appellate courts of last resort

- usually called supreme court

Intermediate appellate courts

- found in half the states
- usually called court of appeals

Trial courts of general jurisdiction

- called district, superior, or circuit court
- prosecute felony cases
- handle major civil disputes, domestic relations (for example, divorces), probate (for example, wills)

Trial courts of limited jurisdiction

- called circuit, district, justice, mayor's, or magistrate's court
- prosecute misdemeanors, traffic and ordinance violations
- handle minor civil disputes

THE STRUCTURE OF AMERICA'S COURTS

It is not an easy task to understand or study America's courts. Instead of a single unified court system, we have a dual system at the federal and state levels (Baum, 1986), as shown in Figure 17.1. The ninety-four federal district courts overlap geographically with state courts but have sole jurisdiction over criminal cases based on federal statutes. Each is headed by a judge, who is appointed by the president with Senate confirmation. Criminal prosecutions, often of white collar offenders, compose just a small part of federal court caseload (Administrative Office of the U.S. Courts, 1985). To initiate these prosecutions, each federal district has an office of the U.S. Attorney, who also is appointed by the President with Senate confirmation. Although U.S. Attorneys are empowered to prosecute violations of federal criminal statutes, they vary considerably in the extent to which they actively pursue criminal cases (Hagan and Bernstein, 1979b).

Within each state are courts that have jurisdiction over criminal cases based on state law. They are more diverse than federal courts because state constitutions and statutes have developed court organizations over time, often adding courts on an ad hoc basis when needed. Over 3,000 major state courts, or courts of general jurisdiction, are responsible for felony cases. The highly decentralized lower courts, or courts of limited jurisdiction, handle the more numerous, less serious criminal cases. Courts in each state tend to be independent of one another and geographically dispersed. Urban areas often are served by one or more lower or municipal courts, some of which may handle only certain types of cases (for example, prostitution or traffic violations). In these jurisdictions, prosecutors manage a large, specialized staff, and decision-making may be left in the hands of deputy district attorneys. In contrast, rural areas typically have a single court and prosecutor located in the county seat. Most state prosecutors are elected, whereas judges obtain their office through partisan or nonpartisan elections, gubernatorial appointment, or legislative election.

THE PROSECUTOR

In the past, the police and judiciary played the major roles during prosecution (McDonald, 1985), and vestiges of these traditional practices persist even today. In some jurisdictions, the police file charges directly with the court (Mellon et al., 1981); in others, prosecutors simply ratify police screening decisions (Feeley and Lazerson, 1983) or negotiate the appropriate charge with officers (Stanko, 1981). In most jurisdictions, though, prosecutors stand at the courthouse door alone, determining which defendants will be overlooked and which will be required to enter. And once in the courthouse, their power continues virtually undiminished.

THE NATURE AND EXTENT OF THE PROSECUTOR'S POWER

Prosecutors determine precisely which charges—whether felonies, misdemeanors, or some combination—are filed against defendants. In order to prosecute, district attorneys must show probable cause in a preliminary hearing before a judge, but these hearings often are ceremonial and may even be waived (Neubauer, 1988). Federal courts and nineteen states also require an indictment from a grand jury; indictments or "true bills" are formal written documents accusing a person or persons of committing a specific offense. Grand juries return indictments if they find enough evidence to warrant convening a jury trial to establish the defendant's guilt beyond a reasonable doubt. As we shall see, indictments are relatively easy to obtain. In many other states, indictments are not required, and prosecutors can begin formal prosecution after filing an "information" with the court (Emerson, 1983). Like an indictment, an information formally accuses an individual of a specific offense. This document usually includes the time, date, and location of the offense, as well as the identity of the victim, if any.

Once formal charges have been filed, prosecutors can decide at any point to cease prosecution entirely, often by submitting to the court a motion to nolle prosequi. Together with the initial screening decision, dismissals account for the "loss" of nearly half of all cases the police bring to the prosecutor (Boland et al., 1989). The amount of loss varies dramatically, but it is usually greater in jurisdictions where prosecutors rigorously screen cases (Boland et al., 1989). Problems with evidence and witnesses are the most often cited reasons for rejecting and dismissing cases.

As the case against the defendant is prepared, prosecutors decide whether to accept a guilty plea or to proceed to trial. In states with capital punishment, they also decide whether to seek the death penalty. Originally discouraged by trial and appellate courts (Alschuler, 1979), guilty pleas are now the preferred method of obtaining convictions, even in smaller, less urban courts (Miller et al., 1978), because the alternative, the jury trial, is more costly, more time consuming, and fraught with uncertainty. To avoid trial, prosecutors tacitly or explicitly offer concessions to induce a guilty plea, and there is considerable room for bargaining the nature and extent of these concessions. Contrary to popular opinion, plea bargaining does not always entail the reduction of charges to less serious offenses (Boland et al., 1989). Instead, prosecutors often negotiate with defense counsel over which charges, if any, will be dropped and which sentence, if any, will be recommended to the judge.

In sum, then, although they are relative newcomers to the courthouse, prosecutors have unparalleled discretion in determining whether and how defendants will be prosecuted (Albonetti, 1987). And few formal or informal limits constrain their discretionary powers. Appellate courts have been reluctant to regulate prosecutorial decisions because they consider intervention a violation of the separation of powers between the executive and judicial branches of government (Gelman, 1982). Instead, the grand jury has been used since colonial times to protect the accused against unfounded charges and oppressive government (Frankel and Naftalis, 1977). Indeed, the Fifth Amendment has enshrined the central role of the grand jury, just as it has the defendant's right to a jury trial.

Unlike trial juries, though, grand juries consist of between six and twenty-three members of the community, and conduct their investigations in secret. Selected at random, grand jurors meet for a designated period, investigating matters of community concern and issuing reports (Alpert and Petersen, 1985). As we noted, they also consider criminal cases brought to them by the prosecutor although their power in this capacity has been much diminished with time. We have noted already that prosecutors can bypass the grand jury entirely in many states, and in others need convene a grand jury only in capital cases. In jurisdictions where an indictment is required, prosecutors are in the powerful position of choosing which witnesses and evidence the grand jury will consider. The defendant and defense counsel may not even be allowed to present their version of the facts, much less to confront and cross-examine witnesses. Not surprisingly, grand jury deliberations are brief. As one appellate court judge colorfully put it, most grand juries would "indict a ham sandwich" if the prosecutor asked them to do so (Carroll, 1985). The consensus seems to be, then, that grand juries are "sleeping watchdogs" that currently serve no meaningful screening or supervisory function. Indeed, calls for reform or outright abolition of the grand jury system are often heard (Emerson, 1983).

Prosecutors are, however, members of courtroom work groups that interact over time and share common interests (Blumberg, 1967a; Lipetz, 1980; Jacob, 1983). These work groups include defense counsel and judges who develop strategies that enable them to dispose of cases with maximum speed and minimal conflict. The prosecutor occupies a position of strength in these groups and hence can strongly determine which strategies will be used. Defense counsel may refuse to cooperate but for a variety of reasons seldom does so. Because about 65 percent of all defendants are unable to retain private counsel, they are represented either by assigned counsel or by a public defender (Neubauer, 1988: 145). Judges assign counsel to these indigent defendants in the majority of counties. To do so, they choose from a list of all attorneys practicing in the jurisdiction or from a shorter list of attorneys who are willing to represent indigents. Several factors hamper assigned counsel's ability or motivation to provide a vigorous defense for the defendant: (1) Compensation is minimal when compared to the fees charged in private practice; (2) criminal cases are handled only sporadically, thus limiting trial court experience; and (3) courts seldom provide the funds assigned counsel needs to conduct investigations or obtain the services of expert witnesses.

Unlike rural counties, most urban jurisdictions use public defenders—court attorneys who receive a salary from the jurisdiction to represent indigents. Sustained experience with criminal cases enables public defenders to prepare a more adequate defense than assigned counsel. However, heavy caseloads and membership in the courtroom work group generate a strong interest in cooperating with the prosecution. Though relationships vary across jurisdictions (Utz, 1978), defense counsel and district attorneys seldom are adversaries, except when the case is a serious one and the issue being contended is the severity of punishment rather than the establishment of guilt (Mileski, 1971; Mather, 1979). Thus, not surprisingly, defense counsel often is considered a co-opted double agent who has few bargaining chips when negotiating with the prosecutor (Blumberg, 1967b; Neubauer, 1988).

What about sentencing judges—can they curb prosecutorial power? The relationship between the judge and prosecutor varies considerably, and in some jurisdictions, the judge dominates the charging and plea bargaining decisions (McIntyre and Lippman, 1970). More typically, though, judges exercise little control over prosecutors. For example, they have no authority during plea negotiations if the concessions offered are solely under the prosecutor's purview, such as the reduction or dropping of charges. Indeed, judges may simply ratify bargains previously negotiated between counsel and prosecution (Ryan and Alfini, 1979). Judicial supervision of plea bargains is seen as crucial to fair and legitimate plea bargains (McDonald, 1985), but the actual participation of judges in the bargaining process is frowned on or prohibited (Ryan and Alfini, 1979). Nevertheless, judges manage to participate, usually during pretrial conferences, although the extent of involvement varies considerably by jurisdiction (Ryan and Alfini, 1979).

Finally, even though prosecutors in state courts are accountable to their constituents, the actual influence of the public is "less than overwhelming" (Baum, 1986). Public preferences and opinions do affect office policy (Mellon et al., 1981), but the daily operations of the prosecutor's office seldom are subjected to sustained scrutiny. In sum, then, there are few effective limits on prosecutorial discretion, and fears of potential abuse are widespread. The obvious question for us to consider, then, is how prosecutors actually exercise their discretionary power. Are they vindictive? Do they unleash their discretion arbitrarily?

To answer these questions, we examine the findings of studies conducted over the past twenty-five years. Researchers have used a variety of techniques to study prosecutors, from observations and interviews to quantitative analyses of actual decisions. Of the more than 3,000 prosecutor offices nationwide, however, only a few dozen, most of them in urban areas, have been examined. Thus, the generalizations that follow must be regarded as provisional.

THE STRONG, SOLID, GOOD CASE

When screening cases or deciding whether full prosecution is warranted, prosecutors compare cases against an ideal that will ensure conviction. This ideal case is variously labeled the "good" (Rauma, 1984), "strong" (Myers and Hagan, 1979), or "solid" (Stanko, 1982) case. The first, and probably most crucial, element of the strong case is a serious offense. One of the most consistent patterns identified by researchers is that prosecutors are more likely to file charges and prosecute fully if the offense is statutorily serious (Jacoby et al., 1982; Albonetti, 1987) or if the victim was injured (Myers, 1982; Rauma, 1984).

Evidence is the second element of the strong case and is particularly important at the initial charging stage (Jacoby et al., 1982). Prosecutors pursue cases more vigorously if there is strong evidence linking the defendant to the crime (Jacoby et al., 1982; Feeney et al., 1983). For example, district attorneys are likely to prosecute fully if eyewitnesses identified the defendant, the police recovered weapons or stolen property, the defendant or accomplice(s) made statements, or numerous witnesses were willing to testify (Myers and Hagan, 1979; Myers and LaFree, 1982). The specific kinds of evidence prosecutors consider depend on which decision is being made (for example, screening or full prosecution; see Albonetti, 1986, 1987), as well as on whether the offense is a felony or misdemeanor (Myers, 1982). Research has yet to establish the relative importance of evidence, in comparison with other elements of the strong case. Some researchers (Jacoby et al., 1982; Feeney et al., 1983) contend that it has the strongest influence on prosecutor decisions, whereas others

(Myers and Hagan, 1979) suggest that the victim's credibility and the seriousness of the offense are more important considerations.

The third element of the strong case is a dangerous and culpable defendant. Prosecutors tend to file charges against and prosecute fully defendants who have a serious prior record or who used a weapon (see, for example, Albonetti, 1986, 1987; Schmidt and Steury, 1989). As we shall see, prosecutorial assessments of how culpable offenders are depend in part on the culpability and credibility of the victim. Part of current concern with prosecutor discretion is the possibility that prosecutors consider attributes of defendants that have little or no direct bearing on their criminal behavior. The most intense concern focuses on discrimination against blacks, particularly in the imposition of the death penalty. We will return to this issue in the next section, which considers the role of the victim during prosecution. For the moment, though, we will note simply that fears about differential treatment are warranted only partially. Some prosecutors pursue cases against blacks (Nakell and Hardy, 1987; Spohn et al., 1987), males (Nagel and Hagan, 1983), and the unemployed (Blumstein et al., 1983) more rigorously, whereas others do not (Albonetti, 1987).

The Stand-Up Victim

The final element of the strong case is a "stand-up" victim, one whom the jury would believe and consider undeserving of victimization (Stanko, 1981–1982, 1982;). From the prosecutor's point of view, believable victims are articulate and consistent when giving testimony; "innocent" victims did nothing to precipitate or provoke their own victimization. Assessments of credibility and culpability are difficult to make, though, and to develop them, prosecutors rely on stereotypic notions about the behavior of certain categories of people, including jurors. For example, prosecutors assume that students usually are law-abiding, and that jurors will doubt the allegations made by disreputable victims or witnesses known to the defendant. These stereotypes transform the social background and behavior of victims into legally relevant factors that become essential when determining whether and how the case should be pursued.

The willingness of victims to cooperate is a paramount consideration. Without victim cooperation, prosecutors are unlikely to file charges and prosecute fully (Myers and Hagan, 1979), particularly if violence was involved or the victim knew the offender (McDonald, 1985). A prior relationship with the offender is particularly problematic, for it leads prosecutors to question whether the victim's testimony is a true depiction of the events (Vera Institute of Justice, 1981). To what extent did the victim precipitate the criminal event? And will the victim cooperate fully during prosecution? This element of uncertainty accounts for the often documented reluctance to file charges or prosecute fully when the victim was acquainted with the offender. This same element of uncertainty helps account for the tendency to reject charges or dismiss cases if the victim was in any way "disreputable"—that is, if the victim had, for example, engaged in deviant or criminal behavior or was unemployed (Myers and LaFree, 1982; Albonetti, 1987).

Do apparently irrelevant attributes such as victim's gender and race enter into prosecution decisions? In some jurisdictions, yes. To assess the credibility of female victims, prosecutors invoke gender stereotypes about how women should act when victimized and how cooperative they are likely to be as witnesses (Stanko, 1982; Frohmann, 1991). Failure to conform to these stereotypes could account for the reluctance of prosecutors in some jurisdictions to accept and prosecute fully cases involving female victims (Myers and Hagan, 1979; Foley and Powell, 1982). Female victims are not perceived universally as less credible, though, because in other jurisdictions, their cases are treated no differently from those involving male victims (Albonetti, 1987).

It also has become increasingly apparent that prosecutors pursue cases more vigorously if the victim is white. Indeed, in cases involving serious violence, prosecutors consider the race of both the defendant and victim. Where homicide is alleged, prosecutors are more likely to upgrade police charges and to seek the death penalty in cases where a black allegedly murdered a white (see Paternoster, 1991, for review). Prosecutors are also more likely to initiate prosecution, to file serious charges, and to prosecute fully if a black allegedly raped a white woman (LaFree, 1989). Before interpreting these trends as evidence of discrimination against black defendants or victims, however, we should emphasize that not all studies controlled adequately for legally relevant factors (such as evidence) with which race might be confounded. Nevertheless, these patterns raise the disturbing possibility that some prosecutors define the victimization of whites, especially when blacks are perpetrators, as more serious criminal events than the comparable victimization of blacks.

PLEA BARGAINING AND THE SPECTER OF A TRIAL

The decision to seek a trial rather than enter a guilty plea is a pivotal one for the defendant. Most research indicates that defendants who exercised their right to a trial and were convicted usually receive a more severe sentence than those who pleaded guilty to the same offense (Blumstein et al., 1983; Peterson and Hagan, 1984; Miethe, 1987b). This decision is a pivotal one for prosecutors and defense counsel as well because a jury trial involves the expenditure of considerable resources in the pursuit of an uncertain outcome. Can a representative and impartial jury be drawn from the community in which the crime occurred? Will jurors understand the evidence? Will they be swayed by sympathy (or hostility) toward the victim or defendant rather than by the evidence? Despite research findings to the contrary (Hans and Vidmar, 1986), prosecutors and defense counsel fear that the answers to these questions will be a resounding no. As a result, jury trials are the exception rather than the rule in most jurisdictions.

◆ **"LIGHT" CASES** ◆   The preferred outcome is a plea bargain, which involves negotiations between the prosecutor and defense counsel. The strength of the evidence and the seriousness of the case are paramount considerations during these negotiations. Most plea bargains are straightforward and implicit because the case is "light" (minor) and evidence of the defendant's guilt is clear (Mather, 1979). In these situations, standardized but unstated "recipes" are available and explicit bargaining is unnecessary (Sudnow, 1965). For example, to determine whether the serious charge of burglary can be reduced to the much less serious offense of petty theft, public defenders examine the case to see if it resembles the routinely encountered or "normal" burglary. What kinds of persons were involved? Where did the offense occur? How much property was taken? Answers to these and other questions determine whether the case is a typical burglary. If it is, the public defender, on the client's behalf, will withdraw the original plea of not guilty and enter a plea of guilty to petty theft, a change the prosecutor usually accepts readily.

◆ **SERIOUS CASES** ◆   Serious cases are different because the nature of the offense and the existence of a prior record make lengthy incarceration a distinct possibility. In these situations, bargaining is more explicit, and the prosecutor and defense counsel may reach a compromise only after protracted negotiations. Attributes of defendants, victims, and the offense are selectively brought into play in an effort to provide what both prosecutor and defense counsel agree is a "just" or deserved outcome (Maynard, 1982). Numerous concessions may be offered: a recommendation from the prosecutor that the judge impose a lenient sentence, a reduction in the severity of the charge, a decision not to prosecute additional charges, or a dismissal of other cases pending against the defendant. More concessions are offered if the evidence is weak (McDonald, 1985) or complex, both of which would consume too many of the court's limited resources (Jacoby et al., 1982). In contrast, fewer concessions are offered if the offense is particularly serious or if the defendant used a weapon or had a long serious prior record (McDonald, 1985; Holmes et al., 1987). Not surprisingly, then, defendants with lengthy prior records are more likely to insist on trial (Myers and LaFree, 1982), especially if they have been charged with a serious offense (Myers, 1982). In these situations, defendants have little to lose if the jury convicts, but much to gain if it acquits. The "Perry Mason" case, with a serious crime and reasonable doubt about the defendant's guilt, rarely is encountered but presents the most difficult situations for defense counsel and prosecutors to resolve (Mather, 1979).

◆ **ADDITIONAL FACTORS** ◆   Apart from the defendant's prior record and offense, do prosecutors consider other factors when offering concessions and assessing the feasibility of trial? Quantitative research indicates that gender and race affect the terms of the plea but not as strongly or consistently as do offense and prior record. In some jurisdictions, male defendants are able to obtain more favorable charge and sentence reductions than are females (Figueira-McDonough, 1985). In New York, charge reductions do not vary by race if the case is disposed of at the first presentation. But if black defendants do not plead guilty at their first presentation, they receive less favorable reductions than comparable whites (Bernstein et al., 1977). However, this is not a consistent pattern; elsewhere, blacks and Mexican-Americans receive more favorable charge reductions than do whites (Holmes et al., 1987). Similarly, research suggests that some types of defendants are more likely than are others to go to trial. These include blacks charged with felonies (Myers, 1982), with property crimes (Myers and LaFree, 1982), or with victimizing whites (Myers, 1980). Prosecutors also appear to prefer going to trial if the attributes of the victim presumably enhance their credibility and blamelessness before the jury. For example, trial is more likely if the victim is a stranger (LaFree, 1980), white (Bienen et al., 1988), employed (Myers and Hagan, 1979), better educated than the defendant (Myers, 1980), and untainted with allegations of misconduct prior to the offense (Myers and Hagan, 1979).

DIVERSITY OF PROSECUTORIAL APPROACHES

Although prosecutors throughout the United States are faced with the same set of decisions, they make them quite differently. Prosecutors vary in the weight they give to evidence (Jacoby et al., 1982; Feeney et al., 1983), the way guilty pleas are negotiated (McDonald, 1985), their use of the death penalty (Paternoster, 1991), and the extent to which they and defense counsel act as adversaries (Utz, 1978). Prosecutorial policies vary markedly across jurisdictions and, to a certain extent, are mandated by the larger environment within which prosecutors, as elected officials, must operate (Mellon et al., 1981).

Researchers have identified several distinct policies, each of which sets the tone for all cases prosecutors subsequently accept (Jacoby et al., 1982). Some of the largest urban offices use a "legal sufficiency" policy and accept cases if the evidence supports the charge; other considerations are irrelevant. Because initial screening in these jurisdictions is not stringent, a variety of dispositions are used extensively, including charge bargaining and dismissals at preliminary hearings and trials. In overloaded courts with scarce resources, prosecutors pursue a "system efficiency" policy, which aims for more stringent screening and early speedy dispositions by whatever means. In these jurisdictions, dismissals are infrequent, and plea bargains to reduced charges are common. Finally, the "defendant rehabilitation" policy emphasizes diversion from the criminal justice system. Decisions are based, therefore, more on characteristics of the defendant than on the offense per se. Few cases are accepted, and those that are, are pursued vigorously.

THE QUEST FOR PLEA BARGAINING REFORM

No prosecutorial decision arouses the concern (and ire) of critics more than the offering of concessions to defendants as inducements to plead guilty. Critics contend that this practice either victimizes defendants or permits them to escape full prosecution (McDonald, 1985). But can plea bargaining be eliminated? Several jurisdictions have attempted to forbid bargaining, but with mixed success (Cohen and Tonry, 1983). In 1985, for example, Alaska's attorney general ordered prosecutors to desist from reducing or dismissing charges as inducements to a guilty plea. To minimize sentence bargaining, prosecutors also were not permitted to recommend sentences to the judge. The ban appears to have been relatively successful although some circumvention in the form of judicial negotiation with defense counsel occurred. But Alaska is hardly a typical state—its felony caseload is small, and the state attorney general sets prosecution policy for the entire state.

Efforts to restrict or eliminate charge bargaining in other jurisdictions have merely shifted discretion to judges, who engage in implicit or explicit bargaining over the sentence (Cohen and Tonry, 1983; McCoy and Tillman, 1987). In Michigan, for example, judges circumvented the mandatory two-year prison sentence for offenders who used a gun to commit a felony by adjusting the sentence for the original felony downward. Whether they are implicit or explicit, concessions at the sentencing stage encourage guilty pleas and serve to perpetuate the use of jury trials only as a last resort.

But what if charge bargaining is restricted or abolished and judges refuse to engage in implicit or explicit sentence bargaining? If the experience of El Paso is indicative, defendants and defense counsel soon will realize there is no penalty for insisting on a jury trial. Jury trials will increase, and clogged dockets will contribute to the quick return of sentence bargaining (McDonald, 1985).

Thus, plea bargaining is the disposition the public "loves to hate" (McCoy and Tillman, 1987); attempts to eliminate it usually are short-lived and ineffective, in large part because the alternative—a jury trial—is simply too uncertain and expensive. We now turn our attention to the second major courthouse figure, the judge, who must face not only the convicted offender and defense attorney but also the public, the prosecutor, and the probation department, all of whom often have strong opinions about the kind of punishment the offender deserves.

THE SENTENCING JUDGE

The most common criticism of judges is that their sentences are too lenient, that they fail to give offenders the punishment they "deserve." This concern with excessive lenience helps explain recent demands for stiffer penalties, mandatory minimum sentences, and restrictions on judicial discretion. Empirical research cannot allay public concerns about excessive lenience because these concerns are based ultimately on value judgments about the punishment offenders should receive. But it can shed light on the way in which judges impose punishment. For decades, critics have feared that the discretion inherent in most sentencing law gives judges the opportunity to discriminate—that is, to base their sentences on factors, such as race or socioeconomic class, that are objectionable on moral or legal grounds. Similarly, critics have feared that judges do not punish consistently—that is, that they treat similar offenders quite differently (Blumstein et al., 1983).

FEDERAL VERSUS STATE AND LOCAL COURTS

Before summarizing what we currently know about judicial sentencing behavior, it is important to note that our knowledge of the process is uneven. Most attention has been devoted to offenders convicted of felonies in state courts. For over fifty years, researchers have grappled with the issue of race discrimination; only more recently have they examined discrimination based on gender and class. Although comparative research across jurisdictions is necessary for a complete understanding of sentencing, it has been hampered by diversity in state sentencing law, court organization, caseload, and community attributes.

In contrast, state courts of limited jurisdiction have received less attention. This neglect is anomalous because judges in lower courts not only sentence the majority of all offenders (that is, misdemeanants) but also make pretrial release decisions involving felons. Comparative descriptive work underscores the diversity of lower courts, and it has become abundantly clear that they bear virtually no resemblance to the Perry Mason stereotype (Feeley, 1979; Ragona and Ryan, 1984). The role of the judge during misdemeanor sentencing varies considerably. Some judges are active participants, whereas others merely ratify agreements reached by the prosecutor, defense counsel, or probation officers. More contextually sensitive than research on felony courts, studies of lower courts show in a general way that the punishment of misdemeanants is shaped by the surrounding community, especially its public attitudes, political culture, and economic resources.

In some lower courts, however, the process of being convicted, which involves being detained in jail, is more punishing than is the actual sanction the judge imposes (Feeley, 1979; Flemming, 1982). Thus, pretrial release decisions are pivotal. For defendants accused of felonies, failure to obtain pretrial release often results in harsher penalties after conviction (Blumstein et al., 1983; Holmes et al., 1987; Miethe, 1987b). Unlike sentencing decisions, however, bail statutes provide judges with explicit guidance about which defendants are eligible for release, which may be released on their own recognizance, and which must pay a set amount prior to release. Judges appear to base pretrial release decisions on factors that statutes have designated as appropriate: the seriousness of the offense, prior record, and the defendant's ties to the community. Nevertheless, inappropriate factors such as race, gender, and socioeconomic status also enter into these decisions, thus raising the same concerns with discrimination as do sentencing outcomes (Patterson and Lynch, 1991).

Finally, federal courts have come under scrutiny only since the early 1980s. More formal and less hurried than are state courts, they handle fewer cases. In 1985, for example, 1.5 million cases were filed in state felony courts, but only 41,000 criminal cases were filed in U.S. district courts (Administrative Office of the U.S. Courts, 1985; Langan, 1988). Yet, these cases are far more significant than their small numbers suggest. A single code governs all federal courts, and this statutory uniformity allows researchers to explore in detail the role the surrounding community plays during sentencing. In addition, the federal code prohibits both "common crimes" (for example, drug use and robbery) and white collar offenses (for example, mail fraud and draft evasion). As a result, researchers can compare the treatment of both types of offenders and assess more accurately the role of class during sentencing.

As is the case with prosecutor activities, judges' sentencing behavior is neither capricious nor arbitrary. Factors commonly regarded as legally relevant consistently and strongly affect sentences. Factors of doubtful legitimacy (for example, gender and age) or of clear illegitimacy (for example, race) play a smaller and less consistent role during sentencing. As alluded to previously, judges also consider previous outcomes and decisions such as recommendations from prosecutors and probation officers, the offender's pretrial release status, and whether the defendant pleaded guilty or was convicted at trial (Blumstein et al., 1983). These previous decisions are especially crucial because they are major conduits through which factors of questionable legitimacy enter the sentencing process.

As elected officials, judges are creatures of their environment, and the significance they attach to the offender's identity and behavior varies across time and space. Judicial and community attributes generally have limited direct effects on outcomes (Gibson, 1983; Myers, 1988). Instead, they indirectly determine the criteria that judges consider appropriate when sentencing and the priorities judges attach to the criteria.

THE ROLE OF LEGALLY RELEVANT FACTORS

Reviewing sentencing research, the National Academy of Sciences has concluded that, "using a variety of different indicators, offense seriousness and offender's prior record emerge consistently as the key determinants of sentences" (Blumstein et al., 1983: 11). This pattern is one of the most striking features of sentencing research. It holds across a wide variety of studies from different jurisdictions, even when diverse measures for offense seriousness and prior record are used.

Outwardly simple, this conclusion requires qualification and elaboration. First, factors of legal relevance are not easily distinguished from those of questionable relevance. States with sentencing guidelines (such as Alaska, Florida, and Minnesota) have the advantage in this respect because their criminal code clearly articulates the legal relevance of prior record and offense (Durham, 1987). Indeed, guidelines specify which types of prior record (for example, convictions or incarcerations) are relevant, as well as the relative weight to give both the offense and prior record. Many guidelines lack the force of law, however, and the majority of states lack guidelines entirely.

In many circumstances, then, statutes offer judges little explicit guidance on which aspects of the offense and offender are appropriate to consider, as well as the weight to give each. As we are well aware, punishment serves many legitimate purposes, including deterrence, rehabilitation, incapacitation, and retribution. And although there may be considerable agreement that race is a morally objectionable criterion on which to base sentences, judges may consider it perfectly acceptable to use other social background information (such as gender, age, or social status) to determine which specific punishment will serve to deter or rehabilitate. In short, most sentencing law fails to specify clearly which factors are legally relevant and which are legally irrelevant.

To complicate matters, factors of legal relevance can mask previous discriminatory actions. In so doing, they operate as conduits through which legally questionable factors indirectly affect sentences. Judicial reliance on "legally relevant" factors does not necessarily imply, then, the absence of discriminatory treatment earlier in the process. Indirect discrimination becomes a more distinct possibility when we realize that judges rely more heavily on the offender's prior record of incarceration rather than arrest, conviction, or misdemeanor record (Welch and Spohn, 1986). Thus, judges weigh most heavily a "legally relevant" factor that is itself the product of a particularly long series of discretionary decisions, including previous sentences. Any decision that led to a prior incarceration could incorporate discrimination based on legally irrelevant factors. In short, then, though the distinction will be used in this review, the line demarcating the legally relevant from the irrelevant factor is neither hard nor fast.

Second, the significance attached to legally relevant factors varies across decisions, offenders, and jurisdictions. In particular, the race of the offender affects which measure of prior record judges use and what weight they give it (Welch et al., 1984). Though not a consistent pattern (Farnworth and Horan, 1980), some evidence suggests that judges weigh both offense seriousness and prior record more heavily if the offender is black (Welch et al., 1984; Miethe and Moore, 1986). In addition to race, the significance of both the type of offense and its seriousness depends on where and when sentencing occurred (Myers and Talarico, 1987).

THE ROLE OF FACTORS
OF DOUBTFUL LEGITIMACY

For most sentencing research, the issue of central importance has been the extent to which sentences are based on factors whose relevance is clearly illegitimate or of doubtful legitimacy. This review will focus on race, gender, and socioeconomic status, as well as on attributes of the victim.

◆ **RACE** ◆ Researchers have attempted for years to estimate the amount of race discrimination in sentencing (Kleck, 1981; Hagan and Bumiller, 1983;

Wilbanks, 1987; Zatz, 1987). Only recently, however, have studies become sophisticated enough to disentangle the effect of race from those legally relevant factors with which it is often confounded. Overall, race now is not consistently important, yet continues to be important in some contexts. Its role depends on other offense and offender attributes, the relationship with and race of the victim, and the nature of the court and surrounding community. For example, Zatz (1984) found no race differences in the treatment of property offenders. Yet among violent offenders, significant race differences exist, and they do not always involve harsher punishment for blacks. Blacks convicted of rape do indeed receive longer sentences than do white rapists, but blacks convicted of homicide receive significantly shorter sentences than do either whites or Chicanos. Peterson and Hagan (1984) document parallel differences in the sentences imposed on drug offenders in federal courts. During the antidrug crusades of the 1970s, black users were sentenced more leniently than were whites because they were perceived as victims of traffickers. Sharp race differences were present, but were reserved for black traffickers, who were seen as doubly villainous for victimizing fellow blacks already disadvantaged socially and economically. In some misdemeanor courts, harsher treatment of blacks also is confined to those who are outsiders to the community (Austin, 1985).

Other studies indicate that the effect of race depends on whom the offender chose to victimize. Based on a sample of offenders convicted in Alaska, Miethe (1987b) found no significant race differences in sentences among offenders who victimized someone they knew. Yet, among offenders who victimized a stranger, blacks were more likely than whites to be incarcerated. In general, blacks who victimize whites seem to receive harsher penalties (Myers and LaFree, 1982; Walsh, 1987). Indeed, in capital homicide cases, the race of the victim is often more significant than the race of the offender (Paternoster, 1991), and may reflect not only the devalued status of black victims but also the presumably greater threat posed by the victimization of members of a socially advantaged group (Kleck, 1981; Hawkins, 1987).

Race differences during sentencing also depend on characteristics of the court and the broader community (Myers and Talarico, 1987). Although early work (Gibson, 1978) found that fundamentalist judges discriminate more against blacks than do nonfundamentalists, more recent research suggests that the nature of the discrimination depends on the penalty in question. Southern Baptist and fundamentalist judges are more likely than their colleagues to incarcerate blacks, but by the same token they impose significantly shorter sentences on them (Myers, 1988). The race of the judge has also interested researchers.

The expectation is that racial discrimination should decline as more black judges are elected or appointed. Consistent evidence of this relationship has yet to emerge. Some researchers (for example, Spohn, 1990) found that black judges do not sentence in a fundamentally different way than do their white colleagues. Others discovered that black judges drew no distinctions based on race until they set prison terms, at which point black judges showed lenience toward blacks by imposing shorter terms than their white colleagues.

Rural–urban differences in discrimination also have been found, but a consistent pattern has yet to emerge. The original expectation was that discrimination would be more likely in rural areas and that the bureaucratization and impersonality of large urban courts would not permit race considerations to intrude. Some evidence supports this expectation (Hagan, 1977), but it is by no means conclusive—other studies have found greater discrimination against blacks in urban or suburban areas (Myers and Talarico, 1986b). In these contexts, the anonymity of large courts might well allow personal preferences to intrude. Race differences are more pronounced in other communities as well, in particular those that are racially unequal (Myers, 1987) and predominantly black (Myers and Talarico, 1986a). Interestingly, however, in these contexts, white rather than black offenders are at a disadvantage.

In sum, then, the significance attached to race varies, and blacks are not consistently punished more severely than whites. Moreover, the effect of race may become apparent only after considering previous outcomes on which judges base their own decisions. Spohn et al. (1981–1982), for example, found instead that blacks are significantly less likely than whites to be released prior to trial and to secure the services of a private attorney. Ultimately, this inability operates to their disadvantage later in the process because judges impose more severe sentences on offenders currently in jail or represented by public counsel. Similar discrimination has been documented through the probation officer's recommendation (Hagan, 1975).

Differences in punishment based on ethnicity have only recently been explored and appear to depend in part on the offense. For example, Hispanics are punished more harshly than Anglo-Americans for drug offenses (Unnever, 1982; Unnever and Hembroff, 1988) but treated more leniently for assaults and homicide (Bienen et al., 1988). More generally, research in some jurisdictions has uncovered no significant differences in treatment regardless of offense (Welch et al., 1985), whereas in other jurisdictions, Hispanics are more likely than Anglo-Americans to be sentenced to both prison and to jail (Farnworth et al., 1991).

◆ **GENDER** ◆ Relatively clear evidence indicates that females are treated more leniently than are males in both state and federal courts, particularly for the initial incarceration decision (Nagel and Hagan, 1983; Kruttschnitt, 1984). Lenient treatment is both a recent (Feeley and Little, 1991; Boritch, 1992) and contingent phenomenon, depending on whether the female offender has dependent children (Daly, 1987a, 1987b; Bickle and Peterson, 1991). "Familial paternalism" derives from judicial assessments of the greater social and actual costs of replacing women's labor in the family. Familial paternalism also could help account for other trends documented in the literature: the greater importance judges place on the marital status of female rather than male offenders (Bernstein et al., 1979) and the lenience some judges extend only to black women (Gruhl et al., 1984).

The significance of gender also varies as a function of characteristics of judges and the surrounding community. Of particular interest is research that examines the extent to which gender differences depend on the sex of the sentencing judge. In one northeastern jurisdiction, male but not female judges sentenced female offenders more leniently (Gruhl et al., 1981). Yet, in Georgia between 1976 and 1985, male judges were harsher toward female offenders than were their female colleagues (Myers and Talarico, 1987). Female offenders were sentenced leniently, primarily in urban areas that could not or did not wish to bear the costs of incarcerating large numbers of women with families (Myers and Talarico, 1986b) or in areas experiencing high income inequality (Myers, 1987) or serious unemployment (Myers and Talarico, 1987).

As was the case for race, gender plays a more diffuse and cumulative role during sentencing because it influences outcomes on which judges base their decisions. In particular, female offenders are more likely than are males to receive probation officer recommendations for lenience (Myers, 1979) and to be released prior to trial (Kruttschnitt and Green, 1984). Both of these outcomes ultimately work to their advantage later in the process because judges impose more lenient sentences on offenders for whom lenience was recommended or pretrial release obtained.

◆ **SOCIOECONOMIC STATUS** ◆ As was the case with gender, researchers only recently have turned their attention to the effect of socioeconomic status on sentences (Blumstein et al., 1983). Most research suggests that status affects sentences, but neither consistently nor strongly. Of greater significance is its adverse effect on previous outcomes on which judges base their decisions, including the defendant's pretrial release status (Lizotte, 1978), the conviction charge (Hagan and Parker, 1985), and the probation officer's recommendation (Unnever et al., 1980; Drass and Spencer, 1987). The adverse effect of status depends on the nature of the victim and the community. For example, unemployed offenders are more severely punished when they victimize a person rather than a corporation (Hagan, 1982). Status differences also are more pronounced in communities experiencing high income inequality (Myers, 1987) and when public attention is focused on certain crimes such as drug trafficking (Peterson and Hagan, 1984).

As noted previously, research in federal courts allows a better estimation of the role of status because the population of offenders sentenced in these courts is more diverse. In general, there is no consistent evidence of lenience toward higher status offenders. Instead, the role status plays depends on the U.S. Attorney's stance toward white collar offenders, political events such as Watergate, and the nature of the offense itself. In research confined to white collar offenders sentenced after Watergate, Wheeler et al. (1982) found that higher-occupational-status offenders are punished more severely. In contrast, offenders with "impeccable backgrounds" (for example, those who have stable marriages or who are active religiously) are treated more leniently. These findings drew on data from large urban districts that prosecute a variety of white collar offenders. Recent work based on a district that more closely approximates the average in size and caseload found that status has no effect on sentencing, and this was true both before and after Watergate (Benson and Walker, 1988).

Contrary to expectations, college-educated white collar offenders reportedly are sentenced no more severely than are less educated common criminals, at least in federal courts. The expected lenience was confined to common criminals, with the college-educated offender receiving slightly shorter sentences than did those with less education (Hagan and Nagel, 1982). It is important to emphasize, however, that these patterns accurately describe the role of status only in districts that initiate few white collar prosecutions. In federal districts where U.S. Attorneys took a more active stance against white collar crime, white collar offenders were punished less severely than common criminals regardless of their educational attainment (Hagan et al., 1980) or income (Hagan et al., 1982).

◆ **VICTIM CHARACTERISTICS** ◆ Although attributes of the victim become less important after conviction (Miethe, 1987b), several remain crucial in certain contexts. As noted previously, the race of the victim is important when sentencing offenders convicted of homicide. Several researchers also have found that offenders who victimize females are punished more severely (Myers, 1979; Hagan, 1982), as are those who victimize strangers (Miethe, 1987b). Finally, the role victim characteristics play during sentencing is not a constant one. It is more prominent in jurisdictions where probation officers recommend sentences to the judge (Myers, 1979) and in cases in which the judge has had contact with the victim during a trial (Myers, 1981).

COMMUNITY CONTEXTS OF SENTENCING

Although generally aware that the social and political environment affects the judge's choice of sanctions, researchers have yet to establish the extent of its impact with any precision. The choice of sanctions for misdemeanants seems to be affected by economic resources in the community (Ragona and Ryan, 1984). For example, fines are preferred in counties with limited economic resources and jail space. Judges in federal courts also are sensitive to community influences (for example, antidrug crusades) and events (for example, Watergate). Events such as war foster more punitive sentences for draft offenders (*Columbia Journal of Law and Social Problems*, 1969), and they influence the relevance of race and religion as well. Hagan and Bernstein (1979a) have characterized the period between 1963 and 1968 as one of uncompromisingly coercive control of draft resisters. Antidraft demonstrations occurred frequently, and editorials advocated strict enforcement of Selective Service laws. During this period, black resisters were more likely than were whites to be incarcerated, as were conscientious objectors such as Jehovah's Witnesses. Between 1969 and 1976, demonstrations became less frequent, and editorials urged draft law reform, noting the wastefulness of imprisoning draft resisters. During this period, judges exercised selective co-optive control, reserving harsh punishment for offenders whose threats were the most obvious and direct: whites who actively resisted. Conscientious objectors, in contrast, were treated much more leniently during this period.

Not all judges are equally responsive to these community pressures. Gibson (1980), for example, found that only certain judges incorporate information about the community crime rate into their sentencing decisions, in particular, those who have greater contact with their constituency, who have experienced electoral defeat, or who have assumed a "delegate" role orientation (which considers it appropriate to be influenced by the environment). Similarly, public preferences for certain sanctions become more important if the judge is elected (Ryan, 1980). Finally, community factors tend to affect judicial sentencing behavior only where sentencing law provides judges with some discretion (Nagel and Geraci, 1983; Miethe and Moore, 1986).

SENTENCING REFORM AND ITS IMPACT

Sentencing reform is hardly a new phenomenon. Instead, it occurs with cyclical regularity (Albanese, 1984b). Within the past twenty years, reforms have been instituted in every state, and their general direction is away from indeterminate or open-ended sentencing and toward determinacy, with explicit standards on the amount of punishment each type of offender receives (Shane-Dubow et al., 1985). These attempts to reduce judicial discretion, it is hoped, will make punishment more certain, uniform, and neutral. Have reforms succeeded? It depends on the nature of the reform. Sentencing guidelines with the force of law appear to be more successful than advisory guidelines in producing more consistent sentences (Tonry, 1988). Although formal compliance with mandatory guidelines appears to be widespread, however, circumvention by both prosecutors and judges does occur (Cohen and Tonry, 1983). For example, where officials consider the required penalties inappropriately harsh, they avoid mandatory minimum sentences by dismissing charges or acquitting defendants.

Minnesota's presumptive guidelines, instituted in 1980, are an excellent example of recent reform efforts. They explicitly designated race, gender, and socioeconomic status as irrelevant during sentencing and sought consistent sentences proportionate to the seriousness of the offense. Early evaluations of these guidelines indicated that they successfully reduced disparity in those decisions regulated by the guidelines. Most notably, judges gave greater weight to prescribed factors such as the weapon and severity of the offense. Differential treatment based on race and employment status declined, as did jurisdictional variation (Miethe and Moore, 1985). Although prosecutors could circumvent guidelines if they wished, no evidence indicated that restrictions on judicial discretion were displaced by enhanced prosecutorial discretion (Miethe and Moore, 1985; Miethe, 1987a).

Even reforms as rigorous as Minnesota's have limits, however. Regulated sentencing outcomes became much more predictable, but the more commonly made decisions outside the guidelines continued to be affected by legally questionable offender characteristics (such as race and marital status) and community attributes (such as urbanization). Thus, discriminatory treatment continued to be a problem for the majority of offenders. Moreover, success in monitoring the regulated decisions was short-lived. Four years after the guidelines went into effect, sentences remained more uniform and neutral than prior to the guidelines, but levels of compliance had diminished. When setting the length of prison sentences, judges relied on the proscribed characteristics of race and employment status (Moore and Miethe, 1986).

CONCLUSION

It is relatively easy to criticize America's prosecutors and judges and to fear that their broad discretionary powers will be abused. But as this review indicates, it is exceedingly difficult to substantiate criticisms and fears with reliable data about how judges and prosecutors actually behave. "Vindictive" prosecutors and "discriminatory" judges surely exist. But the sheer diversity of the American court system makes it extremely difficult to document the precise extent of abuses or to identify exactly where such officials are likely to be found. We do know that they are unlikely to be common. Yet, we must bear in mind that what appears to be an abuse of discretionary power (for example, a race effect) actually may reflect a legitimate reliance on previous outcomes and decisions—be it prior record, the prosecution charge, or the recommendations of other court officials. Such a reliance both cloaks and legitimates early discrimination, thus obviating differential treatment later in the process.

Although the lot of the researcher is not an easy one, the public and its elected representatives face an even more difficult task, for it is their responsibility to develop and monitor policies that prevent or eliminate abuses of discretionary power. Reforms are likely to be unnecessary or unrealistic unless they are grounded in a clear understanding of how prosecutors and judges work. As this chapter has shown, we have only begun to provide that understanding.

DISCUSSION QUESTIONS

1. What is the prosecutor's role in the court system? To what extent do prosecutors influence the work of the grand jury? Discuss the relationship between the judge and the prosecutor in the administration of justice.

2. Myers describes four elements that influence a prosecutor's decision to go forward with a case. Discuss these elements, and comment on the role that characteristics of the victim play in prosecutorial decisions.

3. What is plea bargaining and what influences it? Does it provide just outcomes? Discuss the various attempts that have been made to reform plea bargaining. Can it be eliminated?

4. Judges are criticized often for their sentencing decisions. Discuss the factors that enter into the sentencing process. How important are the guilty party's sociodemographic attributes — gender, race, social class — in influencing the sentence?

CHAPTER 18

◆

ADULT SEGREGATIVE CONFINEMENT

Neal Shover
University of Tennessee

James Inverarity
Western Washington University

SEGREGATIVE CONFINEMENT is second only to the death penalty in the severity of state responses to crime. Although more offenders numerically are controlled by supervised release, the threat of incarceration underlies probation and parole. In 1990, an estimated 2.4 percent of America's adult population, some 4.3 million persons, were being supervised by correctional agencies (U.S. Department of Justice, 1992b: 5). Of this number, approximately 74 percent were on probation or parole; the remaining 26 percent were incarcerated in jails and prisons.

Incarceration as a form of criminal punishment is a product of the Age of Reason, that period of Western history and philosophy in which men and women sought to reorganize political, economic, and social institutions. Empirical observation and logical analysis were to replace irrational impulse and mindless tradition as determinants of penal policies. This way of thinking led Jeremy Bentham, Alexis de Tocqueville, and others to advocate segregative confinement as a practical, effective, and just alternative to then prevailing practices of executing, branding, or exiling criminals.

The sociological analysis of incarceration, in large part, is a sustained examination of why the visions of these reformers failed in practice. Their blueprints for rational organization paid insufficient attention to the dynamics of internal organizations that develop from the interactions among inmates and between the confined and the confiners. Their plans also failed adequately to comprehend the social and fiscal environmental constraints that affect these institutions. This chapter briefly traces how incarceration has developed and outlines the extent of financial and human resources invested in this enterprise. It further summarizes what we know about both the internal and the external social forces that shape segregative confinement.

HISTORICAL DEVELOPMENT

Jails and prisons differ both in function and in origin. Jails are local-level institutions used to detain defendants awaiting trial or placement in other institutions and to incarcerate convicted offenders serving short sentences, usually one year or less. They represent, therefore, a "curious hybrid" combining the traditional function of detaining defendants awaiting trial with the more modern practice of incarceration as a form of punishing convicted offenders (Flynn, 1973: 49). Prisons, by contrast, are operated by state or federal authorities and are used almost exclusively to confine prisoners serving sentences that exceed one year.

The jail is our oldest enduring structure for penal confinement (Moynahan and Stewart, 1980). Although its precise origins are obscure, versions have appeared in England and other countries for several centuries (Flynn, 1983). Before organized jails appeared, prisoners were held pending trial in unscalable pits, dungeons, or suspended cages (Mattick, 1974). In contrast to the jail, the origins of the modern prison are less obscure. Until the late eighteenth century, European nation states sanctioned criminals by fines or corporal punishment. Segregative confinement as a measured punishment for criminal conduct emerged from "houses of correction" established by England and Holland in the 1500s. These institutions housed and disciplined a wide range of disreputable populations, including debtors, criminals, vagrants, and the insane. By the eighteenth century, England and several American states pioneered the prison as a separate institutional strategy for punishing felons; a wave of prison construction swept much of the United States, while separate mental asylums and almshouses were developed to handle the problems posed by noncriminal segments of the disreputable population.

The new prisons, or "penitentiaries," were built on a foundation of good intentions, optimism, and a military model of offender rehabilitation. They were to be models of a disciplined and well-ordered world that would provide the regimentation and routine needed to reform offenders into law-abiding citizens and compliant wage laborers (Rothman, 1971; Ignatieff, 1978; Melossi and Pavarini, 1981). Mundane reality soon departed from these ideals. Throughout much of the nineteenth and twentieth centuries, American convicts were warehoused in overcrowded and underfunded facilities with physically harsh and brutal regimens. Instead of reforming criminals and reducing crime, institutions became notorious for their high rates of recidivism and failure to deter (Rothman, 1971).

These apparent failures led to a series of prison reform movements following a cycle of "conscience and convenience" in which charismatic innovations produced short-term changes that were quickly swamped by administrative and fiscal constraints (Rothman, 1980). Beginning in 1870, for example, the Reformatory movement renewed the effort to transform inmates by concentrating on educational programs for young first offenders. Two key ingredients of this reform were the indeterminate sentence and parole. Because the focus was to be on transforming the individual, success in reform was to be the primary factor determining length of incarceration. To administer this idea, parole — conditional early release from incarceration — was to be administered by review boards that would release inmates who successfully demonstrated reeducation. Although most states constructed new penal institutions designated "reformatories," architecturally they remained indistinguishable from existing prisons, and soon their administration fell into the conventional patterns as well. The innovation of parole became transformed from a tool of reform to an administrative mechanism for relieving prison overcrowding (Sutton, 1985).

Following World War II, an individual treatment model dominated public and professional discourse about crime and corrections. This "medical model" portrayed criminal behavior as symptomatic of internal, emotional conflicts or aberrant personality dynamics. The task for corrections accordingly was to provide therapy, counseling, and other treatment programs to enable offenders to "work through" and eventually to resolve their underlying problems. Political leaders, correctional publicists, and correctional administrators employed a rhetoric of rehabilitation to justify prison programs such as inmate classification, education, and counseling. As convicts became "inmates," the new "treatment" rhetoric was promoted by correctional reformers and mouthed increasingly in the prison world. Inmates now struggled to accumulate and present to parole boards evidence that they were working to overcome their assumed emotional deficiencies. A former prisoner in the California Department of Corrections remarks of his confinement at San Quentin during the heyday of the individual treatment model:

> We quickly learned that we were expected to view this journey through prison as a quest, and the object of our quest was to discover our problem. It was assumed we were here because of psychological problems, and our task now, by which we could expect to be judged, was to isolate and come to terms with them. . . . And no matter what your private opinion, when the . . . remote body authorized to grant parole asked in terms of high seriousness if you had come to grips with your problem, you were willing to concede you might have [one] even if you had to invent [it] on the spot (Braly, 1976: 157–158).

Once again, however, funding was inadequate as reformers either ignored or greatly overestimated the state's willingness to pay for rehabilitative programs. They also underestimated the difficulties involved in accomplishing rehabilitative objectives in an authoritarian, depriving environment.

Disenchantment with the individual treatment model and rehabilitative approaches to offenders increased dramatically in the 1970s, in part due to rising crime rates. As retribution, deterrence, and incapacitation gained in popularity, legislatures began shifting toward determinate sentences of increasing length. A sentencing reform movement swept the nation (Shane-DuBow et al., 1985; Tonry, 1988), often eliminating parole boards and making sentences proportional to offense severity and criminal history.

The sentencing reform movement was accompanied by a boom in prison construction, increasing prison admissions, and longer average sentences. Thus, 39 percent of the 1,037 prisons operating in 1990 were less than twenty years old (Greenfeld, 1992: 4). These changes marked a fundamental shift in correctional ideologies and strategies as well as a change in the dominant style of confinement as the correctional institution was supplanted by the contemporary prison (Irwin, 1980).

SOUTHERN PRISONS

Not all prisons followed a common path of development. The two most important exceptions are Southern prisons and women's prisons. Though many Southern states adopted the penitentiary in the early 1800s, these were rudimentary institutions almost exclusively used to punish white felons (Ayers, 1984). After the Civil War, prison populations expanded enormously, primarily as a means of controlling and exploiting freed slaves (Adamson, 1983). Until the early twentieth century, Southern states employed a convict lease system to minimize the costs of incarceration. While states elsewhere employed prison labor for state or private production, Southern states were unique in the extent to which their prison systems were operated for profit. Railroad construction, mining, and timber industries overcame labor shortages essentially by renting entire state prison populations. The states exercised little supervision over the leasors' labor camps, and rates of death and escape were continual sources of scandal in the late 1800s. Largely because of opposition by organized labor, the convict lease system was abolished in the twentieth century and generally replaced by the use of convict labor on public works (Myers and Massey, 1991).

Although its penitentiaries increasingly have taken on the characteristics of institutions nationally, the South remains distinctive in several ways. Most striking is the propensity to punish. Imprisonment rates, even controlling for crime, have long been higher in the South; this disproportionate use of imprisonment is matched by the relatively liberal use of execution (U.S. Department of Justice, 1989c; see also Chapter 24 of this volume). Another difference is the continued use by Southern states of extremely large plantationlike agricultural prisons such as Parchman (Mississippi) and Angola (Louisiana).

WOMEN'S PRISONS

The history of women's institutions in America both parallels and differs from the history of men's prisons (Freedman, 1981; Rafter, 1983, 1985). Before the development of penitentiaries, men and women generally were confined together in large open rooms or buildings, and officials made little effort to alleviate inmate idleness and despair through organized activities or programs. With the advent of penitentiaries, female prisoners generally were confined to a separate floor, building, or other out-of-the-way area of the men's prison. They were supervised by males, a practice that, not surprisingly, led to abuses and sexual exploitation. Throughout the nineteenth century, female offenders were viewed essentially as depraved persons beyond redemption who fully deserved harsh treatment.

The reformist zeal that fueled the Reformatory movement also extended to female offenders. A new ideological conception of their criminality challenged the notion of willfulness fundamental to the traditional view and, like men, women now were thought to commit crimes for reasons largely beyond their control. A less pessimistic assessment of their rehabilitative potential gained currency as well although the new conception was restrictive in its own way; female offenders now were viewed as childlike persons who needed to be cared for and socialized into their "correct" roles.

The Reformatory movement also sparked the first widespread development of separate institutions for females. Built in the early decades of this century, nearly all remain in operation today. Their open, campuslike grounds and cottage-style housing units differ radically from the fortresslike institutions and cage-filled cell houses common in men's prisons. Moreover, the women's reformatories were staffed almost entirely by females, a reform that virtually ended sexual exploitation of inmates. Originally reserved for misdemeanants, by 1935, women's reformatories had become places of confinement for felons.

Today, many states have two or, at most, three institutions for women to go along with several times this number for men. Approximately 86 percent of the 1,037 state and federal prisons hold males only, and about 7 percent confine females only (Greenfeld, 1992: 2–3). The average population of male-only prisons is about 700 inmates, nearly twice the average daily population of women's prisons. The advantages of confining males and females together are a matter of some debate (Ross et al., 1978; Smykla, 1980), but in practice only 7 percent of American state prisons do so.

THE VARIABLE RATE OF IMPRISONMENT

For over a century, imprisonment rates in America have varied widely both geographically and annually (Garofalo, n.d.; Langan et al., 1988; Cahalan, 1986). On December 31, 1991, for example, state imprisonment rates ranged from a low of 68 in North Dakota to a high of 477 in Nevada (U.S. Department of Justice, 1992f); this range of 7 to 1 in state-level imprisonment rates within the United States matches the range of variation among the nation states of western Europe (Vass, 1990; Christie, 1993). In discussing imprisonment in the United States, therefore, it is important to keep in mind the substantial diversity of its prison systems. This variation can also provide, as we will see later, important clues about the causes and consequences of incarceration.

A narrower but significant range of variation in U.S. imprisonment rates appears over time. Figure 18.1 shows the rate of imprisonment for the period 1925–1990. Except for a sharp but moderate upturn in the late years of the Great Depression and moderate downturns during World War II and the Vietnam War, the figure shows a gradual increase, at least until 1973, when the rate escalated rapidly, nearly tripling by 1990.

Along with regional and temporal variation in the imprisonment rate, the nature of the inmate population varies as well. The most striking variation is

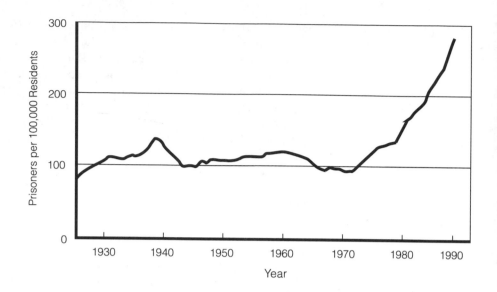

by race and gender. From a record low of 20.7 percent in 1928, the proportion of African-American prisoners increased to 30 percent by World War II and remained close to that level until the 1970s. It then began a steady increase, eventually reaching 48 percent by 1986 before declining to 46 percent in 1991 (U.S. Department of Justice, 1993). Racial composition also varies by region. African-Americans run a substantially greater risk of imprisonment outside the South than they do within the South, even when crime and arrest differentials are controlled (Christianson, 1981; Hawkins, 1985; Innes, 1988; Bridges and Crutchfield, 1988). This pattern is paradoxical because on most other social indicators, such as income inequality or the risk of execution, Southern blacks are more disadvantaged.

In contrast to African-Americans, the proportion of women in the prison population has not changed dramatically, remaining approximately 5 percent of the nation's total imprisoned population over several decades. Both female and male incarceration rates have grown at about the same rate. Between 1925 and 1980, the annual rate of incarceration for women fluctuated in the range of 6 to 10 per 100,000 women age 18 and over in the unincarcerated population. In 1981, it began to increase steadily, reaching a rate of 33 per 100,000 women in 1990 (Greenfeld and Langan, 1987; Greenfeld, 1992).

FACILITIES, POPULATIONS, AND PROGRAMS

The principal difference between jails and prisons we noted earlier. In addition, though both types of facility hold people involuntarily, their structures, population sizes, inmate flows, types of inmates, everyday routines, and control problems differ considerably. Let us examine each facility briefly.

JAILS

America's local jails annually process more citizens than any other component of the correctional apparatus, and few who are arrested and formally charged with criminal offenses can avoid its grasp, however briefly. In the year ending June 28, 1991, the nation's jails admitted approximately 10.1 million persons and released about an equal number (U.S. Department of Justice, 1992b). On an average day in 1991, the nation's jails held 422,609 inmates, an increase of 86 percent over 1983. Like the prison population, the jail population increased dramatically in the 1970s and 1980s (U.S. Department of Justice, 1989c).

The number of prisoners retained in local jails (sometimes for more than a year) because of prison overcrowding has increased as well. Because of lack of bed space in state prisons, on December 31, 1991, 1.5 percent of the nation's prison population (12,225 inmates) were serving felony sentences in local jails (U.S. Department of Justice, 1992d). One unanticipated consequence of America's twenty-year imprisonment binge, therefore, has been overcrowded local jails. The increasing number of jail beds occupied by state prisoners has limited local officials' ability to cope with crimes of local importance. For example, crackdown campaigns against drunk drivers have been hampered by lack of space in local jails. Recent changes in the jail population also reflect America's "war on drugs"; the number of jail inmates held on drug charges increased from 9 percent in 1983 to 23 percent in 1989 (Beck, 1991).

Approximately 53 percent of all adults confined in American jails are awaiting judicial disposition of, typically minor, criminal charges; the remaining 47 percent include prisoners serving misdemeanor sentences and others in a variety of legal statuses (examples include parole violators and prisoners in transit). Some jails continue to be used for pretrial detention of juveniles; nearly 1 percent of the nationwide daily jail population are juveniles (U.S. Department of Justice, 1992b). Largely because they confine a socially homogeneous but legally diverse population, jails have been called the "ultimate ghetto of the criminal justice system" (Goldfarb, 1975).

Based on personal interviews with a nationally representative sample of 5,675 inmates in 525 local jails, Table 18.1 presents social and legal data on jail prisoners. A comparison of these estimates with data on the general population (U.S. Bureau of the Census, 1992) tells us much about the risk factors associated with incarceration. African-Americans are 3.5 times as likely to be in jail on any given day as the general population. Unmarried adults over 18 are 3.2 times as likely to be jailed as the married. Americans age 18–34 are 1.4 times as likely to be in jail, and the risk for the unemployed is 4.5 times that of the employed. These statistical comparisons show that jail inmates are disproportionately poor, undereducated, never-married, African-American, male property offenders. It should not be surprising that they have difficulty finding the resources necessary for pretrial release on bond or for conducting an adequate court defense.

Compared to imprisonment, jail terms are short; the average length of stay in jail is approximately six to eleven days (National Center on Institutions and Alternatives, 1988). Jail confinement can be socially and emotionally traumatic,

TABLE 18.1   SOCIAL, ECONOMIC, AND LEGAL CHARACTERISTICS OF AMERICAN JAIL INMATES, 1989

Percent

Sex
Male	91
Female	9

Race or Ethnicity
White	39
Black	42
Hispanic	14
Other	2

Age
Under 18	1
18–24	33
25–34	43
35 or older	23

Education
Less than 12 years	54
12 or more years	33

Marital Status
Never married	57
Married	19
Other (separated, divorced, widowed)	24

Confinement Status
Convicted	57
Unconvicted	43

Prearrest Employment Status
Full-time employment	53
Part-time employment	11
Unemployed	36

Current Offense
Property*	37
Public order	23
Violent†	17
Drug	23

Prearrest Median Annual Income for Those Free at Least One Year	$7,424
Prearrest Median Monthly Income for Those Free Less Than One Year	$ 736

SOURCE: U.S. Department of Justice (1992g).

* Includes primarily robbery, burglary, auto theft, larceny, stolen property, fraud, forgery, and embezzlement.
† Includes primarily murder, attempted murder, manslaughter, rape, sexual assault, and assault.

however, particularly for those who confront it for the first time (Gibbs, 1982a). New inmates often experience extreme shock and depression:

> I'll never forget it. The place was dim and gray and dirty looking. It had a putrid smell to it. Kind of a mixture of pine oil and dirt. The ceiling was low, and it had a little light that gave off a glow but didn't light up the place. . . . It looked like a concentration camp. Everyone had a sallow look. . . . Man, it was depressing (Irwin, 1985: 63).

Inmates live in a continual state of uncertainty about personal relationships, commitments, and obligations in the outside world, the charges for which they are held, and the stresses of jail life itself. Suicide is a leading cause of death among jail inmates (Winfree, 1987); in the year ending June 30, 1983, for example, nearly 300 suicides were reported in the nation's jails (U.S. Department of Justice, 1988b). Of inmates who commit suicide in jail, 51 percent take their lives within the first twenty-four hours of incarceration (National Center on Institutions and Alternatives, 1988). Even those who pass through the jail repeatedly, such as chronic drunkenness offenders, cannot escape entirely the stress and uncertainty of life in its confines (Wiseman, 1970). Besides being degrading and disorienting, jail confinement hastens the disintegration of inmates' ties with conventional others, identities, and routines in the free world. By eroding their conventional sensibilities, teaching them how to cope successfully with a depriving and dangerous environment, and acclimating them to deviant norms and patterns of adaptation, the jail experience also may undermine its value as a deterrent to future criminal conduct (Irwin, 1985).

Since the time of its adoption in America, the jail has remained a peculiarly local institution. Most of the approximately 3,316 jails in the United States are under the control of the county sheriff or municipal police chief (U.S. Department of Justice, 1992d). On June 28, 1991, 81 percent of the total jail population of the United States were housed in 823 jails located in 505 jurisdictions. Each of these jails had an average daily population of at least 100 inmates. Located in the nation's major cities, the twenty-five largest jail systems had between one and seventeen facilities and populations ranging from 2,076 to 20,779 (U.S. Department of Justice, 1992d). By contrast, 19 percent of America's jail population were confined in 2,493 facilities with an average inmate population of thirty-two. Small jails such as these "typically serve counties of 2,000–3,000 people; tax bases often depend on farming or ranching; and distances are great between population centers or from major cities" (Mays and Thompson, 1988: 425).

Procedures and daily operations in large jails are highly routinized, whereas smaller jails operate more informally. Consequently, although the organizational worlds of small and large jails vary substantially, size and operational variation probably are related inversely. Large jails may employ many specialized personnel, whereas small jails often are understaffed or operated by personnel with little or no training or qualifications for jail duty. As a result, "for small jails . . . it is not unusual for one person to serve as booking officer and turnkey in addition to being the patrol dispatcher or even the courthouse cleaner" (Mays and Thompson, 1988: 427). These staffing patterns contribute to long periods of lockdown for inmates because sheriffs' personnel devote much of their time to law enforcement responsibilities. Many of America's small jails also are among its oldest. Although the post-1975 boom in construction of "new generation" jails has replaced some of these facilities (Zupan, 1991), rural sheriffs often remain saddled with buildings that do not lend themselves easily to humane, secure, and efficient care of prisoners.

The physical facilities, programs, and security of jails reflect all the variations in financing, structure, and operation characteristic of local communities and government in the United States (Wayson et al., 1977; Thompson, 1986; Newman and Price, 1977; Kerle and Ford, 1982; Thompson and Mays, 1991). Some are clean, secure, and well run, whereas others are physically and operationally deficient. This should not obscure the fact that the daily routine in most jails is unrelieved by officially provided programs or facilities. Few jails of any size offer even minimal recreational and educational diversions for inmates. Approximately one-third of all jails have no routine or ready access to professional medical personnel or facilities (U.S. Department of Justice, 1988b). As with state prisons, jails increasingly have come under court order to improve their conditions of confinement and limit their populations (U.S. Department of Justice, 1992b).

Facilities for female jail inmates are extremely limited; many are housed in a "women's unit" in jails designed for and used primarily to confine men. Female prisoners rarely have equal access to jail programs, and even their routine activities are restricted more than is the case for males (Shaw, 1982; Mann, 1984; U.S. Department of Justice, 1992d). In some respects, therefore, jail confinement is more difficult for females than for males. Gender differences notwithstanding, the vast majority of jail prisoners, male and female, pass the days sitting or lying around in their cells, dormitory, or bullpen—usually a large open area where they can congregate, play table games, talk, or watch a communal television set (Spradley, 1972).

Inmates new to jail confinement typically do not know what to expect. They lack detailed understanding of when and how their criminal cases will be processed. They do not know which officials and agencies in the jail and court process are influential or important and which are not. Other inmates become their principal source of information and means of reducing uncertainty and apprehension. Those with previous institutional experience who can explain and clarify jail and court procedures assume positions of high status in the rudimentary inmate hierarchy (Rothman and Kimberly, 1985: 131).

PRISONS

On June 29, 1990, the states and the District of Columbia operated 957 prisons for general adult confinement (Greenfeld, 1992: 2). The federal government operated 80 prisons as well as a handful of military long-term confinement facilities scattered throughout the nation. Two-thirds of America's prisons provide maximum or medium security and house approximately 86 percent of its prison population. By contrast, the remaining third, consisting of minimum security institutions, house only 13 percent of prison inmates. This means a substantial majority of American prison inmates serve all or most of their sentences either in traditional wall-enclosed, fortresslike penitentiaries or in newer "correctional institutions" that are usually surrounded by double chain-link fences.

Prisons provide a variety of recreational and educational programs, their many deficiencies notwithstanding, that contrast sharply with the paucity of programs available in jails. In 1991, 45 percent of all state prison inmates had participated in academic programs, and 31 percent had participated in vocational programs of one kind or another (U.S. Department of Justice, 1993).

Although a nearly equal proportion of male and female state prison inmates are confined for homicide — 15 percent and 12 percent, respectively — they differ substantially in the crimes for which they serve penitentiary time. Generally, a higher proportion of female than male prisoners are imprisoned for less serious, nonconfrontative, and nonviolent crimes. Specifically, proportionately more female prisoners than male prisoners are in prison following conviction for larceny-theft and fraud — 21 percent and 7 percent, respectively — and drug offenses — 33 percent versus 21 percent. Fewer women prisoners are confined for robbery and burglary — 13 percent and 28 percent, respectively (U.S. Department of Justice, 1993).

Generally, men's prisons provide a larger number and wider variety of vocational training and industrial work experience than do women's prisons (Arditi et al., 1973; Glick and Neto, 1977). Much of this disparity results from gender stereotypes held by correctional administrators who believe either that the small numbers of incarcerated women do not justify the expense of duplicate facilities and programs or that women are uninterested in the types of vocational training offered men (U.S. Comptroller General, 1980: 20–21).

In addition to these institutionally imposed handicaps, confined women suffer another deprivation that generally is not shared by their male counterparts: anxiety and guilt over separation from their children. The experience of one is typical:

> I have three children, and I talk to my children. My youngest daughter is with Mary and Joe, who I knew before I came here. . . . [She] calls them "mommy" and "daddy." . . . I'll be holding her when they visit me, and when [she] gets tired of me, she hollers, "Mommy." So you see, for mothers in here, it's hard. . . . [But] I'm more fortunate than most, because I know my child is all right. I don't have to worry about her being abused, neglected, or starving (Fox, 1982b: 216).

Because the population of prison inmates is drawn from local jails, it is hardly surprising that the two populations are strikingly similar in their backgrounds and characteristics. Based on interviews with 13,986 inmates in 277 prisons, Table 18.2 presents data on the social, economic, and legal characteristics of inmates in state prisons in 1991 (U.S. Department of Justice, 1993). It shows that imprisonment is reserved primarily for those convicted of crimes committed disproportionately by the poor and socially disadvantaged. America's prisons, whether for males or females, confine almost exclusively

TABLE 18.2 **SOCIAL, ECONOMIC, AND LEGAL CHARACTERISTICS OF AMERICAN STATE PRISON INMATES, 1991**

	Percent
Sex	
Male	95
Female	5
Race or Ethnicity	
White	35
Black	46
Hispanic	17
Other	2
Age	
17 or younger	1
18–24	21
25–34	46
35–44	23
45 or older	10
Education	
8th grade or less	14
Some high school	27
High school graduate	46
Some college or more	13
Marital Status	
Never married	55
Married	18
Divorced	19
Widowed or separated	8

SOURCE: U.S. Department of Justice (1993).

* Includes robbery, burglary, larceny, auto theft, stolen property, arson, and others.

† Includes murder, manslaughter, rape, other sexual assaults, assault, kidnapping, and others.

undereducated, unskilled, poor, and increasingly, minority citizens. More than one-third of state prison inmates are confined for property crimes. What Table 18.2 does not show is the dramatic change in the prison population in the last years of the 1980s. From 1986 to 1991, the number of state prison inmates serving time for drug offenses increased 281 percent. Those confined for property crimes declined from 52 to 37 percent of the total state prison population (U.S. Department of Justice, 1993).

THE UNDERLIFE OF JAILS AND PRISONS

American prisons have been settings for social research for more than fifty years. Early investigators quickly discovered that confinement in jail or prison means entering a social world sharply distinct from the outside world. For example, Clemmer (1958) and Sykes (1958) sketched a pervasive inmate belief and nor-

	Percent
Current Offense	
Property*	37
Violent†	32
Drug	21
Other	10
Maximum Sentence Length	
1–24 months	10
25–60 months	25
61–120 months	25
121 or more months	30
Life imprisonment or death sentence	10
Prearrest Employment Status	
Full-time employment	55
Part-time employment	12
Unemployed	33
Prearrest Annual Income for Those Free at Least	
One Year	
Less than $3,000	22
$3,000–$4,999	10
$5,000–$9,999	21
$10,000–$14,999	17
$15,000–$24,999	16
$25,000 or more	14

mative system, a complex underground economy for production and distribution of scarce goods and services, and a social structure laced together both by cooperation and conflict. Goffman (1961) coined the concept *underlife* to describe this distinctive, unofficial social organization and culture created by inmates of prisons and similar institutions. As described in now-classic research, the inmate social structure comprised social types or roles, such as "punk," "wolf," "gorilla," and "merchant" (Sykes, 1958) or "square john," "politician," and "outlaw" (Schrag, 1961). Prestige and influence varied with one's position in this social order in which the "right guy" gained respect and informal power:

> Renowned for his unerring loyalty to the inmate code whatever the personal sacrifice or show of official force, [the right guy] holds a position of immense honor and esteem; he is the charismatic leader of the inmate system. He gains prestige among

his fellows largely because he is able to elicit a deferential response from the authorities; because he is capable of mobilizing and employing violence to achieve higher status, they defer to him in order to avert disruptive actions (Cloward, 1960: 34).

The belief system of inmates helped integrate the sub rosa organization and economy. It prescribed how inmates should interpret their personal circumstances, view and interact with staff and with one another, and respond generally to the problems of prison life. By one account, the chief tenets of this code admonished convicts to remain strong in the face of privations and challenges, to "be cool" and to minimize the frictions and irritants of daily life, not to exploit other inmates or interfere with their interests, to be loyal to one another and not to side with prison staff in disputes with inmates (Sykes and Messinger, 1960).

Earlier prison investigators located the principal cause of this unofficial organization and belief system of prisoners in the deprivations of confinement or the "pains of imprisonment." The underlife was seen as a vehicle of relief from the deprivation of liberty, goods and services, heterosexual relations, autonomy, and security (Sykes, 1958; Sykes and Messinger, 1960). Others saw the origins of inmate organization and culture in the distinctive structural characteristics of prisons (Goffman, 1961). Both groups of investigators pointed to the indigenous origins of inmate social organization and culture. In other words, they argued that conditions within the prison itself generated and shaped its underlife. No one disputes that these indigenous factors play a major part in generating the unofficial inmate world.

Research reveals that the behavior and social organization of male and female prisoners differ significantly (Bowker, 1977, 1980, 1981; Burkhart, 1973; Chandler, 1973). Whereas fighting and other forms of physical aggression are common among male prisoners, they are less common among female prisoners, who more often employ verbal aggression to resolve disputes. The underground economy of women's prisons is much less developed than in men's prisons (Ward and Kassebaum, 1965), and collective disturbances and challenges to institutional authority are virtually nonexistent. Gang conflict, common in men's prisons, is absent as well. More important, female prisoners tend to adopt make-believe kinship roles—as "parents," "daughters," "aunts," or other blood relatives—in the relations with one another (Giallombordo, 1966; Ward and Kassebaum, 1965; Heffernan, 1972). These fictive kinship groups are absent from institutions for males. The underlife of womens' prisons in large measure is an interlocking mosaic of inmate family groups and their relationships with institutional staff. The families function as a source of both emotional and material support for inmates and order in the institution.

THE ROLE OF THE STAFF

It would be a mistake to assume that only inmate deprivations and problems shape the sub rosa social order of jails and prisons, for the collective problems of the staff also play a part. Prison work, particularly for correctional officers, is difficult, unpredictable, and cannot be performed satisfactorily without the willing cooperation of inmates. Inmates perform much of the daily work essential to jail and prison operation. They clean the floors, repair the plumbing, and prepare and serve the meals. It is tempting to assume that staff can compel prisoners to work diligently at these assigned labors and to avoid collective threats to institutional order and routines. But the use of threat and force is an extremely crude and ineffective tool for managing resistive human beings. Hierarchical social arrangements operate smoothly and most predictably only when the acquiescence and aid of subordinates (in this case, inmates) can be secured voluntarily. Thus, the staff predicament: despite their monopoly over firearms and other instruments of force, they also must employ "softer" and more humane control procedures. This defect of total power gives rise in all jails and prisons to a system of tacit staff–inmate cooperation and support that reinforces both the official and the unofficial worlds (Sykes, 1958).

Jail and prison staff maintain accommodative relationships with informal inmate leaders in the form, for example, of extra privileges and assignment to preferred work assignments. In the depriving jail and prison environment, this stake in conformity increases commitment by elite inmates to order, the status quo, and staff procedures. The use of inmate leaders as a stabilizing force goes a long way toward explaining the relative infrequency of collective challenges to staff in the face of endemic structural conflict between staff and inmates. In some states and prisons, particularly in the South, elite inmates traditionally occupied quasi-official roles; in Texas prisons, inmate "building tenders" disciplined other prisoners, and in Arkansas, elite inmates actually carried firearms and guarded other prisoners (Murton and Hyams, 1969). But these cases are exceptions. For the most part, the process of co-optation remains unofficial and invisible to the outside world.

The problems and demands of jail work that give rise to tacit cooperation with informal inmate leaders resemble but also differ from the problems of prison guards. In both institutions, staff must secure inmates' cooperation. In contrast to the world of prisons, however, the jail's population is extremely transitory, and during their brief stays, inmates are subject to intense pressures and emotional extremes. The staff may have no knowledge about the vast majority of those who pass through the jail and little time to develop knowledge of them. Identifying stable, compliant inmates to perform the day-to-day work that must be done is one of their main problems. Consequently, jail staff usually select for work details inmates who are known to them from previous stints in jail. These inmates, as we have seen, also rise to positions of informal leadership among their peers (Glaser, 1971). Wise to the ways of institutions and the customs and manners of the staff, their work assignments enable them to move around the jail, thereby minimizing the restrictions and boredom of near-constant cell or dormitory confinement.

THE SOCIAL CONTEXT OF JAILS AND PRISON

Although early investigators studied jails and prisons as self-contained entities largely cut off from the outside world, the discovery of significant differences in the sub rosa organization and culture of institutions for males and females revealed the shortcomings of this approach. Individual and collective responses to the deprivations of imprisonment to a great extent are gender specific. The pains of imprisonment alone clearly cannot explain the diverse and changing worlds created by segregated populations; rather, variables external to the prison—externally grounded identities and interests—are carried into the prison world or in other ways penetrate its walls and help shape the structure and dynamics of its inner world.

This is confirmed by evidence of how recent social and political currents in American life have altered dramatically significant aspects of jail and prison life. Violent urban riots, the formation and activities of urban youth gangs, the emergence and spread of drug use and drug trafficking, and trends in public administration, chiefly unionization of public employees and privatization of government services, all have helped reshape the contemporary prison.

Prison riots provide one of the few occasions when citizens take note of or call into question the peculiar wall-enclosed world of the prison. These large-scale collective challenges to prison authorities involving violence or threatened violence assume a variety of forms and, more important, often follow on the heels of external turmoil and social change that destabilize the prison's administration and fragile internal order. Such destabilizing forces have diverse origins, assume a variety of forms, and fluctuate substantially over time (Useem and Kimball, 1989).

The period 1952–1954, when advocates of the individual treatment model were making inroads in traditional prison practices, saw a wave of prison riots sweep over the nation. Similarly, social and political currents in America during the 1960s and 1970s, particularly urban riots and increasing political consciousness among African-Americans, sparked numerous collective inmate challenges to prison authorities. Distinguished by strong inmate solidarity and political consciousness, the 1971 uprising at New York's Attica State Prison ended after state police and correctional officers mounted an undisciplined armed assault on rebelling prisoners. In the process, they shot and killed ten guard hostages and twenty-nine inmates. Prisoners killed one guard and three of their fellow inmates before the rebellion was suppressed (New York State Special Commission, 1972; Useem and Kimball, 1989). Nine years later, inmates at New Mexico's main prison inflicted savage violence on other inmates, killing thirty-three in the process although no police or guards were killed (Attorney General, 1980; Colvin, 1992; Hirliman, 1982).

Reflecting developments in America's cities, gangs have become a prominent aspect of prison underlife in recent years. As white and Hispanic prisoners organized gangs to resist the growing influence of black inmates, violence, much of it crossing racial or ethnic lines, increased (Davis, 1968; Park, 1975; Bowker, 1982; Lockwood, 1980, 1982; Davidson, 1983; Carroll, 1988). Street gangs carried their activities, allegiances, and recruitment into the prison, thereby adding to the growing sense of disorder and personal insecurity (Jacobs, 1974, 1979). A growing number of inmates retreated from public areas or sought secure niches out of harm's way (Toch, 1977; Bowker, 1977, 1980; Fox, 1982a). The old and largely fictionalized convict code gave way to more numerous and meaner normative adaptations to imprisonment (Irwin and Cressey, 1962; Glaser, 1964). "The old hero of the prison world—the 'right guy'—has been replaced by outlaws and gang members. [They] have raised toughness and mercilessness to the top of prisoners' value systems" (Irwin, 1970: vii). The increasing availability and use of drugs by Americans breached jail and prison walls, and the prisoners' sub rosa economy adapted to take advantage of this highly sought-after commodity (Williams and Fish, 1974; Bowker, 1977).

In the 1960s and 1970s, major changes occurred in the legal status of prisoners. Traditionally, felons lost most of their rights as citizens and, even after serving their sentences, "ex-cons" suffered a host of legal limitations on the right to vote, own firearms, or engage in many occupations. These civil disabilities have eroded in most states (Burton et al., 1987). The most dramatic changes, however, resulted from intervention of federal courts into the administration of jails and prisons. The courts had long adhered to a "hands off" doctrine that left prison administration to legislatures and prison bureaucracies. The major revisions of this doctrine emerged along with the "due process revolution" in criminal procedure that began in the early 1960s. It coincided with the Civil Rights revolution, which extended to black citizens rights previously denied them by the laws of several states (Friedman, 1985). For over a decade, the Court expanded the application of the Bill of Rights to law enforcement practices and correctional administration.

Black prison inmates were the vanguard in mounting successful appellate court challenges to the discretionary practices of prison staff. The resulting federal court decisions produced new formal and procedural restraints on prison administrators and staff, orders to provide a range of inmate programs, and limits on prison population. In Texas and several other states, federal judges appointed "special masters" to oversee ordered prison reforms (Chilton, 1991). These legal victories, in turn, reinforced an emerging conception of prisoners that emphasized their unsurrendered rights as citizens. Along with other forces buffeting the prison world, they helped establish a new, increasingly political, conception of inmates (Stastny and Tyrnauer, 1982). Although federal courts have retreated from their activist stance in recent years, the effects of earlier decisions remain.

The consequences of court decisions and direct intervention in prisons have been widely debated (DiIulio, 1987, 1990). Events in Texas prisons following judicial intervention are illustrative. Ordered to revamp its semifeudal system of using inmate "building tenders" to maintain order, the ensuing power vacuum may have produced a rapid emergence of prison gangs and escalating violence (Martin and Ekland-Olson, 1987; Crouch and Marquart, 1989). In two years, more than fifty inmates were killed by other inmates, and tension and fear remained high even when the level of violence eventually subsided (Press et al., 1986).

The daily world of staff as well as inmates has been reshaped by events beyond the prison walls. Correctional officers—in most states, the formal designation "guard" was discarded years ago—increasingly experienced role ambiguity and feelings of danger while on the job. As work satisfaction decreased, they reacted with increasing militancy (Crouch, 1980; Lombardo, 1981; Jacobs and Crotty, 1983; Cullen et al., 1985; Hepburn, 1985). Unionization efforts met with considerable success, and confrontations with upper-level correctional administrators grew more frequent (Jacobs and Zimmer, 1983). Even as these changes were occurring, growing numbers of minorities and women found employment in guard ranks that once were made up almost entirely of white males from rural or working-class backgrounds. The new mixture proved to be an uneasy one, however, and conflict between guards and supervisors soon was matched by conflict within the guard force (Jacobs, 1979, 1983; Jacobs and Kraft, 1983; Jacobs and Zimmer, 1983; Crouch, 1991). As Jacobs (1988: 3) notes,

> prisons are experiencing stress, even turmoil. The old autocratic system has been abolished by court order. . . . Crowding remains a major problem, and the prisons have deteriorated physically and administratively. . . . [N]ew techniques of control have yet to be successfully developed. While prisoners now enjoy more rights, freer access to the courts, and . . . better health care, they may be more vulnerable to assault by other inmates.

The impact of external social and political events of the 1960s and 1970s show clearly that prisons are inextricable parts of the societies in which they are embedded. Because a number of these developments occurred simultaneously, however, it is difficult to disentangle their individual contributions to changes in prison policies, problems, and underlife.

SOCIETY AND INCARCERATION: EXPLAINING THE CONNECTIONS

The role of jails and prisons in society is less obvious than it appears; like most complex organizations, their operations involve more than their official task of "crime control." In thinking about the other roles, three considerations are primary. First, incarceration is a form of *state* control; only the state can confine citizens involuntarily or empower others to do so. Second, the incarcerated always have been, as we saw earlier, primarily members of a segment of society Karl Marx designated the "lumpen proletariat" and contemporary writers variously have characterized as the "underclass" (Wilson, 1987), "rabble" (Irwin, 1985) or "social refuse" (Spitzer, 1975). Third, because the supply of crime and criminal offenders is extremely large, the agencies and apparatchiks that make up the criminal justice system enjoy considerable discretion in decisionmaking (Christie, 1993). As a result, the proportion of offenders subjected to segregative confinement varies enormously both regionally and temporally.

What explains variation in state use of segregative confinement to control the underclass? Why does Minnesota, for example, have half the incarceration rate of Michigan? Why in recent years has the incarceration rate grown in California but stabilized in Texas (Ekland-Olson et al., 1992)? Why has America's prison population increased steadily for twenty years? Crime rates certainly have something to do with geographic and temporal variation in use of incarceration, but penal policies are influenced by many variables other than crime. Identifying these variables and weighing their impact on rates of prison admissions and releases are important tasks for developing sociological theories of social control (Garland, 1990).

NEOCLASSICAL ECONOMIC PERSPECTIVE

From this perspective, the level and severity of punishment are outcomes of rational choices made by public officials seeking to maximize rewards and minimize costs. As a governmental response to crime, the imprisonment rate varies with the street-crime rate, the public's fear of crime, and the state's responsiveness to public demands. The state balances the costs of crime and crime control through a political process (Becker, 1968; Phillips and Votey, 1981; Wilson, 1975). The imprisonment rate, in turn, affects crime rates either by deterring would-be law violators or by incapacitating convicted criminals.

Viewed in this way, the increasing rate of street crime that began in the 1960s heightened public demand for more severe punishment. Politicians responded by enacting "get tough" legislation that contributed to the explosive growth of prison populations after 1972. The "push to capture and confine" (Gordon, 1990) was produced by the public's anxiety, fears, and demands for action. The increasing use of imprisonment then caused a decline of the crime rate in the 1980s as criminals began to take into account the higher costs imposed by the state (Langan, 1991).

Although this argument is appealing intuitively, research has raised doubts about its major tenets and explanatory adequacy. To begin with, public demands for crime control have little apparent relationship to variations in crime rates, and politicians overestimate public punitiveness. Further, though crime rates and imprisonment are related inversely, deterrence and incapacitation are not the only plausible explanations for this pattern (Blumstein et al., 1978). High crime rates may reduce the rate of imprisonment because jails, courts, and prisons become so overcrowded that relatively fewer felons can be imprisoned (see Krohn, this volume). Calculation of costs and benefits of crime control policy, moreover, is neither straightforward nor clear. Neither the public nor administrators possess requisite knowledge of the costs and consequences of alternative crime control policies. Assessment of the marginal gain of increasing the prison population, for example, requires an accurate estimate of the number and nature of offenses committed by unapprehended offenders. (Surveying prison inmates about their criminal histories yields inflated estimates since inmates are not representative of the offender population.) Furthermore, because the tax burden and potential benefits of crime control are not shared uniformly, the economic perspective obscures the political nature of crime control policy (Greenberg, 1990). Last, advocates of this perspective generally ignore the politically symbolic functions of "get tough" crime control measures and the machinations of crime control bureaucracies (Garland, 1990; Gordon, 1990; Christie, 1993). Other perspectives are efforts to describe and weigh the impact of some of these on incarceration.

WEBERIAN PERSPECTIVE:
ROLE OF FORMAL ORGANIZATIONS

The criminal justice apparatus is made up of specialized bureaucratic organizations that include prosecutors' offices, courts, and correctional organizations that compose an interorganizational network. Both the degree of coordination and the extent to which the network is dominated by any particular agency varies substantially. Like all bureaucracies, they develop autonomous interests, goals, and procedures for processing the flow of defendants and inmates (McCleary, 1978; Pontell, 1984; Shover and Einstadter, 1988). Berk et al. (1983) show that rates of prison admission and release in California from 1850 to 1970 partly reflect the ways correctional agencies control populations to maintain stability within the organization. Balbus (1977) similarly discovered that during riots, felons were *less* likely to go to prison due, in part, to the efforts of administrators to prevent serious overcrowding. Sutton (1987) argues that the growth of such managerial strategies is related to the historical emergence of bureaucratic organization in American states.

The growth in incarcerated populations most likely is influenced by variation in administrative practices and interorganizational relationships. The fact that state prison populations have grown faster than jail or federal prison populations, for example, may be explained by the peculiarities of their administrations. From this perspective, variation in prison populations, at least in part, reflects changes in the relative power and resources of administrative agencies. State prisons are administered and financed at the state level, whereas sentencing decisions are made at the county level. The consequences of this division of administrative responsibilities is illustrated by the "probation subsidy program" in California during the 1960s. Under this plan, California reduced its state prison population by paying counties a subsidy for each felon placed on probation (Lerman, 1975). Jail populations increased, however. The net result was an unintended shift of incarcerated populations from state to local institutions.

DURKHEIMIAN PERSPECTIVE:
RITUALIZED POLITICS

In contrast to the neoclassical economic perspective, others suggest that the most important impact of punishment is not on the criminals but on the general public. Particularly during times of public anxiety and concern over social order, punishment of crime serves to mobilize and reinforce moral sentiments among ordinary members of society (Durkheim, [1893] 1933). In the past, the public participated directly in the collective rituals of punishment. The birth of the prison and the creation of specialized law enforcement agencies eliminated this direct participation, but moral sentiments still may affect indirectly incarceration practices. Perhaps the clearest evidence of this is seen in electoral politics. Local and national candidates often have appealed successfully to the fear of crime (Scheingold, 1984; Gordon, 1990). Unlike the neoclassical economic perspective, the Durkheimian interpretation of the politics of punishment discounts any effect the "wars" on crime and drugs may have on crime rates. Instead, the latter perspective weighs heavily evidence of how public anxiety about crime is based on sensationalized and, therefore, atypical cases rather than rational actuarial calculations of victimization risk .

From the Durkheimian perspective, electoral politics and social movements are critical factors in understanding variation in incarcerated populations. The recent explosion in prison populations, from this perspective, most likely results from legislatures imposing restrictions on plea bargaining and mandatory and longer prison sentences. Moral crusades against drunk drivers, domestic violence, or sexual psychopaths are especially important in explaining the expansion of incarcerated populations.

Investigators, however, generally have not found clear and persuasive evidence that legislative reforms explain much variation in the rates of incarceration. Reforms tend to be offset by the organizational factors outlined earlier and by countervailing social forces of the sort discussed in the next section (Tonry, 1988; Carroll and Cornell, 1985). Keep in mind, though, that many of these legislative reforms have been so recent that it may be difficult to gauge accurately their effects.

MARXIST PERSPECTIVE:
ROLE OF LABOR MARKET

Jails and prisons primarily confine economically marginal people. Though unemployment, poverty, and illiteracy may be related to involvement in street crime, the connection between economic conditions and jail or prison incarceration appears to be more direct. During periods of economic recession, unemployment increases and use of segregative confinement is stepped up as a means to control this potentially restive segment of the labor force. That the risk of incarceration would vary with unemployment might seem odd, but there are several reasons to expect such a connection. First, sentencing is discretionary; only about half of all felons currently receive prison sentences (Langan, 1989). Second, whether a felon gets prison or probation depends in part on an assessment of risk of violation, colored by the offender's history and current prospects of steady employment (Greenberg, 1977b). Third, economic recession may heighten the anxiety of elites, judges, and other decisionmakers about the potential "social dynamite" (Spitzer, 1975) in the form of young, unemployed males (Box, 1985).

Beginning with Rusche and Kirchheimer (1939), an accumulation of evidence links employment demands and imprisonment policy that ebbs and flows independently of the crime rate. In fact, evidence suggests that for individual defendants, pretrial jail time and judicial decisions to incarcerate vary significantly with employment status (Chiricos and Bales, 1991). Studies of the overall rates of crime, unemployment, and imprisonment indicate that the rate of prison admissions is more consistently related to the unemployment rate than the crime rate (Chiricos and Delone, 1992).

The impact of employment on incarceration has been discovered in earlier periods as well. For example, for several decades after the Civil War, the number of young black males incarcerated for minor property offenses in Southern states grew rapidly. This explosive growth seems to be clearly related to the efforts of planters to regain control over the labor of freed slaves (Ayers, 1984). Black imprisonment in Georgia varied systematically with the cotton market, which was not true of white imprisonment rates (Myers, 1991).

Although the four theoretical perspectives we have discussed emphasize the casual significance of different factors, it is a mistake to view them as mutually exclusive or contradictory interpretations of variation in imprisonment rates. As a control strategy, imprisonment can be rational or irrational, economically or politically based, symbolic or pragmatic (Garland, 1990). Cappel and Sykes (1991), for example, find evidence of both a deterrent impact of imprisonment on crime and a direct effect of unemployment on imprisonment. Investigation of variation in jail and prison population must take into account simultaneously political, economic, and organizational factors. To gain an unbiased perspective on incarcerated populations, it is also important to consider potential tradeoffs between incarceration and government policies that function more to placate than repress problem populations. Crime, disorder, and riots have stimulated not only crime control but the creation and expansion of welfare systems (Piven and Cloward, 1971). The military, welfare, educational, and mental institutions may divert populations at risk of incarceration (Inverarity and Grattet, 1989; Lessan, 1991).

We undertake these studies, in part, because the complexity of the phenomena is intellectually challenging. As the costs of incarceration continue to escalate—both for the individuals caught in the machinery and the rest of us who pay in a variety of ways for its operation—it becomes increasingly important to develop a sound understanding of the conditions under which workable alternative state policies emerge. The historical experience of failures of prison reforms, in part, results from inadequacies in our understanding of the external social forces shaping these institutions.

CONCLUSION

The prison was conceived originally as a rational organizational solution to the problem of crime. Increasingly, the prison and the jail have themselves become problems, which seem to be deteriorating at an accelerating rate. Recent years have witnessed unprecedented prison population growth, acute violence in the form of prison riots, and chronic violence in the form of gang conflicts. The social costs of maintaining these institutions extends beyond the fiscal expense of their daily operation. For minority populations, in particular, a substantial proportion of the youth are being processed by the criminal justice system. We have seen a virtual explosion in the numbers of incarcerated drug offenders.

These developments have renewed efforts to understand the scope and bases of these institutions. This chapter has examined some of their historical emergence and the subsequent cycles of reform. In addition, we have gained a sense of the size and content of the inmate population in the past and present. Prisons have changed internally, with staff having consistently less control over inmates, and with inmate gangs, especially those formed along racial lines, having less control over one another. Prisoners no longer simply "do time" since traditional prison culture has given way to continuously more violent conflict. It is tempting to look at this situation solely as a matter of internal prison dynamics, or more broadly, as a function of how much crime we have in society. Yet, we must begin to place what goes on both on the streets and in prisons in the context of larger social issues, especially of governmental attempts to control problems stemming from societal economic policies. Massive and growing institutions of segregative confinement reflect a failure to solve the larger economic issues; there is little reason, therefore, to believe that much will change in correctional institutions in the near future.

DISCUSSION QUESTIONS

1. Compare the early history of prisons and jails. Discuss the factors that shaped the type of prison that we now have in America. How do jails differ from prisons both in concept and in conditions?

2. Discuss the "medical model" of correction of offenders. How does it differ from other prison models? How successful has the medical model been? What appears to be the dominant model today?

3. Discuss the underlife of prison and jails. In what ways can we speak of prisons having cultures of their own? Do prison cultures depend on whether prisons house males or females? If so, why?

4. What social factors seem to influence both the growth rate and the composition of inmates in prison? Are these simply a matter of the amount of crime we have? Discuss the larger implications of social control for this society.

CHAPTER 19

CORRECTION
BEYOND PRISON
WALLS

Todd Clear

Rutgers, The State University of New Jersey, Campus at Newark

PRISON CROWDING in the United States has been and remains a chronic problem of a general penal policy that equates punishment with incarceration (Sherman and Hawkins, 1981). Any account of nonincarcerative forms of punishment in the United States must begin with a frank realization that this country has a firmly established history of apprehending and processing far more offenders than its cell space allows.

The existence of nonincarcerative correction is much like the 80 percent of the iceberg that floats below the surface of the water—its vast presence remains hidden beneath the tip that is perceived by the casual observer as "the iceberg." The figures are somewhat startling. Of all offenders under correctional care on any given day, nearly three-fourths are under some form of community supervision (U.S. Department of Justice, 1988c). To secure prison or jail space for these individuals in a system already suffering extreme crowding is simply to fantasize; to create new space for them would require public funds of unprecedented proportions. Nonincarcerative correction is much more than the most common (and most frequently experienced) form of correctional intervention; it is the very foundation on which our postadjudication system of social control rests. This chapter examines the major issues surrounding nonincarcerative correction.

THE QUESTION OF PHILOSOPHY

Scholars may debate the finer points of the philosophy of imprisonment, but one glaring fact remains central: The prison represents fundamentally a loss of freedom. What, by contrast, is the philosophy of the nonincarcerative alternative? Is the intention to provide a type of correction without loss of freedom?

The very phrasing of the question exposes the analytical problem: Nonincarcerative methods are described as *alternatives* to incarceration. In practice, however, nonincarcerative methods operate as the correctional method of choice, and incarceration stands as the alternative. That is why authors recently have begun referring to nonincarcerative versions of correction as "intermediate sanctions" rather than as "alternatives to incarceration" (McCarthy, 1987; Morris and Tonry, 1990). By intermediate sanctions, they mean the many correctional approaches falling between traditional prison and traditional probation.

TYPES OF PROGRAMS

In this chapter, the term *subincarcerative correction* will be used to denote all the forms of correction that exist short of full-scale sentences to prison or jail. Many types of programs, in addition to traditional probation and parole, fit this definition. Among the most common are:

Intensive supervision. Operating either in probation or parole settings, intensive supervision programs provide increased scrutiny over the offender's behavior by maintaining enhanced levels of contact. Usually, correction workers have at least weekly contact and sometimes as much as daily personal contact under these programs.

House arrest. Some offenders are sentenced to loss of freedom via staying in their own homes. There are several versions of this type of sanction; some call for curfews at night and weekend lockup (to allow for employment), whereas others call for continual, twenty-four-hour home detention.

Electronic monitoring. Frequently used in conjunction with a house arrest or intensive supervision program, electronic monitoring mandates that an offender be fitted with a device that gives off a signal. This increases the accuracy of knowledge of the offender's whereabouts by indicating times when the offender has not been within proximity to a homing device, normally located in the home.

Urine screening. By testing urine samples, correctional authorities are able to determine if an offender has been using drugs or alcohol.

Fines. It is ironic that in a country priding itself on its capitalist values, money as a negative sanction is so seldom used, especially as a sole sanction. Instead, it is normally assessed in conjunction with another type of punishment, such as probation.

Community service. Also used as a companion sanction to probation, community service orders require the offender to work a specified number of hours without compensation on some project providing general benefit to the community.

Halfway houses and work release centers. Usually, these types of semi-incarcerative programs allow a person to be free during working hours in order to obtain or keep a job but require a return to the facility overnight.

Shock probation. These programs provide a very brief incarcerative term (usually a month or less) as a way of demonstrating the seriousness of the criminal law and the hardships of confinement, in the hope that the experience will convince the offender to forego further criminal activity. The "shock" term is followed by a period of probation.

Treatment programs. Often, offenders with special types of problems (for example, sexual adjustment, substance abuse, or emotional adjustment problems) will be sentenced to enter special treatment programs designed to help them overcome their difficulties. Inpatient programs provide treatment to offenders while they are residents in the program; outpatient programs provide treatment while the offender continues to reside at home.

To this limited selection of special approaches can be added the traditional forms of probation and parole supervision. This array of programs is so varied that it is difficult even to find a name that encompasses them all. They are primarily nonincarcerative, but many rely on intermittent or short-term stays in secure facilities. They all involve community supervision, but some include residential supervision as well. For that same reason, the commonly used term *field services* often is misleading.

PROGRAM ORIENTATION: CONTROL VERSUS CHANGE

In terms of overall philosophy, these programs can be divided into two general classes of orientation. Some programs seek primarily to *change* offenders by helping them overcome some problem or attitude that contributes to criminal behavior. Others seek to establish effective *control* over the offender's predilections toward criminality by reducing the opportunity for criminal behavior. The programs in both classes are utilitarian in that they seek to reduce the instance of crime. In fact, all subincarcerative programs engage in both control and change strategies; the difference is that some programs are more compatible with one philosophical approach than the other. For example, intensive supervision and electronic monitoring programs emphasize the use of surveillance to reduce or eliminate opportunities for crime. By contrast, treatment and semi-incarcerative programs help the offender develop and strengthen a crime-free lifestyle.

It should be obvious that the claims of control and change made by these programs are no different from similar claims made in behalf of the incarcerative sanction. Years ago, subincarcerative programs could be distinguished by the fact that they were less punitive than was confinement, and this was often their stated intention. However, recent experience with the programs finds that, because of the surveillance and treatment requirements, they have grown sufficiently onerous that a significant number of offenders prefer regular incarceration to a community alternative (Clear et al., 1988). Therefore, subincarcerative programs may be thought of rightfully as at least potentially punitive.

Just as the dual aims of control and change mix poorly in the context of the coercive environment of the prison, so it is also commonly the case for subincarcerative programs. One example illustrates the problem: How should an offender be handled who drinks to the point of intoxication and then drives? Obviously, such an offender represents a risk to the community, and it is incumbent on the correctional authorities to control the risk. This would suggest such measures as coercive antabuse (a drug that, when ingested with alcohol, makes the user ill), loss of driving privileges, or even house arrest to prevent driving at night. On the other hand, the problem of alcohol abuse will never be overcome fully until the person makes a change in personal lifestyle, and this approach would connote treatment such as Alcoholics Anonymous or other counseling. Although in the short run, it may be logical to try both approaches, at some point the desire for change requires a relaxation of the requirements of control so that the offender can test out the newly established lifestyle. Indeed, this competition between control and change characterizes the process of influencing behavior in any setting (Kelman, 1961).

Perhaps the main distinction of these programs is that they uniformly claim to be cheaper than confinement. Incarceration is without question an expensive government program. By comparison, all subincarcerative programs require considerably less investment of tax dollars to operate, at least on the face of it, than does prison, a fact that has not been lost on the tax-conscious public in the post–Vietnam War era. A second claim these programs make is that their presence helps obviate incarceration. This latter claim reflects a concept often referred to as "diversion" and deserves greater discussion.

THE QUESTION OF DIVERSION

The dictionary defines the word *divert* as "to turn aside from a course or direction." When correctional authorities say they are "diverting" an offender, they mean they are altering a course of action that ordinarily would lead to prison or jail. Yet, because the vast majority of offenders can never really be candidates for extended incarceration of any kind, simply because that resource is so scarce, it stretches the meaning of the term to call all these programs "diversionary." For most offenders, the existence of subincarcerative programs means correctional authorities may adopt some form of change or control in the face of limited institutional resources.

The question of diversion in the subincarcerative arena can be divided into three areas of inquiry: conceptual (diversion from what?), substantive (how does diversion work?), and effectual (how many are diverted?).

CONCEPTUAL ISSUES

In its original usage, the idea of diversion meant to avoid involvement in the formal criminal justice system, mostly by avoiding prosecution. However, many of the early diversion programs failed to demonstrate a significant potential for this approach (Zimring, 1974) although nearly every major jurisdiction in the United States now has a diversionary program allowing certain defendants to take steps that will result in charges being dropped.

More recently, the concept of diversion has come to include the intentional avoidance of any more serious consequence. For example, a man who has been convicted of a serious crime would be eligible for prison, but authorities might seek to divert him to some less onerous sanction. This more general meaning of diversion therefore can apply to any stage in the criminal justice system, even the postadjudication stage. Some convicted offenders might be diverted from any correctional intervention (through a fine, court costs, or some reduced type of community service). More serious offenders might be diverted from jail through treatment programs. The most serious offenders might be diverted from prison through intensive supervision or work release programs. For all these offenders bound for some form of correctional control, the system intervenes to divert them to a lesser level of control.

SUBSTANTIVE ISSUES

Two questions arise: (1) How is it known where an offender is bound? and (2) How does the system reroute the offender to less onerous subinstitutional correction?

The first question is not as simple as it sounds, for it is a what-if question: What would have happened if the diversion program had not been in existence? The approach of many of the subincarcerative programs is to set up a new diversionary program (such as house arrest) and to extend eligibility to those offenders whose crimes qualify them for a prison or jail term (normally excluding violent, predatory, or repetitive offenders). This is an intuitively attractive approach: Excluding the violent offender maintains public confidence, and diversion presumably is achieved by accepting only prison eligibles.

Unfortunately, research has shown this approach to be seriously flawed. Most penal codes establish eligibility for incarceration very broadly — few felons actually are ineligible for prison. Yet, in nearly every jurisdiction, a large proportion — even a majority — of ordinary felons never end up in custody for any length of time. One study in Oregon (Clear et al., 1986) found that only those who posed the highest risk (that is, violent repeaters) *and* those convicted of the most serious criminal conduct (such as forcible rape, arson, and homicide) had high rates of imprisonment. The low-risk, low-seriousness offenders — those ordinarily eligible for subincarcerative programs — were already being placed on probation 85 percent of the time. In fact, offenders who fell in the group in between the two extremes — sometimes excluded from consideration for special diversion programs — already received probation 55 percent of the time. Studies of probation caseloads in California (Petersilia, 1985), New York (New York City Department of Probation, 1973), Tennessee (Fox et al., 1987), and Georgia (Erwin, 1987) have found large numbers of serious, high-risk offenders already on regular probation.

This poses a serious challenge to the diversion movement. To divert offenders who ordinarily would receive probation would be to give them a sanction *less* than probation, and no serious current diversion proposal seeks to do that. Instead of diverting, these programs run the risk of doing what often is called "widening the net of social control"—that is, increasing the level of control for offenders beyond the probation they ordinarily would have received. Often, in order to target a group of offenders that is truly confinement-bound, the eligibility criteria have to allow offenders whose crimes are so serious as to call into question the wisdom of diversion.

Some critics of the diversion movement argue that too much attention is given to the problem of net widening. Instead, they argue, the institutions of social control have broken down in some areas of the country to the point that "net repairing" is needed (Petersilia, 1987). These critics believe that true diversion is unwise, and that the system should expand its current methods and make them more control oriented. Whatever the merits of this argument, the point remains that in order truly to divert, subincarcerative programs face serious problems in framing the description of eligible offenders. If the criteria are drawn too restrictively, the program risks diverting people from probation rather than prison. If the program taps a highly concentrated group of confinement-bound offenders, there is a real risk of loss of public and political support.

Many programs have approached this problem by focusing on *how* the offender gets admitted to the program as much as on *who* is eligible. The usual technique is to develop elaborate admission criteria. One of the steps is to establish, often through the court or the plea bargaining process, that the person is truly bound for confinement. In Georgia, for example, judges sign a statement that they would have placed the person in prison without the diversion program (Erwin, 1987). In New Jersey, judges actually sentence offenders to prison and then later modify their sentence order (Pearson, 1988). Such careful screening helps guarantee high true diversion rates. A second step is to assess the offender and determine whether he or she is likely to be successful in the program. Diversion programs that do careful offender assessments often have high rates of rejection (Erwin, 1987; Clear et al., 1988; Pearson, 1988).

EFFECTIVENESS ISSUES

The problem of the target group has been a difficult one for correction leaders to solve and has limited the effectiveness of the diversion movement. An overview evaluation of numerous diversion efforts by Krisberg and Austin (1980) concluded that on the whole, little evidence supports the belief that they have not merely widened the net. This is true mainly because most programs have not been able to target offenders correctly; instead, they serve as alternatives to lesser sanctions.

This finding has ominous implications for program costs. Most advocates of subincarceration point out that these programs are cheaper to run than the confinement alternative, with the implication that their use saves tax dollars. Although the programs are indeed cheaper than incarceration, they do not actually save money unless they are truly used as alternatives to confinement. The fact that so many programs have not been used this way must be viewed as a major failure of the subincarcerative movement. Their addition to the correctional arsenal actually *adds* to the correctional costs, because they almost always are more expensive than the less severe sanction they are replacing for most offenders.

This does not mean these programs have been total failures, however. Saving public funds is merely one of several goals often attributed to them. They also can be evaluated in terms of achieving the dual aims of control and change. In the sections that follow, specific types of subincarcerative programs are assessed. A fair summary of all these evaluations taken together would be that the difference in long-term rates of criminality between offenders sentenced to average periods of confinement and those diverted to most types of subincarceration is negligible or even favors the latter programs. This suggests that, viewed in the long range, the subincarcerative methods fare about as well or better than prison in changing and controlling offenders. Yet, this general summary also reflects a web of evaluation problems and issues.

TRADITIONAL FIELD SERVICES PROGRAMS

The two traditional field services programs are probation and parole supervision. The issues in each program are similar although they have different administrative patterns and programmatic histories.

PROBATION

Probation began in the United States in 1841, when John Augustus, the famous Boston shoemaker and philanthropist, first "stood bail" for inebriates in order to avoid what he considered worthless jail sentences (National Probation Association, 1939). Formal probation was first instituted in the Commonwealth of Massachusetts in 1869. By 1925, when the U.S. Congress established adult probation, nearly all states had formal adult and juvenile probation systems. In 1956, Mississippi became the last state to enact a juvenile probation system (Hussey and Duffee, 1980).

Because the organization of probation in the United States is a hodgepodge of arrangements (U.S. Department of Justice, 1978a), the probation system has been slow to change and has represented a weak political link in the correction process. In days when tax dollars are difficult to find, underorganized probation departments often find it difficult to compete with other government services for support. In the last two decades, probation caseloads have grown considerably faster than have probation resources. Only recently has probation begun to respond to the challenge of increasingly serious cases (Harlow and Nelson, 1984).

PAROLE

The harshness of English criminal law was responsible for the development of the parole system. By the late 1700s, the English penal system was characterized mainly by overcrowding, disease, and brutality—and at a high cost to the government. A policy of transportation of criminals was undertaken to rid Great Britain of the thousands of English poor who literally had been stuffed into old jails and "hulks"—unserviceable ships anchored in London harbor. The English courts sentenced offenders to extremely lengthy terms of confinement to be served under cruel conditions, but even these sentences were less feared by the poor than was the imposition of "transportation."

During the 1700s, 40,000 convicts were sent to the American colonies and the Caribbean, a practice that was abandoned after the American Revolution. From the 1780s until 1868, nearly 150,000 convicts were sent to Australia and its environs (Hughes, 1987). These offenders were subjected to penal servitude and to whippings, starvation, and other forms of privation. In reaction to the brutish penal systems of the day, a remarkable reformer, Alexander Maconochie, advocated leading convicts to a better life through example and teaching, not corporal punishment. In 1840, he established the "mark" system in Australia's dreaded Norfolk Prison, which allowed convicts to earn their way out of prison through good behavior. This was followed by Sir Walter Crofton's similar "ticket-of-leave" system in Ireland in 1854 (Barnes and Teeters, 1959). These systems were the predecessors of modern parole.

In the United States, indeterminate sentencing first was established in New York in 1869, and formal parole administered in Elmira Reformatory in 1876 (Barnes and Teeters, 1959). The idea of the indeterminate sentence was that the duration of the prisoner's punishment would be determined by his or her behavior *after* sentencing as much as by the crime itself. Those offenders showing initiative and reformation would be released earliest; those who resisted authority would pay the price in longer time served. By 1944, every state in the United States had a parole law.

The U.S. parole system differed in several respects from the programs of Maconochie and Crofton, but one difference was critical. Under the earlier systems, convicts earned release by following a published set of rules and earning marks according to an established formula. In contrast, the U.S. system required the convict to apply to prison authorities for release and to demonstrate reformation. The difference was momentous. The earlier system left control of the release decision in the inmate's hands, whereas the American innovation placed it in the hands of correctional administrators. The difference was to play a major role in the sentencing reform movements of the 1970s (Hussey and Duffee, 1980).

Organizationally, parole in the United States is always operated at the state level of government under the executive branch. In the majority of jurisdictions, parole supervision is distinguished from release, with the former operated by a parole board, and the latter by the department of correction. In other jurisdictions, parole supervision is administered by the releasing authority. The advent of the determinate sentencing movement of the 1970s challenged the idea of parole release in many states, but the supervision of released offenders was a concept that survived challenge nearly everywhere.

ISSUES IN TRADITIONAL SUPERVISION

The basic transaction of traditional correctional field services is "field supervision"—the maintenance of contact between the offender and the probation or parole worker as a means of service and surveillance (Studt, 1978). Considerable research has investigated the supervision relationship in field services and has identified a number of controversies in field supervision.

THE RELATIONSHIP

Probation and parole officers often emphasize the importance of the relationship they are able to establish with their clients. Through this relationship, they are able to influence the attitudes and behaviors of the clients assigned to them. Studies of the relationship show its dynamics to be a complicated process. McCleary (1978) spent six months observing a parole office in 1974 and found that, based on their experiences, the caseworkers formed general stereotypes of clients early in the supervision relationship. Some of the "types" were pejorative ("criminals"); others were related to the goals of control ("dangerous man") and change ("sincere client"). The parole officer selected a supervision approach that fit the client type, and established a relationship designed to pursue supervision goals.

Observers agree that the relationship between the caseworker and the client does not always develop the way the officer believes it should, however, because the organization's bureaucracy also has an impact on the supervision effort. McCleary found that the bureaucracy operated as a constraint on the flexibility of the relationship. Similarly, Takagi (1976) evaluated a sample of parole failures to find that "organizational variables" such as office policy and bureaucratic pressures for consistency resulted in cases being unnecessarily classified as failures.

Klockars (1972) has theorized that the bureaucracy and its requirements are so important that they constitute a third element in the supervision relationship. He proposes that the supervision relationship actually is a process in which the attachment gradually strengthens between the officer and the client, while the bond between officer and bureaucracy grows weaker by contrast. Therefore, in successful relationships, the caseworker–client bond is stronger and more important than the caseworker–organization bond. This allows the worker to use authority to influence the client and helps the officer justify ignoring minor misbehavior.

SUPERVISION ROLES

The relationship also is constrained by officer attitudes. Studt (1978) observed parole work in California and found that officers had personalized approaches to conducting the work. These individualized supervision rationales resulted in wide differences in supervision strategies, to the point that, in effect, each parole officer constituted his or her own agency.

Several researchers have classified officers in terms of the roles they undertake, based on their philosophies. One of the first such studies was conducted by Glaser (1964), who identified two dimensions of supervision philosophy: (1) concern for assistance (analogous to "change") and (2) concern for control based on four stereotypic "officer types." Subsequent research (Clear and O'Leary, 1982) found that these types of officers tended to develop different supervision plans for offenders.

Most researchers have treated the concerns for control and change as though they are in conflict—a caseworker must choose between one or the other because they are incompatible (Stanley, 1976). Based on this idea, Georgia recently experimented with a "team" caseload approach in which a surveillance officer was paired with a probation officer, with the former responsible for control and the latter for assistance. Authorities believed such a system would help avoid role confusion by separating the roles. In practice, however, the teams reported that their roles tended to meld, and studies of their casework practices showed little distinction between the way officers carried out the assigned roles (Erwin and Clear, 1987). The researchers concluded that even though officers differ in their role philosophies, the roles of control and change may be mutually supportive and not as contradictory as is ordinarily believed.

CLASSIFICATION

Because of differences in officer attitudes, the typing process is unreliable. Studies of officers' attempts to classify offenders find that substantial disagreement often arises over the client's risk to the community and responsiveness to supervision (Clear and O'Leary, 1982). When officer classifications are unreliable, it is difficult to establish officer accountability for judgments made about cases without simply second-guessing. In order to achieve greater reliability and to enhance accountability, it has become common practice to develop classification instruments that provide a set of variables with weights that will be used to "score" the supervision class of the offender. The use of quantitatively established classification instruments has helped increase greatly the reliability of classification decisions (Baird, 1981).

Most classification systems in use today are multidimensional. Often, they combine two instruments—"risk" assessment (the predicting of the likelihood of a new offense) and "needs" assessment (a summary measure of the overall degree of problems in an offender's life)—to determine the amount of supervision a case will require.

Some people have pointed out that the use of objective risk and needs devices is not without problems (Clear and Gallagher, 1985; Clear, 1988). As a result, some more qualitative approaches to classification have been developed, based on an attempt to use interpersonal methods to determine supervision strategies (Warren, 1971; Jesness and Wedge, 1985).

CASELOAD SIZE

One of the most controversial areas of study is "the search for the magic number" (Carter and Wilkins, 1976), or the attempt to determine the optimal caseload size for field supervision. Despite the frequency in the literature of numbers cited as "standards" for caseload size, such as sixty or thirty-five, there is no empirical basis for any prescribed caseload size as being optimal. In fact, studies of caseload size have found consistently that simply reducing the size of the caseload does not increase the effectiveness of supervision (Banks et al., 1976; Albanese et al., 1985). Although such findings are difficult to understand or explain, the uniformity of the evidence is persuasive: Smaller caseloads do not result in greater success.

The most plausible explanation for this phenomenon is that there is an "interaction effect"—that the same supervision technique will help some offenders, hurt others, and when applied across the board, have no overall effect. Summary reviews of field supervision strategies find much support for the existence of the interaction effect (Warren, 1973; Palmer, 1975; Gendreau and Ross, 1981). If the interaction hypothesis is correct, the solution is to specialize supervision, taking different approaches for different types of cases, and not merely do the same thing, although more intensively, with everybody.

This approach, often called "differential supervision," has been found consistently to produce results superior to the traditional approach of equal supervision for all clients (Baird et al., 1986; Andrews, 1987). The success of the differential supervision approach has led researchers to abandon the search for the "magic number" of cases in favor of a "workload" model that measures the *time* a case requires under differential supervision (National Institute of Corrections, 1981). Workload systems have been more differentially effective in determining the best staffing level for supervision (Harlow and Nelson, 1984).

CONDITIONS OF SUPERVISION

The formal conditions of supervision are established by the requisite sentencing authority (the court or the parole board), and they define binding requirements placed on the offender. In fact, because case law consistently has held that the supervision officer does not have the discretion to alter the conditions of supervision, they may also be thought of as binding on the supervision officer.

Despite the centrality of conditions to the supervision process, there have been few studies of them. Given the dearth of research on conditions, several writers have attempted to define the policy that should apply to conditions. The generally accepted standard for setting conditions is that they should be reasonably related to the circumstances that produced the original criminal behavior. Unfortunately, this is such a narrow standard that many experts question its usefulness.

In addressing the narrowness problem, attention should be given to three general types of conditions (O'Leary and Clear, 1982):

1. **Punitive** conditions, such as community service and restitution, are designed to demonstrate to the offender community disapproval of the criminal conduct.

2. **Risk** conditions, such as drug treatment, are designed to reduce the probability of future conduct through ameliorating specific problems in the offender's situation.

3. **Management** conditions, such as reporting address changes, are designed to provide basic support for the supervision process.

Under this logic, only the minimum number of conditions needed to carry out these three functions should be imposed: Punitive conditions should be commensurate with the crime's seriousness, and risk conditions should be the least drastic needed to control the risk.

REVOCATION

The offender's status in the community is ended through revocation. Despite much controversy about whether the freedom granted an offender under probation or parole is a legal entitlement (Newman, 1985), the courts have held that federal probation is a privilege and not a right (*U.S.* v. *Birnbaum,* 1970) that, once granted, can only be removed with just cause and due process (*Morrissey* v. *Brewer,* 1972; *Gagnon* v. *Scarpelli,* 1973).

There are two general types of revocation. When an offender is convicted of a new crime, this constitutes a violation of the requirement to remain law-abiding, and serves as a *prima facie* (at first view) basis for revocation. When an offender fails to abide by the conditions of supervision, even if the misbehavior does not constitute a violation of the law, the person's status may be revoked. This is called a "technical" revocation.

In practice, a great deal of discretion may be exercised in making the revocation decision. When offenders under supervision for traditional felonies commit minor offenses (such as shoplifting), a revocation may not result. Technical violations often are followed by a warning or by lesser sanctions such as forty-eight hours in jail, with a revision in conditions. By the same token, if a condition is considered central to supervision, especially if it relates to risk (such as required therapy for a child molester), violation often will result in removal from the community and confinement.

One study of revocations compared patterns of client misbehavior and response in five jurisdictions (Baird et al., 1986). The major finding was that practices vary widely, both within and among jurisdictions. This disparity in response to violations was further complicated by the fact that virtually no relationship seemed to exist between the type of violation, the type of response, and subsequent misbehavior, including criminal behavior. In other words, there was no support for the idea that rules violations are flags for impending criminal behavior.

Crowded institutions since the 1980s have placed a premium on dealing with violations short of full revocation and confinement. At the same time, revoked offenders make up a significant proportion of all prison and jail intakes. So long as discretion attaches to the decisions to impose conditions and enforce them, this area will remain controversial.

EFFECTIVENESS

The effectiveness of traditional supervision methods remains a controversial subject. Many experts find little basis for confidence that supervision accomplishes much, and a few would agree with Martinson's (1976) classic assessment that probation supervision in some areas is "a kind of a standing joke." Certainly, the reputation of supervision is not what its advocates would wish.

But the real question about the effectiveness of supervision is: Compared to what? Only a few studies have tried to compare supervision to other alternatives. Saks and Logan (1984) matched a sample of Connecticut mandatory releases (without supervision) with a similar sample of parolees released during the same period. There was an initial advantage in favor of the parolees, but within three years, the records of criminal activity looked nearly identical. They concluded that parole did not prevent criminal activity but instead retarded it; their study played a significant role in the parole abolition movement in Connecticut.

By contrast, Petersilia (1987) measured a sample of serious California felons sentenced to prison against a matched sample of offenders (with similar characteristics) sentenced to probation. Here, the prison group showed an initial advantage, but after four years, there was no difference in criminal activity between the groups. Using similar methodologies, comparisons of prison to probation have shown little difference in rates of arrest or numbers of arrests across time (Barry and Clear, 1984; Clear et al., 1988). Other studies have shown that persons who receive supervision after brief periods of incarceration appear to fare no differently than those who receive only supervision (Vaughan, 1980). The only comparative study to show a major difference in performance (Murray and Cox, 1979) indicated that young serious offenders placed on probation performed slightly worse than a similar sample of offenders placed in training schools. This study has been criticized, however, for overestimating the criminal behavior rates of the training school sample before training school (McCleary, 1981).

Based on studies such as these, it would be easy to conclude that traditional supervision makes little or no difference. That would be stretching the interpretation of these studies, however, because none represents a tightly controlled experiment, and all have been criticized for their methodological flaws. The more significant point is this: If supervision appears not to be markedly superior to nonsupervision, it also appears to be little different from confinement. Based on this conclusion, the best approach would seem to be to do nothing to offenders because supervision is not more effective than doing nothing, and incarceration is not more effective than supervision. Obviously, this is an exceedingly unlikely policy, and the research results are simply not convincing enough to justify eradication of either supervision or confinement.

NONTRADITIONAL FIELD SERVICES

Since the middle of the 1980s, nontraditional methods of supervision have proliferated. The main impetus for this has been the tremendous crowding found in virtually all the traditional correctional realms in the decade. Numerous programs have been developed to help address this problem, but three primary types can be identified: intensive supervision, house arrest with electronic monitoring, and partial release. Each type of program raises particular issues about its use.

INTENSIVE SUPERVISION

Intensive supervision programs (ISPs) have become perhaps the most common response to institutional crowding across the country. The claims of the intensive supervision programs are ambitious: Protect the community, reduce crowding, save tax dollars, demonstrate probation effectiveness, and rehabilitate clients. It is small wonder the new ISPs are so popular; their claims are spectacular.

The two major studies on the new ISPs, in Georgia (Erwin, 1986) and in New Jersey (Pearson, 1987), have produced some significant findings. Offenders placed in the program did as well as or better than those with other sentences on several performance criteria, including new arrests. The results suggest that ISPs can perform a useful role in overcoming the crowded conditions that plague most prison and jail systems. When the evaluations of a series of controlled ISP experiments now under way are completed, a fuller picture of the effectiveness of ISPs will emerge.

The picture for ISPs is not completely rosy, however. One problem, related to diversion, was discussed previously. The Georgia and New Jersey programs appear to have been successful in achieving high rates of diversion, and this is their main reason for existence. But this is by no means the uniform experience of other ISPs around the country. In fact, in the experiments mentioned previously, it proved difficult to identify appropriate diversion cases for ISP.

In New Jersey and Georgia, the diversion emphasis has meant that these programs have been exceedingly careful in the kind of offenders admitted to supervision. The result has been that both programs have provided intensified supervision to "the best of the bad"—low-risk offenders who were in prison or prison-bound. Although this has helped ensure high rates of program success, it also has resulted in an ironic reversal of appropriation of correctional resources. The ISPs in these states represent the toughest level of supervision the states can provide. Undoubtedly, the quality of supervision provided by these programs is far superior to traditional supervision programs, as a result of greater resources, more effective staff, and better management. Because of the careful selection of offenders for diversion, this heightened supervision practice is applied to a clientele that in Georgia is nearly 40 percent low-risk, and in New Jersey around 50 percent. In other words, the toughest supervision in the subincarcerative arsenal is used to control a population of offenders that is not markedly different in risk to the community than a caseload of regular probationers.

How can this be? The reason is that the prisons in New Jersey and Georgia contain large numbers of low- and moderate-risk offenders—enough to fill their ISPs. The ISP provides the rationale for their release from incarceration. Yet, because probation has such a mediocre reputation, it seems that from a public viewpoint, something *more* than regular probation is needed, if release is to be feasible. So the ISP is made to be tough and serious even though the cases it supervises are, for the most part, not much different from typical community supervision cases. The fact that far more serious offenders come out of prison each day onto regular parole caseloads three to five times as large is an irony the system has not yet addressed.

The placement of better risks in an ISP is not entirely benign, however. The requirements of the ISPs are more strict than those of regular probation, and are much more strictly enforced. As a result, even though ISP clients commit fewer crimes than their probation counterparts, they have a considerably higher failure rate (Erwin, 1986; Pearson, 1987). They may not commit crimes, but they certainly fail to meet the enhanced program requirements and often go to prison as a result. Some critics have asked whether the ISP movement creates failures by selecting the best cases and then holding them accountable for extreme performance requirements. This is not an idle question. The typical ISP requires twice weekly contacts (one a surprise home visit), periodic urine screening for drugs or alcohol, community service, payment of fines and program fees, and attendance at treatment programs—as well as full-time employment. It is unlikely that many people could survive these requirements without incident for six to nine months.

The final issue is historical. The ISP movement of the 1980s follows an earlier version in the 1960s, one based on treatment and assistance. Once its conceptual rationale fell out of favor, the older ISP movement disintegrated. It remains an interesting question whether the current movement will survive its ironies and achieve its apparent potential. If prison crowding ended tomorrow, would ISP survive?

HOUSE ARREST WITH ELECTRONIC MONITORING

Another response to institutional crowding has been the sentencing of offenders to serve time in their own homes instead of institutions. The use of the home has considerable appeal—it is cheaper than prison or jail, it keeps families intact, and it ensures a loss of freedom without the brutalizing aspects of the custodial facility. The problem, of course, is assuring that the offender will stay home.

For years, court-ordered home detention has been a legal possibility with little practical support because of problems in enforcement. Technological advances in surveillance devices have made home detention a practical reality, and by 1987, it was an operating aspect of correctional processes in nearly two dozen jurisdictions (Petersilia, 1987).

Several versions of electronic monitoring now are available on the market. They work on the basis of a three-way communication between a stable device that sends and receives signals, a bodily device (worn by the offender on the wrist or the ankle) that sends signals to the stable device, and a centralized computer that records the communication between the other two. In order for the device to record an answer, the offender wearing the "bracelet" must be nearby. All monitoring systems have a single intention: to indicate whether an offender is in a particular spot at a particular time. Some monitors work only intermittently, checking for the offender's presence at preprogrammed intervals. Other, more costly versions provide a constant monitoring of the location of the person wearing the monitor.

Even though the technology remains relatively new, advances in monitoring devices are being made every day. The problems with electronic monitoring systems are not so much technical as programmatic. First, electronic monitoring requires a heavy investment of staff resources. Whenever the machine indicates the offender is AWOL, authorities must respond immediately if the electronic supervision approach is to have any credibility. Second, there is the problem of what to do in response to violations. Given the serious prison crowding that gives electronic monitoring systems their impetus, it seems incredible that mere absence from the house would result in any significant confinement without additional evidence that some criminal behavior was involved. Yet, if the monitor is to deter, disobedience of a home arrest order must be punished somehow. Finally, and more fundamental, what is the appropriate target group for monitors? The use of the equipment is helpful only when the offender is unlikely to obey the order without it or when there is a substantial risk of criminal activity to be avoided through home detention (Clear, 1988). In other words, electronic monitoring makes sense only when the offender is at risk of some harmful behavior; otherwise, the monitor is superfluous. Yet, the equipment is so new that most programs have extensive eligibility exclusions. These result in a pool of offenders for monitoring who represent low-risk, reasonably compliant clients. Whether these offenders would seriously violate home detention orders without monitoring devices—indeed, whether they would receive custodial sentences in the first place—remains an unanswered question.

RELEASE PROGRAMS

Numerous types of release programs have been developed to counteract prison crowding, including work release programs, halfway houses, treatment facilities, and the relatively new restitution centers. Nearly all these programs have two characteristics in common: (1) They incarcerate the offender only during limited hours of the day, usually when he or she is not working, and (2) they provide special treatment programs to help the offender deal with adjustment problems prior to release to the community.

Unfortunately, few evaluations of these programs, especially the newer ones, have been done. Evaluations of halfway houses find that offenders do at least as well after release from them as they do after release from traditional prisons (Sullivan et al., 1974). However, whether these programs really represent an improvement over regular supervision has not been tested effectively. Perhaps their most valuable contribution to the system is to provide an enforcement sanction for field services violators short of complete confinement.

THE COST-EFFECTIVENESS OF SUBINCARCERATION

Many observers are impressed with the comparative humaneness of subincarcerative approaches to correction. The original rationale for the development of these correctional approaches, to mitigate the abusive harshness of imprisonment, remains important today. But it is probably true that subincarceration receives most of its support because it is cheaper than confinement—the public dollar talks loudest when public values and priorities are confused.

The argument for the relative cheapness of these programs is persuasive. Housing an offender in prison costs $15,000–$20,000 per year. By contrast, regular probation costs about $500 per year, and intensive probation $3,000–$5,000 per year. Building a prison cell costs $70,000–$100,000, whereas a community supervision worker, with the capacity to handle 20 to 100 offenders a year, costs $20,000–$40,000 a year. A work release facility costs $20,000–$40,000 per bed to build and $10,000–$20,000 per bed to operate. Without question, when choosing on the basis of cost alone, subincarcerative methods are far preferable (Funke and Wayson, 1975).

These figures do not mean that growth in the subincarcerative apparatus has resulted in cost savings. First, in order for these programs to be cost savers, they must be used *instead of* confinement. America's jails and prisons are full to the brim. It is difficult to imagine that many more bodies could be stuffed into existing facilities, and this suggests that the growth of subincarcerative systems has enabled the corrections process to continue operating despite overcrowding, rather than reducing crowding. If so, the new correctional approaches actually are more expensive because their programs have not reduced appreciably the costs of running prisons (Clear et al., 1982).

Advocates of the efficiency of subincarceration argue that these systems have helped avoid expensive prison and jail expansion. Perhaps so, but this argument loses some of its persuasiveness in the face of two facts: Even as the United States is in a period of unprecedented expansion of subincarcerative programs, it also is enjoying the greatest national program of expansion of secure facilities since the invention of the penitentiary (Gibbons, 1988). Moreover, under the tighter fiscal policies of the early 1970s, wholesale increases in imprisonment rates *and* community supervision rates were accomplished while there was a relative reduction in dollars spent on traditional probation and parole services in most areas. If there is a relationship between the growth of subincarceration and the reduction in the costs of social control, it is a complex one.

There is also a problem of secondary costs. The new subincarcerative approaches make an express point of advertising their toughness (Petersilia, 1987). For this to be credible, there must be follow-up that includes enforcement of the "tough" requirements. Anything else makes a mockery of the new program's touted toughness. This often can mean an expensive imposition of confinement for rules violations that fall far short of new criminal activity. It is ironic indeed that after careful consideration by authorities, the original criminal behavior does not result in incarceration, but subsequent misbehaviors that are not illegal force the offender into confinement. An illustration is provided by a diversion program in Oregon, in which a burglar was placed on probation in lieu of 180 days in jail. When he failed to attend drug treatment, he was given five years in prison (Clear et al., 1986). Whatever savings were created by the original decision were totally voided by the tough enforcement.

In sum, the costs of correction are very difficult to calculate, and new programs designed to save money may not always do so, regardless of their advantages in "per offender" costs (McDonald, 1980). No one can argue with the desirability of saving money on correction, but simply expanding the use of subincarcerative methods will not necessarily save dollars.

CONCLUSION

The discussion in this chapter has highlighted several areas of controversy for which improved policy information is needed. However, four broad areas of inquiry suggest themselves as particularly necessary for those interested in developing useful knowledge.

First, much better information is needed about how and how well traditional programs work. This is particularly true of the semi-incarcerative methods such as work release programs and treatment centers. These programs are widely used simply because they seem to make sense in the face of the overwhelming presence of the prison as an alternative. But compared to the prison, little is known about them and their consequences. Does the use of the residential method reduce the rate of return to crime? For whom and under what circumstances?

Second, the same types of questions apply to traditional supervision, but they have a greater research base on which to build. The models need to specify types of offenders, types of interventions, and types of intervenors: What kinds of supervision methods work best for which types of offenders? What types of supervision worker attitudes are associated with success? Researchers have made a great deal of headway on this topic, but much more remains to be done.

Third, information comparing the relative success of different correctional approaches needs to be generated. Carefully established experimental programs need to compare the effectiveness of probation to prison, probation to intensive probation, and so forth, not only in terms of the costs but also in terms of the impacts of these programs.

Finally, the public policy context of correction must be better understood. Most policymakers infer public values, but the few public surveys that have been done show the public to be far less punitive than is ordinarily believed. Why, then, is it so difficult to implement reasoned policies through the political process? Do policymakers influence the public, or vice versa?

Underlying any research agenda must be one central fact: There has always been an interplay between the harshness of the formal correction system and the need to mitigate that harshness through less onerous methods. It is as though we design a penal system in the abstract for the image we have of offenders — depraved and dangerous, unknown predators — and then implement a system that takes into account the neighbors, family members, and friends we actually process in it.

DISCUSSION QUESTIONS

1. Discuss the concept of subincarcerative correction. What does it mean, and what are the most common types of subincarcerative programs? What is the orientation of these programs, control or change of the offender?

2. We often hear about diversionary programs operating in place of incarceration. What is diversion? Does it seem to work? How many and what kinds of offenders are diverted?

3. Discuss the concept of parole, including its history. Many people think of parole as the careless return of dangerous persons to society. Among the more common complaints is that paroled offenders are poorly supervised in the communities to which they are returned. What does the evidence actually suggest?

4. Is subincarcerative correction cost effective? Discuss the problems encountered in trying to measure cost effectiveness in this context.

PART SIX

CRIME CONTROL ISSUES

Much of the public has its mind made up about two "causes" of crime in America today: drugs and guns. Politicians and editorialists argue that illegal drug sales and use are behind a majority of contemporary property crime and a significant amount of contemporary violent crime. In Chapter 20, "Crime Control Through Drug Control," Cynthia Gentry examines the adequacy of the evidence for this position. She notes first that the notion of a drug–crime connection is not new—only the drugs of interest seem to change. The exception to this is an almost constant interest for several decades in heroin and its link to criminal behavior. Gentry is careful not to dismiss out of hand such a potential connection. But her review of the literature makes obvious that the public's picture of the heroin–crime connection is not a clear one. After examining the role of class in heroin use and taking into account the many sampling problems in studies of such use, she concludes that a subset of poor, urban users commits considerable crime. Yet, users from other class backgrounds do not display the same criminal patterns. Looking beyond heroin, Gentry points to the paucity of evidence to link PCP and amphetamines to significant portions of today's crime. She notes that the relationship of alcohol use to crime is only now receiving the serious attention it deserves. Finally, she examines cocaine use and crime; popular notions notwithstanding, there is as yet little evidence of a link of any greater proportions than that between heroin and crime.

The contemporary public also believes that we would eliminate a major portion of crime were we to outlaw guns. Those who oppose gun control claim that it penalizes the noncriminal owner for the abuse of guns by criminals. James Wright reviews the pertinent research evidence bearing on the conventional wisdom of gun control in Chapter 21, "Guns, Crime, and Violence." He begins by noting the variety of definitions of gun control, ranging from registration to prohibition of ownership. Some seem reasonable and pose few problems for persons on either side of the debate. Others are quite restrictive and, gun control opponents argue, represent major infringements on individual liberty without offering gains in the area of crime control. Wright focuses on this last claim, and ultimately agrees that proponents of gun control are on the weaker ground. Felons will not be deterred from carrying guns even in the face of severe penalties—especially when the supply of guns in America currently is immense. Deaths due to crimes of passion likely will decrease little with gun control in a society that has not yet addressed the issue of why we have so much dispute-oriented violence. Wright warns against the deceptively simple notion that the crime rate will fall if we outlaw the cheap handgun (the Saturday Night Special). Criminals, especially more serious ones, have little use for such guns, nor would they be likely to give up on guns were cheap ones less available. In the final analysis, Wright concludes, those looking to control crime through controlling guns will have to look elsewhere for a solution to the crime problem.

One contemporary school of thought regarding crime control suggests that if solutions depend on identifying the causes of crime, we shall be waiting forever for them. But if by *solution* we mean addressing the fact that crime is an inexplicable given for which the only remedy is "getting tough" with criminals, then perhaps something can be done: Criminals who are caught will be given no more chances to violate the law, and those not caught will be deterred from further crime by the fate of their unsuccessful peers.

This rather simplistic approach has focused its attention particularly on *career* felons. Considerable evidence indicates that a significant proportion of serious crimes are committed by a relatively small number of particularly dangerous individuals. Proponents of *selective incapacitation* policies advocate a greater concentration on repeat offenders by police and prosecutors, longer prison terms for convicted persons, and a reduction in probations and paroles given to offenders. Christy Visher examines this issue in considerable depth in Chapter 22, "Career Offenders and Crime Control." She describes the career offender as commonly in his twenties, violating the law weekly if not daily, having a long record of juvenile and adult crimes, committing multiple types of offenses, and consuming large quantities of illicit drugs. But Visher also notes that knowledge of this profile in no sense makes selective incapacitation of people who fit it easy. Predictive scales to this point have been fairly inaccurate. The information on which those scales often are based does not serve well, and information that may serve well is available less often. Visher concludes that we are far from able to put selective incapacitation policy to work. She also raises a number of ethical and constitutional issues that must be addressed in any discussion of such a crime control strategy.

A common response to the problem of crime is the proposed elimination of legal "technicalities" that seem to stand in the way of arrest and prosecution of suspected offenders. As Susan Herman points out in Chapter 23, "Crime Control and Civil Liberties," the "technicalities" in question are, in fact, constitutional rights that protect citizens from such governmental excesses as unreasonable search and seizure and denial of counsel at the time of arrest. Herman effectively uses the exclusionary rule as a vehicle by which to demonstrate the Supreme Court's attempts to balance the competing demands of crime control and civil liberties. She argues that providing adequate protection for our civil liberties is not likely to expose us to more crime but that limiting those liberties is likely to precipitate government intrusion into our lives.

Finally, in discussions of "getting tough" with criminals, no more passionate crime control issue exists than that of capital punishment. For some, the death penalty is a simple matter of justice: To take a life is to lose one's life. In purer crime control terms, however, the major death penalty issue is whether or not capital punishment deters criminal behavior. Can convicted murderers be prevented from future criminal behavior by other means? Are potential murderers swayed from such crimes by the fact that convicted murderers are put to death? In Chapter 24, "The Death Penalty in America," M. Dwayne Smith addresses these issues with available empirical evidence and finds little support for the deterrence doctrine. He also raises an important issue that should be confronted by all who debate capital punishment's worth: racial discrimination in assignment of the death penalty. This matter once was of such significance that it brought executions to a standstill in this country. States have rewritten their laws to eliminate discriminatory and arbitrary death sentences, and many people believe the issue is no longer pertinent. Smith suggests that we have been less than successful in eliminating race as a variable in death sentences; it is simply more subtly embedded in the assignment of capital punishment. He presents evidence for this position, raises other provocative questions about capital punishment, and speculates about the death penalty in the future.

◆ The Hypotheses

◆ Heroin

Recent Data on Use and Crime
The Pharmacological Model
The Heroin–Crime Relationship: Which Comes First?
Sampling Issues

◆ PCP

◆ Amphetamines

◆ Alcohol

The Alcohol–Violence Relationship

◆ Cocaine

Recent Data on Use and Crime
The Cocaine–Crime Relationship
Crack

◆ Conclusion

CHAPTER 20

CRIME CONTROL THROUGH DRUG CONTROL

Cynthia Gentry
Trinity University

T HE FIVE QUOTES on the previous page indicate that our current "war on drugs" actually is only one more in a long series of battles fueled by the assumption of a link between drugs and crime. This chapter reviews research that has examined the connection between crime and heroin, PCP, amphetamines, alcohol, and cocaine, respectively.

THE HYPOTHESES

The alleged relationship between drugs and crime can be stated most simply in terms of a "drug use causes crime" hypothesis, a "crime causes drug use" hypothesis, and a "criminalization of drug use causes crime" hypothesis. The first hypothesis, that drug use causes crime, has two derivatives: (1) that the pharmacological effects of certain drugs can induce violent (criminal) acts and (2) that the prohibitive price of some drugs causes addicts to turn to criminal activities as a source of income. The second hypothesis, that crime causes drug use, is based on the argument that the involvement in criminal activity provides a context conducive to drug use (Watters et al., 1985). The third hypothesis, that criminalization of drugs causes crime, centers on the argument that the criminal justice response to certain drugs has exacerbated, if not created, a drugs–crime connection (Schur, 1962; Nadelmann, 1988). A derivative of this hypothesis is a systemic model suggesting that violence may be intrinsic to the use and distribution of illegal drugs (Goldstein, 1985). There also is the argument that any correlation between drugs and crime is spurious in that drug use and criminal involvement may have the same etiology (Watters et al., 1985; Speckart and Anglin, 1985).

HEROIN

One of the first major pieces of federal legislation regarding narcotics was the 1914 Harrison Act, passed essentially without fanfare, which focused on the regulation and taxation of opiates. The Harrison Act ultimately made criminal the use of heroin and other opiate derivatives (Clausen, 1977; Dickson, 1977; Conrad and Schneider, 1980). Although the "criminalization causes crime" argument implies that this legislation suddenly caused otherwise law-abiding addicts to become criminals, a more convincing argument is that the criminal-creation process was the result of legislation *combined* with a new class of users from the criminal underclass (Inciardi, 1986; Goode, 1972). Intravenous heroin use apparently began, in any significant numbers, in urban areas after 1945 (Inciardi, 1986). By the 1950s, heroin use became increasingly associated with ghetto life. During the 1960s, a purported heroin epidemic began to threaten more affluent sectors of society (Conrad and Schneider, 1980).

RECENT DATA ON USE AND CRIME

In the 1970s, media coverage and government expenditure on the "drug crisis" skyrocketed with considerable emphasis on the distribution of heroin and treatment of addicts (Lidz and Walker, 1980). Was there in fact a heroin "epidemic"? No one really knows because nationwide survey techniques did not become popular until the mid–1970s. Once the results of these surveys were published, the clear indication was that among the general population, even among youths, the use of heroin was very infrequent. For example, since 1979, the annual prevalence of heroin use among young adults and college students has remained stable at around 0.2 percent (Johnston et al., 1991). Similar low rates of use are reported among the general public (National Institute on Drug Abuse, 1991). Even government estimates of heroin addiction, relative to estimates regarding other drugs, are modest and stable at about 500,000 throughout the past decade. Some consider even this estimate to be inflated and "mythical" (Reuter, 1984). However, despite relatively low levels of use, literature on the drug–crime connection remains disproportionately focused on heroin use and its relationship to criminal activity.

One source of information regarding this relationship has been a biased, but nonetheless convenient, sample of incarcerated populations. Heroin use among prisoners is consistently and dramatically higher than among the general population. For example, recent reports suggest that approximately 18 to 25 percent of prisoners and jail inmates report having ever used heroin (Bureau of Justice Statistics, 1988c, 1991). Among arrestees, the percent testing positive for heroin range from 1 percent in Miami to 24 percent in New York (National Institute of Justice, 1990).

Recognition of the biases inherent in data derived from incarcerated populations led to efforts to examine the drug–crime relationship in nonincarcerated populations. Typically, these studies either have used a nonrandom "snowball" technique, in which respondents are asked to identify other potential respondents, or have selected subjects from drug treatment programs. Because these studies are situated in low-income neighborhoods, subjects overwhelmingly are poor and minorities are disproportionately represented. Still, these sampling strategies represent a marked improvement over a sole dependence on prisoner data.

The research by Inciardi (1979, 1986) and by Ball et al. (1981) is frequently cited as evidence of the high levels of criminality among nonincarcerated heroin users. For example, Inciardi (1979, 1986) reports results from interviews with current narcotics users in Miami located via snowball sampling. The 573 users included in the study reported committing over 215,000 offenses in the year prior to the interview. Although about 60 percent of the offenses involved drug sales or other "victimless crimes," these respondents claimed responsibility for approximately 6,000 robberies and assaults, 6,700 burglaries, 900 stolen vehicles, 25,000 instances of shoplifting, 17 crimes of arson, 240 instances of extortion, 800 cases of loansharking, and over 46,000 other instances of larceny and fraud. Even though the level of criminal involvement was extremely high, the incidence of arrest was very low: one arrest for every 353 crimes.

Ball et al. (1981) report results from interviews with nonincarcerated opiate addicts identified by the Baltimore Police Department. The difficulty in operationalizing criminality was resolved with the formulation of a "crimedays per year" measure. This is a count of any twenty-four-hour period in which an individual commits at least one crime and, accordingly, can range from 0 to 365 days per year. Since the onset of addiction, these addicts averaged 178 crime-days per year. Since most had first become addicted over ten years prior to the interview, over 470,000 crime-days were amassed by the 243 addicts included in the study. Subsequent research has found similarly high rates of criminal activity among narcotics users (see, for example, Nurco et al., 1988; Strung et al., 1984; Hanson et al., 1985; Chaiken and Chaiken, 1990).

THE PHARMACOLOGICAL MODEL

Given that there is a strong and consistent relationship between narcotics addiction and crime when research is limited to incarcerated or inner-city samples, investigators also have addressed the explanatory power of the various hypotheses of a drugs–crime relationship. For example, as noted in the introduction, the pharmacological model suggests that the effects of a particular drug can exacerbate violent or criminal activity. There are several convincing indications, however, that this model is not valid regarding heroin. Only a minority of inmates, even if we consider only those with a drug history, were high on heroin at the time they committed the offense for which they were incarcerated. For example, approximately 5 percent of jail inmates reported they were under the influence of heroin at the time of their offense (Bureau of Justice Statistics, 1991a). There is also evidence that this percentage has been declining over the past several decades (Bureau of Justice Statistics, 1988c). In addition, ethnographic studies suggest that addicts separate drug taking and "hustling" activities (Hanson et al., 1985).

THE HEROIN–CRIME RELATIONSHIP: WHICH COMES FIRST?

The pharmacological model aside, the arguments suggesting "drugs cause crime" versus "crime causes drug use" have dominated the literature on heroin use. Efforts have centered on a variety of retrospective analyses in order to determine "which came first." Does criminal behavior precede heroin use, or does heroin use lead to crime? The literature suggests that the answer to either question is a confident yes—when the referent is the contemporary, lower-class addict.

Studies that have examined the history of addicts prior to the 1950s indicate little criminal activity before addiction (O'Donnell, 1966; Greenberg and Adler, 1974; Kolb, 1925a, 1925b). However, these early narcotics addicts were also more likely to have become addicted as a result of prescribed drugs. Beginning in the 1950s, a new type of narcotics user emerged: one who voluntarily used heroin and likely had some prior involvement in crime (Faupel and Klockars, 1987; Wish and Johnson, 1986). Among contemporary narcotics users, arrests and criminal activity precede the use of narcotics. However, an increase in the frequency and seriousness of criminal activity also parallels an increase in the frequency and the level of narcotics use. Further, during treatment or abstinence cycles, criminality continues, but at lower levels when compared with drug-using periods (Fields and Walters, 1985; Nurco et al., 1988; Ball et al., 1981; Bennett and Wright, 1986; McGlothlin and Anglin, 1981; Hunt et al., 1984; Anglin and Speckart, 1988; Chaiken and Chaiken, 1990).

Given the argument that the prohibitive price of narcotics contributes to crime, opiate users traditionally have been characterized as more likely than their nonusing counterparts to engage in income-generating property crimes (Goldstein, 1981; Nurco et al., 1988; Fields and Walters, 1985; Greenberg and Adler, 1974; Collins et al., 1985; Parker and Newcombe, 1987; Faupel and Klockars, 1987). Other research focuses on the possibility that violence may be more characteristic of young abusers of multiple drugs (Miller and Welte, 1986) or of those most deeply involved in narcotics use (Chaiken and Chaiken, 1990), or may stem from changes in illegal drug distribution systems (Wish and Johnson, 1986; Mieczkowski, 1986).

Additional attempts have been made to clarify addict "types" (see, for example, Parker and Newcombe, 1987; White et al., 1987), "stages" in addict careers (see, for example, Faupel, 1987; Faupel and Klockars, 1987; Nurco et al., 1988; Anglin and Speckart, 1988), and gender or ethnic differences in the criminality of addicts (see, for example, Ball et al., 1975; Weissman and File, 1978; Pettiway, 1987; Anglin et al., 1987). Although important differences have been noted, the general conclusions remain the same and bear repeating: Most of the narcotics addicts studied had criminal involvement prior to heroin use, *and* addiction is associated with an increase in the frequency and seriousness of criminal involvement. Some observers argue that further efforts to clarify "which came first" are not only overly simplistic but also unproductive because it has been effectively shown that narcotics use "drives" or "amplifies" criminal behavior (Wish and Johnson, 1986; Speckart and Anglin, 1985).

SAMPLING ISSUES

However, this apparent consistency of findings suffers from a near-fatal flaw. What is missing in the current literature is any serious consideration of the sampling bias in most of the research examining the heroin–crime nexus. Sampling limitations are given only the obligatory qualifications and, then typically, ignored when conclusions are presented. Curiously, detailed demographics (beyond age and race) are rare in most studies. When they are noted, the deficiencies in sampling become obvious. For example, in one study of street users of narcotics, 81 percent were unemployed and 2 percent were white (Johnson, 1988). Among a sample of female drug users, 82 percent were unemployed (Pettiway, 1987). An ethnography of heroin users noted that over 60 percent defined their economic status as poor or very poor, and although approximately 33 percent reported they were "usually employed," those who were unemployed at the time of the interview had been so for an average of two and a half years (Hanson et al., 1985). In another study of active heroin users, almost all (95 percent) had not worked legally on the day of the interview; those who had worked earned less than $10 (Strung et al., 1984). Over 40 percent of the subjects recruited for a study on the relationship between drugs and violence were living in shelters (Goldstein et al., 1991).

Those few studies that do not use treatment or inner-city street samples consistently paint a different portrait of the heroin–crime connection. For example, Winick (1964) presented results of interviews with physicians who were narcotics addicts. Typically, they had been confronted by narcotics law enforcement officials and turned over to state licensing authorities. These physician-addicts did not associate with other addicts because they diverted opiates from legal channels. None had smoked marijuana.

A second example is found in a study commissioned to assess the opiate-using patterns of Army enlisted men who returned from Vietnam in late 1971 (Robins, 1973; Robins et al., 1980). In contrast to the samples of most studies of opiate users, 80 percent of the Vietnam sample was white, 70 percent had been employed at the time of induction, and 70 percent had no civilian arrest. Only 2 percent reported having used heroin prior to their military career.

The impression that drug use, particularly opiate use, was widespread in Vietnam was supported by this research. Over 40 percent of the veterans had used narcotics while in Vietnam, and 20 percent believed they had been addicted. However, the drug use patterns of these veterans changed markedly with their return to the United States. There was a decline in all drug use, but the decline in the use of narcotics was particularly dramatic. Only 10 percent of narcotics users had continued use within eight to twelve months of their return home, and their usage patterns tended to be more casual and infrequent (although typically via injection) than was the case in Vietnam. In addition, half of those who had ceased narcotics use had used nothing stronger than marijuana since their return home. It should be noted that those who had used drugs in Vietnam did have more arrests, more psychiatric treatment, more unemployment, and more marital problems after returning home. For those who continued using narcotics, the differences were more dramatic. Still, the levels of criminality among ex-users and those who continued use did not approximate the levels documented in studies dependent on inner-city or treatment samples.

The few studies that move beyond sampling the poorest and most marginal representatives of narcotics addicts present a very different picture of the heroin–crime connection; indeed, they present a different picture of narcotics use. Given these different results, it appears that poverty may be a critical qualifier for the conclusion that heroin "drives" crime. This is not to argue for some kind of "inevitability hypothesis" suggesting that all poor heroin users are driven to crime and all upper-class users are otherwise law-abiding. However, based on the literature, class appears to be an important but neglected consideration (Goldman, 1981; Watters et al., 1985).

PCP

Phencyclidine, more commonly known as PCP, and amphetamine abuse were briefly a focus of political and academic attention in the 1960s and early 1970s. Although little contemporary research examines the relationship between these drugs and crime, a review may provide lessons regarding current and future policy debates and research agendas.

PCP was introduced as a potential anesthetic and analgesic, but experiments on humans in the 1950s indicated serious side effects. As a result, PCP was limited to use in veterinary medicine until illegal diversion led to the discontinuation of production in 1978 (Lerner and Burns, 1978). However, PCP is produced cheaply and easily in illegal laboratories (Abadinsky, 1989).

PCP was introduced into the drug culture during the late 1960s and, in some cases, falsely marketed as tetrahydrocannabinol (THC), the active ingredient in marijuana. Between 1973 and 1975, PCP earned a poor reputation in terms of unpredictable and extreme effects. Thereafter, there was a shift to smoking or inhaling (snorting) PCP in order that effects could be more easily monitored (Feldman, 1979; Inciardi, 1986; Lerner and Burns, 1978).

The introduction and spread of PCP was paralleled by media attention and government concern regarding the potential relationship between PCP use and violent behavior (Beschner and Feldman, 1979; Linder, 1981). Media reports noted psychotic behaviors, the potential for "instant addiction," and a new "number one drug problem" (Inciardi, 1986; *People*, 1978). Concern over PCP provoked special hearings in Congress in the late 1970s wherein the drug was described as one of the most insidious drugs known and a potential threat to national security (Beschner and Feldman, 1979). The underlying paradigm of this concern apparently was a pharmacological model, in that the effects of PCP were seen as so disorienting and profound that individuals would engage in irrational and sometimes violent behavior.

Research and subsequent drug use trends indicated that this level of panic was unwarranted. Indeed, users often appeared puzzled about the public assumption of a link between PCP and violence (Feldman, 1979). This perception was supported by clinical research that found no relationship between the levels of PCP in urine samples and violent behavior (Walker et al., 1981).

Once PCP had spread into the drug culture, use of the drug stabilized and then declined as users became concerned about the potential for "burning out" and other possible harmful effects. The use of PCP became concentrated among drug aficionados who emphasized a recognition of the drug's power and the importance of knowledge about how to use it in a controlled fashion (Feldman, 1979). Indeed, among these drug-using groups, the expectation was that PCP would be abandoned as one left adolescence (Feldman, 1979). Further, the research indicates that PCP is typically taken sporadically and is generally not preferred over other drugs (Lerner and Burns, 1978; Siegel, 1977; Pope et al., 1981; Graeven, 1978; Fauman and Fauman, 1978).

National surveys report that the use of PCP among high school seniors has remained low for several years; the annual prevalence was 1.2 percent in 1990, down from a high of 7 percent in 1979 (Johnston et al., 1991). Although inmates are less likely to have used PCP than cocaine or heroin, prevalence rates of PCP use among prisoners are higher than rates among the general population (Bureau of Justice Statistics, 1988c; National Institute of Justice, 1987). However, the available research suggests that the percentage of PCP users who commit violent acts while under the influence of the drug is probably very small (Wish and Johnson, 1986).

AMPHETAMINES

The term *amphetamine* will be used here to refer to amphetamines (for example, Benzedrine, Dexedrine, and methamphetamine), as well as analogs, derivatives, and substitutes (Spotts and Spotts, 1980).

As was the case with PCP, the focus on amphetamine abuse and crime was similarly brief and apparently unfounded. In the 1930s, amphetamine was marketed as a nonprescription inhalant for the relief of nasal congestion and in tablet form as a prescription drug for the treatment of narcolepsy (McGlothlin, 1973). There are suggestions that in the 1940s and 1950s, "amphetamine abuse was regarded by most as something like the 'Coke and aspirin' habit, a little naughty but nothing serious" (Rawlin, 1968: 57). Ray (1978) notes that this was a period when people wore charm bracelets with attached pillboxes; they were advertised to carry Benzedrine for fun and aspirin in case of a headache. During the 1940s and 1950s, amphetamines were also prescribed by physicians for a wide array of maladies (Spotts and Spotts, 1980). In the 1960s, a third to a half of the amphetamines produced legally (estimates range in the *billions* of doses) ended up in illicit channels (Kramer and Pinco, 1973; Byles, 1968; Sandusk, 1966).

Concern about amphetamine abuse and crime did not appear until the 1960s with the first reports of high-dose intravenous use. In several cases, a shortage of heroin appeared to be as responsible as was the new drug-oriented youth subculture (Shick et al., 1973; Kramer and Pinco, 1973; Greene and Dupont, 1973). Accordingly, there was a growing concern that amphetamines could produce psychosis and exacerbate violent behaviors in some individuals (Kramer and Pinco, 1973; Connell, 1966; Ellinwood et al., 1973). As was the case with PCP, special congressional hearings were convened that centered on extreme users and (for the time being) confirmed the public's worst fears (Inciardi, 1986; Graham, 1972). Medical community recognition of the therapeutic limits of amphetamines and public concern over possible widespread illicit use led to tighter controls for prescription, production, and distribution (Kramer and Pinco, 1973).

During the late 1960s and early 1970s, researchers also began to explore the amphetamine–crime connection within a rough pharmacological model that linked amphetamine use to violent behaviors. However, evidence of this link was not forthcoming (Research Triangle Institute, 1976). For example, researchers found no evidence that the amphetamine abusers were more likely than nonamphetamine abusers to have been incarcerated for a violent crime (Greene, 1973; Eckerman et al., 1971). Most amphetamine-related violence that did occur appeared to be confined to the drug marketplace or those relative few who used the drug in extreme doses (Smith, 1969; Carey and Mandel, 1968).

Amphetamine abuse, particularly heavy IV use, quickly fell out of favor in the drug culture (Scott and Buckell, 1971; Davis and Munroe, 1968). Even underground publications, which generally reported positively regarding the use of LSD and marijuana, frowned on and warned of the dangers of amphetamine use (Siegel, 1973). Recent surveys in the United States indicate that since the early 1980s, the annual prevalence of the use of stimulants has declined to 9 percent among high school seniors and about 5 percent among college students (Johnston et al., 1991). It should be noted that intravenous methamphetamine use remains common among certain subgroups. For example, Waldorf and Murphy (1990) found that half of their sample of male prostitutes in San Francisco reported having injected methamphetamine over 250 times. However, as Inciardi (1992) suggests, although there probably were (and are) persons abusing amphetamines and "speed freaks" who are prone to violence, the actual prevalence of these kinds of individuals was always far from epidemic.

There have been recent reports of a "highly addictive" form of smokable, crystalline methamphetamine, or "ice," surfacing in Hawaii and on the West Coast (*Winston–Salem Journal*, 1989b). If crack was supposed to be the drug plague of the 1980s, ice was the expected menace for the 1990s (Inciardi, 1992). The drug's effects can last from seven to twenty-four hours and are reported to cause psychoses and violent behavior (Inciardi, 1992). To date, however, there is no evidence of ice becoming a popular drug. In 1990, among nineteen-year-old to twenty-eight-year-old respondents, there was an annual prevalence of only 0.4 percent in the use of crystal methamphetamine (Johnston et al., 1991).

ALCOHOL

The first federal law regarding alcohol, passed in 1790, authorized giving every soldier a daily ration of a fourth of a pint of rum, brandy, or whiskey (Ray, 1978). Moderate drinking in the new nation was widespread, and drunkenness was far from rare (Conrad and Schneider, 1980). At the turn of the twentieth century, however, the nation was going through many changes — in drinking patterns as well as demographic patterns related to urbanization and immigration — that led to the great experiment of Prohibition. Gusfield (1963) has convincingly interpreted Prohibition as a moral crusade, an effort to maintain middle-class Protestant values within a context of rapid social change. Alcohol continues to be the drug of choice of most Americans and the only legal substance to receive a substantial amount of attention within the drug–crime research.

As is the case with other drugs, the prevalence of alcohol abuse among inmates is much higher than in the general population, a finding that has been documented for decades (Goodwin et al., 1971). Studies indicate that almost 50 percent of the male inmates in state prisons consumed the equivalent of at least two drinks daily in the year before incarceration. In contrast, an estimated 14 percent of the general male population consumed a similar amount. For women, the differences are more dramatic: Over 20 percent of female inmates reported a daily intake of an ounce or more of pure alcohol, compared to an estimated 4 percent of the general female population (Bureau of Justice Statistics, 1983a). In a study of over 200 individuals associated with the criminal justice system (incarcerated, paroled, and so on), over 40 percent were found to be alcoholic, and another 11 percent were suspected to be (Guze et al., 1962).

THE ALCOHOL–VIOLENCE RELATIONSHIP

The alcohol–crime literature focuses on the relationship between alcohol consumption and its role in the commission of violent crimes. For example, in the United States, alcohol use is involved in half to two-thirds of homicides and serious assaults (Collins and Schlenger, 1988; Virkkunen, 1974). Based on a census of state prisons, half of the inmates reported drinking just prior to their offense, a third heavily (Bureau of Justice Statistics, 1983a). Over a fourth of the victims of violent crimes report their offenders to have been under the influence of alcohol (Bureau of Justice Statistics, 1991a). Miller and Welte (1986) reported that alcohol involvement, particularly in combination with other drugs, was related to an increased probability of incarceration for a violent offense. Similarly, in a multivariate analysis, Collins and Schlenger (1988) found that drinking, particularly moderate drinking, prior to the offense was significantly related to incarceration for a violent crime. Bohman et al. (1982) suggested that alcohol-related criminality is more often violent and repetitive.

One popular "third variable" explanation in the alcohol–violence relationship is a predisposition to aggression in some individuals that may be exacerbated by alcohol. For example, Jaffe et al. (1988) suggest that childhood aggression may be a significant predictor of aggression while drinking in adulthood. Similarly, Boyatzis (1975), using subjects from the general public, found that certain personality traits appeared to be associated with alcohol-related interpersonal aggression. Tamerin et al. (1970) concluded that alcoholics may have more of a tendency to lose control when intoxicated. However, other research (see, for example, Collins and Schlenger, 1988) has found that chronic alcohol abuse (as opposed to drinking prior to the commission of a crime) is not significantly associated with incarceration for a violent offense.

A dominant model for explaining the correlation between alcohol use and violent crime is a derivative of the pharmacological model outlined in the introduction. The disinhibition model suggests that alcohol reduces inhibitions to act on aggressive impulses. Thus, alcohol consumption increases the probability of socially undesirable and, by extension, violent behaviors that normally would be suppressed. This hypothesis is indeed part of "what everyone knows" about alcohol and, until recently, was the unchallenged paradigm in the academic community for explaining the relationship between alcohol and violent behaviors (Conrad and Schneider, 1992).

Accordingly, a variety of experimental studies have been designed to test the disinhibition model. These studies, reported primarily in the psychiatric or treatment literature, have yielded equivocal results. For example, some research has documented a relationship between aggressiveness and alcohol under certain laboratory conditions (Taylor, 1983; Shuntich and Taylor, 1972; Taylor and Gammon, 1975). However, an additional finding is that the *belief* that one was receiving alcohol (not whether the subject actually did or did not) was related to aggression under experimental conditions (Lang et al., 1975; Marlatt and Rohsenow, 1981). Clearly, experimental tests of the disinhibition model are contradictory and far from convincing (Fagan, 1990).

In addition to the inconsistent results from laboratory studies, the disinhibition model also has been criticized on theoretical grounds. These critiques, primarily from social scientists, center on arguments that the effects of alcohol on social conduct cannot be understood adequately without considering the cultural meanings and expectations attached to drinking and drinkers in a variety of situations (Levinson, 1983; Heath, 1983). MacAndrew and Edgerton (1969), for example, argue that "drunken comportment" is essentially a social phenomenon and not simply pharmacologically determined. Pernanen (1976) labels the disinhibition model a "pseudoexplanation" that disguises what is likely a conceptual, symbolic activity associated with many conditional and cultural factors. In other words, there are calls for efforts directed toward understanding what distinguishes drinking situations that lead to violence or other kinds of crime from the vast majority that do not.

In summary, research seems to have moved from a focus on the pharmacological or predisposition models to a clarification of many other potentially critical variables that require attention if the apparent relationship between alcohol and violence is to become clarified (Collins, 1981; Gottheil et al., 1983). If the quality of these theoretical efforts is any indication, the research on alcohol soon will surpass other research on the relationship between drugs and crime.

COCAINE

The early history of cocaine use in the United States parallels that of narcotics. Cocaine initially was assumed to be a wonder drug within the medical profession and, by 1883, had been indexed in fifty scientific papers (Murray, 1986). Among the best-known champions of cocaine was Sigmund Freud, who proposed the drug as a treatment for morphine addiction and alcoholism, a claim he later withdrew although he still thought cocaine itself was not dangerous (Murray, 1986). In the late nineteenth century, cocaine was also a frequent ingredient in patent medicines; the initial recipe for Coca-Cola contained traces of cocaine (Abadinsky, 1989). However, though pharmacologically not a narcotic, cocaine was included in the provisions of the Harrison Act (McGlothlin, 1973).

RECENT DATA ON USE AND CRIME

During the first part of the twentieth century, occasional unsubstantiated reports surfaced of heinous crimes involving cocaine-crazed blacks (Petersen, 1977; Musto, 1973). Otherwise, until the early 1970s, cocaine use and abuse was rare and limited to celebrities, musicians, the wealthy, and pockets of the drug-using underworld (Gold et al., 1986; Grinspoon and Bakalar, 1985). However, during the 1970s, an increase in the use of cocaine extended beyond the small number of upper-income users and the narcotic addict population (Hunt et al., 1987; Newcomb and Bentler, 1986; Gottheil, 1986). Although cocaine use became "democratized," with users representing all social strata, it maintains an elite, glamorous reputation whether used by lawyers or methadone treatment clients (Hunt et al., 1987; McGlothlin, 1973; Murray, 1986; Adams et al., 1986).

Despite the apparent increase of cocaine use in the 1970s, the popularity of the drug has been waning. Use among young people peaked around 1980 and then began to decline. By 1990, the annual prevalence of cocaine use was 5 percent among high school seniors, 6 percent among college students, and 9 percent among young adults (Johnston et al., 1991). Similar trends are revealed in national surveys. For example, in 1990, 7.5 percent of persons age 18 to 25 reported cocaine use in the past year, down from a high of about 20 percent in 1979 (National Institute on Drug Abuse, 1991). It should be noted that although sustained and controlled use of cocaine is possible (Murphy et al.,

1989), for a minority of users, the drug appears to produce a severe "psychic" dependence with corresponding physical damage (Murphy, 1986; Weiss and Mirin, 1987; Mittleman and Wetli, 1984).

THE COCAINE–CRIME RELATIONSHIP

Despite widespread use relative to heroin, little research has investigated the relationship between cocaine use and crime. Of the research that does focus on this relationship within treatment and incarcerated populations, results parallel those found in studies of opiate users. Again, relative to the general population, much higher levels of cocaine use are found among incarcerated populations (Bureau of Justice Statistics, 1988c, 1991a).

Research using treatment populations also indicates high levels of criminal involvement. A study based on a sample of methadone treatment clients and a nontreatment sample of narcotics users found a higher level of criminal activity among those who also used cocaine. In addition, the amount of criminal involvement increased with the frequency of cocaine use (Hunt et al., 1987). Using data collected from over 3,500 people in drug treatment programs, Collins et al. (1985) found a direct relationship between the frequency of cocaine use and the amount of illegal income. Based on anonymous calls to a cocaine hotline, 45 percent reported stealing from employers and from family or friends, over 33 percent sold cocaine to help support their habit, and 12 percent had been arrested for a drug-related crime (Washton and Gold, 1986). Most of the research supports the assumption that the cost of cocaine drives users to resort to illegal sources of income (Hunt et al., 1987). Regarding violence, Goldstein et al. (1991) found that though heavy users of cocaine reported more involvement, most of this violence was not drug related. They noted that among their street sample, heavy use of cocaine and involvement with violence were more likely characteristics of a particular lifestyle and not causally related.

Studies looking at cocaine users who are more economically advantaged again weaken arguments that link cocaine and crime. Waldorf and his associates (Waldorf, 1983; Waldorf et al., 1991; Waldorf and Murphy, 1990) have made an impressive effort to study more representative samples than those found in most of the drug literature. For example, in a study of current and past users of cocaine, approximately 90 percent of their sample had at least a high school education, 72 percent were white, and 56 percent held middle-class or upper-middle-class jobs. There was little evidence that these heavy users became immersed in a criminal subculture. In fact, 60 percent had never been arrested as an adult; only 22 percent had ever been incarcerated, typically for a few days (Waldorf et al., 1991). A similar portrait of social-recreational users of cocaine has been presented by Siegel (1977). Finally, Harrison and Gfroerer (1992) found that though cocaine use was correlated with involvement in both violent and property offenses, age was an even stronger predictor of criminal activity among the general public.

The evidence of a drugs–crime relationship is not only challenged among nonpoor users, it extends to dealers with middle-class backgrounds. Interviews with demographically diverse cocaine sellers found them to be the antithesis of the common portrayals of cocaine dealers as ruthless, violent individuals—indeed, the biggest fear seemed to be that they might be *victims* of violence or robbery attempts (Waldorf and Murphy, 1990). Adler (1985) presented similar results based on an ethnographic study of midlevel cocaine dealers. She found the lifestyle of these dealers was characterized by hedonism, self-indulgence, drugs, freedom, and money but, again, very little violence or criminal activity beyond drug sales.

CRACK

If the relationship between heroin and crime dominates the professional literature, the relationship between *crack* and crime recently dominated the mass media. Crack, a crystalline form of cocaine base that is sold in the form of relatively inexpensive "rocks," made inroads into the drug culture during the early 1980s (Klein et al., 1991). Media reports have portrayed crack as highly addictive and the crack–cocaine marketplace as plagued with violence to the degree that entire neighborhoods, indeed cities, are threatened (*U.S. News & World Report*, 1989; Reinarman and Levine, 1989). In less than a year, several major newspapers, magazines, and wire services provided the nation with over 1,000 crack-related stories (Inciardi, 1992). Treatment literature mirrored the concern regarding "a major crisis due to crack cocaine" (Allen and Jekel, 1991). There was also the assumption that gang involvement, particularly those gangs formed explicitly for coordinating drug sales, dramatically increased the amount of violence associated with crack distribution (U.S. Department of Justice, 1989e). It appeared that the low cost, the intense high, and the addictive potential of crack would lead to unprecedented chaos and violence and create a new generation of drug users and sellers. Crack, it was argued, was different.

Given that crack-cocaine is a new addition to the illicit drug scene, research regarding use is limited. However, based on the evidence that is available, media and law enforcement assessments of the prevalence of crack and its association with violence apparently are overestimated. Results from recent national surveys indicate an annual prevalence of crack use at about 2 percent among high school seniors and young adults (Johnston et al., 1991). Among the general population, the lifetime prevalence of crack is 1.4 percent; annual prevalence is 0.5 percent (National Institute on Drug Abuse, 1991).

Given that 98 percent of the public has never tried crack, it is highly improbable that crack has, as media reports suggest, become America's new drug of choice (Reinarman and Levine, 1989). In addition, there is evidence that the minor inroads made by crack are already beginning to decline (Johnston et al., 1991). Other evidence contradicts the assumption that crack-cocaine is instantly addicting. For example, although 25 percent of arrestees in Manhattan in 1986 admitted to having used crack, only 7 percent felt they were dependent (National Institute of Justice, 1987). Similarly, Mieczkowski (1989) noted that arrestees in Detroit typically reported moderate and controlled use of crack. Furthermore, although 3.5 percent of high school seniors report ever using crack, only 0.7 percent report use in the past month. This represents noncontinuation by 80 percent of those who try crack (Johnston et al., 1991).

In addition, reports of a unique drug–gang-violence connection in the crack marketplace have been contradicted by some recent research. In Detroit, the crack subculture, with multiple units of small user-entrepreneurs responsible for most sales, apparently is not dramatically different from other drug subcultures (Mieczkowski, 1990). Based on results of a study of crack-related arrests in New York City, Fagan and Chin (1989) reject the recent portrayals of crack sellers as uniquely disciplined and prone to instrumental violence. They suggest that any increases in crack-related violence may be more a function of a volatile drug market in destabilized inner-city neighborhoods than due to any unique property of crack itself.

Goldstein et al. (1989) examined the relationship between the use and trafficking of crack and homicide in New York City in 1988. They found that 33 percent of all homicides (60 percent of drug-related homicides) were related to crack. Most of these crack homicides were systemic—that is, they occurred in the context of the drug distribution system. However, the authors concluded that the crack phenomenon did not appear to have influenced the overall homicide rate in New York City. Rather, crack-related homicides simply may have replaced other kinds of homicide. A similar finding was presented by Klein et al. (1991) who failed to find any unique gang-violence–crack nexus; they concluded that the crack marketplace has simply merged with the traditional illegal market and has not become the domain of gangs.

In sum, we know very little about crack and hardly anything about the relationship between crack and crime. In the meantime, most of the discussion regarding this drug is heavily laced with terrifying but unsubstantiated statistics and shocking anecdotes. The few studies that do focus on crack (and cocaine) and crime parallel the conclusions of research on heroin. Among poor, inner-city users, an increase in use is matched by a corresponding increase in criminal activity. In addition, preliminary research on crack has failed to document that this drug has a unique association with violence. To date, evidence suggests that the crack subculture looks remarkably similar to other drug subcultures. As Mieczkowski (1990, p. 25) has suggested, "crack represents a variation on a theme rather than a radical departure from a historical pattern of a persistent and even ancient social behavior."

CONCLUSION

Given that the level of concern regarding crime, PCP, and amphetamines appears to have been exaggerated, what, if any, lessons can be learned? First, it is reasonable to assume that media attention to and clinical studies of extreme cases hardly represent a valid indicator of the consequences of the use of particular substances. Second, because these drugs are relatively inexpensive to purchase and easy to produce, it appears unlikely that legal restrictions did much to reduce supply or increase cost. Third, unlike heroin or crack, perhaps these drugs typically are used in the context of (time-bound) adolescence rather than within the desperate and unpromising world of what Wilson (1987) calls "the truly disadvantaged."

Research on the relationship between alcohol and crime has, until recently, been conducted primarily by psychologists and treatment personnel. For this reason, the literature remains somewhat separated from other research on drugs and crime. However, the movement away from dependence on a simple pharmacological or disinhibition model has been facilitated by the contributions of sociologists and criminologists. In some ways, theoretical refinements in this area have surpassed the sophistication of, for example, research on heroin and crime, with a movement toward consideration of biological, psychological, and (sub)cultural factors. Although at present there are no firm answers regarding a connection between alcohol and crime, the quality of the questions that have been developed is cause for optimism.

As we noted, much of the research on the relationship between drugs and crime has centered on the use of heroin and, more recently, cocaine. Contemporary, poor, inner-city narcotics addicts and heavy consumers of cocaine are likely to have been criminal prior to addiction, and addiction "drives" crime in terms of increasing the frequency and seriousness of criminal activity. Furthermore, there is evidence that involvement in drug sales intensifies the drug–crime relationship, particularly regarding crimes of violence (Altschuler and Brounstein, 1991; Callahan and Rivara, 1992). For example, Inciardi and Pottieger (1991) suggest that involvement in crack sales may be criminogenic in that it exacerbates crime among already serious delinquents. Ending narcotics or cocaine use will not eliminate the criminal activity of these kinds of users and dealers but could reduce the amount of criminal activity when funds for the purchase of drugs are no longer needed and involvement in the drug marketplace is diminished.

However, the assumption that drugs and crime are causally related weakens when more representative or nonpoor subjects are considered. In his study of heroin addicts who recovered without treatment, Biernacki (1986) found that commitments and involvements in conventional activities gave his respondents an identity to embrace as they abandoned the role of addict. Among middle-class subjects, even heavy users and dealers of cocaine and crack appear to escape the "inevitable" decline into addiction and crime. As to this finding, Waldorf et al. (1991: 137) note "if freebasers and crack users who have resources rarely get violent or become street criminals, then the crack–crime connection may be as much a function of finances as of pharmacology." In other words, correlations between drug use and crime may be more a reflection of a lifestyle than evidence of a causal relationship (Chaiken and Chaiken, 1990).

Certainly, sufficient evidence indicates that a subset of drug users—specifically, a subset of poor inner-city drug users—do commit an alarming amount of crime, though they do not commit most crimes (Reuter, 1984). Yet, when confronted with the need for explanations for crime, it is tempting and easy to blame illegal drugs. There may be some comfort in perpetuating the assumption that we need correct only the drug-abusing habits of some marginal members of society to combat crime. There are more potentially threatening, expensive, and radical implications in the search for the causes of both drug abuse and crime in those neighborhoods where many researchers collect their respondents and from which much of the prison population is drawn (McBride and McCoy, 1981).

It is hoped that this review does not appear simply to represent the rather dated (but nonetheless heuristic) position that only criminologists and sociologists understand what the "real" problems are and that policy recommendations and majority opinion are consistently misdirected. The use of illicit drugs apparently is declining, but it remains a critical issue. Drugs can and do take a devastating toll on some (but far from all) users and on some (but far from all) neighborhoods, schools, and so on.

On the other hand, it is also hoped that this review highlights the politics (and research) that encourage the perception of the drug problem primarily in terms of the crime problem and vice versa. Indeed, much of the contemporary research has moved beyond simple correlational analysis to the recognition that any relationship between drugs and crime is considerably more complex. However, there is almost no consideration of class, race, and age issues in recent research, particularly the research on the link between crime and heroin or cocaine (Reinarman and Levine, 1989). There is little recognition of the less robust drugs–crime relationship among countries that minimize criminal justice involvement (Grapendaal et al., 1992; Pearson, 1992; Reuband, 1992; Mugford, 1992). Yet, policy decisions, indirectly shaped by the traditional research, continue to target heroin, cocaine, and more recently, crack as important contributors to crime. Inequality, poverty, half-hearted efforts at reform, racism, underfunded and neglected drug treatment programs, and an enthusiastic criminal justice response to drugs may be more criminogenic than heroin and crack (Johns, 1992; Johnson et al., 1990). However, investigations of such factors are rare in the contemporary drugs–crime research, and they are ignored in the current cohort of "moral entrepreneurs" attempting yet another war on drugs.

DISCUSSION QUESTIONS

1. The public is greatly concerned about the relationship between drug activity and criminal behavior. Discuss research findings that address this possible relationship, and describe the types of crime committed by traditional and contemporary heroin addicts.

2. What about other types of drugs? Do PCP and amphetamine abuse lead to increased criminal activity? To what extent have these drugs been used by the populace?

3. Discuss the role that alcohol plays in the commission of violent crime. What does the research evidence tell us concerning the disinhibition model as it relates to crime and alcohol use?

4. What do we know about cocaine and crack and their relation to criminal activity? Discuss the relationship between social class and criminal activity by cocaine and crack users.

◆   The author is grateful to Philip Perricone, John Earle, Kenneth Bechtel, and Joseph Sheley for careful reviews of earlier drafts. Jeffrey Fagan, Cheryl Maxson, Paul Goldstein, Craig Reinarman, Tom Mieczkowski, and Dan Waldorf were particularly generous with suggestions and drafts of forthcoming articles.

CHAPTER 21

◆

GUNS, CRIME, AND VIOLENCE

James D. Wright
Tulane University

T**HE** CONVENTIONAL wisdom about gun control in the United States is very familiar and resurfaces in nearly every public policy debate about the topic. The essentials are these: Guns are plentiful and easy to obtain in this country, and they are involved in an enormous number of crimes and other acts of violence. In other countries with stricter gun laws and fewer guns in circulation, gun-related crime and violence are rare. Most of the firearms involved in crime, it is said, are of the sort for which no legitimate use or need exists — small, cheap handguns (as the argument once went) or military-style automatic and semiautomatic weapons (the argument heard more frequently today). Thus, firearms of the sort preferred by criminals could be banned without seriously infringing on the rights or prerogatives of legitimate gun owners. Many families buy guns because they feel the need to protect themselves; instead, they end up shooting one another. If there were fewer guns around, there also would be less crime and less violence.

Most of the public understands this and has supported stricter gun control for as long as pollsters have been asking the question. And yet, Congress has so far refused to act in meaningful ways, owing mainly to the powerful gun lobby, chiefly, the National Rifle Association (NRA). Were the power of this lobby somehow effectively countered — for example, by mobilizing public opinion — stricter gun laws would follow quickly, and we would have embarked, at long last, on the road to a safer, more civilized society (Anderson, 1985; National Coalition to Ban Handguns, 1988; Zimring and Hawkins, 1987).

This chapter reviews the pertinent research evidence bearing on the various particulars of the conventional wisdom about gun control. Many of the key points seem self-evident but are in fact not supported by research; there is, indeed, at least some reason to question nearly every element of the conventional

◆ 495

wisdom. A careful review of the research literature suggests that a compelling case for stricter gun controls is difficult to make on empirical grounds and that solutions to the problems of crime and violence in this nation will have to be found elsewhere.

GUN CONTROL

Gun control is itself a very nebulous concept. To say that one favors, or opposes, gun control is to speak in ambiguities. In the present-day American political context, "stricter gun control" can mean anything from federal registration of private firearms, to mandatory sentences for gun use when committing crime, to outright bans on the manufacture, sale, or possession of certain types of firearms. One can control the manufacturers, the importers, the wholesalers, the retailers, or the purchasers of firearms. One can control firearms themselves, or the ammunition they require, or the uses to which they are put. And one can likewise control their purchase, their carrying, or their mere possession. Gun control thus covers a very wide range of specific policy interventions, each focused on a different aspect of the problem.

There are approximately 20,000 gun laws of various sorts already on the books in the United States (Wright et al., 1983: Chapter 12). A few of these are federal laws, such as the Gun Control Act (GCA) of 1968 or the Firearms Owners' Protection Act of 1986, but most are state and local regulations. It is erroneous to say, as gun control advocates sometimes do, that the United States has no meaningful gun control legislation. The problem, rather, is that the gun regulations in force vary enormously from one jurisdiction to the next (such that one state's laws can be circumvented by driving to a neighboring state), or in many cases, that the regulations being carried on the books are not or cannot be enforced (Zimring, 1975; Leff and Leff, 1981; Kleck, 1991: 347–358).

Much of the gun control now in force, whether enacted by federal, state, or local statute, falls into the category of reasonable precaution and is neither more nor less stringent than measures taken to safeguard against abuses of other potentially life-threatening products, such as automobiles. Included within the category of reasonable precaution are such measures as requiring permits to carry concealed weapons; bans on the ownership of automatic weapons without special permits; and bans on gun acquisition by felons, drug addicts, and alcoholics. Mandatory registration of new handgun purchases and screening of new gun buyers are other widely adopted precautionary measures; Cook (1979; see also Cook and Blose, 1981) has estimated that about two-thirds of the American population live in jurisdictions where some sort of handgun registration or permit is required by either state or local ordinances. Many jurisdictions also have enacted "waiting" or "cooling off" periods. These, too, seem reasonable at first glance since few legitimate purposes to which a firearm might be put would be thwarted if the user had to wait a few days, or even a few weeks, between filing the application and actually acquiring the weapon. The much-debated Brady Law (after James Brady, the press secretary who was nearly killed in the assassination attempt on President Reagan) enacted a national waiting period of five days.

Thus, to state that a compelling case for stricter gun controls cannot be made on empirical grounds is not meant to rule out obvious, reasonable precautions of the general sort just discussed. Most of these precautionary measures are noncontroversial (waiting periods are certainly an exception) and widely supported, even by most gun owners. The reference, rather, is to measures distinctly more restrictive than those presently on the books throughout most of the nation, and even more particularly, to measures that would deny or seriously restrict the right of the population at large to own firearms, or that would ban the sale or possession of certain kinds of firearms, such as handguns, the restricted class of handguns known as Saturday night specials, or the so-called military-style firearms.

EFFECTS OF GUN LAWS

None of the 20,000 firearms regulations so far enacted has reduced the incidence of criminal violence by any appreciable amount. One of the strictest gun regulations to be found anywhere in the country is New York's Sullivan Law, which makes it illegal to own a handgun without a difficult-to-obtain permit. That law has been on the books for more than fifty years. And yet, New York City alone contributes about 20 percent of all the armed robberies that occur *anywhere* in the nation in an average year and accounts for about 13 percent of all the nation's violent crimes. The New York City police also speculate that there may be as many as 2 million illegally owned handguns in the city although this is probably an exaggeration. Another exceptionally stringent local handgun law is the Washington, D.C., law that, in effect, outlaws the civilian possession of handguns by D.C. residents. And yet in recent years, Washington has been cursed with the highest homicide rate of any city in the nation. It is obviously one thing to enact legislation and quite another thereby to influence people's behavior.

Regarding the crime-reductive effects of various gun laws (Wright et al., 1983: Chapter 13; Kleck, 1991: Chapter 10), studies have been done of the Bartley-Fox law in Massachusetts (Pierce and Bowers, 1981), the District of Columbia's gun law, sometimes said to be "the toughest in the nation" (Jones, 1981), Detroit's "One with a Gun Gets You Two" law (Loftin and McDowall, 1981; Loftin et al., 1983), the 1980 New York gun law (Margarita, 1985), and many other laws in other jurisdictions. None of these studies provides compelling evidence that gun laws, in whatever form, have had anything more than very marginal effects on the rates of violent crime. One of the most recent and sophisticated analyses of the issue is published in Kleck (1991: 394–402). Based on multivariate analyses of applicable gun laws in 170 cities with populations greater than 100,000, Kleck concludes that none of the laws examined consistently reduced levels of gun ownership and that "gun restrictions appear to exert no significant negative effect on total violence rates" (1991: 398). Consistent with many previous studies, "these results generally do not support the idea that existing gun controls reduce city gun ownership or violence rates" (p. 402).

Both sides of the gun control debate now more or less grant the point that existing laws have little or no effect on rates of crime and violence but have very different interpretations of the reasons. The progun position is that gun laws do not work because they *cannot* work. They are often unenforceable or unenforced, widely ignored (especially by criminals), and go about the problem in the wrong way. For this reason, many progun organizations, such as the NRA, have long supported mandatory sentences for the use of firearms in felonies, just as they have long opposed stricter regulations on the legitimate ownership and use of guns. (As a matter of fact, several studies of mandatory sentence enhancements for gun use in crime have failed to show significant crime-reductive effects; the NRA's support for such measures is largely rhetorical.)

The procontrol argument is that gun laws do not work because there are too many of them, because they are indifferently enforced, and because the laws that are in effect vary wildly from one jurisdiction to the next. States with very restrictive firearms laws often are bordered by states with very lax laws, and so existing laws in any jurisdiction are readily circumvented. To illustrate, the District of Columbia's Firearms Control Regulations Act of 1975 essentially prohibits the purchase, sale, transfer, and possession of handguns by D.C. residents; across the city boundaries, in Virginia, however, handguns can be obtained easily. Massachusetts has relatively strict laws governing the ownership of handguns, and is bordered by New Hampshire and Vermont, which have some of the least restrictive handgun laws in the nation. What we need, gun control advocates argue, are strict *federal* firearms regulations that are uniform across all states and local jurisdictions. Lacking an aggressive national firearms policy, it is no wonder that the morass of state and local regulations has had no notable effect. In this sense, they argue (not without justification) that we have never given gun control a fair test.

Has gun control reduced crime and violence in the United States? The answer, clearly, is no. Would stronger controls, enacted on a national level, do so? This has to be considered an open empirical question. As we shall see, however, many of the arguments that stricter national controls *would* work to reduce crime and violence fare poorly in the light of current research.

GUNS, CRIMES, AND NUMBERS

From the onset of the twentieth century up through about 1978, some 180–200 *million* firearms were manufactured in or imported into the United States. Domestic manufacture has averaged about 4.5 million units annually since 1978 (Howe, 1987: 102), which brings the total for the century to well more than 250 million weapons. Of these, the number now remaining in private hands is not very accurately known—some 200 million is a reasonable guess. Survey evidence dating to at least 1959 shows routinely that about 50 percent of all U.S. households possess at least one firearm, with the average number owned (among those owning at least one) being just over three guns (Wright et al., 1983: Chapters 2 and 5).

Of the total firearms, roughly a third are handguns (this proportion has risen in the past decades); in other words, there are some 60–70 million handguns now in private possession in the United States. The remainder are shoulder weapons: rifles and shotguns. The most commonly owned handgun is a .38 caliber revolver, a powerful piece of weaponry; next to the .38, the .22 is the most popular. Among shoulder weapons, rifles are preferred over shotguns by a thin margin.

What is the annual firearms toll in this country? How many people are killed, injured, victimized, or intimidated by firearms in the average year? Some components of the annual toll — particularly the deaths — are known quite precisely, others considerably less so. In recent years, the total number of homicides in the United States has been right around 25,000. Expressed as a rate, this is about 10 homicides per 100,000 population. Of the 25,000 annual homicides, approximately 60 percent are committed with firearms, and of those committed with firearms, some half to three-quarters are committed with handguns.

There are also about 30,000 suicides committed in an average recent year, of which about half involve a firearm. Of these, the proportion involving a handgun is unknown. Death from firearms accidents has represented about 2 percent of the total accidental death toll in the nation for as long as data have been collected. In absolute numbers, fatal firearms accidents contribute approximately 1,000–1,500 deaths per year, of which about 40 percent are hunting accidents; fewer than half the total accidental deaths involve handguns (Morrow and Hudson, 1986).

If we add it all up, we find that the number of deaths from firearms in our society in an average recent year is right around 30,000: about 15,000 homicides, 15,000 suicides, and 1,000 or so fatal accidents. Keeping things in perspective, this would amount, in an average year, to some 1.5 percent of all deaths from any cause.

The affection of all sides in the gun control debate for rhetorical formulations is legendary. In the case of gun deaths, the progun forces will often stress that the total deaths from firearms in any year are but a fraction of the total deaths due to, say, automobile accidents (about 50,000) — but nobody wants to ban cars. To counter, the procontrol forces often will express the gun toll as a number of deaths per unit of time. The resulting figure is dramatic, to be sure: On the average, someone in the United States is killed by a firearm every seventeen or eighteen minutes.

Death, of course, is an incomplete indicator of the overall firearms toll. One must also include nonfatal but injurious firearms accidents, crimes other than homicide or suicide committed with guns, unsuccessful suicide attempts with firearms, armed encounters between citizens and criminals, and so on. Although precise figures for these types of incidents are not available, rough estimates can be made.

The number of nonfatal firearms accidents is much higher than the number of fatal ones, but the actual number is known only very imprecisely. Kleck (1991: Chapter 7; 1986c) has reviewed a variety of data on the topic and concludes that the number of nonfatal but injurious firearms accidents is around 100,000 per annum.

Concerning gun crimes other than homicide and suicide, the numbers again are highly uncertain. The FBI's *Uniform Crime Reports* provide data only on crimes known to the police, and dozens of criminal victimization surveys have made it plain that this represents but a fraction of all crimes; at the same time, the victimization surveys are not entirely reliable either. The rough consensus is that there are perhaps 300,000 chargeable gun crimes committed in the United States each year (see Cook, 1985), not including "victimless" gun crimes such as illegal carrying of firearms (Kessler, 1980).

The total firearms toll also would have to factor in many additional components, none of them known to any useful degree of precision. Taking the (roughly) 300,000 annual chargeable gun crimes and adding plausible guesses about nonfatal firearms accidents and the other sorts of incidents, we would arrive at a final tally of something definitely fewer than a million total "gun incidents"—that is, incidents where a firearm of some sort was involved in some way in some kind of violent or criminal act (whether intentional or accidental, serious or trivial, fatal or nonfatal)—or perhaps two million if self-defensive uses are considered (see p. 509).

IS STRICT GUN CONTROL A PLAUSIBLE POLICY?

Thirty thousand annual deaths add up, without doubt, to a serious toll, and it is very much in society's best interests to reduce that number. The question is whether stricter gun control would do so. Let us consider the various types of gun-related deaths.

SUICIDES AND ACCIDENTS

The argument that stricter gun controls would reduce death by suicide stems from the well-known fact that many suicide attempts are not "attempts in earnest" but rather cries for help or attention from emotionally disturbed or depressed individuals. Firearms, it is argued, are extremely lethal. Many of these attempts to "cry for help" result in self-destruction not because that was the actual intent but because of the extreme lethality of the chosen method. If firearms were not available, people would "cry out" with different means, and because these other means are generally less lethal, fewer of them would be successful; the number of suicide *attempts* might remain the same, but the number of successful suicides would decline dramatically.

This argument assumes, however, that the intentionality of a suicide attempt is not correlated with the method chosen. Certainly, many people who swallow a bottle of pills are not really trying to kill themselves; they are, rather, trying to get somebody's attention. But people who kill themselves with guns can be assumed to be quite serious about it, and it is not unreasonable to assume that they would find a way to accomplish the task whether firearms were at hand or not. As a matter of fact, the apparent lethalities (relative "success rates") of several methods of suicide, among them hanging, carbon monoxide poisoning, and drowning, are nearly as high as for suicide attempts with firearms (see Kleck, 1991: Chapter 6, for an extensive analysis of the many complex issues involved).

The rate of accidental gun death may be more amenable to policy intervention, but this is the least important source of gun death, by far, and the rate of accidental gun death already is falling. About 40 percent of gun-related fatal accidents are hunting accidents, and there is little to be done about them so long as hunters have the right to their sport. If, in other words, people are to be allowed to hunt, then *some* accidental deaths will be the result, just as *some* accidental death is the inevitable result of people being allowed to pursue other recreational activities: boating, swimming, racing cars, hang-gliding, sky-diving, skiing, football, and so on.

GUN CONFISCATION

For these more or less obvious reasons, much of the gun control debate has focused on gun homicides, especially those that occur in the heat of the moment. To be sure, if there were no guns at all, then no crimes or other acts of violence could ever be committed with them. A very practical question, however, remains to be asked: Can a "no-guns" condition ever be achieved in a nation that already possesses perhaps 200 million guns? If we take the highest plausible value for the number of gun incidents in a year—1 million—and the lowest conceivable value for the number of guns presently owned—say, 150 million—we see that the guns now owned exceed the annual incident count by a factor of about 150. In other words, the existing stock is adequate to supply all conceivable nefarious purposes for at least the next century and a half.

These numbers can be considered in another way. Suppose that, as a society, we did embark on a program of firearms confiscation, with the aim of achieving the no-guns condition. We would have to confiscate 100 or 200 guns to get just one that, in any typical year, would be involved in any kind of gun incident; maybe 500 to get just one that would otherwise be involved in a chargeable gun crime; and several thousand to get just one that would otherwise be used to bring about someone's death. Whatever else might be said about such a policy, it is certainly not a very *efficient* way to reduce the level of crime and violence in the country.

FELONS AND GUNS

It is not unreasonable, incidentally, to assume that the existing stock of privately owned firearms constitutes a potential source of guns for illicit or criminal use—not because anyone who owns a gun is potentially a criminal but because the gun can be stolen by someone who is. Several hundred thousand firearms are stolen from private residences alone each year (Wright et al., 1983: Chapter 9); to that figure one would have to add an unknown but possibly very large number stolen from retail or wholesale outlets, or from shippers and importers, or from manufacturers themselves. A survey of nearly 2,000 men doing felony time in ten state prisons all around the country found that *half* had stolen at least one gun at some time in their criminal careers; somewhere between 40 and 70 percent of the most recent handguns these men possessed were stolen weapons—the 30 percent gap representing many inmates' own uncertainties about the ultimate source of their guns (Wright and Rossi, 1986: Chapter 10).

Results from the felon survey indicated that to the average criminal, a gun was both a means of survival in a hostile environment and an income-producing tool. In both cases, the consequent value of the gun to a felon is many times greater than its purchase price. Analysis of victimization data by Cook (1976) suggested that the average "take" in a robbery committed with a firearm was something more than $150 (in 1976 dollars) and was three times the take for a robbery committed with any other weapon. (One major reason for the difference is that criminals armed with a firearm rob more lucrative targets.) This being the case, the average robber apparently could "afford" to spend many hundreds of dollars, perhaps even a few thousand, on a handgun and still recover his investment in the first week of "business." Consider, too, that results from the felon survey showed clearly that many criminals carry guns because they dread the prospect of life on the streets without one. In this light, price would be of lesser concern.

Demand, it is said, creates its own supply. Just as cocaine will always be available so long as there are people willing to pay $200 a gram for it, so too will guns always be available to anyone willing to spend, let us say, $1,000 to obtain one, especially when, failing all else, one need only walk into any second home and steal one. Given the economics of crime in this country, the perceived and rather urgent need felt by many felons to be armed with a gun, and the immense supply of guns already in private hands, the possibility of somehow disarming the criminal population of this country seems very unlikely.

Crimes of Passion

Many advocates on both sides of the gun control debate would grant the preceding points. No one seriously expects stricter gun controls to solve the problem of hard-core criminal violence or even make much of a dent in it. Much of the argument thus has shifted away from hard-core criminal violence and toward violence perpetrated not for economic gain, or for any other preconceived reason, but rather in the heat of the moment. These are the so-called crimes of passion, crimes that turn injurious or lethal not so much because anyone intended them to but because, in a moment of rage, a firearm was at hand. And perhaps, if there were fewer firearms at hand, fewer incidents of this sort would occur.

CHARACTERISTICS OF CRIMES OF PASSION

Crimes of passion or rage certainly happen; it is also certain that in at least some cases, their consequences are strongly exacerbated because of an available firearm. But just how common are they? The fact is nobody knows. The pro-control assumption, that they are very common (see, for example, Zimring, 1968) is usually inferred from the well-known fact that most homicides involve persons known to one another before the event—typically, family members, friends, or other acquaintances. (The proportion of "acquaintance homicides" to the total has dropped in recent years because of the increasing frequency of robbery-connected murders [Block, 1977; Zimring, 1977], but they still constitute a majority.) But it does not follow that they are, ipso facto, crimes of passion committed in the heat of the moment. Ordinarily, the only people one would ever have any good reason to kill would be people known to oneself. Contrary to the common assumption, prior acquaintance does *not* rule out willful, murderous intent.

Possibly the strongest case for the crime of passion scenario is the killing of family members by one another, the so-called family homicides. Unfortunately, this is another topic about which we know much less than we should. One pertinent study, conducted in Kansas City, looked into every family homicide that occurred in a single year. In 85 percent of the cases examined, the police had been called to the family residence within the previous five years to break up a domestic quarrel; in half the cases, the police had been there five or more times. Generalizing from this pattern, it would be seriously misleading to view these homicides as isolated and unfortunate outbursts occurring among normally placid and loving individuals. They are, rather, the culminating episodes in a long history of interpersonal violence and abuse between the parties, a history whose causes and precipitants are far more complex than the mere presence or absence of a gun.

Interesting differences exist between men who kill women and women who kill men. Women who kill men tend disproportionately to use a firearm for the purpose; men who kill women seem to prefer other, more brutalizing means, such as stabbing. The reason for the difference seems reasonably obvious: Women typically do not command the physical strength necessary to get the job done with any weapon other than a gun. Further, many of the women who kill men presumably do so because they have suffered repeated episodes of physical and mental abuse (Howard, 1986). The resulting killings are tragic, certainly, but no more tragic than the history of abuse that leads up to them. Thus, in the extreme, one could argue that firearms equalize the differences between men and women; gun control puts women at an even further disadvantage relative to men, so far as interpersonal violence is concerned (Silver and Kates, 1978).

The number of homicides involving family members has been exaggerated in many presentations. Evidence on victim–offender relationships in homicide is published annually by the FBI, in their *Uniform Crime Reports*. These data make it plain that homicides by outright strangers (as for example, in a robbery-motivated homicide) compose only a small fraction of the total, approximately one in every eight. But this assuredly does *not* imply that the remaining seven in every eight involve loved ones slaying one another. In many cases—nearly a third of the total—the relationship between victim and offender is simply unknown (as would be the case for unsolved homicides). Next to "unknown," the largest category is "acquaintance," accounting for approximately one additional third of the murders. Absent additional details, one might think that acquaintance refers to friends, neighbors, and other reasonably close associates, but in fact neighbors, friends, boyfriends, girlfriends, and all categories of relatives are tallied in their own separate categories. Thus, almost *any* degree of intimacy or closeness between "acquaintances" would cause the homicide to be tallied elsewhere in the FBI reports. *All* categories of family and relatives combined account for only about one murder in every six. Contrary to a common depiction, then, it is definitely not the case that most murders involve persons who share some degree of intimacy or closeness. Most murders, some three-quarters of them, are committed by casual acquaintances (about 30 percent), perfect strangers (about 15 percent), or persons unknown (30 percent) (see Wright, 1990, for further discussion).

GUNS AS CATALYSTS TO VIOLENCE

Another facet of the crime of passion argument deserves comment, the argument that guns give people the psychic strength to do things of which they otherwise would not be capable. With a gun, harm can be inflicted at a comfortable distance, and this, it is said, is easier than assaulting somebody "up close and personal"—with a knife, for example. In the same vein, it is also sometimes argued that even the casual sight of a gun can "catalyze violence" (Berkowitz, 1968).

These arguments are not consistent with several research findings. First, studies by Cook (1981b, 1983) found no significant differences in the rates of armed robbery between cities where guns were widely available and cities where they were not; in cities with a low "gun density," armed robbers simply robbed with other weapons. (To be sure, robbery-connected murder was somewhat less frequent in the low-density cities, but armed robbery itself was not.) Armed robbers, at least, apparently do not *need* firearms to work up the requisite courage. Second, concerning interpersonal violence not strictly committed for economic gain, assaults with a knife are already some three times more common than assaults with a firearm of any sort (Curtis, 1974; Zimring, 1968), even though guns are readily available in half of all households. Here, too, most people with assaultive intentions seemingly manage to work up the requisite courage even without a gun. Finally, the hypothesis that guns somehow catalyze violence has spawned a fairly extensive experimental literature though the principle findings are mixed and inconclusive (Kleck and Bordua, 1984).

Many crimes of passion are exactly that, but many are crimes of hatred whose outcomes depend less on the available equipment than on lethal, murderous intent. In some cases, the outcomes of these crimes would be less devastating if guns were less available; in other cases, the outcomes would be just the same. In any case, the problem goes far deeper than the presence or absence of firearms; it is a problem rooted in a culture that glorifies, or at least condones, physical violence as a means of resolving disputes. Until this more basic cultural problem is addressed, it is not clear that stricter gun controls would make much, if any, difference.

GEOGRAPHIC COMPARISONS

A common theme in the gun control literature, one frequently offered as a rejoinder to many of the themes expressed here, is the comparison of the U.S. experience with that of other industrialized Western nations. There are, in the United States, no strict federal controls over civilian arms, vast numbers of firearms in private hands, and an enormous amount of gun crime and gun violence. By contrast, other nations have very strict national controls, very few guns, and little or no gun crime. Is this not compelling evidence that strong laws reduce the number of guns and that a reduced number of guns means less crime and violence?

In the absence of more detailed analyses, such comparisons are highly problematic. Any two nations will differ along many dimensions — history, culture, social structure, and legal precedent, for example — and any of these differences (no less than the difference in gun laws or in the number of guns available) might well be the "real" cause of the difference in violent crime rates. Without some examination of these other potentially relevant factors, attributing the crime difference to the gun law or gun availability difference is gratuitous.

The English case is among the more commonly cited in this connection. However, it is well established that the rates of firearms ownership and of violent crime were both extremely low in England for decades *before* that nation's strict gun laws were passed (Greenwood, 1972). England's gun control laws also have *not* prevented a very sharp increase in armed crime in that nation over the past two decades (Greenwood, 1983). The Japanese case also is commonly cited. In fact, the rate of *nongun* homicide in the United States is many times higher than the total homicide rate of Japan. So there is obviously more to the U.S.–Japan difference than first meets the eye.

In at least a few nations, such as Norway and Switzerland, the proportional presence of guns among the civilian population at least rivals that of the United States, but gun crime and violence are exceptionally rare. (In both cases, the degree of armament is a result of the nation's policy with respect to a standing reserve militia.) It may well be that guns are a necessary condition for high rates of violent crime, but these nations make it plain that they are not a sufficient condition.

The most detailed comparison yet published of gun laws and crime rates across nations is Kopel (1992), which provides in-depth analyses of the applicable gun laws and other social circumstances in Japan, Great Britain, Canada, Australia, New Zealand, Jamaica, Switzerland, and the United States. Kopel's basic conclusion is that gun control is irrelevant in peaceful nations and ineffective in violent nations, and that any effort to model U.S. gun laws on those of other advanced industrialized societies would probably prove fruitless. "Broader cultural forces, of which gun policy is only one element, are more important" than gun control per se (1992: 406).

What is true of comparisons among nations is equally true of comparisons among other geographic aggregates, for example, among regions of the country, or states, or counties. Any two states or regions, like any two countries, will differ in a number of ways, and all those various ways must somehow be held constant in an analysis of differences in gun laws, gun availability, and crime rates. One seemingly "obvious" way to examine the effects of gun laws is to compare states or cities that have very restrictive gun laws to states or cities whose laws are less restrictive; several studies of that sort have been done (see, for example, Geisel et al., 1969; Murray, 1975; DeZee, 1983; Kleck, 1991).

The results are predictably contradictory. Some find that gun laws reduce crime; others find that they do not. The relatively cruder analyses tend to fall in the former category; more sophisticated analyses tend to fall in the latter. The problem in drawing inferences from such studies is exactly that of knowing what to hold constant in the analysis so that one can be confident that the crime difference results from the difference in gun laws and not from some other unexamined factor (see Kleck, 1984a, 1991, for additional discussion).

To illustrate, it has been known for some time that rates of firearms ownership are higher in the South than elsewhere in the country (Erskine, 1972; Wright and Marston, 1975). It is also well known that the homicide rate is higher in the South than elsewhere (Harries, 1974). Some cite these facts as proof that guns cause crime. In fact, the high homicide rates in the South result mostly from the generally lower socioeconomic conditions that prevail in that region and apparently have little to do with the somewhat higher availability of guns (see Loftin and Hill, 1974; Erlanger, 1975; O'Connor and Lizotte, 1978; Bangston et al., 1986; see also Chapter 7 of this volume).

Just as there are regional differences in gun ownership, so too are there differences by city size. Gun ownership is highest in small-town and rural areas and falls off sharply as city size increases (Wright et al., 1983: Chapter 6). The violent crime problem, in contrast, shows just the opposite pattern, being highest in the major urban centers and dropping off sharply in the more rural areas. We should not conclude, from this evidence alone, that guns are *not* the cause of crime or that guns somehow reduce crime. Rather, we need something more from the analysis. Without that something more, nothing of value can be inferred, and so too with crude comparisons between the United States and other nations.

PUBLIC OPINION

Public opinion always has figured prominently in the gun control debate. "An important part of the gun control lobby's political construct is the idea that the public 'wants' gun control and is prevented from getting it by the 'gun lobby'" (Bordua, 1984: 54; see also Schuman and Presser, 1981). If the effectiveness of stricter gun control in reducing crime is in some doubt, at least little apparent harm would be done by such controls, and the public, it is said, is long since on the record as favoring them.

So far as can be told, the first gun control question in a national poll was asked in the 1930s. Even at that early date, large majorities said they were "in favor." In 1959, Gallup instituted what is now the standard gun control question: whether one would favor or oppose a law that required a person to acquire a police permit before purchasing a gun. In the original study, and in many subsequent iterations, the proportions favoring such a law seldom have been less than 70 percent (Wright, 1981).

These large majorities are interpreted by many as evidence of widespread popular demand for "stricter" gun controls. This may well be a misinterpretation; as noted previously, Cook has shown that about three-quarters of the U.S. population now reside in political jurisdictions where something very similar to the Gallup "police permit" mechanism is already in force. The strong majorities registered on this item, in other words, may represent more an endorsement of the status quo than a demand for new and stricter regulations.

Most questions in most polls asking about registration and permit mechanisms receive substantial majority support. It is, as suggested, a plausible guess that much of this majority comes from persons residing in jurisdictions where such measures are presently in force. Other gun control measures that sometimes are asked about, those substantially more stringent than registration or permit requirements, do not, in general, curry much popular favor. Bans on the manufacture, sale, or ownership of handguns, for example, are rejected by good-sized majorities; having the government use public funds to buy back and destroy guns is rejected by an even larger majority. Apparently, a small majority favors a ban on "cheap, low-quality" handguns. Mandatory sentencing for the use of a firearm in committing a crime is very popular; mandatory sentencing for the illegal carrying or possession of a firearm is less so. In general, the available evidence suggests that most people support most of the "reasonable social precautions" discussed at the outset of this chapter but are not anxious to see government go much further. Not incidentally, very large majorities of the population, approaching 90 percent, believe (rightly or wrongly) that the Constitution guarantees them the right to own a gun—again, a topic beyond the scope of this chapter (Wright, 1981). The most recent review of poll evidence on public opinion and gun control is by Kleck (1991: Chapter 9), which also concludes that majorities support a wide range of weak-to-moderate controls but that "this support does not, however, extend to stronger controls" (1991: 369).

GUN OWNERSHIP AND SELF-DEFENSE

The ownership of guns for self-defense also figures prominently in the gun control debate. The progun forces routinely invoke the specter of an unarmed population defenseless against the ravages of crime and violence. The procontrol theme also is well known: Crime is on the rise, and to cope with their fear, people buy guns. In fact, their odds of deterring any crime with a gun are essentially nil; the odds are far better that they will end up shooting one another, either by accident or in the heat of some lamentable moment. To quote briefly from one procontrol pamphlet, "Ownership of handguns by private citizens for self-protection against crime appears to provide more a psychological belief in safety than actual deterrence to criminal behavior" (Yeager et al., 1976: 35).

MOTIVATIONS FOR OWNING A GUN

To begin, it is not at all clear that "fear of crime" is an important motivation to buy a gun. Many studies have examined the question, but most fail to show any significant correlation between fear of crime and gun ownership (Wright and Marston, 1975; Williams and McGrath, 1976; DeFronzo, 1979; Northwood et al., 1978; Stinchcombe et al., 1980; Young, 1985); a few studies show small but significant effects (see, for example, Lizotte and Bordua, 1980; McDowall and Loftin, 1983; Smith and Uchida, 1988). The best that could be said about the topic is that the research is highly ambiguous and supports, at best, the conclusion of a weak relationship between fear and gun possession.

Despite an apparently widespread impression to the contrary, owning a firearm primarily for self-defense is itself relatively uncommon (Wright, 1984). Approximately three firearms in four (conceivably, four in five) are owned mainly for other reasons, sport and recreational reasons being the most common. Even among *handgun* owners, sport and recreational reasons are mentioned about as often as defense or self-protection. Thus, guns owned primarily for self-defense are outnumbered by sport and recreational guns by roughly three or four to one. And because only about half the households in the nation own *any* gun for any reason, the proportion owning a weapon primarily for self-defense is about 10 to 15 percent. (To be sure, the proportions citing "defense" as a secondary or tertiary reason are higher but still below 50 percent.)

CHARACTERISTICS OF "SELF-DEFENDING" GUN OWNERS

We do not know very much about the people who own guns for self-defense. For example, we do not know what they intend the weapon to protect them *against*. We assume that it is for protection against other humans, but some evidence indicates that about half the actual *uses* of guns in "defense" are in defense against animals (Wright, 1984), which makes some sense in that guns are far more commonly owned in rural than in urban areas. If half the defensive ownership of firearms turns out to be for defense against aggressive fauna, the proportion of households owning a firearm primarily for defense against other humans would then be around 5 percent.

We also have little or no reliable information on how these defensive firearms are kept—whether loaded and ready for use or disassembled and locked away in storage cabinets. We do not know how many gun-owning households keep ammunition for the weapon in the home, or how many members of the average gun-owning household would know how to fire the weapon even if they wanted to. We do not know whether defensive owners tend to own just the one firearm or whether, on the average, they own many firearms and have been gun owners all of their lives. We do not know whether they are "nervous and paranoid" about guns or familiar and comfortable with small arms and well versed in their safe operation.

THE EXTENT OF CRIME DETERRENCE

We also do not know very much about the rate at which privately owned firearms actually are used to deter crimes—most of the evidence cited in this connection is episodic or journalistic. It is frequently claimed that a private firearm is six times more likely to be involved in a firearms accident than to be used in deterring a crime. The "six-to-one" finding originates with a study in

Cleveland by Rushford et al. (1975; see also Kellerman and Reay, 1986), a study that has been severely and rightly criticized (Silver and Kates, 1978). The fact is, we have some data on firearms accidents, but very little useful data on the actual deterrence of crime by armed citizens. Kleck (1986a, 1988, 1991) has reviewed what little data there are; he concludes that civilians frequently use guns against criminals (perhaps as often as a million times a year) and that civilian weapons use is effective as a deterrent to crime (see also Green, 1986). In fact, there appear to be some 1,500–2,800 felons killed in the act of committing a crime annually by gun-using civilians, far more than are killed by the police (Kleck, 1988).

A "best guess" about the annual number of firearms accidents, fatal and nonfatal, would be around 100,000. Given the total number of firearms "out there," the percentage of firearms involved in an accident in a typical year has to be on the order of a tenth of 1 percent. The average gun-owning household possesses three guns, but even if we therefore multiply by three, the annual risk per gun-owning household is still considerably less than 0.5 percent per year. Survey evidence for 1978, in contrast, shows that about 15 percent of the population (which would amount to 30 percent of the gun-owning population) claim to have used a gun for self-defense (of which about half was in defense against animals), and the proportion that appears actually to have *fired* a gun in self-defense ranges from 2 to 6 percent (Wright, 1984). The idea that there are many times more firearms accidents than incidents where firearms are used in self-defense is not consistent with these data and, indeed, is not sustained in any available evidence. If Kleck's rough estimates of the annual number of firearms accidents (some 100,000) and the annual number of times civilians use firearms to defend themselves against crime (close to a million) are even approximately correct, then self-defensive uses far outnumber accidental misuses, perhaps by an order of magnitude.

It *is* clear that much crime occurs in circumstances where the victim's ownership of a gun would be irrelevant: for example, the burglary of an unoccupied residence, or the "crime on the street" (which presumably would catch most gun owners far away from their weapons). But evidence from the criminal victimization surveys also suggests that in the cases where having a gun is not irrelevant, it can be an effective crime deterrent in some cases. Indeed, the probability of a successful victimization appears to go down — although, to stress a critical point, the probability of injury or death to the victim goes up (Cook, 1986) — if resistance of any sort is offered, and of the various means of resistance available, resisting with a gun appears to be the most effective (Kleck and Bordua, 1984: 34–39).

In general, the arguments against gun ownership for self-defense fare poorly. It is not at all clear that crime or fear of crime is responsible for much gun ownership in the first place; most guns are owned for reasons having little to do with self-defense. It is also by no means clear that the actual uses of guns in self-defense are vastly outnumbered by their accidental misuse (in fact, the precise opposite may be true) or that using a gun to deter crime is somehow ineffective.

The small, cheap handgun known as the Saturday night special (SNS) was once singled out for much special attention. The term is used very loosely: variously, it refers to low price, or inferior quality, or a small caliber, or a short barrel length, or some combination thereof. One problem, as Cook (1981a; see also McClain, 1984) has pointed out, is that the Saturday night special has not been defined with enough precision to allow special policies to be enacted for its regulation.

The special attention that was at one time given to the SNS typically was justified on two grounds: (1) that these guns have no legitimate sport or recreational use and (2) that they are the preferred firearm in crime. Thus, if we could just ban their manufacture or importation altogether, we would reduce directly the number of crime guns available and not infringe on anyone's legitimate ownership rights.

SERIOUS CRIMINALS AND THE SNS

Until recently, the only systematic evidence available on the firearms used in crime was that derived from analyses of the firearms confiscated by police in the course of criminal investigations. The confiscation studies did not present a very clear picture. One of the largest and most systematic of them (Brill, 1977) reports, based on probable cost, that the proportion of SNSs among confiscated crime handguns is less than 50 percent. Contrary to the common claim, these data do *not* establish the SNS as the preferred crime gun.

More recent and perhaps more telling data, based on direct surveys of imprisoned felons, are reported in Wright and Rossi (1986: Chapter 8). The conclusion was that "felons neither preferred to own, nor did they actually own, small, cheap, low-quality handguns. The strong preference, rather, was for large, well-made guns" (p. 180). Only about 14 percent of the most recent handguns owned by this sample would qualify as SNSs, and most of these were owned by men who had not used guns to commit crimes; the more serious the criminal history, the stronger the preference for large, well-made handguns. Felons in this survey were given a list of desirable handgun traits and asked to rate their importance; the top three choices, in order, were that the handgun be accurate, untraceable, and well made. Similar results have also been reported for samples of incarcerated *juvenile* offenders (Sheley and Wright, 1993).

A later item sequence spoke more directly, perhaps, to the advisability of an SNS ban. The felons in the survey were asked to imagine that "the handgun you really wanted was a small, cheap, low caliber little gun, but that there just weren't any of them around for you to get." A large majority of the gun criminals in the survey said they would respond to this situation by obtaining bigger, more expensive (or in other words, more lethal) handguns. Another item asked them to imagine the complete absence of handguns; a large majority of the gun criminals said they would carry sawed-off shotguns instead. At least one scholar (Kleck, 1984b) infers from these and related data that a handgun-only ban would be a "policy disaster in the making."

The conclusion is that criminals, especially serious criminals, have relatively little use for the SNS; indeed, it seems obvious that they prefer to be at least as well armed as their most likely adversary, namely, the police; data on the handguns felons actually own suggest that most of them are successful to this end. Moreover, even if they did have some preference for the smaller, cheaper handguns, the absence of those guns would *not* cause them to go unarmed, but to "move up" to bigger, more lethal equipment—to bigger and better handguns in the absence of small, cheap ones, and to sawed-off rifles and shotguns in the complete absence of handguns of all sorts. Given what is known about the comparative lethality of big-caliber versus small-caliber guns (Zimring, 1972), not to mention the lethality of sawed-off shotguns, an SNS ban seemingly has virtually nothing to recommend it (see also Kleck, 1985, 1986b).

NONCRIMINALS AND THE SNS

What about the other side of the argument, that these small, cheap guns have no legitimate use and should therefore be banned on those grounds alone, irrespective of the possible criminal response? It is obviously doubtful whether many SNSs are purchased for sporting purposes; most, in all likelihood, are purchased for self-defense by households of modest means. Whether "self-protection" from crime is a legitimate or illegitimate reason to own a handgun also can be disputed. But surely, all would agree that people at the highest risk from crime have the best reasons to protect themselves against it. Those at highest risk in the United States are the poor, blacks, and central-city residents—exactly those segments of society that can least afford large, well-made, expensive handguns. The often-urged SNS ban might well deny the means of self-protection to those most evidently in need of it, or in the words of the Congress of Racial Equality, "deny the law-abiding poor, including the law-abiding black poor, access to weapons for the defense of their families. That effect is doubly discriminatory because the poor, and especially the black poor, are the primary victims of crime and in many areas lack the political power to command as much police protection as better neighborhoods" (Innis, 1987).

ASSAULT WEAPONS

The concern expressed a decade ago about small, cheap handguns has been replaced more recently by a concern with so-called military-style assault weapons, and a complete ban on the sale, purchase, and ownership of these weapons is now a common policy recommendation. (In fact, several states have recently enacted such bans, among them California.) The attention now being given to assault weapons illustrates what Kleck (1991: Chapter 3) calls "Searching for 'Bad' Guns," the persistent hope among gun control advocates that if we can just find a way to ban "bad guns" and leave "good guns" alone, then we will reduce the level of crime and violence but not infringe on the rights of legitimate gun owners. Since the "goodness" or "badness" of a gun inheres entirely in the motivations and intentions of its user, and certainly not in the gun itself, this approach, although commonly urged, is bound to be unproductive.

Just as SNS handguns were once said to be the weapon of choice for criminals (but turned out not to be), assault weapons are now commonly said to be the weapons of choice, especially for drug dealers and youth gangs. There is practically no systematic evidence to support such an assertion. The fraction of guns confiscated from criminals by police that could be called assault weapons, even using liberal definitions, is not more than 1 or 2 percent (Kleck, 1991: 73). Large-caliber handguns, not assault rifles or other military-style weapons, remain the overwhelming weapon of choice among both adult and juvenile criminals (Sheley and Wright, 1993).

CONCLUSION

Attempts to control crime by regulating the ownership or use of firearms are attempts to regulate the artifacts and activities of a culture that, in its own way, is as unique as any of the myriad other cultures that compose the American ethnic mosaic. This is the American gun culture, about which Hofstadter (1970), Sherrill (1973), Tonso (1982), and others have written, and it remains among the least understood of any of the various subcultural strands that make up modern American society.

There is no question that a "gun culture" exists, one that amply fulfills any definition of a "culture." The best evidence we have on its status as a culture is that the most important predictor of whether a person owns a gun is whether his or her father owned one, which means that gun owning is a tradition transmitted across generations (Wright et al., 1983). Most gun owners report that there were firearms in their homes when they were growing up; this is true even of criminal gun users (Wright and Rossi, 1986: Chapter 5; Sheley and Wright, 1993).

The existence and characteristics of a gun culture have implications that rarely are appreciated. For one, gun control deals with matters that people feel strongly about, that are integral to their upbringing and their worldview. Gun control advocates frequently are taken aback by the stridency with which their proposals are attacked, but from the gun culture's viewpoint, restrictions on the right to "keep and bear arms" amount to the systematic destruction of a valued way of life.

The gun evokes powerful, emotive imagery that often stands in the way of intelligent debate. To the procontrol point of view, the gun is a symbol of much that is wrong in American culture. It symbolizes violence, aggression, and male dominance, and its use is seen as an acting out of our most regressive and infantile fantasies. To the gun culture's way of thinking, the same gun symbolizes much that is right in the culture. It symbolizes manliness, self-sufficiency, and independence, and its use is an affirmation of man's relationship to nature and to history. The "Great American Gun War," as Bruce-Briggs (1976) has described it, is far more than a contentious debate over crime and the equipment with which it is committed. It is a battle over fundamental values. Scholars and criminologists who study the problem of guns and crime would do well to conceptualize the problem in terms of this battle between cultures.

DISCUSSION QUESTIONS

1. Describe the various positions regarding gun control taken by interested parties. To what extent have past efforts at gun control succeeded in decreasing criminal violence? What problems make such an assessment difficult?

2. Who kills whom with guns in America? Is most gun-related crime the work of felons, or are most firearm incidents crimes of passion? Is the argument that guns promote violence supported by research findings?

3. Is fear of crime the reason so many people possess guns in this society? Do guns figure in many acts of self-defense? Discuss the proposition that increased gun ownership would deter crime in America.

4. What is a Saturday night special? Is this type of gun at the heart of the relationship between guns and crime in this society? How about the military-style assault weapons that we hear so much about lately? Are they driving up the crime rate?

CHAPTER 22

CAREER OFFENDERS AND CRIME CONTROL

Christy A. Visher
National Institute of Justice, Washington, D.C.

FACED WITH high crime rates, crowded jails and prisons, and increasing public demand for action, the criminal justice system longs for solutions that will reduce crime and keep criminals off the streets. Many victims' groups and policymakers are calling for stiffer prison sentences that would remove criminals from our communities for longer periods. But this crime control strategy, often referred to as "incapacitation," if directed at all offenders, would require large increases in the numbers of those who are incarcerated at a time when prisons in most states are under court order to reduce their populations.

To some, one solution to this dilemma is to reserve the scarce prison space primarily for "career offenders," those serious, persistent criminals who are likely to continue to commit serious crimes frequently. The momentum for these notions derives from research indicating that not all offenders are equally active and that a small group of criminals is responsible for a majority of serious crime, particularly robbery, burglary, theft, and assault. The direct implication of this knowledge for crime control is that crime may be reduced substantially if these career offenders could be identified.

In the 1980s, criminal justice researchers and policymakers debated the merits of "selective incapacitation" as a crime control strategy. Many states increased mandatory sentences for some types of offenders, particularly drug offenders and those with previous convictions. As a result, state and federal prison populations *more than doubled* from 1982 to 1992 (Bureau of Justice Statistics, 1993: 10). It is estimated that incarcerations for drug offenses accounted for more than half of the growth in prison populations (Bureau of Justice Statistics, 1992: 7). Offenders convicted of a violent crime account for only 45 percent of all state prison inmates (Bureau of Justice Statistics, 1992d: 16).

These skyrocketing prison populations coupled with changing attitudes about crime and punishment are likely to lead to a more multifaceted approach to crime control in the 1990s. In fact, President Clinton in his 1993 State of the Union address simultaneously called for using boot camps for first-time, nonviolent offenders and putting "hardened criminals behind bars." Encouraging the criminal justice system carefully to distinguish serious offenders from less serious ones is also an outgrowth of increasing research attention during the 1980s on different types of criminal careers (Blumstein et al., 1986). This research has permitted more systematic attention to the characteristics of the most serious group of criminals, career offenders.

But is there a small group of "career offenders" or "superfelons"? Can they be identified? Does removing them from the community eliminate their crimes? This chapter describes what is known about career offenders and their characteristics. We will examine common perceptions of career offenders held by the public, the criminal justice system, and the researchers who study these offenders and how they differ from other offenders. These perceptions generally overlap, but they often diverge in important respects. The chapter also will consider incapacitation strategies to reduce crime, practical problems in identifying career offenders, and the limitations of incapacitation as a crime control strategy.

UNDERSTANDING DIFFERENCES AMONG OFFENDERS

In the past fifteen years, research increasingly has shown that a small group of criminals commits the majority of all serious crime. In a study of 9,945 males born in 1945 in Philadelphia, 627 (or 6.3 percent) had at least five contacts with the police before age 18. This group accounted for 18 percent of the delinquents in the sample, but they committed 52 percent of all officially recorded crimes in the juvenile years, including 70 percent of all robberies (Wolfgang et al., 1972). In a similar study of 1,369 males born in 1955 in Racine, Wisconsin, the 6.5 percent of the cohort who had at least four police contacts involving a felony accounted for 70 percent of all felony crimes (Shannon, 1988: Chapter 9).

Some observers claim that these patterns reflect only repeated police attention to some offenders and do not depict a unique group of very active, serious offenders. However, data gathered through a survey of 624 California inmates in 1977 dispute this view (Peterson and Braiker, 1980). The inmates were asked to report the frequency with which they had committed ten types of crimes in the three years prior to being incarcerated. Twenty-five percent of these offenders reported committing about 60 percent of the armed robberies, burglaries, and auto thefts, and about 50 percent of the assaults and drug deals.

A larger study carried out by the Rand Corporation questioned over 2,000 inmates in California, Michigan, and Texas prisons and jails about seven types of crimes they had committed prior to incarceration (Chaiken and Chaiken, 1982; Chaiken, 1987). Analysis of these self-report data revealed wide variation among offenders in the number of crimes they committed annually. Fifty percent of the inmates in the Rand survey reported committing fewer than five crimes per year for each crime type. Considering all crimes included in the survey (except drug deals), the typical offender reported committing less than fifteen crimes per year.

However, there was another, smaller group of offenders in the survey who reported committing crimes much more frequently. For example, the most active 10 percent of all inmates who had committed robbery reported committing at least 58 robberies per year, and the most active 10 percent of the burglars reported committing 187 or more burglaries per year. Overall, the most active 10 percent of the inmates reported committing about 600 of the seven survey crimes in the two-year period prior to their incarceration—more than 10 crimes per week. (Rape, kidnapping, and arson were not included in the survey.)

Taken together, many studies of delinquents and surveys of inmates indicate that most juvenile and adult offenders actually commit few crimes. Very active offenders represent a small portion of the criminal population, but they appear to commit the majority of the crimes. These findings have surprised both researchers and law enforcement officials. They have also fostered the need for profiles of frequent offenders so that the criminal justice system can identify them.

DIMENSIONS OF CRIMINAL CAREERS

As we have seen in the preceding discussion, clear distinctions among offenders are evident when examining the annual number of crimes they commit. Individual crime frequencies, however, are just one dimension of an offender's "criminal career"—that is, the longitudinal sequence of offenses committed by an individual offender. In an exhaustive review of research on criminal careers (Blumstein et al., 1986: 13–14), the notion of a criminal career is further clarified: "Criminal careers may vary substantially among offenders. At one extreme are offenders whose careers consist of only one offense. At the other extreme are 'career criminals' . . . who commit serious offenses with high frequency over extended periods of time."

In describing the criminal careers of active offenders, three characteristics have become particularly instructive: (1) the individual frequency rate, (2) the seriousness of crimes committed and the combination of offense types, and (3) the length of the criminal career. We have already seen how individual frequency rates vary among active offenders. Other important issues in studying criminal careers include the age of initiation into criminal activity (often called "age at onset") and the relationship between juvenile delinquency and adult crime. In the next section, these characteristics will be used to distinguish career offenders from other types of criminals.

JUVENILE PATTERNS

A common image gleaned from news reports and television is that juvenile delinquents mature into adult professional criminals and pursue crime as a preferred occupation, becoming more specialized and sophisticated in their criminal activities. To what extent is this image accurate?

Most juvenile delinquents do not become adult criminals. According to one review of many studies of juvenile participation in crime, at least one-third of all U.S. males are detained by the police or arrested before age 18 (Visher and Roth, 1986). However, the majority of these delinquents (perhaps two-thirds) are arrested only once or twice and do not have adult arrest records. A small group of chronic juvenile offenders is much more likely to persist in criminal activity. In the Philadelphia study, half of these chronic offenders (those with five or more arrests) were arrested at least four times between ages 18 and 30 (Wolfgang et al., 1972, 1987).

Most criminal careers, especially those of persistent, career offenders, begin at or before age 16. And juveniles who engage in serious crime at an early age are likely to become serious adult offenders. In studies of juvenile offenders followed into adulthood, the most serious adult offenders typically began committing crimes or experienced their first arrest when they were between ages 11 and 14. These early starters accumulate more crimes during their criminal careers and are less likely to terminate their criminal activity than are offenders who began criminal activity at a later age (Petersilia, 1980; Wolfgang et al., 1972: Chapter 8; Wolfgang et al., 1987: Chapter 5).

Studies of adult inmates who were asked to recall their juvenile activity also show that age at onset is an important predictor of serious, persistent criminal activity as an adult (Chaiken and Chaiken, 1982). Other juvenile patterns also characterize adult career offenders: (1) a history of committing violent crimes, particularly robbery, before age 16; (2) frequent property offenses; (3) convictions before age 16; and (4) multiple sentences to juvenile institutions.

OFFENDER TYPES

One influential study of inmates used self-reports of crimes committed prior to incarceration to classify inmates into one of ten offender types depending on the specific combination of crimes they reported: (1) violent predators (those who committed robbery, assault, *and* drug deals), (2) robber-assaulters, (3) robber-dealers, (4) low-level robbers, (5) "mere assaulters," (6) burglar-dealers, (7) low-level burglars, (8) property and drug offenders, (9) low-level property offenders, and (10) drug dealers (Chaiken and Chaiken, 1982).

The offender types are listed in order of severity, with those at the top of the list generally more serious than those at the bottom. The least serious offender types, primarily those who committed only property and drug offenses, committed crimes less often. The most serious category of offenders, those called violent predators, both committed robbery and assault *and* sold drugs at very high frequencies. In the survey, violent predators comprised 15 percent of the inmates committing the crimes.

The different levels of seriousness implied by the ten offender categories are supported by self-reported information about the annual number of robberies, burglaries, and thefts committed (see Table 22.1). Offenders classified as violent predators committed an average of 70 robberies, 144 burglaries, and

TABLE 22.1 AVERAGE ANNUAL NUMBER OF ROBBERIES, BURGLARIES, AND THEFTS COMMITTED BY SIX OFFENDER TYPES

Offender Type	Robbery	Burglary	Theft*
Violent predators†	70	144	229
Robber-assaulters	50	48	127
Robber-dealers	32	93	132
Low-level robbers	10	31	54
Burglar-dealers	—	42	140
Low-level burglars	—	36	25
Low-level property offenders	—	—	369

SOURCE: Chaiken and Chaiken, 1982: 219–221.

* Includes larceny, auto theft, bad checks and credit cards, and fraud.

† Defined as offenders concurrently committing robbery, assault, and drug deals.

229 thefts in one year. They also committed more burglaries than the burglar-dealers or the low-level burglars. This relatively small group of serious, high-rate offenders accounted for the majority of all robberies, assaults, burglaries, and drug deals committed by the entire inmate sample.

SPECIALIZATION

The findings on offender types also are important to the question of whether offenders specialize in the types of crimes they commit. Contrary to popular beliefs held by the public and by law enforcement officials, the Rand study found that offenders—at least, incarcerated offenders—are much more often "generalists" than "specialists." Among inmates in the Rand study, only 20 percent reported committing just one of the seven types of crime in the two years preceding their incarceration. Although the ten offender types can be thought of as "specialities," offenders within each type committed many different types of crimes. For example, most robbers also committed burglary, and most inmates who reported committing burglary or robbery also engaged in some form of theft, forgery, or fraud (Chaiken and Chaiken, 1982: 55–63; see also Petersilia et al., 1978; Peterson and Braiker, 1980).

Analysis of juvenile and adult official arrest histories provides a slightly different picture of offense specialization (see Cohen, 1986, for a discussion of problems with arrest data in studies of offense specialization). Among all juveniles, the type of prior offense in the arrest record is not very helpful in predicting the next arrest charge although some evidence of specialization exists for runaway and theft. However, persistent juvenile offenders—those with numerous arrests—tend to become more specialized with each additional offense, particularly within the broad categories of violence and theft, and for robbery, drugs, and liquor offenses. Specialization among juveniles is weakest for offenses involving injury (Cohen, 1986: 366–406; Farrington et al., 1988).

Among adult offenders, some specialization is evident for all offense types when arrest records are analyzed carefully, but it is stronger for drugs, fraud, and auto theft. Specialization may occur more frequently for these offenses because they are often committed in conjunction with an organized criminal network. Violent and property offenses form distinct clusters, and adult offenders are more likely to commit offenses *within* a cluster than to switch to offenses *outside* a cluster. Offenders committing robbery are somewhat more likely to switch to other violent offenses than to property offenses. Drug offenders, however, do not consistently switch to either violent or property offenses (Cohen, 1986: 366–406; Blumstein et al., 1988).

Both types of studies—inmate surveys and analyses of arrest histories—indicate that adult offenders specialize in clusters of offenses rather than in specific offense types although the clusters are defined somewhat differently depending on the source of the data. Juveniles are less likely to specialize. Finally, higher levels of specialization for adult offenders suggest that offenders who remain criminally active until older ages are also more specialized in their offending patterns.

SERIOUSNESS

Another dimension of criminal careers is the seriousness of offenses, particularly the extent to which offenders commit crimes of increasing seriousness over the course of their careers. Most of the research on offense seriousness and escalation is based on analyses of arrest histories. During the juvenile years, the seriousness of arrests does not steadily increase over successive arrests. However, for juveniles who remain active, some escalation occurs after a large number of arrests, particularly increases in switches to robbery and injury offenses.

For most adult offenders, offense seriousness generally is stable over successive arrests or *decreases* slightly. A different picture emerges if the analysis takes into account the length of the arrest record and excludes minor offenses such as public drunkenness. Comparing offenders with few arrests to those with many arrests confounds the experiences of less serious offenders with the experiences of more serious offenders. In one comprehensive study of offenders' criminal careers in Michigan, average seriousness is stable over the career among black offenders with ten arrests for serious crimes, whereas similar white offenders show increases in seriousness over successive arrests (Blumstein et al., 1988). The dominant pattern, however, is one of little change in seriousness over the adult career. Only a small group of offenders are likely to engage in increasingly serious criminal behavior.

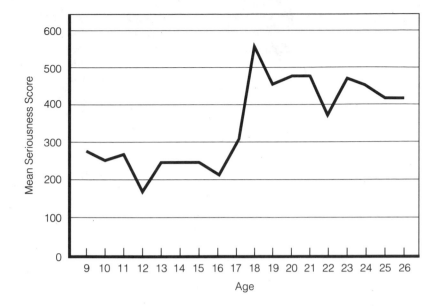

These juvenile and adult patterns are compatible with one study that has examined offense seriousness for a sample of juveniles followed into adulthood using official arrest records (Rand, 1987). Figure 22.1 displays the mean offense seriousness score (based on methods discussed in Sellin and Wolfgang, 1978) from ages 9 to 26 for 106 offenders in the Philadelphia study who committed Index or other serious crimes. A total of 315 offenses are represented. The average seriousness score (243) is relatively stable during the juvenile years. Then, during the juvenile–adult transition period, a marked increase in offense seriousness occurs between ages 16 and 18. In the adult period, the mean seriousness score (444) is again relatively stable although seriousness scores are about 200 points higher for adults than juveniles.

The dramatic jump in offense seriousness in the late teen years is puzzling. Although strictly juvenile offenses (for example, runaway and underage drinking) and other minor offenses are excluded, the change in offense seriousness might reflect differences in the official arrest charges for juveniles and adults. For example, a juvenile offender may be arrested for breaking and entering, whereas an adult offender may be charged with burglary. Alternatively, it may reflect a shift into organized criminal activities as former juvenile delinquents become more committed to a deviant lifestyle.

CAREER LENGTH

An important dimension of criminal careers is their length. Research on career length is scarce, in part because it is difficult to determine exactly when an offender's criminal activity ends. The popular belief is that certainly by age 30, offenders terminate their criminal careers. As a consequence, prosecutors and judges hesitate to sentence such offenders to long prison terms because they are thought to be near the end of their life of crime anyway.

Estimates of the average length of adult criminal careers involving Index offenses range from five to fifteen years (see Blumstein et al., 1986: 91–94). However, these career length estimates include only adult careers, so overall career length may be longer if the offender started criminal activity as a juvenile. This average length pertains to offenders who drop out quickly and to those who remain criminally active for much longer periods.

Another way to study career length is to ask how many years are left in a criminal career given the time that has already been spent committing crimes, or the *residual* career length. The pattern of residual career lengths in one study of males in Washington, D.C., displayed three segments: (1) a "break-in" period, in which many offenders in their twenties are dropping out of crime and the remaining years in crime for nondropouts increase from five to ten years; (2) a "stable" period beginning around age 30 and extending up to age 39 or 40, in which time remaining in a career is about ten years; and (3) a "burnout" period beginning about age 41 (or after twenty-three years in active adult careers), in which careers terminate rapidly (Blumstein et al., 1986; Blumstein and Cohen, 1987). Thus, persistent offenders who begin their adult careers at age 18 (or before) and who are still active in their thirties are likely to continue to commit crimes for another ten years.

Different patterns emerge for property and violent offenses. Offenders who are arrested for the violent offenses of murder, aggravated assault, and rape are less likely than are property offenders (including robbers) to drop out during the early years of their careers. In this context, robbery was more similar to property crimes than to violent crimes. Thus, persistent career offenders less often are simply property offenders and more often have criminal histories that include arrests for violent offenses. However, *older* property offenders with long careers likely will continue committing crimes into their forties.

DRUG USE

The consumption of illicit drugs is linked closely by the public and by law enforcement officials to the commission of property and violent crimes, but the nature of those links is the subject of extensive study in the research community. Some drug users never begin committing crimes; some criminals never begin using drugs; and among those who engage in both behaviors, drug use typically begins *at the same time* or *shortly after* criminal activity. The drug–crime relationship may also differ depending on the extent of drug use and criminal activity (see Chaiken and Chaiken, 1990).

Most adult drug-involved offenders are not violent and commit crimes infrequently (see Chapter 20). However, we do know that the persistent, career offender who commits hundreds of crimes a year usually is also a drug user. Offenders who use multiple types of illicit drugs in large amounts commit at least twice, and perhaps ten times, as many crimes per year as do other offenders. The regularity of drug use is related to the frequency of offending—daily drug users commit more crimes than do occasional users. Offenders who reduce their consumption of illicit drugs often show a sharp reduction in their frequency of criminal activity, particularly robbery, burglary, and drug dealing. But drug-involved offenders who committed crimes frequently *before* developing heavy drug habits show less reductions in criminal activity when they are not using drugs. (For a review of several relevant studies, see Chaiken and Chaiken, 1990; Cohen, 1986: 349–352).

Specific types and combinations of drugs, including alcohol, also seem linked to particular patterns of offending and offender types. For example, offenders who have expensive heroin addictions are not especially assaultive, whereas offenders who use both alcohol and barbiturates are likely to commit violent offenses frequently. Offenders who were classified as violent predators in the Rand study were habitual users of heroin and cocaine, but they also used other combinations of drugs, particularly the alcohol–barbiturate combination, in large quantities. The frequent commission of robbery, burglary, and other forms of theft, but not auto theft, is common among offenders with expensive heroin habits. It is also significant that some heroin and cocaine addicts with less expensive habits primarily deal drugs and rarely commit violent or serious property crimes (Chaiken and Chaiken, 1982: 156–178; Chaiken and Johnson, 1988; Wish and Johnson, 1986). The chronic use of alcohol has also been linked to repeated involvement in violent crimes (Reiss and Roth, 1993). Thus, many different types of linkages exist between alcohol use, illicit drug use and crime, and the relationship may vary depending on the nature of the drug use, the type of offense, and other personal or situational factors.

Several cities have begun urinalysis tests to detect recent use of illicit drugs by persons who are arrested. Although criminal justice officials suspected that a substantial proportion of those arrested were drug users, few realized the extent of drug use among arrested persons. In 1991, for example, at least half of a sample of males arrested in twenty-four large urban areas tested positive for illegal drugs, primarily cocaine (U.S. Department of Justice, 1992). However, a single positive urine test detects only the *presence* of a specific drug; it does not indicate intensity of use and hence cannot be used to distinguish career offenders from less serious criminals.

Finally, career offenders are likely to have used multiple types of illicit drugs as juveniles, especially frequent use of serious drugs such as heroin, cocaine, and barbiturates (Chaiken and Chaiken, 1982). In fact, among multiple-drug users, girls are as likely as boys, whites as likely as blacks, and middle-class suburban youths as likely as lower-class youths raised in the city to become serious, frequent drug-involved offenders (Chaiken and Johnson, 1988). But experimentation with hard drugs or use of marijuana only does not appear to lead to serious adult criminal activity (Chaiken and Chaiken, 1982; Wish and Johnson, 1986). Thus, it is not drug use per se, but the frequency and intensity of drug use that is strongly related to serious, peristent, and frequent criminal behavior.

INCAPACITATION AS A CRIME CONTROL STRATEGY

Incapacitation is one of the principle methods employed by the criminal justice system to control crime. Simply stated, putting offenders in prison physically prevents them from committing crimes in the community.

Two strategies based on incapacitation exist. The common approach, known as *collective incapacitation*, incarcerates offenders on the basis of the crime they have committed. Occasionally, the judge also considers the offender's prior criminal record in setting a sentence. For example, under a collective incapacitation strategy, most convicted robbers receive the same sentence. A second approach, which received considerable attention in the 1980s, is called *selective incapacitation*. This strategy was designed to reduce crime by sentencing offenders according to predictions about whether they are likely to commit serious crimes frequently in the future. For example, under a selective incapacitation strategy, convicted robbers who were predicted to be very active offenders in the future would be sentenced to longer terms in prison; convicted robbers who were predicted to be better risks would receive more lenient sentences. Not surprisingly, this proposed strategy generated much debate in the research and policy communities. The remainder of this chapter discusses the impact of incapacitation strategies, including selective incapacitation, on crime and operational concerns involved in improving our ability to achieve crime reduction through incapacitation.

INCAPACITATION, CRIME RATES, AND PRISON POPULATIONS

Interest in incapacitation is motivated by rising crime rates, increasing public fear of crime, and the perceived inadequacy of rehabilitation and deterrence strategies. Further, the greater use of incarceration in general during the 1970s and 1980s led to dramatic increases in prison populations, but it did not bring about any significant reduction in serious crime. In fact, the evidence indicates that general incarceration strategies are not as effective as one might think.

Several studies have estimated the amount of crime that is prevented by different sentencing practices (for reviews see Cohen, 1983; Visher, 1987). One particularly interesting study of how collective incapacitation has worked took advantage of the fact that the U.S. prison population nearly doubled in the period between 1973 and 1982, from 204,211 to 396,072 inmates (Blumstein et al., 1986: 123–128). This study attempted to answer the question, How much crime was prevented by incarcerating inmates between 1973 and 1982? The conclusions were that doubling prison populations prevented only an additional 6 percent each of all robberies and burglaries that would have been committed if the inmates had been free in the community. The total number of robberies recorded by the police in 1982 was 536,890, and the number of burglaries was 3,415,500; in 1973, robberies numbered 384,220, and burglaries numbered 2,565,500 (McGarrell and Flanagan, 1985: Table 3.81). Thus, incarcerating about 192,000 additional persons prevented approximately 9,160 robberies and 51,000 burglaries.

Furthermore, a recent examination of the effects of incarceration on *violent* crime shows that increasing prison populations had little effect on levels of violent crime between 1975 and 1989 (Cohen and Canela-Cacho, 1993). Although average prison time served per violent crime tripled during this period, primarily because of statutes mandating minimum sentences, there has been no appreciable decline in the rate of violent crime. Clearly, incapacitation prevented some violent crimes, but this crime control effect has been overwhelmed by other factors that have increased the number of criminals still on the street (Reiss and Roth, 1993). This study further suggested that additional increases in incarceration are not likely to bring about meaningful crime control effects.

An increasingly popular collective sentencing strategy in the 1980s and 1990s is the use of mandatory minimum sentences, which require that offenders be incarcerated for a minimum period with no sentence reduction for good behavior. Proponents believe that such sentences reduce crime significantly because they guarantee a longer period of incarceration. The likely impact on crime rates of imposing mandatory minimum sentences, however, also is much smaller than expected. Five-year mandatory prison terms for convicted offenders with at least one prior felony conviction would prevent between 5 and 15 percent of all Index offenses, but prison populations would need to expand still more to accommodate the additional offenders serving longer prison terms. Moreover, mandatory minimum sentencing policies are regularly circumvented by prosecutors and judges, reduce defendant's incentives to plead guilty, and increase case processing time, all of which reduce their potential effectiveness in controlling crime (Tonry, 1992).

Targeting these collective incapacitation strategies at a new group of offenders in the 1980s—persons convicted of selling and possessing illicit drugs—led to large increases in our prison populations. As mentioned earlier, state and federal prison populations doubled again between 1982 and 1992. And, at year end 1991, the Bureau of Justice Statistics estimated that state prisons were operating from 16 to 31 percent above their capacities (Bureau of Justice Statistics, 1992d: 1).

Thus, during the height of increasing prison populations, an innovative control strategy—selective incapacitation—which purported to reduce crime without increasing the prison population by reserving lengthy prison sentences for the most serious, active offenders, received considerable attention. The next section discusses an influential study that claimed a selective incapacitation strategy could reduce robbery by a fifth with no increase in incarcerated populations.

GREENWOOD'S SELECTIVE INCAPACITATION STUDY

In 1982, Peter Greenwood, one of the researchers involved in the Rand survey of prison and jail inmates, presented some provocative findings in a report that explored whether greater reductions in crime would occur if prison sentences were based, in part, on predictions of the offender's future criminal activity. Building on the initial findings of the inmate survey—that a small minority of offenders, by their own admission, committed most of the crimes—Greenwood created a prediction scale that he thought would identify these offenders (Greenwood and Abrahamse, 1982).

Seven characteristics emerged that were strongly related to high annual frequencies of robbery and burglary: (1) prior conviction for robbery or burglary, (2) incarceration for more than half of the preceding two years, (3) juvenile conviction prior to age 16, (4) commitment to a state or federal juvenile institution, (5) heroin or barbiturate use in the preceding two years, (6) heroin or barbiturate use as a juvenile, and (7) employment for less than half of the preceding two years.

In assigning scores to estimate offenders' potential for future crime, each of the seven characteristics merited 1 point, and thus, each inmate could be given a score ranging from 0 to 7. In Greenwood's analysis, inmates with a scale score of 0–1 were likely to be "low-rate" offenders in the future, those with scores of 2–3 were likely to be "medium-rate" offenders, and those with scores of 4–7 were the probable "high-rate" offenders. Using a statistical model that estimated the amount of crime prevented by incarceration, Greenwood calculated that if predicted high-rate robbers in California served prison terms of eight years and all other robbers served one-year jail terms, the robbery rate could be reduced by 20 percent without increasing the prison population.

Greenwood's study received considerable attention from the research community (Cohen, 1983; von Hirsch and Gottfredson, 1984; Visher, 1986). Technical reviews of his work generally agree that Greenwood's claim of a potential 20 percent reduction in robbery with no prison population increase *overstates* the likely effects of selective incapacitation for several reasons. The two most important qualifications concern assumptions about the length of criminal careers and the fact that the study was based on California robbers.

First, Greenwood's analysis implicitly assumes that the length of a criminal career is *longer* than the prison sentence imposed. As discussed previously, however, evidence indicates that the total criminal career is short, averaging five to ten years. Many offenders sentenced to long prison terms under a selective incapacitation policy would likely have ended their careers within a few years anyway if they had not been incarcerated. Thus, part of the time spent incarcerated would not prevent any crimes.

Second, in Greenwood's study, the dramatic reduction in crime resulting from selective incapacitation was limited to California, and was for robbery only, not for burglary. A similar sentencing policy would not reduce robbery at all in Michigan or Texas. Apparently, robbers in California prisons and jails were much more serious criminals than were their counterparts in the other two states and longer sentences would prevent more crimes in California than they would in Michigan or Texas.

Greenwood's study of the likely impact of selective incapacitation forced researchers and policymakers to take a more realistic look at crime control strategies targeted at career offenders. The next section addresses some specific problems associated with targeting career offenders, including criminal justice decisions such as sentencing that explicitly take into account predictions of future criminal activity.

TARGETING CAREER OFFENDERS: LEGAL AND ETHICAL ISSUES

An analysis of potential legal and constitutional impediments to prediction-based crime control strategies (which includes selective incapacitation) reveals that state statutes and the U.S. Constitution have virtually nothing to say about limits on uses of predictions in criminal justice decisions (Tonry, 1987). Predictions or classifications based on race, ethnicity, religion, or gender generally, of course, are prohibited. But predictions based on other factors are nearly always permitted, even if they result in differential impact on racial groups, so long as that effect is unintentional. Moreover, in several criminal cases, the U.S. Supreme Court has upheld the use of predictions of dangerousness to set sentences or to detain suspects before trial (Tonry, 1987).

Indeed, other segments of the criminal justice system are already implementing special procedures designed to enhance the apprehension and conviction of career offenders. For example, many large cities have "career criminal" prosecution units or "repeat offender" policing divisions that target offenders thought to be engaging in frequent, serious criminal activity. During prosecution, cases involving these types of offenders generally receive more attention, often using "vertical prosecution" methods that require a single prosecutor to handle the case from arraignment to trial (see Blumstein et al., 1986: Chapter 6; Chaiken and Chaiken, 1990).

Because criminal justice policy is largely independent of federal regulation, decisions about specific procedures for targeting career offenders ultimately fall to the states. Most of the controversy about criminal justice decisions aimed at career offenders centers not on legal limitations but on ethical questions. The ethical issue raised most often concerns whether or not such strategies are fair.

The primary ethical objection to criminal justice strategies aimed at career offenders is their use in sentencing decisions. For example, some critics argue that a sentencing policy such as that proposed by Greenwood, which includes predictions about *future* criminal behavior, is unfair because it punishes people for crimes they have not yet committed and may never commit. Selective incapacitation also is thought to be unjust because two persons who have committed the same offense deserve equal punishment. Today, offenders generally are sentenced according to the seriousness of the crimes they commit: More serious crimes receive more serious punishment, and similar crimes usually receive similar punishment.

Proponents of selective incapacitation, however, do not believe that it necessarily would be unfair or unjust. Most states permit a wide range of sentences for a particular offense, for example, five to fifteen years for armed robbery.

The choice of a particular sentence in that range could be based on predictions of future criminality (Morris and Miller, 1985). Offenders likely to commit future crimes at high rates could receive a sentence in the upper range; low-risk offenders could receive a sentence in the lower end. It is also argued that selective incapacitation would merely formalize and improve current decisions in the criminal justice system because many judges' decisions are based in part on their own intuitive predictions of future dangerousness.

IDENTIFYING SERIOUS, FREQUENT OFFENDERS

Predictions about an offender's future criminal activity cannot be perfectly accurate. Errors will be made in deciding which offenders are likely to be serious offenders in the future. In fact, research shows that accurate prediction of criminal behavior is very difficult. Predictions commonly are made about the likelihood of violent behavior among released mental patients or criminal behavior by released prisoners out on parole. But as many as one-half to two-thirds of these predictions have been shown to be wrong in research on prediction (Blumstein et al., 1986; Chaiken et al., 1993; Farrington, 1987).

Four possible results of a prediction decision about the likelihood of recidivism must be considered:

1. **True positives:** The offender is predicted to recidivate, and in fact, the offender commits a new crime.
2. **True negatives:** The offender is not predicted to recidivate, and in fact, no new crime is committed.
3. **False positives:** The offender is predicted to recidivate, but no new crime is committed.
4. **False negatives:** The offender is not predicted to recidivate, but the offender commits a new crime.

Prediction errors — false negatives and false positives — affect the community in different ways. Criminal justice officials and the public are most worried, for example, about the rapist out on bail who commits a new crime or the robber on parole who shoots a convenience store clerk during another robbery. These are false negative prediction errors — they cause emotional harm and personal loss to victims of crime and increase the public's dissatisfaction with the criminal justice system.

But false positive errors also are costly. These erroneous predictions unfairly extend the incarceration of offenders who actually are good risks. Not only do the offenders and their families suffer needlessly, society suffers because of the high cost of the wasted incarceration. Most criminal justice officials would rather err on the side of caution than risk releasing potential robbers or rapists, but this "overprediction" has resulted in many unnecessary

TABLE 22.2   **ACCURACY OF GREENWOOD SCALE FOR PREDICTING FUTURE CRIMINAL ACTIVITY**

	Predicted to Be Low to Moderate Offender	Predicted to Be Frequent Offender
Percent arrested within twenty-four months	65–70	80–83
Percent with "safety" arrest within twenty-four months*	47	55
Percent reincarcerated within twenty-four months	32	55
Percent "failed" during entire follow-up†	75	86

SOURCE: Visher, 1987: Table 5.

*Murder, aggravated assault, rape, robbery, and burglary are referred to as "safety" crimes.
†A failure is either an arrest, a jail term, or a prison term. Offenders could be returned to prison without an arrest.

incarcerations. Thus, crowding in America's prisons may be due partly to the substantial number of incarcerated offenders who are unlikely to reoffend (Clear, 1988).

Using Greenwood's seven-item scale, two studies have assessed the extent to which persons predicted to be high-rate offenders were in fact frequent, serious offenders after their release from prison. Criminal history information was gathered on the California inmates from the original study who had been out of prison for two years (Greenwood and Turner, 1987; Klein and Caggiano, 1986). Unfortunately, the scale was unable to predict very accurately which inmates would commit new crimes, much less which ones would become career offenders. Table 22.2 provides the results of these studies. Of the inmates predicted by the scale to be low or moderate offenders, 65 to 70 percent were arrested within twenty-four months, compared to 80 to 83 percent of the predicted high-rate offenders.

Even focusing on the most serious offenses—the "safety" crimes of murder, aggravated assault, rape, robbery, and burglary—the predicted high-rate offenders were only slightly more likely to be arrested than were the predicted low- or moderate-rate offenders (55 percent for high-rate, 47 percent for others). Over half (55 percent) of the inmates thought to be the highest risks were reincarcerated, but 32 percent of the lower risks also were sent back to prison or jail.

The ability of the criminal justice system to identify frequent offenders accurately rests on the information available to criminal justice officials who make decisions. The next section discusses some issues about the types of information that are acceptable and useful.

OFFENDER CHARACTERISTICS

Many critics of Greenwood's study objected to the choice of some offender characteristics in the prediction formula, specifically employment information and aspects of juvenile criminal history. Some believe that this information should not influence sentencing because it is irrelevant to the seriousness of the offense and the offender's legal culpability for that offense. Employment and other factors such as education and length of residence are inappropriate because they may discriminate against poor offenders. Information related to social class may result in more severe punishment for black and Hispanic offenders.

Indicators of past behavior — for example, youthful criminal activities — are objectionable to others because these behaviors are beyond the offender's current control. For this reason, many states allow juvenile records to be sealed permanently or destroyed so as not to stigmatize forever those who had a few encounters with the law during their youth. In addressing the issue of juvenile records, an influential report on career offenders suggested that these records be available to criminal justice officials only if a person continues to commit crimes as an adult (Blumstein et al., 1986: Chapter 6). In that situation, the juvenile official record can provide useful information about the nature and extent of prior criminal activity, especially for young adult offenders who may appear to have no prior record.

Research discussed previously in this chapter on the characteristics of career offenders is based largely on studies of offenders who are known to be career offenders. However, prosecutors and judges must make decisions on the basis of information available to the criminal justice system at the time of sentencing. Recent studies show that some information used by police, prosecutors, and judges to identify career offenders is a weak predictor of future offending. For example, the seriousness of the current offense is not a good indicator of future criminal activity (Clear, 1988; Gottfredson and Gottfredson, 1986). Those who commit the most vicious crimes are not necessarily the most frequent offenders with the longest careers in crime. Of course, brutal murderers and rapists usually are given long prison sentences because of the nature of the crime and the desire for appropriate punishment.

The number of prior arrests, convictions, or prison terms is also not a good predictor of serious, frequent offending. This information is misleading because two types of offenders often are involved with the criminal justice system: (1) offenders whose high rates of criminal activity result in frequent apprehensions and convictions and (2) infrequent offenders who are basically inept, unsophisticated criminals.

Many states have some sort of "habitual offender" statute that permits the judge to add twenty or thirty years to an offender's sentence if he has a certain number of previous convictions, usually at least three felonies. But these habitual offenders may not be the serious, frequent, drug-involved offenders that are responsible for large numbers of crimes. They are likely to be more inept criminals, and their long incarceration may limit available prison space for more serious offenders.

If the overall length of an offender's criminal record is not a good indicator of the frequency of criminal activity, what other characteristics predict serious frequent offending? Given two offenders with equal numbers of arrests, the one who has accumulated those arrests more rapidly is more likely the career offender. Further, in addition to information about drug use patterns, *specific* information about previous offenses, juvenile criminal history, and so on often included in arrest and presentence reports (but rarely in official criminal history records) is the most useful.

In a more detailed study based on the inmate survey, three broad types of offenders emerged: (1) "low-rate losers," who reported low crime frequencies and high arrest rates; (2) "high-rate losers," who reported high crime frequencies and high arrest rates; and (3) "high-rate winners," who reported high crime frequencies and low arrest rates (Chaiken and Chaiken, 1985; Chaiken and Johnson, 1988). Both types of high-rate criminals may be career offenders, but the "winners" apparently are evading detection by the criminal justice system. Closer study reveals that the winners are younger, have a history of committing crime since adolescence, use illicit drugs (but not heroin), are more careful about planning their crimes, often work with partners, have never been married, and hold jobs longer.

Unfortunately, much of this information is not readily available to police or prosecutors in official criminal records. When relying on official records to distinguish between career offenders and inept criminals, the following criteria may be particularly useful: (1) a prior conviction for robbery, burglary, arson, forcible rape, sex crime involving a child, kidnapping, or murder; (2) an escape from prison or failure to complete parole successfully; (3) currently on bail or free awaiting trial for another crime when arrested; (4) convictions for robbery as a juvenile; and (5) indications of *persistent* and *frequent* use of drugs (Chaiken and Johnson, 1988; Chaiken and Chaiken, 1990). The last two items of information are less readily available.

In summary, the criminal justice system's ability to identify career offenders is limited by a lack of relevant information in existing official records. First, these offenders usually are young, and their adult criminal records do not reveal the extent of their criminal activity. Second, juvenile records, when available, often are inadequate because court records may not reflect the extent of culpability or the nature of the crimes committed. The inmates in the Rand survey actually reported more juvenile arrests and incarcerations than appeared in their official records. Third, some frequent offenders successfully evade arrest and conviction for the crimes they commit for many years; hence, their criminal record gives an inaccurate picture of their criminal activity. Finally, official records rarely contain detailed information about drug involvement.

Other sources, such as arrest and presentence investigation reports, might contain predictive information about current probation or parole status, the number of offenders involved in specific crimes, employment history, specific drug use (types of drug use, drug combinations, and frequency of use), and juvenile criminal activity. These materials could be an important source of information for use in identifying career offenders.

CONCLUSION

Researchers' attention to identifying career offenders and Greenwood's controversial selective incapacitation strategy during the 1980s led the criminal justice system to experiment with new strategies for reducing crime. Armed with the knowledge that not all offenders commit crimes frequently and that a small number of criminals—career offenders—may account for the majority of serious crimes, the criminal justice system has developed a system of "intermediate sanctions" that can be tailored to specific offenders (see Clear, in this volume). Boot camps, intensive supervision probation, electronic monitoring, and house arrest are some of the innovative programs being implemented around the country for less serious offenders.

Meanwhile, the notion of career offenders has crept into media reports, political speeches, and everyday conversation. Criminal justice officials are becoming more knowledgeable about how to identify career offenders. Sentencing guidelines increasingly incorporate research findings about career offenders into legislation. A striking example is the implementation of Federal Sentencing Guidelines in 1990, which are the basis for judges' sentencing decisions for all offenders convicted of federal crimes. In developing these guidelines, the United States Sentencing Commission explicitly incorporated a defendant's past criminal record into the determination of the sentence. The term of imprisonment is increased depending on prior sentences of imprisonment and the recency of those sentences and whether the offender was under criminal justice supervision at the time of the offense (probation, parole, work release, and so on).

The commission also noted that the guidelines "are consistent with the extant empirical research assessing correlates of recidivism and patterns of career criminal behavior" (United States Sentencing Commission, 1990: 4.1). The commission's approach is a step forward; however, they chose not to include other indicators of career involvement such as juvenile convictions or incarcerations and drug abuse. As of 1992, an evaluation of the effectiveness of these guidelines in identifying career offenders had not yet been completed.

But attempts at crime reduction based on targeting career offenders (including incapacitation strategies) may be hampered for a number of reasons. The problems involved in identifying high-rate offenders using existing information in criminal justice records discussed earlier limits the impact of these strategies on reducing crime. Moreover, crimes will not be prevented if the incarcerated career offender simply is replaced by another offender recruited to take his place, especially if the offender is a drug dealer or part of an organized burglary or auto theft network. Further, if the incarcerated offender is a member of a gang or other offending group, the group may continue committing the same number of crimes without him.

In conclusion, aggressively targeting career offenders for prosecution, conviction, and incarceration may have some effect on the volume of crime in some states. However, the success of this strategy depends on the ability of the criminal justice system to identify career offenders accurately and early in their criminal careers. Better information needs to be gathered and made available to the criminal justice officials who arrest, prosecute, and sentence these offenders. Targeting career offenders will not likely provide the "magic bullet" for substantial reductions in crime that politicans, the public, and the criminal justice system seek. A multifaceted approach to crime control that reserves incapacitation for career offenders or for those offenders convicted of truly heinous crimes and expands the use of intermediate sanctions with other types of offenders is likely to be the most effective crime control strategy for the 1990s.

DISCUSSION QUESTIONS

1. Construct a profile of the average criminal offender. Will he be a juvenile or an adult? If an adult, will that offender likely have been a serious offender as a juvenile? Do offenders usually specialize in certain types of crime, or are they more generalistic?

2. Discuss the concept of criminal career. Describe career in terms of the three segments of residual career length. Are there differences in career patterns between violent and property offenders? To what extent does drug use influence career patterns?

3. Discuss the notion of incapacitation as a crime control strategy. Why have most uses of this strategy centered on selective instead of collective incapacitation? What problems face selective incapacitation efforts, and how effective do they seem to have been?

4. Selective incapacitation depends on our ability to identify offenders who will engage in criminal behavior in the future. Why is that so difficult?

◆ The points of view expressed in this chapter are solely those of the author and do not represent the official position of either the National Institute of Justice or the U.S. Department of Justice.

CHAPTER 23

CRIME CONTROL AND CIVIL LIBERTIES

Susan N. Herman
Brooklyn Law School

T HE COMPLAINT allege[d] that 13 Chicago police officers broke into [the Monroe family's] home in the early morning, routed them from bed, made them stand naked in the living room, and ransacked every room, emptying drawers and ripping mattress covers . . . that Mr. Monroe was taken to the police station and detained on "open" charges for 10 hours, while he was interrogated about a two-day-old murder, that he was not taken before a magistrate, though one was accessible, that he was not permitted to call his family or attorney, that he was subsequently released without criminal charges being preferred against him . . . that the officers had no search warrant and no arrest warrant.

The crime of which James Monroe was suspected was a serious one, but the Chicago police had the wrong man. The Supreme Court, in *Monroe* v. *Pape*, decided in 1961 that Monroe and his family could bring a federal civil rights action to seek monetary damages from the Chicago police officers who subjected him to the many violations of constitutional rights described in this nightmarish incident. The Fourth Amendment, for example, guarantees the right of the people to be "secure against unreasonable searches and seizures." In order to prevent unreasonable searches and arrests, the Fourth Amendment provides a warrant procedure whereby, as a general rule, the police must ask a neutral and detached magistrate to review their reasoning and to decide whether "probable cause" exists to believe that the suspect has committed a crime before they can enter a home to conduct a search or to make an arrest. Such a review could have shown that Monroe was the wrong man before, rather than after, he and his family were subjected to a humiliating and traumatic ordeal.

CIVIL LIBERTIES

The Bill of Rights limits the manner in which searches, arrests, and interrogations are conducted in order to protect innocent citizens against police error and to prevent the police from intruding on the privacy of anyone, guilty or innocent, without sufficient justification. The Fifth Amendment's privilege against self-incrimination gave Monroe a right to decline to answer questions during his interrogation; the Sixth Amendment's right to the assistance of counsel meant that, once he was charged, he would have been entitled to consult an attorney.

These civil liberties are so integral a part of the traditional American conception of what it means to live in a free society that few Americans would question their importance. In one recent study, for example, 79 percent of those surveyed opposed the idea of allowing the police to search a home without a warrant (Gallup, 1989). Without the protections of the Fourth and Fifth Amendments, we would risk the excesses of a police state; stories like that of James Monroe would become more frequent.

When the rights of innocent people are at stake, few would disagree with the Supreme Court that these rights should be respected and that government officials should be held responsible if they are not. But what if James Monroe had not been the wrong man? Would the intrusion into his home, the humiliating treatment of him and his family, and the incommunicado interrogation be as offensive? The courts have held, as is logically necessary, that constitutional limitations on police conduct are the same whether the suspect is innocent or guilty. After all, there is no way for the police to know in advance whether their suspicions are correct and whether a suspect will prove to be innocent or guilty. It is for that reason that the Fourth Amendment focuses on what the police knew *at the time of their actions* in evaluating whether they acted constitutionally. Even if, in hindsight, Monroe was guilty, the police still acted illegally in failing to obtain a warrant before entering his home.

These constitutional guarantees necessarily allow some people to escape detection or conviction. Suspects who in fact may have committed the crime in question may well go free because the police do not have probable cause to arrest them or because the police are not permitted to compel a suspect to confess. All Americans share the right to remain free unless their guilt is fairly and constitutionally established. The Bill of Rights treats these limitations on the investigation of crime as integral parts of our valued right to be let alone, not as mere "technicalities." Although a majority of Americans clearly do value these rights, there is less consensus about the extent to which the need for detection and prevention of crime should provide a counterweight to our desire to enjoy our freedom. Should we sacrifice some of our right to be free of government intrusion in the interest of law and order? If so, how much?

CRIME CONTROL VERSUS DUE PROCESS

When the legislature makes decisions about what to criminalize and how to define crimes, those decisions often pit individual freedom against interests of public security. Vagrancy laws, for example, limit an individual's freedom to frequent public places in order to allow the police to ask questions of anyone they deem suspicious or to tell those individuals to move on. Such broad discretion carries the danger that individual officers may behave in an arbitrary or racially discriminatory manner. To what extent are these costs justifiable?

Those who subscribe to what is sometimes called the *Crime Control Model* would be likely to respond that some such risk is acceptable because of our need to safeguard society. The Crime Control Model focuses primarily on security from outlawry and secondarily on individual freedom from the state. In contrast, the *Due Process Model* focuses primarily on the scope of the individual liberties guaranteed by the Constitution and secondarily on crime control (Packer, 1964, 1968). Whereas adherents to the Crime Control Model might be willing to see some number of innocent people, like James Monroe, searched, arrested, possibly even convicted erroneously in order to prevent actual criminals from escaping, adherents to the Due Process Model, in one classic formulation, would rather let ten guilty individuals go free than unjustly punish one who is innocent.

These two different starting points can lead to different conclusions about levels of acceptable risk and whether a risk is described as the threat to individual liberty or to individual safety. But this difference is not the only significant one between the two polar positions. Crime control advocates are more willing to assume that defining civil liberties narrowly, sometimes described as not "handcuffing" the police, can decrease the number of crimes committed; due process advocates question whether demanding compliance with Bill of Rights guarantees—like the warrant requirement, for example—would have any measurable impact on the crime rate at all.

Both sides might agree that defining civil liberties narrowly could increase the number of successful prosecutions for crimes already committed, even if the crime rate itself were not affected. But given the uncertainty surrounding studies of deterrence and the multiplicity of theories about the purposes of punishment (see Chapter 14), it is debatable what would be achieved by a higher conviction rate. Would additional crimes in fact be deterred? Would it be worth curtailing constitutional freedoms, even if no additional measure of deterrence were achieved, in order to further other goals of punishment, like retribution?

DETERRING POLICE MISCONDUCT

Both sides agree that we should deter law enforcement officials from violating the constitutional rights of suspects but disagree about how that goal should be accomplished. Due process advocates fear that certain nonrestrictive judicial decisions might encourage the police to believe that they can get away with violating, for example, the Fourth Amendment. Crime control advocates respond that a few permissive judicial decisions are not likely to undermine other forces that deter unconstitutional actions. This debate reflects not only a difference of opinion regarding the urgency of deterring undesirable police conduct but also a fundamental disagreement about *who* should have primary responsibility for deciding how the balance should be struck in particular contexts. Because such decisions obviously depend so heavily on the point of view of the individuals making the decisions, choosing a decisionmaker can be critical. Crime control advocates believe that legislatures should make these decisions because there are so many important policy questions involved. They also favor allowing decisions to be made at local levels (state as opposed to federal, municipal as opposed to state) on the theory that the needs of law enforcement vary widely across different jurisdictions. Due process champions, on the other hand, favor a greater role for the courts and argue that decisions should be made at a national level, in the belief that broader-based decisions promote consistency and strengthen the efficacy of the Constitution.

In fact, the Constitution gives the last word on this subject to the judiciary, ultimately to the United States Supreme Court. Legislatures do make many decisions concerning the content of substantive criminal law and criminal procedure law, but their decisions are always subject to judicial review concerning whether or not the legislation is unconstitutional. If the courts find a criminal statute unconstitutional, that statute may not be enforced; if the courts find a particular criminal procedure unconstitutional (a state statute allowing the police to arrest persons in their homes without a warrant, for example), the state may be ordered to follow whatever procedure the Supreme Court finds the Constitution to require. Therefore, although debates about how to balance the conflicting demands of crime control and due process do take place in the legislature, the most noteworthy struggles with these issues are contained in judicial opinions, and the most consequential of these in the opinions of the Supreme Court.

DUE PROCESS BATTLEGROUND: THE EXCLUSIONARY RULE

One of the most significant, least understood, and least popular decisions the Supreme Court has made in the area of criminal justice has been to enforce the Constitution by adopting an exclusionary rule. Under the exclusionary rule, evidence that was obtained illegally by the police cannot be used in court. Sometimes this rule will serve to exclude unreliable evidence, like a confession the police have beaten out of a suspect. On other occasions, the rule will exclude evidence obtained by police who did not have probable cause or who did not obtain a necessary search warrant. The latter application of the exclusionary rule makes particularly good media copy. It is easy to understand why unreliable evidence should be excluded, but it is less apparent why the courts find it necessary to exclude reliable physical evidence, even if the suspect will then go free because there is no longer sufficient admissible evidence for a conviction. Ronald Reagan argued through the media during his years as president that the exclusionary rule rests "on the absurd proposition that a law enforcement error, no matter how technical, can be used to justify throwing an entire case out of court, no matter how guilty the defendant or how heinous the crime" (U.S. Department of Justice, 1981: 1). The remainder of this chapter examines the merits of his claim (see also Kamisar, 1982) and, in so doing, examines the more general case for the importance of due process.

In 1914, the Supreme Court in *Weeks* v. *United States* fashioned an exclusionary rule in order to deter violations of the Fourth Amendment by federal law enforcement agents. The Court held that illegally seized evidence was not to be used "at all" in federal criminal trials because, as Justice Oliver Wendell Holmes later would state in *Silverthorne Lumber Co.* v. *United States*, without this exclusionary remedy the Fourth Amendment would be nothing more than a "form of words." For decades, however, the Court declined to impose the exclusionary rule on the state courts. During that era, it was possible to interpret a constitutional guarantee, like the Fourth Amendment, as imposing different requirements on federal and state courts because the Bill of Rights had been found to apply directly only to the federal government and not to the states.

The states' ability to declare their own criminal laws and procedures was limited only by the Fourteenth Amendment, which (among other provisions) prohibits the states from denying an individual life, liberty, or property without due process of law. Instead of applying the Fourth Amendment to state proceedings, therefore, the Court had to decide whether or not the Due Process Clause of the Fourteenth Amendment, like the Fourth Amendment, also required an exclusionary rule with respect to illegally seized evidence. Although in 1949, in *Wolf* v. *Colorado*, the Court decided that the Due Process Clause did "incorporate" the Fourth Amendment—that is, state law enforcement officials were also bound by the Fourth Amendment's regime of warrants and probable cause—the Court decided at that time that the exclusionary rule was optional, describing the rule as a matter of "judicial implication" rather than as something derived from the explicit requirements of the Fourth Amendment. Thus, it may have been illegal for state or city police to search a home without a warrant, and evidence of a crime found during an illegal entry would have been unconstitutionally obtained evidence. But, unlike the federal authorities, the city or state authorities would have been permitted to use that evidence to prosecute or convict a suspect.

In 1961, the same year in which *Monroe* v. *Pape* was decided, the Supreme Court reconsidered this disparity. In *Mapp* v. *Ohio*, petitioner Dollree Mapp had been discovered in possession of some allegedly obscene publications when the Cleveland police illegally forced their way into her apartment. Mapp had called her attorney when three police officers wanted to enter her home and was advised that she had the right under the Fourth Amendment to demand that the police first get a search warrant from a magistrate. She told the police that she would let them search her home only if they could show her a search warrant.

The police left and returned several hours later, with four more officers, and again asked to search Mapp's home. In response to her demand that they show her a warrant, one of the officers waved a piece of paper at her but would not let her read it. Determined to know whether the paper was actually a warrant, Mapp grabbed it and, to keep the officers from taking it away, stuffed it down her bosom. The police wrestled the paper away from her, handcuffed her to a bannister for being "belligerent," and proceeded to search her home. In one sense, Mapp, too, was the wrong person. The police had come to her two-family dwelling to search for another individual who was wanted for questioning in connection with a recent bombing. When they did not find the suspect they sought in Mapp's home, they continued to search anyway, ransacking papers, cabinets, and luggage, until they finally came upon a trunk in the basement that contained what they decided was obscene literature.

Mapp never got to see whether the police had a search warrant. During the subsequent judicial proceedings, all the parties assumed that the search of her home had been unconstitutional. No search warrant was ever produced. However, the state claimed the right to use the evidence from the trunk in an obscenity prosecution against Mapp, regardless of whether the search was legal. The Supreme Court decided, reversing its earlier decisions, that the Fourth Amendment's protection against unreasonable searches and seizures, combined with the Fourteenth Amendment's guarantee that no state shall deprive any citizen of life, liberty, or property without due process of law, did prohibit the state from relying on illegally seized evidence in a criminal proceeding.

The Court based its landmark decision in the *Mapp* case on a number of factors. First, the Court concluded that the exclusionary rule would "compel respect for the constitutional guaranty in the only effective way—by removing the incentive to disregard it." The Court also believed that "the imperative of judicial integrity" demanded that illegally obtained evidence not be used in judicial proceedings. As Justice Louis Brandeis had said in a stirring opinion written in *Olmstead* v. *United States* in 1928: "Our government is the potent, the omnipresent teacher. . . . If the government becomes a lawbreaker, it breeds contempt for law; it invites every man to become a law unto himself; it invites anarchy."

It is no coincidence that *Monroe* and *Mapp* were decided in the same year. The two cases both involve questions about what remedies will be provided to give substance to the same constitutional guarantees. The remedies at issue were different because there was evidence seized in one case but not in the other. Some argued that this distinction should have been irrelevant in *Mapp* and that the civil remedy provided in Monroe's case was an adequate deterrent in cases like Mapp's too, making it unnecessary for the Court to adopt an exclusionary rule. One critical issue in *Mapp*, therefore, was whether the exclusionary rule is actually necessary to deter violations of the Fourth Amendment or whether alternative remedies can be equally effective.

In a 1932 case in New York, *People* v. *Defore*, Judge (later Justice) Benjamin Cardozo, had refused to impose an exclusionary rule on New York courts, deploring the notion that "[t]he criminal is to go free because the constable has blundered." Opponents of the exclusionary rule were anxious to believe that alternative remedies, like civil litigation, would suffice to deter constitutional violations because they were reluctant to exclude reliable evidence of a crime and thereby risk allowing someone who was demonstrably a criminal to escape punishment. But by the time that *Mapp* was decided three decades later, many states had already reached the conclusion that the Supreme Court had reached in *Weeks*—that other remedies could not reasonably be expected to be effective in securing compliance with constitutional guarantees and that only "clos[ing] the . . . courtroom door to evidence secured by official lawlessness" could actually promote the opportunity to enjoy the "right to be let alone."

Mapp, like *Monroe* v. *Pape*, was decided at the beginning of the 1960s when, under the leadership of Chief Justice Earl Warren, the Supreme Court began to expand previous interpretations of constitutional rights involving both liberty and equality. The Warren Court became known for its commitment to promoting fair and equal justice for criminal suspects as well as for racial minorities and civil rights demonstrators. One justification for judicial review of the constitutionality of legislative and executive actions is that the life tenure of federal judges, including Supreme Court Justices, insulates them from political pressures and enables them to protect the rights of minorities whose interests are not likely to prevail in the legislature. The Warren Court accepted this responsibility, believing that racial minorities are entitled to especially solicitous judicial review.

The need for a countermajoritarian force in interpreting the rights involved in the criminal process seemed just as compelling to the Warren Court. Legislators and executive officers who are subject to election usually seem to believe, probably accurately, that a "tough on crime" stance will win them more votes than advocating the rights of criminal suspects. This fact of political life makes the intervention of the courts necessary for those whose rights are at stake. It is perhaps even welcome to politicians who can enact popular "tough on crime" legislation on the assumption that the courts will invalidate the legislation if they go too far.

For these reasons, it is not surprising that courts adopt exclusionary rules more often than legislatures do. Long before *Mapp*, the Court had applied an exclusionary rule to prohibit a state's use of a confession that had been beaten out of a suspect with a metal studded belt, in violation of the Due Process Clause's ban on coerced confessions (*Brown* v. *Mississippi*, 1936). The Warren Court, after adopting an exclusionary rule for evidence seized in violation of the Fourth Amendment, in a number of cases in the mid-1960s went on to extend this exclusionary remedy to evidence seized in violation of the Sixth Amendment right to counsel (*Massiah* v. *United States*, 1964), to evidence seized in violation of the Fifth Amendment right to remain silent (*Miranda* v. *Arizona*, 1967), and to evidence seized in violation of the Due Process Clause's prohibition of suggestive identification procedures — whereby police unduly influenced witnesses' identifications of suspects (*Stovall* v. *Denno*, 1967).

As the Warren Court expanded the scope of the remedies available to vindicate constitutional rights, the Court also expanded the definition of the rights protected. In *Miranda*, for example, the Court held that the Fifth Amendment privilege against self-incrimination confers a right to remain silent, which must be respected by law enforcement agents interrogating suspects in their custody. To ensure that the right would be respected, the Court required that the police follow certain procedures (including the now famous *Miranda* warnings) and also provided that the suspect had a right to counsel during interrogation; if the suspect invoked either the right to remain silent or the right to counsel, interrogation was to cease. These rules were regarded by the Court as necessary to prevent the police from badgering a suspect into abandoning what the Court had just described as a constitutional right.

ATTEMPTS AT REPEALING THE EXCLUSIONARY RULE

Critics have complained that the Court's actions were antidemocratic. The Court's decisions did not always correspond with the general public's conclusions about how to balance the needs of crime control and due process. The Warren Court recognized the general public's views but believed that its very mission was sometimes to thwart what the majority wished, particularly where the public may not have been fully educated about all the interests involved. It is easy to understand that if evidence is suppressed, a criminal may go free, and to find grounds for concern in that prospect. It is more difficult to understand why the Constitution has provided the rights leading to that potential result, why those rights apply to the guilty as well as to the innocent, and why those rights must often be vindicated by the most guilty. The fact that elected officials often find it convenient to shape the debate on these issues by simplifying and sloganeering rather than by presenting a thoughtful and balanced discussion makes it more likely that members of the public will not have enough information to analyze whether, on balance, they actually would agree with what the courts are doing.

The difference between the Court's perspective on these issues and that of popularly elected representatives was revealed dramatically in several instances where Congress tried to shrink the scope of rights the Court had just declared. In Title II of the Omnibus Crime Control and Safe Streets Act of 1968, for example, Congress tried to "repeal" *Miranda*, by declaring that confessions should be admissible as long as they are voluntarily given, even if the interrogators did not respect the suspect's right to remain silent in the manner prescribed by *Miranda*. (Federal prosecutors have not relied on this provision in their prosecutions, so the Supreme Court has not been called on to decide whether or not this legislation is constitutional.)

On other occasions, partly at President Ronald Reagan's urging, Congress considered whether to "repeal" or sharply limit the exclusionary rule with respect to physical evidence seized in violation of the Fourth Amendment. The exclusionary rule was open to criticism because, in addition to being, in all likelihood, counter to the intuitions of a majority of the public, it is not explicitly required by the language of the Constitution. The Court was accused of usurping the role of the legislature by making what were actually policy decisions in the guise of constitutional interpretation. Therefore, Congress considered that it might be entitled to modify, if not to repeal entirely, the Fourth Amendment exclusionary rule.

In Oversight Hearings on the Exclusionary Rule in Criminal Trials held in March and April of 1983, the House Judiciary Committee of the Ninety-Eighth Congress considered whether to adopt a legislative good faith exception to the exclusionary rule. This exception would allow the use of evidence illegally seized as long as the police seizing the evidence reasonably believed that they were acting in accordance with the Constitution. The Committee (Oversight Hearings, 1983, at 2–3) summarized the issues to be addressed in debating the proposed legislation:

> First we must assess the costs to society of the rule. Is the existence of the exclusionary rule a serious impediment to law enforcement? How frequently are cases

not brought because of police misconduct? How often do suppression motions lead to the dismissal of cases against guilty defendants? What is the nature of the cases in which the exclusionary rule becomes an issue?

Secondly, we must examine the benefits derived from the exclusionary rule. Is it a deterrent to police misconduct? Has it promoted greater concern by the police for the constitutional rights of citizens? Are there other purposes served by the rule?

Third, we must examine alternative methods of enforcing Fourth Amendment rights. How effective would they be? What would be the impact upon the courts, and upon criminal trials in particular, of alternative enforcement mechanisms?

Congress did not enact legislation on the subject of the exclusionary rule. The Court itself mooted this particular debate by adopting a good faith exception to the exclusionary rule, as described next. But as long as the wisdom and necessity of the exclusionary rule is debated, in legislatures, courts, or classrooms, this representative list of questions is useful. Unfortunately, many of them do not yield precise or reliable answers.

COSTS OF THE EXCLUSIONARY RULE

If evidence is excluded because it was obtained in violation of a defendant's rights, it is possible that the prosecutor will no longer have enough evidence to obtain a conviction against the defendant. There have been several attempts to measure *how many* criminals go free under the exclusionary rule because the constable blundered. The first and best known major study was performed by the General Accounting Office (1979) at the request of Congress. The GAO concluded that motions to suppress evidence were made in approximately 10.5 percent of the federal criminal cases surveyed and that 80 to 90 percent of those motions were denied. Evidence was actually excluded in 1.3 percent of the cases studied, and the exclusion of evidence resulted in acquittals or dismissals of a case in 0.7 percent of the cases. Federal prosecutors declined to prosecute because of concerns about the admissibility of evidence in 0.4 percent of the cases that they declined, or 0.2 percent of federal felony arrests.

Other studies have yielded more or less comparable statistics. A study based on data from nine mid-sized counties in Illinois, Michigan, and Pennsylvania showed motions to suppress made in 5 percent of the 7,500 cases studied (Nardulli, 1983). These motions led to the exclusion of evidence in 0.7 percent of the cases and to acquittals or dismissals in 0.6 percent of cases. Data from 1978–1979 studies in San Diego and Jacksonville showed 1 percent of cases resulting in nonconviction because of the exclusion of evidence (Feeney et al., 1983).

Another frequently cited study (Stewart, 1982), based on data gathered in California from 1976–1979, found that 4.8 percent of all cases declined for prosecution in California were rejected because of illegally seized evidence. Another way to state this figure is that 0.8 percent of all arrests were rejected for prosecution due to illegally seized evidence. One author has estimated the frequency of nonprosecution or nonconviction nationwide due to exclusions of evidence as between 0.6 and 2.35 percent of individuals arrested for felonies

(Davies, 1983). The researchers in these studies generally characterized the impact of the exclusionary rule on conviction rates as insubstantial.

These studies have been the subjects of intense debate (see Davies, 1983; Mertens & Wasserstrom, 1984). Some point out that the cost of the exclusionary rule may be greater than case studies can reflect because the police may not even bring charges against some individuals if they know that the evidence they have seized will not be admissible. But even if all observers could agree on the validity of particular studies or particular percentages, there would still be little agreement about whether the cost of the exclusionary rule is great or insignificant. For example, some Supreme Court justices, in the 1984 case of *United States* v. *Leon*, observed that these "small percentages . . . mask a large absolute number of felons who are released because the cases against them were based in part on illegal searches." Other justices argued conversely that the "costs" of the exclusionary rule in terms of dropped prosecutions and lost convictions were "quite low" and that prosecutions were "very rarely" dropped because of illegal search problems.

More trenchantly, Justice Brennan's opinion in the *Leon* case called into question the whole idea that nonprosecution or acquittal is a "cost" of the exclusionary rule. "[S]ome criminals will go free *not* . . . 'because the constable has blundered,' but rather because official compliance with Fourth Amendment requirements makes it more difficult to catch criminals. . . . [I]t is not the exclusionary rule, but the Amendment itself that has imposed this cost." From this point of view, the fact that some defendants cannot be prosecuted because the evidence against them was illegally seized should be charged not to the exclusionary rule but to the law enforcement officials who violated the Fourth Amendment in seizing the evidence. If the illegality was indeed a procedural "technicality," like a failure to obtain a warrant, the police could easily have complied with the requirements of the Fourth Amendment and the evidence would not then have been illegally seized. If the police could not obtain the evidence without violating the Fourth Amendment, it could be only because they did not have sufficient information to justify the intrusion they proposed. In fact, rather than positing that high "costs" should lead to a narrowing or abandonment of the exclusionary rule, the numbers should be read to favor continuing or strengthening sanctions against rampant violations of the Fourth Amendment: The greater the number of motions to suppress evidence made and the greater the number of incidents in which evidence is excluded, the greater the lawlessness of the police in that jurisdiction.

In answer to another of the Judiciary Committee's questions, the exclusionary rule seems to have a greater impact in drug prosecutions than in other types of cases. One estimate of the loss of prosecutions due to nonprosecution or nonconviction via the exclusion of illegally seized evidence in felony drug cases is 2.8 to 7.1 percent, compared to the nonprosecution estimate of 0.6 to 2.35 percent in all cases (Davies, 1983:680). Again, it is impossible to state objectively whether these figures show that the costs of the exclusionary rule should be regarded as heightened, as observers dedicated to the war against drugs might believe, or ameliorated by the fact that evidence is excluded more often in nonviolent offenses than in prosecutions for violent felonies.

A more subtle cost of the exclusionary rule is exacted precisely because of the rule's effectiveness. Fourth Amendment guarantees are interpreted almost exclusively in the context of criminal cases, in which the person whose rights have been violated has moved to suppress evidence. When judges, students, law enforcement agents, and the general public learn about the Fourth Amendment in this limited context, it is difficult to ignore the subliminal message of these cases: that police constantly violate the Fourth Amendment but that their suspicions are always correct. Every exclusionary rule case is one in which there was at least an arguable violation of the Fourth Amendment, and in which incriminating evidence was found. The many cases in which the police complied with the Fourth Amendment become invisible. So do the cases in which the police were wrong and found no evidence, except for the rare case, like *Monroe* v. *Pape*, in which the constitutionality of police actions is litigated in a noncriminal proceeding.

BENEFITS OF THE EXCLUSIONARY RULE

The principal aim of the exclusionary rule is to deter the police from violating the Fourth Amendment in order to promote enjoyment of the right to be let alone. This form of deterrence is resistant to measurement; it is difficult toconstruct studies to determine whether law enforcement agents obtain search warrants that they would not obtain if the exclusionary rule were to be repealed. Outcomes of earlier attempts to study deterrence of police violations of the Fourth Amendment have varied, but more recent studies claim that the exclusionary rule does create a system of incentives for individual officers, reinforced by supervisory practices also prompted by the rule, that does deter unlawful searches (Orfield, 1987; see also Oaks, 1970; Spiotto, 1973; Cannon, 1973–1974).

One easily measurable, positive outcome of the exclusionary rule is that after *Mapp*, law enforcement agencies instituted training programs to teach agents what the Constitution requires of them. Former New York City Police Commissioner Patrick Murphy (1966: 941) described the impact of *Mapp* in a jurisdiction where, previously, under Cardozo's version of the law, there had been no exclusionary rule:

> I can think of no decision in recent times in the field of law enforcement which had such a dramatic and traumatic effect as this. . . . I was immediately caught up in the entire program of reevaluating our procedures which had followed the *Defore* rule [precluding an exclusionary rule], and modifying, amending, and creating new policies and new instructions for the implementation of Mapp. . . . Retraining sessions had to be held from the very top administrators down to each of the thousands of foot patrolmen.
>
> *Judicial Review of Police Methods in Law Enforcement: The Problem of Compliance by Police Departments, 44 Tex L. Rev. 939, 941 (1966).*

Mapp, of course, had not changed the rules—only the remedies for violation of the rules of the Fourth Amendment. This testimony to the difference the exclusionary remedy made in how seriously a police department took the requirements of the Fourth Amendment suggests that the exclusionary rule has promoted implementation of the requirements of the Fourth Amendment.

Another benefit of the exclusionary rule stems from the involvement of prosecutors. Because prosecutors have an interest in the admissibility of evidence seized by law enforcement agents, they will have an incentive to work more closely with those agents to ensure that their conduct complies with constitutional dictates. Prosecutors, unlike most police officers, are trained in law and have the skills as well as the incentive to absorb and explain case law interpreting constitutional rights.

Of course, what happened before *Mapp* also happened before *Monroe* v. *Pape*, so it is once again difficult to be conclusive about whether the expansion of police educational programs is attributable only to *Mapp* and not also to *Monroe*. If the police are told that they will be sued and held liable in damages, this prospect too could cause renewed attention to the requirements of the Fourth Amendment. This leads to the question of the effectiveness of alternative remedies.

ALTERNATIVE REMEDIES

CIVIL LITIGATION

The civil rights action that was the subject of *Monroe* v. *Pape* is sometimes viewed as a remedy of limited effectiveness. Most of those who are illegally searched or arrested will not be able to afford to hire an attorney or maintain an expensive lawsuit to establish whether or not their rights were violated. If persons illegally searched or arrested are released, as James Monroe was, most will breathe a sigh of relief and will have little desire to litigate whether or not their rights had been violated. If the police have happened on a person who, like Dollree Mapp, can be charged with a crime based on evidence found during an illegal search, it will be difficult for that person to maintain or win a civil lawsuit, for a number of reasons.

First, the individual will have pending criminal charges that will probably seem more pressing than a civil lawsuit. If the individual can afford to hire an attorney, it is likely that the attorney will be hired to defend the criminal action. Second, even if persons in Mapp's situation have the stamina to prosecute a civil action in addition to defending against a criminal charge, they will be handicapped by the fact that the police did find evidence. One reason for the Fourth Amendment's requirement that a neutral and detached magistrate evaluate probable cause beforehand is that hindsight is distorting. It is a great challenge to ask jurors to forget that they now know that Mapp had illegal materials in her possession and to concentrate only on what the police knew at the time. In cases where a heinous crime is at issue (the murder of which Monroe was suspected, for example), the jurors may also be reluctant to accept the testimony of a known lawbreaker over conflicting testimony of a law enforcement agent. It is only in a very unusual case that a civil rights plaintiff will not suffer from these handicaps. James Monroe ultimately was able to win $13,000 after five years of litigating his civil rights action, but no evidence had been found in his home, and the complainant whose testimony had led the police to Monroe later recanted and admitted her own responsibility for the crime for which Monroe was questioned.

One additional problem with relying on civil litigation to influence police conduct is that many jurisdictions indemnify their employees for acts performed within the course of their employment and provide lawyers to represent them if they are sued for actions taken while on duty. If police know that they will be given free lawyers to defend them, and that any monetary verdict against them will be paid by their employer, will the prospect of a civil lawsuit actually deter them from violating the Fourth Amendment rights of a suspect they wish to search or arrest?

CRIMINAL PROSECUTION

Police misconduct sometimes also violates the criminal law. Among the unreasonable "seizures" the Fourth Amendment prohibits are shooting at fleeing suspects and unprovoked physical brutality, actions that may constitute assault or even homicide. Criminal prosecution is not likely to be available as a remedy for violations of the warrant clause or for searches conducted without probable cause, for the very reason discussed earlier — legislatures are not likely to value those rights highly enough to criminalize their violation. But even when police misconduct is covered by criminal statutes of general applicability, like homicide or assault statutes, that does not necessarily mean that prosecution will be an effective remedy. Some critics contend that, given the close working relationship of law enforcement agents and prosecutors, it is unlikely that criminal prosecution will take place except in occasional highly publicized cases. As in civil litigation, a jury may tend to value the word of a police officer who testifies that he believed that the force used was necessary, over the testimony of a known criminal.

The recent state court trial of the officers who were captured on videotape beating Rodney King demonstrates that credibility is not the only problematic issue. Even when the physical facts are clear, the implications to be drawn from those facts are still subjective: How much force is excessive? When does a suspect seem sufficiently dangerous to justify a baton blow to the head? The fact that criminal charges must be proved beyond a reasonable doubt makes it even less likely that criminal convictions will provide an effective means for deterring police brutality. And again, criminal prosecution cannot address most varieties of police misconduct covered by the Fourth Amendment, like warrantless searches or arrests without probable cause.

ADMINISTRATIVE SANCTIONS

Most sizeable law enforcement agencies impose administrative sanctions on those who do not follow the department's rules and regulations. These sanctions can be mild (a disfavored work assignment, for instance) or severe (a suspension or dismissal). Some observers, like Kenneth Culp Davis (1975, 1977), one of the preeminent students of the art of limiting discretion, argue that administrative guidelines constitute one of the most effective means of limiting discretion, by structuring behavioral and decision-making authority instead of merely second-guessing uses of that authority after the fact. On the one hand, law enforcement agencies know best how investigations operate and should have the most expertise to bring to bear on the problem. On the other hand, law enforcement agencies may not be objective in balancing the needs of law enforcement agents and the rights of suspects. In the pressured, competitive world of catching criminals, is arguing that the police can best police themselves like putting foxes in charge of the foxes who run the chicken coop?

THE EXCLUSIONARY RULE IN THE POST-WARREN COURT

The Supreme Court, like Congress, has not seriously considered abolishing the exclusionary rule but, as the Court grew more conservative after the Warren Court era, various decisions sharply limited the reach of the exclusionary rule and of the Fourth Amendment itself. President Richard Nixon was elected at the end of the 1960s on a platform of "law and order." He took as one of his goals changing the Supreme Court's attitudes toward crime control and due process. As the Justices of the Warren Court retired, they were replaced with Justices like Warren Burger (successor to Earl Warren as Chief Justice) who valued the needs of crime control more highly, who were willing to balance constitutional guarantees, who wished to allow the states more leeway in making decisions about criminal procedure, and who believed that the costs of a broadly applied exclusionary rule outweighed any benefits (see Whitebread, 1985; Schulhofer, 1988; Graham, 1970; Israel, 1977).

LIMITING CONTEXTS

First, the Burger Court began to limit the contexts in which the exclusionary rule would apply. Beyond criminal proceedings, the rule was held not to apply in civil proceedings (*United States* v. *Janis*, 1976), in the grand jury (*United States* v. *Calandra*, 1974), or in forfeiture proceedings (*One 1958 Plymouth Sedan* v. *Pennsylvania*, 1965). Despite the earlier assertion of the Court that evidence illegally seized was not to be used "at all," the Court permitted illegally seized evidence to be used to impeach defendants who testified in their own behalf (*United States* v. *Havens*, 1980). The Court also decided that claims that a defendant's conviction was based on unconstitutionally obtained evidence generally may not be raised in federal court habeas corpus proceedings (the forum where petitioners usually receive federal court hearings on all other claims that their state convictions were obtained in disregard of their federal constitutional rights) (*Stone* v. *Powell*, 1976).

The Court's rationale in all these cases was that the exclusionary rule is not really a constitutional right, but merely a judge-made prophylactic device, and that therefore the Court is free to decide how much application of the exclusionary rule is required to achieve adequate deterrence of constitutional violations. In each of these cases, the Court decided that the "incremental deterrence" that would be accomplished by applying the exclusionary rule in that one particular context would not be great. This determination was part of a new cost–benefit approach to such questions, whereby the Court balanced the amount of deterrence effected through a particular application of the exclusionary rule against the fact that a criminal might escape punishment.

Justices who had joined the decision in *Mapp* protested that *Mapp* had not been based only on notions of deterrence. The Court had also been concerned about judicial integrity, concluding that it is as unconstitutional for the courts to use illegally seized evidence against an individual as it is for the police to seize it. The new majority of the Court personalized the exclusionary rule debate, however, describing the exclusionary rule as a punishment for police officers who make mistakes rather than as a rule about how the courts conduct their own business.

As part of its campaign to minimize the costs of the exclusionary rule, the Court also adopted a doctrine under which a defendant is not considered to have "standing" to challenge the use of illegally seized evidence in his own criminal trial if the evidence was seized in violation of someone else's rights. In the case of *United States* v. *Payner* (1980), Internal Revenue Service agents who suspected Payner of income tax violations illegally stole and searched the briefcase of a banker at a bank where Payner was a customer in order to look at Payner's bank records. The violation of the Fourth Amendment was flagrant—a female agent lured the bank officer out of his hotel room so that other agents could break into the room and search his briefcase, all without a warrant. The prosecution used evidence from these purloined records as part of its case against Payner. However, the Supreme Court held that because Payner's own Fourth Amendment rights had not been violated by this illegal search, the exclusionary rule could not be invoked. The dissenters charged that this decision seriously undermined the deterrent effect of the exclusionary rule and encouraged Fourth Amendment violations because illegally seized evidence could be used after all. Law enforcement officials are particularly encouraged to violate the Fourth Amendment rights of people they do not suspect of wrongdoing at all in order to obtain what will, after the *Payner* decision, be admissible evidence against people whom they do suspect.

In addition, the Burger Court in 1984 took the action Congress had been debating: It created a good faith exception to the exclusionary rule in the case of *United States* v. *Leon*. Under *Leon*, if law enforcement officials rely on search warrants that are invalid, the evidence can nevertheless be admissible. The theory of the majority opinion was that a law enforcement agent who believes that he is acting legally cannot be deterred from effecting the constitutional violation that is actually taking place—because he does not know that he is doing anything wrong—and that, therefore, the "cost" of the exclusionary rule in such a case is not justifiable.

This case marked the pinnacle of the Court's cost–benefit analysis and of its narrow view of the purposes of the exclusionary rule. The Court did not go on to apply this good faith exception to cases in which the police had not obtained a warrant. (In some circumstances, usually involving exigency, the police are permitted to conduct searches without a search warrant as long as they have probable cause. If the Court had extended the good faith exception created in *Leon*, the police might have been able to render admissible evidence seized in a search that was not even based on probable cause simply because they believed, incorrectly but sincerely, that they had probable cause) (see Dripps, 1986). Because of its personalization of the Fourth Amendment as a contest between guilty defendants and well-meaning police, the Court no longer was concerned about whether the magistrate who issued the defective warrant had erred or about whether innocent people might be subject to unnecessary searches or arrests because a magistrate incorrectly believed that the police had probable cause.

LIMITING THE SCOPE OF THE FOURTH AMENDMENT

Perhaps also due to a desire to limit the costs of excluding evidence obtained in violation of the Fourth Amendment, the post-Warren Supreme Court, under Chief Justice Burger and then under Chief Justice Rehnquist, also narrowed the circumstances in which the Fourth Amendment can be said to have been violated. One way in which the Court narrowed the Fourth Amendment was by creating new exceptions to the warrant requirement: Warrants are no longer required, for example, to search cars or packages within cars (*California* v. *Acevedo*, 1991); nor are they required to search mobile homes (*California* v. *Carney*, 1985) (see Wasserstrom, 1984). A more dramatic method of narrowing the scope of the Fourth Amendment lay in the Court's approach to interpreting the Fourth Amendment's reference to "searches" and "seizures." The Court interpreted these words as limiting language, reasoning that if a police activity does not constitute a "search" or a "seizure," then the Fourth Amendment does not apply at all and cannot be violated even if the police have no warrant, no probable cause, and act completely unreasonably. The Court explained that no "search" takes place when the police merely observe something that an individual has exposed to the public because the police then are not intruding on any meaningful privacy interest (*Katz* v. *United States*, 1967; see Amsterdam, 1974).

This theory stretched in its succeeding applications, however, since the Court held that it is not a "search" when the police use trained dogs to sniff luggage (*United States* v. *Place*, 1983) or student lockers (*New Jersey* v. *T.L.O.*, 1985); that it is not a search when the police trespass on "open fields," even if those fields are fenced and posted with no trespassing signs (*Oliver* v. *United States*, 1984); that it is not a search when the police fly helicopters over homes (*Florida* v. *Riley*, 1989) or when the police seize an individual's bank or telephone company records (*United States* v. *Miller*, 1976; *Smith* v. *Maryland*, 1979).

In each of these cases, the Court reasoned that what the police observed had been potentially exposed to at least some members of the public, even if the exposure was limited and even if members of the public would have had to act illegally in order to observe the activity at issue. One of the most extreme examples of this theory came in the case of *California* v. *Greenwood* (1988), when the Court held that the police could seize and pore over the contents of a suspect's garbage can even if the garbage can was on the suspect's property. The trash inside the garbage can, the Court held, had been exposed to the public because a neighboring child or animal might have knocked over the garbage can, or because the contents of the can could have been exposed to those who picked up and disposed of the trash.

Although in the context of the exclusionary rule, the Court has been inclined to view searches and seizures as a clash between suspect and police, in the context of cases defining what constitutes a "search" for purposes of the Fourth Amendment, the Court seems to depart from this adversarial portrayal and to regard the police as standing in exactly the same relationship to a suspect as any other person might. The result is that the Court often finds that individuals have no reasonable expectation of privacy concerning potential police intrusion. The first attempt to study empirically the Supreme Court's conclusions what members of the public reasonably expect, and what privacy interests the public would be prepared to honor and protect, found that the Court decisions do not reflect societal understandings (Slobogin and Schumacher, 1993).

Just as the Court has narrowed the application of the Fourth Amendment by restricting the definition of the word *search*, it has also been cutting back the definition of the word *seizure*. A seizure does not have to be a full-blown arrest, as the Court explained during the 1960s and 1970s. A seizure takes place any time law enforcement officials interfere with an individual's freedom (by asking questions, detaining, or transporting that person) to such an extent and in such a manner that a reasonable person would not feel free to leave. If a seizure has taken place, the police must comply with the requirements of the Fourth Amendment—that they have probable cause if they wish to make an arrest or at least reasonable suspicion that criminal activity is afoot if they wish temporarily to detain an individual for investigation.

Some recent cases have carved exceptions to what used to be a general rule. When the Oakland police cornered a teenage boy in a dark alley, according to the Court he was not "seized," even though he obviously did not feel free to leave because he had not yet stopped trying to escape (*California* v. *Hodari D.*, 1991). So now the Fourth Amendment does not apply, and the police need not follow Fourth Amendment requirements, unless they have physically touched a suspect or unless the suspect has already submitted to their authority. In another case, the Court acknowledged that a bus passenger probably would not reasonably have felt free to leave when law enforcement agents, performing a "sweep" of the buses during a temporary stop of his long-distance bus, stood blocking the aisle between him and the door and asked to search his luggage. Nevertheless, the Court held that the passenger's feeling that he was not free to leave was not because of the police but because he wanted to continue his bus trip to his destination. Otherwise, the Court reasoned, he was free to get off of the bus rather than submit to the search and therefore was not "seized" (*Florida* v. *Bostick*, 1991).

With the Fourth Amendment shrinking in this way, there are fewer possibilities for violations; and with the application of the exclusionary rule simultaneously being cut back, even the violations that can still be found are not often redressed. That the Supreme Court has narrowed the Fourth Amendment in recent decades is beyond debate. But what is still debatable is whether these narrow interpretations are justifiable or wise—whether the enhanced license afforded law enforcement agencies will undermine their incentive to comply with the letter or spirit of the Bill of Rights or whether these decisions still accomplish enough deterrence while removing unwanted handcuffs from those who enforce our criminal laws.

THE EXCLUSIONARY RULE AND CONFESSIONS

Many of the themes characterizing search and seizure issues are also apparent in the Supreme Court's treatment of the problem of police interrogation. As we described, the Warren Court translated its concern about the inherent coerciveness of police interrogation into the prophylactic rules of *Miranda*. But the Supreme Court in the post-Warren Court era has, in many respects, been narrowing the circumstances in which confessions will be found inadmissible. For example, *Miranda* provides rights and procedures applicable to "custodial interrogation." This prerequisite could be interpreted broadly or narrowly; recently, it has been interpreted narrowly. Must the police give *Miranda* warnings and rights to a suspect whose car is stopped and who is then questioned next to the road at night? The Court, in *Berkemer* v. *McCarty* (1984), found that *Miranda* did not apply to this situation because the defendant was not in "custody." The dangers of coercion next to a road are different from the dangers at the police station, according to the Court, because the interrogation is less likely to be prolonged and because the interrogation may be open to public view.

Similarly, the Court has found, in other cases, that *Miranda* should not apply because there was no "interrogation." Interrogation need not, the Court recognized, always take the form of sentences with question marks at the end directed to the suspect; *Miranda* will apply whenever the police act in a way reasonably likely to elicit a response from the suspect. Yet the Court, in *Rhode Island* v. *Innis* (1980), found that police officers traveling to the stationhouse with an arrested defendant did not "interrogate" the defendant by talking, ostensibly among themselves, about their need to find the gun the defendant was believed to have used, and speculating that it would be a shame if a little handicapped girl were to find the gun. The suspect rose to the bait and showed the police where he had hidden the gun. The Court ruled that this evidence could be admitted even though the defendant had not been told of his right to remain silent as *Miranda* would have required, because *Miranda* did not apply.

The Court also has created exceptions to *Miranda*, even where the Court agrees that there has been custodial interrogation. Under a "public safety" exception, police may question a defendant without advising him of his rights if they want to interrogate him for some pressing reason other than their desire to obtain evidence—for example, about the whereabouts of a gun (*New York* v. *Quarles*, 1984). Under an "administrative questioning" exception, the police also may ask a suspect general questions related to booking (name, address, and so on) without providing the *Miranda* warnings.

Miranda has also been held not to apply when the police act fraudulently rather than coercively. The suspect whose rights were at issue in *Moran* v.

Burbine (1986) did not actually request an attorney, as would have been his right under *Miranda*. However, his sister, learning of his arrest, called an attorney on his behalf. The attorney asked to see Burbine but was not permitted to do so; he asked the police not to interrogate Burbine until he had a chance to speak with him and was promised that they would not. Without telling Burbine that this attorney had been trying to speak with him, however, the police did interrogate Burbine, and elicited a confession. The Court refused to suppress the confession, holding that *Miranda* did not apply to prohibit police trickery but only police coercion.

On the other hand, the Court has not trimmed the scope of *Miranda* or the applicability of the exclusionary rule in this context as extensively as it has the Fourth Amendment and its exclusionary rule (see Kamisar, 1983; Schulhofer, 1988), perhaps because coerced confessions pose a danger of unreliable evidence being used as the basis of conviction. During the 1980s, the Burger Court created some additional prophylactic rules to implement *Miranda*'s guarantee that interrogation will cease if a defendant invokes his right to remain silent or right to counsel. The police are not permitted to try to persuade a defendant who has invoked his rights to change his mind (*Edwards* v. *Arizona*, 1981) or to resume questioning of a defendant who has consulted counsel but whose counsel is not present (*Minnick* v. *Mississippi*, 1990). Finally, in *Withrow* v. *Williams* (1993), the Court held that defendants may raise *Miranda* claims, unlike Fourth Amendment claims, on habeas corpus.

As in the area of search and seizure, there are preventive measures that can be taken to ensure that the police observe appropriate standards of behavior. The Fourth Amendment relies on the judgment of neutral and detached magistrates to review and license police activity. Under the Fifth and Sixth Amendments, the Court has relied on the right to counsel. A suspect who might otherwise feel overwhelmed and intimidated is given the right to seek legal advice from a lawyer who understands the criminal process and who knows what rights suspects have. Among the rights the Court prescribed in *Miranda* was the right of indigent defendants to have counsel assigned if they cannot afford to hire their own attorney so that there will not be two standards of justice, one for the affluent and another for the poor.

IDENTIFICATION PROCEEDINGS

Another situation in which the Court has relied on the provision of counsel to protect the rights of an accused person is when that person is required to submit to a line-up or other pretrial identification procedure. The Warren Court was concerned about pretrial identification procedures because eyewitness identifications are not nearly as reliable as many would believe and because those conducting identification procedures could, purposely or even unconsciously, act suggestively.

If the police ask a complainant to identify a suspect they have arrested, for example, by just presenting the suspect to the complainant and telling the complainant that they believe they have found the person who committed the robbery, the complainant may, in all good faith, mistakenly decide that the suspect is the same person as the robber. Even if the police conduct a line-up, if only the suspect the police have arrested matches a description of the robber provided by the victim, then the line-up will be suggestive. At the line-up, the police might, either purposely or inadvertently, focus the witness's attention on one particular suspect. The danger of suggestion in this context is that a witness's memory of the face of the person who committed the crime in question may be permanently and irrevocably replaced by a memory of the face of the person the police have arrested. There is a particularly grave danger that the person arrested may be incorrectly identified if the witness or victim did not have a good opportunity to observe the actual criminal—if a robbery was fleeting, if the robber stood behind the victim, or if there was not much light, for example. There is an even greater danger here than in the interrogation context that improper police behavior could cause an innocent person to be convicted.

To ensure the fairness of line-ups, therefore, the Supreme Court in 1967 held that criminal defendants have a right to counsel at a line-up (*United States* v. *Wade*). In a familiar progression, however, the Court later narrowed the applicability of this right to counsel by holding that if an identification procedure takes place *before* the suspect has been formally charged, there is no right to counsel (*Kirby* v. *Illinois*, 1972). The danger of misidentification is just as great at line-ups that take place before a defendant has been formally indicted. But the Burger Court narrowed the scope of the right declared by the Warren Court, and thereby reduced the number of occasions on which convictions might have to be reversed because they were obtained in violation of a defendant's rights.

CONCLUSION

Our examination of the exclusionary rule serves as a vehicle by which to understand the Supreme Court's attempts to balance the competing demands of crime control and civil liberties. Most judges, like most people who do not sit on the bench, are not attracted to either of the polar extremes of the Crime Control or the Due Process Models. It is easy to say, in the abstract, that we want our criminal laws and procedures to allow us to protect ourselves against crime but also to preserve the freedoms that the Constitution was designed to guarantee. It is more difficult, as the discussion suggests, to know how to draw lines in particular cases to accomplish both of these goals.

Because legislatures tend to veer too far in the direction of the Crime Control Model, it is left to the courts to give content to what appear to be the rights of an unattractive minority: criminal suspects. But if we consider the ideas underlying the Fourth Amendment, the right to remain silent, the right to counsel, and the right not to be convicted unfairly, it becomes apparent that many of these rights—and those emanating from other Amendments—guard the freedom not only of criminals but of all the innocent people who, like James Monroe, can find themselves the object of suspicion. Among our civil liberties are the right not to be arrested, interrogated, or convicted unfairly and the right to be let alone unless the government is justified in curtailing our freedom or privacy. A presidential commission once charged with considering the criminal justice system entitled its report, "The Challenge of Crime in a Free Society" (President's Commission, 1967b). Perhaps the most important safeguard of the freedom of our society lies in educating the people who vote for the legislatures, judges, or those who appoint judges so that they can make the balanced decisions that most elected officials do not expect the public to make. Providing adequate protection for our civil liberties is not likely to expose us to more crime, but if we limit those protections for fear of crime, we run the risk of a greater evil—a government that controls the people rather than a government of, by, and for the people.

DISCUSSION QUESTIONS

1. Attempts to control crime often are pitted against the important constitutional guarantee of due process. Discuss both of these concepts. To what extent could we expect a decrease in societal crime rates were we to move away from due process?

2. Using the exclusionary rule as your example, discuss the problems we encounter when we try to control police misconduct in this society. Why is it that we simply do not bring criminal charges against police who violate procedural law? How about civil litigation?

3. Has the exclusionary rule meant that more criminals now roam our streets? Herman discusses a number of costs and benefits accruing from the exclusionary rule. Describe these.

4. In recent years, the Supreme Court has attempted to limit the reach of the exclusionary rule. Describe these efforts, and comment on the extent to which they actually seem to have contributed to crime control.

CHAPTER 24

THE DEATH PENALTY IN AMERICA

M. Dwayne Smith
Tulane University

CAPITAL PUNISHMENT is an exceptionally controversial issue, and the ongoing debate concerning it frequently spawns confusing and, at times, erroneous information. This chapter explores specific issues in the capital punishment debate and summarizes the empirical evidence pertinent to those issues. We begin with an examination of the history and current status of capital punishment in the United States.

CAPITAL PUNISHMENT IN THE UNITED STATES

For much of our history, capital punishment was seen as an appropriate and justifiable response to crime. The English settlers of this country imported a justice system wherein death sentences were imposed for a variety of offenses; consequently, executions were regular events in the early colonial settlements (Bedeau, 1982). Subsequently, in prohibiting "cruel and unusual punishment" through the inclusion of the Eighth Amendment in the Bill of Rights, the framers of the Constitution clearly did not intend to ban capital punishment but only to limit the methods by which it might be administered (Inciardi, 1987). As a result, individual states had considerable latitude in structuring their capital punishment statutes. Although murder was the most commonly cited offense, crimes such as rape, kidnapping, treason, robbery, and even train wrecking were punishable by the death penalty in some states (Bedeau, 1982).

Since 1930, when the federal government began collecting data on state-sanctioned executions, over 3,900 executions have been recorded. The 1930s appear to have been the most active period of capital punishment in contemporary U.S. history; 1,520 executions were recorded during that decade. With 199 executions, 1935 remains the year in which the largest number of death sentences were carried out (U.S. Department of Justice, 1978b).

Executions decreased following the 1930s, a trend accelerated by the Civil Rights movement of the late 1950s and early 1960s. During this period, perhaps for the first time, serious concerns regarding the constitutionality of the death penalty were raised (White, 1984). Ultimately, this led to an unofficial moratorium on capital punishment beginning in 1968. The moratorium became official four years later when a bitterly divided U.S. Supreme Court ruled in *Furman* v. *Georgia* that the existing practice of capital punishment violated the Eighth and Fourteenth Amendments of the Constitution. However, the Court left open the possibility that the death penalty could be reinstated by states instituting safeguards against such constitutional violations.

Seizing this opportunity, a number of states quickly rewrote their capital punishment statutes. These efforts succeeded in 1976 when the Supreme Court, in *Gregg* v. *Georgia*, approved a revamped set of death penalty laws, thus establishing a model for states to pursue. Following refinement based on several subsequent Court decisions, states were required to limit the death penalty to cases involving murder and to spell out clearly under what circumstances the penalty could be imposed. However, considerable variation in state laws has been allowed. States differ considerably not only in the number of circumstances for which capital punishment can be administered but even in the age at which one becomes legally eligible for execution: no age limits in three states, between 10 and 17 years of age in twenty states, and 18 years of age in fourteen states (Streib, 1987).

In resuming the practice of capital punishment, the United States has assumed a rather odd position among nations of similar social and cultural composition. Although the death penalty is a common feature throughout the world (Otterbein, 1986), virtually all Western industrial nations have abandoned its use. Those major nations that continue the practice — Russia, the People's Republic of China, South Africa, and most countries of the Mideast, especially Iran — tend to be nations culturally and politically dissimilar to the United States. Further, Zimring and Hawkins (1986) point to a general correlation between a nation's utilization of capital punishment and a disregard for human rights. This is a position adopted by Amnesty International, the worldwide organization dedicated to the protection of human rights (Amnesty International, 1989). Primarily because of the United States' use of the death penalty, Amnesty International now lists it as a nation with governmental policies violating human rights.

CAPITAL PUNISHMENT IN THE POST-*GREGG* ERA

On January 17, 1977, in a widely publicized event, Gary Mark Gilmore was executed by firing squad in Utah. Thus, the moratorium on capital punishment ended, and what has become known as the "post-*Gregg*" era was ushered in (White, 1984).

Opponents of capital punishment feared that Gilmore's execution would lead to a rush of executions unparalleled in the twentieth century. Yet, this did not occur, and the few initial persons to be executed represented rather atypical cases (Jolly and Sagarin, 1984; Streib, 1984). In part, this situation can be attributed to the abnormally large number of reversals of death sentences by federal courts in the years following *Gregg*, many of which were due to ambiguities in state laws that required Supreme Court interpretation. However, by 1983, a discernible shift in attitude toward capital punishment was evident among a majority of the Court's justices. Deliberations on individual cases became less measured, and a greater tolerance for "imperfection" in states' efforts to execute emerged (White, 1987). Consequently, the pace of executions quickened in 1984, and by mid-1993, over 200 persons had been put to death. Still, this number pales in comparison to the large number of persons sentenced to death and awaiting execution: At present, this ever-increasing figure exceeds 2,700, the largest "death row" population in U.S. history. Of this population, 51 percent are white, 39 percent are black, and 10 percent are from other racial or ethnic backgrounds; 98 percent are male, and thirty-four of the persons awaiting death were under age 18 at the time of their offense (NAACP Legal Defense and Educational Fund, 1993).

Table 24.1 details states' death penalty status and methods of execution, as well as the number of persons awaiting execution and already put to death. Thirty-eight jurisdictions (thirty-six states, the U.S. military, and the U.S. government) have capital punishment statutes, and fifteen (fourteen states and the District of Columbia) do not. Those states with the largest death row populations (also those most likely to execute) are concentrated in the southern and western regions of the country. For example, well over half of death row inmates are in the sixteen southern states (as defined by the U.S. Bureau of the Census); two states, Texas and Florida, account for a quarter of the nation's death row population and nearly half of its executions.

Zimring and Hawkins (1986) contend that the current picture suggested by Table 24.1 closely resembles that existing prior to *Furman*. That is, those states previously prohibiting capital punishment, with the exception of Oregon, continue to do so, whereas those few states pursuing capital punishment with zeal, and whose practices are most likely to produce constitutional abuses, have again assumed that position.

PUBLIC OPINION CONCERNING THE DEATH PENALTY

Many state legislators rewriting their states' laws so that death penalties could be assessed believed that their constituents supported, and even demanded, such action. Erskine (1970), in an analysis of three decades of opinion polls, concluded that a general decrease in support for capital punishment occurred from 1936 to 1966, a year in which less than 50 percent of the population favored this sanction. However, an upswing in support began in the late 1960s, accelerated following the *Furman* decision, and has continued until the present. By the late 1980s, polls were recording some of the highest percentages ever of those who approve of use of the death penalty (Bohm, 1987). Although some racial differences remain, support for the death penalty now extends across virtually all segments of the population, even in those regions of the country where death sentences are relatively rare (Smith and Wright, 1992; for a discussion of race differences, see Young, 1991). Only the execution of juveniles seems to lack the general approval of the American public (Skovron et al., 1989).

TABLE 24.1   INMATES ON DEATH ROW, NUMBER OF EXECUTIONS SINCE 1976, AND METHOD OF EXECUTION, BY STATE*

State	Death Row Population	Number of Executions	Method of Execution[†]
Alabama	117	10	Electrocution
Alaska	No death penalty		
Arizona	111	3	Lethal injection or gas chamber
Arkansas	33	4	Lethal injection or gas chamber
California	356	1	Lethal injection or gas chamber
Colorado	3	0	Lethal injection
Connecticut	4	0	Electrocution
Delaware	11	1	Lethal injection or hanging
District of Columbia	No death penalty		
Florida	317	30	Electrocution
Georgia	107	15	Electrocution
Hawaii	No death penalty		
Idaho	23	0	Lethal injection or firing squad
Illinois	153	1	Lethal injection
Indiana	55	2	Electrocution
Iowa	No death penalty		
Kansas	No death penalty		
Kentucky	29	0	Electrocution
Louisiana	41	21	Lethal injection
Maine	No death penalty		
Maryland	16	0	Gas chamber
Massachusetts	No death penalty		
Michigan	No death penalty		
Minnesota	No death penalty		
Mississippi	52	4	Lethal injection or gas chamber

Source: NAACP Legal Defense and Educational Fund, *Death Row U.S.A.* (Spring 1993).

*Through Spring 1993.

†Method currently in use; in some states, convicted persons have choice of methods.

Much of the research concerning public opinion has been directed toward the issue of *why* support (or nonsupport) for capital punishment exists. Some researchers have linked the shift toward approval to an increasing concern about crime (Rankin, 1979; Thomas and Foster, 1975), whereas others have viewed it as reflective of support for a punitive, retributive model of crim-

TABLE 24.1
(continued)

State	Death Row Population	Number of Executions	Method of Execution[†]
Missouri	87	8	Lethal injection
Montana	8	0	Hanging or lethal injection
Nebraska	11	0	Electrocution
Nevada	61	5	Lethal injection
New Hampshire	0	0	Hanging
New Jersey	7	0	Lethal injection
New Mexico	1	0	Lethal injection
New York	No death penalty		
North Carolina	111	5	Lethal injection or gas chamber
North Dakota	No death penalty		
Ohio	127	0	Electrocution
Oklahoma	124	3	Lethal injection
Oregon	13	0	Lethal injection
Pennsylvania	152	0	Lethal injection
Rhode Island	No death penalty		
South Carolina	46	4	Lethal injection
South Dakota	0	0	Lethal injection
Tennessee	105	0	Electrocution
Texas	376	56	Lethal injection
Utah	10	4	Lethal injection or firing squad
Vermont	No death penalty		
Virginia	48	19	Electrocution
Washington	11	1	Lethal injection or hanging
Wyoming	0	1	Lethal injection
U.S. Government	4	0	Lethal injection
U.S. Military	6	0	Lethal injection
Totals	2,729	199	

inal justice (Bohm, 1992; Neapolitan, 1983; Tyler and Weber, 1982; Gelles and Straus, 1975). However, Ellsworth and Ross (1983), in an extensive study of the issue, found that support for or opposition to capital punishment is not strongly correlated with any set of reasoned beliefs. Bohm (1987) affirms this position by noting that most respondents have little information by which to formulate their opinions and frequently express contradictory positions.

Further complicating matters is the finding that support for the *principle* of capital punishment does not necessarily translate into support for the way in which the penalty actually is administered. In one study (M. D. Smith, 1987a), a majority of respondents supported capital punishment; however, most thought it should be applied on a limited basis and expressed disagreement with a number of actual cases in which the death penalty was assessed. Conversely, several respondents who opposed the death penalty reversed themselves when presented with details of some cases in which individuals escaped the sentence (also see Williams et al., 1988).

In sum, a majority of the American public currently supports the existence of death penalty laws. However, studies of public opinion regarding capital punishment have found that the public is neither particularly informed nor thoughtful concerning death penalty issues, leading researchers such as Bohm et al. (1991) to question the advisability of allowing public opinion to serve as a basis for public policy on this issue.

DEBATING THE MAJOR ISSUES

The debate over capital punishment in the United States dates back to the eighteenth century (Carrington, 1978b). However, this exchange was largely academic until the 1960s when serious legal challenges were mounted against the practice of capital punishment. It was not until this time that a substantial body of social science research, much of it controversial in itself, emerged to supplement the debate. Although any list of the issues framing this debate may omit concerns that some believe to be important, at least four areas addressed by recent research — and at least one crucial area beyond empirical investigation — merit discussion.

CAPITAL PUNISHMENT AS A DETERRENT TO CRIME

Perhaps the most hotly contested issue involving capital punishment is whether or not it serves to restrain people from committing murder, thereby sparing the lives of countless potential victims. Many people strongly believe this to be the case, adopting the classical view that individuals rationally weigh the consequences of their actions before engaging in crime. Conceding that this model may not be appropriate for "crimes of passion" (murders resulting from heated disputes with loved ones or acquaintances), proponents point out that capital punishment now is reserved only for the most heinous of homicides, especially those committed in the course of another felony such as rape or robbery. Quite rightly, they point out that murders under these conditions are frequently committed with little cause or a viciousness that defies explanation. They argue that executing those who engage in such violations may cause other potential offenders to reconsider their actions.

Although this reasoning may sound logical, does evidence support the argument? Some notable studies have purported to show a pronounced deterrent effect (Ehrlich, 1975; Yunker, 1976), whereas others (Cover and Thistle, 1988; Peterson and Bailey, 1988; Shin, 1978; Bowers and Pierce, 1975) dispute such a finding. In extensive reviews of the deterrence literature, both Klein et al. (1978) and Waldo (1981) conclude that no substantial evidence supports the position that the death penalty deters criminal homicide. However, given the methodological complexities involved in addressing the issue, they question whether it can be resolved through empirical investigation (see also Gibbs, 1982).

For now, we can state that those imputing a general deterrence effect to capital punishment have yet to prove their case, leaving them with little cause to justify its retention on this basis. In response, advocates might contend rightly that neither has its efficacy been disproved (see Ehrlich and Mark, 1977) and that, at the very least, capital punishment operates to ensure that individual offenders will not escape from prison at a later date and repeat their violent offenses. Opponents of capital punishment acknowledge the possibility of a repeat offense, but stress its improbability (see Marquart and Sorensen, 1988), and are unmoved by this argument as a justification for continuing to assess death sentences.

Assuming for a moment that a deterrent effect, though empirically elusive, somehow actually is operating to dampen people's propensity for murder, some difficult and potentially discomforting questions remain. For instance, historically, those states that have been the most avid practitioners of capital punishment have consistently had among the highest homicide rates in the nation (Glaser and Zeigler, 1974). In contrast, those states without the death penalty tend to be those with low homicide rates. At first glance, this may suggest simply that some states "need" capital punishment, and thus have it. But if not the threat of death, then what controls the populations of states with low homicide rates and no death penalty? And what are the characteristics of some states that cause them to "need" capital punishment as a deterrent, especially those states that already have bulging death row populations? On an even larger scale, why does the United States continue to have shockingly higher rates of murder than do Western European nations, none of which practice capital punishment (Archer and Gartner, 1984)? Answers to these kinds of questions come no more easily than do answers to those questions that have been addressed so far; at the same time, at least asking such questions may take discussions of deterrence and the death penalty in different directions than are now being pursued.

DISCRIMINATION AND CAPITAL PUNISHMENT

Critics of capital punishment in the United States long have contended that it is practiced in a discriminatory fashion (Black, 1978). More specifically, they believe that minorities (especially blacks) and the poor are at greater risk of receiving a death sentence than are their white, more affluent counterparts.

TABLE 24.2

Case	Implication of Ruling
Furman v. *Georgia* (1972)	Capital punishment ruled to be capricious and arbitrary in application, thereby violating Eighth and Fourteenth Amendments of the U.S. Constitution
Gregg v. *Georgia* (1976) *Proffitt* v. *Florida* (1976) *Jurek* v. *Texas* (1976)	Death penalty statutes approved; circumstances qualifying for death sentence must be clearly defined; established bifurcated trial system
Woodson v. *North Carolina* (1976)	Mandatory death penalty for first-degree murder is unconstitutional; penalty must be left to jury discretion
Roberts v. *Louisiana* (1977)	Mandatory death penalty for killing a law enforcement officer on duty is unconstitutional; penalty must be left to jury discretion
Coker v. *Georgia* (1977)	Death penalty for rape ruled unconstitutional, limiting its application to capital murder
Spanzio v. *Florida* (1984)	Upheld right of state to allow presiding judge to override jury's decision in penalty phase of trial
Lockhart v. *McCree* (1986)	Upheld right of prosecution to exclude from a jury those who say they could never vote for a death sentence; rejected evidence that this created a conviction-prone jury at the trial phase (see Bersoff, 1987)
McClesky v. *Kemp* (1987)	Rejected arguments that disproportionate imposition of death penalty for cases involving white victims was unconstitutional application of capital punishment; held that social science data were insufficient evidence to demonstrate unconstitutional patterns of discrimination
Stanford v. *Kentucky* (1989) *Wilkins* v. *Missouri* (1989)	Permits the execution of persons convicted of capital murder who were under the age of 18 at the time of their offense
Penry v. *Lynaugh* (1989)	Permits the execution of mentally retarded persons convicted of capital murder

◆ **CAPRICIOUSNESS AND ARBITRARINESS** ◆ This contention was a central feature of arguments presented in the *Furman* case and an issue that strongly influenced several of the justices' opinions. Ultimately, the majority, by a slim 5–4 margin, held that capital punishment, as then practiced, violated the Eighth Amendment protection against "cruel and unusual punishment" because it was administered in a manner that was both *capricious* and *arbitrary*. That is, there seemed to be very few features distinguishing those convicted persons assessed the death penalty from those granted prison terms (the capricious component), giving it what some justices termed a "freakish" or "lottery-like" quality (Bowers, 1984). Further, among the very few factors that might distinguish those receiving a death sentence, several, such as race, were "extra-legal" factors (the arbitrary component).

Only two of the justices (Brennan and Marshall) in *Furman* believed that capital punishment, in itself, was cruel and unusual and should be prohibited. The remainder of the majority, though particularly concerned with the discrimination issue, left the door open for a return to capital punishment. Responding to the challenge, and aided by a number of subsequent Court decisions (see Table 24.2) that defined the parameters of what would be allowed, most states have developed a bifurcated (two-part) trial system for charges of "capital murder" — those homicides that meet specific criteria ("aggravating circumstances") and thus are subject to the death penalty. In the trial phase, guilt or innocence of the defendant is determined by a jury that has been "death qualified" — that is, there are no members who oppose the death penalty. (See Hans, 1988, for a discussion of the implications of death qualification.) If a guilty verdict is returned, a penalty phase begins in which the jury has the option of assessing a life term in prison or the death penalty. (In some states, the jury has the option of finding the defendant guilty of a lesser charge whereby a death sentence would not be applicable.) At this time, counsel for the defense can present any "mitigating circumstances" that might argue against the imposition of the death penalty. In rebuttal, prosecuting attorneys can present arguments, including evidence not admissible during the trial phase (such as the defendant's prior convictions), to buttress their appeal for the death penalty. In most states, the jury's decision determines the penalty; in a few states, it is considered advisory, and final authority for sentencing rests with the presiding judge. For example, in Florida, one of the leading death penalty states, it is not unusual for judges to override jury decisions that call for prison terms and instead impose death sentences (Radelet, 1989).

◆ **RACE** ◆   In the *Gregg* decision that established a model for capital murder trials, a majority of the justices seemingly felt that revisions in the sentencing process could either eliminate or, at least, significantly reduce the influence of arbitrary factors in the capital punishment process. Once death sentences began to be assessed under this approved model, researchers sought to measure the extent to which these expectations were being met. Studies conducted on sentencing patterns in a number of states, especially southern states, have produced similar results despite a variety of databases and methods of analysis (Kiel and Vito, 1992; Baldus, 1990; Gross and Mauro, 1989; Nakell and Hardy, 1987; M. D. Smith, 1987b; Bentele, 1985; Paternoster, 1984; Jacoby and Paternoster, 1982; Radelet, 1981; Zeisel, 1981; Arkin, 1980; Bowers and Pierce, 1975). In brief, a rather uniform pattern of discrimination based on *race of the victim* has been found; offenders killing whites were more likely to be assessed the death penalty than those killing blacks, even when a host of circumstances that might alter this relationship were controlled (Gross, 1985). The strength of this relationship, however, varied considerably by state. Further, the rather capricious nature of death sentences remained relatively intact, with few factors, legal or extralegal, distinguishing those few offenders assigned the death penalty from those who were not. In contrast, evidence for discrimination by *race of offender*, a focus in the *Furman* decision, was quite mixed, suggesting that it is not a factor of significant magnitude in most states (see especially Kiel and Vito, 1992).

Why does race continue to play a part in death penalty decisions, even though more subtly than in the past? Some suggest that the criminal justice system still is very much dominated by whites — from prosecutors to judges to juries — who tend to show greater concern over the murder of other whites, regardless of who kills them (Gross and Mauro, 1984). It is noteworthy that the "race-of-victim" effect is due largely to the relative infrequency of death sentences for blacks who kill other blacks, though that category of murder tends to be rather large (Lempert, 1983; Kleck, 1981). This has led to charges that the lives of black victims simply have less value in the criminal justice system than do those of whites. Several studies (Paternoster and Kazyaka, 1988; Nakell and Hardy, 1987; Radelet and Pierce, 1985; Paternoster, 1983, 1984) lend some credibility to this idea but in rather odd fashion. It is not only the decisions of jurors that produce this effect, these studies find, but the discretion afforded prosecutors in seeking the death penalty. Quite simply, seeking the death penalty for the killers of whites appears to have more political value for prosecutors. Because many prosecutors hold elected positions, successful death penalty cases, especially those involving white victims, represent political as well as legal victories. And as Mello (1984) suggests, the more "aggravating circumstances" provided prosecutors by a state's death penalty laws, the more capriciousness and arbitrariness may creep into their decisions. In particular, several states prescribe death sentences for murders that are "unusually cruel or heinous." Such a designation is sufficiently ambiguous to allow considerable latitude in pressing for capital murder charges.

As studies emerged indicating that the concerns raised in *Furman* may not have been addressed sufficiently, new challenges to death penalty practices developed. This culminated in 1987 with *McCleskey* v. *Kemp*, in which the Supreme Court heard arguments that Georgia, despite reforms in its capital punishment statutes, continued to display patterns of arbitrariness. A central focus of the case was a complex, sophisticated study by Baldus et al. (1983, 1985) that demonstrated a rather pronounced race-of-victim effect in Georgia's death-sentencing patterns. *McClesky* was particularly important because, given the Court's more relaxed attitude, the case represented the last major "systemic" attack that opponents could mount against the nation's capital punishment practices. By a 5–4 vote, the Court rejected McClesky's appeal, reaffirming the practice of capital punishment. In so doing, the majority opinion, while noting the Baldus team's effort, and even acknowledging the probable validity of their findings, viewed as inadequate studies utilizing "aggregate" statistics to demonstrate effects on individual cases (Bynam, 1988, and Acker, 1987, provide detailed discussion of the decision). Consequently, an entire body of social scientific literature used to reveal patterns of discrimination was, in effect, dismissed from future consideration (Ellsworth, 1988).

In fairness, some studies (for example, Heilbrun et al., 1989, and Barnett, 1985) have critiqued the Baldus research by providing findings suggesting that the race-of-victim effect could be accounted for through a more careful consideration of the total circumstances (especially the heinousness of the crime) surrounding each murder case used in the analysis. However, responses by Baldus et al. (1985), as well as by Kiel and Vito (1989), have presented evidence that disputes this contention.

◆ **SOCIAL CLASS** ◆ Although the majority of research concerning discrimination in death sentences focuses on race, a more important, though less easily studied, source of discrimination may be operative. The factor is that of social class. A number of observers have noted that a vast majority of those sentenced to death live under conditions of poverty at the time they are accused of their offense. Consequently, as they move through the criminal justice system, they have limited resources with which to fight their conviction (Bowers, 1983). Unable to hire attorneys, indigent defendants are assigned either a public defender (employed by the state) or a court-appointed attorney, usually drawn from a pool of private attorneys who agree or are assigned to work for limited compensation from the state. Though many indigent defendants receive admirable representation (public defenders in large metropolitan jurisdictions, for instance, may be quite skilled), cases abound of capital murder defendants represented by overworked and inexperienced counsel, many of whom are unfamiliar with the unique and complex nature of capital murder trials (Goodpaster, 1983). The Supreme Court has expressed sympathy with this plight, but has issued several rulings making it extremely difficult to overturn a case on the basis of incompetent counsel, even if defendants had no choice in their representation (see *Strickland* v. *Washington*, 1984).

A further difficulty lies in the appeals process. If convicted, defendants are entitled automatically to a set of appeals; however, the state is not obligated to provide an attorney for these appeals beyond the state level. If appeals for indigent offenders are carried forward to the federal level, at which they traditionally have received more sympathetic hearings, it is usually by volunteer attorneys who are willing to take a case as a matter of conscience or as a public service (Dayan, 1986). Such appeals can become time consuming and costly for these attorneys, leaving their numbers in short supply. In the South, especially, such service is sorely needed but frequently is discouraged by public opinion and even fellow attorneys (Wallace, 1987; Stout, 1988).

◆ **THE CURRENT SITUATION** ◆   Does discrimination still exist in the practice of capital punishment in this country? On the basis of available evidence, the answer is a qualified yes. Race remains a factor, though apparently not so grievously as in the pre-*Furman* years. And, though difficult to assess its impact apart from other factors, being economically disadvantaged appears to increase the likelihood that defendants will be assessed a death sentence.

Could this discrimination be reduced further? The answer here is possibly. By holding to a minimum their aggravating circumstances, states can reduce potential sources of arbitrariness. To the extent states conduct regular studies of their death sentences to identify problematic patterns of arbitrariness and send observers to jurisdictions disproportionately contributing to any objectionable patterns, judges and prosecutors must be more conscious of patterns in their death penalty decisions. And by creating pools of specially prepared private attorneys or public defenders to handle capital murder trials involving indigent defendants, assurances of adequate representation would be more likely than at present.

Ideally, state supreme court justices could do much to monitor the arbitrariness of sentences in their states. Yet, as Inciardi (1987) mentions, state appeals courts generally are reluctant to overturn the decisions of trial courts. In the case of capital punishment, it can be speculated also that the fact that the justices in many states are elected may influence their (un)willingness to interfere with death sentences.

A remaining issue is whether states presently are under any legal obligation to be particularly concerned about discrimination, except for its most overt forms, in their systems of capital punishment. Realistically, given the tenor of recent Supreme Court decisions, the answer is no, a situation of which many states seem inclined to take full advantage.

THE COST OF LIFE IMPRISONMENT

The cost of maintaining convicted murderers for the duration of their lives frequently is cited as a factor in support of capital punishment. Advocates of the death penalty maintain that, faced with an already overcrowded penal system, the lifetime care of thousands of convicted persons, many of them guilty of heinous murders, is an unnecessary and, in some ways, tauntingly cruel burden on taxpayers. Further, they suggest that the expenditures made on behalf of these individuals could be used more productively.

Traditionally, those opposed to the death penalty have responded that the principles involved in the issue do not lend themselves to financial considerations. More recently, however, studies have emerged that challenge the assumption that capital punishment is necessarily a fiscally conservative crime measure. Both Garey (1985) and Nakell (1978), for example, argue persuasively that a criminal justice system that utilizes the death penalty simply costs more than a system restricting its maximum punishment to life imprisonment (see also Keve, 1992).

Given the expense of housing prisoners, such a claim flies in the face of conventional wisdom. Yet, as several writers have made clear, "death is different," and the imposition of capital punishment requires a legal system whose safeguards far exceed those of conventional trials (Bedeau, 1987). As Garey found, capital murder cases involve a disproportionate number of legal maneuvers, from pretrial motions to appeals on behalf of the defendant. Such extraordinary efforts are rare in noncapital cases, especially because many of the appeals in capital cases emanate from the penalty phase of the trial. Estimates vary on actual cost benefits, but a conservative figure places the cost per individual at two to three times greater for capital punishment (Gradess, 1988).

When confronted with such statistics, supporters of the death penalty point to the seemingly endless number of appeals available to death row inmates (Berger, 1982), and suggest that a reduction in appeals (for instance, a limitation of one court appearance in which all appeals are considered together) would reduce considerably the cost associated with executing persons. Although some cost reduction might be realized, the significance of the reduction is debatable. As Garey has shown, appeals are only a part of the overall cost of capital punishment, and one that varies considerably across defendants. As mentioned previously, the bulk of the appeals process is handled by *volunteer* attorneys or is funded by organizations aiding indigent defendants (such as the American Civil Liberties Union, NAACP Legal Defense Fund, or Southern Poverty Law Center), thereby effectively subsidizing states' expenditures. Thus, a recent federal judicial panel recommended a reduction in appeals available to individuals under a death sentence but warned that states will have to spend considerably more money in providing adequate counsel for defendants, including the reduced appeals phase (Greenhouse, 1989).

Based on available research, capital punishment apparently cannot be rationalized as a cost-saving measure. The only realistic methods of equalizing the cost difference would mandate substantially less aggressive defenses of those accused of capital murder, thus minimizing constitutional safeguards designed to ensure a fair trial and careful review of a verdict. As the next section reveals, such outcomes are not to be taken for granted.

WRONGFUL EXECUTIONS

Opponents of the death penalty consistently note the possibility that a person may be executed for a crime he or she did not commit. Thus, in an ironic twist, the state would assume the role of "murderer," an offense for which there are no specified sanctions. Supporters of capital punishment acknowledge such a possibility, but using a strategy employed by the opposition regarding further murders by escaped "lifers," stress the improbability of this occurrence. Though begrudging the extended appeals process available to convicted persons, supporters see this as a safeguard that makes the "innocent man theory" a contrived argument, pointing out that there are virtually no verified cases in which such a miscarriage of justice actually happened (Carrington, 1978b).

Responding to that challenge, Bedeau and Radelet (1987), using narrowly defined criteria for "innocence," were able to assemble 350 cases in which defendants were wrongfully convicted of homicide for which they could have received a death sentence or of a rape for which a death penalty was assessed. Of these persons, 139 actually were sentenced to die; 23 ultimately were executed. An additional 22 persons came within seventy-two hours of being executed; 2, in fact, already were strapped in the electric chair before news of their vindication stopped the execution.

Bedeau and Radelet stress that their figures should be considered very conservative estimates because of their stringent criteria for inclusion of cases and because it becomes extremely difficult to prove innocence after an individual has been executed. Further, they report that the "system"—that is, the appeals process—was rarely the source of correction of the judicial error. At best, the appeals process, frequently criticized as too extensive by death penalty supporters, bought time for information to surface that exonerated the wrongfully convicted person.

In a later, expanded version of this work, Radelet et al. (1992) have discovered a number of additional cases of wrongful convictions (though not executions), including a number during the post-*Gregg* era. Consequently, it would be erroneous to assume that wrongful convictions and possible executions have been eliminated under contemporary death-sentencing laws.

Responding to findings of this nature, Ernst van den Haag, reflecting the views of many supporters of capital punishment, asserts that these cases simply represent an unfortunate price that must be paid in order to enjoy the advantages that capital punishment offers a society (Margolick, 1985; van den Haag, 1985). This position brings us to perhaps the crucial issue in the capital punishment debate, the morality of government-sanctioned executions.

CAPITAL PUNISHMENT AS A MORAL AND SYMBOLIC ISSUE

Although empirical evidence, however controversial, can be brought to bear on the assertions of either side of the capital punishment debate, such evidence is rarely the basis for people's intense feelings on the issue (Bohm, 1992; Ellsworth and Ross, 1983). Instead, positions more often reflect deeply held convictions regarding the morality of taking the lives of other people, except in the extreme conditions of self-defense and war.

Ultimately, the moral debate about capital punishment centers on the appropriate role of retribution in a modern criminal justice system (Reiman, 1988; Dolinko, 1986). There was considerable discussion in both *Furman* and *Gregg* about whether "evolving standards of decency" in the United States continue to stress the retribution aspect of capital punishment. In justifying a return to capital punishment, the majority opinion in *Gregg* noted the popularity of capital punishment in opinion polls as well as the continued willingness of juries to impose death sentences. Thus, they concluded that retribution was among the appropriate functions that capital punishment could serve, one falling well within the boundaries of current "standards of decency" in the United States.

Supporters of the death penalty heartily agree (van den Haag and Conrad, 1983; Berns, 1979), and have argued that the death penalty is crucially symbolic in expressing, in the strongest terms possible, the collective moral outrage over the unlawful taking of human life. In their view, anything less than responding with the most extreme penalty available suggests a tolerance for those activities, a threat to the fundamental trust that binds members of a society. From this perspective, it is virtually *immoral* to oppose such a sanction, especially in deference to concerns for offenders over those of victims.

Opponents of capital punishment agree that it is symbolic of society's outrage but maintain that the abolition of capital punishment also is symbolic. The abolition of capital punishment, they argue, represents society's affirmation of the sanctity of human life, a sanctity that even the state should not violate. Ideally, in their opinion, as a society progresses in its moral as well as cultural development, it abandons the hypocritical practice of engaging in precisely those activities it seeks to condemn (Gorecki, 1983; Kohlberg and Elfenbein, 1975). Life imprisonment, opponents claim, inflicting as it does a kind of "social" death, represents an adequate, appropriate, and symbolic response to those who take the lives of others (Bedeau, 1987; van den Haag and Conrad, 1983).

In discussing patterns of abolition in European countries, Zimring and Hawkins (1986) report that the United States' case was similar, even in the public's outcry for the death penalty's return once it was halted. What distinguishes the United States, they argue, was the lack of highly placed "moral leadership" that stood firm against its return. In other countries, resistance by "moral leadership" to the immediate demands for the restoration of capital punishment ultimately led to a shift in public opinion to an abolitionist position. In contrast, no such leadership emerged after *Furman*. Ideally, the Supreme Court, insulated from the political pressures of election, would have served this function. Instead, it was bitterly divided in *Furman*, leaving open the possibility of a return to capital punishment. Ultimately, the Court abandoned an opportunity for moral leadership in *Gregg*, bending, as Zimring and Hawkins see it, before the politics of public opinion.

For all practical purposes, the moral debate regarding capital punishment is unresolvable, with both sides holding passionately to their beliefs. At present, supporters of capital punishment have carried the day, both politically and in terms of public sentiment. Barring unforeseen events that would dramatically alter public opinion, this situation is not likely to change in the near future.

CONCLUSION

Given recent developments, it is safe to say that the death penalty will be a part of the American criminal justice system for the duration of this century. Capital punishment received strong support during the 1980s from the administrations of Presidents Reagan and Bush. President Clinton also supports it. The Reagen and Bush support included efforts to expand the types of crimes under federal jurisdiction for which executions may be performed. In addition, they were committed to the appointment of federal judges whose records indicated approval of the death penalty. Not the least of these appointments were four Supreme Court justices whose support for capital punishment was an implicit (some would say explicit) requirement for their nomination. A notable result of this restructured court is a retreat from the "death is different" philosophy, resulting in a considerably reduced set of judicial safeguards afforded those accused or convicted of capital murder (Denno, 1992; Bilionis, 1991; White, 1991). The commitment of the new appointees to capital punishment is illustrated by a recent case (*Herrera* v. *Collins*, 1993) in which the Court ruled that if established judicial procedures were followed, states are not obligated to overturn a death sentence even if after-trial evidence emerges indicating that the convicted person is innocent.

Faced with these prospects, abolitionists probably will be forced to shift their reform efforts from the courts to the legislatures of death penalty states. Given current public sentiment, success at this level, particularly in the most active states, is unlikely. However, the relative success of capital punishment supporters in recent years may have created some unique problems. Several writers have identified an impending crisis that will demand attention in the near future. The crisis stems from the fact that, since *Gregg*, executions have been outpaced greatly by admissions to death rows around the country. Simultaneously, the judicial appeals of death row inmates are being denied in more rapid fashion than previously (Levinson, 1993). This has created an unprecedented death row population awaiting execution, though that population is concentrated largely in about ten states (see Table 24.1).

Cheatwood (1985) has suggested that to restore some type of stability to these states' penal systems, the rate of executions will have to be increased to a magnitude not seen in this country in the twentieth century. For instance, he projects the need for at least one execution per weekday for a period of approximately six to seven years, and thereafter for the number of executions to approximate the death sentences assessed per year (currently about 200). Such a rate would be unheard of in the current Western world and the international standing of the United States could suffer considerable damage. Cheatwood believes that even supporters of capital punishment are reluctant to embark on such a venture for fear that it might inspire a backlash that would revive abolitionist sentiments in the public, especially if a dreaded "wrong man" execution should occur (Haines, 1992).

Zimring and Hawkins (1986) describe the current situation as a perverse game of "chicken." As they see it, state politicians, aware of the popularity of the death penalty, insist on its retention. Yet, while lashing out at various components of the criminal justice system for blocking executions (though the Supreme Court is not nearly the convenient target it once was), many of these same politicians, aware of the potential consequences, are reluctant to see executions proceed at the pace necessary to reduce their states' burdensome death row populations. A stalemate has resulted that will soon demand an expanded rate of execution (the most likely short-term response), a slowed rate of death sentences via state legislative reform, a commutation of many current death sentences to life imprisonment, or some combination of these approaches. All these strategies have practical and political drawbacks that will sorely test policymakers and may well affect the long-term future of capital punishment in this country. One thing is certain: The debate regarding capital punishment and all its attendant issues, as one-sided as it is presently, is far from over.

DISCUSSION QUESTIONS

1. Is the United States in the mainstream of developed nations in its use of the death penalty? Discuss capital punishment's history in this country. To what extent has public opinion about capital punishment changed in recent years? What accounts for such changes?

2. Many supporters of the death penalty argue that it deters crime. What does the research evidence have to say concerning this position?

3. Have we succeeded in eliminating discrimination from the application of the death sentence in this country? Discuss the ways in which the death penalty may still be assigned unfairly. What have the courts ruled regarding current evidence of discrimination in capital punishment?

4. Both sides of the capital punishment debate see great symbolism in the use of such punishment. Discuss the symbolic effects of the death penalty. Why do Americans not perceive the same symbolism in the assignment of a life sentence in place of death?

References

Aarronson, D. E., C. T. Dienes, and M. C. Musheno. 1978. "Changing the Public Drunkenness Laws: The Impact of Decriminalization." *Law and Society Review* 12: 405–416.

———. 1984. *Public Policy and Police Discretion.* New York: Clark Boardmen.

Abadinsky, H. 1981. *The Mafia in America: An Oral History.* New York: Praeger.

———. 1989. *Drug Abuse: An Introduction.* Chicago: Nelson-Hall.

Abel, R. 1990. "The Contradictions of Legal Professionalism." In *New Directions in the Study of Justice, Law, and Social Control.* Edited by School of Justice Studies. New York: Plenum.

Acker, J. R. 1987. "Capital Punishment by the Numbers—An Analysis of *McClesky v. Kemp.*" *Criminal Law Bulletin* 23: 454–482.

Adams, E. H., J. C. Groerer, B. A. Rouse, and N. J. Kozel. 1986. "Trends in Prevalence and Consequences of Cocaine Use." *Advances in Alcohol and Substance Abuse* 6: 49–72.

Adamson, C. R. 1983. "Punishment After Slavery: Southern State Penal Systems, 1865-1890." *Social Problems* 30: 555–569.

———. 1984. "Toward a Marxian Penology: Captive Criminal Populations as Economic Threats and Resources." *Social Problems* 31: 435–458.

Adler, P. A. 1985. *Wheeling and Dealing: An Ethnography of an Upper-Level Drug Dealing and Smuggling Community.* New York: Columbia University Press.

Adler, P. A., and P. Adler. 1983. "Shifts and Oscillations in Deviant Careers: The Case of Upper-Level Drug Dealers and Smugglers." *Social Problems* 31: 195–207.

Administrative Office of the U.S. Courts. 1985. *Federal Judicial Workload Statistics.* Washington, DC: Statistical Analysis and Reports Divisions.

Ageton, S., and D. S. Elliott. 1974. "The Effects of Legal Processing on Self Concept." *Social Problems* 22: 87–100.

Agnew, R. 1984a. "The Effect of Appearance on Personality and Behavior: Are the Beautiful Really Good?" *Youth and Society* 15: 285–303.

———. 1984b. "Autonomy and Delinquency." *Sociological Perspectives* 27: 219–240.

———. 1984c. "The Work Ethic and Delinquency." *Sociological Focus* 17: 337–346.

———. 1985a. "A Revised Strain Theory of Delinquency." *Social Forces* 64: 151–167.

———. 1985b. "Social Control Theory and Delinquency: A Longitudinal Test." *Criminology* 23: 47–61.

———. 1987a. "Challenging Strain Theory: An Examination of Goals and Goal-Blockage in an Adolescent Sample." Paper presented at the 1987 meeting of the American Society of Criminology, Montreal.

———. 1987b. "On 'Testing Structural Strain Theories.'" *Journal of Research in Crime and Delinquency* 24: 281–286.

———. 1989. "A Longitudinal Test of the Revised Strain Theory." *Journal of Quantitative Criminology* 5: 373-387.

———. 1991. "A Longitudinal Test of Social Control Theory and Delinquency." *Journal of Research in Crime and Delinquency* 28: 126–156.

———. 1992. "Foundation for a General Strain Theory of Crime and Delinquency." *Criminology* 30: 47–87.

Agnew, R., and D. Jones. 1988. "Adapting to Deprivation: An Examination of Inflated Educational Expectations." *Sociological Quarterly* 29: 315–337.

Agnew, R., and A. Peters. 1985. "The Techniques of Neutralization: An Analysis of Predisposing and Situational Factors." *Criminal Justice and Behavior* 12: 221–239.

Agnew, R., and H. R. White. 1992. "An Empirical Test of General Strain Theory." *Criminology* 30: 475–499.

Ainlay, J. 1975. "Book Review: The New Criminology and Critical Criminology." *Telos* 26: 213–225.

Ainslie, G., and R. J. Herrnstein. 1981. "Preference Reversal and Delayed Reinforcement." *Animal Learning and Behavior* 9: 476–482.

Akers, R. 1979. "Theory and Ideology in Marxist Criminology." *Criminology* 16: 527–544.

———. 1985. *Deviant Behavior: A Social Learning Approach.* Belmont, CA: Wadsworth.

Albanese, J. S. 1983. *God & the Mafia Revisited: From Valachi to Fratianno.* In *Career Criminals.* Edited by G. Waldo. Beverly Hills, CA: Sage.

———. 1984a. *Justice, Privacy, and Crime Control.* Lanham, MD: University Press of America.

———. 1984b. "Concern About Variation in Criminal Sentences: A Cyclical History of Reform." *Journal of Criminal Law and Criminology* 75: 260–271.

———. 1987a. "Predicting the Incidence of Organized Crime." In *Organized Crime in America: Concepts and Controversies.* Edited by T. Bynum. Monsey, NY: Willow Tree Press.

———. 1987b. *Organizational Offenders: Understanding Corporate Crime.* Niagara Falls, NY: Apocalypse.

———. 1989. *Organized Crime in America.* 2d ed. Cincinnati: Anderson.

———. 1993. "Models of Organized Crime." *Handbook of Organized Crime in the United States.* Edited by R. Kelly, K. Chin, and R. Schatzberg. Westport, CT: Greenwood Publishing.

Albanese, J. S., B. A. Fiore, J. H. Porwell, and J. R. Storit. 1985. *Is Probation Working? A Guide for Managers and Methodologists.* Lanham, MD: University Press of America.

Albini, J. L. 1971. *The American Mafia: Genesis of a Legend.* New York: Irvington.

Albonetti, C. A. 1986. "Criminality, Prosecutorial Screening, and Uncertainty: Toward a Theory of Discretionary Decision-Making in Felony Cases." *Criminology* 24: 623–644.

———. 1987. "Prosecutorial Discretion: The Effects of Uncertainty." *Law & Society Review* 21: 291–313.

Albrecht, S., and M. Green. 1977. "Attitudes Toward Police and the Larger Attitude Complex." *Criminology* 15: 485–494.

Allan, E., and D. Steffensmeier. 1989. "Youth, Unemployment, and Property Crime: Differential Effects of Job Availability and Job Quality on Juvenile and Young Adult Arrest Rates." *American Sociological Review* 54: 107–123.

Allen, D. F., and J. F. Jekel. 1991. *Crack: The Broken Promise.* New York: St. Martin's Press.

Allen, D. N. 1982. "Police Supervision on the Street." *Journal of Criminal Justice* 10: 91–109.

Allen, M. P. 1991. "Capitalist Response to State Intervention: Political Finance in the New Deal." *American Sociological Review* 56: 679–689.

Alper, B., and L. Nichols. 1981. *Beyond the Courtroom.* Lexington, MA: Lexington Books.

Alpert, G., and P. Anderson. 1986. "The Most Deadly Force: Police Pursuits." *Justice Quarterly* 3: 1–15.

Alpert, G. P., and T. K. Petersen. 1985. "The Grand Jury Report: A Magic Lantern or an Agent of Social Control?" *Justice Quarterly* 2: 23–49.

Alschuler, A. W. 1979. "Plea Bargaining and Its History." *Columbia Law Review* 79: 1–43.

Alston, L. 1986. *Crime and Older Americans.* Springfield, IL: Thomas.

Altheide, D. 1978. "Newsworkers and Newsmakers: A Study in News Use." *Urban Life* 7: 359–378.

Altschuler, M., and J. Brounstein. "Patterns of Drug Use, Drug Trafficking, and other Delinquency among Inner-City Adolescent Males in Washington, D.C." *Criminology* 29: 4: 589–622.

American Correctional Association. 1983. *Female Classification: An Examination of the Issues.* National Institute of Corrections. Washington, DC: U.S. Government Printing Office.

American Friends Service Committee. 1971. *Struggle for Justice.* New York: Hill & Wang.

American Psychiatric Association. 1987. *Diagnostic and Statistical Manual.* 3d ed., rev. Washington, DC: American Psychiatric Association.

Amir, M. 1967. "Victim Precipitated Forcible Rape." *Journal of Criminal Law, Criminology and Police Science* 58: 439–502.

Amnesty International. 1989. *When the State Kills: The Death Penalty vs. Human Rights.* London: Amnesty International.

Amsterdam, A. 1974. "Perspectives on the Fourth Amendment." *Minnesota Law Review* 58: 349–477.

Anderson, A. G. 1979. *The Business of Organized Crime.* Stanford, CA: Hoover Institution Press.

Anderson, J. 1985. *Guns in American Life.* New York: Random House.

Anderson, L. S., T. G. Chiricos, and G. P. Waldo. 1977. "Formal and Informal Sanctions: A Comparison of Deterrent Effects." *Social Problems* 25: 103–114.

Andrews, D. M. 1987. "Differential Supervision of Offenders." Paper presented at the annual meeting of the American Probation and Parole Association, Salt Lake City. August.

Anglin, M. D., Y. Hser, and T. Booth. 1987. "Addicted Women and Crime." *Criminology* 25: 359–397.

Anglin, M. D., and G. Speckart. 1988. "Narcotics Use and Crime: A Multisample, Multimethod Analysis." *Criminology* 26: 197–234.

Archer, D., and R. Gartner. 1984. *Violence and Crime in Cross-National Perspective.* New Haven, CT: Yale University Press.

Arditi, R. R., F. Goldberg, Jr., M. M. Hartle, J. H. Peters, and W. R. Phelps. 1973. "The Sexual Segregation of American Prisons." *Yale Law Journal* 82: 1229–1273.

Arkin, S. D. 1980. "Discrimination and Arbitrariness in Capital Punishment: An Analysis of Post-*Furman* Murder Cases in Dade County, Florida, 1973–1976." *Stanford Law Review* 33: 75–101.

Arlacchi, P. 1986. *Mafia Business: The Mafia Ethic and the Spirit of Capitalism.* London: Verso.

Armor, D. J., J. M. Polich, and H. B. Stambul. 1976. *Alcoholism and Treatment.* Santa Monica, CA: Rand Corporation.

Attorney General. 1980. *Report of the Attorney General on the Feb. 2 & 3, 1980 Riot.* Albuquerque: Attorney General, State of New Mexico.

Attorney General's Commission on Pornography. 1986. *Final Report of the Attorney General's Commission on Pornography.* Washington, DC: U.S. Department of Justice.

Austern, D. 1987. *The Crime Victim's Handbook.* New York: Penguin Books.

Austern, D., B. Galaway, R. Godegast, R. Gross, R. Hofrichter, J. Hudson, T. Hutchinson, and M. Young-Rifai. 1979. *Compensating Victims of Crime—Participant's Handbook: Criminal Justice Utilization Program.* Washington, DC: University Research Corporation.

Austin, R. L. 1978. "Race, Father-Absence, and Female Delinquency." *Criminology* 15: 487–504.

Austin, T. L. 1985. "Does Where You Live Determine What You Get? A Case Study of Misdemeanant Sentencing." *Journal of Criminal Law and Criminology* 76: 490–511.

Axenroth, J. B. 1983. "Social Class and Delinquency in Cross-Cultural Perspective." *Journal of Research in Crime and Delinquency* 20: 164–182.

Ayers, E. L. 1984. *Crime and Punishment in the Nineteenth Century South.* New York: Oxford University Press.

Bailey, J. M. 1989. "A Critique and Reinterpretation of Gordon's IQ-Commensurability Property." *International Journal of Sociology and Social Policy* 9: 64–74.

Bailey, W., J. D. Martin, and L. Gray. 1974. "Crime and Deterrence: A Correlational Analysis." *Journal of Research in Crime and Delinquency* 11: 124–143.

Bailey, W. C. 1984. "Poverty, Inequality, and City Homicide Rates: Some Not So Unexpected Results." *Criminology* 22: 531–550.

Baird, C. S. 1981. "Probation and Parole Classification: The Wisconsin Model." *Corrections Today* 43: 36.

Baird, C. S., T. R. Clear, and P. M. Harris. 1986. *The Behavior Control Tools of Probation Officers.* Report to the National Institute of Justice. April.

Balbus, I. 1977. "Commodity Form and Legal Form: An Essay on the 'Relative Autonomy' of the Law." *Law & Society Review* 11: 571–587.

———. 1983. *The Dialectics of Legal Repression.* New York: Russell Sage.

Baldus, D. C. 1990. *Equal Justice and the Death Penalty: A Legal and Empirical Analysis.* Boston: Northeastern University Press.

Baldus, D. C., C. Pulaski, and G. Woodworth. 1983. "Comparative Review of Death Sentences: An Empirical Study of the Georgia Experience." *Journal of Criminal Law and Criminology* 74: 661–753.

Baldus, D. C., G. Woodworth, and C. A. Pulaski, Jr. 1985. "Monitoring and Evaluating Contemporary Death Sentencing Systems: Lessons from Georgia." *U.C. Davis Law Review* 18: 1375–1407.

Balkan, S., R. J. Berger, and J. Schmidt. 1980. *Crime and Deviance in America: A Critical Approach*. Belmont, CA: Wadsworth.

Balkwell, J. W. 1990. "Ethnic Inequality and the Rate of Homicide." *Social Forces* 69: 53–70.

Ball, J. C., B. K. Levine, R. G. Demaree, and J. F. Neman. 1975. "Pretreatment Criminality of Male and Female Drug Abuse Patients in the United States." *Addictive Diseases* 1: 481–489.

Ball, J. C., L. Rosen, J. A. Flueck, and D. N. Nurco. 1981. "The Criminality of Heroin Addicts: When Addicted and When off Opiates." Pp. 39–66 in *The Drugs-Crime Connection*. Edited by J. A. Inciardi. Beverly Hills, CA: Sage.

Ball, R. A., and R. A. Lilly. 1986. "The Potential Use of Home Incarceration for Drunken Drivers." *Crime and Delinquency* 32: 224–247.

Bankowski, Z., G. Mungham, and P. Young. 1977. "Radical Criminology or Radical Criminologist?" *Contemporary Crises* 1: 37–52.

Banks, J., et al. 1976. *An Evaluation of Special and Intensive Probation Programs*. Washington, DC: National Institute of Justice.

Bankston, W., C. Thompson, Q. Jenkins, and C. Forsyth. 1986. "Carrying Firearms: The Influence of Southern Culture and Fear of Crime." Paper presented at the 1986 meeting of the American Society of Criminology, Atlanta.

Banton, M. 1964. *The Police in the Community*. New York: Basic Books.

Barak, G. 1980. *In Defense of Whom? A Critique of Criminal Justice Reform*. Cincinnati: Anderson.

Barber, D. F. 1972. *Pornography and Society*. London: Skilton.

Barlow, H. 1987. *Introduction to Criminology*. Boston: Little, Brown.

Barnes, H. E., and N. D. Teeters. 1959. *New Horizons in Criminology*. Englewood Cliffs, NJ: Prentice-Hall.

Barnett, A. 1985. "Some Distribution Patterns for the Georgia Death Sentence." *U.C. Davis Law Review* 18: 1327–1374.

Barnett, H. 1979. "Wealth, Crime and Capital Accumulation." *Contemporary Crises* 3: 171–186.

Barnett, H. C. 1984. "Branch Culture and Economic Structure: Correlates of Tax Noncompliance in Sweden." Revised version of a paper presented at the 1984 meeting of the American Society of Criminology, Cincinnati.

Baron, L., and M. A. Straus. 1987. "Four Theories of Rape: A Macrosociological Analysis." *Social Problems* 34: 467–489.

———. 1989. *Four Theories of Rape in American Society: A State-Level Analysis*. New Haven: Yale University Press.

Barr, R., and Pease, K. 1990. "Crime Placement, Displacement, and Deflection." Vol. 11, pp. 277–318 in *Crime and Justice: An Annual Review of Research*. Edited by M. Tonry and N. Morris. Chicago: University of Chicago Press.

Barron, F., and D. M. Harrington. 1981. "Creativity, Intelligence, and Personality." *Annual Review of Psychology* 32: 439–476.

Barry, D., and T. R. Clear. 1984. *The Effects of Criminal Sanctions*. Report to the National Institute of Justice. April.

Bastion, L. 1992a: *Criminal Victimization 1991*. Wash., D.C.: Bureau of Justice Statistics.

———. 1992b: *Crime and The Nation's Households, 1991*. Wash., D.C.: Bureau of Justice Statistics.

Battle, B. P., and P. B. Weston. 1978. *Arson: Detection and Investigation*. New York: Arco.

Baum, L. 1986. *American Courts: Process and Policy*. Boston: Houghton Mifflin.

Baunach, P. J. 1985. *Mothers in Prison*. New Brunswick, NJ: Transaction.

Bayley, D. 1975. "The Police and Political Development in Europe." Pp. 1328–1379 in *The Formation of National States in Europe*. Edited by C. Tilly. Princeton, NJ: Princeton University Press.

———. 1979. "Police Function, Structure and Control in Western Europe." Pp. 109–144 in *Crime and Justice: An Annual Review of Research*. Edited by N. Morris and M. Tonry. Chicago: University of Chicago Press.

———. 1985. *Patterns of Policing*. New Brunswick, NJ: Rutgers University Press.

———. 1986. "The Tactical Choices of Police Patrol Officers." *Journal of Criminal Justice* 14: 329–348.

———. 1988. "Community Policing: Rhetoric or Reality." Edited by J. R. Greene and S. Mastrofski. New York: Praeger.

Bayley, D., and E. Bittner. 1984. "Learning the Skills of Policing." *Law and Contemporary Problems* 47: 35–59.

Bayley, D., and J. Garofalo. 1989. "Community Police Officers and Control." *Criminology* 27: 1–25.

Bean, P. 1976. *Rehabilitation and Deviance*. London: Routledge & Kegan Paul.

Beare, M. 1987. "The Police and Ideological Work." Paper presented at the 1987 meeting of the American Society of Criminology, Montreal.

Becarria, C. 1764. *An Essay on Crimes and Punishments*. Philadelphia: Nicklin.

Beck, A. J. 1991. *Profile of Jail Inmates, 1989*. Washington, DC: U. S. Department of Justice, Bureau of Justice Statistics.

Beck, E. M., and S. E. Tolnay. 1990. "The Killing Fields of the Deep South: The Market for Cotton and the Lynching of Blacks, 1882–1930." *American Sociological Review* 55: 526–539.

Becker, G. S. 1968. "Crime and Punishment: An Economic Approach." *Journal of Political Economy* 76: 169–217.

Becker, H. 1960. "Notes on the Concept of Commitment." *American Journal of Sociology* 66: 32–40.

———. 1963. *Outsiders: Studies in the Sociology of Deviance*. New York: Free Press.

———. 1967. "Whose Side Are We On?" *Social Problems* 14: 239–247.

———. 1974. "Labelling Theory Reconsidered." Pp. 41–66 in *Deviance and Social Control*. Edited by P. Rock and M. McIntoch. London: Tavistock.

Becker, H., and I. Horowitz. 1972. "Radical Politics and Sociological Research: Observations on Methodology and Ideology." *American Journal of Sociology* 78: 48–66.

Beckwith, J. 1976. "Social and Political Uses of Genetics in the United States: Past and Present." In *Ethical and Social Issues Posed by Human Uses of Molecular Genetics*. Edited by M. Lapp. New York: Annals of the New York Academy of Sciences.

Bedeau, H. A. 1974. "Are There Really 'Crimes Without Victims'?" Pp. 66–76 in *Victimless Crimes: Two Sides of a Controversy*. Edited by M. Schur and H. A. Bedeau. Englewood Cliffs, NJ: Prentice-Hall.

———. 1975. "Physical Intervention to Alter Behavior in a Punitive Environment: Some Moral Reflections in New Technology." *American Behavioral Scientist* 18(5): 657–678.

———. 1982. "Background and Development." In *The Death Penalty in America*. 3d ed. Edited by H. A. Bedeau. New York: Oxford University Press.

———. 1987. *Death Is Different: Studies in the Morality, Law, and Politics of Capital Punishment*. Boston: Northeastern University Press.

Bedeau, H. A., and M. L. Radelet. 1987. "Miscarriages of Justice in Potentially Capital Cases." *Stanford Law Review* 40: 21–179.

Bell, D. 1953. "Crime as an American Way of Life." *The Antioch Review* 13: 131–154.

Bennett, T., and R. Wright. 1984. "Constraints to Burglary: The Offender's Perspective." Pp. 181–200 in *Coping With Burglary*. Edited by R. Clarke and T. Hope. Boston: Nijhoff.

———. 1986. "The Impact of Prescribing on the Crimes of Opioid Users." *British Journal of Addiction* 81: 265–273.

Benson, M. L. 1985. "Denying the Guilty Mind: Accounting for Involvement in White Collar Crime." *Criminology* 23: 585–607.

Benson, M. L., and E. Walker. 1988. "Sentencing the White-Collar Offender." *American Sociological Review* 53: 294–302.

Bentele, U. 1985. "The Death Penalty in Georgia: Still Arbitrary." *Washington University Law Quarterly* 62: 573–646.

Bentham, J. 1892. *Introduction to the Principles of Morals and Legislation*. Oxford: Clarendon Press.

Berger, R. 1982. *Death Penalties: The Supreme Court's Obstacle Course*. Cambridge, MA: Harvard University Press.

Berk, R. A., S. Messinger, D. Rauma, and J. E. Berecochea. 1983. "Prisons as Self-Regulating Systems: A Comparison of Historical Patterns in California for Male and Female Offenders." *Law & Society Review* 17: 547–586.

Berk, R. A., and S. C. Ray. 1982. "Selection Biases in Sociological Data." *Social Science Research* 11: 352–398.

Berkowitz, E., and K. McQuaid. 1980. *Creating the Welfare State: The Political Economy of Twentieth Century Reform*. New York: Praeger.

Berkowitz, L. 1968. "Impulse, Aggression, and the Gun." *Psychology Today* 2: 19–24.

Berlin, F., and F. W. Schaef. 1985. "Laboratory Assessment of the Paraphilias and Their Treatment with

Antandrogenic Moderation." Pp. 273–305 in *Handbook of Psychiatric Diagnostic Procedures*. Vol. 2. Edited by R. C. W. Hall and T. P. Beresford. New York: Spectrum.

Berman, D. M. 1978. *Death on the Job*. New York: Monthly Review Press.

Berman, J. 1987. *Police Administration and Progressive Reform*. New York: Greenwood.

Bernard, T. 1981. "The Distinction Between Conflict and Radical Criminology." *The Journal of Criminal Law and Criminology* 72: 362–379.

———. 1984. "Control Criticisms of Strain Theories: An Assessment of Theoretical and Empirical Adequacy." *Journal of Research in Crime and Delinquency* 21: 353–372.

———. 1990. "Angry Aggression Among the 'Truly Disadvantaged.'" *Criminology* 28: 73–96.

Berns, W. 1979. *For Capital Punishment: Crime and the Morality of the Death Penalty*. New York: Basic Books.

Bernstein, I. N., J. Cardascia, and C. E. Ross. 1979. "Defendant's Sex and Criminal Court Decisions." Pp. 329–354 in *Discrimination in Organizations*. Edited by R. Alvarez, K. Lutterman, and associates. San Francisco: Jossey-Bass.

Bernstein, I. N., E. Kick, J. T. Leung, and B. Schulz. 1977. "Charge Reduction: An Intermediary Stage in the Process of Labelling Criminal Defendants." *Social Forces* 56: 362–384.

Beschner, G. M., and H. W. Feldman. 1979. "Introduction." Pp. 1–17 in *Angel Dust: An Ethnographic Study of PCP Users*. Edited by H. W. Feldman, M. H. Agar, and G. M. Beschner. Lexington, MA: Lexington Books.

Bickle, G. S., and R. D. Peterson. 1991. "The Impact of Gender-Based Family Roles on Criminal Sentencing." *Social Problems* 38: 372–394.

Biderman, A., L. Johnson, J. McIntyre, and A. Wier. 1967. *Report on a Pilot Study in the District of Columbia on Victimization and Attitudes toward Law Enforcement. Field Surveys I of the President's Commission on Law Enforcement and Administration of Justice*. Washington, DC: U.S. Government Printing Office.

Biderman, A. D., J. P. Lynch, and J. L. Peterson. 1991. *Understanding Crime Incidence Statistics: Why the UCR Diverges from the NCS*. New York: Springer-Verlag.

Bieck, W., W. Spelmen, and T. Sweeney. 1991. "The Police Function." Pp. 59–95 in *Local Government Police Management*. Edited by W. Geller. Washington, DC: International City Management Association.

Bienen, L., N. Weiner, D. Denno, P. Allison, and D. Mills. 1988. "The Reimposition of Capital Punishment in New Jersey: The Role of Prosecutorial Discretion." *Rutgers Law Review* 41: 27–37.

Biernacki, Patrick. 1986. *Pathways from Heroin Addiction: Recovery Without Treatment*. Philadelphia: Temple University Press.

Bilionis, L. D. 1991. "Moral Appropriateness, Capital Punishment, and the *Lockett* Doctrine." *Journal of Criminal Law and Criminology* 82: 283–333.

Bittner, E. 1970. *The Functions of Police in Modern Society*. Bethesda, MD: U.S. National Institute of Mental Health.

———. 1983. "Legality and Workmanship." In *Control in the Police Organization*. Edited by M. Punch. Cambridge, MA: MIT Press.

———. 1974. "A Theory of Police: Florence Nightingale in Pursuit of Willie Sutton." Pp. 17–44 in *The Potential for Reform of Criminal Justice*. Edited by H. Jacob. Newbury Park, CA: Sage.

Black, C. L., Jr. 1978. *Capital Punishment: The Inevitability of Caprice and Mistake*. 2d ed. New York: Norton.

Black, D. J. 1970. "The Production of Crime Rates." *American Sociological Review* 35: 733–748.

———. 1976. *The Behavior of Law*. New York: Academic Press.

———. 1980. *The Manners and Customs of the Police*. New York: Academic Press.

Blackmore, J., and J. Welsh. 1983. "Selective Incapacitation: Sentencing According to Risk." *Crime and Delinquency* 29: 504–528.

Blackstock, N. 1975. *COINTELPRO: The FBI's Secret War on Political Freedom*. New York: Vintage Books.

Blaszczynski, A., and N. McConaghy, 1992. *Pathological Gambling and Criminal Behaviour*. Report to the Criminology Research Council. Canberra, Australia.

Blau, J. R., and P. M. Blau. 1982. "The Cost of Inequality: Metropolitan Structure and Violent Crime." *American Sociological Review* 47: 114–129.

Bloch, H., and A. Niederhoffer. 1958. *The Gang*. New York: Philosophical Library.

Block, A. A. 1978. "History and the Study of Organized Crime." *Urban Life* 6: 455–474.

————. 1979. "The Snowman Cometh: Coke in Progressive New York." *Criminology* 17 (May): 75–99.

Block, A. A., and W. J. Chambliss. 1981. *Organizing Crime*. New York: Elsevier North Holland.

Block, R. 1977. *Violent Crime*. Lexington, MA: Lexington Books.

Block, R., and C. R. Block, 1980. "Decisions and Data: The Transformation of Robbery Incidents into Official Robbery Statistics." *Journal of Criminal Law and Criminology* 71: 622–636.

Blok, A. 1974. *The Mafia of a Sicilian Village, 1860–1960*. New York: Harper & Row.

Blum-West, S., and T. J. Carter. 1983. "Bringing White-Collar Crimes Back in: An Examination of Crimes and Torts." *Social Problems* 30: 545–554.

Blumberg, A. S. 1967a. *Criminal Justice*. Chicago: Quadrangle Press.

————. 1967b. "The Practice of Law as a Confidence Game." *Law & Society Review* 1: 15–39.

Blumenthal, M. D., R. L. Kahn, F. M. Andrews, and K. B. Head. 1972. *Justifying Violence: Attitudes of American Men*. Ann Arbor, MI: Institute for Social Research.

Blumstein, A., and J. Cohen. 1980. "Sentencing Convicted Offenders: An Analysis of the Public's View." *Law and Society Review* 14: 223–261.

————. 1987. "Characterizing Criminal Careers." *Science* 237 (August): 985–991.

Blumstein, A., J. Cohen, and D. Nagin. 1978. *Deterrence and Incapacitation: Estimating the Effects of Criminal Sanctions on Crime Rates*. Washington, DC: National Academy of Sciences.

Blumstein, A., J. Cohen, S. Das, and S. Moitra. 1988. "Specialization and Seriousness During Adult Criminal Careers." *Journal of Quantitative Criminology* 4: 303–345.

Blumstein, A., J. Cohen, S. E. Martin, and M. Tonry. 1983. *Research on Sentencing: The Search for Reform*. Vol. 1. Washington, DC: National Academy Press.

Blumstein, A., J. Cohen, and R. Rosenfeld. 1991. "Trend and Deviation in Crime Rates: A Comparison of UCR and NCS Data for Burglary and Robbery." *Criminology* 29: 237–263.

Blumstein, A., J. Cohen, J. Roth, and C. Visher. 1986. *Criminal Careers and "Career Criminals."* Vols. 1 and 2. Washington, DC: National Academy Press.

Blumstein, A., J. Cohen, and A. M. Williams. 1993. *"The Racial Disproportionality of United States' Prison Populations."* Working draft, Unpublished manuscript, Heinz School, Carnegie-Mellon University, Pittsburgh, PA.

Blumstein, A., and E. Graddy. 1982. "Prevalence and Recidivism in Index Arrests: A Feedback Model." *Law & Society Review* 16: 265–290.

Blundell, W. E. 1978. "Equity Funding: I Did It for Jollies." In *Crime at the Top*. Edited by J. Johnson and J. Douglas. Philadelphia: Lippincott.

Bock, G. 1987. "Blood, Sweat and Fears." *Time*, September 28, 50–51.

Boggs, S. L. 1965. "Urban Crime Patterns." *American Sociological Review* 30: 899–908.

Bohannan, P. 1960. *African Homicide and Suicide*. Princeton, NJ: Princeton University Press.

Bohm, R. M. 1987. "American Death Penalty Attitudes: A Critical Examination of Recent Evidence." *Criminal Justice and Behavior* 14: 380–396.

————. 1992. "Retribution and Capital Punishment: Toward a Better Understanding of Death Penalty Opinion." *Journal of Criminal Justice* 20: 227–236.

Bohm, R. M., L. J. Clark, and A. F. Aveni. 1991. "Knowledge and Death Penalty Opinion: A Test of the Marshall Hypothesis." *Journal of Research in Crime and Delinquency* 28: 360–387.

Bohman, M. 1978. "Some Genetic Aspects of Alcoholism and Criminality: A Population of Adoptees." *Archives of General Psychiatry* 35: 269–276.

Bohman, M., C. R. Cloniger, S. Siguardsson, and A. L. von Knorring. 1982. "Predisposition to Petty Criminality in Swedish Adoptees." *Archives of General Psychiatry* 39: 1233–1241.

Boland, B., C. H. Conly, L. Warner, R. Sones, and W. Martin. 1989. *The Prosecution of Felony Arrests, 1986*. Washington, DC: U.S. Department of Justice, Bureau of Justice Statistics.

Bonanno, J. 1984. *A Man of Honor*. New York: Pocket Books.

Booth, A., D. R. Johnson, and H. M. Choldin. 1977. "Correlates of City Crime Rates: Victimization Surveys Versus Official Statistics." *Social Problems* 25: 187–197.

Bordua, D. 1958. "Juvenile Delinquency and 'Anomie': An Attempt at Replication." *Social Problems* 6 (Winter): 230–238.

————. 1984. "Gun Control and Opinion Measurement: Adversary Polling and Construction of Meaning." Pp. 51–70 in *Firearms and Violence: Issues of Public Policy.* Edited by D. B. Kates. Cambridge, MA: Ballinger.

Bordua, D., and E. Haurek. 1971. "The Police Budget's Lot: Components of the Increase in Local Police Expenditures, 1902–1960." Pp. 57–70 in *The Police in Urban Society.* Edited by H. Hahn. Beverly Hills, CA: Sage.

Bordua, D., and A. J. Reiss, Jr. 1967. "Law Enforcement." Pp.275–303 in *The Uses of Sociology.* Edited by P. Lazarsfeld, W. Sewell, and H. Wilensky. New York: Basic Books.

Boritch, H. 1992. "Gender and Criminal Court Outcomes: An Historical Analysis." *Criminology* 30: 293–325.

Bowers, W. J. 1983. "The Pervasiveness of Arbitrariness and Discrimination Under Post-*Furman* Statutes." *Journal of Criminal Law and Criminology* 74: 1067–1100.

————. 1984. *Legal Homicide: Death as Punishment in America, 1864–1982.* Boston: Northeastern University Press.

Bowers, W. J., and G. L. Pierce. 1975. "The Illusion of Deterrence in Isaac Ehrlich's Research on Capital Punishment." *Yale Law Journal* 85: 187–208.

Bowker, L. H. 1977. *Prisoner Subcultures.* Lexington, MA: Heath.

————. 1978. "Menstruation and Female Criminality: A New Look at the Data." Paper presented at the 1978 meeting of the American Society of Criminology, Dallas. November.

————. 1980. *Prison Victimization.* New York: Elsevier.

————. 1981. "Gender Differences in Prisoner Subcultures." Pp. 409–419 in *Women and Crime in America.* Edited by L. Bowker. New York: Macmillan.

————. 1982. "Victimizers and Victims in American Correctional Institutions." Pp. 63–76 in *Pains of Imprisonment.* Edited by R. Johnson and H. Toch. Beverly Hills, CA: Sage.

————. 1985. "Unemployment, Imprisonment, and Prison Overcrowding." *Contemporary Crises* 9: 209–228.

Box, S. 1987. *Recession, Crime and Punishment.* Totawa, NJ: Barnes and Noble.

Boyatzis, R. E. 1975. "The Predisposition Toward Alcohol-Related Interpersonal Aggression in Men." *Journal of Studies on Alcohol* 36: 1196–1207.

Boyer, Paul S. 1968. *Purity in Print: The Vice Society Movement and Book Censorship in America.* New York: Charles Scribner's Sons.

Bradley, R. J. 1984. "Trends in State Crime-Control Legislation." In Search Group, Inc. *Information Policy and Crime Control Strategies.* Washington, DC: U.S. Department of Justice.

Brady, J. P. 1983. "Arson, Urban Economy and Organized Crime: The Case of Boston." *Social Problems* 31: 1–27.

————. 1984. "The Social Economy of Arson: Vandals, Gangsters, Bankers and Officials in the Making of an Urban Problem." *Research in Law, Deviance and Social Control.* Edited by S. Spitzer and A. Scull. Greenwich, CT: JAI Press. 6: 199–242.

Braithwaite, J. 1981. "The Myth of Social Class and Criminality Reconsidered." *American Sociological Review* 46: 36–57.

————. 1984. *Corporate Crime in the Pharmaceutical Industry.* London: Routledge & Kegan Paul.

Braly, M. 1976. *False Starts.* Boston: Little, Brown.

Brandl, S., and F. Horvath. 1991. "Crime Victim Evaluation Of Police Investigative Performance." *Journal of Criminal Justice* 19: 2: 109–121.

Brandl, S., J. Frank, R. Worden, and T. Bynum. 1993. "Global and Incident Specific Attitudes Toward the Police." Unpublished manuscript. Cincinnati, OH: University of Cincinnati.

Branfman, F. 1978. "The Secret Wars of the CIA." Pp. 90–100 in *Uncloaking the CIA.* Edited by H. Frazier. New York: Macmillan.

Brantingham, P. J., and P. L. Brantingham. 1984. *Patterns in Crime.* New York: Macmillan.

Brecher, E. M., and the editors of *Consumer Reports.* 1972. *Licit & Illicit Drugs.* Boston: Little, Brown.

Breggin, P. 1975. "Psychosurgery for the Control of Violence: A Critical Review." Pp. 350–391 in *Neural Bases of Violence and Aggression.* Edited by W. Field and W. Sweed. St. Louis: Green.

Breggin, P. R. 1979. *Electroshock: Its Brain-Disabling Effects.* New York: Springer.

Briar, S., and I. Piliavin. 1965. "Delinquency, Situational Inducements, and Commitment to Conformity." *Social Problems* 13: 33–45.

Bridges, G., and R. Crutchfield. 1988. "Law, Social Standing and Racial Disparities in Imprisonment." *Social Forces* 66: 699–724.

Brill, S. 1977. *Firearms Abuse: A Research and Policy Report.* Washington, DC: The Police Foundation.

Brod, H. 1988. "Pornography and the Alienation of Male Sexuality." *Social Theory and Practice* 14: 3: 265–284.

Boderick, J. 1987. *Police in a Time of Change.* 2d ed. Prospect Heights, IL: Waveland Press.

Brodeur, P. 1974. *Expendable Americans.* New York: Viking Press.

Brody, J. 1976. "Incompetent Surgery Is Found Not Isolated." *New York Times,* January 27, 1 *passim.*

Brown, J. W., D. Glaser, E. Waxer, and G. Geis. 1974. "Turning Off: Cessation of Marijuana Use After College." *Social Problems* 21 (April): 527–538.

Brown, M. 1981. *Working the Streets.* New York: Russell Sage Foundation.

Brown, R. 1975. *Strain of Violence: Historical Studies of American Violence and Vigilantism.* New York: Oxford University Press.

Brown, R. I. F. 1987. "Pathological Gambling and Associated Patterns of Crime: Comparisons with Alcohol and Other Drug Addictions." *Journal of Gambling Behavior* 3: 98–114.

Browne, A. 1987. *When Battered Women Kill.* New York: Free Press.

Brownmiller, S. 1975. *Against Our Will: Men, Women, and Rape.* New York: Simon & Schuster.

Bruce-Briggs, B. 1976. "The Great American Gun War." *The Public Interest* 45: 37–62.

Bryan, J. H. 1965. "Apprenticeships in Prostitution." *Social Problems* 12: 287–297.

Buffalo, M. D., and J. W. Rogers. 1971. "Behavioral Norms, Moral Norms, and Attachment: Problems of Deviance and Conformity." *Social Problems* 19: 101–113.

Buikhuisen, W. 1987. "Cerebral Dysfunction and Persistent Juvenile Delinquency." In *The Causes of Crime.* Edited by S. A. Mednick, T. E. Moffitt, and S. A. Stack. New York: Cambridge University Press.

Buikhuisen, W., and S. A. Mednick. 1988. *Explaining Criminal Behavior.* New York: Brill.

Bullogh, V. 1980. *Sexual Variance in Society and History.* Chicago: University of Chicago Press.

Bureau of Justice Statistics. 1982. *Households Touched by Crime, 1981.* Washington, DC: U.S. Department of Justice.

———. 1983a. *Prisoners and Alcohol.* Washington, DC: U.S. Department of Justice.

———. 1983b. *Prisoners and Drugs.* Washington, DC: U.S. Department of Justice.

———. 1985. *Jail Inmates.* Washington, DC: U.S. Department of Justice.

———. 1986a. *Criminal Victimization in the U.S., 1984.* Washington, DC: U.S. Government Printing Office.

———. 1986b. *Electronic Fund Transfer Systems Fraud.* Washington, DC: U.S. Government Printing Office.

———. 1987a. *Bureau of Justice Statistics Annual Report, 1986.* Washington, DC: U.S. Government Printing Office.

———. 1987b. *Criminal Victimization, 1986.* Washington, DC: U.S. Department of Justice.

———. 1987c. *Federal Offenses and Offenders: White Collar Crime.* Washington, DC: U.S. Government Printing Office.

———. 1988a. *Households Touched by Crime, 1987.* Washington, DC: U.S. Department of Justice.

———. 1988b. *Criminal Victimization, 1987.* Washington, DC: U.S. Department of Justice.

———. 1988c. *Drug Use and Crime.* Washington, DC: U.S. Department of Justice. July.

———. 1989. *Criminal Victimization in the United States, 1987.* Washington, DC: U.S. Department of Justice.

———. 1990. *Criminal Victimization in the US, 1988.* Washington, DC: US Government Printing Office.

———. 1991a. *Drugs and Crime Facts, 1991.* Rockville, MD: U.S. Department of Justice.

———. 1991b. *Correctional Populations in the United States, 1989.* Washington, DC: Bureau of Justice Statistics.

———. 1992a. *Justice Expenditure and Employment, 1990.* Washington, DC: U.S. Department of Justice.

———. 1992b. *Criminal Victimization In The United States, 1991.* Washington, DC: Dept. of Justice.

———. 1992c. *Prisoners in 1991.* Washington, DC: U.S. Department of Justice.

———. 1992d. *Prisons and Prisoners in the United States.* Washington, DC: U.S. Department of Justice.

———. 1993. *National Update.* Volume II, No. 3. Washington, DC: U.S. Department of Justice.

Bureau of Labor Statistics. 1987. *Employment and Earnings.* Washington, DC: U.S. Department of Labor.

———. 1989. *Employment and Earnings. Bulletin 2307.* Washington, DC: U.S. Department of Labor.

Bureau of National Affairs. 1976. "White-Collar Justice: A BNA Special Report on White-Collar Crime." *United States Law Weekly* 44: 38–53.

Burgess, E. W. 1925. "The Growth of the City." Pp. 47–62 in *The City.* Edited by R. E. Park and E. W. Burgess. Chicago: University of Chicago Press.

Burkett, S. R., and B. O. Warren. 1987. "Religiosity, Peer Associations, and Adolescent Marijuana Use: A Panel Study of Underlying Causal Structures." *Criminology* 25: 109–131.

Burkhart, K. W. 1973. *Women in Prison.* Garden City, NY: Doubleday.

Burrows, W. 1976. *Vigilante!* New York: Harcourt Brace Jovanovich.

Bursik, R. J., Jr., and H. G. Grasmick. 1993. "Economic Deprivation and Neighborhood Crime Rates, 1960–1980." *Law and Society Review* forthcoming.

Burton, J. F. 1966. "An Economic Analysis of Sherman Act Criminal Cases." In *Sherman Act Indictments 1955–1965.* Edited by J. M. Clabault and J. F. Burton. New York: Federal Legal Publications.

Burton, V., F. T. Cullen, and L. F. Travis III. 1987. "The Collateral Consequences of a Felony Conviction: A National Study of State Statutes." *Federal Probation* 51: 52–60.

Business Week. 1981. "The Spreading Danger of Computer Crime." April 20.

Buzawa, E. 1982. "Police Officer Response to Domestic Legislation in Michigan." *Journal of Police Science and Administration* 10: 415–424.

Byles, D. W. 1968. "Abuse Control Laws and the Drug Industry." Pp. 39–50 in *Amphetamine Abuse.* Edited by J. R. Russo. Springfield, IL: Thomas.

Bynam, A. E. 1988. "Eighth and Fourteenth Amendments—The Death Penalty Survives." *Journal of Criminal Law and Criminology* 78: 1080–1118.

Byrne, J., and R. Sampson. 1984. *The Social Ecology of Crime: Theory, Research and Public Policy.* Chicago: University of Chicago Press.

Cahalan, M. W., 1986. *Historical Corrections Statistics in the United States, 1850–1984.* Washington, DC: U.S. Department of Justice, Bureau of Justice Statistics.

Cain, M. 1979. "Trends in the Sociology of Police Work." *International Journal of the Sociology of Law* 7: 143–167.

Calevita, K. 1983. "The Demise of the Occupational Safety and Health Administration: A Case Study in Symbolic Action." *Social Problems* 30: 437–448.

California Assembly Committee on Criminal Procedure. 1968. *Deterrent Effects of Criminal Sanctions.* Sacramento: Assembly of the State of California.

Callahan, C., and F. Rivara. 1992. "Urban High School Youth and Handguns." *Journal of the American Medical Association* 267: 3038–3042.

Campbell, J., and L. Lindberg. 1990. "Property Rights and the Organization of Economic Activity by the State." *American Sociological Review* 55: 634–647.

Cameron, M. O. 1964. *The Booster and the Snitch: Department Store Shoplifting.* Glencoe, IL: Free Press.

Campagna, D. S., and D. L. Poffenberger. 1988. *The Sexual Trafficking in Children.* Dover, MA: Auburn.

Cannon, B. 1973–1974. "Is the Exclusionary Rule in Failing Health? Some New Data and a Plea Against a Precipitous Conclusion." *Kentucky Law Journal* 62: 681–730.

Cantor, D., and K. C. Land. 1985. "Unemployment and Crime Rates in the Post-World War II U.S.: A Theoretical and Empirical Analysis." *American Sociological Review* 50: 317–332.

———. 1991. "Exploring Possible Temporal Relationships of Unemployment and Crime: A Comment on Hale and Sabbagh." *Journal of Research in Crime and Delinquency* 28: 418–425.

Cappell, C. L., and G. Sykes. 1991. "Prison Commitments, Crime and Unemployment: A Theoretical and Empirical Specification for the U.S., 1933–1985." *Journal of Quantitative Criminology* 7: 155–199.

Carey, J. T., and J. Mandel. 1968. "San Francisco Bay Area 'Speed' Scene." *Journal of Health and Social Behavior* 9: 164–174.

Carrington, F. 1977. "Victim's Rights Litigation: A Wave of the Future?" *University of Richmond Law Review* 11: 447–470.

———. 1978a. "Victim's Rights: A New Tort." *Trial* (June): 39–41.

———. 1978b. *Neither Cruel Nor Unusual.* New Rochelle, NY: Arlington Press.

Carroll, L. 1988 (originally published in 1974). *Hacks, Blacks and Cons.* Prospect Heights, IL: Waveland Press.

Carroll, L., and C. P. Cornell. 1985. "Racial Composition, Sentencing Reforms and Rates of Incarceration, 1970–1980." *Justice Quarterly* 2: 473–490.

Carroll, L., and P. I. Jackson. 1983. "Inequality, Opportunity, and Crime Rates in Central Cities." *Criminology* 21: 178–194.

Carroll, M. 1985. "Wachtler Urges Legislators to Approve Court Changes." *New York Times*, April 23, B2.

Carrow, D. 1980. *Crime Victims Compensation: U.S. Department of Justice Program Model.* Washington, DC: U.S. Government Printing Office.

Carter, B. 1987. "The Roles of Peers in Sex Role Socialization." In *Current Conceptions of Sex Roles and Sex Typing: Theory and Research.* Edited by B. Carter. New York: Praeger.

Carter, D., and A. Sapp. 1991. *Police Education and Minority Recruitment.* Washington, DC: Police Executive Research Forum.

Carter, D., A. Sapp, and D. Stephens. 1988. "Higher Education as a Bona Fide Occupational Qualification for Police." *American Journal of Police* 7: 1–27.

———. 1989. *The State of Police Education.* Washington, DC: Police Executive Research Forum.

Carter, R. L. 1974. *The Criminal's Image of the City.* Unpublished dissertation. University of Oklahoma, Department of Geography.

Carter, R. M., and L. T. Wilkins. 1976. "Caseloads: Some Conceptual Models." In *Probation, Parole and Community Corrections.* Edited by R. M. Carter and L. T. Wilkins. New York: Wiley.

Cates, J. A. 1989. "Adolescent Male Prostitution by Choice." *Child and Adolescent Social Work* 6 (2) 151–156.

Cernkovich, S. A. 1978. "Value Orientation and Delinquency Involvement." *Criminology* 15: 443–458.

Cernkovich, S. A., P. Giordano, and M. Pugh. 1985. "Chronic Offenders: The Missing Cases in Self-Report Delinquency Research." *Journal of Criminal Law and Criminology* 71: 56–67.

Chaiken, J. 1987. "Tabulations of Adjusted Crime Commission Rates." Appendix A in *Identifying High-Rate Serious Criminals from Official Records.* By J. Rolph and J. Chaiken. Rand Report R-3433-NIJ. Santa Monica, CA: Rand Corporation.

Chaiken, J., and M. Chaiken. 1982. *Varieties of Criminal Behavior.* Rand Report R-2814-NIJ. Santa Monica, CA: Rand Corporation.

———. 1990. "Drugs and Predatory Crime." In *Drugs and Crime.* Edited by M. Tonry and J. Wilson. Chicago: University of Chicago Press. 203–240.

Chaiken, J., M. Chaiken, and W. Rhodes. 1993. "Predicting Violent Behavior and Classifying Violent Offenders." In *Understanding and Preventing Violence, Volume 4.* Edited by Albert J. Reiss and Jeffrey A. Roth. Washington, DC: National Academy Press.

Chaiken, J., P. Greenwood, and J. Petersilia. 1977. "The Criminal Investigation Process." *Policy Analysis* 3: 187–217.

Chaiken, M., and J. Chaiken. 1985. *Who Gets Caught Doing Crime?* Final Report to the Bureau of Justice Statistics, Grant No. 84-BJ-CX-0003. Los Angeles: Hamilton, Rabinovitz, Szanton, and Alschuler.

———. 1990. *Redefining the Career Criminal: Priority Prosecution of High-Rate Dangerous Offenders.* Washington, DC: National Institute of Justice.

Chaiken, M., and B. Johnson. 1988. *Characteristics of Different Types of Drug-Involved Offenders.* Washington, DC: National Institute of Justice.

Chambliss, W. J. 1964. "A Sociological Analysis of the Law of Vagrancy." *Social Problems* 12: 67–77.

———. 1971. "Vice, Corruption, Bureaucracy, and Power." *Wisconsin Law Review* 4: 1150–1173.

———. 1974. "The State, the Law, and the Definition of Behavior as Criminal or Delinquent." In *Handbook of Criminology.* Edited by D. Glaser. Chicago: Rand McNally.

———. 1976. "Functional and Conflict Theories of Crime." Pp. 1–28 in *Whose Law? What Order?* Edited by W. Chambliss and M. Mankoff. New York: Wiley.

———. 1984. "Crime Rates and Crime Myths." Pp. 167–177 in *Criminal Law in Action.* Edited by W. J. Chambliss. New York: John Wiley.

———. 1988. *On the Take: From Petty Crooks to Presidents.* 2d ed. Bloomington: Indiana University Press.

Chambliss, W. J., and R. Seidman. 1982. *Law, Order, and Power.* 2d ed. Reading, MA: Addison-Wesley.

Chandler, E. W. 1973. *Women in Prison.* Indianapolis, IN: Bobbs-Merrill.

Chatterton, M. 1983. "Police Work and Assault Charges." Pp. 194–222 in *Control in the Police Organization*. Edited by M. Punch. Cambridge, MA: MIT Press.

Cheatwood, D. 1985. "Capital Punishment and Corrections: Is There an Impending Crisis?" *Crime and Delinquency* 31: 461–479.

Chesney–Lind, M. 1973. "Judicial Enforcement of the Female Sex Role: The Family Court and the Female Delinquent." *Issues in Criminology* 8: 51–69.

———. 1986. "Women and Crime: The Female Offender." *Signs: Journal of Women in Culture and Society* 12: 78–96.

Chevigny, P. 1969. *Police Power*. New York: Vintage Books.

Chibnall, S., and P. Saunders. 1977. "Worlds Apart: Notes on the Social Relativity of Corruption." *British Journal of Sociology* 8: 138–153.

Chilton, B. S. 1991. *Prisons under the Gavel: The Federal Court Takeover of Georgia Prisons*. Columbus: Ohio State University Press.

Chilton, R. 1964. "Continuity in Delinquency Area Research: A Comparison for Baltimore, Detroit and Indianapolis." *American Sociological Review* 24 (February): 71–83.

———. 1980. "Criminal Statistics in the United States." *Journal of Criminal Law and Criminology* 71: 56–67.

———. 1986. "Age, Sex, Race, and Arrest Trends for Twelve of the Nation's Largest Central Cities." In *The Social Ecology of Crime: Theory, Research, and Public Policy*. Edited by J. Byrne and R. Sampson. New York: Springer-Verlag.

Chilton, R., and J. Galvin. 1985. "Race, Crime, and Criminal Justice." *Crime and Delinquency* 31: 3–14.

Chilton, R., and A. Spielberger. 1971. "Is Delinquency Increasing? Age Structure and the Crime Rate." *Social Forces* 49: 487–493.

Chiricos, T. G. 1987. "Rates of Crime and Unemployment: An Analysis of Aggregate Research Evidence." *Social Problems* 34: 187–212.

Chiricos, T. G., and W. D. Bales. 1991. "Unemployment and Punishment: An Empirical Assessment." *Criminology* 29: 701–724.

Chiricos, T., and M. Delone. 1992. "Labor Surplus and Punishment: A Review and Assessment of Theory and Evidence." *Social Problems* 39: 421–446.

Chomsky, N. 1975. "Introduction." In *COINTELPRO*. Edited by N. Blackstock. New York: Vintage Books.

———. 1979. *From Genesis to Genocide*. Cambridge, MA: MIT Press.

Chorover, S. 1980. "Violence: A Localizable Problem." In *The Psychosurgery Debate*. Edited by E. Valenstein. San Francisco: Freeman.

Christenson, J. A., and C. Yang. 1976. "Dominant Values in American Society: An Exploratory Analysis." *Sociology and Social Research* 60: 461–473.

Christiansen, E. M. 1988. "1987 U.S. Gross Annual Wager." *Gaming & Wagering Business* 9 (July 15): 7–20, 37.

Christiansen, E. M., and P. A. McQueen. 1992. "The Gross Annual Wager of the United States — Part I: Handle." *Gaming and Wagering Business* 13: 22–37.

Christiansen, K. O. 1977a. "A Preliminary Study of Criminality Among Twins." In *Biosocial Bases of Criminal Behavior*. Edited by S. A. Mednick and K. O. Christiansen. New York: Gardner Press.

———. 1977b. "A Review of Studies of Criminality Among Twins." In *Biosocial Bases of Criminal Behavior*. Edited by S. A. Mednick and K. O. Christiansen. New York: Gardner Press.

Christianson, S. 1981. "Our Black Prisons." *Crime and Delinquency* 27: 364–375.

Christie, N. 1993. *Crime Control as Industry*. London: Routledge.

Civil Liberties. 1992–1993. 378 (Winter): 7.

Clark, J., and E. Wenninger. 1963. "Goal Orientations and Illegal Behavior Among Juveniles." *Social Forces* 42: 49–59.

Clark, J. P., and R. Sykes. 1974. "Some Determinants of Police Organization and Practice in a Modern Industrial Democracy." Pp. 445–494 in *Handbook of Criminology*. Edited by D. Glaser. Chicago: Rand McNally.

Clausen, J. A. 1977. "Early History of Narcotics Use and Narcotics Legislation in the United States." Pp. 23–29 in *Drugs and Politics*. Edited by P. E. Rock. New Brunswick, NJ: Transaction Books.

———. 1986. *The Life Course: A Sociological Perspective*. New York: Prentice-Hall.

Clear, T. R. 1987. "Punishment and Control in Probation and Parole Supervision." Paper presented to the American Society of Criminology, Montreal. November.

_____. 1988. *Statistical Prediction in Corrections*. Santa Monica, CA: Rand Corporation.

Clear, T. R., and K. W. Gallagher. 1985. "Probation and Parole Supervision: A Review of Current Classification Practices." *Crime and Delinquency* 31: 423.

Clear, T. R., P. Harris, and A. Record. 1982. "Managing the Costs of Incarceration." *The Prison Journal* 62: 1.

Clear, T. R., and V. O'Leary. 1982. *Controlling the Offender in the Community*. Lexington, MA: Lexington Books.

Clear, T. R., C. A. Shapiro, and S. Flynn. 1986. "Identifying High–Risk Offenders for Intensive Supervision." *Federal Probation* 40: 24.

Clear, T. R., C. A. Shapiro, S. Flynn, and E. Chayet. 1988. *Final Report of the Probation Development Project*. New Brunswick, NJ: Rutgers University Program Resources Center.

Cleckley, H. 1976. *The Mask of Sanity*. St. Louis: Mosby.

Clemmer, D. 1958 (originally published in 1940). *The Prison Community*. New York: Holt, Rinehart & Winston.

Clinard, M. B. 1964. *Anomie and Deviant Behavior*. New York: Free Press.

Clinard, M. B., and R. Quinney. 1986. *Criminal Behavior Systems: A Typology*. 2d ed. Cincinnati: Anderson.

Clinard, M. B., and P. C. Yeager. 1980. *Corporate Crime*. New York: Free Press.

Clinard, M. B., P. C. Yeager, J. Brissette, D. Petrashek, and E. Harries. 1979. *Illegal Corporate Behavior*. Washington, DC: U.S. Government Printing Office.

Cloward, R. A. 1960. "Social Control in the Prison." In *Theoretical Studies in Social Organization of the Prison*. Edited by R. A. Cloward et al. Social Science Research Pamphlet 15. New York: Social Science Research Council.

Cloward, R. A., and L. E. Ohlin. 1960. *Delinquency and Opportunity*. New York: Free Press.

Cohen, A. 1955. *Delinquent Boys*. New York: Free Press.

_____. 1990. "Criminal Actors: Natural Persons and Collectivities." In *New Directions in the Study of Justice, Law, and Social Control*. Edited by School of Justice Studies. New York: Plenum.

Cohen, J. 1983. "Incapacitation as a Strategy for Crime Control: Possibilities and Pitfalls." Pp. 1–84 in *Crime and Justice: An Annual Review of Research*. Vol. 5. Edited by M. Tonry and N. Morris. Chicago: University of Chicago Press.

_____. 1986. "Research on Criminal Careers: Individual Frequency Rates and Offense Seriousness." Appendix B in *Criminal Careers and "Career Criminals."* Vol. 1. Edited by A. Blumstein, J. Cohen, J. Roth, and C. Visher. Washington, DC: National Academy Press.

Cohen, Jacqueline, and J. Canela-Cacho. Forthcoming. "Incarceration and Violent Crime: 1965–88" *Understanding and Preventing Violence, Vol. 4*. Edited by Albert J. Reiss, Jr., and Jeffrey A. Roth. Washington, DC: National Academy Press.

Cohen, J., P. Alexander, and C. Wofsky. 1988. "Prostitution and AIDS: Public Policy Issues." *AIDS & Public Policy Journal* 3 (2) 16–22.

Cohen, J., and M. Lichbach. 1982. "Alternative Measures of Crime: A Statistical Evaluation." *Sociological Quarterly* 23: 253–266.

Cohen, J., and M. H. Tonry. 1983. "Sentencing Reforms and Their Impacts." Pp. 305–459 in *Research on Sentencing: The Search for Reform*. Vol. 2. Edited by A. Blumstein, J. Cohen, S. E. Martin, and M. H. Tonry. Washington, DC: National Academy Press.

Cohen, L. E. 1981. "Modeling Crime Trends: A Criminal Opportunity Perspective." *Journal of Research in Crime and Delinquency* 18: 138–164.

Cohen, L. E., and M. Felson. 1979. "Social Change and Crime Rates Trends: A Routine Activities Approach." *American Sociological Review* 44: 588–608.

Cohen, L. E., M. Felson, and K. C. Land. 1980. "Property Crime Rates in the U.S.: A Macrodynamics Analysis 1947-1977 With Ex Ante Forecasts for the Mid 1980's." *American Journal of Sociology* 86: 90–118.

Cohen, L. E., J. Kluegal, and K. Land. 1981. "Social Inequality and Criminal Victimization." *American Sociological Review* 46: 505–524.

Cohen, R. L. 1992. *1989 Survey of Inmates of Local Jails: Drunk Driving*. Washington, DC: Bureau of Justice Statistics.

Cohn, E., L. Kidder, and J. Harvey. 1978. "Crime Prevention vs. Victimization Prevention: The Psychology of Two Different Reactions." *Victimology* 3: 285–296.

Cohn, S. F., and J. E. Gallagher. 1984. "Gay Movements and Legal Change: Some Aspects of the Dynamics of a Social Problem." *Social Problems* 32: 72–86.

Cole, S. 1975. "The Growth of Scientific Knowledge: Theories of Deviance as a Case Study." Pp. 175–220 in *The Idea of Social Structure: Papers in Honor of Robert K. Merton.* Edited by L. A. Coser. New York: Harcourt Brace Jovanovich.

Coleman, J. W. 1985a. "Law and Power: The Sherman Antitrust Act and Its Enforcement in the Petroleum Industry." *Social Problems* 32: 264–274.

———. 1985b. *The Criminal Elite: The Sociology of White Collar Crime.* New York: St. Martin's Press.

———. 1987. "Toward an Integrated Theory of White Collar Crime." *American Journal of Sociology* 93: 406–439.

———. 1989. *The Criminal Elite: The Sociology of White Collar Crime.* 2d ed. New York: St. Martin's Press.

Coleman, L. 1974. "Perspectives on the Medical Research of Violence." *American Journal of Orthopsychiatry* 44: 675–687.

Collins, J. J. 1981. *Drinking and Crime: Perspectives on the Relationship between Alcohol Consumption and Criminal Behavior.* New York: Guilford Press.

Collins, J. J., and W. E. Schlenger. 1988. "Acute and Chronic Effects of Alcohol Use on Violence." *Journal of Studies on Alcohol* 49: 516–521.

Collins, J. J., R. L. Hubbard, and J. V. Rachal. 1985. "Expensive Drug Use and Illegal Income: A Test of Explanatory Hypotheses." *Criminology* 23: 743–764.

Colton, K. W. 1978. *Police Computer Technology.* Lexington, MA: Heath.

Coltrane, S., and N. Hickman. 1992. "The Rhetoric of Rights and Needs: Moral Discourse in the Reform of Child Custody and Child Support Laws." *Social Problems* 39: 400–420.

Columbia Journal of Law and Social Problems. 1969. "Sentencing Selective Service Violators: A Judicial Wheel of Fortune." 5: 164–196.

Colvin, M. 1992. *The Penitentiary in Crisis.* Albany: State University of New York Press, 1992.

Colvin, M., and J. Pauly. 1983. "A Critique of Criminology: Toward an Integrated Structural-Marxist Theory of Delinquency Production." *American Journal of Sociology* 89: 513–551.

Commission on Obscenity and Pornography. 1970. *The Report of the Commission on Obscenity and Pornography.* New York: Bantam Books.

Commission on the Review of the National Policy Towards Gambling. 1976. *Gambling in America.* Washington, DC: U.S. Government Printing Office.

Conklin, J. E. 1971. "Criminal Environment and Support for the Law." *Law & Society Review* 6: 247–259.

———. 1972. *Robbery and the Criminal Justice System.* Philadelphia: Lippincott.

———. 1975. *The Impact of Crime.* New York: Macmillan.

———. 1977. *Illegal But Not Criminal: Business Crime in America.* Englewood Cliffs, NJ: Prentice–Hall.

———. 1986. *Criminology.* 2d ed. New York: Macmillan.

———. 1992. *Criminology.* 4th ed. New York: Macmillan.

Connell, P. H. 1966. "Clinical Manifestations of the Treatment of Amphetamine Type of Dependence." *Journal of the American Medical Association* 196: 130–135.

Conrad, P., and J. W. Schneider. 1980. *Deviance and Medicalization: From Badness to Sickness.* St. Louis: Mosby.

———. 1992. *Deviance and Medicalization: From Badness to Sickness.* 3d ed. Columbus, OH: Merrill.

Cook, P. J. 1976. "A Strategic Choice Analysis of Robbery." Pp. 173–187 in *Sample Surveys of the Victims of Crime.* Edited by W. Skogan. Cambridge, MA: Ballinger.

———. 1979. "An Overview of Federal, State, and Local Firearms Regulations." Unpublished manuscript, Institute of Policy Sciences, Duke University.

———. 1981a. "The Saturday Night Special: An Assessment of Alternative Definitions from a Policy Perspective." *Journal of Criminal Law and Criminology* 72: 1735–1745.

———. 1981b. "The Effect of Gun Availability on Violent Crime Patterns." *The Annals of the American Academy of Political and Social Science* 455: 63–79.

———. 1983. "The Influence of Gun Availability on Violent Crime Patterns." Pp. 49–89 in *Crime and Justice: An Annual Review of Research.* Edited by M. Tonry and N. Morris. Chicago: University of Chicago Press.

———. 1985. "The Case of the Missing Victims: Gunshot Woundings in the National Crime Survey." *Journal of Quantitative Criminology* 1: 91–102.

———. 1986. "The Relationship Between Victim Resistance and Injury in Noncommercial Robbery." *Journal of Legal Studies* 15: 405–416.

Cook, P. J., and J. Blose. 1981. "State Programs for Screening Handgun Buyers." *The Annals of the American Academy of Political and Social Science* 455: 80–91.

Cooper, R. C., and P. E. Steiger. 1976. "Occupational Health Hazards — A National Crisis." *Los Angeles Times*, June 27, I1 *passim*.

Cordner, G. 1982. "While on Routine Patrol . . ." *American Journal of Police* 2: 94–112.

Cornish, D. B., and R. V. Clarke. 1986. *The Reasoning Criminal: Rational Choice Perspectives on Offending*. New York: Springer-Verlag.

Corporate Crime Reporter. 1987. "IRS Not Set Up to Monitor Whether Interest and Dividend Income to Business Is Being Reported." April 13, 5–6.

Corzine, J., and L. Huff-Corzine. 1992. "Racial Inequality and Black Homicide: An Analysis of Felony, Non-felony and Total Rates." *Journal of Contemporary Criminal Justice* 8: 150–165.

Coser, L. 1956. *The Functions of Social Conflict*. Glencoe, IL: Free Press.

Cover, J. P., and P. D. Thistle. 1988. "Time Series, Homicide, and the Deterrent Effect of Capital Punishment." *Southern Economic Journal* 54: 615–622.

Covington, J. 1985. "Gender Differences in Criminality Among Heroin Users." *Journal of Research in Crime and Delinquency* 22: 329–353.

Coyners, J. 1980. "Corporate and White-Collar Crime: A View by the Chairman of the House Subcommittee on Crime." *American Criminal Law Review* 17: 287–300.

Craft, M. 1978. "The Current States of XYY and XXY Syndromes: A Review of Treatment Implications." *International Journal of Law and Psychiatry* 1.

Crank, J. 1990. "The Influence of Environmental and Organizational Factors on Police Style." *Journal of Research in Crime and Delinquency* 27: 166–189.

Crank, J. and R. Langworthy. 1992. "An Institutional Perspective on Policing." *Journal of Criminal Law and Criminology* 83: 338–363.

Cressey, D. 1971. *Other People's Money*. Belmont, CA: Wadsworth.

———. 1976. "Restraints of Trade, Recidivism, and Delinquent Neighborhoods." In *Delinquency, Crime and Society*. Edited by J. Short. Chicago: University of Chicago Press.

Cressey, D. R. 1960. "Epidemiology and Individual Conduct: A Case from Criminology." *Pacific Sociological Review* 3: 47–58.

Crites, L. 1976. *The Female Offender*. Lexington, MA: Heath.

Cromwell, P. F., J. N. Olson, and D. W. Avary. 1991. *Breaking and Entering: An Ethnographic Analysis of Burglary*. Newbury Park, CA: Sage.

Crouch, B. M. 1980. *The Keepers: Prison Guards and Contemporary Corrections*. Springfield, IL: Thomas.

———. 1991. "Guard Work in Transition." *Dilemmas of Punishment. Rev. ed*. Edited by K. C. Haas and G. P. Alpert. Prospect Heights, IL: Waveland Press. 164–183.

Crouch, B. M., and J. W. Marquart. 1989. *An Appeal to Justice: Litigated Reform of Texas Prisons*. Austin: University of Texas Press.

Crowe, R. 1974. "An Adoption Study of Antisocial Personality." *Archives of General Psychiatry* 31: 785–791.

———. 1975. "An Adoptive Study of Psychopathy: Preliminary Results from Arrest Records and Psychiatric Hospital Records." In *Genetic Research in Psychiatry*. Edited by R. R. Fieve, D. Rosenthal, and H. Brill. Baltimore: Johns Hopkins University Press.

Cullen, F. T., B. G. Link, N. T. Wolfe, and J. Frank. 1985. "Social Dimensions of Correctional Officer Stress." *Justice Quarterly* 2: 505–534.

Cunningham, W., and T. Taylor. 1985. *The Hall-Crest Report*. Portland, OR: Chancellor.

Curtis, L. A. 1974. *Criminal Violence: National Patterns and Behavior*. Lexington, MA: Lexington Books.

Curtis, L. A. 1975. Violence, Race, and Culture. Lexington, MA: Lexington.

Daggett, L. R., and E. J. Rolde. 1980. "Decriminalization of Drunkenness: Effects on the Work of Suburban Police." *Journal of Studies on Alcohol* 41: 819–828.

Dahl, T. S. 1977. "State Intervention and Social Control in Nineteenth-Century Europe." *Contemporary Crises* 1: 163–187.

Dahrendorf, R. 1959. *Class and Class Conflict in Industrial Society*. Palo Alto, CA: Stanford University Press.

Dalton, K. 1961. "Menstruation and Crime." *British Medical Journal* 2: 1752–1753.

Daly, K. 1986. "Gender and White-Collar Crime." Paper presented at the 1986 meeting of the American Society of Criminology, Atlanta.

———. 1987a. "Structure and Practice of Familial-Based Justice in a Criminal Court." *Law & Society Review* 21: 267–290.

———. 1987b. "Discrimination in the Criminal Courts: Family, Gender and the Problem of Equal Treatment." *Social Forces* 66: 152–175.

———. 1989. "Gender and Varieties of White-Collar Crime." *Criminology* 27: 769–793.

Damon, A., H. W. Stoudt, and R. A. McFarland. 1966. *The Human Body in Equipment Design*. Cambridge, MA: Harvard University Press.

Damon, A., H. K. Bleibtreu, O. Elliot, and E. Giles. 1962. "Predicting Somatype from Body Measurements." *American Journal of Physical Anthropology* 20: 461–474.

D'Angelo, R. 1984. *The Social Organization of Sports Gambling: A Study in Conventionality and Deviance*. Ph.D. dissertation, Bryn Mawr College.

———. 1987. "Sports Gambling and the Media." *Arena Review* 11: 1–4.

Davidson, T. R. 1983. *Chicano Prisoners: The Key to San Quentin*. Prospect Heights, IL: Waveland Press.

Davies, T. 1983. "A Hard Look at What We Know (and Still Need to Learn) About the 'Costs' of the Exclusionary Rule: The NIJ Study and Other Studies of 'Lost' Arrests." *American Bar Foundation Research Journal* 1983: 611–690.

Davis, A. J. 1968. "Sexual Assaults in the Philadelphia Prison System and Sheriff's Vans." *Transaction* 6: 8–16.

Davis, F., and L. Munroe. 1968. "Head and Freaks: Patterns and Meanings of Drug Use among Hippies." *Journal of Health and Social Behavior* 9: 156–163.

Davis, K. 1961. "Prostitution." Pp. 275–276 in *Contemporary Social Problems*. Edited by R. K. Merton and R. A. Nisbet. New York: Harcourt, Brace & World.

Davis, K. C. 1975. *Police Discretion*. St. Paul: West.

———. 1977. *Discretionary Justice: A Preliminary Inquiry*. Chicago: University of Illinois Press.

Davis, N. 1972. "Labelling Theory in Deviance Research: A Critique and Reconsideration." *The Sociological Quarterly* 13: 447–474.

———. 1978. "Prostitution: Identity, Career, and Legal Economic Enterprise." Pp. 195–222 in *The Sociology of Sex*. Edited by J. Henslin and E. Sagarin. New York: Schocken Books.

———. 1980. *Sociological Constructions of Deviance*. 2d ed. Dubuque, IA: Brown.

———. 1986. "Abortion and Legal Policy." *Contemporary Crises* 10: 373–397.

Davis, S. 1983. "Restoring the Semblance of Order: Police Strategies in the Domestic Dispute." *Symbolic Interaction* 6: 261–278.

Dayan, M. 1986. "Payment of Costs in Death Penalty Cases." *Criminal Law Bulletin* 22: 18–28.

Decker, S. H. 1977. "Official Crime Rates and Victim Surveys: An Empirical Comparison." *Journal of Criminal Justice* 5: 47–54.

Defleur, L. B. 1975. "Biasing Influences on Drug Arrest Records: Implications for Deviance Research." *American Sociological Review* 40: 88–103.

DeFleur, M. L., and S. Ball-Rokeach. 1975. *Theories of Mass Communication*. New York: McKay.

DeFronzo, J. 1979. "Fear of Crime and Handgun Ownership." *Criminology* 17: 331–339.

Delgardo, E. A., et al. 1981. "Special Report: The Nature of Aggression During Epileptic Seizures." *New England Journal of Medicine* 30S: 711–716.

Denno, D. W. 1992. "'Death is Different' and Other Twists of Fate." *Journal of Criminal Law and Criminology* 83: 437–467.

Dentan, R. N. 1968. *The Semai: A Nonviolent People of Malaya*. New York: Holt, Rinehart & Winston.

Department of Health and Human Services. 1984. *Drug Abuse and Drug Abuse Research*. Rockville, MD: National Institute on Drug Abuse.

Department of Justice. 1977. *Uniform Crime Reports*. Washington, DC: U.S. Government Printing Office.

———. 1987. *Uniform Crime Reports*. Washington, DC: U.S. Government Printing Office.

Dershowitz, A. M. 1987. "Gotti Case Shows Flaws of Buying Witnesses." *The Buffalo News*, March 20, C3.

Devine, J., J. Sheley, and D. Smith. 1988. "Macroeconomic and Social-Control Policy Influences on Crime Rate Changes, 1948-1985." *American Sociological Review* 53: 407–420.

Devlin, P. 1965. *The Enforcement of Morals*. London: Oxford University Press.

DeZee, M. 1983. "Gun Control Legislation: Impact and Ideology." *Law and Policy Quarterly* 5: 367–379.

Dickson, D. T. 1977. "Bureaucracy and Morality: An Organizational Perspective on a Moral Crusade."

Pp. 31–34 in *Drugs and Politics.* Edited by P. E. Rock. New Brunswick, NJ: Transaction Books.

DiIulio, J. J., Jr. 1987. *Governing Prisons.* New York: Free Press.

_____. 1990. *Courts, Corrections, and the Constitution.* New York: Oxford University Press.

Dixon, D. 1980. " 'Class Law': The Street Betting Act of 1906." *International Journal of the Sociology of Law* 8: 101–128.

Doerner, W. G. 1983. "Why Does Johnny Reb Die When Shot? The Impact of Medical Resources Upon Lethality." *Sociological Inquiry* 53: 1–15.

Doerner, W. G., and J. C. Speir. 1986. "Stitch and Sew: The Impact of Medical Resources Upon Criminally Induced Lethality." *Criminology* 24: 319–330.

Dolinko, D. 1986. "Supreme Court Review—Forward: How to Criticize the Death Penalty." *Journal of Criminal Law and Criminology* 77: 546–601.

Domhoff, G. W. 1967. *Who Rules America?* Englewood Cliffs, NJ: Prentice-Hall.

_____. 1978. *The Powers That Be.* New York: Random House.

Dominick, J. R. 1973. "Crime and Law Enforcement on Prime Time Television." *Public Opinion Quarterly* 37: 241–250.

_____. 1978. "Crime and Law Enforcement in the Mass Media." Pp. 105–128 in *Deviance and Mass Media.* Edited by C. Winick. Beverly Hills, CA: Sage.

Donnerstein, E. 1984. "Erotica and Human Aggression." Pp. 127–154 in *Aggression: Theoretical and Empirical Reviews.* Edited by R. E. Geen and E. I. Donnerstein. New York: Academic Press.

Donnerstein, E. I., and D. G. Linz. 1986. "The Question of Pornography: It Is Not Sex, but Violence That Is an Obscenity in Our Society." *Psychology Today,* December, 56–59.

Donnerstein, E. I., D. G. Linz, and S. Pernod. 1987. *The Question of Pornography: Research Findings and Policy Implications.* New York: Free Press.

Dorn, D. S. 1969. "A Partial Test of the Delinquency Continuum Typology: Contracultures and Subcultures." *Social Forces* 47: 305–314.

Dowie, M. 1979. "Pinto Madness." In *Crisis in American Institutions.* 4th ed. Edited by J. Skolnick and E. Currie. Boston: Little, Brown.

Drass, K. A., and J. W. Spencer. 1987. "Accounting for Pre-sentencing Recommendations: Typologies and Probation Officers' Theory of Office." *Social Problems* 34: 277–293.

Dripps, D. 1986. "Living with *Leon.*" *Yale Law Journal* 95: 1405–1423.

Drug Enforcement Administration. 1985. *Drugs of Abuse.* Washington, DC: U.S. Department of Justice.

DuBow, F., E. McCabe, and G. Kaplan. 1979. *Reactions to Crime: A Critical Review of the Literature.* Washington, DC: U.S. Government Printing Office.

Dubro, J. 1986. *Mob Rule: Inside the Canadian Mafia.* Toronto: Totem Books.

Dugdale, R. 1970 (originally published in 1877). *The Jukes.* New York: Arno Press.

Duncan, D., and R. Gold. 1982. *Drugs and the Whole Person.* New York: Wiley.

Durham III, A. M. 1987. "Justice in Sentencing: The Role of Prior Record of Criminal Involvement." *Journal of Criminal Law and Criminology* 78: 614–643.

Durkheim, E. [1893] 1933. *The Division of Labor in Society.* Translated by G. Simpson. New York: Free Press.

_____. [1897] 1951. *Suicide.* Translated by G. Simpson. New York: Free Press.

_____. [1895] 1958. *The Rules of Sociological Method.* Translated by S. A. Soloway and J. H. Mueller. Glencoe, IL: Free Press.

Duster, T. 1970. *The Legislation of Morality.* New York: Free Press.

Dutton, D., and J. J. Browning. 1984. "Power Struggles and Intimacy Anxieties as Causative Factors of Wife Assault." In *Violence in Intimate Adult Relationships.* Edited by G. Russell. New York: Spectrum.

Dworkin, A. 1981. *Pornography: Men Possessing Women.* New York: Putnam.

_____. 1985. "Against the Male Flood: Censorship, Pornography and Equality." *Harvard Women's Law Journal* 8: 1–29.

Easterlin, R. 1978. "What Will 1984 Be Like? Socio-economic Implications of Recent Twists in Age Structure." *Demography* 15: 397–421.

Eck, J. 1983. *Solving Crimes.* Washington, DC: Police Executive Research Forum.

Eckerman, W. C., J. D. Gates, J. V. Rachel, and W. K. Poole. 1971. *Drug Usage and Arrest Charges: A Study of Drug Usage and Arrest Charges among Arrestees in Six Metropolitan Areas of the United States.* Washington, DC: U.S. Department of Justice.

Edelhertz, H. 1970. *The Nature, Impact, and Prosecution of White Collar Crime.* Washington, DC: U.S. Government Printing Office.

Edelman, M. 1964. *The Symbolic Uses of Politics.* Urbana: University of Illinois Press.

———. 1977. *Political Language.* New York: Academic Press.

———. 1988. *Constructing the Political Spectacle.* Chicago: University of Chicago Press.

Ehrlich, I. 1975. "The Deterrent Effect of Capital Punishment: A Question of Life and Death." *American Economic Review* 65: 397–417.

Ehrlich, I., and R. M. Mark. 1977. "Fear of Deterrence." *Journal of Legal Studies* 6: 293–316.

Ekland-Olson, S., W. R. Kelly, and M. Eisenbert. 1992. "Crime and Incarceration: Some Comparative Findings from the 1980s." *Crime and Delinquency* 38: 392–416.

Elias, R. 1983. *Victims of the System.* New Brunswick, NJ: Transaction Books.

———. 1986. *The Politics of Victimization: Victims, Victimology, and Human Rights.* New York: Oxford University Press.

———. 1990. "Which Victim Movement: The Politics of Victim Policy." Pp. 226–250 in *Victims of Crime: Problems, Policies, and Programs.* Edited by A. Lurigio, W. Skogan, and R. Davis. Newbury Park, CA: Sage.

Ellenberger, H. 1955. "Psychological Relationships Between the Criminal and His Victim." *Archives of Criminal Psychodynamics* 2: 257–290.

Ellenwood, H., A. Sudilovsky, and L. M. Nelson. 1973. "Evolving Behavior in the Clinical and Experimental Amphetamine (Model) Psychosis." *American Journal of Psychiatry* 130: 1088–1093.

Elliott, D., and S. Ageton. 1980. "Reconciling Race and Class Differences in Self-reported and Official Estimates of Delinquency." *American Sociological Review* 45: 95–110.

Elliott, D., S. Ageton, and R. Canter. 1979. "An Integrated Theoretical Perspective on Delinquent Behavior." *Journal of Research in Crime and Delinquency* 16: 3–27.

Elliott, D., S. Ageton, and D. Huizinga. Forthcoming. *Social Correlates of Delinquent Behavior.*

Elliott, D. S., S. S. Ageton, D. Huizinga, B. A. Knowles, and R. J. Canter. 1983. *The Prevalence and Incidence of Delinquent Behavior: 1976–1980: National Estimates of Delinquent Behavior by Sex, Race, Social Class and Other Selected Variables.* Boulder, CO: Behavioral Research Institute.

Elliott, D., D. Huizinga, and S. S. Ageton. 1985. *Explaining Delinquency and Drug Use.* Beverly Hills, CA: Sage.

Elliott, D., and H. Voss. 1974. *Delinquency and Dropout.* Lexington, MA: Lexington Books.

Ellis, L. 1982. "Genetics and Criminal Behavior: Evidence Through the End of the 1970s." *Criminology* 20: 43–66.

———. 1986. "Evidence of Neuroandrogenic Etiology of Sex Roles from a Combined Analysis of Human, Nonhuman Primate, and Nonprimate Mammalian Studies." *Personality and Individual Differences* 7: 519–552.

Ellsworth, P. C. 1988. "Unpleasant Facts: The Supreme Court's Response to Empirical Research on Capital Punishment." In *Challenging Capital Punishment: Legal and Social Science Approaches.* Edited by K. C. Haas and J. A. Inciardi. Newbury Park, CA: Sage.

Ellsworth, P. C., and L. Ross. 1983. "Public Opinion and Capital Punishment: A Close Examination of the Views of Abolitionists and Retentionists." *Crime and Delinquency* 29: 116–169.

Emerson, D. D. 1983. *Grand Jury Reform: A Review of Key Issues.* Washington, DC: U.S. Department of Justice, National Institute of Justice.

Emerson, R., and S. Messinger. 1977. "The Micro-Politics of Trouble." *Social Problems* 25: 121–134.

Empey, L. 1956. "Social Class and Occupational Aspirations: A Comparison of Absolute and Relative Measurement." *American Sociological Review* 45: 95–110.

———. 1982. *American Delinquency: Its Meaning and Construction.* Homewood, IL: Dorsey.

Empey, L. T., and S. G. Lubeck. 1971. *Explaining Delinquency.* Lexington, MA: Heath.

Empey, L. T., and M. C. Stafford. 1991. *American Delinquency: Its Meaning and Construction.* Belmont, CA: Wadsworth.

England, R. W. 1960. "A Theory of Middle Class Juvenile Delinquency." *Journal of Criminal Law, Criminology and Police Science* 50: 535–540.

English, T. J. 1991. *The Westies.* New York: St. Martin's.

Ennis, P. H. 1967. *Criminal Victimization in the United States: A Report of a National Survey. President's Commission on Law Enforcement and the Administration of*

Justice. Field Surveys II. Washington, DC: U.S. Government Printing Office.

Erickson, M., and L. T. Empey. 1963. "Court Records, Undetected Delinquency and Decision-Making." *Journal of Criminal Law, Criminology, and Police Science* 54: 456–569.

Erickson, M. L., and J. P. Gibbs. 1978. "Objective and Perceptual Properties of Legal Punishment and the Deterrence Doctrine." *Social Problems* 25: 253–264.

——. 1979. "Community Tolerance and Measures of Delinquency." *Journal of Research in Crime and Delinquency* 17: 55–79.

Erickson, M. L., J. P. Gibbs, and G. F. Jensen. 1977. "The Deterrence Doctrine and Perceived Certainty of Legal Punishments." *American Sociological Review* 42: 305–317.

Ericson, R. V. 1981. *Making Crime.* Toronto: Butterworth.

——. 1982. *Reproducing Order.* Toronto: University of Toronto Press.

Ericson, R. V., P. M. Baranek, and J. B. L. Chan. 1987. *Visualizing Deviance: A Study of News Organization.* Toronto: University of Toronto Press.

Ericson, R. V., and C. D. Shearing. 1986. "The Scientification of Police Work." Pp. 129–159 in *The Knowledge Society.* Edited by G. Bohme and N. Stehr. Dordrecht, Netherlands, and Boston: Reidel.

Erikson, K. 1962. "Notes on the Sociology of Deviance." *Social Problems* 9: 307–314.

——. 1966. *Wayward Puritans.* New York: Wiley.

Erlanger, H. S. 1974. "The Empirical Status of the Subculture of Violence Thesis." *Social Problems* 22: 280–292.

——. 1975. "Is There a 'Subculture of Violence' in the South?" *Journal of Criminal Law and Criminology* 66: 483–490.

Erskine, H. 1970. "The Polls: Capital Punishment." *Public Opinion Quarterly* 34: 290–307.

——. 1972. "The Polls: Gun Control." *Public Opinion Quarterly* 36: 455–469.

Erwin, B. S. 1986. *An Evaluation of Georgia's Intensive Probation Supervision Program.* Atlanta: Georgia Department of Corrections.

——. 1987. *Evaluation of Intensive Probation Supervision in Georgia.* Atlanta: Georgia Department of Corrections.

Erwin, B. S., and T. R. Clear. 1987. "Rethinking Role Conflict in Community Supervision." *Perspectives* 11: 21.

Eve, R. 1975. "'Adolescent Culture,' Convenient Myth or Reality? A Comparison of Students and Their Teachers." *Sociology of Education* 48: 152–167.

Eysenck, H. 1964. *Crime and Personality.* Boston: Houghton Mifflin.

Eysenck, H., and L. Kamin. 1981. *The Intelligence Controversy.* New York: Wiley.

Fagan, J. 1990. "Intoxication and Aggression." Pp. 241–320 in *Drugs and Crime.* Edited by Michael Tonry and James Q. Wilson. Chicago: The University of Chicago Press. 241–320.

Fagan, J., and K. Chin. 1989. "Violence as Regulation and Social Control in the Distribution of Crack." Paper presented at the Technical Review on "Drugs and Violence." National Institute on Drug Abuse, Rockville, Maryland.

Fagot, B., and M. Leinbach. 1983. "Play Styles in Early Childhood: Social Consequences for Boys and Girls." Pp. 93–116 in *Social and Cognitive Skills: Sex Roles and Children's Play.* Edited by M. Liss. New York: Academic Press.

Farberman, H. A. 1975. "A Criminogenic Market Structure: The Automobile Industry." *Sociological Quarterly* 16: 438–457.

Farnworth, M. 1984. "Male-Female Differences in Delinquency in a Minority-Group Sample." *Journal of Research in Crime and Delinquency* 21: 191–213.

Farnworth, M., and P. M. Horan. 1980. "Separate Justice: An Analysis of Race Differences in Court Outcomes." *Social Science Research* 9: 381–399.

Farnworth, M., and M. J. Leiber. 1989. "Strain Theory Revisited: Economic Goals, Educational Means, and Delinquency." *American Sociological Review* 54: 263–274.

Farnworth, M., R. Teske, and G. Thurman. 1991. "Ethnic, Racial, and Minority Disparity in Felony Court Processing." Pp. 54–70 in *Race and Criminal Justice.* Edited by M. J. Lynch and E. B. Patterson. New York: Harrow and Heston.

Farrington, D. 1987. "Predicting Individual Crime Rates." Pp. 53–101 in *Prediction and Classification: Criminal Justice Decision Making.* Edited by D. Gottfredson and M. Tonry. Chicago: University of Chicago Press.

Farrington, D., H. Synder, and T. Finnegan. 1988. "Specialization in Juvenile Court Careers." *Criminology* 26: 461–488.

Farrington, D. P. 1988. "Social Psychological and Biological Influences on Juvenile Delinquency and Adult Crime." In *Explaining Criminal Behavior.* Edited by W. Buikhuisen and S. A. Mednick. Leiden, Netherlands: Brill.

Fauman, M. A., and B. J. Fauman. 1978. "The Psychiatric Aspects of Chronic Phencyclidine Use: A Study of Chronic PCP Users." Pp. 183–200 in *Phencyclidine (PCP) Abuse: An Appraisal.* NIDA Research Monograph 21. Edited by R. C. Petersen and R. C. Stillman. Rockville, MD: Department of Health, Education, and Welfare.

Faupel, C. E. 1987. "Heroin Use and Criminal Careers." *Qualitative Sociology* 10: 115–131.

Faupel, C. E., and C. B. Klockars. 1987. "Drugs-Crime Connections: Elaborations for the Life Histories of Hard-Core Heroin Addicts." *Social Problems* 34: 54–68.

Federal Bureau of Investigation. 1966. *Manual of Police Records.* Washington, DC: U.S. Government Printing Office.

———. 1980. *Crime in the United States—1979.* Washington, DC: U.S. Government Printing Office.

———. 1985. *Blueprint for the Future of the Uniform Crime Reporting Program.* Washington, DC: U.S. Government Printing Office.

———. 1985. *Uniform Crime Reporting Handbook.* Washington, DC: U.S. Government Printing Office.

———. 1988. *Crime in the United States—1981.* Washington, DC: U.S. Government Printing Office.

———. 1989. *Crime in the United States—1988.* Washington, DC: U.S. Government Printing Office.

———. 1991. *Crime in the United States—1990.* Washington, DC: U.S. Government Printing Office.

———. 1992. *Crime in the United States—1991.* Washington, DC: US Government Printing Office.

Federal Bureau of Prisons. 1963. *Prisoners Released from State and Federal Institutions, 1960.* Washington, DC: U.S. Government Printing Office.

Feeley, M. M. 1979. *The Process Is the Punishment: Handling Cases in a Lower Criminal Court.* New York: Russell Sage Foundation.

Feeley, M. M., and M. H. Lazerson. 1983. "Police-Prosecutor Relationships: An Interorganizational Perspective." Pp. 216–243 in *Empirical Theories about Courts.* Edited by K. O. Boyum and L. Mather. New York: Longman.

Feeley, M. M., and D. L. Little. 1991. "The Vanishing Female: The Decline of Women in the Criminal Process, 1687-1912." *Law & Society Review* 25: 719–757.

Feeley, M. M., and A. Sarat. 1980. *LEAA: Crime Control the Futile Myth.* Minneapolis: University of Minnesota Press.

Feeney, F., F. Dill, and A. Weir. 1983. *Arrests Without Conviction: How Often They Occur and Why.* Washington, DC: Department of Justice, National Institute of Justice.

Feldman, H. W. 1979. "PCP Use in Four Cities: An Overview." Pp. 29–51 in *Angel Dust: An Ethnographic Study of PCP Users.* Edited by H. W. Feldman, M. H. Agar, and G. M. Beschner. Lexington, MA: Lexington Books.

Felson, M. 1986. "Linking Criminal Choices, Routine Activities, Informal Control and Criminal Outcomes." Pp. 119–128 in *The Reasoning Criminal.* Edited by D. Cornish and R. Clarke. New York: Springer-Verlag.

Felson, M., and L. E. Cohen. 1980. "Human Ecology and Crime: A Routine Activity Approach." *Human Ecology* 8: 389–406.

Felson, R. B., and H. J. Steadman. 1983. "Situational Factors in Disputes Leading to Criminal Violence." *Criminology* 21: 59–74.

Ferdinand, T. 1970. "Demographic Shifts and Criminality: An Inquiry." *British Journal of Criminology* 10: 169–175.

Fielding, N. 1988. *Joining Forces.* London: Tavistock.

Fields, A., and J. M. Walters. 1985. "Hustling: Supporting a Heroin Habit." Pp. 49–74 in *Life with Heroin: Voices from the Inner City.* Edited by B. Hanson, G. Beschner, J. M. Walters, and E. Bovelle. Lexington, MA: Lexington Books.

Figueira-McDonough, J. 1985. "Gender Differences in Informal Processing: A Look at Charge Bargaining and Sentence Reduction in Washington, D.C." *Journal of Research in Crime and Delinquency* 22: 101–133.

Finestone, H. 1976. *Victims of Change.* Westport, CT: Greenwood Press.

Fishbach, S., and N. Malamuth. 1978. "Sex and Aggression: Proving the Link." *Psychology Today* 12: 112–122.

Fishbein, D. H. "Biological Perspectives in Criminology," *Criminology* 28 (1) 27–72.

Fishman, M. 1978. "Crime Waves as Ideology." *Social Problems* 25: 531–543.

———. 1981. "Police News: Constructing an Image of Crime." *Urban Life* 9: 371–394.

Flanagan, T. J., and Maguire, K. 1992. *Sourcebook of Criminal Justice Statistics—1991.* Washington, DC: U.S. Department of Justice, Bureau of Justice Statistics.

Flanagan, T. J., D. van Alstyne, and M. Gottfredson. 1982. *Sourcebook of Criminal Justice Statistics, 1981.* Washington, DC: U.S. Department of Justice.

Fleming, T. 1983. "Criminalizing a Marginal Community: The Bawdy House Raids." Pp. 37–60 in *Deviant Designations: Crime, Law and Deviance in Canada.* Edited by T. Fleming and L. A. Visano. Toronto: Butterworth.

Flemming, R. B. 1982. *Punishment Before Trial: An Organizational Perspective on Felony Bail Processes.* New York: Longman.

Flynn, E. E. 1973. "Jail and Criminal Justice." Pp. 49–88 in *Prisoners in America.* Edited by L. E. Ohlin. Englewood Cliffs, NJ: Prentice–Hall.

———. 1983. "Jails." Pp. 915–922 in *Encyclopedia of Crime and Justice.* Edited by S. H. Kadish. New York: Macmillan.

Foley, L. A., and R. S. Powell. 1982. "The Discretion of Prosecutors, Judges, and Juries in Capital Cases." *Criminal Justice Review* 7: 16–22.

Forcier, M. W., N. R. Kurtz, D. G. Parent, and M. D. Corrigan. 1986. "Deterrence of Drunk Driving in Massachusetts: Criminal Justice System Impacts." *The International Journal of the Addictions* 21: 1197–1220.

Fox, J., et al. 1987. *Final Report on the Tennessee Intensive Supervision Project.* Richmond, KY: Eastern Kentucky State Press.

Fox, J. G. 1982a. *Organizational and Racial Conflict in Maximum Security Prisons.* Lexington, MA: D. C. Heath.

———. 1982b. "Women in Prison: A Case Study in the Social Reality of Stress." *The Pains of Imprisonment.* Edited by R. Johnson and H. Toch. Beverly Hills, CA: Sage. 205–220.

Fox, R. 1971. "The XYY Offender: A Modern Myth." *Journal of Criminal Law, Criminology and Policy Science* 62: 59–73.

Frankel, M. E., and G. P. Naftalis. 1977. *The Grand Jury: An Institution on Trial.* New York: Hill & Wang.

Franklin, C., and A. Franklin. 1976. "Victimology Revisited." *Criminology* 14: 125–136.

Freedman, E. 1981. *Their Sisters' Keepers: Women's Prison Reform in America, 1830–1930.* Ann Arbor: University of Michigan Press.

Freeman, R. B. 1983. "Crime and Unemployment." Pp. 89–106 in *Crime and Public Policy.* Edited by J. Q. Wilson. San Francisco: ICS Press.

Freitag, P. J. 1983. "The Myth of Corporate Capture: Regulatory Commissions in the United States." *Social Problems* 30: 480–491.

Frey, J. H., and I. N. Rose. 1987. "The Role of Sports Information Services in the World of Sports Gambling." *Arena Review* 11: 44–51.

Friday, P., and J. Hage. 1976. "Youth Crime in Postindustrial Societies." *Criminology* 14: 347–368.

Friedman, L. 1985. *Total Justice.* Boston: Beacon Press.

Friedman, W. 1972. *Law in a Changing Society.* Harmondsworth, England: Penguin Books.

Friedrich, R. 1977. "The Impact of Organizational, Individual, and Situational Factors on Police Behavior." Unpublished Ph.D. dissertation, University of Michigan.

———. 1980. "Police Use of Force: Individuals, Situations, and Organizations." *Annals of the American Academy of Political and Social Science* 452: 82–97.

Friedrichs, D. 1980. "The Legitimacy Crisis in the United States: A Conceptual Analysis." *Social Problems* 27: 540–555.

Frieze, I., and Browne, A. 1989. "Violence in Marriage." Vol. 10, pp. 163–218 in *Crime and Justice: An Annual Review of Research.* Chicago: Univ. of Chicago Press.

Frohmann, L. 1991. "Discrediting Victims' Allegations of Sexual Assault: Prosecutorial Accounts of Case Rejections." *Social Problems* 38: 213–226.

Funke, G. S., and B. L. Wayson. 1975. *Comparative Costs of State and Local Facilities*. Washington, DC: Correctional Economics Center.

Furst, P. 1972. *Flesh of the Gods: The Ritual Use of Hallucinogens*. New York: Praeger.

Fyfe, J. 1979. "Administrative Interventions on Police Shooting Discretion." *Journal of Criminal Justice* 7: 309–323.

———. 1988. "Police Use of Deadly Force: Research and Reform." *Justice Quarterly* 5: 165–205.

Galaway, B., and J. Hudson. 1979. *Victims, Offenders, and Restitutive Sanctions*. Lexington, MA: Lexington Books.

Galaway, B., and J. Hudson (eds.). 1990. *Criminal Justice, Restitution, and Reconciliation*. Monsey, NY: Willow Tree Press.

Galliher, J. F., and J. R. Cross. 1982. "Symbolic Severity in the Land of Easy Virtue: Nevada's High Marijuana Penalty." *Social Problems* 29: 380–386.

———. 1983. *Moral Legislation Without Morality*. New Brunswick, NJ: Rutgers University Press.

Gallup, G. 1989. *The Gallup Poll*, Report No. 285 (June) Princeton, NJ: The Gallup Poll.

———. 1991. *The Gallup Poll Monthly*. Report No. 313 (October) Princeton, NJ: The Gallup Poll.

Garbarino, J. 1989. "The Incidence and Prevalence of Child Maltreatment." Vol. 10, pp. 219–261 in *Crime and Justice: An Annual Review of Research*. Edited by M. Tonry and N. Morris. Chicago: U. of Chicago Press.

Gardiner, J. 1969. *Traffic and the Police*. Cambridge, MA: Harvard University Press.

Garey, M. 1985. "The Cost of Taking a Life: Dollars and Sense of the Death Penalty." *U.C. Davis Law Review* 18: 1221–1273.

Garfinkel, H. 1956. "Conditions of Successful Degradation Ceremonies." *American Journal of Sociology* 61: 420–424.

Garland, D. 1990. *Punishment and Modern Society*. Chicago: University of Chicago Press.

Garofalo, J. n.d. *Measuring the Use of Imprisonment*. Washington, DC: U.S. Department of Justice, National Institute of Justice.

———. 1977. *Public Opinion About Crime*. Washington, DC: U.S. Government Printing Office.

———. 1981. "Victimization Surveys: An Overview." Pp. 98–103 in *Perspectives on Crime Victims*. Edited by B. Galaway and J. Hudson. St. Louis: Mosby.

———. 1986. "Lifestyles and Victimization: An Update." Pp. 135–155 in *From Crime Policy to Victim Policy*. Edited by E. Fattah. New York: St. Martin's Press.

———. 1987. "Reassessing the Lifestyle Model of Criminal Victimization." Pp. 23–42 in *Positive Criminology*. Edited by M. R. Gottfredson and T. Hirschi. Beverly Hills, CA: Sage.

Garofalo, J., and M. J. Hindelang. 1977. *An Introduction to the National Crime Survey*. Washington, DC: Criminal Justice Research Center, U.S. Department of Justice.

Geerken, M. R., and W. R. Gove. 1977. "Deterrence, Overload and Incapacitation: An Empirical Evaluation." *Social Forces* 56: 424–447.

Geis, G. 1967. "The Heavy Electrical Equipment Antitrust Cases of 1961." Pp. 139–150 in *Criminal Behavior Systems*. Edited by M. Clinard and R. Quinney. New York: Holt, Rinehart & Winston.

———. 1976. "Compensation to Victims of Violent Crime." Pp. 90–115 in *Contemporary Issues in Criminal Justice*. Edited by R. Gerber. Port Washington, NY: Kennikat.

———. 1979. *Not the Law's Business*. New York: Schocken Books.

Geisel, M. S., R. Roll, and R. S. Wettick. 1969. "The Effectiveness of State and Local Regulation of Handguns: A Statistical Analysis." *Duke Law Review* 4: 647–676.

Geller, W. and N. Morris. 1992. "Relations Between Federal and Local Police." Pp. 231–348 in *Modern Policing*. Edited by M. Tonry and N. Morris. Chicago: University of Chicago Press.

Gelles, R. J., and M. A. Straus. 1975. "Family Experience and Public Support of the Death Penalty." *American Journal of Orthopsychiatry* 45: 596–613.

Gelman, A. M. 1982. "Prosecutorial Decision-Making: The Screening Process." Pp. 235–255 in *The Criminal Justice System: A Social-Psychological Analysis*. Edited by V. J. Konecni and E. B. Ebbesen. San Francisco: Freeman.

Gendreau, P., and B. Ross. 1981. *Effective Corrections*. Toronto: Butterworth.

———. 1987. "Revivification of Rehabilitation: Evidence from the 1980's." *Justice Quarterly* 3: 349–408.

General Accounting Office. 1979. *The Impact of the Exclusionary Rule on Federal Criminal Prosecutions.* Washington, DC: General Accounting Office.

Gentry, C. 1988. "The Social Construction of Abducted Children as a Social Problem." *Sociological Inquiry* 58: 413–425.

———. 1991. "Pornography and Rape: An Empirical Analysis." *Deviant Behavior: An Interdisciplinary Journal.* 12: 277–288.

Giallombordo, R. 1966. *Society of Women.* New York: Wiley.

Gibbons, D. C. 1975. *The Criminological Enterprise.* Englewood Cliffs, NJ: Prentice-Hall.

———. 1988. *The Limits of Punishment as Social Policy.* San Francisco: National Council of Crime and Delinquency.

Gibbons, D. C., and J. F. Jones. 1975. *The Study of Deviance: Perspectives and Problems.* Englewood Cliffs, NJ: Prentice-Hall.

Gibbs, J. J. 1982a. "Disruption and Distress: Going from the Street to Jail." Pp. 29–44 in *Coping with Imprisonment.* Edited by N. Parisi. Beverly Hills, CA: Sage.

———. 1982b. "The First Cut is the Deepest: Psychological Breakdown and Survival in the Detention Setting." Pp. 97–114 in *The Pains of Imprisonment.* Edited by R. Johnson and H. Toch. Beverly Hills, CA: Sage.

Gibbs, J. P. 1966. "Conceptions of Deviant Behavior: The Old and the New." *Pacific Sociological Review* 9: 9–14.

———. 1975. *Crime, Punishment and Deterrence.* New York: Elsevier.

———. 1982. "Preventive Effects of Capital Punishment Other Than Deterrence." In *The Death Penalty in America.* 3d ed. Edited by H. A. Bedeau. New York: Oxford University Press.

Gibbs, J. P., and M. L. Erickson. 1979. "Conceptions of Criminal and Delinquent Acts." *Deviant Behavior* 1: 71–100.

Gibson, J. L. 1978. "Race as a Determinant of Criminal Sentences: A Methodological Critique and a Case Study." *Law & Society Review* 12: 455–478.

———. 1980. "Environmental Constraints on the Behavior of Judges: A Representational Model of Judicial Decision Making." *Law & Society Review* 14: 343–370.

———. 1983. "From Simplicity to Complexity: The Development of Theory in the Study of Judicial Behavior." *Political Behavior* 5: 7–49.

Gilfoyle, T. J. 1992. *New York City, Prostitution, and the Commercialization of Sex, 1790–1920.* New York: W. W. Norton & Company.

Gilfus, M. 1988. "Seasoned by Violence, Tempered by Love: A Relational Theory of Women's Crime." Paper presented at the annual meeting of the American Society of Criminology, Chicago.

Gilgi, G. L., et al. 1981. "Epilessia, Aggressivita E. Criminalita" (Epilepsy, Aggression and Criminality). *Archivio di Psicologia Neurologia e Psichiatria* 42: 273–284.

Gillespie, R. W. 1978. "Economic Factors in Crime and Delinquency: A Critical Review of the Empirical Evidence." Pp. 601–626 in *Unemployment and Crime: Hearings Before the Subcommittee on Crime of the Committee on the Judiciary.* House of Representatives. Washington, DC: U.S. Government Printing Office.

Gilligan, C. 1982. *In a Different Voice.* Cambridge, MA: Harvard University Press.

Giordano, P., S. Cernkovich, and M. D. Pugh. 1986. "Friendships and Delinquency." *American Journal of Sociology* 91: 1170–1202.

Glaser, D. 1964. *Effectiveness of a Prison and Parole System.* Indianapolis, IN: Bobbs-Merrill.

———. 1971. "Some Notes on Urban Jails." Pp. 236–244 in *Crime in the City.* Edited by D. Glaser. New York: Harper & Row.

———. 1978. *Crime in Our Changing Society.* New York: Holt, Rinehart & Winston.

Glaser, D., and M. S. Zeigler. 1974. "The Use of the Death Penalty v. Outrage at Murder." *Crime and Delinquency* 20: 333–338.

Glick, R. M., and V. V. Neto. 1977. *National Study of Women's Correctional Programs.* Washington, DC: U.S. Department of Justice, National Institute of Law Enforcement and Criminal Justice.

Globetti, E., G. Globetti, C. L. Brown, and J. T. Stem. 1992. "Campus Attitudes Toward Alcohol and Drugs in a Deep Southern University." *Journal of Drug Education.* 22: 203–213.

Goddard, H. H. 1923. *The Kallikak Family.* New York: Macmillan.

Goffman, E. 1959. *The Presentation of Self in Everyday Life.* New York: Doubleday/Anchor Books.

———. 1961. *Asylums*. Garden City, NY: Anchor.

———. 1963. *Stigma: Notes on the Management of Spoiled Identity*. Englewood Cliffs, NJ: Prentice-Hall.

———. 1974. *Frame Analysis*. Cambridge, MA: Harvard University Press.

Gold, M. 1970. *Delinquent Behavior in an American City*. Belmont, CA: Brooks/Cole.

Gold, M. S., C. A. Dackis, A. L. C. Pottash, I. Extein, and A. Washton. 1986. "Cocaine Update: From Bench to Bedside." *Advances in Alcohol and Substance Abuse* 5: 35–60.

Golden, R. M., and S. F. Messner. 1987. "Dimensions of Racial Inequality and Rates of Violent Crime." *Criminology* 25: 525–542.

Goldfarb, R. 1975. *Jails*. Garden City, NY: Anchor.

Goldman, F. 1981. "Drug Abuse, Crime, and Economics: The Dismal Limits of Social Choice." Pp. 155–182 in *The Drugs-Crime Connection*. Edited by J. A. Inciardi. Beverly Hills, CA: Sage.

Goldstein, H. 1977. *Policing a Free Society*. Cambridge, MA: Ballinger.

———. 1979. "Improving Policing: A Problem-oriented Approach." *Journal of Crime and Delinquency* 25: 236–258.

———. 1987. "Toward Community-oriented Policing: Potential, Basic Requirements and Threshold Questions." *Crime and Delinquency* 33: 6–33.

———. 1990. *Problem-Oriented Policing*. New York: McGraw-Hill.

Goldstein, J. 1960. "Police Discretion Not To Invoke the Criminal Process." *Yale Law Journal* 69: 543–588.

Goldstein, P. J. 1981. "Getting Over: Economic Alternatives to Predatory Crime among Street Drug Users." Pp. 67–84 in *The Drugs-Crime Connection*. Edited by J. A. Inciardi. Beverly Hills, CA: Sage.

———. 1983. "Occupational Mobility in the World of Prostitution: Becoming a Madam." *Deviant Behavior* 3–4: 267–279.

———. 1985. "The Drugs/Violence Nexus: A Tripartite Conceptual Framework." *Journal of Drug Issues* 14: 493–506.

Goldstein, P. J., P. A. Bellucci, B. J. Spunt, and T. Miller. 1991. "Volume of Cocaine Use and Violence: A Comparison between Men and Women." *Journal of Drug Issues* 21 (2): 345–367.

Goldstein, P. J., H. H. Brownstein, P. J. Ryan, and P. A. Bellucci. 1989. "Crack and Homicide in New York City: A Conceptually Based Event Analysis." *Contemporary Drug Problems* 16 (4): 651–687.

Goode, E. 1972. *Drugs in American Society*. New York: Knopf.

———. 1984. *Drugs in American Society*. 2d ed. New York: Knopf.

———. 1993. *Drugs in American Society*. New York: McGraw-Hill.

Goodpaster, G. 1983. "The Trial for Life: Effective Assistance of Counsel in Death Penalty Cases." *New York University Law Review* 58: 299–362.

Goodwin, D. W., J. B. Crane, and S. B. Guze. 1971. "Felons Who Drink: An 8-Year Follow-Up." *Quarterly Journal of Studies on Alcohol* 32: 136–147.

Gordon, D. 1973. "Capitalism, Class, and Crime in America." *Crime and Delinquency* 19: 163–186.

Gordon, D. R. 1990. *The Justice Juggernaut*. New Brunswick, NJ: Rutgers University Press.

Gordon, M., and L. Heath. 1981. "The News Business, Crime and Fear." Pp. 227–250 in *Reactions to Crime*. Edited by D. A. Lewis. Beverly Hills, CA: Sage.

Gordon, R. A. 1967. "Issues in the Ecological Study of Delinquency." *American Sociological Review* 32: 927–944.

———. 1980. "Research on IQ, Race and Delinquency." Pp. 37–66 in *Taboos in Criminology*. Edited by E. Sagarin. Beverly Hills, CA: Sage.

Gorecki, J. 1983. *Capital Punishment: Criminal Law and Social Evolution*. New York: Columbia University Press.

Gottfredson, D. M., M. G. Neithercutt, P. S. Venezia, and E. A. Wenk. 1970. *A National Uniform Parole Reporting System*. Washington, DC: U.S. Government Printing Office.

Gottfredson, M. 1981. "On the Etiology of Criminal Victimization." *Journal of Criminal Law and Criminology* 72: 714–726.

Gottfredson, M., and D. M. Gottfredson. 1988. *Decision Making in Criminal Justice: Toward the Rational Exercise of Discretion*. 2d ed. New York: Plenum.

Gottfredson, S., and D. Gottfredson. 1986. "Accuracy of Prediction Models." Pp. 212–290 in *Criminal Careers and "Career Criminals."* Vol. 2. Edited by A. Blumstein, J. Cohen, J. Roth, and C. Visher. Washington, DC: National Academy Press.

Gottheil, E. 1986. "Cocaine Abuse and Dependence: The Scope of the Problem." *Advances in Alcohol and Substance Abuse* 6: 23–30.

Gottheil, E., K. A. Druley, T. E. Skloda, and H. M. Waxman. 1983. *Alcohol, Drug Abuse and Aggression.* Springfield, IL: Thomas.

Gould, L. C. 1969. "The Changing Structure of Property Crime in an Affluent Society." *Social Forces* 48: 50–59.

Gould, S. J. 1976. "Biological Potential vs. Biological Determinism." *Natural History Magazine* (May).

———. 1981. *The Mismeasure of Man.* New York: Norton.

Gouldner, A. 1968. "The Sociologists as Partisan: Sociology and the Welfare State." *The American Sociologist* 3: 103–116.

Gove, W. 1970. "Societal Reaction as an Explanation of Mental Illness: An Evaluation." *American Sociological Review* 35: 873–884.

———. 1985. "The Effect of Age and Gender on Deviant Behavior: A Biopsychosocial Perspective." In *Gender and the Life Course.* Edited by A. Rossi. New York: Aldine.

Graber, D. A. 1980. *Crime News and the Public.* New York: Praeger.

Gradess, J. 1988. "Which Is More Expensive? Execution or a Life Sentence?" *Washington Post National Weekly Edition*, May 2–8, 23.

Graeven, D. B. 1978. "Patterns of Phencyclidine Use." Pp. 176–183 in *Phencyclidine (PCP) Abuse: An Appraisal.* NIDA Research Monograph 21. Edited by R. C. Petersen and R. C. Stillman. Rockville, MD: Department of Health, Education, and Welfare.

Graham, F. 1970. *The Due Process Revolution: The Warren Court's Impact on Criminal Law.* New York: Hayden Book Co.

Graham, J. M. 1972. "Amphetamine Politics on Capitol Hill." *Society* 9: 14–23.

Grapendaal, Martin, Ed Leuw, and Nelen. 1992. "Drugs and Crime in an Accommodating Social Context: The Situation in Amsterdam." *Contemporary Drug Problems* 19(2): 279–301.

Grasmick, H. G., and G. J. Bryjak. 1980. "The Deterrent Effect of Perceived Severity of Punishment." *Social Forces* 59: 471–491.

Grawunder, R., and M. Steinman. *Life and Health.* New York: Random House.

Gray, S. H. 1982. "Exposure to Pornography and Aggression Toward Women: The Case of the Angry Male." *Social Problems* 29: 387–398.

Green, G. S. 1986. "Reflections on Citizen Gun Ownership and Criminal Deterrence: Theory, Research and Policy." Paper presented at the annual meeting of the American Society of Criminology, Atlanta.

Green, M. J., B. L. Moore, and B. Wasserstein. 1972. *The Closed Enterprise System.* New York: Grossman.

Greenberg, D. 1977a. "Delinquency and the Age Structure of Society." *Contemporary Crises* 1: 66–86.

———. 1977b. "The Dynamics of Oscillatory Punishment Policies." *Journal of Criminal Law and Criminology* 68: 643–651.

———. 1979. *Mathematical Criminology.* New Brunswick, NJ: Rutgers University Press.

———. 1981. *Crime and Capitalism: Readings in Marxist Criminology.* Palo Alto, CA: Mayfield.

———. 1990. "The Cost-Benefit Analysis of Imprisonment." *Social Justice* 17: 49–75.

Greenberg, D., R. Kessler, and C. Logan. 1979. "A Panel Model of Crime Rates and Arrest Rates." *American Sociological Review* 44: 843–850.

Greenberg, S. W., and F. Adler. 1974. "Crime and Addiction: An Empirical Analysis of the Literature, 1920–1973." *Contemporary Drug Problems* 3: 221–261.

Greene, J., and C. Klockars. 1987. "Police Workload: Some New Findings." Paper presented at the annual meeting of the American Society of Criminology, Montreal.

Greene, J., and S. Mastrofski. 1988. *Community Policing.* New York: Praeger.

Greene, M. H. 1973. "Amphetamines in the District of Columbia: Patterns of Abuse in an Arrestee Population." *Archives of General Psychiatry* 29: 773–776.

Greene, M. H., and R. L. DuPont. 1973. "Amphetamines in the District of Columbia: Identification and Resolution of an Abuse Epidemic." *Journal of the American Medical Association* 226: 1437–1440.

Greenfeld, L. 1981. *Measuring the Application and Use of Punishment.* Washington, DC: National Institute of Justice.

———. 1988. "Drunk Driving." *Bureau of Justice Statistics Special Report.* Washington, DC: U.S. Department of Justice.

———. 1992. *Prisons and Prisoners in the United States.* Washington, DC: U.S. Department of Justice, Bureau of Justice Statistics.

Greenfeld, L. A., and P. A. Langan. 1987. *Trends in Prison Populations.* Paper prepared for the National Conference on Punishment for Criminal Offenses, Ann Arbor, Michigan. November.

Greenhouse, L. 1989. "Judicial Panel Urges Limit on Death Row Appeals." *New York Times*, September 22, 13.

Greenwood, C. 1972. *Firearms Control: A Study of Armed Crime and Firearms in England and Wales.* London: Routledge & Kegan Paul.

———. 1983. "Armed Crime in Britain." *Handgunner* 19: 37ff.

Greenwood, P., and A. Abrahamse. 1982. *Selective Incapacitation.* Rand Report R-2815-NIJ. Santa Monica, CA: Rand Corporation.

Greenwood, P., J. Chaiken, and J. Petersilia. 1977. *The Criminal Investigation Process.* Lexington, MA: Heath.

Greenwood, P., and S. Turner. 1987. *Selective Incapacitation Revisited: Why the High-Rate Offenders Are Hard to Predict.* Rand Report R-3397-NIJ. Santa Monica, CA: Rand Corporation.

Grinspoon, L., and J. B. Bakalar. 1985. *Cocaine: A Drug and Its Social Evolution.* New York: Basic Books.

Gross, S. R. 1985. "Race and Death: The Judicial Evaluation of Discrimination in Capital Sentencing." *U.C. Davis Law Review* 18: 1275–1325.

Gross, S. R., and R. Mauro. 1984. "Patterns of Death: An Analysis of Racial Disparities in Capital Sentencing and Homicide Victimization." *Stanford Law Review* 37: 27–153.

———. 1989. *Death and Discrimination: Racial Disparities in Capital Sentencing.* Boston: Northeastern University Press.

Grosser, G. 1952. *Juvenile Delinquency and Contemporary American Sex Roles.* Ph.D. dissertation, Harvard University.

Groves, B. 1985. "Marxism and Positivism." *Crime and Social Justice* 23: 129–150.

Groves, B., and R. Sampson. 1986. "Critical Theory and Criminology." *Social Problems* 33: S58–S80.

Gruhl, J., C. Spohn, and S. Welch. 1981. "Women as Policymakers: The Case of Trial Judges." *American Journal of Political Science* 25: 308–322.

———. 1984. "Women as Criminal Defendants: A Test for Paternalism." *Western Political Quarterly* 37: 456–467.

Gunn, J. 1977. "Criminal Behavior and Mental Disorder." *British Journal of Psychiatry* 130: 317–329.

Gusfield, J. R. 1963. *Symbolic Crusade.* Urbana: University of Illinois Press.

———. 1981. *The Culture of Public Problems: Drinking-Driving and the Symbolic Order.* Chicago: University of Chicago Press.

Guze, S. B., V. V. Tuason, P. D. Gatfield, M. A. Stewart, and B. Picken. 1962. "Psychiatric Illness and Crime with Particular Reference to Alcoholism: A Study of 223 Criminals." *Journal of Nervous and Mental Disease* 134: 512–521.

Haberman, P. W. 1987. "Alcohol Use and Alcoholism among Motor Vehicle Driver Fatalities." *The International Journal of the Addictions* 22: 1119–1128.

Hagan, F. E. 1986. *Introduction to Criminology: Theories, Methods, and Criminal Behavior.* Chicago: Nelson-Hall.

———. 1987. *Introduction to Criminology.* Chicago: Nelson-Hall.

Hagan, J. 1975. "The Social and Legal Construction of Criminal Justice: A Study of the Pre-sentencing Process." *Social Problems* 22: 620–637.

———. 1977. "Criminal Justice and Rural and Urban Communities: A Study of the Bureaucratization of Justice." *Social Forces* 55: 597–612.

———. 1982. "The Corporate Advantage: A Study of the Involvement of Corporate and Individual Victims in a Criminal Justice System." *Social Forces* 60: 993–1022.

———. 1991. "Destiny and Drift: Subcultural Preferences, Status Attainments, and the Risks and Rewards of Youth." *American Sociological Review* 56 (Oct.): 567–582.

———. 1992. "The Poverty of a Classless Criminology." *Criminology* 30: 1–19.

Hagan, J., and I. N. Bernstein. 1979a. "Conflict in Context: The Sanctioning of Draft Resisters, 1963–1976." *Social Problems* 29: 109–122.

———. 1979b. "The Sentence Bargaining of Upperworld and Underworld Crime in Ten Federal District Courts." *Law & Society Review* 13: 467–478.

Hagan, J., and K. Bumiller. 1983. "Making Sense of Sentencing: A Review and Critique of Sentencing

Research." Pp. 1–54 in *Research on Sentencing: The Search for Reform.* Vol. 2. Edited by A. Blumstein, J. Cohen, S. E. Martin, and M. H. Tonry. Washington, DC: National Academy Press.

Hagan, J., M. Huxter, and P. Parker. 1988. "Class Structure and Legal Practice: Inequality and Mobility Among Toronto Lawyers." *Law & Society Review* 22: 9–55.

Hagan, J., I. H. Nagel, and C. Albonetti. 1980. "The Differential Sentencing of White-Collar Offenders in Ten Federal District Courts." *American Sociological Review* 45: 802–820.

———. 1982. "The Social Organization of White-collar Sanctions: A Study of Prosecution and Punishment in the Federal Courts." Pp. 259–275 in *White-Collar and Economic Crime.* Edited by P. M. Wickman and T. Dailey. Lexington, MA: Heath.

Hagan, J., and P. Parker. 1985. "White-collar Crime and Punishment: The Class Structure and Legal Sanctioning of Securities Violations." *American Sociological Review* 50: 302–317.

Hagan, J., J. Simpson, and A. R. Gillis. 1987. "Class in the Household: A Power-Control Theory of Gender and Delinquency." *American Journal of Sociology* 92: 788–816.

Hagan, J. L., and I. H. Nagel. 1982. "White-collar Crime, White-collar Time: The Sentencing of White-collar Offenders in the Southern District of New York." *American Criminal Law Review* 20: 259–290.

Haines, H. 1992. "Flawed Executions, the Anti-Death Penalty Movement, and the Politics of Capital Punishment." *Social Problems* 39: 125–138.

Hale, C., and D. Sabbagh. 1991. "Testing the Relationship Between Unemployment and Crime: A Methodological Comment and Empirical Analysis Using Time Series Data From England and Wales." *Journal of Research in Crime and Delinquency* 28: 400–417.

Hales, D., and R. E. Hales. 1982. "The Bonding Hormone." *American Health Magazine*, November–December, 1–14.

Hall, J. 1952. *Theft, Law and Society.* 2d ed. Indianapolis, IN: Bobbs-Merrill.

Hall, S., C. Critcher, T. Jefferson, J. Clarke, and B. Roberts. 1978. *Policing the Crisis: Mugging, the State, and Law and Order.* London: Macmillan.

Haller, M. 1963. *Eugenics.* New Brunswick, NJ: Rutgers University Press.

Haller, M. H. 1992. "Bureaucracy and the Mafia: An Alternative View." *Journal of Contemporary Criminal Justice* 8: 1–10.

Hamilton, V. L., and S. Rytina. 1980. "Social Consensus on Norms of Justice: Should the Punishment Fit the Crime?" *American Journal of Sociology* 85: 1117–1144.

Hans, V. P. 1988. "Death by Jury." In *Challenging Capital Punishment: Legal and Social Science Approaches.* Edited by K. C. Haas and J. A. Inciardi. Newbury Park, CA: Sage.

Hans, V. P., and N. Vidmar. 1986. *Judging the Jury.* New York: Plenum.

Hanson, B., G. Beschner, J. M. Walters, and E. Bovelle. 1985. *Life with Heroin: Voices from the Inner City.* Lexington, MA: Lexington Books.

Hardt, R. H. and S. Peterson-Hardt. 1977. "On Determining the Quality of the Delinquency Self-Report Method." *Journal of Research in Crime and Delinquency* 14: 247–261.

Harer, M. D., and D. Steffensmeier. 1992. "The Differing Effects of Economic Inequality on Black and White Rates of Violence." *Social Forces* 70: 1035–1054.

Harland, A. 1981. *Restitution to Victims of Personal and Household Crimes.* Washington, DC: U.S. Department of Justice.

Harlow, C. 1985. *Reporting Crime to the Police: Bureau of Justice Statistics Special Report.* Washington, DC: U.S. Department of Justice.

———. 1987. *Robbery Victims: Bureau of Justice Statistics Special Report.* Washington, DC: U.S. Department of Justice.

Harlow, M., and K. Nelson. 1984. *Managing Probation and Parole Services in an Era of Fiscal Restraint.* Washington, DC: National Institute of Corrections.

Harries, K. D. 1974. *The Geography of Crime and Justice.* New York: McGraw-Hill.

Harring, S. 1977. "Class Conflict and the Suppression of Tramps in Buffalo, 1892–1894." *Law & Society Review* 11: 873–912.

Harris, A. R. 1976. "Race, Commitment to Deviance, and Spoiled Identity." *American Sociological Review* 41: 432–442.

———. 1977. "Sex and Theories of Deviance: Toward a Functional Theory of Deviant Type-scripts." *American Sociological Review* 42: 3–16.

———. 1988. "Self-esteem Among Black and White Prisoners: A Secondary Analysis of the 'Rand Inmate Survey' Data." Unpublished report, Department of Sociology, University of Massachusetts, Amherst.

———. 1989. "Caste and Crime: Opportunity Theory Revisited." Unpublished manuscript, Department of Sociology, University of Massachusetts, Amherst.

Harris, A. R., and G. D. Hill. 1982. "The Social Psychology of Deviance: Toward a Reconciliation with Social Structure." *Annual Review of Sociology* 8: 161–186.

Harrison, L. and J. Gfroerer. 1992. "The Intersection of Drug Use and Criminal Behavior: Results From the National Household Survey on Drug Abuse." *Crime and Delinquency* 38 (4): 422–443.

Hart, H. L. A. 1963. *Law, Liberty and Morality.* Palo Alto, CA: Stanford University Press.

Hartnagel, T. 1982. "Modernization, Female Social Roles, and Female Crime: A Cross-national Investigation." *Sociological Quarterly* 23: 477–490.

Hastings Center Group. 1980. "The XYY Controversy: Researching Violence and Genetics." *Hastings Center Report* 10(4).

Hauser, R. M., W. H. Sewell, and D. Alwin. 1976. "High School Effects on Achievement." Pp. 309–343 in *Schooling and Achievement in American Society.* Edited by W. H. Sewell, R. M. Hauser, and D. L. Featherman. New York: Academic Press.

Hawkins, D. 1985. "Trends in Black-White Imprisonment: Changing Conceptions of Race or Changing Patterns of Social Control?" *Crime and Social Justice* 24: 187–209.

———. 1987. "Beyond Anomalies: Rethinking the Conflict Perspective on Race and Criminal Punishment." *Social Forces* 65: 719–745.

Hawkins, G. 1969. "God and the Mafia." *Public Interest* 14: 24–51.

Hawley, A. 1950. *Human Ecology: A Theory of Community Structure.* New York: Ronald.

Hawley, F. F., and S. F. Messner. 1989. "The Southern Violence Construct: A Review of Arguments, Evidence, and the Normative Context." *Justice Quarterly* 6: 481–511.

Hay, D. 1975. "Property, Authority and the Criminal Law." Pp. 17–63 in *Albion's Fatal Tree.* Edited by D. Hay, P. Linebaugh, J. Rule, E. P. Thompson, and C. Winslow. New York: Pantheon.

Heath, D. B. 1983. "Alcohol and Aggression: A 'Missing Link' in Worldwide Perspective." Pp. 89–103 in *Alcohol, Drug Abuse and Aggression.* Edited by E. Gottheil, K. A. Druley, T. E. Skoloda, and H. M. Waxman. Springfield, IL: Thomas.

Heath, L. 1984. "Impact of Newspaper Crime Reports on Fear of Crime: Multimethodological Investigation." *Journal of Personality and Social Psychology* 47: 263–276.

Heffernan, E. 1972. *Making It in Prison.* New York: Wiley.

Heilbrun, A.B. Jr., A. Foster, and J. Golden. 1989. "The Death Sentence in Georgia, 1974–84." *Criminal Justice and Behavior* 16: 139–154.

Heninger, B. L., and J. Urbanek. 1983. "Civilianization of the American Police: 1970–1980." *Journal of Police Science and Administration* 11: 200–205.

Henley, J. R., and L. D. Adams. 1973. "Marijuana Use in Postcollegiate Cohorts: Correlates of Use, Prevalence Patterns and Factors Associated with Cessation." *Social Problems* 20 (Spring): 514–520.

Henry, A. F., and J. F. Short, Jr. 1954. *Suicide and Homicide: Some Economic, Sociological and Psychological Aspects of Aggression.* New York: Free Press.

Henry, S. 1978. *The Hidden Economy.* Oxford: Martin Robertson.

———. 1985. "Community Justice, Capitalist Society, and Human Agency: The Dialectics of Collective Law in the Cooperative." *Law & Society Review* 19: 303–327.

Hepburn, J. R. 1984. "Occasional Property Crime." Pp. 73–94 in *Major Forms of Crime.* Edited by R. F. Meier. Beverly Hills, CA: Sage.

———. 1985. "The Exercise of Power in Coercive Organizations: A Study of Prison Guards." *Criminology* 23: 145–164.

Herek, G., and K. Berrill. 1992. *Hate Crime: Confronting Violence Against Lesbians and Gay Men.* Newbury Park, CA: Sage.

Hess, H. 1973. *Mafia and Mafiosi: The Structure of Power.* Lexington, MA: Heath.

Heyl, B. 1979. "Prostitution: An Extreme Case of Sex Stratification." In *The Criminology of Deviant Women.*

Edited by F. Adler and R. J. Simon. Boston: Houghton Mifflin.

Hill, G. D., and E. Crawford. 1990. "Women, Race, and Crime." *Criminology* 28: 601–626.

Hill, G. D., and A. R. Harris. 1982 "Changes in the Gender-Patterning of Crime, 1953-1977: Opportunity vs. Identity." *Social Science Quarterly* 62: 658–671.

Hill, J. 1975. *Class Analysis: United States in the 1970s.* Emeryville, CA: Class Analysis.

Hillenbrand, S. "Restitution and Victim Rights in the 1980s." Pp. 188–204 in *Victims of Crime: Problems, Policies, and Programs.* Edited by A. Lurigio, W. Skogan, and R. Davis. Newbury Park, CA: Sage.

Hiltzik, M. A. 1984. "Laws Against Monopolies Under Attack." *Los Angeles Times,* March 19, I1 *passim.*

———. 1987. "Inside Trader to Pay Penalty of $100 Million." *Los Angeles Times,* November 15, 1, 30.

Himmelstein, J. L. 1986. "The Continuing Career of Marijuana: Backlash . . . Within Limits." *Contemporary Drug Problems* 13: 1–21.

Hindelang, M. J. 1970. "The Commitment of Delinquents to Their Misdeeds: Do Delinquents Drift?" *Social Problems* 17: 502–509.

———. 1973. "Causes of Delinquency: A Partial Replication and Extension." *Social Problems* 20 (Spring): 471–487.

———. 1974. "Moral Evaluations of Illegal Behaviors." *Social Problems* 21: 370–385.

———. 1978. "Race and Involvement in Common Law Personal Crimes." *American Sociological Review* 43: 93–109.

———. 1979. "Sex Differences in Criminal Activity." *Social Problems* 27: 143–156.

———. 1981. "Variations in Sex-Race-Age-Specific Incidence Rates of Offending." *American Sociological Review* 46: 461–474.

Hindelang, M. J., M. R. Gottfredson, and J. Garofalo. 1978. *Victims of Personal Crime: An Empirical Foundation for a Theory of Personal Victimization.* Cambridge, MA: Ballinger.

Hindelang, M. J., T. Hirschi, and J. Weis. 1979. "Correlates of Delinquency: The Illusion of Discrepancy Between Self-report and Official Measures." *American Sociological Review* 44: 995–1014.

———. 1981. *Measuring Delinquency.* Beverly Hills, CA: Sage.

Hingson, R., and Howland, J. 1990. "Use of Laws to Deter Drinking and Driving." *Alcohol Health and Research World.* 14: 36–43.

Hippchen, L. 1978. *Ecologic-Biochemical Approaches to Treatment of Delinquents and Criminals.* New York: Van Nostrand Reinhold.

Hirliman, I. 1982. *The Hate Factory.* Agoura, CA: Paisano.

Hirschi, T. 1969. *Causes of Delinquency.* Berkeley: University of California Press.

———. 1975. "Labelling Theory and Juvenile Delinquency: An Assessment of the Evidence." Pp. 181–203 in *The Labeling of Deviance: Evaluating a Perspective.* Edited by W. Gove. Beverly Hills, CA: Sage.

———. 1979. "Separate and Unequal Is Better." *Journal of Research in Crime and Delinquency* 16: 34–38.

———. 1986. "On the Compatibility of Rational Choice and Social Control Theories of Crime." Pp. 105–118 in *The Reasoning Criminal.* Edited by D. Cornish and R. Clarke. New York: Springer-Verlag.

———. 1987. "Exploring Alternatives to Integrated Theory." Paper presented at the Albany Conference on Theoretical Integration in the Study of Deviance and Crime, Albany, New York.

Hirschi, T., and M. R. Gottfredson. 1983. "Age and the Explanation of Crime." *American Journal of Sociology* 89: 552–584.

———. 1987. "Causes of White-collar Crime." *Criminology* 25: 949–974.

———. 1989. "The Significance of White-collar Crime for a General Theory of Crime." *Criminology* 27: 359–371.

Hirschi, T., and M. J. Hindelang. 1977. "Intelligence and Delinquency: A Revisionist View." *American Sociological Review* 42: 571–587.

Hirst, P. 1975. "Marx and Engels on Law, Crime, and Morality." Pp. 203–232 in *Critical Criminology.* Edited by I. Taylor, P. Walton, and J. Young. London: Routledge & Kegan Paul.

Hofstadter, R. 1970. "America as a Gun Culture." *American Heritage* 21: 4ff.

Hogg, R. 1979. "Imprisonment and Society Under Early British Capitalism." *Crime and Social Justice* 12: 4–17.

Holdaway, S. 1979. *British Police*. London: Edward Arnold.

———. 1980. "The Occupational Culture of Urban Policing: An Ethnographic Study." Unpublished Ph.D. thesis, University of Sheffield.

———. 1983. *Inside the British Police*. Oxford: Basil Blackwell.

Hollinger, R., and J. Clark. 1983. *Theft by Employees*. Lexington, MA: Lexington Books.

———. 1983b. "Deterrence in the Workplace: Perceived Certainty, Perceived Severity and Employee Theft." *Social Forces* 62: 398–419.

Hollinger, R. C., and L. Lanza-Kaduce. 1988. "The Process of Criminalization: The Case of Computer Crime Laws." *Criminology* 26: 101–126.

Holmes, M. D., H. C. Daudistel, and R. A. Farrell. 1987. "Determinants of Charge Reductions and Final Dispositions in Cases of Burglary and Robbery." *Journal of Research in Crime and Delinquency* 24: 233–254.

Hook, E. B. 1973. "Behavioral Implications of the Human XYY Genotype." *Science* 5: 139–150.

Horan, P. M., and P. G. Hargis. 1991. "Children's Work and Schooling in the Late Nineteenth-Century Family Economy." *American Sociological Review* 56: 583–596.

Horney, J. 1978. "Menstrual Cycles and Criminal Responsibility." *Law and Human Behavior* 2: 25–36.

Horning, D. N. M. 1970. "Blue Collar Theft: Conceptions of Property Attitudes Toward Pilfering and Work Group Norms in a Modern Industrial Plant." In *Crime Against Bureaucracy*. Edited by E. O. Smigel and H. L. Ross. New York: Van Nostrand Reinhold.

Horowitz, I., and M. Liebowitz. 1968. "Social Deviance and Political Marginality: Toward a Redefinition of the Relation Between Sociology and Politics." *Social Problems* 15: 280–296.

Horowitz, R. Forthcoming. *Identity and Organization*.

Horrock, N. 1976. "Car Burnings and Assaults on Radicals Linked to FBI Agents in Last Five Years." *The New York Times*, July 11, 20.

Horton, J. 1969. "Order and Conflict Theories of Social Problems as Competing Ideologies." *American Journal of Sociology* 71: 701–713.

Hough, J. M. 1980. "Managing with Less Technology." *British Journal of Criminology* 20: 344–357.

Howard, M. 1986. "Husband-Wife Homicide: An Essay from a Family Law Perspective." *Law and Contemporary Problems* 49: 63–88.

Howe, W. J. 1987. "Firearms Production by U.S. Manufacturers, 1973–1985." *Shooting Industry*: 101–112.

Hoyenga, K., and K. T. Hoyenga. 1979. *The Question of Sex Differences*. Boston: Little, Brown.

Hudson, J., and B. Galaway. 1977. *Restitution in Criminal Justice*. Lexington, MA: Lexington Books.

Huff-Corzine, L., J. Corzine, and D. C. Moore. 1986. "Southern Exposure: Deciphering the South's Influence on Homicide Rates." *Social Forces* 64: 906–924.

Hughes, E. 1945. "Dilemmas and Contradictions of Status." *American Journal of Sociology* 50: 353–359.

———. 1962. "Good People and Dirty Work." *Social Problems* 10: 3–11.

Hughes, E. C. 1971. *The Sociological Eye*. Chicago: Aldine.

Hughes, M., and T. J. Carter. 1981. "A Declining Economy and Sociological Theories of Crime: Predictions and Explications." Pp. 5–26 in *Crime and Criminal Justice in a Declining Economy*. Edited by K. N. Wright. Cambridge, MA: Oelgeschlager, Gunn and Hain.

Hughes, R. 1987. *Fatal Shore*. New York: Knopf.

Huizinga, D., and D. S. Elliott. 1987. "Juvenile Offenders: Prevalence, Offender Incidence, and Arrest Rates by Race." *Crime and Delinquency* 33: 206–223.

Humphreys, L. 1970. *Tearoom Trade: Impersonal Sex in Public Places*. Chicago: Aldine.

Hunt, A. 1985. "The Ideology of Law: Advances and Problems in Recent Applications of the Concept of Ideology to the Analysis of Law." *Law & Society Review* 19: 11–37.

———. 1987. "The Critique of Law: What Is 'Critical' about Critical Legal Theory?" In *Critical Legal Studies*. Edited by P. Fitzpatrick and A. Hunt. Oxford: Basil Blackwell.

Hunt, D., B. Spunt, D. Lipton, D. Goldsmith, and D. Strung. 1987. "The Costly Bonus: Cocaine Related Crime Among Methadone Treatment Clients." *Advances in Alcohol and Substance Abuse* 6: 107–122.

Hunt, D. E., D. S. Lipton, and B. Spunt. 1984. "Patterns of Criminal Activity Among Methadone Clients and Current Narcotics Users Not in Treatment." *Journal of Drug Issues* 14: 687–702.

Hunt, M. 1974. *Sexual Behavior in the 1970's*. New York: Dell.

Hussey, F. A., and D. E. Duffee. 1980. *Probation, Parole and Community Field Services: Policy Structure and Practice*. New York: Harper & Row.

Hyman, H. 1953. "The Value Systems of the Different Classes: A Social-Psychological Contribution to the Analysis of Stratification." Pp. 488–499 in *Class, Status, and Power*. Edited by R. Bendix and S. M. Lipset. New York: Free Press.

Ianni, E., and F. Ianni. 1983. "Street Cops and Management Cops: Two Cultures of Policing." Pp. 251–274 in *Control in the Police Organization*. Edited by M. Punch. Cambridge, MA: MIT Press.

Ianni, F. A. J. 1974. *Black Mafia*. New York: Simon & Schuster.

Ianni, F. A. J., and E. Reuss-Ianni. 1973. *A Family Business: Kinship and Social Control in Organized Crime*. New York: New American Library.

Ignatieff, M. 1978. *A Just Measure of Pain*. New York: Pantheon.

Inbau, F., J. Thompson, and J. Zagel. 1974. *Criminal Law and Its Administration*. Mineola, NY: Foundation Press.

Inciardi, J. A. 1979. "Heroin Use and Street Crime." *Crime and Delinquency* 25: 335–346.

———. 1986. *The War on Drugs: Heroin, Cocaine, Crime, and Public Policy*. Palo Alto, CA: Mayfield.

———. 1987. *Criminal Justice*. 2d ed. San Diego: Harcourt.

———. 1989. "Trading Sex for Crack Among Juvenile Drug Users: A Research Note." *Contemporary Drug Problems* 16: 689–700.

———. 1992. *The War on Drugs II*. Mountain View, CA: Mayfield Publishing Company.

Inciardi, J. A., A. E. Potteiger, M. A. Forney, D. D. Chitwood, and D. C. McBride. 1991. "Prostitution, IV Drug Use, and Sex-For-Crack Exchanges Among Serious Delinquents: Risks For HIV Infection." *Criminology* 29(2): 221–236.

Incove, D. J., V. B. Wherry, and J. D. Shroeder. 1979. *Combatting Arson-for-Profit*. Columbus, OH: Battelle Press.

Innes, C. A. 1988. *Profile of State Prison Inmates, 1986*. Washington, DC: U.S. Department of Justice, Bureau of Justice Statistics.

Innis, R. 1987. "Memorandum of Law of Roy Innis and the Congress of Racial Equality." Amici Curia Brief, Brooklyn, New York.

Institute for Law and Social Research (INSLAW). 1975. *PROMIS Briefing Series, Interface with Other CJIS, INSLAW*. Washington, DC: U.S. Social Security Office.

International Association of Chiefs of Police. 1929. *Uniform Crime Reporting: A Complete Manual for Police*. New York: Little & Ives.

Inverarity, J. 1976. "Populism and Lynching in Louisiana: A Test of Erikson's Theory of the Relationship Between Boundary Crises and Repressive Justice." *American Sociological Review* 41: 262–280.

Inverarity, J., and R. Grattet. 1989. "Institutional Responses to Unemployment: A Comparative Analysis of Criminal Justice, Welfare, and Mental Health Trends in the U.S., 1940-1985." *Contemporary Crises* 13: 351–370.

Irwin, J. 1970. *The Felon*. Englewood Cliffs, NJ: Prentice-Hall.

———. 1980. *Prisons in Turmoil*. Boston: Little, Brown.

———. 1985. *The Jail*. Berkeley: University of California Press.

Irwin, J., and D. R. Cressey. 1962. "Thieves, Convicts and the Inmate Subculture." *Social Problems* 10: 142–155.

Israel, J. 1977. "Criminal Procedure, The Burger Court, and the Legacy of the Warren Court." *Michigan Law Review* 75: 1319–1425.

Jackson, P. G. 1988. "Assessing the Validity of Official Data on Arson." *Criminology* 26: 181–195.

Jackson, P. I. 1986. "Black Visibility, City Size, and Social Control." *Sociological Quarterly* 27: 185–203.

Jackson, P. I., and L. Carroll. 1981. "Race and the War on Crime." *American Sociological Review* 46: 290–305.

Jacob, H. 1983. "Courts as Organizations." Pp. 191–215 in *Empirical Theories About Courts*. Edited by K. O. Boyum and L. Mather. New York: Longman.

Jacobs, D. 1979. "Inequality and Police Strength: Conflict Theory and Coercive Control in Metropolitan Areas." *American Sociological Review* 44: 913–925.

Jacobs, D., and D. Britt. 1979. "Inequality and Police Use of Deadly Force: An Empirical Assessment of a Conflict Hypothesis." *Social Problems* 26: 403–412.

Jacobs, J. B. 1974. "Street Gangs Behind Bars." *Social Problems* 21: 395–409.

———. 1979. "Race Relations and the Prisoner Subculture." Pp. 1–27 in *Crime and Justice.* Vol. 1. Edited by N. Morris and M. Tonry. Chicago: University of Chicago Press.

———. 1983. "Female Guards in Men's Prison." Pp. 178–202 in *New Perspectives on Prisons and Imprisonment.* Edited by J.B. Jacobs. Ithaca, NY: Cornell University Press.

———. 1988. *Inside Prisons.* Washington, DC: U.S. Department of Justice, National Institute of Justice.

Jacobs, J. B., and N. Crotty. 1983. "The Guard's World." Pp. 133–141 in *New Perspectives on Prisons and Imprisonment.* Edited by J. B. Jacobs. Ithaca, NY: Cornell University Press.

Jacobs, J. B., and L. J. Kraft. 1983. "Race Relations and the Guard Subculture." Pp. 160–178 in *New Perspectives on Prisons and Imprisonment.* Edited by J. B. Jacobs. Ithaca, NY: Cornell University Press.

Jacobs, J. B., and L. Zimmer. 1983. "Collective Bargaining and Labor Unrest." Pp. 142–160 in *New Perspectives on Prisons and Imprisonment.* Edited by J. B. Jacobs. Ithaca, NY: Cornell University Press.

Jacobs, P., et al. 1965. "Aggressive Behavior, Mental Subnormality and the XYY Male." *Nature* 208: 1351–1352.

Jacoby, J. E., and C. S. Dunn. 1987. "National Survey on Punishment for Criminal Offenses: Executive Summary." Paper prepared for the National Conference for Criminal Offenses, Ann Arbor, Michigan.

Jacoby, J. E., L. Mellon, E. Ratledge, and S. Turner. 1982. *Prosecutorial Decisionmaking: A National Study.* Washington, DC: U.S. Department of Justice, National Institute of Justice.

Jacoby, J. E., and R. Paternoster. 1982. "Sentencing Disparity and Jury Packing: Further Challenges to the Death Penalty." *Journal of Criminal Law and Criminology* 73: 379–387.

Jacoby, T. 1988. "Going After Dissidents." *Newsweek,* February 8, 29.

Jaffe, J., T. F. Babor, and D. H. Fishbein. 1988. "Alcoholics, Aggression and Antisocial Personality." *Journal of Studies on Alcohol* 49: 211–218.

James, J. 1976. "Motivations for Entrance into Prostitution." In *The Female Offender.* Edited by L. Crites. Lexington, MA: Lexington Books.

———. 1977. "Prostitutes and Prostitution." In *Deviants: Voluntary Action in a Hostile World.* Edited by E. Sagarin and F. Montanino. New York: Scott, Foresman.

Jamieson, K. M., and T. J. Flanagan. 1987. *Sourcebook of Criminal Justice Statistics—1986.* Washington, DC: U.S. Government Printing Office.

———. 1988. *Sourcebook of Criminal Justice Statistics—1987.* Washington, DC: U.S. Government Printing Office.

Jankovic, I. 1977. "Labor Market and Imprisonment." *Crime and Social Justice* 8: 17–31.

Jankowski, M. S. 1991. *Islands in the Street: Gangs and American Urban Society.* Berkeley, CA: University of California Press.

Jaquith, S. M. 1981. "Adolescent Marijuana and Alcohol Use: An Empirical Test of Differential Association Theory." *Criminology* 19: 271–280.

Jeffery, C. R. 1957. "The Development of Crime in Early English Society." *Journal of Criminology, Law Criminology and Political Science* 47: 647–666.

———. 1971. *Crime Prevention Through Environmental Design.* Beverly Hills, CA: Sage.

———. 1978. "Criminology as an Interdisciplinary Behavioral Science." *Criminology* 16 (2).

———. 1985. *Attacks on the Insanity Defense.* Springfield, IL: Thomas.

Jenness, V. 1990. "From Sex as Sin to Sex as Work: COYOTE and the Reorganization of Prostitution as a Social Problem." *Social Problems* 37: 403–420.

Jensen, G. F. 1972a. "Delinquency and Adolescent Self-conceptions: A Study of the Personal Relevance of Infraction." *Social Problems* 20: 84–102.

———. 1972b. "Parents, Peers, and Delinquent Action: A Test of the Differential Association Perspective." *American Journal of Sociology* 78: 562–575.

———. 1973. "Inner Containment and Delinquency." *Journal of Criminal Law and Criminology* 64: 46–70.

Jensen, G. F., M. Erickson, and J. Gibbs. 1978. "Perceived Risk of Punishment and Self-Reported Delinquency." *Social Forces* 57: 57–78.

Jermeir, J., and L. Berkes. 1979. "Leader Behavior in a Police Command Bureaucracy: A Closer Look at the Quasi-military Model." *Administrative Science Quarterly* 24: 1–23.

Jesness, C. F., and R. F. Wedge. 1985. *Jesness Inventory Classification System.* Palo Alto, CA: Consulting Psychologists Press.

Joey (with D. Fisher). 1974. *Killer.* New York: Pocket Books.

Johns, C. J. 1992. *Power, Ideology, and the War on Drugs: Nothing Succeeds Like Failure.* New York: Praeger.

Johnson, B. 1988. "A Day in the Life of 105 Drug Addicts and Abusers: Crimes Committed and How the Money Was Spent." *Sociology and Social Research* 72: 185–191.

Johnson, B. D., T. Williams, K. A. Dei, and H. Sanabria. 1990. "Drug Abuse in the Inner City: Impact on Hard-Drug Users and the Community." Pp. 9–67 in *Drugs and Crime.* Edited by Michael Tonry and James Q. Wilson. Chicago: University of Chicago Press.

Johnson, R. E. 1979. *Juvenile Delinquency and Its Origins.* Cambridge, MA: Harvard University Press.

Johnson, R. E., A. C. Marcos, and S. J. Bahr. 1987. "The Role of Peers in the Complex Etiology of Adolescent Drug Use." *Criminology* 25: 323–340.

Johnston, L. 1973. *Drugs and American Youth.* Ann Arbor, MI: Institute for Social Research.

Johnston, L. D., P. M. O'Malley, and J. G. Bachman. 1987. *National Trends in Drug Use and Related Factors among American High School Students and Young Adults, 1975-1986.* Rockville, MD: National Institute of Drug Abuse.

———. 1991. *Drug Use Among American High School Seniors, College Students and Young Adults, 1975-1990.* Rockville, MD: National Institute on Drug Abuse.

———. 1992a. *Smoking, Drinking and Illicit Drug Use Among American Secondary School Students, College Students and Young Adults, 1975-1991: Volume I, Secondary School Students.* Rockville, MD: National Institute on Drug Abuse.

———. 1992b. *Smoking, Drinking and Illicit Drug Use Among American Secondary School Students, College Students and Young Adults, 1975-1991: Volume II, College Students and Young Adults.* Rockville, MD: National Institute on Drug Abuse.

Johnston, L. D., P. M. O'Malley, and L. K. Eveland. 1978. "Drugs and Delinquency: A Search for Causal Connections." Pp. 137–156 in *Longitudinal Research on Drug Use: Empirical Findings and Methodological Issues.* Washington, DC: Hemisphere.

Jolin, A., and D. Gibbons. 1987. "Age Patterns in Criminal Involvement." *International Journal of Offender Therapy and Comparative Criminology* 31: 237–260.

Jolly, R. W., Jr., and E. Sagarin. 1984. "The First Eight Executed after Furman: Who Was Executed with the Return of the Death Penalty?" *Crime and Delinquency* 30: 610–623.

Jones, A. 1981. *Women Who Kill.* New York: Fawcett Books.

Jones, F. D. 1926. "Historical Development of the Law of Business Competition." *Yale Law Journal* 35: 905.

Jones, G. 1990. "Prison Gambling." *The National Association for Gambling Studies* 2: 5–15.

Juth, C. L. 1987. "The Role of the Founder(s) in the Direct Selling Corporation." Paper presented at the 1987 meeting of the American Society of Criminology, Montreal.

Kadish, S. H. 1967. "The Crisis of Overcriminalization." *The Annals of the American Academy of Political and Social Science* 374: 158–170.

Kamin, L. J. 1985. "Criminality and Adoption." *Science* 227: 982.

———. 1986. "Is Crime in the Genes? The Answer May Depend on Who Chooses What Evidence." *Scientific American*, February, 22–27.

Kamisar, Y. 1982. "How We Got the Fourth Amendment Exclusionary Rule and Why We Need It." *Criminal Justice Ethics* 1: 4–15.

———. 1983. "Does (Did) (Should) the Exclusionary Rule Rest on a 'Principled Basis' Rather than an 'Empirical Proposition'?" *Creighton Law Review* 16: 565–667.

Kandel, D. B., and D. R. Maloff. 1983. "Commonalities in Drug Use: A Sociological Perspective." Pp. 3–28 in *Commonalities in Subtance Abuse and Habitual Behavior.* Edited by P. K. Levinson, D. R. Gerstein, and D. R. Maloff. Lexington, MA: Lexington Books.

Kaplan, H. B. 1972. "Toward a General Theory of Psychosocial Deviance: The Case of Aggressive Behavior." *Social Science and Medicine* 6: 593–617.

———. 1980. *Deviant Behavior in Defense of Self.* New York: Academic Press.

Kaplan, H. B., S. S. Martin, and R. J. Johnson. 1986. "Self-Rejection and the Explanation of Deviance: Specification of the Structure Among Latent Constructs." *American Journal of Sociology* 92: 384–411.

Kaplan, H. B., S. S. Martin, and C. Rubbins. 1982. "Application of a General Theory of Deviant Behavior: Self-Derogation and Adolescent Drug

Use." *Journal of Health and Social Behavior* 23: 274–294.

Kaplan, J. 1970. *Marijuana — The New Prohibition.* New York: World.

Karacki, L., and J. Toby. 1962. "The Uncommitted Adolescent: Candidate for Gang Socialization." *Sociological Inquiry* 32: 203–215.

Karlen, A. 1971. *Sexuality and Homosexuality.* New York: Norton.

Karmen, A. 1979. "Victim Facilitation: The Case of Auto Theft." *Victimology* 4: 361–370.

_____. 1980. "Auto Theft: Beyond Victim Blaming." *Victimology* 5: 161–174.

_____. 1981. "Auto Theft and Corporate Irresponsibility." *Contemporary Crises* 5: 63–81.

_____. 1990. *Crime Victims: An Introduction to Victimology.* 2d ed. Pacific Grove, CA: Brooks/Cole.

_____. 1991. "The Controversy Over Shared Responsibility: Is Victim-Blaming Ever Justified?" Pp. 395–408 in *To Be A Victim: Encounters With Crime And Injustice.* Edited by D. Sank and D. Caplan. New York: Plenum Press.

Karmin, A. 1980. "Race Inferiority, Crime and Research Taboos." Pp. 188–214 in *Taboos in Criminology.* Edited by E. Sagarin. Beverly Hills, CA: Sage.

Katz, G. 1983. "Police Bugs Could Tap City for Millions." *USA Today,* April 29, 3.

Katz, J. 1976. *Gay American History: Lesbians and Gay Men in the USA.* New York: Avon Books.

Katz, J., and C. Abel. 1984. "The Medicalization of Repression." *Contemporary Crises* 8: 227–241.

Keil, T. J., and G. F. Vito. 1989. "Race, Homicide Severity, and Application of the Death Penalty: A Consideration of the Barnett Scale." *Criminology* 27: 511–535.

Kellam, S. G., R. G. Adams, C. H. Brown, and M. E. Ensminger. 1982. "The Long-term Evolution of the Family Structure of Teenage and Older Mothers." *Journal of Marriage and the Family* 44: 539–554.

Kellerman, A. L., and D. T. Reay. 1986. "Protection or Peril? An Analysis of Firearms-Related Deaths in the Home." *New England Journal of Medicine* 314: 1557–1560.

Kelling, G. 1988. "Police and Communities: The Quiet Revolution." *Perspectives on Policing.* U.S. Department of Justice, National Institute of Justice.

Kelly, D. 1990. "Victim Participation in the Criminal Justice System." Pp. 172–187 in *Victims of Crime: Problems, Policies, and Programs.* Edited by A. Lurigio, W. Skogan, and R. Davis. Newbury Park, CA: Sage.

Kelman, H. 1961. "Processes of Opinion Change." *Public Opinion Quarterly* 25: 57.

Kerle, K. E., and F. R. Ford. 1982. *State of Our Nation's Jails.* Washington, DC: National Sheriffs' Association.

Kerstetter, W. 1985. "Who Disciplines the Police?" In *Police Leadership: Crisis and Opportunity.* Edited by W. Geller. New York: Praeger.

Kessler, R. G. 1980. "Enforcement Problems of Gun Control: A Victimless Crimes Analysis." *Criminal Law Bulletin* 16: 131–148.

Keve, P. W. 1992. "The Costliest Punishment — A Corrections Administrator Contemplates the Death Penalty." *Federal Probation* 56: 11–15.

Kiel, T. J., and F. G. Vito. 1989. "Race, Homicide Severity, and Application of the Death Penalty: A Consideration of the Barnett Scale." *Criminology* 27: 511–531.

_____. 1992. "The Effects of the *Furman* and Gregg Decisions on Black-White Execution Ratios in the South." *Journal of Criminal Justice* 20: 217–226.

Kifner, J. 1974. "FBI Gave Chicago Police Plan of Slain Panther's Apartment." *New York Times,* May 24.

Kinsey, A., W. B. Pomeroy, and C. E. Martin. 1948. *Sexual Behavior in the Human Male.* Philadelphia and London: Saunders.

_____. 1953. *Sexual Behavior in the Human Female.* Philadelphia and London: Saunders.

Kitsuse, J. 1962. "Societal Reaction to Deviant Behavior: Problems of Theory and Method." *Social Problems* 9: 247–256.

_____. 1975. "The 'New Conception of Deviance' and Its Critics." Pp. 273–284 in *The Labelling of Deviance: Evaluating a Perspective.* Edited by W. Gove. Beverly Hills, CA: Sage.

Kitsuse, J. I., and A. V. Cicourel. 1963. "A Note on the Use of Official Statistics." *Social Problems* 11: 131–138.

Kittrie, N. N. 1971. *The Right to Be Different: Deviance and Enforced Therapy.* Baltimore: Johns Hopkins University Press.

Klebba, J. A. 1975. "Homicide Trends in the United States: 1900-74." *Public Health Reports* 90: 195–204.

Kleck, G. 1981. "Racial Discrimination in Criminal Sentencing: A Critical Evaluation of the Evidence on the Death Penalty." *American Sociological Review* 46: 783–805.

———. 1984a. "The Relationship Between Gun Ownership Levels and Rates of Violence in the United States." Pp. 99–132 in *Firearms and Violence: Issues of Public Policy*. Edited by D. B. Kates. Cambridge, MA: Ballinger.

———. 1984b. "Handgun Control Only: A Policy Disaster in the Making." Pp. 167–200 in *Firearms and Violence: Issues in Public Policy*. Edited by D. B. Kates. Cambridge, MA: Ballinger.

———. 1985. "Handguns and Violence: Is the 'Saturday Night Special' the Problem?" Unpublished manuscript.

———. 1986a. "Policy Lessons From Recent Gun Control Research." *Law and Contemporary Problems* 49: 35–62.

———. 1986b. "Evidence That 'Saturday Night Specials' Not Very Important for Crime." *Sociology and Social Research* 70: 303–307.

———. 1986c. "Firearms Accidents." Unpublished manuscript.

———. 1988. "Crime Control through the Private Use of Armed Force." *Social Problems* 35: 1–21.

———. 1991. *Point Blank: Guns and Violence in America*. Hawthorne, NY: Aldine de Gruyter.

Kleck, G., and D. Bordua. 1984. "The Assumptions of Gun Control." Pp. 23–44 in *Firearms and Violence: Issues of Public Policy*. Edited by D. Kates. Cambridge, MA: Ballinger.

Klein, L., B. Forst, and V. Filatov. 1978. "The Deterrent Effect of Capital Punishment: An Assessment of the Estimates." In *Deterrence and Incapacitation: Estimating the Effects of Criminal Sanctions on Crime Rates*. Edited by A. Blumstein, J. Cohen, and D. Nagin. Washington, DC: National Academy of Sciences.

Klein, Malcolm W., Cheryl L. Maxson, and Lea C. Cunningham. 1991. "'Crack,' Street Gangs, and Violence." *Criminology* 29(4): 623–650.

Klein, S., and M. Caggiano. 1986. *The Prevalence, Predictability, and Policy Implications of Recidivism*. Rand Report R-3413-BJS. Santa Monica, CA: Rand Corporation.

Kline, G., and P. Tichenor. 1972. *Current Perspectives in Mass Communication Research*. Beverly Hills, CA: Sage.

Klinger, D. 1983. "Demeanor or Crime? An Inquiry into Why 'Hostile' Suspects Are More Likely To Be Arrested." Unpublished manuscript. University of Houston.

Klockars, C. B. 1972. "A Theory of Probation Supervision." *Journal of Criminal Law, Criminology and Police Science* 63: 550.

———. 1974. *The Professional Fence*. New York: Free Press.

———. 1979. "The Contemporary Crises of Marxist Criminology." *Criminology* 16: 477–515.

———. 1984. "Blue Lies and Police Placebos: The Moralities of Police Lying." *American Behavioral Scientist* 27: 529–544.

———. 1985. *The Idea of Police*. Newbury Park, CA: Sage.

———. 1988. "The Rhetoric of Community Policing." In *Community Policing: Rhetoric or Reality*. Edited by J. R. Greene and S. D. Mastrofski. New York: Praeger.

Klockars, C. B., and W. E. Harver. 1993. "The Production and Consumption of Research in Police Agencies in the United States." Report to the National Institute of Justice. Unversity of Delaware.

Knapp Commission. 1972. *Knapp Commission on Police Corruption*. New York: Braziller.

Kohlberg, L., and D. Elfenbein. 1975. "The Development of Moral Judgements Concerning Capital Punishment." *American Journal of Orthopsychiatry* 45: 614–640.

Kolb, L. 1925a. "Drug Addiction and Its Relation to Crime." *Mental Hygiene* 9: 74–89.

———. 1925b. "Types and Characteristics of Drug Addicts." *Mental Hygiene* 9: 300–313.

Kopel, D. B. 1992. *The Samurai, the Mountie, and the Cowboy: Should America Adopt the Gun Controls of Other Democracies?* Buffalo, NY: Prometheus.

Koppel, H. 1987. *Lifetime Likelihood of Victimization: Bureau of Justice Statistics Technical Report*. Washington, DC: Department of Justice.

Kornhauser, R. R. 1978. *Social Sources of Delinquency*. Chicago: University of Chicago Press.

Koss, M. 1992. "The Underdetection Of Rape: Methodological Choices Influence Incidence Estimates." *Journal of Social Issues* 48 (1): 61–75.

Kotarba, J. 1980. "Labelling Theory and Everyday Deviance." Pp. 82–112 in *Introduction to the Sociologies of Everyday Life*. Edited by J. Douglas. Boston: Allyn and Bacon.

Krahn, H., T. F. Hartnagel, and J. W. Gartrell. 1986. "Income Inequality and Homicide Rates: Cross-national Data and Criminological Theories." *Criminology* 24: 269–295.

Krajick, K. 1983. "Should Police Wiretap?: States Don't Agree." *Police Magazine* (May).

Kramer, J. C., and R. G. Pinco. 1973. "Amphetamine Use and Misuse: A Medicolegal View." Pp. 9–22 in *Uppers and Downers*. Edited by D. E. Smith and D. R. Wesson. Englewood Cliffs, NJ: Prentice-Hall.

Krantz, S., B. Gilman, and C. Benda, et al. 1979. *Police Policymaking*. Lexington, MA: Lexington Books.

Krisberg, B. 1975. *Crime and Privilege*. Englewood Cliffs, NJ: Prentice-Hall.

Krisberg, B., and J. Austin. 1980. *The Unmet Promise of Alternatives to Incarceration*. San Francisco: National Council on Crime and Delinquency.

Krisberg, B., I. Schwartz, G. Fishman, Z. Eisikovits, E. Guttman, and K. Joe. 1987. "The Incarceration of Minority Youth." *Crime and Delinquency* 33: 173–205.

Krohn, M. 1986. "The Web of Conformity: A Network Approach to the Explanation of Delinquent Behavior." *Social Problems* 33: 81–93.

Krohn, M., and J. Massey. 1980. "Social Control and Delinquent Behavior: An Examination of the Elements of the Social Bond." *Sociological Quarterly* 21: 529–543.

Krohn, M., W. F. Skinner, J. L. Massey, and R. Akers. 1985. "Social Learning Theory and Adolescent Cigarette Smoking: A Longitudinal Study." *Social Problems* 32: 455–471.

Kruttschnitt, C. 1984. "Sex and Criminal Court Dispositions: The Unresolved Controversy." *Journal of Research in Crime and Delinquency* 21: 213–232.

Kruttschnitt, C., and D. E. Green. 1984. "The Sex-Sanctioning Issue: Is It History?" *American Sociological Review* 49: 541–551.

Kugel, Y., and G. W. Gruenberg. 1977. *International Payoffs*. Lexington, MA: Lexington Books.

Kunstler, W. T., and M. L. Ratner. 1988. "FBI Goes Snooping: Liberties Burned Again." *Los Angeles Times*, February 3.

Kutchinsky, B. 1973. "The Effect of Easy Availability of Pornography on the Incidence of Sex Crimes." *Journal of Social Issues* 29: 95–112.

———. 1991. "Pornography and Rape: Theory and Practice? Evidence from Crime Data in Four Countries where Pornography is Easily Available." (Paper presented at the 14th International Congress on Law and Mental Health, Montreal, Canada.) Published in *International Journal of Law and Psychiatry*. 14 (1–2): 47–64.

LaFave, W. 1965. *Arrest*. Boston: Little, Brown.

LaFave, W., and J. Israel. 1992. *Criminal Procedure* (2d ed.) St. Paul: West.

LaFleur, T., and P. Hevener. 1992. "U.S. Gaming at a Glance." *Gaming and Wagering Business* 13: September 15–October 14: 34.

LaFree, G. D. 1980. "Variables Affecting Guilty Pleas and Convictions in Rape Cases: Toward a Social Theory of Rape Processing." *Social Forces* 58: 833–850.

———. 1989. *Rape and Criminal Justice: The Social Construction of Sexual Assault*. Belmont, CA: Wadsworth.

LaFree, G., K. A. Drass, and P. O'Day. 1992. "Race and Crime in Postwar America: Determinants of African-American and White Rates, 1957-1988." *Criminology* 30: 157–185.

LaGrange, R. L., and H. R. White. 1985. "Age Differences in Delinquency: A Test of Theory." *Criminology* 23: 19–45.

Land, K. C., P. L. McCall, and L. E. Cohen. 1990. "Structural Covariates of Homicide Rates: Are There Any Invariances Across Time and Space?" *American Journal of Sociology* 95: 922–963.

Lander, B. 1954. *Toward an Understanding of Juvenile Delinquency*. New York: Columbia University Press.

Landesco, J. 1929. *Organized Crime in Chicago*. Part III of the Illinois Crime Survey. Chicago: University of Chicago Press.

Lane, R. 1979. *Violent Death in the City: Suicide, Accident, and Murder in 19th Century Philadelphia*. Cambridge, MA: Harvard University Press.

———. 1992. "Urban Police and Crime in Nineteenth-Century America." In *Modern Policing*. Edited by M. Tonry and N. Morris. Chicago: University of Chicago Press.

Lane, R. E. 1954. *The Regulation of Businessmen*. New Haven, CT: Yale University Press.

Lang, A. R., D. J. Goeckner, V. J. Adesso, and G. A. Marlatt. 1975. "Effects of Alcohol on Aggression in Male Social Drinkers." *Journal of Abnormal Psychology* 84: 508–518.

Langan, P. 1988. *State Felony Courts and Felony Laws.* Ann Arbor, MI: Criminal Justice Archive and Information Network.

———. 1989. *Race of Prisoners Admitted to State and Federal Institutions, 1926-86.* Washington, DC: U.S. Department of Justice, Bureau of Justice Statistics.

———. 1991. "America's Soaring Prison Population." *Science* 251: 1568-1573.

Langan, P. A., J. V. Fundis, L. A. Greenfeld, and V. W. Schneider. 1988. *Historical Statistics on Prisoners in State and Federal Institutions, Yearend 1925-86.* Washington, DC: U.S. Department of Justice, Bureau of Justice Statistics.

Lange, J. 1929. *Crime as Destiny.* New York: Boni.

Langworthy, D. 1986. *The Structure of Police Organizations.* New York: Praeger.

Lauderdale, P. 1976. "Deviance and Moral Boundaries." *American Sociological Review* 41: 660–676.

Lawrence, P., and J. Lorsch. 1969. *Organization and Environment.* Homewood, IL: Irwin.

Lee, R. B. 1979. *The Kung San: Men, Women, and Work in a Foraging Society.* Cambridge: Cambridge University Press.

Leff, C., and M. Leff. 1981. "The Politics of Ineffectiveness: Federal Firearms Legislation, 1919-1938." *The Annals of the American Academy of Political and Social Science* 455: 48–62.

Lemert, E. 1951. *Social Pathology.* New York: McGraw-Hill.

———. 1974. "Beyond Mead: The Societal Reaction to Deviance." *Social Problems* 21: 457–468.

———. 1981. "Issues in the Study of Deviance." *The Sociological Quarterly* 22: 285–305.

Lempert, R. 1983. "Capital Punishment in the 80's: Reflection on the Symposium." *Journal of Criminal Law and Criminology* 74: 1101–1114.

Lengermann, P. M. 1979. "The Founding of the American Sociological Review." *American Sociological Review* 44: 185–198.

Leo, R. 1992. "From Coercion to Deception." *Crime, Law, and Social Change* 18: 35–59.

Leonard, E. 1982. *Women, Crime, and Society.* New York: Longman.

Leonard, W. N., and M. G. Weber. 1970. "Automakers and Dealers: Study of Criminogenic Market Forces." *Law & Society Review* 4: 407–424.

Lerman, P. 1968. "Individual Values, Peer Values, and Subcultural Delinquency." *American Sociological Review* 33: 219–235.

———. 1975. *Community Treatment and Social Control.* Chicago: University of Chicago Press.

Lerner, S. E., and R. S. Burns. 1978. "Phencyclidine Use Among Youth: History, Epidemiology, and Acute and Chronic Intoxication." Pp. 66–118 in *Phencyclidine (PCP) Abuse: An Appraisal.* NIDA Research Monograph 21. Edited by R. C. Petersen and R. C. Stillman. Rockville, MD: Department of Health, Education, and Welfare.

Lesieur, H. R. 1984. *The Chase: Career of the Compulsive Gambler.* Cambridge: Schenkman.

———. 1987. "The Female Pathological Gambler." In *Gambling Research: Proceedings of the Seventh International Conference on Gambling and Risk Taking.* Edited by W. R. Eadington. Reno, NE: Bureau of Business and Economic Research.

Lesieur, H. R., and R. Klein. 1985. *Prisoners, Gambling and Crime.* Paper presented at the annual meeting of the Academy of Criminal Justice Sciences, Las Vegas, Nevada. April.

Lesieur, H. R., S. B. Blume, and R. M. Zoppa. 1985. "Alcoholism, Drug Abuse, and Gambling." *Alcoholism: Clinical and Experimental Research* 10: 33–38.

Lesieur, H. R., and J. F. Sheley. 1987. "Illegal Appended Enterprises: Selling the Lines." *Social Problems* 34: 249–260.

Lessan, G. T. 1991. "Macro-Economic Determinants of Penal Policy: Estimating the Unemployment and Inflation Influences on Imprisonment Rate Changes in the United States, 1948-1985." *Crime, Law and Social Change* 16: 177–198.

Leuptow, L. 1980. "Social Change and Sex Role Change in Orientations Toward Life, Work, and Achievement." *Social Psychology Quarterly* 43: 48–59.

Levine, J. 1976. "The Potential for Crime Overreporting in Criminal Victimization Surveys." *Criminology* 14: 307–331.

Levinson, A. 1993. "Pace of Executions Quickens Since 1977." *Houston Post* (May 9): A–14.

Levinson, D. 1983. "Social Setting, Cultural Factors, and Alcohol-Related Aggression." Pp. 41–48 in *Alcohol, Drug Abuse and Aggression*. Edited by E. Gottheil, K. A. Druley, T. E. Skoloda, and H. M. Waxman. Springfield, IL: Thomas.

Lewis, O. 1968. *La Vida*. New York: Vintage Books.

Lewontin, R. C., S. Rose, and L. J. Kamin. 1984. *Not in Our Genes*. New York: Pantheon Books.

Liazos, A. 1972. "The Poverty of the Sociology of Deviance: Nuts, Sluts, and Perverts." *Social Problems* 20: 103–120.

Lichter, L., and S. R. Lichter. 1983. *Prime Time Crime*. Washington, DC: The Media Institute.

Lidz, C. W., and A. L. Walker, with assistance of L. C. Gould. 1980. *Heroin, Deviance and Morality*. Beverly Hills, CA: Sage.

Liker, J. 1982. "Wage and Status Effects of Employment on Affective Well-Being Among Ex-felons." *American Sociological Review* 47: 264–283.

Lilly, R., and R. Ball. 1982. "A Critical Analysis of the Changing Concept of Criminal Responsibility." *Criminology* 20: 169–184.

Linder, R. L. 1981. *PCP: The Devil's Dust*. Belmont, CA: Wadsworth.

Lindesmith, A. R. 1965. *The Addict and the Law*. New York: Vintage Books.

Lipetz, M. A. 1980. "Routine and Deviations: The Strength of the Courtroom Workgroup in a Misdemeanor Court." *International Journal of the Sociology of Law* 8: 47–60.

Lipsky, M. 1980. *Street-Level Bureaucracies*. New York: Russell Sage Foundation.

Lipton, D., R. Martinson, and J. Wilks. 1975. *The Effectiveness of Correctional Treatment: A Survey of Treatment Evaluation Studies*. New York: Praeger.

Liska, A. 1987. *Perspectives on Deviance*. 2d ed. Englewood Cliffs, NJ: Prentice-Hall.

Liska, A., and M. B. Chamblin. 1984. "Social Structure and Crime Control Among Macrosocial Units." *American Journal of Sociology* 90: 383–395.

Liska, A., J. Laurence, and M. Benson. 1981. "Perspectives on the Legal Order: The Capacity for Social Control." *American Journal of Sociology* 87: 413–426.

Liska, A., and M. D. Reed. 1985. "Ties to Conventional Institutions and Delinquency: Estimating Reciprocal Effects." *American Sociological Review* 50: 547–560.

Liska, A., and B. Warner. 1991. "Functions of Crime: A Paradoxical Process." *American Journal of Sociology* 96: 1441–1463.

Livingston, J. 1974. *Compulsive Gamblers: Observations on Action and Abstinence*. New York: Harper Torchbooks.

Lizotte, A. 1978. "Extra-legal Factors in Chicago's Criminal Courts: Testing the Conflict Model of Criminal Justice." *Social Problems* 25: 564–580.

Lizotte, A., and D. Bordua. 1980. "Firearms Ownership for Sport and Protection: Two Divergent Models." *American Sociological Review* 45: 229–244.

Lockwood, D. 1980. *Prison Sexual Violence*. New York: Elsevier.

———. 1982. "Stress, Change and Collective Violence in Prison." In *Pains of Imprisonment*. Edited by R. Johnson and H. Toch. Beverly Hills, CA: Sage.

Loftin, C., and R. Hill. 1974. "Regional Subculture and Homicide." *American Sociological Review* 39: 714–724.

Loftin, C., and D. McDowall. 1981. "'One With a Gun Gets You Two': Mandatory Sentencing and Firearms Violence in Detroit." *The Annals of the American Academy of Political and Social Science* 455: 150–168.

Loftin, C., and R. N. Parker. 1985. "The Effect of Poverty on Urban Homicide Rates: An Error in Variables Approach." *Criminology* 23: 269–287.

Loftin, C., M. Heumann, and D. McDowall. 1983. "Mandatory Sentencing and Firearms Violence: Evaluating an Alternative to Gun Control." *Law & Society Review* 17 (2): 287–318.

Loftus, E. 1979. *Eyewitness Testimony*.

Logan, C. H. 1972. "General Deterrence Effects of Imprisonment." *Social Forces* 51: 63–72.

Lombardo, L. X. 1981. *Guards Imprisoned*. New York: Elsevier.

Long, S. K., and A. D. Witte. 1981. "Current Economic Trends: Implications for Crime and Criminal Justice." Pp. 69–143 in *Crime and Criminal Justice in a Declining Economy*. Edited by K. N. Wright. Cambridge, MA: Oelgeschlager, Gunn and Hain.

Lorenz, V. C., and I. N. Rose. 1988. "Compulsive Gambling and the Law." Special issue of *Journal of Gambling Behavior* 5: 4.

Los Angeles Times. 1979. "U.S. Drops Park Influence Case." August 17.

Lubash, A. H. 1985. "Mafia Member Testifies on Sicily 'Commission'." *The New York Times*, November 1, B3.

_____. 1986. "Persico Asks Jury Not to Be Duped by Mafia Label." *The New York Times*, September 19, 1, 24.

Luckenbill, D. F. 1977. "Homicide as a Situated Transaction." *Social Problems* 25: 176–186.

_____. 1986. "Deviant Career Mobility: The Case of Male Prostitutes." *Social Problems* 33: 283–296.

Luckenbill, D. F., and D. P. Doyle. 1989. "Structural Position and Violence: Developing a Cultural Explanation." *Criminology* 27: 419–436.

Lukes, S. 1975. "Political Ritual and Social Integration." *Sociology* 9: 289–308.

Lynn, W. 1981. "What Scientists Really Mean by 'Acceptable Risk.'" *U.S. News & World Report* 90: 60.

MacAndrew, C., and R. B. Edgerton. 1969. *Drunken Comportment*. Chicago: Aldine.

Maccoby, E. 1985. "Social Groupings in Childhood: Their Relationship to Prosocial and Antisocial Behavior in Boys and Girls." In *Development of Antisocial and Prosocial Behavior: Theories, Research and Issues*. Edited by D. Olwens, J. Block, and M. Radke-Yarrow. San Diego: Academic Press.

Maccoby, E. E., J. P. Johnson, and R. M. Church. 1958. "Community Integration and the Social Control of Juvenile Delinquency." *Journal of Social Issues* 14: 38–51.

MacKinnon, C. 1984. "Not a Moral Issue." *Yale Law and Policy Review* 2: 321–345.

MacPherson, C. B. 1978. "The Meaning of Property." Pp. 1–14 in *Property: Mainstream and Critical Positions*. Edited by C. B. MacPherson. Toronto: University of Toronto Press.

Maeder, T. 1985. *Crime and Madness*. New York: Harper and Row.

Magnuson, E. 1986. "Hitting the Mafia." *Time*, September 29, 14–22.

Malamuth, N. M., and E. Donnerstein. 1983. "The Effects of Aggressive-Pornographic Mass Media Stimuli." Vol. 15, pp. 103–196 in *Advances in Experimental Social Psychology*. Edited by L. Berkowitz. New York: Academic Press.

Malina, R. M. 1973. "Biological Substrata." *Comparative Studies of Blacks and Whites in the United States*. Edited by K. S. Miller and R. M. Dreger. New York: Seminar Press.

Malina, R. M., and G. L. Rarick. 1973. "Growth, Physique, and Motor Performance." *Physical Activity,*

Human Growth and Development. Edited by G. L. Rarick. New York: Academic Press.

Mankoff, M. 1971. "Societal Reaction and Career Deviance: A Critical Analysis." *The Sociological Quarterly* 12: 204–217.

_____. 1978. "On the Responsibility of Marxist Criminologists: A Reply to Quinney." *Contemporary Crises* 2: 293–301.

Mann, C. R. 1984. *Female Crime and Delinquency*. Tuscaloosa: University of Alabama Press.

Manning, P. K. 1977. *Police Work*. Cambridge, MA: MIT Press.

_____. 1979a. "The Social Control of Police Work." Pp. 41–65 in *The British Police*. Edited by S. Holdaway. London: Edward Arnold.

_____. 1979b. "The Reflexivity and Facticity of Knowledge." *American Behavioral Scientist* 22 (July/August): 697–732.

_____. 1980. *Narcs' Game*. Cambridge, MA: MIT Press.

_____. 1988. "Community Policing as a Drama of Control." In *Community Policing: Rhetoric or Reality*. Edited by J. R. Greene and S. D. Mastrofski. New York: Praeger.

_____. 1989. "The Occupational Culture of the Police." In *The Encyclopedia of Police Science*. Edited by L. Hoover et al. Dallas: Garland Press.

_____. 1991. "The Police." In *Criminology: A Contemporary Handbook*. Edited by J. F. Sheley. Belmont, CA: Wadsworth.

_____. 1992a. "Technological Dramas and the Police: Statement and Counterstatement in Organizational Analysis." *Criminology* 30: 327–346.

_____. 1992b. "Information Technologies and the Police." In *Modern Policing*. Edited by M. Tonry and N. Morris. Chicago: University of Chicago Press.

_____. 1993. "Toward a Theory of Police Organization Polarities and Change." Paper delivered at the International Conference on Social Change in Policing. Central Police University of R.O.C., Taipei (August).

Margarita, M. 1985. *The 1980 New York Gun Law: An Evaluation of Its Implementation and Impact*. Washington, DC: National Institute of Justice.

Margolick, D. 1985. "25 Wrongfully Executed in U.S., Study Finds." *The New York Times*, November 14, A19.

Mark, V., and F. R. Ervin. 1970. *Violence and the Brain*. New York: Harper & Row.

Mark, V., W. Sweet, and F. Ervin. 1967. "Role of Brain Disease in Riots and Urban Violence." *Journal of the American Medical Association* 201: 895.

Marlatt, G. A., and D. J. Rohsenow. 1981. "The Think-Drink Effect." *Psychology Today*, December, 60–69, 93.

Marquart, J. W., and J. R. Sorensen. 1988. "Institutional and Postrelease Behavior of *Furman*-Commuted Inmates in Texas." *Criminology* 26: 677–693.

Marshall, G. 1965. *The Police and Government.* London: Methuen.

Martin, S. 1989. *Women on the Move?: A Report on the Status of Women in Policing.* Washington, DC: The Police Foundation.

Martin, S. J., and S. Ekland-Olson. 1987. *Texas Prisons: The Walls Came Tumbling Down.* Austin: Texas Monthly Press.

Martindale, D. 1960. *The Nature and Types of Sociological Theory.* Boston: Houghton Mifflin.

Martinson, R. 1976. "California Research at the Crossroads." *Crime and Delinquency* 22: 180.

Marx, G. T. 1974. "Thoughts on a Neglected Category of Social Movement Participant: The Agent Provocateur and the Informant." *American Journal of Sociology* 80: 402–422.

———. 1987. "Interweaving of Public and Private Police in Undercover Work." Pp. 172–193 in *Private Policing.* Edited by C. Shearing and P. Stenning. Newbury Park, CA: Sage.

Mash, E., and D. Wolfe. 1991. "Methodological Issues In Research On Physical Child Abuse." *Criminal Justice and Behavior* 18 (1): 8–29.

Massey, J. L., and M. D. Krohn. 1986. "A Longitudinal Examination of an Integrated Social Process Model of Deviant Behavior." *Social Forces* 65: 106–134.

Mastrofski, S. 1981. "Policing the Beat: The Impact of Organizational Scale on Patrol Officer Behavior in Urban Residential Neighborhoods." *Journal of Criminal Justice* 9:343–358.

———. 1983. "The Police and Non-Crime Services." Pp. 33–61 in *Evaluating the Performance of Criminal Justice Agencies.* Edited by G. P. Whitaker and C. D. Phillips. Newbury Park, CA: Sage.

———. 1986. "Police Agency Accreditation: The Prospects of Reform." *American Journal of Police* 5: 45–81.

———. 1988. "Community Policing as Reform: A Cautionary Tale." In *Community Policing: Rhetoric or Real-*

ity. Edited by J. R. Greene and S. D. Mastrofski. New York: Praeger.

———. 1989. "Police Agency Consolidation: Lessons from a Case Study." In *Police Management Today.* Edited by J. J. Fyfe. Washington DC: International City Mangement Association.

———. 1990. "The Prospects of Change in Police Patrol: A Decade in Review." *American Journal of Police* 9:1–79.

Mastrofski, S. D., and R. Ritti. 1992. "You Can Lead a Horse to Water...: A Case Study of a Police Department's Response to Stricter Drunk-Driving Laws." *Justice Quarterly* 9:465–491.

Mastrofski, S. D., and J. Snipes. 1993. "A Task-Time Analysis of Community Policing in Richmond, Virginia." Unpublished manuscript. University Park, PA: Pennsylvania State University.

Mastrofski, S. D., R. Ritti, and D. Hoffmaster. 1987. "Organizational Determinants of Police Discretion: The Case of Drinking Driving." *Journal or Criminal Justice* 15: 387–402.

Mastrofski, S. D., R. Ritti, and J. Snipes. 1994. "Expectancy Theory and Police Productivity in DUI Enforcement." *Law and Society Review* (forthcoming).

Mastrofski, S. D., and C. Uchida. 1993. "Transforming the Police." *Journal of Research in Crime and Delinquency* 30: 330–358.

Mastrofski, S. D., R. Worden, and J. Snipes. 1993. "Law Enforcement in a Time of Community Policing." Paper delivered at the annual meeting of the American Society of Criminology, Phoenix.

Mather, L. M. 1979. *Plea Bargaining or Trial?* Lexington, MA: Heath.

Mathews, J. 1986. "Lottery Rush Strikes California." *The Washington Post*, January 13, A3.

Matsueda, R. L. 1982. "Testing Control Theory and Differential Association: A Causal Modeling Approach." *American Sociological Review* 47: 489–504.

———. 1988. "The Current State of Differential Association Theory." *Crime and Delinquency* 34: 277–306.

Matsueda, R. L., R. Gartner, I. Piliavin, and M. Polakowski. 1992. "The Prestige of Criminal and Conventional Occupations: A Subcultural Model of Criminal Activity." *American Sociological Review* 57: 752–770.

Matsueda, R. L., and K. Heimer. 1987. "Race, Family Structure, and Delinquency: A Test of Differential

Association and Social Control Theories." *American Sociological Review* 52: 826–840.

Mattick, H. W. 1974. "The Contemporary Jails of the United States: An Unknown and Neglected Area of Justice." Pp. 777–848 in *Handbook of Criminology*. Edited by D. Glaser. Chicago: Rand McNally.

Matza, D. 1964. *Delinquency and Drift*. New York: Wiley.

———. 1969. *Becoming Deviant*. Englewood Cliffs, NJ: Prentice-Hall.

Matza, D., and G. M. Sykes. 1961. "Juvenile Delinquency and Subterranean Values." *American Sociological Review* 26: 712–720.

Mauer, D. 1939. "Prostitutes and Criminal Argots." *American Journal of Sociology* 44: 546–550.

Mauer, M. 1990. "Young Black Men and the Criminal Justice System: A Growing National Problem." Washington, DC: The Sentencing Project.

Maurer, D. 1974. *The American Confidence Man*. Springfield, IL: Thomas.

Maxfield, M. G. 1987. "Lifestyles and Routine Activity Theories of Crime: Empirical Studies of Victimization, Delinquency, and Offender Decision-making." *Journal of Quantitative Criminology* 3: 275–281.

Maxim, P. 1985. "Cohort Size and Juvenile Delinquency: A Test of the Easterlin Hypothesis." *Social Forces* 63: 661–679.

Maynard, D. W. 1982. "Defendant Attributes in Plea Bargaining: Notes on the Modeling of Sentencing Decisions." *Social Problems* 29: 347–360.

Mays, G. L., and J. A. Thompson. 1988. "Mayberry Revisited: The Characteristics and Operations of America's Small Jails." *Justice Quarterly* 5: 421–440.

Mazur, A. 1986. "U.S. Trends in Feminine Beauty and Overadaptation." *The Journal of Sex Research* 22: 281–303.

McBride, D. C., and C. B. McCoy. 1981. "Crime and Drug-Using Behavior: An Areal Analysis." *Criminology* 19: 281–301.

McCaghy, C. H. 1987. *Deviant Behavior: Crime, Conflict, and Interest Groups*. New York: Macmillan.

McCandless, B. R., W. S. Persons III, and A. Roberts. 1972. "Perceived Opportunity, Delinquency, Race, and Body Build Among Delinquent Youth." *Journal of Consulting and Clinical Psychology* 38: 281–287.

McCarthy, B. R. 1987. *Intermediate Punishments*. Monsey, NY: Willow Tree.

McCarthy, J. D., and D. R. Hoge. 1984. "The Dynamics of Self-Esteem and Delinquency." *American Journal of Sociology* 90: 396–410.

McCarthy, S. 1982. "Pornography, Rape, and the Cult of Macho." Pp. 218–232 in *Crisis in American Institutions*. Edited by J. H. Skolnick and E. Currie. Boston: Little, Brown.

McClain, P. 1984. "Prohibiting the 'Saturday Night Special': A Feasible Policy Option?" Pp. 201–217 in *Firearms and Violence: Issues of Public Policy*. Edited by D. B. Kates. Cambridge, MA: Ballinger.

McCleary, R. 1978. *Dangerous Men: The Sociology of Parole*. Beverly Hills, CA: Sage.

———. 1981. *Time Series Analysis for the Social Sciences*. Beverly Hills, CA: Sage.

McCleary, R., B. Nienstedt, and J. M. Erven. 1982. "Uniform Crime Reports as Organizational Outcomes." *Social Problems* 29 (April): 361–372.

McCord, W., and J. Sanchez. 1983. "The Treatment of Deviant Children: A Twenty-five Year Follow-up Study." *Crime and Delinquency* 29: 238–253.

McCormick, A. E. 1977. "Rule Enforcement and Moral Indignation: Some Observations on the Effects of Criminal Antitrust Convictions." *Social Problems* 25: 30–39.

McCoy, C. 1984. "Lawsuits Against the Police." *Criminal Law Bulletin* 20:49–56.

———. 1987. "Constitutional Tort Litigation." Paper delivered at the annual meeting of the American Political Science Association, Chicago.

McCoy, C., and R. Tillman. 1987. *The Impact of the Victim's Bill of Rights on Plea Bargaining in California*. Sacramento: Department of Justice, Bureau of Crime Statistics.

McDonald, D. 1980. *The Price of Punishment*. Boulder, CO: Westview Press.

———. 1987. *Restitution and Community Service: National Institute of Justice Crime File Study Guide*. Washington, DC: U.S. Department of Justice.

McDonald, W. 1976. *Criminal Justice and the Victim*. Newbury Park, CA: Sage.

McDonald, W. F. 1985. *Plea Bargaining: Critical Issues and Common Practices*. Washington, DC: U.S. Department of Justice, National Institute of Justice.

McDowall, D., and C. Loftin. 1983. "Collective Security and the Demand for Legal Handguns." *American Journal of Sociology* 88: 1146–1161.

———. 1992. "Comparing the UCR and NCS Over Time." *Criminology* 30: 125–132.

McGahey, R. 1986. "Economic Conditions, Neighborhood Organization, and Urban Crime." In *Communities and Crime*. Edited by A. Reiss, Jr., and M. Tonry. Chicago: University of Chicago Press.

McGarrell, E., and T. Flanagan. 1985. *Sourcebook of Criminal Justice Statistics, 1984*. U.S. Department of Justice, Bureau of Justice Statistics. Washington, DC: U.S. Government Printing Office.

McGillis, D. 1982. "Minor Dispute Processing: A Review of Recent Developments." Pp. 60–76 in *Neighborhood Justice: Assessment of an Emerging Idea*. Edited by R. Tomasic and M. Freeley. New York: Longman.

———. 1986. *Crime Victims Restitution: An Analysis of Approaches*. Washington, DC: National Institute of Justice.

McGillis, D., and P. Smith. 1983. *Compensating Victims of Crime: An Analysis of American Programs*. Washington, DC: U.S. Department of Justice.

McGlothlin, W. H. 1973. *Amphetamines, Barbiturates and Hallucinogens: An Analysis of Use, Distribution and Control*. Department of Justice, Bureau of Narcotics and Dangerous Drugs. Washington, DC: U.S. Government Printing Office.

McGlothlin, W. H., and D. Anglin. 1981. "Shutting Off Methadone." *Archives of General Psychiatry* 38: 885–892.

McIntosh, M. 1975. *The Organization of Crime*. London: Macmillan.

McIntyre, D., and D. Lippman. 1970. "Prosecutors and Disposition of Felony Cases." *American Bar Association Journal* 56: 1156.

McIver, J. P. 1981. "Criminal Mobility: A Review of Empirical Studies." Pp. 20–47 in *Crime Spillover*. Edited by S. Hakim and G. F. Rengert. Beverly Hills, CA: Sage.

McNamara, J. 1967. "Uncertainties in Police Work: The Relevance of Recruits' Background and Training." Pp. 163–252 in *The Police*. Edited by D. Bordua. New York: Wiley.

McNeely, R. L., and C. E. Pope. 1981. *Race, Crime, and Criminal Justice*. Beverly Hills, CA: Sage.

Mead, G. H. 1918. "The Psychology of Punitive Justice." *American Journal of Sociology* 23: 577–602.

Medalie, R., L. Zeitz, and P. Alexander. 1968. "Custodial Police Interrogation in our Nation's Capitol." *Michigan Law Review* 66: 1347–1422.

Mednick, S. A. 1979. "Biosocial Factors and Primary Prevention of Antisocial Behavior." In *New Paths in Criminology*. Edited by S. Mednick and S. G. Shaham. Lexington, MA: Heath.

Mednick, S. A., and J. Volavka. 1980. "Biology and Crime." Pp. 85–158 in *Criminal Justice: An Annual Review of Research*. Vol. 2. Edited by N. Morris and M. Tonry. Chicago: University of Chicago Press.

Mednick, S. A., et al. 1981. "EEG as a Predictor of Antisocial Behavior." *Criminology* 19: 219–230.

———. 1982. "Biology and Violence." In *Criminal Violence*. Edited by M. Wolfgang and N. A. Weiner. Beverly Hills, CA: Sage.

Mednick, S. A., W. F. Gabrielli, and B. Hutchings. 1984. "Genetic Influences in Criminal Convictions: Evidence from an Adoption Cohort." *Science* 224: 891–894.

Meier, R. 1976. "The New Criminology: Continuity in Criminological Theory." *Journal of Criminal Law and Criminology* 67: 461–469.

Meier, R. F., and W. T. Johnson. 1977. "Deterrence as Social Control: The Legal and Extralegal Production of Conformity." *American Sociological Review* 42: 292–304.

Meiners, R. 1978. *Victim Compensation: Economic, Political, and Legal Aspects*. Lexington, MA: Heath.

Meisenhelder, T. 1977. "An Exploratory Study of Exiting From Criminal Careers." *Criminology* 15: 319–334.

Mello, M. 1984. "Florida's 'Heinous, Atrocious, or Cruel' Aggravating Circumstance: Narrowing the Class of Death-Eligible Cases Without Making It Smaller." *Stetson Law Review* 13: 523–554.

Mellon, L. R., J. E. Jacoby, and M. A. Brewer. 1981. "The Prosecutor Constrained by His Environment: A New Look at Discretionary Justice in the United States." *Journal of Criminal Law and Criminology* 72: 52–81.

Melossi, D. 1985. "Overcoming the Crisis in Critical Criminology: Toward a Grounded Labelling Theory." *Criminology* 23: 193–208.

Melossi, D., and M. Pavarini. 1981. *Prison and the Factory: Origins of the Penitentiary System*. Totowa, NJ: Barnes & Noble Books.

Menard, S. 1992. "Residual Gains, Reliability, and the UCR-NCS Relationship: A Comment on Blumstein, Cohen and Rosenfeld." *Criminology* 30: 105–113.

Mertens, A., and S. Wasserstrom. 1984. "The Exclusionary Rule on the Scaffold: But Was It a Fair Trial?" *American Criminal Law Review* 22: 85–179.

Merton, R. 1938. "Social Structure and Anomie." *American Sociological Review* 3: 672–682.

———. 1964. "Anomie, Anomia, and Social Interaction: Contexts of Deviant Behavior." Pp. 213–242 in *Anomie and Deviant Behavior*. Edited by M. B. Clinard. New York: Free Press.

———. 1968. *Social Theory and Social Structure*. New York: Free Press.

Messerschmidt, J. 1986. *Capitalism, Patriarchy, and Crime: Toward a Socialist Feminist Criminology*. Totowa, NJ: Rowman & Littlefield.

Messner, S. F. 1983a. "Regional and Racial Effects on the Urban Homicide Rate: The Subculture of Violence Revisited." *American Journal of Sociology* 88: 997–1007.

———. 1983b. "Regional Differences in the Economic Correlates of the Urban Homicide Rate: Some Evidence on the Importance of Context." *Criminology* 21: 477–488.

———. 1988. "Research on Cultural and Socioeconomic Factors in Criminal Violence." *The Psychiatric Clinics of North America* 11: 511–525.

———. 1989. "Economic Discrimination and Societal Homicide Rates: Further Evidence on the Cost of Inequality." *American Sociological Review* 54: 597–611.

Messner, S. F., and K. Tardiff. 1985. "The Social Ecology of Urban Homicide: An Application of the Routine Activities Approach." *Criminology* 23: 241–267.

———. 1986. "Economic Inequality and Levels of Homicide: An Analysis of Urban Neighborhoods." *Criminology* 24: 297–318.

Methvin, E. 1986. "The Proven Key to Crime Control." *Reader's Digest*, May, 97–101.

Meyer, G., and T. Fabian. 1992. "Delinquency Among Pathological Gamblers: A Causal Approach." *Journal of Gambling Studies* 8: 61–77.

Michalowski, R. 1985. *Order, Law and Crime*. New York: Random House.

Michalowski, R., and E. Bohlander. 1976. "Repression and Criminal Justice in Capitalist America." *Sociological Inquiry* 46: 95–106.

Mieczkowski, T. 1986. "Geeking Up and Throwing Down: Heroin Street Life in Detroit." *Criminology* 24: 645–666.

———. 1989. "Understanding Life in the Crack Culture: The Investigative Utility of the Drug Use Forecast System." National Institute of Justice. Washington, DC: U.S. Government Printing Office.

———. 1990. "Crack Distribution in Detroit." *Contemporary Drug Problems* 17 (1): 9–30.

Miethe, T. D. 1987a. "Charging and Plea Bargaining Practices Under Determinate Sentencing: An Investigation of the Hydraulic Displacement of Discretion." *Journal of Criminal Law and Criminology* 78: 101–122.

———. 1987b. "Stereotypical Conceptions and Criminal Processing: The Case of the Victim-Offender Relationship." *Justice Quarterly* 4: 571–593.

Miethe, T. D., and C. A. Moore. 1985. "Socioeconomic Disparities Under Determinate Sentencing Systems: A Comparison of Preguideline and Postguideline Practices in Minnesota." *Criminology* 23: 337–363.

———. 1986. "Racial Differences in Criminal Processing: The Consequences of Model Selection on Conclusions about Differential Treatment." *Sociological Quarterly* 27: 217–237.

Miethe, T. D., M. C. Stafford, and J. S. Long. 1987. "Social Differentiation in Criminal Victimization: A Test of Routine Activities/Lifestyle Theories." *American Sociological Review* 52: 184–194.

Miethe, T., M. Stafford, and D. Sloane. 1990. "Lifestyle Changes and Risks of Criminal Victimization." *Journal of Quantitative Criminology* 6 (4): 357–375.

Mileski, M. 1971. "Courtroom Encounters: An Observation Study of a Lower Criminal Court." *Law & Society Review* 5: 473–538.

Mill, J. S. 1892 (originally published in 1859). *On Liberty*. London: Longmans, Green.

Miller, B., and J. W. Welte. 1986. "Comparisons of Incarcerated Offenders According to Use of Alcohol and/or Drugs Prior to Offense." *Criminal Justice and Behavior* 13: 366–392.

Miller, E. 1986. *Street Woman*. Philadelphia: Temple University Press.

Miller, H. S., W. F. McDonald, and J. A. Cramer. 1978. *Plea Bargaining in the United States.* Washington, DC: National Institute of Law Enforcement and Criminal Justice, Law Enforcement Assistance Administration.

Miller, W. 1958. "Lower Class Culture as a Generating Milieu of Gang Delinquency." *Journal of Social Issues* 14: 5–19.

———. 1973. "The Molls." *Society* 11: 32–35.

Miller, W. R. 1977. *Cops and Bobbies.* Chicago: University of Chicago Press.

Millett, K. 1973. *The Prostitution Papers.* New York: Ballantine.

Mills, C. W. 1956. *The Power Elite.* New York: Oxford University Press.

Milner, N. 1971. *The Court and Local Law Enforcement.* Beverly Hills, CA: Sage.

Milton, C., et al. 1977. *Police Use of Deadly Force.* Washington, DC: The Police Foundation.

Minor, W. W. 1981. "Techniques of Neutralization: A Reconceptualization and Empirical Examination." *Journal of Research in Crime and Delinquency* 18: 295–318.

———. 1984. "Neutralization as a Hardening Process: Considerations in the Modeling of Change." *Social Forces* 62: 995–1019.

Mittleman, R. E., and C. V. Wetli. 1984. "Death Caused by Recreational Cocaine Use." *Journal of the American Medical Association* 252: 1889–1893.

Mizruchi, E. 1964. *Success and Opportunity.* New York: Free Press.

Mokhiber, R. 1986. "Greedy Corporations: Criminal by Any Other Name." *Los Angeles Daily Journal,* February 28, 4.

Molotch, H. 1970. "Oil in Santa Barbara and Power in America." *Sociological Inquiry* 40: 131–144.

Monkkonen, E. 1981. *Police in Urban America: 1860–1920.* Cambridge: Cambridge University Press.

Montague, A. 1980. "The Biologist Looks at Crime." *Annals of the American Academy of Political and Social Sciences* 217: 46–57.

Montare, A., and S. L. Boone. 1980. "Aggression and Paternal Absence: Racial-Ethnic Differences Among Inner-City Boys." *Journal of Genetic Psychology* 137: 223–232.

Moore, C. A., and T. D. Miethe. 1986. "Regulated and Unregulated Sentencing Decisions: An Analysis of First-Year Practices Under Minnesota's Felony Sentencing Guidelines." *Law & Society Review* 20: 254–277.

Moore, M. H., and R. C. Trojanowicz. 1988. "Corporate Strategies for Policing." *Perspectives on Policing.* No. 6 NIJ/Kennedy School.

Moore, W. H. 1974. *The Kefauver Committee and the Politics of Crime, 1950-1952.* Columbia: University of Missouri Press.

Morash, M. 1986. "Gender, Peer Groups and Delinquency." *Journal of Research in Crime and Delinquency* 23: 43–67.

Morgan, R. 1980. "Theory and Practice: Pornography and Rape." Pp. 125–132 in *Take Back the Night: Women on Pornography.* Edited by L. Lederer. New York: Morrow.

Morris, N., and G. Hawkins. 1970. *The Honest Politician's Guide to Crime Control.* Chicago: University of Chicago Press.

Morris, N., and M. Miller. 1985. "On 'Dangerousness' in the Judicial Process." Pp. 1–50 in *Crime and Justice: An Annual Review of Research.* Vol. 6. Edited by M. Tonry and N. Morris. Chicago: University of Chicago Press.

Morris, N., and M. Tonry. 1990. *Between Prison and Probation: Intermediate Punishment in a Rational Sentencing System.* New York: Oxford.

Morris, T. 1957. *The Criminal Area: A Study in Social Ecology.* London: Routledge & Kegan Paul.

Morrow, P., and P. Hudson. 1986. "Accidental Firearm Fatalities in North Carolina, 1976-1980." *American Journal of Public Health* 76: 1120–1123.

Moynahan, J. M., and E. K. Stewart. 1980. *The American Jail.* Chicago: Nelson-Hall.

Mugford, S. 1992. "Licit and Illicit Drug Use, Health Costs and the 'Crime Connection' in Australia: Public Views and Policy Implications." *Contemporary Drug Problems* 19 (2): 351–385.

Muir, W. K., Jr. 1977. *The Police: Street Corner Politicians.* Chicago: University of Chicago Press.

Muir, W. K., and D. Perez. 1992. "Administrative Review of Alleged Police Brutality." In *And Justice for All.* Edited by W. Geller and H. Toch. Washington, DC: Police Executive Research Forum.

Munger, F., and C. Seron. 1984. "Critical Legal Studies versus Critical Legal Theory: A Comment on Method." *Law & Policy* 6: 257–297.

Murphy, L. R., and R. W. Dodge. 1981. "The Baltimore Recall Study." *The National Crime Survey: Working Papers. Vol. 1: Current and Historical Perspectives.* Edited by R. G. Lehnen and W. G. Skogan. Washington, DC: U.S. Government Printing Office. 16–21.

Murphy, P. 1966. "Judicial Review of Police Methods in Law Enforcement: The Problem of Compliance by Police Departments." *Texas Law Review* 44: 939–964.

Murphy, S. B., C. Reinarman, and D. Waldorf. 1989. "An 11-year Follow-up of a Network of Cocaine Users." *British Journal of Addictions* 84: 427–436.

Murphy, S. E. 1986. *Marijuana Decriminalization: The Unfinished Reform.* Ph.D. dissertation, University of Missouri, Columbia.

Murray, C. A., and L. A. Cox. 1979. *Beyond Probation: Juvenile Corrections and Chronic Delinquents.* Beverly Hills, CA: Sage.

Murray, D. 1975. "Handguns, Gun Control Laws, and Firearms Violence." *Social Problems* 23: 81–93.

Murray, J. B. 1986. "An Overview of Cocaine Use and Abuse." *Psychological Reports* 59: 243–264.

Murton, T., and J. Hyams. 1969. *Accomplices to the Crime.* New York: Grove Press.

Musto, D. F. 1973. *The American Disease: Origins of Narcotic Control.* New Haven, CT: Yale University Press.

Myers, M. 1990. "Black Threat and Incarceration in Postbellum Georgia." *Social Forces* 69: 373–393.

Myers, M. A. 1979. "Offended Parties and Official Reactions: Victims and the Sentencing of Criminal Defendants." *Sociological Quarterly* 20: 529–540.

———. 1980. "Predicting the Behavior of Law: A Test of Two Models." *Law & Society Review* 14: 835–857.

———. 1981. "Judges, Juries and the Decision to Convict." *Journal of Criminal Justice* 9: 289–303.

———. 1982. "Common Law in Action: The Prosecution of Felonies and Misdemeanors." *Sociological Inquiry* 52: 1–15.

———. 1987. "Economic Inequality and Discrimination in Sentencing." *Social Forces* 65: 746–766.

———. 1988. "Social Background and the Sentencing Behavior of Judges." *Criminology* 26: 649–675.

———. 1991. "Economic Conditions and Punishment in Postbellum Georgia." *Journal of Quantitative Criminology* 7: 99–121.

Myers, M. A., and J. Hagan. 1979. "Private and Public Trouble: Prosecutors and the Allocation of Court Resources." *Social Problems* 26: 439–451.

Myers, M. A., and G. D. LaFree. 1982. "Sexual Assault and Its Prosecution: A Comparison with Other Crimes." *Journal of Criminal Law and Criminology* 73: 1282–1305.

Myers, M. A., and J. L. Massey. 1991. "Race, Labor and Punishment in Postbellum Georgia." *Social Problems* 38: 267–286.

Myers, M. A., and S. M. Talarico. 1986a. "The Social Contexts of Racial Discrimination in Sentencing." *Social Problems* 33: 236–251.

———. 1986b. "Urban Justice, Rural Justice? Urbanization and Its Effect on Sentencing." *Criminology* 24: 367–391.

———. 1987. *The Social Contexts of Criminal Sentencing.* New York: Springer-Verlag.

NAACP Legal and Educational Defense Fund. 1993. *Death Row USA.* (Spring).

Nadelmann, E. A. 1988. "The Case for Legalization." *The Public Interest:* 923–931.

Nader, R., M. J. Green, and J. Segilman. 1976. *Taming the Giant Corporation.* New York: Norton.

Nagel, I. H. 1983. "The Legal/Extra-Legal Controversy: Judicial Decisions in Pretrial Release." *Law & Society Review* 17: 481–515.

Nagel, I. H., and J. Hagan. 1983. "Gender and Crime: Offense Patterns and Criminal Court Sanctions." Pp. 91–144 in *Crime and Justice: An Annual Review of Research.* Vol. 4. Edited by M. Tonry and N. Morris. Chicago: University of Chicago Press.

Nagel, S., and R. Geraci. 1983. "Effects of Reducing Judicial Sentencing Discretion." *Criminology* 21: 309–331.

Nagin, D. 1978. "General Deterrence: A Review of the Empirical Evidence." Pp. 95–139 in *Deterrence and Incapacitation: Estimating the Effects of Criminal Sanctions on Crime Rates.* Edited by A. Blumstein, J. Cohen, and D. Nagin. Washington, DC: National Academy of Sciences.

Nakell, B. 1978. "The Cost of the Death Penalty." *Criminal Law Bulletin* 14: 69–80.

Nakell, B., and K. A. Hardy. 1987. *The Arbitrariness of the Death Penalty*. Philadelphia: Temple University Press.

Nardulli. 1983. "The Societal Cost of the Exclusionary Rule: An Empirical Assessment." 1983. *American Bar Foundation Research Journal* 1983: 585–609.

Nassi, A., and S. I. Abramowitz. 1976. "From Phrenology to Psychosurgery and Back Again: Biological Studies of Criminality." *American Journal of Orthopsychiatry* 46: 591.

National Center for Health Statistics. 1968. *International Classification of Diseases, Eighth Revision, Adapted for Use in the United States*. PHS Publication No. 593D. Washington, DC: U.S. Government Printing Office.

———. 1971. *Medical Examiners' and Coroners' Handbook on Death and Fetal Death Registration*. PHS Publication No. 1693. Washington, DC: U.S. Government Printing Office.

———. 1976. *Funeral Directors' Handbook on Death and Fetal Death Registration*. PHS Publication No. 593c. Washington, DC: U.S. Government Printing Office.

National Center on Institutions and Alternatives. 1988. *National Study of Jail Suicides: Seven Years Later*. Alexandria, VA: National Center on Institutions and Alternatives.

National Coalition to Ban Handguns. 1988. *Membership solicitation letter*. no date.

National Commission for the Protection of Human Subjects of Biomedical and Behavioral Research. 1977. *Report and Recommendations: Psychosurgery*. Department of Health and Welfare Publication No. (OS) 77-0002. Washington, DC: U.S. Government Printing Office.

National Commission on Law Observance and Enforcement. 1931. *Report on Criminal Statistics*. Washington, DC: U.S. Government Printing Office.

National Commission on Marijuana and Drug Abuse. 1973. *Patterns and Consequences of Drug Use*. Washington, DC: U.S. Government Printing Office.

National Commission on the Causes and Prevention of Violence (NCCPV). 1969. *The Offender and His Victim*. Washington, DC: U.S. Government Printing Office.

National Commission on Violence. 1967. *The Kerner Report*. Washington, DC: U.S. Government Printing Office.

National Crime Information Center (NCIC). 1976. *Computerized Criminal History Program: Background, Concept and Policy*. Washington, DC: U.S. Department of Justice.

National Crime Prevention Institute (NCPI). 1978. *Understanding Crime Prevention*. Louisville, KY: National Crime Prevention Institute.

National Criminal Justice Information and Statistics Service. 1973. *Description of National Crime Panel*. Washington, DC: U.S. Justice Department, LEAA.

———. 1976. *Criminal Victimization in the United States*. Washington, DC: U.S. Department of Justice, LEAA.

National Highway Traffic Safety Administration (NHTSA). 1983. *Tracking the Alcohol Involvement Problem in U.S. Highway Crashes*. National Center for Statistics and Analysis. Washington, DC: Author.

———. 1991. *Fatal Accident Reporting System 1990: A Decade of Progress*. Washington, DC: U.S. Government Printing Office.

National Indian Gaming Association. 1992. *Issues and Facts*. Washington, DC: Author.

National Institute of Corrections. 1981. *Model Probation and Parole Management Project*. Washington, DC: National Institute of Corrections.

National Institute of Justice. 1982. *The Effects of the Exclusionary Rule*. Washington, DC: U.S. Government Printing Office.

———. 1987 (February). *Drug Use Forecasting: New York 1984 to 1986*. Washington, DC: U.S. Department of Justice.

———. 1990. *Drug Use Forecasting Annual Report: Drugs and Crime in America*. Washington, DC: U.S. Department of Justice.

National Institute on Drug Abuse. 1991. *National Household Survey on Drug Abuse: Main Findings 1990*. Rockville, MD: U.S. Department of Health and Human Services.

———. 1992. *Annual Medical Examiner Data, 1991: Data from the Drug Abuse Warning Network (DAWN)*. Statistical Series. Series 1: Number 11-B. Rockville, MD: NIDA.

National Opinion Research Center (NORC). 1987. *General Social Surveys, 1972-1987: Cumulative Codebook*. Chicago: National Opinion Research Center.

National Opinion Research Center (NORC). 1991. *General Social Survey, 1991: Codebook*. Chicago: National Opinion Research Center.

National Organization for Victim Assistance (NOVA). 1988. *Victim Rights and Services: A Legislative Directory*. Washington, DC: National Organization for Victim Assistance.

National Probation Association. 1939. *John Augustus: First Probation Officer*. New York: National Probation Association.

National Victim Center. 1988. "Constitutional Amendment." *Networks* (Spring): 6.

National Wiretap Commission. 1976. *Electronic Surveillance Report*. National Commission for the Review of Federal and State Laws Relating to Wiretapping and Electronic Surveillance. Washington, DC: U.S. Government Printing Office.

Neapolitan, J. 1983. "Support for and Opposition to Capital Punishment: Some Associated Social-Psychological Factors." *Criminal Justice and Behavior* 10: 195–208.

Nelkin, D., and J. Swazey. 1982. "Science and Social Control: Controversies over Research on Violence." In *Violence and Politics of Research*. Edited by W. Gaylin. New York: Plenum.

Nelli, H. S. 1981. *The Business of Crime: Italians and Syndicate Crime in the United States*. Chicago: University of Chicago Press.

Nelson, E. 1982. "Pornography and Sexual Aggression." Pp. 171–248 in *The Influence of Pornography on Behavior*. Edited by M. Yaffe and E. C. Nelson. New York: Academic Press.

Nelson, J. F. 1978. *Alternative Measures of Crime: A Comparison of the Uniform Crime Report and the National Crime Survey in 26 American Cities*. Presented at the American Society of Criminology meeting in Dallas.

———. 1979. "Implications for the Ecological Study of Crime: A Research Note." Pp. 21–28 in *Perspectives on Victimology*. Edited by W. H. Parsonage. Beverly Hills, CA: Sage.

Nettler, G. 1978. *Explaining Crime*. New York: McGraw-Hill.

———. 1982. *Criminal Careers*. 4 vols. Cincinnati: Anderson.

———. 1984. *Explaining Crime*. 3d ed. New York: McGraw-Hill.

Neubauer, D. W. 1988. *America's Courts and the Criminal Justice System*. 3d ed. Pacific Grove, CA: Brooks/Cole.

Newcomb, M. D., and P. M. Bentler. 1986. "Cocaine Use Among Adolescents: Longitudinal Associations with Social Context, Psychopathology, and Use of Other Substances." *Addictive Behaviors* 11: 263–273.

Newman, C. L., and B. R. Price. 1977. "Jails and Services for Inmates: A Pespective on Some Critical Issues." *Criminology* 14: 501–512.

Newman, D. J. 1985. *Introduction to Criminal Justice*. New York: Random House.

Newman, G. 1979. *Understanding Violence*. New York: Lippincott.

Newman, O. 1972. *Defensible Space*. New York: Macmillan.

Newsweek. 1982. "End of a Sleazy Affair." March 22, 18–21.

———. 1985. "The War Against Pornography." March 18, 58–67.

———. 1987. "Brothers." March 23, 54–86.

———. 1988. "Black and White in America." March 7, 18–23.

———. 1988. New York Academy of Medicine. 1963. "Report on Drug Addiction." *Bulletin of the New York Academy of Medicine* 39: 417–473.

New York City Department of Probation. 1973. *Differential Supervision of Offenders*. New York: New York City Department of Probation.

New York State Special Commission on Attica. 1972. *Attica: The Official Report of the New York State Special Commission on Attica*. New York: Bantam.

New York Times. 1969. "Text of Nixon's Message to Congress Proposing 10 Steps in Fight on Narcotics." July 15, 18.

Nicholson, T., and D. F. Duncan. 1991. "Pornography as a Source of Sex Information for Students at a Southwestern State University." *Psychological Reports*. 68 (3): 802.

Nicodemus, C. 1979. "Anti-Dissent Techniques Varied Widely." *Los Angeles Times*, August 22, I4–I6.

Nienstedt, B. C. 1986. *Testing Deterrence: The Effects of a DWI Law and Publicity Campaigns*. Unpublished dissertation, Arizona State University, Tempe.

Nobile, P., and E. Nadler. 1986. *United States of America vs. Sex: How the Meese Commission Lied About Pornography*. New York: Minotaur Press.

Nora, R. 1984. *Profile Survey on Pathological Gamblers.* Paper presented at the Sixth National Conference on Gambling and Risk Taking, Atlantic City, New Jersey. December.

Normandeau, A. 1966. "The Measurement of Delinquency in Montreal." *Journal of Criminal Law, Criminology, and Police Science* 57: 172–177.

Northwood, L. K., R. Westgard, and C. Barb. 1978. "Law Abiding One Man Armies." *Society* 16: 69–74.

Nurco, D., T. Hanlon, T. Kinlock, and K. Duszynksi. 1988. "Differential Criminal Patterns of Narcotic Addicts Over an Addiction Career." *Criminology* 26: 407–424.

Nye, F. I. 1958. *Family Relationships and Delinquent Behavior.* New York: Wiley.

Oaks, D. 1970. "Studying the Exclusionary Rule in Search and Seizure." *University of Chicago Law Review* 37: 665–757.

O'Brien, J. F., and A. Kurins. 1991. *Boss of Bosses: The FBI and Paul Castellano.* New York: Simon and Schuster.

O'Brien, R. 1983. "Metropolitan Structure and Violent Crime: Which Measure of Crime?" *American Sociological Review* 48: 434–437.

———. 1985. *Crime and Victimization Data.* Beverly Hills, CA: Sage.

———. 1991. "Sex Ratios and Rape Rates: A Power-Control Theory." *Criminology* 29: 99–114.

O'Brien, R. M., D. Shichor, and D. L. Decker. 1980. "An Empirical Comparison of the Validity of UCR and NCS Crime Rates." *Sociological Quarterly* 21: 301–401.

O'Connor, J. F., and A. J. Lizotte. 1978. "The 'Southern Subculture of Violence' Thesis and Patterns of Gun Ownership." *Social Problems* 25: 420–429.

O'Donnell, J. A. 1966. "Narcotic Addiction and Crime." *Social Problems* 13: 374–385.

Ohlin, L. E. 1951. *Selection for Parole.* New York: Russell Sage Foundation.

O'Leary, V., and T. R. Clear. 1982. *Controlling the Offender in the Community.* Lexington, MA: Lexington Books.

Oliver, M. J. 1980. "Epilepsy, Crime and Delinquency: A Sociological Account." *Sociology* 14: 417–440.

Olweus, D. 1988. "Environmental and Biological Factors in the Development of Aggressive Behavior." In *Explaining Criminal Behavior.* Edited by W. Buikhuisen and S. A. Mednick. Leiden, Netherlands: Brill.

Olweus, D., A. Matlsson, D. Schalling, and H. Low. 1980. "Testosterone, Aggression, Physical and Personality Dimensions in Normal Adolescent Males." *Psychosomatic Medicine* 42: 253–269.

O'Malley, P. 1988. "The Purpose of Knowledge: Pragmatism and the Praxis of Marxist Criminology." *Contemporary Crises* 12: 65–79.

Orcutt, J. D. 1970. "Self-concept and Insulation Against Delinquency: Some Critical Notes." *Sociological Quarterly* 2: 381–390.

Oreskes, M. 1986. "Commission Trial Illustrates Changes in Attitude on Mafia." *The New York Times,* September 20, B29.

Orfield, M. 1987. "The Exclusionary Rule and Deterrence: An Empirical Study of Chicago Narcotics Officers." *University of Chicago Law Review* 54: 1016–1069.

Osborne, R. T. 1980. *Twins: Black and White.* Athens, GA: Foundation for Human Understanding.

Ostrom, E., R. Parks, and G. Whitaker. 1978. *Patterns of Metropolitan Policing.* Cambridge, MA: Ballinger.

Otterbein, K. F. 1986. *The Ultimate Coercive Sanction: A Cross Cultural Study of Capital Punishment.* New Haven, CT: HRAF Press.

Oversight Hearings before the Subcommittee on Criminal Justice of the House Committee on the Judiciary on the Exclusionary Rule in Criminal Trials, 98th Cong., 1st Sess. 1983.

Packer, H. 1964. "Two Models of the Criminal Process." *Pennsylvania Law Review* 118: 1–68.

Packer, H. L. 1968. *The Limits of the Criminal Sanction.* Stanford, CA: Stanford University Press.

Pagelow, M. "The Incidence And Prevalence Of Criminal Abuse Of Other Family Members." Vol. 10, pp. 263–313 in *Crime and Justice: An Annual Review of Research.* Edited by M. Tonry and N. Morris. Chicago: University of Chicago Press.

Palamara, F., F. Cullen, and J. Gersten. 1986. "The Effect of Police and Mental Health Intervention on Juvenile Deviance: Specifying Contingencies in the Impact of Formal Reaction." *Journal of Health and Social Behavior* 27: 90–105.

Palmer, T. 1975. "Martinson Revisited." *Journal of Research in Crime and Delinquency* 12: 133–152.

Park, J. W. L. 1975. "The Organization of Prison Violence." In *Prison Violence*. Edited by A. K. Cohen, G. F. Cole, and R. Bailey. Lexington, MA: Heath.

Park, R. E., E. W. Burgess, and R. D. McKenzie. 1925. *The City*. Chicago: University of Chicago Press.

Parker, H., and R. Newcombe. 1987. "Heroin Use and Acquisitive Crime in an English Community." *British Journal of Sociology* 38: 331–350.

Parker, R. N. 1985. "Aggregation Ratio Variables, and Measurement Problems in Criminological Research." *Journal of Quantitative Criminology* 1: 269–280.

———. 1989. "Poverty, Subculture of Violence, and Type of Homicide." *Social Forces* 67: 983–1007.

Parker, R. N., and M. D. Smith. 1979. "Deterrence, Poverty, and Type of Homicide." *American Journal of Sociology* 85: 614–624.

Parmelee, M. 1918. *Criminology*. New York: Macmillan.

Parsonage, W. 1979. *Perspectives on Victimology*. Beverly Hills, CA: Sage.

Parsons, T. 1962. "The Law and Social Control." In *The Law and Sociology*. Edited by W. M. Evan. New York: Free Press.

Pateman, C. 1988. *The Sexual Contract*. Stanford, CA: Stanford University Press.

Paternoster, R. 1983. "Race of Victim and Location of Crime: The Decision to Seek the Death Penalty in South Carolina." *Journal of Criminal Law and Criminology* 74: 754–785.

———. 1984. "Prosecutorial Discretion in Requesting the Death Penalty: A Case of Victim-Based Racial Discrimination." *Law & Society Review* 18: 437–478.

———. 1991. *Capital Punishment in America*. New York: Lexington Books.

Paternoster, R., and A. Kazyaka. 1988. "Racial Considerations in Capital Punishment: The Failure of Evenhanded Justice." In *Challenging Capital Punishment: Legal and Social Science Approaches*. Edited by K. C. Haas and J. A. Inciardi. Newbury Park, CA: Sage.

Paternoster, R., L. E. Saltzman, G. P. Waldo, and T. G. Chiricos. 1985. "Assessments of Risk and Behavioral Experience: An Exploratory Study of Change." *Criminology* 23: 417–436.

Paternoster, R., and R. Triplett. 1988. "Disaggregating Self-Reported Delinquency and Its Implication for Theory." *Criminology* 26: 591–625.

Patterson, E. B., and M. J. Lynch. 1991. "Biases in Formalized Bail Procedures." Pp. 36–53 in *Race and Criminal Justice*. Edited by M. J. Lynch and E. B. Patterson. New York: Harrow and Heston.

Pearson, F. S. 1988. *Final Findings of Research on New Jersey's Intensive Supervision Program*. New Brunswick, NJ: Rutgers University Institute of Criminology.

Pearson, G. 1978. "Goths and Vandals — Crime in History." *Contemporary Crises* 2: 119–139.

———. 1992. "Drug Problems and Criminal Justice Policy in Britain." *Contemporary Drug Problems* 19 (2): 279–301.

Pennsylvania Crime Commission. 1989. *Organized Crime, 1989 Report*. St. Davids, PA: Commonwealth of Pennsylvania.

Pennsylvania Crime Commission. 1991. *1990 Report — Organized Crime in Pennsylvania: A Decade of Change*. Commonwealth of Pennsylvania.

People. 1978. September 4, 46–48.

Pepinsky, H., and R. Quinney. 1991. *Criminology As Peacemaking*. Indianapolis: Indiana University Press.

Pernanen, K. 1976. "Alcohol and Crimes of Violence." In *Biology of Alcoholism*. Edited by B. Kissen and H. Beleiter. New York: Plenum.

Perrucci, R. 1969. "The Neighborhood 'Bookmaker': Entrepreneur and Mobility Model." In *Urbanism, Urbanization and Change: Comparative Perspectives*. Edited by P. Meadows and E. H. Mizruchi. Reading, MA: Addison-Wesley.

Petchesky, R. 1979. "Reproduction, Ethics and Public Policy: The Federal Sterilization Regulations." *Hastings Center Report* 1.

Petersen, R. C. 1977. "History of Cocaine." Pp. 17–34 in *Cocaine: 1977*. Edited by R. C. Petersen and R. C. Stillman. Rockville, MD: National Institute on Drug Abuse.

Petersilia, J. 1980. "Criminal Career Research: A Review of Recent Evidence." Pp. 321–379 in *Crime and Justice: An Annual Review of Research*. Vol. 2. Edited by N. Morris and M. Tonry. Chicago: University of Chicago Press.

———. 1985. "Racial Disparities in the Criminal Justice System: A Summary." *Crime & Delinquency* 31: 15–34.

———. 1987. *Extending Options for Criminal Sentencing*. Santa Monica, CA: Rand Corporation.

Petersilia, J., P. Greenwood, and M. Lavin. 1978. *Criminal Careers of Habitual Felons*. Santa Monica, CA: Rand Corporation.

Peterson, M., and H. Braiker. 1980. *Doing Crime: A Survey of California Prison Inmates.* Rand Report R-2200-DOJ. Santa Monica, CA: Rand Corporation.

Peterson, M., H. Braiker, and S. Polich. 1981. *Who Commits Crimes: A Survey of Prison Inmates.* Boston: Oelgeschlager, Gunn & Hain.

Peterson, R. D., and W. C. Bailey. 1988. "Murder and Capital Punishment in the Evolving Context of the Post-*Furman* Era." *Social Forces* 66: 774–807.

Peterson, R. D., and J. Hagan. 1984. "Changing Conceptions of Race: Towards an Account of Anomalous Findings of Sentencing Research." *American Sociological Review* 49: 56–70.

Pettiway, L. 1987. "Participation in Crime Partnerships by Female Drug Users: The Effects of Domestic Arrangements, Drug Use, and Criminal Involvement." *Criminology* 25: 741–767.

Pfeffer, J., and G. R. Salancik. 1978. *The External Control of Organizations.* New York: Harper & Row.

Pfohl, S. 1977. "The Discovery of Child Abuse." *Social Problems* 24: 310–323.

———. 1985. *Images of Deviance and Social Control.* New York: McGraw-Hill.

Phillips, L., and H. F. Votey, Jr. 1981. *The Economics of Crime Control.* Beverly Hills, CA: Sage.

Piaget, J. 1932. *The Moral Judgement of the Child.* London: Kegan Paul.

Pierce, G. L., and W. J. Bowers. 1981. "The Bartley-Fox Gun Law's Impact on Crime in Boston." *The Annals of the American Academy of Political and Social Science* 455: 40–47.

Piliavin, I., R. Gartner, C. Thorton, and R. L. Matsueda. 1986. "Crime, Deterrence and Rational Choice." *American Sociological Review* 51: 101–119.

Piven, F. F., and R. A. Cloward. 1971. *Regulating the Poor.* New York: Random House.

Platt, A. 1974. "Prospects for a Radical Criminology in the U.S." *Crime & Social Justice* 1: 2–10.

———. 1977. *The Child Savers: The Invention of Delinquency.* 2d ed. Chicago: University of Chicago Press.

Pogue, T. F. 1986. "Offender Expectations and Identification of Crime Supply Functions." *Evaluation Review* 10: 455–482.

Poklemba, J., and P. Crusco. 1982. "Public Enterprises and RICO: The Aftermath of United States v. Turkette." *Criminal Law Bulletin* 18: 197–203.

Polsky, N. 1969. *Hustlers, Beats and Others.* Garden City, NY: Doubleday Anchor.

Pontell, H. N. 1984. *A Capacity to Punish.* Bloomington: Indiana University Press.

Pontell, H. N., P. D. Jesilow, and G. Geis. 1982. "Policing Physicians: Practitioner Fraud and Abuse in a Government Medical Program." *Social Problems* 30: 117–125.

Pope, C. E. 1975. "Offender-Based Transaction Statistics: New Directions in Data Collection and Reporting." *Utilization of Criminal Justice Statistics.* Analytic Report 5, National Criminal Justice Information and Statistics Service. Washington, DC: U.S. Government Printing Office.

———. 1980. "Patterns in Burglary: An Empirical Examination of Offense and Offender Characteristics." *Journal of Criminal Justice* 8: 39–52.

Pope, H., M. Ionescu-Pioggia, and J. D. Cole. 1981. "Drug Use and Life Style among College Undergraduates." *Archives of General Psychiatry* 38: 588–591.

Pope, W., and C. Ragin. 1977. "Mechanical Solidarity, Repressive Justice, and Lynchings in Louisiana." *American Sociological Review* 42: 363–368.

Posner, R. 1970. "A Statistical Study of Antitrust Enforcement." *Journal of Law and Economics* 13: 365–420.

Potts, L. 1983. *Responsible Police Administration: Issues and Approaches.* University, AL: University of Alabama Press.

Pound, R. 1943. "A Survey of Social Interests." *Harvard Law Review* 57: 1–39.

Powell, S., S. Enerson, O. Kelly, D. Collins, and B. Quick. 1986. "Busting the Mob." *U.S. News & World Report*, February 3, 24–31.

Prechel, H. 1990. "Steel and the State: Industry Politics and Business Policy Formation, 1940-1989." *American Sociological Review* 55: 648–668.

Prentky, R. 1985. "The Neurochemistry and Neuroendocrinology of Sexual Aggression." Pp. 7–56 in *Aggression and Dangerousness.* Edited by D. F. Farrington and J. Gunn. Chichester, England: Wiley.

President's Commission on Drunk Driving. 1983. *Final Report.* Washington, DC: U.S. Government Printing Office.

President's Commission on Law Enforcement and Administration of Justice. 1967a. *Task Force Report:*

Organized Crime. Washington, DC: U.S. Government Printing Office.

———. 1967b. *The Challenge of Crime in a Free Society*. Washington, DC: U.S. Government Printing Office.

———. 1967c. *Task Force Report: Crime and Its Impact — An Assessment*. Washington, DC: U.S. Government Printing Office.

President's Commission on Organized Crime. 1987. *The Impact: Organized Crime Today*. Washington, DC: U.S. Government Printing Office.

President's Task Force on Victims of Crime. 1982. *Final Report*. Washington, DC: U.S. Government Printing Office.

Press, A., D. Pedersen, D. Shapiro, and A. McDaniel. 1986. "Inside America's Toughest Prison." *Newsweek*, October 6, 46–61.

Prottas, J. 1978. "The Power of the Street-Level Bureaucrat in Public Service Bureaucracies." *Urban Affairs Quarterly* 13: 285–312.

Pruitt, C. R., and J. Q. Wilson. 1983. "A Longitudinal Study of the Effect of Race on Sentencing." *Law & Society Review* 17: 613–635.

Prus, R., and S. Irini. 1980. *Hookers, Rounders and Desk Clerks*. Toronto: Gage.

Prus, R., and C. Sharper. 1977. *Road Hustler*. Toronto: Gage.

Punch, M. 1986. *Conduct Unbecoming*. London: Tavistock.

Punch, M., and T. Naylor. 1973. "The Police: A Social Service." *New Society* 24.

Pyeritz, R., et al. 1977. "The XYY Male: The Making of a Myth." In *Biology as a Social Weapon*. Minneapolis, MN: Burgess.

Quadagno, J. 1984. "Welfare Capitalism and the Social Security Act of 1935." *American Sociological Review* 49: 632–647.

Quicker, J. 1974. "The Effect of Goal Discrepancy on Delinquency." *Social Problems* 22: 76–86.

Quinney, R. 1970. *The Social Reality of Crime*. Boston: Little, Brown.

———. 1974. *Critique of the Legal Order*. Boston: Little, Brown.

———. 1977. *Class, State and Crime*. New York: McKay.

———. 1980. *Class, State and Crime*. 2d ed. New York: Longman.

Radelet, M. L. 1981. "Racial Characteristics and the Imposition of the Death Penalty." *American Sociological Review* 46: 918–927.

———. 1989. "Introduction and Overview." In *Facing the Death Penalty: Essays on a Cruel and Unusual Punishment*. Edited by M. L. Radelet. Philadelphia: Temple University Press.

Radelet, M. L., H. A. Bedau, and C. E. Putnam. 1992. *In Spite of Innocence: Erroneous Convictions in Capital Cases*. Boston: Northeastern University Press.

Radelet, M. L., and G. L. Pierce. 1985. "Race and Prosecutorial Discretion in Homicide Cases." *Law and Society Review* 19: 587–621.

Radelet, M. L., and M. Vandiver. 1986. "Race and Capital Punishment: An Overview of the Issues." *Crime and Social Justice* 25: 94–113.

Radzinowicz, L. 1968. *The Reform of the Police*. (The History of English Criminal Law. Vol. 4.) London: Stevens.

Rafter, N. H. 1983. "Prisons for Women 1790-1980." Pp. 129–181 in *Crime and Justice*. Vol. 5. Edited by M. Tonry and N. Morris. Chicago: University of Chicago Press.

———. 1985. *Partial Justice*. Boston: Northeastern University Press.

Rafter, N. H. 1992. "Criminal Anthropology in the United States." *Criminology* 30 (4): 525–546.

Ragona, A. J., and J. P. Ryan. 1984. *Beyond the Courtroom: A Comparative Analysis of Misdemeanor Sentencing*. Washington, DC: U.S. Department of Justice, National Institute of Justice.

Rand, A. 1987. "Transitional Life Events and Desistance from Delinquency and Crime." Pp. 134–162 in *From Boy to Man, from Delinquency to Crime*. Edited by M. Wolfgang, T. Thornberry, and R. Figlio. Chicago: University of Chicago Press.

Rand, M. 1985. *Household Burglary. BJS Bulletin*. Washington, DC: U.S. Department of Justice.

Rankin, J. H. 1979. "Changing Attitudes Toward Capital Punishment." *Social Forces* 58: 194–211.

Rathus, S. 1983. *Human Sexuality*. New York: Holt, Rinehart & Winston.

Ratterman, D. 1982. "Pornography: The Spectrum of Harm." *Aegis* (Autumn): 42–52.

Rauma, D. 1984. "Going for the Gold: Prosecutorial Decision Making in Cases of Wife Assault." *Social Science Research* 13: 321–351.

Rawlin, J. W. 1968. "Street Level Abuse of Amphetamines." Pp. 51–65 in *Amphetamine Abuse*. Edited by J. R. Russo. Springfield, IL: Thomas.

Ray, O. 1978. *Drugs, Society, and Human Behavior.* St. Louis: Mosby.

Reaves, B. 1992a. *Law Enforcement Management and Administrative Statistics, 1990.* Washington, DC: Bureau of Justice Statistics.

———. 1992. *Sheriffs' Departments, 1990.* Washington, DC: Bureau of Justice Statistics.

———. 1992c. *State and Local Police Departments, 1990.* Washington, DC: Bureau of Justice Statistics.

Reckless, W. 1950. *The Crime Problem.* New York: Appleton-Century.

———. 1961. "A New Theory of Delinquency and Crime." *Federal Probation* 25: 42–46.

———. 1973. *The Crime Problem.* 5th ed. Santa Monica, CA: Goodyear.

Reckless, W. C., and S. Dinitz. 1972. *The Prevention of Juvenile Delinquency: An Experiment.* Columbus: Ohio University Press.

Reckless, W. C., S. Dinitz, and B. Kay. 1957a. "The Self-component in Potential Delinquency and Potential Nondelinquency." *American Sociological Review* 21: 744–756.

———. 1957b. "The 'Good Boy' in a High Delinquency Area." *Journal of Criminal Law, Criminology and Police Science* 68: 18–25.

Reckless, W. C., S. Dinitz, and E. Murray. 1956. "Self Concept as an Insulator Against Delinquency." *American Sociological Review* 21: 744–746.

Reed, J. S. 1971. "To Live — and Die — in Dixie: A Contribution to the Study of Southern Violence." *Political Science Quarterly* 86: 429–443.

Regoli, R., E. Poole, and F. Esbensen. 1985. "Labelling Deviance: Another Look." *Sociological Focus* 18: 18–28.

Reid, I. D. 1939. *The Negro Immigrant: His Background, Characteristics and Social Adjustment, 1899-1937.* New York: Columbia University Press.

Reiff, R. 1979. *The Invisible Victim.* New York: Basic Books.

Reiman, J. 1984. *The Rich Get Richer and the Poor Get Prison.* 2d ed. New York: Wiley.

———. 1988. "The Justice of the Death Penalty in an Unjust World." In *Challenging Capital Punishment: Legal and Social Science Approaches.* Edited by K. C. Haas and J. A. Inciardi. Newbury Park, CA: Sage.

Reinarman, C., and H. G. Levine. 1989. "The Crack Attack: Politics and Media in America's Latest Drug Scare." Pp. 115–137 in *Images of Issues: Typifying Contemporary Social Problems.* Edited by J. Best. New York: Aldine de Gruyter.

Reiner, R. 1985. *The Politics of the Police.* Brighton, England: Wheatsheaf.

Reiss, A. 1971. *The Police and the Public.* New Haven, CT: Yale University Press.

———. 1974. "Discretionary Justice." Pp. 679–699 in *Handbook of Criminology.* Edited by D. Glaser. Chicago: Rand McNally.

———. 1986. "Official Survey Statistics." Pp. 53–79 in *From Crime Policy to Victim Policy.* Edited by E. Fattah. New York: St. Martin's Press.

———. 1987. "The Legitimacy of Intrusion into Private Space." In *Private Policing.* Edited by C. D. Shearing and P. C. Stenning. Newbury Park, CA: Sage.

———. 1988. "Private Employment of Public Police." Research in Brief. Washington, DC: National Institute of Justice.

———. 1992. "Police Organization in the Twentieth Century." In *Modern Policing.* Edited by M. Tonry and N. Morris. Chicago: University of Chicago Press.

———. 1993. "Towards a Theoretical Perspective on Enforcing Law and Maintaining Domestic Order." Paper delivered at the annual meeting of the American Society of Criminology, Phoenix.

Reiss, A. J., and A. L. Rhodes. 1961. "The Distribution of Juvenile Delinquency in the Social Class Structure." *American Sociological Review* 26: 720–732.

———. 1963. "Status Deprivation and Delinquent Behavior." *Sociological Quarterly* 4: 135–149.

Reiss, A. J., Jr., and J. A. Roth, eds. 1993. *Understanding and Preventing Violence.* Panel on the Understanding and Control of Violent Behavior, National Research Council. Washington, DC: National Academy Press.

Reiss, A. J., Jr., and M. Tonry. 1986. *Communities and Crime.* Chicago: University of Chicago Press.

Rengert, G. F. 1989. "Behavioral Geography and Criminal Behavior." Pp. 161–175 in *The Geography of*

Crime. Edited by D. J. Evans and D. T. Herbert. London: Routledge.

Rengert, G., and J. Wasilchick. 1985. *Suburban Burglary: A Time and a Place for Everything*. Springfield, IL: Thomas.

Rensberger, B. 1976. "Thousands a Year Killed by Faulty Prescriptions." *New York Times*, June 27, 1 *passim*.

Report of the Special Committee on Pornography and Prostitution. 1985. *Pornography and Prostitution in Canada*. Ottawa: Canadian Government Publishing Centre.

Reppetto, T. J. 1974. *Residential Crime*. Cambridge, MA: Ballinger.

———. 1978. *The Blue Parade*. New York: Macmillan.

Research and Forecasts. 1980. *The Figgie Report on Fear of Crime, Part 1: The General Public*. Willoughby, Ohio: ATO, Inc.

Research Triangle Institute. 1976. *Drug Use and Crime: Report of the Panel on Drug Use and Criminal Behavior*. Springfield, VA: National Technical Information Service.

Reuband, K. 1992. "Drug Addiction and Crime in West Germany: A Review of the Empirical Evidence." *Contemporary Drug Problems* 19 (2): 327–339.

Reuss-Ianni, E. 1983. *The Two Cultures of Policing*. New Brunswick, NJ: Transaction Books.

Reuter, P. 1983. *Disorganized Crime: The Economics of the Visible Hand*. Cambridge, MA: MIT Press.

———. 1984. "The (Continued) Vitality of Mythical Numbers." *Public Interest* 75: 135–147.

Reuter, P., and M. Kleiman. 1986. "Risks and Prices: An Economic Analysis of Drug Enforcement." In *Crime and Justice*. Edited by M. Tonry and N. Morris.

Reuter, P., J. Rubinstein, and S. Wynn. 1983. *Racketeering in Legitimate Industries: Two Case Studies*. Washington, DC: National Institute of Justice.

Reynolds, Q. 1953. *I, Willie Sutton*. New York: Farrar, Straus & Young.

Rhode, Deborah. 1989. *Gender and Justice*. Cambridge, MA: Harvard University Press.

Rhodes, R. P. 1984. *Organized Crime: Crime Control vs. Civil Liberties*. New York: Random House.

Rich, R. M. 1978. "Sociological Paradigms and the Sociology of Law." In *The Sociology of Law*. Edited by C. E. Reasons and R. M. Rich. Toronto: Butterworth.

Riedel, M. 1968. "Corporate Crime and Interfirm Organization." *Graduate Sociology Club Journal* 8: 74–97.

Riksheim, E., and S. Chernak. 1993. "Causes of Police Behavior Revisited." *Journal of Criminal Justice*. 21: 353–382.

Roberts, N. 1992. *Whores in History*. New York: Harper Collins.

Robins, L. N. 1973. *The Vietnam Drug User Returns*. Washington, DC: U.S. Government Printing Office.

Robins, L. N., and S. Y. Hill. 1966. "Assessing the Contributions of Family Structure, Class and Peer Groups to Juvenile Delinquency." *Journal of Criminal Law, Criminology, and Police Science* 57: 325–334.

Robins, L. N., J. E. Helzer, M. Hesselbrock, and E. Wish. 1980. Vol. 2, pp. 213–230 "Vietnam Veterans: Three Years After Vietnam: How Our Study Changed Our View of Heroin." in *The Yearbook of Substance Use and Abuse*. Edited by L. Brill and C. Winick. New York: Human Sciences Press.

Robinson, L. N. 1922. *History and Organization of Criminal Statistics in the United States*. New York: Hart, Schaffner & Marx.

Robinson, M. 1990. "Social Science and the Citizen: A Third of Homeless Teenagers Survive by Prostitution." *Society*. 28 (1): 2.

Roby, P. A. 1969. "Politics and Criminal Law: Revision of the New York State Penal Law on Prostitution." *Social Problems* 17: 83–109.

Rock, P. 1979. "Feature Review Symposium of 'The New Criminology': For a Social Theory of Deviance." *The Sociological Quarterly* 14: 594–599.

Rogers, J. W., and M. D. Buffalo. 1974. "Neutralization Techniques: Toward a Simplified Measurement Scale." *Pacific Sociological Review* 17: 313–331.

Rokeach, M. 1973. *The Nature of Human Values*. New York: Free Press.

Romenesko, K., and E. M. Miller. 1989. "The Second Step in Double-Jeopardy: Appropriating the Labor of Female Street Hustlers." *Crime and Delinquency*. 35 (1): 109–135.

Rose, H. M., and P. D. McClain. 1990. *Race, Place, and Risk: Black Homicide in Urban America*. Albany, NY: State University of New York Press.

Rose, S. 1986. "Stalking the Criminal Chromosome." *The Nation*, May 24, 732–736.

Rosecrance, J. 1988a. *Gambling Without Guilt: The Legitimation of an American Pastime*. Pacific Grove, CA: Brooks/Cole.

———. 1988b. "Maintaining the Myth of Individualized Justice: Probation Presentence Reports." *Justice Quarterly* 5: 235–256.

Rosen, L. 1969. "Matriarchy and Lower-class Negro Male Delinquency." *Social Problems* 17: 175–189.

Rosenbaum, J., and P. Sederberg. 1976. *Vigilante Politics*. Philadelphia: University of Pennsylvania Press.

Rosenbaum, M. 1981. *Women on Heroin*. New Brunswick, NJ: Rutgers University Press.

Roshier, B. 1973. "The Selection of Crime News by the Press." Pp. 28–39 in *The Manufacture of News*. Edited by S. Cohen and J. Young. Beverly Hills, CA: Sage.

Ross, J. G., E. Heffernan, J. R. Sevik, and F. T. Johnson. 1978. *Assessment of Coeducational Corrections*. Washington, DC: U.S. Department of Justice, National Institute of Law Enforcement and Criminal Justice.

Rossi, P. H., R. A. Berk, and B. K. Eidson. 1974a. *The Roots of Urban Discontent*. New York: Wiley.

Rossi, P. H., E. Waite, C. E. Bose, and R. Berk. 1974b. "The Seriousness of Crimes: Normative Structure and Individual Differences." *American Sociological Review* 39: 224–237.

Rothman, D. B., and R. Kimberly. 1985. "The Social Context of Jails." Pp. 125–139 in *Correctional Institutions*. 3d ed. Edited by R. M. Carter, D. Glaser, and L. T. Wilkins. New York: Harper & Row.

Rothman, D. J. 1971. *Discovery of the Asylum*. Boston: Little, Brown.

———. 1980. *Conscience and Convenience*. Boston: Little, Brown.

Rothman, J., L. Ehrlich, and J. G. Theresa. 1976. *Planning and Implementing Change in Organizations and Communities*. New York: Wiley.

Rowe, A., and C. Tittle. 1977. "Life Cycle Changes and Criminal Propensity." *Sociological Quarterly* 18: 223–236.

Rowe, D. 1985. "Sibling Interaction and Self-Reported Delinquent Behavior: A Study of 265 Twin Pairs." *Criminology* 23: 223–240.

Rubinstein, J. 1973. *City Police*. New York: Farrar, Straus & Giroux.

Rusche, G., and O. Kirchheimer. 1939. *Punishment and Social Structure*. New York: Columbia University Press.

Rushford, N. C., A. F. Hirsch, and L. Adelson. 1975. "Accidental Firearms Fatalities in a Metropolitan County (1958-1973)." *American Journal of Epidemiology* 100: 499–505.

Rustigan, M. 1980. "A Reinterpretation of Criminal Law Reform in Nineteenth-Century England." *Journal of Criminal Justice* 8: 205–219.

Ryan, J. P. 1980. "Adjudication and Sentencing in a Misdemeanor Court: The Outcome Is the Punishment." *Law & Society Review* 15: 79–108.

Ryan, J. P., and J. J. Alfini. 1979. "Trial Judges' Participation in Plea Bargaining: An Empirical Perspective." *Law & Society Review* 13: 479–507.

Ryder, N. 1965. "The Cohort as a Concept in the Study of Social Change." *American Sociological Review* 47: 774–787.

Sagarin, E. 1969. *Odd Man In: Societies of Deviants in America*. Chicago: Quadrangle Books.

Sagi, P. C., and C. F. Wellford. 1968. "Age Composition and Patterns of Change in Criminal Statistics." *Journal of Criminal Law, Criminology and Police Science* 59: 29–36.

Saks, H. R., and C. H. Logan. 1984. "Does Parole Make a Lasting Difference?" In *Criminal Justice: Law and Politics*. 4th ed. Edited by G. F. Cole. Monterey, CA: Brooks/Cole.

Saltzman, L., R. Paternaster, G. P. Waldo, and T. G. Chiricos. 1982. "Deterrent and Experiential Effects: The Problem of Causal Order in Perceptual Deterrence Research." *Journal of Research in Crime and Delinquency* 19: 172–189.

Sampson, R. J. 1985a. "Neighborhood and Crime: The Structural Determinants of Personal Victimization." *Journal of Research in Crime and Delinquency* 22: 7–40.

———. 1985b. "Structural Sources of Variation in Race-Age Specific Rates of Offending Across Major U.S. Cities." *Criminology* 23: 647–673.

———. 1987. "Urban Black Violence: The Effect of Male Joblessness and Family Disruption." *American Journal of Sociology* 93: 348–382.

Sampson, R. J., and J. H. Laub. 1990. "Crime and Deviance Over the Life Course: The Salience of Adult Social Bonds." *American Sociological Review* 55 (Oct.): 609–627.

Sampson, R. J., and J. D. Wooldredge. 1987. "Linking the Micro- and Macro- Level Dimensions of Lifestyle-Routine Activity and Opportunity Models of Predatory Victimization." *Journal of Quantitative Criminology* 3: 371–393.

Sampson, W. A., and P. H. Rossi. 1975. "Race and Family Social Standing." *American Sociological Review* 40: 201–215.

San Antonio Express-News. 1993. "Islands Among Drug Assets taken in Puerto Rico 'Al Capone' Raids." February 27, 10A.

Sandusk, J. F. 1966. "Amphetamines: Size and Extent of the Problem." *Journal of the American Medical Association* 196: 707–709.

Santos, B. D. S. 1980. "Law and Community: The Changing Nature of State Power in Late Capitalism." *International Journal of the Sociology of Law* 8: 379–397.

———. 1985. "On Modes of Production of Law and Social Power." *International Journal of the Sociology of Law* 13: 299–336.

Sarbin, T. R., and J. E. Miller. 1971. "Demonism Revisited: The XYY Chromosomal Abnormality." *Issues in Criminology* 5(2).

Schafer, S. 1968. *The Victim and His Criminal.* New York: Random House.

———. 1977. *Victimology: The Victim and His Criminal.* Reston, VA: Reston Publishing.

Schauss, A., and C. Simonson. 1979. "A Critical Analysis of the Diets of Chronic Juvenile Offenders." *Journal of Orthomolecular Psychiatry* 8: 1949-1957.

Scheff, T. 1974. "The Labelling Theory of Mental Illness." *American Sociological Review* 39: 444–452.

Scheingold, S. 1984. *The Politics of Law and Order: Street Crime and Public Policy.* New York: Longman.

Schlegel, K. 1988. "Life Imitating Art: Interpreting Information from Electronic Surveillances." Pp. 101–112 in *Critical Issues in Criminal Investigation,* 2d ed. Edited by M. J. Palmiotto. Cincinnati: Pilgrimage Press.

Schmidt, J., and E. H. Steury. 1989. "Prosecutorial Discretion in Filing Charges in Domestic Violence Cases." *Criminology* 27: 487–510.

Schmidt, W. 1974. "A Proposal for a Statewide Law Enforcement Administrative Law Council." *Journal of Police Science and Administration* 2: 330–338.

Schneider, H. 1982. *The Victim in International Perspective.* New York: de Gruyter.

Schrag, C. 1961. "Some Foundations for a Theory of Corrections." Pp. 309–358 in *The Prison.* Edited by D. R. Cressey. New York: Holt, Rinehart & Winston.

———. 1972. *Crime and Justice: American Style.* Washington, DC: U.S. Government Printing Office.

Schrag, P. G. 1972. *Counsel for the Deceived.* New York: Pantheon Books.

Schuerman, L., and S. Kobrin. 1986. "Community Careers in Crime." Pp. 67–100 in *Communities and Crime.* Edited by A. J. Reiss, Jr., and M. Tonry. Chicago: University of Chicago Press.

Schulhofer, S. 1988. "The Constitution and the Police: Individual Rights and Law Enforcement." *Washington University Law Quarterly* 66: 11–32.

Schuman, H., and S. Presser. 1981. "The Attitude-Action Connection and the Issue of Gun Control." *The Annals of the American Academy of Political and Social Science* 455: 40–47.

Schur, E. M. 1962. *Narcotic Addiction in Britain and America.* Bloomington: Indiana University Press.

———. 1965. *Crime Without Victims.* Englewood Cliffs, NJ: Prentice-Hall.

———. 1969. "Reactions to Deviance: A Critical Assessment." *American Journal of Sociology* 75: 309–322.

———. 1971. *Labelling Deviant Behavior.* New York: Harper & Row.

———. 1973. *Radical Non-Intervention: Rethinking the Delinquency Problem.* Englewood Cliffs, NJ: Prentice-Hall.

———. 1975. "Comments." Pp. 285–294 in *The Labelling of Deviance: Evaluating a Perspective.* Edited by W. Gove. Beverly Hills, CA: Sage.

———. 1984. *Labeling Women Deviant: Gender, Stigma, and Social Control.* New York: Random House.

Schwartz, M., and S. Stryker. 1970. *Deviance, Selves, and Others.* Washington, DC: American Sociological Association.

Schwartz, M., and S. S. Tangri. 1965. "A Note on Self-concept as an Insulator Against Delinquency." *American Sociological Review* 30: 922–926.

Schwendinger, H., and J. Schwendinger. 1970. "Defenders of Order or Guardians of Human Rights." *Issues in Criminology* 5: 113–146.

————. 1985. *Adolescent Subcultures and Delinquency.* New York: Praeger.

Scott, E. 1981. *Police Referral in Metropolitan Areas to NIJ.* Bloomington: University of Indiana Workshop in Political Theory and Policy Analysis.

Scott, E., and S. Percy. 1983. "Gatekeeping Police Services." Pp. 127–144 in *Police at Work.* Edited by R. Bennett. Beverly Hills, CA: Sage.

Scott, P. D., and M. Buckell. 1971. "Delinquency and Amphetamines." *British Journal of Psychiatry* 119: 179–182.

Scott, W. R. 1992. *Organizations.* Englewood Cliffs, NJ: Prentice-Hall.

Scull, A. 1984. *Decarceration: Community Treatment and the Deviant—A Radical View.* Englewood Cliffs, NJ: Prentice-Hall.

Secretary of Health and Human Services. 1983. *Fifth Special Report to the U.S. Congress on Alcohol and Health.* Washington, DC: U.S. Government Printing Office.

————. 1990. *Seventh Special Report to the U.S. Congress on Alcohol and Health.* Rockville, MD: National Institute on Alcohol Abuse and Alcoholism.

Seidman, D., and M. Couzens. 1974. "Getting the Crime Rate Down: Political Pressure and Crime Reporting." *Law and Society Review* 8: 457–493.

Select Committee to Study Governmental Operations With Respect to Intelligence Activities. 1975. *Alleged Assassination Plots Involving Foreign Leaders.* Washington, DC: U.S. Government Printing Office.

Selke, W. L., and H. E. Pepinsky. 1982. "The Politics of Police Reporting in Indianapolis, 1948-1978." *Law and Human Behavior* 6: 327–342.

Sellin, T. 1938. *Culture, Conflict, and Crime.* New York: Social Science Research Council.

Sellin, T., and M. Wolfgang. 1978. *The Measurement of Delinquency.* Montclair, NJ: Patterson Smith.

Seng, M. J. 1989. "Child Sexual Abuse and Adolescent Prostitution: A Comparative Analysis." *Adolescence.* 24: 95: 665–675.

Servadio, G. 1978. *Mafioso: A History of the Mafia from Its Origins to the Present Day.* New York: Dell.

Seymour, W. N. 1973. *Why Justice Fails.* New York: Morrow.

Shah, S., and L. Roth. 1974. "Biological and Psychophysiological Factors in Criminality." Pp. 101–174 in *Handbook of Criminology.* Edited by D. Glaser. Chicago: Rand McNally.

Shane-DuBow, S., S. P. Crown, and E. Olsen. 1985. *Sentencing Reform in the United States.* Washington, DC: U.S. Department of Justice, National Institute of Justice.

Shannon, L. 1988. *Criminal Career Continuity: Its Social Context.* New York: Human Sciences Press.

Shapiro, S. 1984. *Wayward Capitalists: Target of the Securities and Exchange Commission.* New Haven, CT: Yale University Press.

Shaw, C. R. (with the collaboration of F. M. Zorbaugh, H. D. McKay, and L. S. Cottrell). 1929. *Delinquency Areas.* Chicago: University of Chicago Press.

Shaw, C. R., and H. D. McKay. 1931. *Social Factors in Juvenile Delinquency.* Vol. 2 of *Report of the Causes of Crime.* National Commission of Law Observance and Enforcement. Washington, DC: U.S. Government Printing Office.

————. 1942. *Juvenile Delinquency and Urban Areas.* Rev. ed. Chicago: University of Chicago Press.

Shaw, G. B. 1905. *Author's Apology From Mrs. Warren's Profession.* New York: Brentano's Press.

Shaw, N. S. 1982. "Female Patients and the Medical Profession in Jails and Prisons: A Case Study of Quintuple Jeopardy." In *Judge, Lawyer, Victim, Thief.* Edited by N. H. Rafter and E. Stanko. Boston: Northeastern University Press.

Sheehy, G. 1973. *Hustling: Prostitution in Our Wide Open Society.* New York: Delacorte Press.

Sheldon, W. H. 1949. *Varieties of Delinquent Youth: An Introduction to Constitutional Psychiatry.* New York: Harper & Brothers.

Sheley, J. F. 1979. *Understanding Crime: Concepts, Issues, Decisions.* Belmont, CA: Wadsworth.

————. 1980. "Is Neutralization Necessary for Criminal Behavior?" *Deviant Behavior* 2: 49–72.

————. 1983. "Critical Elements of Criminal Behavior." *Sociological Quarterly* 24: 509–525.

————. 1985. *America's "Crime Problem."* Belmont, CA: Wadsworth.

Sheley, J. F., and C. D. Ashkins. 1981. "Crime, Crime News, and Crime Views." *Public Opinion Quarterly* 45: 492–506.

Sheley, J. F., and J. J. Hanlon. 1978. "Unintended Effects of Police Decisions to Actively Enforce Laws: Implications for Analysis of Crime Trends." *Contemporary Crises* 2: 265–275.

Sheley, J. F., and A. R. Harris. 1976. "A Rejoinder to Wiley and Hudik's 'Police-Citizen Encounters.'" *Social Problems* 23: 630–631.

Sheley, J. F., and J. D. Wright. 1993. "Gun Acquisition and Possession in Selected Juvenile Samples." *Research in Brief* (December). Washington, DC: National Institute of Justice.

Sherizen, S. 1978. "Social Creation of Crime News: All the News Fitted to Print." Pp. 203–224 in *Deviance and Mass Media*. Edited by C. Winick. Beverly Hills, CA: Sage.

Sherman, L. W. 1974. "Police Corruption Control: New York, London, Paris." In *Police Corruption: A Sociological Perspective*. Edited by L. W. Sherman. Garden City: Anchor Books.

———. 1983. "Reducing Gun Use: Critical Events, Administrative Policy, and Organizational Change." In *Control in the Police Organization*. Edited by M. Punch. Cambridge, MA: MIT Press.

———. 1986. "Policing Communities: What Works?" In *Communities and Crime*. Edited by A. J. Reiss, Jr., and M. Tonry. Chicago: University of Chicago Press.

———. 1990. "Police Crackdowns: Initial and Residual Deterrence." In *Crime and Justice*. Edited by M. Tonry and N. Morris. Chicago: University of Chicago Press.

———. 1992a. "Attacking Crime: Policing and Crime Control." In *Modern Policing*. Edited by M. Tonry and N. Morris. Chicago: University of Chicago Press.

———. 1992b. *Policing Domestic Violence: Experiments and Dilemas*. New York: Free Press.

———. 1993. "Why Crime Control is Not Reactionary." In *Police Innovation and Control of the Police: Problems of Law, Order, and Community*. Edited by D. Weisburd and C. Uchida. New York: Springer-Verlag.

Sherman, L., Gartin, P., and Buerger, M. 1989. "Hot Spots of Predatory Crime: Routine Activities and the Criminology Of Place." *Criminology* 27 (1): 27–40.

Sherman, M., and G. Hawkins. 1981. *Imprisonment in America: Choosing the Future*. Chicago: University of Chicago Press.

Sherrill, R. 1973. *The Saturday Night Special*. New York: Charterhouse.

Shick, J., D. E. Smith, and D. R. Wesson. 1973. "An Analysis of Amphetamine Toxicity and Patterns of Use." Pp. 23–61 in *Uppers and Downers*. Edited by D. E. Smith and D. R. Wesson. Englewood Cliffs, NJ: Prentice-Hall.

Shideler, E. H. 1918. "Family Disintegration and the Delinquent Boy in the United States." *Journal of Criminal Law and Criminology* 8: 709–732.

Shin, K. 1978. *Death Penalty and Crime: Empirical Studies*. Fairfax, VA: Center for Economic Analysis.

Shinn, M. 1978. "Father Absence and Children's Cognitive Development." *Psychological Bulletin* 85: 295–324.

Shock, N. 1984. *Normal Human Aging: The Baltimore Longitudinal Study of Aging*. Washington, DC: U.S. Government Printing Office.

Short, J. F. 1957. "Differential Association and Delinquency." *Social Problems* 4: 233–239.

Short, J. F., and F. I. Nye. 1957. "Reported Behavior as a Criterion of Deviant Behavior." *Social Problems* 5: 207–213.

———. 1958. "Extent of Unrecorded Juvenile Delinquency: Tentative Conclusions." *Journal of Criminal Law and Criminology* 49: 296–302.

Short, J. F., and F. L. Strodtbeck. 1965. *Group Process and Gang Delinquency*. Chicago: University of Chicago Press.

Shover, N. 1973. "The Social Organization of Burglary." *Social Problems* 20: 499–513.

———. 1983. "The Later Stages of Ordinary Property Offender Careers." *Social Problems* 30: 208–218.

Shover, N., and W. J. Einstadter. 1988. *Analyzing American Corrections*. Belmont, CA: Wadsworth.

Shuey, A. M. 1966. *The Testing of Negro Intelligence*. New York: Social Science Press.

Shuntich, R. J., and S. P. Taylor. 1972. "The Effects of Alcohol on Human Physical Aggression." *Journal of Experimental Research in Personality* 6: 34–38.

Siegel, A. J. 1973. "Appendix D: An Analysis of the Frequency and Content of Drug-Related Material Published in the Underground Press." Pp. D1–D50 in *Amphetamines, Barbiturates and Hallucinogens: An Analysis of Use, Distribution and Control*. By William H. McGlothlin. Department of Justice, Bureau of Narcotics and Dangerous Drugs. Washington, DC: U.S. Government Printing Office.

Siegel, B. 1985. "One Man's Efforts to Tell Dalkon Story." *Los Angeles Times*, August 22, I1 *passim*.

Siegel, L. G. 1986. *Criminology*. 2d ed. St. Paul, MN: West.

Siegel, L. J., S. A. Rathus, and C. A. Ruppert. 1973. "Values and Delinquent Youth: An Empirical Re-examination of Theories of Delinquency." *British Journal of Criminology* 13: 237–244.

Siegel, R. K. 1977. "Cocaine: Recreational Use and Intoxication." Pp. 119–136 in *Cocaine: 1977*. Edited by R. C. Petersen and R. C. Stillman. Rockville, MD: National Institute on Drug Abuse.

Silberman, C. E. 1978. *Criminal Violence, Criminal Justice*. New York: Random House.

Silberman, M. 1976. "Toward a Theory of Criminal Deterrence." *American Sociological Review* 41: 442–461.

Silver, A. 1967. "The Demand for Order in Civil Society: A Review of Some Themes in the History of Urban Crime, Police and Riots." In *The Police*. Edited by D. Bordua. New York: Wiley.

Silver, C. R., and D. B. Kates. 1978. "Self-Defense, Handgun Ownership, and the Independence of Women in a Violent, Sexist Society." Pp. 139–196 in *Restricting Handguns: The Liberal Skeptics Speak Out*. Edited by D. B. Kates. Croton-on-Hudson, NY: North River Press.

Silverman, I. J., and S. Dinitz. 1974. "Compulsive Masculinity and Delinquency." *Criminology* 11: 498–515.

Simmons, R., and D. Blyth. 1987. *Moving Into Adolescence*. New York: Aldine de Gruyter.

Simons, R. L., and L. B. Whitbeck. 1991. "Sexual Abuse as a Precursor to Prostitution and Victimization Among Adolescent and Adult Homeless Women." *Journal of Family Issues*. 12 (3): 361–379.

Simpson, S. 1986. "The Decomposition of Antitrust: Testing a Multi-Level Longitudinal Model of Profit Squeeze." *American Sociological Review* 51: 859–875.

———. 1991. "Caste, Class, and Violent Crime: Explaining Difference in Female Offending." *Criminology* 29: 115–135.

Skocpol, T. 1980. "Political Response to Capitalist Crisis: Neo-Marxist Theories of the State and the Case of the New Deal." *Politics and Society* 10: 155–201.

Skogan, W. G. 1986. "Methodological Issues in the Study of Victimization." Pp. 80–116 in *From Crime Policy to Victim Policy*. Edited by E. Fattah. New York: St. Martin's Press.

———. 1990. *Disorder and Decline*. New York: Free Press.

Skogan, W. G., and M. G. Maxfield. 1981. *Coping with Crime: Individual and Neighborhood Reactions*. Beverly Hills, CA: Sage.

Skolnick, J. 1966. *Justice Without Trial*. New York: Wiley.

Skolnick, J., and D. Bayley. 1986. *The New Blue Line*. New York: Free Press.

Skolnick, J. H. 1968. "Coercion to Virtue." *Southern California Law Review* 41: 3.

———. 1971. "Neighborhood Police." *The Nation* (March 22): 372–373.

Skovron, S. E., J. E. Scott, and F. T. Cullen. 1989. "The Death Penalty for Juveniles: An Assessment of Public Support." *Crime and Delinquency* 35: 546–561.

Sloan, I. J. 1984. *The Computer and the Law*. London: Oceana Publications.

Slobogin, C., and J. Schumacher. 1993. "Reasonable Expectations of Privacy and Autonomy in Fourth Amendment Cases: An Empirical Look at 'Understandings Recognized and Permitted by Society.'" *Duke Law Journal* 42: 727–775.

Slovak, J. 1986. *Styles of Urban Policing*. New York: New York University Press.

Smart, C. 1976. *Women, Crime and Criminology*. London: Routledge & Kegan Paul.

Smith, D. 1987. "Police Response to Interpersonal Violence." *Social Forces* 65: 767–782.

Smith D., and J. Gray. 1983. *The Police and People in London*. 4 vols. London: Policy Studies Institute.

Smith, D. A. 1986. "The Neighborhood Context of Police Behavior." In *Communities and Crime*. Edited by A. Reiss and M. Tonry. Chicago: University of Chicago Press.

Smith, D. A., and G. R. Jarjoura. 1988. "Social Structure and Criminal Victimization." *Journal of Research in Crime and Delinquency* 25: 27–52.

Smith, D. A., and J. Klein. 1983. "Police Agency and Characteristics and Arrest Decisions." In *Evaluating Performance of Criminal Justice Agencies*. Edited by G. Whitaker and C. Phillips. Beverly Hills, CA: Sage.

Smith, D. A., and R. Paternoster. 1987. "The Gender Gap in Theories of Deviance: Issues and Evidence." *Journal of Research in Crime and Delinquency* 24: 140–172.

Smith, D. A., and C. D. Uchida. 1988. "The Social Organization of Self-Help." *American Sociological Review* 53: 94–102.

Smith, D. A., and C. Visher. 1980. "Gender and Crime: An Empirical Assessment of Research Findings." *American Sociological Review* 48: 509–514.

Smith, D. A., and C. A. Visher. 1981. "Street Level Justice: Situational Determinants of Police Arrest Decisions." *Social Problems* 29: 167–177.

Smith, D. A., C. A. Visher, and L. A. Davidson. 1984. "Equity and Discretionary Justice: The Influence of Race on Police Arrest Decisions." *Journal of Criminal Law and Criminology* 75: 234–249.

Smith, D. C. 1978. "Organized Crime and Entrepreneurship." *International Journal of Criminology and Penology* 6: 161–177.

———. 1980. "Paragons, Pariahs, and Pirates: A Spectrum-Based Theory of Enterprise." *Crime and Delinquency* 26: 358–386.

———. 1990. *The Mafia Mystique, Revised Edition.* Lanham, MD: University Press of America.

Smith, J., and W. Fried. 1974. *The Uses of the American Prison.* Lexington, MA: Lexington Books.

Smith, M. D. 1986. "The Era of Increased Violence in the United States: Age, Period, or Cohort Effect?" *Sociological Quarterly* 27: 239–251.

Smith, M. D. 1987a. "General Versus Specific Support for Capital Punishment." *Journal of Crime and Justice* 15: 279–286.

———. 1987b. "Patterns of Discrimination in Assessments of the Death Penalty: The Case of Louisiana." *Journal of Criminal Justice* 15: 279–286.

———. 1992. "Variation in Correlates of Race-Specific Urban Homicide Rates." *Journal of Contemporary Criminal Justice* 8: 137–149.

Smith, M. D., and N. Bennett. 1985. "Poverty, Inequality, and Theories of Forcible Rape." *Crime and Delinquency* 31: 295–305.

Smith, M. D., and J. D. Wright. 1992. "Capital Punishment and Public Opinion in the Post-*Furman* Era: Trends and Analyses." *Sociological Spectrum* 12: 127–144.

Smith, R. 1969. "Traffic in Speed: Illegal Manufacture and Distribution." *Journal of Psychedelic Drugs* 2: 20–24.

Smith, S., and M. Jepson. 1993. "Big Fish, Little Fish: Politics and Power in the Regulation of Florida's Marine Resources." *Social Problems* 40: 39–49.

Smothers, R. 1986. "Tapes Played at Mob Trial Focus on Money and Power." *The New York Times*, January 26, 20.

Smykla, J. D. 1980. *Coed Prison.* New York: Human Sciences Press.

Snell, T. L. 1992. *Women in Jail 1989.* Washington, DC: U.S. Department of Justice, Bureau of Justice Statistics.

Snow, R. L. 1990. "Funding by Offenders." *Law and Order* 38 (4): 67–70.

Sobel, L. 1977. *Corruption in Business.* New York: Facts on File.

Sokoloff, N. 1988. "Contributions of Marxism and Feminism to the Sociology of Women and Work." P. 116 in *Women Working.* Edited by A. Stromberg and H. Harkness. Mountain View, CA: Mayfield.

Soule, S. A. 1992. "Populism and Black Lynching in Georgia, 1890-1900." *Social Forces* 71: 431–449.

Sparks, R. 1980. "A Critique of Marxist Criminology." Pp. 159–210 in *Crime and Justice: An Annual Review of Research.* Vol. 2. Edited by N. Morris and M. Tonry. Chicago: University of Chicago Press, Mayfield.

Sparks, R., H. Genn, and D. Dodd. 1977. *Surveying Victims.* New York: Wiley.

Special Committee on Pornography and Prostitution in Canada. 1985. *Pornography and Prostitution in Canada.* Ottawa: Canadian Government Publishing Centre.

Speckart, G., and M. D. Anglin. 1985. "Narcotics and Crime: An Analysis of Existing Evidence for a Causal Relationship." *Behavioral Sciences and the Law* 3: 259–282.

Spector, M., and J. I. Kitsuse. 1975. *Constructing Social Problems.* Menlo Park, CA: Cummings.

———. 1977. *Constructing Social Problems.* 2d ed. Menlo Park, CA: Benjamin/Cummings.

Speigelman, R., and F. D. Wittman. 1983. "Urban Redevelopment and Public Drunkenness in Fresno: A California Move Toward Recriminalization." *Research in Law, Deviance and Social Control* 5: 141–170.

Spierenburg, P. 1984. *The Spectacle of Suffering: Executions and the Evolution of Repression.* Cambridge: Cambridge University Press.

Spiotto, J. 1973. "Search and Seizure: An Empirical Study of the Exclusionary Rule and Its Alternatives." *Journal of Legal Studies* 2: 243–278.

Spitzer, S. 1975. "Toward a Marxian Theory of Deviance." *Social Problems* 22: 638–651.

Spohn, C. 1990. "The Sentencing Decisions of Black and White Judges: Expected and Unexpected Similarities." *Law & Society Review* 24: 1197–1216.

Spohn, C., J. Gruhl, and S. Welch. 1981–1982. "The Effect of Race on Sentencing: A Reexamination of an Unsettled Question." *Law & Society Review* 16: 71–88.

———. 1987. "The Impact of the Ethnicity and Gender of Defendants on the Decision to Reject or Dismiss Felony Charges." *Criminology* 25: 175–191.

Spotts, J. V., and C. A. Spotts. 1980. *Use and Abuse of Amphetamine and Its Substitutes*. Rockville, MD: National Institute on Drug Abuse.

Spradley, J. P. 1972. "An Ethnographic Approach to the Study of Organizations: The City Jail." Pp. 94–105 in *Organizations and Their Environments*. Edited by M. Brinkerhoff and P. Kunz. Dubuque, IA: Brown.

SRI International. 1983. *Final Report of the Seattle-Denver Income Maintenance Experiment. Vol. 1: Design and Results*. Washington, DC: U.S. Government Printing Office.

Stafford, M. C., and O. R. Galle. 1984. "Victimization Rates, Exposure to Risk, and Fear of Crime." *Criminology* 22: 173–185.

Stanko, E. A. 1981. "The Arrest Versus the Case: Some Observations on Police/District Attorney Interaction." *Urban Life* 9: 395–414.

———. 1981–1982. "The Impact of Victim Assessment on Prosecutors' Screening Decisions: The Case of the New York County District Attorney's Office." *Law & Society Review* 16: 225–239.

———. 1982. "Would You Believe This Woman? Prosecutorial Screening for 'Credible' Witnesses and a Problem of Justice." Pp. 63–82 in *Judge, Lawyer, Victim, Thief: Women, Gender Roles, and Criminal Justice*. Edited by N. Rafter and E. Stanko. Boston: Northeastern University Press.

Stanley, D. T. 1976. *Prisoners Among Us*. Washington, DC: Brodangs.

Stark, J., and H. Goldstein. 1985. *The Rights of Crime Victims*. Chicago: Southern Illinois University Press.

Stastny, C., and G. Tyrnauer. 1982. *Who Rules the Joint?* Lexington, MA: Lexington Books.

Staw, B., and E. Szwajkowski. 1975. "The Scarcity-Munificence Component of Organizational Environments and the Commission of Illegal Acts." *Administrative Science Quarterly* 20: 345–354.

Stead, J. 1977. *Pioneers in Policing*. Montclair, NJ: Patterson Smith.

Steel, K., P. M. Gertman, C. Crescenzl, and J. Anderson. 1981. "Iatrogenic Illness on a General Medical Service at a University Hospital." *New England Journal of Medicine* 304: 638–642.

Steffensmeier, D. 1980. "Sex Differences in Patterns of Adult Crime, 1965-77: A Review and Assessment." *Social Forces* 58: 1080–1108.

———. 1983. "Organization Properties and Sex-Segregation in the Underworld: Building a Sociological Theory of Sex Differences in Crime." *Social Forces* 61: 1010–1132.

———. 1986. *The Fence: In the Shadow of Two Worlds*. Totowa, NJ: Rowman & Littlefield.

———. 1987. "Invention of the 'New' Senior Citizen Criminal." *Research on Aging* 9: 281–311.

———. 1989. "On the Causes of White-collar Crime: An Assessment of Hirschi and Hindelang's Claims." *Criminology* 27: 345–358.

———. 1992. "More Pennslvania Prisons Did Not Reduce Violent Crime." *Overcrowded Times* 3 (6): 1–7.

———. Forthcoming. "Trends in Female Criminality, 1960-1990." *Journal of Quantitative Criminology*.

Steffensmeier, D., and E. Allan. 1988. "Sex Disparities in Arrests by Residence, Race, and Age: An Assessment of the Gender Convergence/Crime Hypothesis." *Justice Quarterly* 5: 53–80.

———. 1993. "Age-Inequality and Property Crime." In John Hagan and Ruth Peterson (eds), *Age Stratification and Crime*. University of Chicago Press.

Steffensmeier, D., E. Allan, and C. Streifel. 1989. "Development and Female Crime: A Cross-National Test of Alternative Explanations." *Social Forces* 68: 262–283.

Steffensmeier, D., and M. Harer. 1987. "Is the Crime Rate Really Falling? An 'Aging' U.S. Population and Its Impact on the Nation's Crime Rate, 1980-84." *Journal of Research in Crime and Delinquency* 24: 23–48.

———. 1991. "Did Crime Rise or Fall During the Reagan Presidency? The Effects of an 'Aging' U.S.

Population on the Nation's Crime Rate." *Journal of Research in Crime and Delinquency* 28: 330–359.

Steffensmeier, D., and C. Streifel. 1991. "The Distribution of Crime by Age and Gender Across Three Historical Periods — 1935, 1960, 1985." *Social Forces* 69: 869–894.

———. 1992. "Time-Series Analysis of the Female Percentage of Arrests for Property Crimes, 1960-1985: A Test of Alternative Explanations." *Justice Quarterly* 9: 78–103.

———. Forthcoming. "The Distribution of Crime by Age and Sex." *Social Forces.*

Steffensmeier, D., and R. Terry. 1986. "Institutional Sexism in the Underworld: A View from the Inside." *Sociological Inquiry* 56: 304–323.

Steinert, H. 1978. "Can Socialism Be Advanced by Radical Rhetoric and Sloppy Data: Some Remarks on Richard Quinney's Latest Output." *Contemporary Crises* 2: 303–313.

Steinmetz, A. 1969 (originally published in 1870). *The Gaming Table.* Montclair, NJ: Patterson Smith.

Steinmetz, S. K., and M. A. Straus. 1974. *Violence in the Family.* New York: Dodd, Mead.

Stewart, J. 1982. *The Effects of the Exclusionary Rule: A Study in California.* Washington, DC: National Institute of Justice.

Stinchcombe, A., R. Adams, C. A. Heimer, K. L. Scheppelle, T. W. Smith, and D. G. Taylor. 1980. *Crime and Punishment — Changing Attitudes in America.* San Francisco: Jossey-Bass.

Stone, A. 1985. "The Place of Law in the Marxian Structure-Superstructure Archetype." *Law & Society Review* 19: 39–67.

Stoneman, Z., G. Brody, and C. MacKinnon. 1984. "Naturalistic Observations of Children's Activities and Roles While Playing with their Siblings and Friends." *Child Development* 55: 617–627.

Stout, D. G. 1988. "The Lawyers of Death Row." *New York Times Magazine*, February 14, 46–54.

Straus, M. A., and R. J. Gelles. 1986. "Societal Change and Change in Family Violence From 1975 to 1985 as Revealed by Two National Surveys." *Journal of Marriage and the Family* 48: 465–479.

Streib, V. L. 1984. "Executions Under the Post-*Furman* Capital Punishment Statutes: The Halting Progression from 'Let's Do It' to 'Hey, There Ain't No Point

in Pulling So Tight." *Rutgers Law Journal* 15: 443–487.

———. 1987. *Death Penalty for Juveniles.* Bloomington: Indiana University Press.

Strung, D., E. Wish, B. Johnson, K. Anderson, T. Miller, and A. Sears. 1984. "The Role of Alcohol in the Crimes of Active Heroin Users." *Crime and Delinquency* 30: 551–567.

Studt, E. 1978. *Surveillance and Service in Parole.* Washington, DC: National Institute of Corrections.

Sudnow, D. 1965. "Normal Crimes: Sociological Features of the Penal Code in a Public Defender Office." *Social Problems* 12: 255–276.

Sullivan, D. C., L. J. Seigel, and T. R. Clear. 1974. "The Halfway House, Ten Years Later." *Canadian Journal of Corrections* 16: 3.

Sullivan, M. 1989. *"Getting Paid": Youth Crime and Work in the Inner City.* Ithaca: Cornell University Press.

Sullivan, W. 1980. "Violent Pornography Elevates Aggression, Researchers Say." *The New York Times*, September 30, C1, C3.

Sumner, C. 1979. *Reading Ideologies: An Investigation into the Marxist Theory of Ideology and Law.* New York: Academic Press.

Surette, R. 1992. *Media, Crime, and Justice.* Pacific Grove, CA: Brooks/Cole.

Sutherland, E. H. 1949. *White Collar Crime.* New York: Dryden.

———. 1983. *White Collar Crime: The Uncut Version.* New Haven, CT: Yale University Press.

Sutherland, E. H., and D. R. Cressey. 1978. *Criminology.* Philadelphia: Lippincott.

Sutton, J. 1987. "Doing Time: Dynamics of Imprisonment in the Reformist State." *American Sociological Review* 52: 612–630.

Swidler, A. 1984. "Culture in Action: Symbols and Strategems." *American Sociological Review* 51: 273–286.

Sykes, G. 1958. *Society of Captives.* Princeton, NJ: Princeton University Press.

———. 1974. "The Rise of Critical Criminology." *The Journal of Criminal Law and Criminology* 65: 206–213.

Sykes, G., and D. Matza. 1957. "Techniques of Neutralization: A Theory of Delinquency." *American Sociological Review* 22: 664–670.

Sykes, G., and S. L. Messinger. 1960. "The Inmate Social System." Pp. 5–19 in *Theoretical Studies in Social Organization of the Prison.* Edited by R. A. Cloward et al. New York: Social Science Research.

Sykes, R. E., and E. E. Brent. 1983. *Policing: A Social Behaviorist Perspective.* New Brunswick, NJ: Rutgers University Press.

Szasz, A. 1984. "Industrial Resistance to Occupational Safety and Health Legislation: 1971-1981." *Social Problems* 32: 103–116.

Takagi, P. 1976. "The Parole Violators Organizational Reject." In *Probation, Parole, and Community Corrections.* Edited by R. M. Carter and L. T. Wilkins. New York: Wiley.

Tamerin, J. S., S. Weiner, and J. H. Mendelson. 1970. "Alcoholics' Expectancies and Recall of Experiences During Intoxication." *American Journal of Psychiatry* 126: 1697–1704.

Tangri, S. S., and M. Schwartz. 1967. "Delinquency Research and the Self-concept Variable." *Journal of Criminal Law, Criminology and Police Science* 58: 182–190.

Tausky, C., and R. Dubin. 1965. "Career Anchorages: Managerial Mobility Orientations." *American Sociological Review* 30: 725–735.

Taylor, I., P. Walton, and J. Young. 1973. *The New Criminology: For a Social Theory of Deviance.* New York: Harper & Row.

Taylor, S. 1983. "Alcohol and Human Physical Aggression." Pp. 280–291 in *Alcohol, Drug Abuse and Aggression.* Edited by E. Gottheil, K. A. Druley, T. E. Skoloda, and H. M. Waxman. Springfield, IL: Thomas.

Taylor, S., and C. B. Gammon. 1975. "Effects of Type and Dose of Alcohol on Human Physical Aggression." *Journal of Personality and Social Psychology* 32: 169–175.

Teplin, L. 1986. *Keeping the Peace.* Washington, DC: U.S. Government Printing Office.

Theilgaard, A. 1983. "Aggression and the XYY Personality." *International Journal of Law and Psychiatry* 6: 413–421.

Theresa, V., and T. C. Renner. 1973. *My Life in the Mafia.* Greenwich, CT: Fawcett.

Thomas, C. W., and S. C. Foster. 1975. "A Sociological Perspective on Public Support for Capital Punishment." *American Journal of Orthopsychiatry* 45: 641–657.

Thompson, E. P. 1975. *Whigs and Hunters: The Origin of the Black Act.* New York: Pantheon.

Thompson, J. A. 1986. "The American Jail: Problems, Politics, and Prospects." *American Journal of Criminal Justice* 10: 205–221.

Thompson, J. A., and G. L. Mays. 1991. *American Jails: Public Policy Issues.* Chicago: Nelson-Hall.

Thompson, J. D. 1967. *Organizations in Action.* New York: McGraw-Hill.

Thornberry, T. 1987. "Toward an Interactional Theory of Delinquency." *Criminology* 25 (November): 863–892.

Thornberry, T. P., and R. L. Christenson. 1984. "Unemployment and Criminal Involvement: An Investigation of Reciprocal Causal Structures." *American Sociological Review* 49: 398–411.

Thornberry, T. P., and M. Farnworth. 1982. "Social Correlates of Criminal Involvement: Further Evidence on the Relationship Between Social Status and Criminal Behavior." *American Sociological Review* 47: 505–518.

Thrasher, F. 1927. *The Gang: A Study of 1,313 Gangs in Chicago.* Chicago: University of Chicago Press.

Tierney, K. J. 1982. "The Battered Women Movement and the Creation of the Wife Beating Problem." *Social Problems* 29: 207–220.

Time. 1930. "Heroin Trade." October 13, 28.

———. 1976. "Gambling Goes Legit." December 6, 70.

———. 1979. "Forewarning of Fatal Flaws." June 25.

———. 1981. "Abscam's Toll." August 10.

Tittle, C. R. 1969. "Crime Rates and Legal Sanctions." *Social Problems* 16: 408–423.

———. 1975. "Labelling and Crime: An Empirical Evaluation." Pp. 157–179 in *The Labelling of Deviance: Evaluating a Perspective.* Edited by W. Gove. Beverly Hills, CA: Sage.

———. 1988. "Two Explanatory Regularities (maybe) in Search of an Explanation: Commentary on the Age/Crime Debate." *Criminology* 26: 75–85.

Tittle, C. R., and R. F. Meier. 1990. "Specifying the SES Delinquency Relationship." *Criminology* 28: 271–299.

Tittle, C. R., and A. R. Rowe. 1974. "Certainty of Arrest and Crime Rates: A Further Test of the Deterrence Hypothesis." *Social Forces* 52: 455–462.

Tittle, C. R., W. J. Villemez, and D. A. Smith. 1978. "The Myth of Social Class and Criminality: An Empirical Assessment of the Empirical Evidence." *American Sociological Review* 43: 643–656.

Toby, J. 1979. "The New Criminology Is the Old Sentimentality." *Criminology* 16: 516–526.

Toch, H. 1977. *Living in Prison.* New York: Free Press.

Tonry, M. 1987. "Prediction and Classification: Legal and Ethical Issues." Pp. 367–413 in *Prediction and Classification: Criminal Justice Decision Making.* Edited by D. Gottfredson and M. Tonry. Chicago: University of Chicago Press.

———. 1988. "Structuring Sentencing." Pp. 267–337 in *Crime and Justice: A Review of Research.* Vol. 10. Edited by M. Tonry and N. Morris. Chicago: University of Chicago Press.

———. 1992. "Mandatory Penalties." Pp. 243–274 in *Crime and Justice: A Review of Research*, Michael Tonry (ed.). Volume 16. Chicago: University of Chicago Press.

Tonso, W. R. 1982. *Guns and Society: The Social and Existential Roots of the American Attachment to Firearms.* Washington, DC: University Press of America.

Tracey, P., M. Wolfgang, and R. Figlio. 1990. *Delinquency Careers in Two Birth Cohorts.* New York: Plenum.

Tracy, C. 1980. "Race, Crime and Social Policy: The Chinese in Oregon, 1871-1885." *Crime and Social Justice* 14: 11–25.

Troyer, R. J., and G. E. Markle. 1982. "Creating Deviant Rules: A Macroscopic Model." *Sociological Inquiry* 23: 157–169.

Tunnell, K. D. 1992. *Choosing Crime: The Criminal Calculus of Property Offenders.* Chicago: Nelson-Hall.

Turk, A. 1969. *Criminality and Legal Order.* Chicago: Rand McNally.

———. 1976. "Law as a Weapon in Social Conflict." *Social Problems* 23: 276–291.

———. 1979. "Analyzing Official Deviance: For Nonpartisan Conflict Analyses in Criminology." *Criminology* 16: 459–476.

Turkington, C. 1986. "Pornography and Violence." *American Psychological Association's Monitor* (August): 8–9.

Turkus, B. B., and S. Feder. 1951. *Murder, Inc.* New York: Manor Books.

Turner, A. G. 1972. *The San Jose Methods Test of Known Crime Victims.* National Criminal Justice Information and Statistics Service, Law Enforcement Assistance Administration. Washington, DC: U.S. Government Printing Office.

Turner, R. 1969. "The Public Perception of Protest." *American Sociological Review* 34: 815–831.

Tyler, T. R., and R. Weber. 1982. "Support for the Death Penalty: Instrumental Response to Crime or Symbolic Attitude?" *Law & Society Review* 17: 21–45.

U.S. Bureau of Census. 1992. *Statistical Abstract of the United States.* Washington, DC: U.S. Government Printing Office.

U.S. Comptroller General. 1980. *Women in Prison.* Washington, DC: U.S. Government Printing Office.

———. 1984. *Witness Security Program: Prosecutive Results and Participant Arrest Data.* Washington, DC: U.S. General Accounting Office.

U.S. Department of Justice. 1978a. *State and Local Probation and Parole Systems.* Washington, DC: U.S. Government Printing Office.

———. 1978b. *Capital Punishment, 1976.* Washington, DC: U.S. Government Printing Office.

———. 1981. *Justice Assistance News.* Vol. 2, No. 9 (November). Washington, DC: U.S. Department of Justice.

———. 1986. "Uniform Crime Reports." Federal Bureau of Investigation. Washington, DC: U.S. Government Printing Office.

———. 1987a. *Jail Inmates, 1986.* Washington, DC: Bureau of Justice Statistics.

———. 1987b. *1984 Census of State Adult Correctional Facilities.* Washington, DC: Bureau of Justice Statistics.

———. 1987c. *Prisoners in 1986.* Washington, DC: Bureau of Justice Statistics.

———. 1988a. *Census of Local Jails, 1983.* Vol. 5. Selected Findings and Methodology. Washington, DC: Bureau of Justice Statistics.

———. 1988b. *Prisoners in 1987.* Washington, DC: Bureau of Justice Statistics.

———. 1988c. *Report to the Nation on Crime and Justice.* Bureau of Justice Statistics. Washington, DC: U.S. Government Printing Office.

———. 1989a. *BJS Data Reports, 1988.* Washington, DC: Bureau of Justice Statistics.

———. 1989b. *Sourcebook of Criminal Justice Statistics—1988.* Washington, DC: U.S. Government Printing Office.

———. 1989c. *Prisoners in 1988.* Washington, DC: Bureau of Justice Statistics.

———. 1989d. "The Police and Drugs." *Perspectives on Policing, No. 11.* Washington, DC: National Institute of Justice.

———. 1989e. *Drug Use Forecasting: January to March 1989.* National Institute of Justice Research in Action Series. Washington, DC: U.S. Department of Justice.

———. 1991. *Uniform Crime Reports.* Federal Bureau of Investigation. Washington, DC: U.S. Government Printing Office.

———. 1992a. *Criminal Victimization in the United States—1991.* Washington, DC: U.S. Government Printing Office.

———. 1992b. *Correctional Populations in the United States, 1990.* Washington, DC: Bureau of Justice Statistics.

———. 1992c. *Drug Use Forecasting 1991 Annual Report.* Washington, DC: National Institute of Justice.

———. 1992d. *Jail Inmates 1991.* Washington, DC: Bureau of Justice Statistics.

———. 1992e. *National Update.* Washington, DC: Bureau of Justice Statistics.

———. 1992f. *Prisoners in 1991.* Washington, DC: Bureau of Justice Statistics.

———. 1992g. *Profile of Jail Inmates, 1989.* Washington, DC: Bureau of Justice Statistics.

———. 1993. *Survey of State Prison Inmates, 1991.* Washington, DC: Bureau of Justice Statistics.

U.S. News & World Report. 1951. "Teenage Dope Addicts: New Problem?" June 29, 18.

———. 1980. "Congress Feels the Sting." February 18, 14–19.

———. 1989. "Dead Zones." April 10, 20–32.

U.S. Senate. 1963. *Organized Crime and Illicit Traffic in Narcotics: Hearings Part I.* Committee on Government Operations Permanent Subcommittee on Investigations. 88th Congress, 1st Session. Washington, DC: U.S. Government Printing Office.

———. 1965. *Report on Organized Crime and Illicit Traffic in Narcotics.* Committee on Government Operations Permanent Subcommittee on Investigations. 89th Congress, 1st Session. Washington, DC: U.S. Government Printing Office.

United States Sentencing Commission. 1990. *Guidelines Manual.* Washington, DC: United States Sentencing Commission.

Unnever, J. D. 1982. "Direct and Organizational Discrimination in the Sentencing of Drug Offenders." *Social Problems* 30: 212–225.

Unnever, J. D., C. E. Frazier, and J. C. Henretta. 1980. "Race Differences in Criminal Sentencing." *Sociological Quarterly* 21: 197–205.

Unnever, J. D., and L. A. Hembroff. 1988. "The Prediction of Racial/Ethnic Sentencing Disparities: An Expectation States Approach." *Journal of Research in Crime and Delinquency* 25: 53–82.

Urban Institute. 1988. *Growth of the Underclass 1970-1980.* Urban Institute Discussion Paper, April 1988. Washington, DC: Urban Institute.

Useem, B., and P. Kimball. 1989. *States of Siege: U.S. Prison Riots, 1971-1986.* New York: Oxford University Press.

Utz, P. J. 1978. *Settling the Facts: Discretion and Negotiation in Criminal Court.* Lexington, MA: Heath.

Valentine, B. 1978. *Hustling and Other Hard Work: Lifestyles in the Ghetto.* New York: Free Press.

van den Haag, E. 1985. "The Death Penalty Once More." *U.C. Davis Law Review* 18: 957–972.

van den Haag, E., and J. P. Conrad. 1983. *The Death Penalty: A Debate.* New York: Plenum Press.

Van Maanen, J. 1974. "Working the Street." Pp. 83–130 in *Prospects for Reform in Criminal Justice.* Edited by H. Jacob. Beverly Hills, CA: Sage.

———. 1983. "The Boss: A Portrait of the American Police Sergeant." In *The Control of the Police.* Edited by M. Punch. Cambridge, MA: MIT Press.

Vass, A. A. 1990. *Alternatives to Prison: Punishment, Custody and the Community.* London: Sage.

Vaughan, D. 1980. "Shock Probation and Shock Parole: The Impact of Changing Correctional Ideology." In *Corrections: Problems and Prospects.* Edited by D. M. Peterson and C. W. Thomas. Englewood Cliffs, NJ: Prentice-Hall.

Vaz, E. W. 1967. "Juvenile Delinquency in the Middle-Class Youth Culture." Pp. 131–147 in *Middle-Class Juvenile Delinquency.* Edited by E. Vas. New York: Harper & Row.

Vera Institute of Justice. 1981. *Felony Arrests: Their Prosecution and Disposition in New York City's Courts.* Rev. ed. New York: Longman.

Viano, E. 1976. *Victims and Society.* Washington, DC: Visage.

Vidmar, N., and P. C. Ellsworth. 1982. "Research on Attitudes Toward Capital Punishment." Pp. 68–84 in *The Death Penalty in America.* Edited by H. A. Bedeau. Oxford: Oxford University Press.

Villmoore, E., and V. Neto. 1987. *Victim Appearances at Sentencing Under California's Victims' Bill of Rights.* NIJ Research in Brief. Washington, DC: U.S. Department of Justice.

Virkkunen, M. 1974. "Alcohol as a Factor Precipitating Aggression and Conflict Behaviour Leading to Homicide." *British Journal of Addiction* 69: 149–154.

Visher, C. A. 1983. "Gender, Police, Arrest Decisions, and Notions of Chivalry." *Criminology* 21: 5–28.

———. 1986. "The Rand Second Inmate Survey: A Reanalysis." Pp. 161–211 in *Criminal Careers and "Career Criminals."* Vol. 2. Edited by A. Blumstein, J. Cohen, J. Roth, and C. Visher. Washington, DC: National Academy Press.

———. 1987. "Incapacitation and Crime Control: Does a 'Lock 'em Up' Strategy Reduce Crime?" *Justice Quarterly* 4: 513–543.

Visher, C. A., and J. Roth. 1986. "Participation in Criminal Careers." Appendix A in *Criminal Careers and "Career Criminals."* Vol. 1. Edited by A. Blumstein, J. Cohen, J. Roth, and C. Visher. Washington, DC: National Academy Press.

Vold, G., and T. J. Bernard. 1986. *Theoretical Criminology.* 3d ed. New York: Oxford University Press.

Volkman, R., and D. R. Cressey. 1963. "Differential Association and the Rehabilitation of Drug Addicts." *American Journal of Sociology* 29: 129–142.

Von Hentig, H. 1941. "Remarks on the Interaction of Perpetrator and Victim." *Journal of Criminal Law, Criminology, and Police Science* 31: 303–309.

———. 1948. *The Criminal and His Victim.* New Haven, CT: Yale University Press.

von Hirsch, A., and D. Gottfredson. 1984. "Selective Incapacitation: Some Queries on Research Design and Equity." *New York University Review of Law and Social Change* 12: 11–51.

Voss, H. 1964. "Differential Association and Reported Delinquent Behavior: A Replication." *Social Problems* 12: 78–85.

Voss, H., and J. Hepburn. 1968. "Patterns in Criminal Homicide in Chicago." *Journal of Criminal Law, Criminology, and Police Science* 59: 499–508.

Waldo, G. P. 1981. "The Death Penalty and Deterrence: A Review of Recent Research." In *The Mad, the Bad, and the Different.* Edited by I. L. Barak-Glantz and C. R. Huff. Lexington, MA: Lexington Books.

Waldo, G. P., and T. G. Chiricos. 1972. "Perceived Penal Sanction and Self-reported Criminology: A Neglected Approach to Deterrence Research." *Social Problems* 19: 522–540.

Waldorf, D. 1983. "Natural Recovery from Opiate Addiction: Some Social Psychological Processes of Untreated Recovery." *Journal of Drug Issues* 13: 237–280.

Waldorf, D., and S. Murphy. 1990. "IV Drug Use and Syringe Sharing Practices of Call Men and Hustlers." In *Prostitutes, Drugs and AIDS.* Edited by M. Plant. London: Routledge & Kegan Paul.

Waldorf, D., C. Reinarman, and S. Murphy. 1991. *Cocaine Changes: The Experience of Using and Quitting.* Philadelphia: Temple University Press.

Walker, S. 1977. *A Critical History of Police Reform.* Lexington, MA: Lexington Books.

———. 1985. "Racial Minority and Female Employment in Policing: The Implications of 'Glacial' Change." *Crime and Delinquency* (October): 555–572.

———. 1986. "Controlling the Cops: A Legislative Approach to Police Rulemaking." *University of Detroit Law Review* (Spring): 361–391.

———. 1989. *Sense and Nonsense About Crime: A Policy Guide,* 2d ed. Pacific Grove, CA: Brooks/Cole.

———. 1992. *The Police in America: An Introduction.* New York: McGraw-Hill.

———. 1993. "Historical Roots of the Legal Control of Police Behavior." In *Police Innovation and Control of the Police: Problems of Law, Order and Community.* Edited by D. Weisburd and C. Uchida. New York: Springer-Verlag.

Walker, S., J. A. Yesavage, and J. R. Tinklenberg. 1981. "Acute Phencyclidine (PCP) Intoxication: Quantitative Urine Levels and Clinical Management." *American Journal of Psychiatry* 138: 674–675.

Wallace, A. 1987. "Wanted: Attorneys for Death-Row Inmates." *Atlanta Journal-Constitution*, October 11, B1, B10.

Walsh, A. 1987. "The Sexual Stratification Hypothesis and Sexual Assault in Light of the Changing Conceptions of Race." *Criminology* 25: 153–173.

Walsh, J. 1977. "Career Styles and Police Behavior." Pp. 149–167 in *Police and Society*. Edited by D. Bayley. Beverly Hills, CA: Sage.

Walters, G. D. 1992. "A Meta-Analysis of the Gene-Crime Relationship," *Criminology* 30 (4): 595–613.

Walters, G., and T. White. "Heredity and Crime: Bad Genes or Bad Research." *Criminology* 27 (3): 455–486.

Ward, D. A., and G. Kassebaum. 1965. *Women's Prison*. Chicago: Aldine.

Warr, M. 1980. "The Accuracy of Public Beliefs About Crime." *Social Forces* 59: 456–470.

———. 1981. "Which Norms of Justice? A Commentary on Hamilton and Rytina." *American Journal of Sociology* 85 (September): 433–435.

———. 1982. "The Accuracy of Public Beliefs About Crime: Further Evidence." *Criminology* 20 (August): 185–204.

———. 1984. "Fear of Victimization: Why Are Women and the Elderly More Afraid?" *Social Science Quarterly* 65 (September): 681–702.

———. 1985. "Fear of Rape Among Urban Women." *Social Problems* 32 (February): 238–250.

———. 1987. "Fear of Victimization and Sensitivity to Risk." *Journal of Quantitative Criminology* 3 (March): 29–46.

———. 1990. "Dangerous Situations: Social Context and Fear of Criminal Victimization." *Social Forces* 68: 891–907.

———. 1992. "Altruistic Fear of Victimization in Households." *Social Science Quarterly*. In press.

———. 1993. "Age, Peers, and Delinquency." *Criminology* 31: 17–40.

Warr, M., J. P. Gibbs, and M. L. Erickson. 1982. "Contending Theories of Criminal Law: Statutory Penalties Versus Public Preferences." *Journal of Research in Crime and Delinquency* 19: 25–46.

Warr, M., R. F. Meier, and M. L. Erickson. 1983. "Norms, Theories of Punishment, and Publicly Preferred Penalties for Crimes." *Sociological Quarterly* 24 (Winter): 75–91.

Warr, M., and M. C. Stafford. 1983. "Fear of Victimization: A Look at the Proximate Causes." *Social Forces* 61 (June): 1033–1043.

———. 1984. "Public Goals of Punishment and Support for the Death Penalty." *Journal of Research in Crime and Delinquency* 21 (May): 95–111.

Warren, C., and J. Johnson. 1972. "A Critique of Labelling Theory from the Phenomenological Perspective." Pp. 69–92 in *Theoretical Perspectives on Deviance*. Edited by R. Scott and J. Douglas. New York: Basic Books.

Warren, M. Q. 1971. "Classification as an Aide to Efficient Management and Effective Treatment." *Journal of Criminal Law, Criminology and Police Science* 2: 239.

———. 1973. "All Things Not Being Equal . . ." *Criminal Law Bulletin* 9 (4): 483.

Washington Post. 1992a. "University of Maryland Cancels Conference on Genetic Link to Crime." September 5, A1.

———. 1992b. "Controversy Flares Over Crime, Heredity," August 19, A4.

Washton, A. M., and M. S. Gold. 1986. "Recent Trends in Cocaine Abuse: A View from the National Hotline, '800-COCAINE.'" *Advances in Alcohol and Substance Abuse* 6: 31–48.

Wasserman, I. M. 1977. "Southern Violence and the Political Process." *American Sociological Review* 42: 359–362.

Wasserstrom, S. 1984. "The Incredible Shrinking Fourth Amendment." *American Criminal Law Review* 21: 257–401.

Watters, J. K., C. Reinarman, and J. Fagan. 1985. "Causality, Context, and Contingency: Relationships Between Drug Abuse and Delinquency." *Contemporary Drug Problems* 12: 351–373.

Wayson, B. L., G. S. Funke, S. F. Hamilton, and P. B. Meyer. 1977. *Local Jails: The New Correctional Dilemma*. Lexington, MA: Heath.

Webster, W. 1980. "An Examination of FBI Theory and Methodology Regarding White-collar Crime Investigation and Prevention." *American Criminal Law Review* 17: 275–286.

Webster, W., and H. Williams. 1992. *The City in Crisis*. Report by the Special Advisor to the Police Commissioners on the Civil Disorder in Los Angeles. Los Angeles, CA.

Weick, K. 1979. *The Social Psychology of Organizing.* 2d ed. Reading, MA: Addison-Wesley.

Weinstein, H. 1978. "Did Asbestos Industry Suppress Data?" *Los Angeles Times*, October 23, Il *passim.*

Weis, K., and S. Borges. 1973. "Victimology and Rape: The Case of the Legitimate Victim." *Issues in Criminology* 8: 71–115.

Weisburd, D., F. Gajewski, L. Green, and C. Bellucci. 1991. *Preliminary Report: Jersey City Community Survey.* Newark, NJ: Center for Crime Prevention Studies, Rutgers University.

Weiss, R. D., and S. M. Mirin. 1987. *Cocaine.* Washington, DC: American Psychiatric Press.

Weissman, J. C., and K. N. File. 1978. "Criminal Behavior Patterns of Female Addicts: A Comparison of Findings in Two Cities." Pp. 1082–1096 in *Drug Abuse: Modern Trends, Issues, and Perspectives.* Edited by A. Schecter, H. Alksne, and E. Kaufman. New York: Marcel Dekker.

Weitzer, R. 1991. "Prostitutes' Rights in the United States: The Failure of a Movement." *Sociological Quarterly.* 32 (1): 23–41.

Welch, M. 1988. "The Contradiction and Deception of the Meese Report on Pornography: Avoiding the Real Issue of Violence." Paper presented at the annual meeting of the American Society of Criminology, Chicago.

———. Forthcoming. "Jail Overcrowding: Social Sanitation and the Warehousing of the Urban Underclass." *Critical Issues in Crime and Justice.* Edited by Albert Roberts.

Welch, S., and C. Spohn. 1986. "Evaluating the Impact of Prior Record on Judges' Sentencing Decisions: A Seven-City Comparison." *Justice Quarterly* 3: 389–407.

Welch, S., J. Gruhl, and C. Spohn. 1984. "Sentencing: The Influence of Alternative Measures of Prior Record." *Criminology* 22: 215–227.

Welch, S., C. Spohn, and J. Gruhl. 1985. "Convicting and Sentencing Differences Among Black, Hispanic, and White Males in Six Localities." *Justice Quarterly* 2: 67–80.

Wellford, C. 1975. "Labelling Theory and Criminology: An Assessment." *Social Problems* 22: 332–345.

Wells, R. T., and T. S. Smith. 1970. "Development of Preference for Delayed Reinforcement in Disadvantaged Children." *Journal of Educational Psychology* 61: 118–123.

Weppner, R. S., and J. A. Inciardi. 1978. "Decriminalizing Marijuana." *International Journal of Offender Therapy and Comparative Criminology* 22: 115–126.

West, D. J. 1982. *Delinquency: Its Roots, Careers and Prospects.* Cambridge, MA: Harvard University Press.

Westley, W. 1970. *Violence and the Police.* Cambridge, MA: MIT Press.

Wetheritt, M. 1987. *Police Research.* Farnborough, England: Gower.

Wheeler, S., D. Weisburd, and N. Bode. 1982. "Sentencing the White-collar Offender: Rhetoric and Reality." *American Sociology Review* 47: 641–659.

Wheeler, S., D. Weisburd, N. Bode, and E. Waring. 1988. "White Collar Crime and Criminals." *American Criminal Law Review* 25: 331–357.

White, H. R., R. J. Pandina, and R. L. LaGrange. 1987. "Longitudinal Predictors of Serious Substance Use and Delinquency." *Criminology* 25: 715–740.

White, S. 1972. "A Perspective on Police Professionalism." *Law and Society Review* 7: 61–85.

White, W. S. 1984. *Life in the Balance: Procedural Safeguards in Capital Cases.* Ann Arbor: University of Michigan Press.

———. 1987. *The Death Penalty in the Eighties.* Ann Arbor: University of Michigan Press.

———. 1991. *The Death Penalty in the Nineties: An Examination of the Modern System of Capital Punishment.* Ann Arbor: University of Michigan Press.

Whitebread, C. 1985. "The Burger Court's Counter-Revolution in Criminal Procedure: The Recent Criminal Decisions of the United States Supreme Court." *Washburn Law Journal* 24: 471–498.

Whitford, D. 1983. "Getting Police off the Skid Row Merry-Go-Round." *Police* 6: 12–22.

Wiatrowski, M. D., D. B. Griswold, and G. Elder. 1981. "Social Control Theory and Delinquency." *American Sociological Review* 46: 525–541.

Wilbanks, W. 1987. *The Myth of a Racist Criminal Justice System.* Monterey, CA: Brooks/Cole.

Williams, F. P., D. R. Longmire, and D. B. Gulick. 1988. "The Public and the Death Penalty: Opinion as an Artifact of Question Type." *Criminal Justice Research Bulletin* 3: 1–5.

Williams, J. S., and J. H. McGrath. 1976. "Why People Own Guns." *Journal of Communication* 26: 22–30.

Williams, K. 1978. *The Effects of Victim Characteristics on Judicial Decisions*. PROMIS Research Project Report. Washington, DC: Institute for Law and Social Research.

Williams, K. R. 1984. "Economic Sources of Homicide: Reestimating the Effects of Poverty and Inequality." *American Sociological Review* 49: 283–289.

Williams, K. R., and R. L. Flewelling. 1987. "Family Acquaintance, and Stranger Homicide: Alternative Procedures for Rate Calculation." *Criminology* 25: 543–560.

———. 1988. "The Social Production of Criminal Homicide: A Comparative Study of Disaggregated Rates in American Cities." *American Sociological Review* 53: 421–431.

Williams, K. R., J. P. Gibbs, and M. L. Erickson. 1980. "Public Knowledge of Statutory Penalties: The Extent and Basis of Accurate Perception." *Pacific Sociological Review* 23 (January): 105–128.

Williams, R. 1977. *Marxism and Literature*. Oxford: Oxford University Press.

Williams, V. L., and M. Fish. 1974. *Convicts, Codes and Contraband*. Cambridge, MA: Ballinger.

Wilson, E. 1975. *Sociobiology*. Cambridge, MA: Harvard University Press.

Wilson, J. Q. 1968. *Varieties of Police Behavior*. Cambridge, MA: Harvard University Press.

———. 1975. *Thinking About Crime*. New York: Basic Books.

———. 1978. *Varieties of Police Behavior: The Management of Law and Order in Eight Communities*. Cambridge, MA: Harvard University Press.

———. 1986. *"Forward" to Reducing Fear of Crime in Houston and Newark*. Summary report. Washington, DC: Police Foundation.

Wilson, J. Q. and B. Boland. 1978. "The Effect of the Police on Crime." *Law and Society Review* 12: 267–390.

Wilson, J. Q., and R. Herrnstein. 1985. *Crime and Human Nature*. New York: Simon & Schuster.

Wilson, W. J. 1978 [1980]. *The Declining Significance of Race*. Second edition. Chicago: University of Chicago Press.

———. 1987. *The Truly Disadvantaged: The Inner City, the Underclass, and Public Policy*. Chicago: University of Chicago Press.

Winfree, L. T. 1987. "Toward Understanding State-Level Jail Mortality." *Justice Quarterly* 4: 51–71.

Winick, C. 1964. "Physician Narcotic Addicts." Pp. 261–279 in *The Other Side: Perspectives on Deviance*. Edited by H. S. Becker. New York: Free Press.

Winick, C., and P. M. Kinsie. 1971. *The Lively Commerce: Prostitution in the U.S.* Chicago: Quadrangle Books.

Winston-Salem Journal. 1989a. "Bush Proposes $7.9 Billion in Drug War." September 6, 1.

———. 1989b. "Highly Addictive Drug Is Heading for the Mainland, Hawaiians Warn." September 24, A8.

Wise, D. 1976. "The Campaign to Destroy Martin Luther King." *New York Review of Books* 23: 38–42.

Wiseman, J. P. 1970. *Stations of the Lost*. Englewood Cliffs, NJ: Prentice-Hall.

Wish, E., and B. Johnson. 1986. "The Impact of Substance Abuse on Criminal Careers." Pp. 52–88 in *Criminal Careers and "Career Criminals."* Vol. 2. Edited by A. Blumstein, J. Cohen, J. Roth, and C. Visher. Washington, DC: National Academy Press.

Wolf, D. 1991. *The Rebels: A Brotherhood of Outlaw Bikers*. University of Toronto Press.

Wolfgang, M. 1958. *Patterns in Criminal Homicide*. Philadelphia: University of Pennsylvania Press.

Wolfgang, M. E., and F. Ferracuti. 1967. *The Subculture of Violence: Towards an Integrated Theory in Criminology*. Beverly Hills, CA: Sage.

Wolfgang, M., R. M. Figlio, and T. Sellin. 1972. *Delinquency in a Birth Cohort*. Chicago: University of Chicago Press.

Wolfgang, M., R. M. Figlio, P. E. Tracy, and S. I. Singer. 1985. *The National Survey of Crime Severity*. Washington, DC: U.S. Department of Justice, Bureau of Justice Statistics.

Wolfgang, M., and N. A. Werner (eds.). 1982. *Criminal Violence*. Beverly Hills, CA: Sage.

Wolfgang, M., T. Thornberry, and R. Figlio. 1987. *From Boy to Man, From Delinquency to Crime*. Chicago: University of Chicago Press.

Woltman, H. F., and J. M. Bushery. 1975. *A panel bias study in the National Crime Survey*. Proceedings of the Social Statistics Section of the American Statistical Association.

Worden, R. 1984. "Patrol Officer Attitudes and the Distribution of Police Services: A Preliminary Analysis." In *Understanding Police Agency Performance*. Edited by G. P. Whitaker. Washington DC: National Institute of Justice.

———. 1989. "Situational and Attitudinal Explanations of Police Behavior: A Theoretical Reapprasial and Empirical Assessment." *Law and Society Review* 23: 667–671.

———. 1992. "The 'Causes' of Police Brutality." In *And Justice for All: A National Agenda for Understanding and Controlling Police Abuse of Force*. Edited by W. A. Geller and H. Toch. Unpublished manuscript. Washington, DC: Police Executive Research Forum.

Worden, R., and S. Mastrofski. 1989. "Varieties of Police Subcultures: A Preliminary Investigation." Unpublished paper presented to the Law and Society Association, Madison, Wisconsin. June.

Worden, R., and A. Pollitz. 1984. "Police Arrests in Domestic Disturbances: A Further Look." *Law & Society Review* 18: 105–119.

Wright, E. O. 1973. *The Politics of Punishment*. New York: Harper Colophon Books.

Wright, J. D. 1981. "Public Opinion and Gun Control: A Comparison of Results from Two Recent National Surveys." *The Annals of the American Academy of Political and Social Science* 455: 24–39.

———. 1984. "The Ownership of Firearms for Reasons of Self-Defense." Pp. 301–328. in *Firearms and Violence: Issues of Public Policy*. Edited by D. B. Kates. Cambridge, MA: Ballinger.

———. 1990. "In the Heat of the Moment." *Reason* 22 (4): 44–45.

Wright, J. D., and L. L. Marston. 1975. "The Ownership of the Means of Destruction: Weapons in the United States." *Social Problems* 23: 93–107.

Wright, J. D., and P. Rossi. 1986. *Armed and Considered Dangerous: A Survey of Felons and Their Firearms*. Hawthorne, NY: Aldine.

Wright, J. D., P. Rossi, and K. Daly. 1983. *Under the Gun: Weapons, Crime, and Violence in America*. Hawthorne, NY: Aldine.

Wright, M., 1991. *Justice For Victims And Offenders*. Philadelphia: Open University Press.

Wright, M., and B. Galaway. 1989. *Mediation and Criminal Justice: Victims, Offenders and Community*. Newbury Park, CA: Sage.

Wykes, A. 1964. *The Complete Illustrated Guide to Gambling*. Garden City, NY: Doubleday.

Yamaguchi, K., and D. B. Kandel. 1985. "On the Resolution of Role Incompatability: A Life Event History Analysis of Family Roles and Marijuana Use." *American Journal of Sociology* 90: 1284–1325.

Yaryura-Tobias, J. A., and F. Neziroglu. 1975. "Violent Behavior, Brain Dysrhythmia and Glucose Dysfunction and New Syndrome." *Journal of Orthopsychiatry* 4: 182–188.

Yeager, M. G., J. D. Alviani, and N. Loving. 1976. *How Well Does the Handgun Protect You and Your Family?* Washington, DC: U.S. Conference of Mayors.

Yeager, P. C. 1987. "Structural Bias in Regulatory Law Enforcement: The Case of the U.S. Environmental Protection Agency." *Social Problems* 34: 330–344.

Young, J. 1975. "Working-Class Criminology." Pp. 63–94 in *Critical Criminology*. Edited by I. Taylor, P. Walton, and J. Young. London: Routledge & Kegan Paul.

Young, R. L. 1985. "Perceptions of Crime, Racial Attitudes, and Firearms Ownership." *Social Forces* 64: 473–486.

———. 1991. "Race Conceptions of Crime and Justice, and Support for the Death Penalty." *Social Psychology Quarterly* 54: 67–75.

Yunker, J. A. 1976. "Is the Death Penalty a Deterrent to Homicide? Some Time Series Evidence." *Journal of Behavioral Economics* 5: 45–81.

Zatz, M. S. 1984. "Race, Ethnicity, and Determinate Sentencing." *Criminolgy* 22: 147–171.

———. 1987. "The Changing Forms of Racial/ Ethnic Biases in Sentencing." *Journal of Research in Crime and Delinquency* 24: 69–92.

Zatz, M. S., and J. Hagan. 1985. "Crime, Time, and Punishment: An Exploration of Selection Bias in Sentencing Research." *Journal of Quantitative Criminology* 1: 103–126.

Zedlewski, E.W. 1983. "Deterrence Findings and Data Sources: A Comparison of Uniform Crime Reports and National Crime Surveys." *Journal of Research on Crime and Delinquency* 20: 262–276.

Zeisel, H. 1981. "Race Bias in the Administration of the Death Penalty: The Florida Experience." *Harvard Law Review* 95: 456–468.

Zeitz, D. 1981. *Women Who Embezzle or Defraud: A Study of Convicted Felons*. New York: Praeger.

Zimring, F. E. 1968. "Is Gun Control Likely to Reduce Violent Killings?" *University of Chicago Law Review* 35: 721–737.

———. 1972. "The Medium Is the Message: Firearm Caliber as a Determinant of Death from Assault." *Journal of Legal Studies* 1: 97–123.

———. 1974. "Measuring the Impact of Pre-Trial Diversion from the Criminal Justice System." *University of Chicago Law Review* 31 (2) (May): 241.

———. 1975. "Firearms and Federal Law: The Gun Control Act of 1968." *Journal of Legal Studies* 4 (1) (January): 133–198.

———. 1977. "Determinants of the Death Rate from Robbery: A Detroit Time Study." *Journal of Legal Studies* 6 (June): 317–332.

Zimring, F. E., and G. Hawkins. 1986. *Capital Punishment and the American Agenda.* Cambridge: Cambridge University Press.

———. 1987. *The Citizen's Guide to Gun Control.* New York: Macmillan.

Zupan, L. L. 1991. *Jails: Reform and the New Generation Philosophy.* Cincinnati: Anderson.

Zurcher, L. A., R. George, R. G. Cushing, et al. 1971. "The Anti-pornography Campaign: A Symbolic Crusade." *Social Problems* 19: 217–238.

Name Index

◆

Aarronson, D. E., 226, 389, 391, 392, 393, 405
Abadinsky, H., 82, 237, 240, 487
Abel, C., 276
Abel, R., 365
Abrahamse, A., 526
Abramowitz, S. I., 284, 291
Acker, J. R., 566
Adams, E. H., 487
Adams, L. D., 338
Adamson, C. R., 365, 423
Adler, F., 480
Adler, P. A., 109, 240, 489
Administrative Office of the U.S. Courts, 408, 419
Ageton, S., 78, 79, 121, 124, 125, 126, 139
Agnew, R., 305, 306, 309, 310, 311, 313, 314, 315, 323, 325, 326, 338
Aguirre, A., Jr., 385
Ainlay, J., 363
Ainslie, G., 133
Akers, R. L., 321, 325, 363
Albanese, J. S., 239, 240, 241, 244, 246, 424, 463
Albini, J. L., 233, 236, 237, 240
Albonetti, C. A., 410, 412, 413, 414
Albrecht, S. L., 398
Alfini, J. J., 411, 412
Allan, E., 87, 101, 104, 105, 194
Allen, D. F., 489
Allen, D. N., 381, 392
Allen, M. P., 43, 46
Alper, B., 163
Alpert, G. P., 410
Alschuler, A. W., 410
Alston, L., 110
Altheide, D., 357
Altschuler, D. M., 491
American Correctional Association, 92
American Friends Service Committee, 362
American Psychiatric Association, 205
Amir, M., 155
Amnesty International, 558

Amsterdam, A., 550
Anderson, A. G., 240, 246
Anderson, J., 495
Anderson, L. S., 344
Andrews, D. M., 463
Anglin, M. D., 96, 477, 480, 481
Archer, D., 563
Arditi, R. R., 439
Arkin, S. D., 565
Arlacchi, P., 233, 239, 240
Armor, D. J., 206
Ashkins, C. D., 25, 26
Attorney General, 444
Attorney General's Commission on Pornography, 215
Austern, D., 159, 160
Austin, R. L., 131
Austin, T. L., 421
Axenroth, J. B., 124
Ayers, E. L., 432, 450

Bailey, J. M., 128
Bailey, W. C., 179, 343, 563
Baird, C. S., 462, 463, 464
Bakalar, J. B., 223, 224, 487
Baker, D. V., 385
Balbus, I., 364, 448
Baldus, D. C., 565, 566
Bales, W. D., 449
Balkan, S., 44, 212
Balkwell, J. W., 136
Ball, J. C., 479, 480
Ball, R., 364
Ball, R. A., 227
Ball-Rokeach, S., 28
Bankowski, Z., 363
Banks, J., 463
Bankston, W., 506
Barak, G., 361
Barber, D. F., 213
Barlow, H., 218
Barnes, H. E., 460
Barnett, A., 566
Barnett, H. C., 263, 360

Baron, L., 215, 216
Barr, R., 157
Barron, F., 313
Barry, D., 465
Bastion, L., 148, 149, 150, 151
Battle, B. P., 189
Baum, L., 408, 412
Bayley, D. H., 382, 394, 395, 400
Bean, P., 350, 362
Beccaria, C., 341, 342
Beck, A. J., 435
Beck, E. M., 37
Becker, G. S., 447
Becker, H. S., 338, 353, 354, 356, 357, 359
Beckwith, J., 277
Bedeau, H. A., 202, 302, 557, 568, 569, 570
Bell, D., 235
Bennett, N., 182
Bennett, T., 197, 198, 480
Benson, M. L., 265, 424
Bentele, U., 565
Bentham, J., 341, 342
Bentler, P. M., 487
Berger, R., 568
Berk, R. A., 127, 448
Berkowitz, E., 44
Berkowitz, L., 504
Berlin, F., 292
Berman, D. M., 261
Berman, J. S., 378, 379
Bernard, T., 134, 310, 326, 359, 363
Berns, W., 570
Bernstein, I. N., 408, 416, 422, 424
Berrill, K., 49
Beschner, G. M., 482, 483
Bickle, G. S., 422
Biderman, A. D., 27, 191
Bieck, W. H., 378
Bienen, L., 416, 422
Biernacki, P., 491
Bilionis, L. D., 571
Biomedical and Behavioral Research, 285

◆ 643

SUBJECT INDEX

◆